# CANNON
# BALL

Publishers Tom Kaczynski
Design & Production by Kelsey Wroten, Tom Kaczynski & Jordan Shiveley

**Uncivilized Books**
P.O. Box 6534
Minneapolis, MN 55406
USA
uncivilizedbooks.com

ISBN: 978-1-941250-33-4

DISTRIBUTED TO THE TRADE BY:
**Consortium Book Sales & Distribution, LLC.**
34 Thirteenth Avenue NE, Suite 101
Minneapolis, MN 55413-1007
cbsd.com
Orders: (800) 283-3572

First Edition, April 2019

10 9 8 7 6 5 4 3 2 1

Printed in China

KELSEY WROTEN

# CANNON BALL

UNCIVILIZED BOOKS

# PROLOGUE

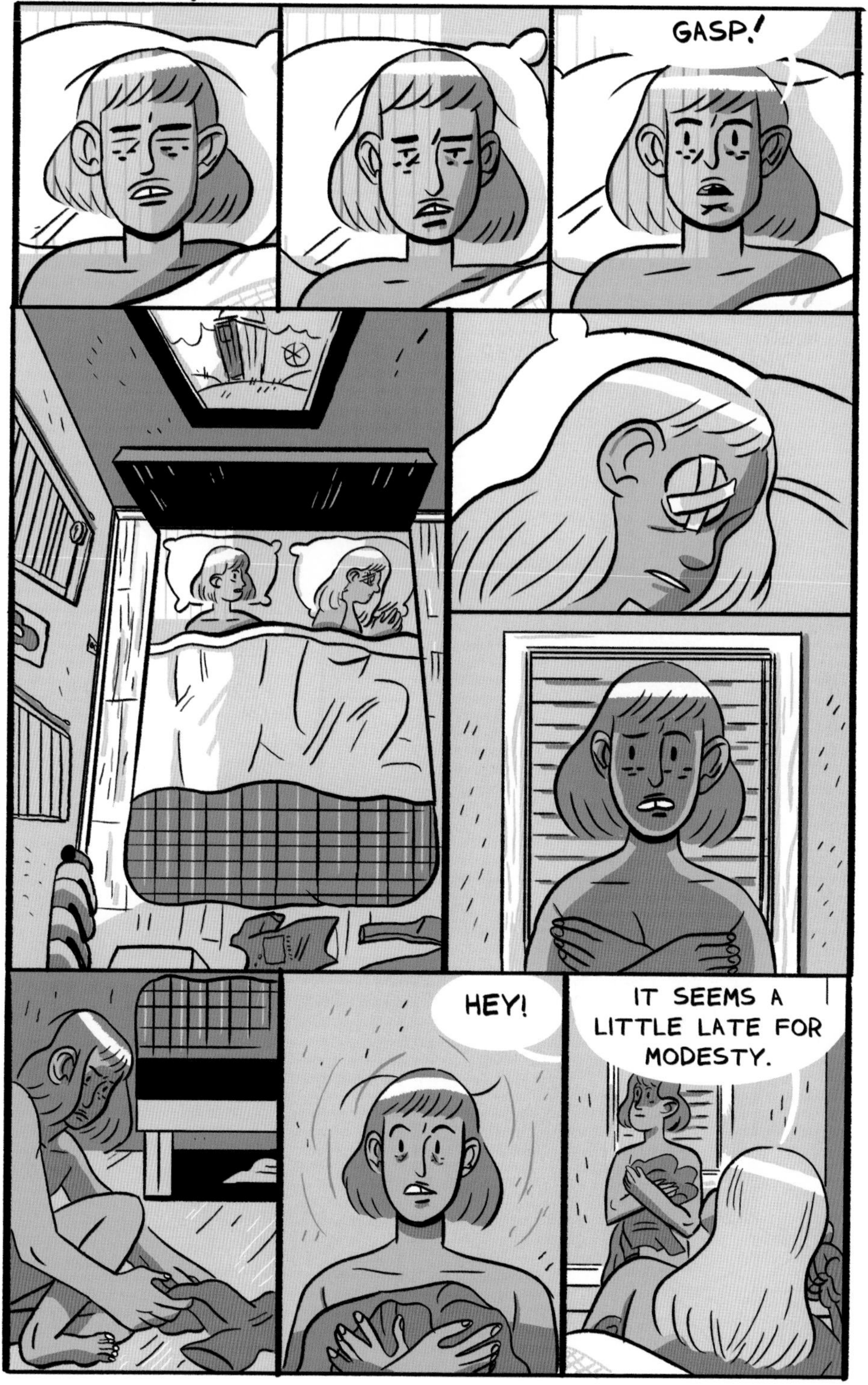
GASP!
HEY!
IT SEEMS A LITTLE LATE FOR MODESTY.

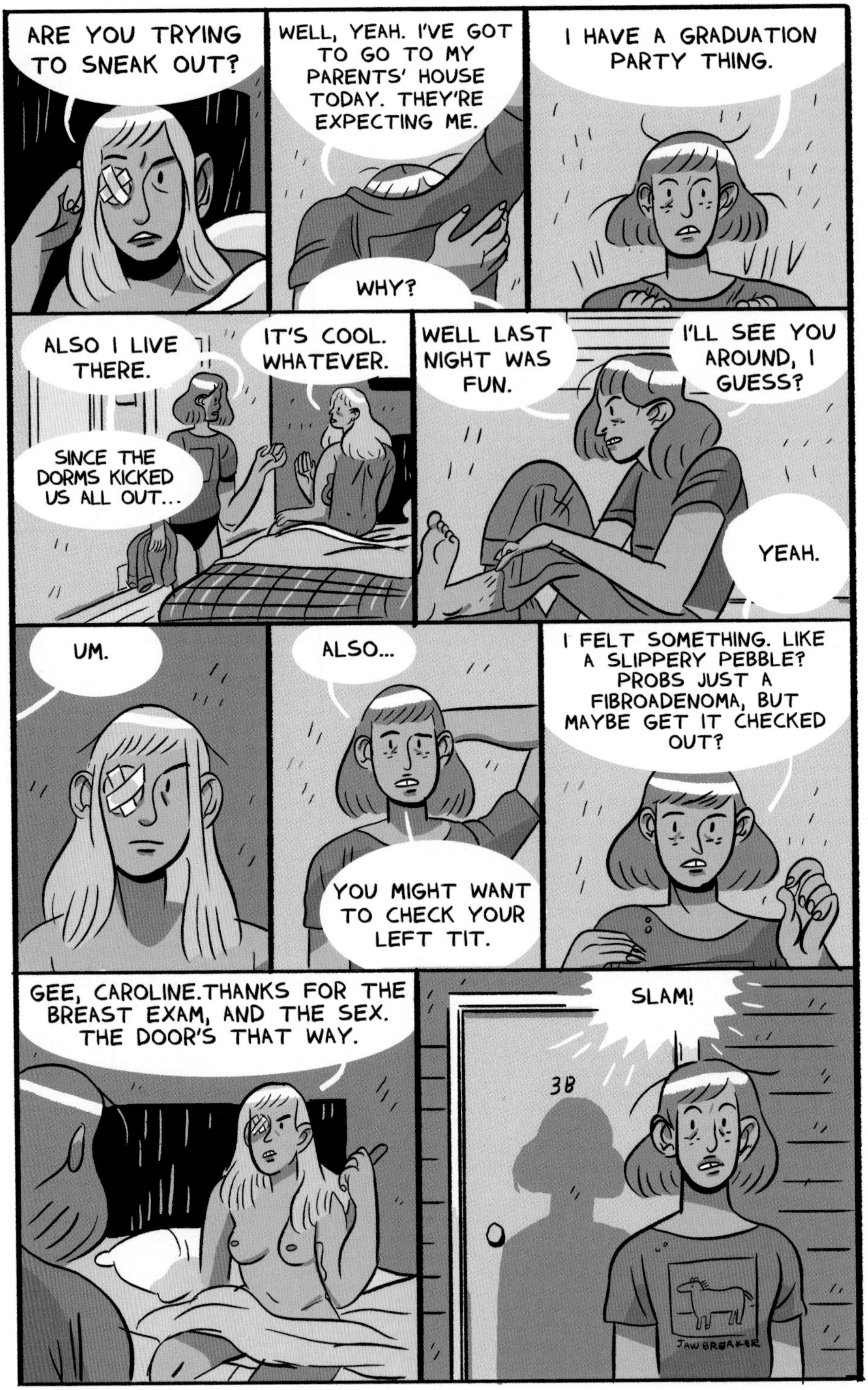
ARE YOU TRYING TO SNEAK OUT?
WELL, YEAH. I'VE GOT TO GO TO MY PARENTS' HOUSE TODAY. THEY'RE EXPECTING ME.
WHY?
I HAVE A GRADUATION PARTY THING.
ALSO I LIVE THERE.
SINCE THE DORMS KICKED US ALL OUT...
IT'S COOL. WHATEVER.
WELL LAST NIGHT WAS FUN.
I'LL SEE YOU AROUND, I GUESS?
YEAH.
UM.
ALSO...
YOU MIGHT WANT TO CHECK YOUR LEFT TIT.
I FELT SOMETHING. LIKE A SLIPPERY PEBBLE? PROBS JUST A FIBROADENOMA, BUT MAYBE GET IT CHECKED OUT?
GEE, CAROLINE. THANKS FOR THE BREAST EXAM, AND THE SEX. THE DOOR'S THAT WAY.
SLAM!
3B
JAWBREAKER

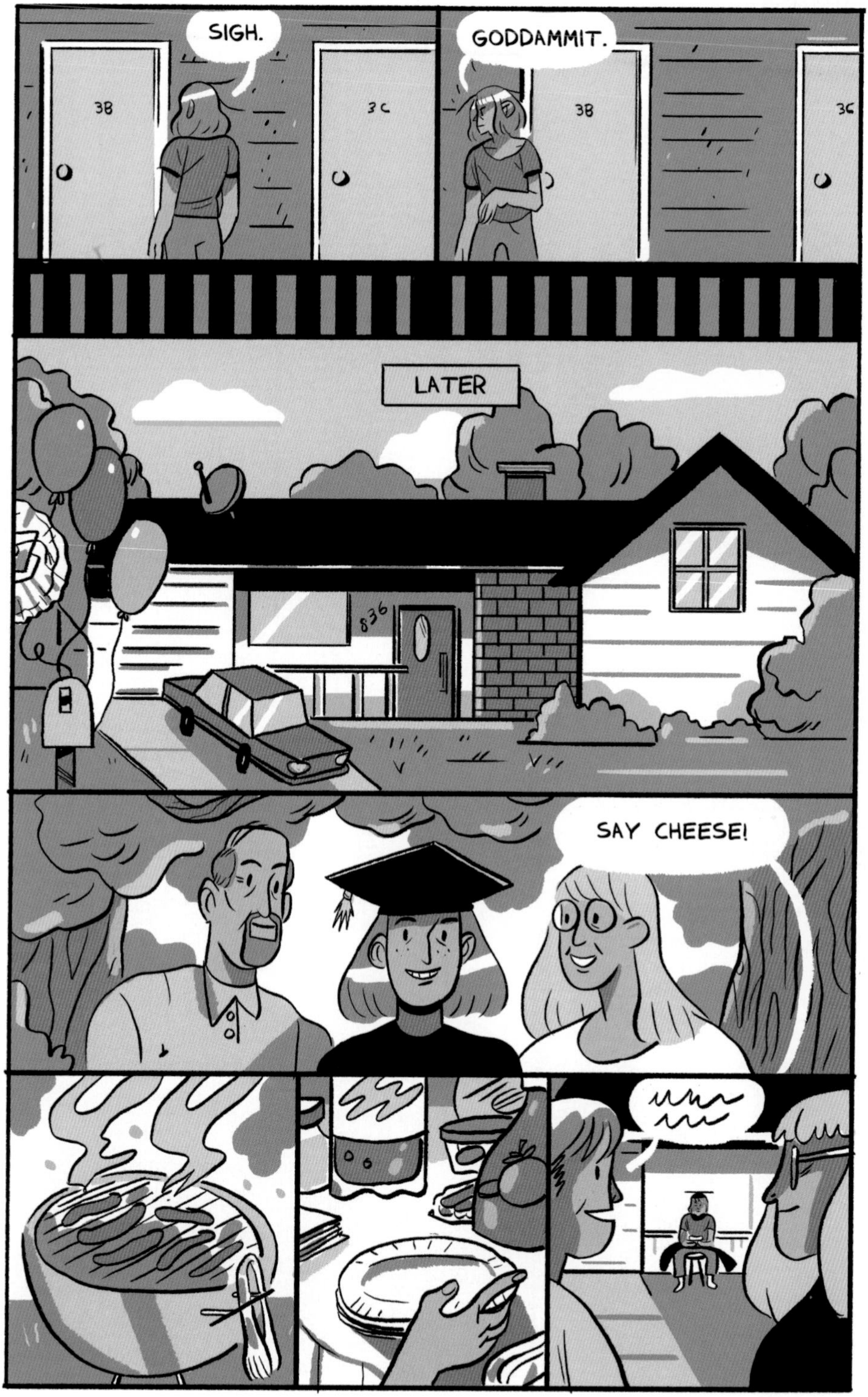

SIGH.
GODDAMMIT.
LATER
SAY CHEESE!

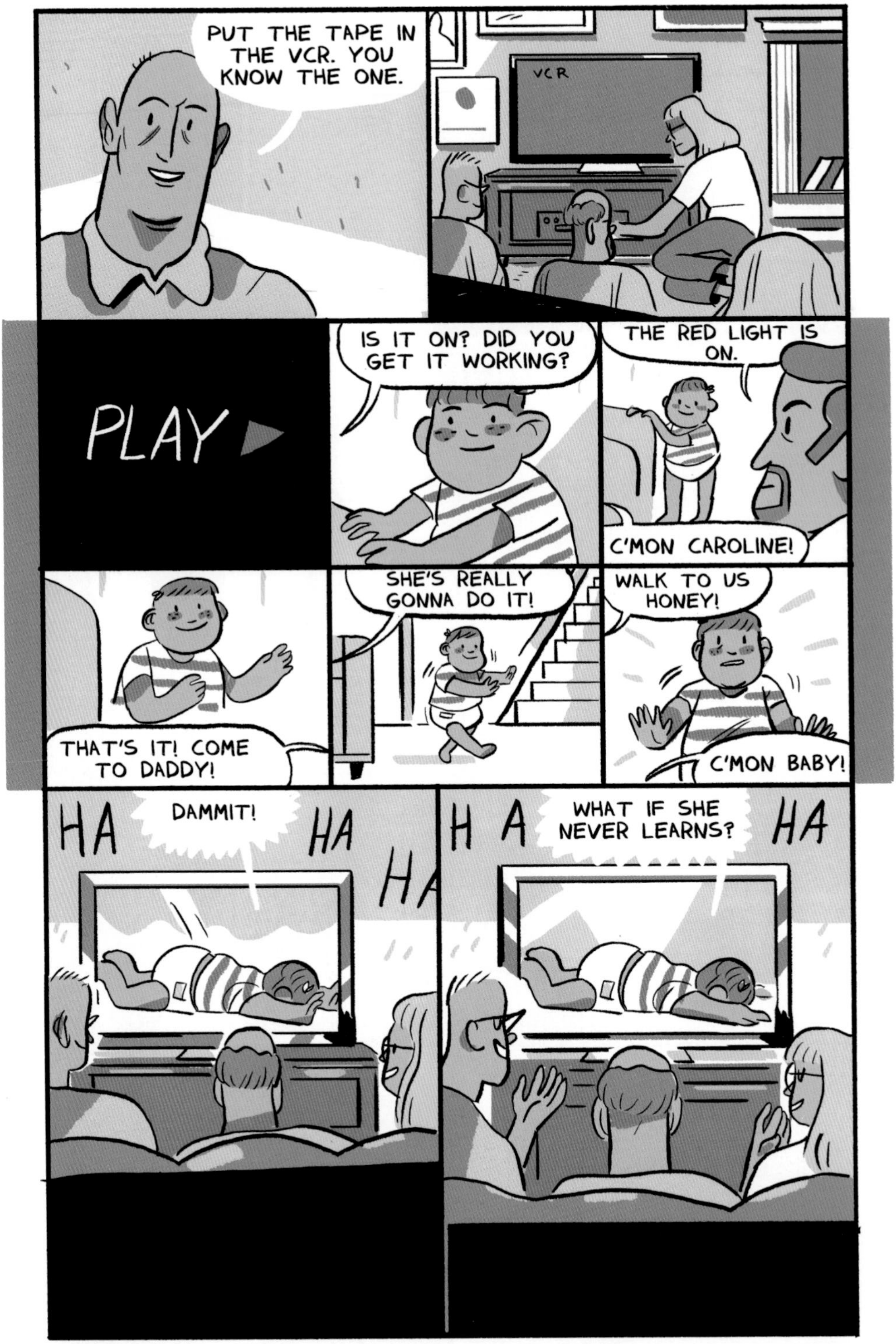
PUT THE TAPE IN THE VCR. YOU KNOW THE ONE.
VCR
PLAY
IS IT ON? DID YOU GET IT WORKING?
THE RED LIGHT IS ON.
C'MON CAROLINE!
THAT'S IT! COME TO DADDY!
SHE'S REALLY GONNA DO IT!
WALK TO US HONEY!
C'MON BABY!
HA
DAMMIT!
HA
HA
H A
WHAT IF SHE NEVER LEARNS?
HA

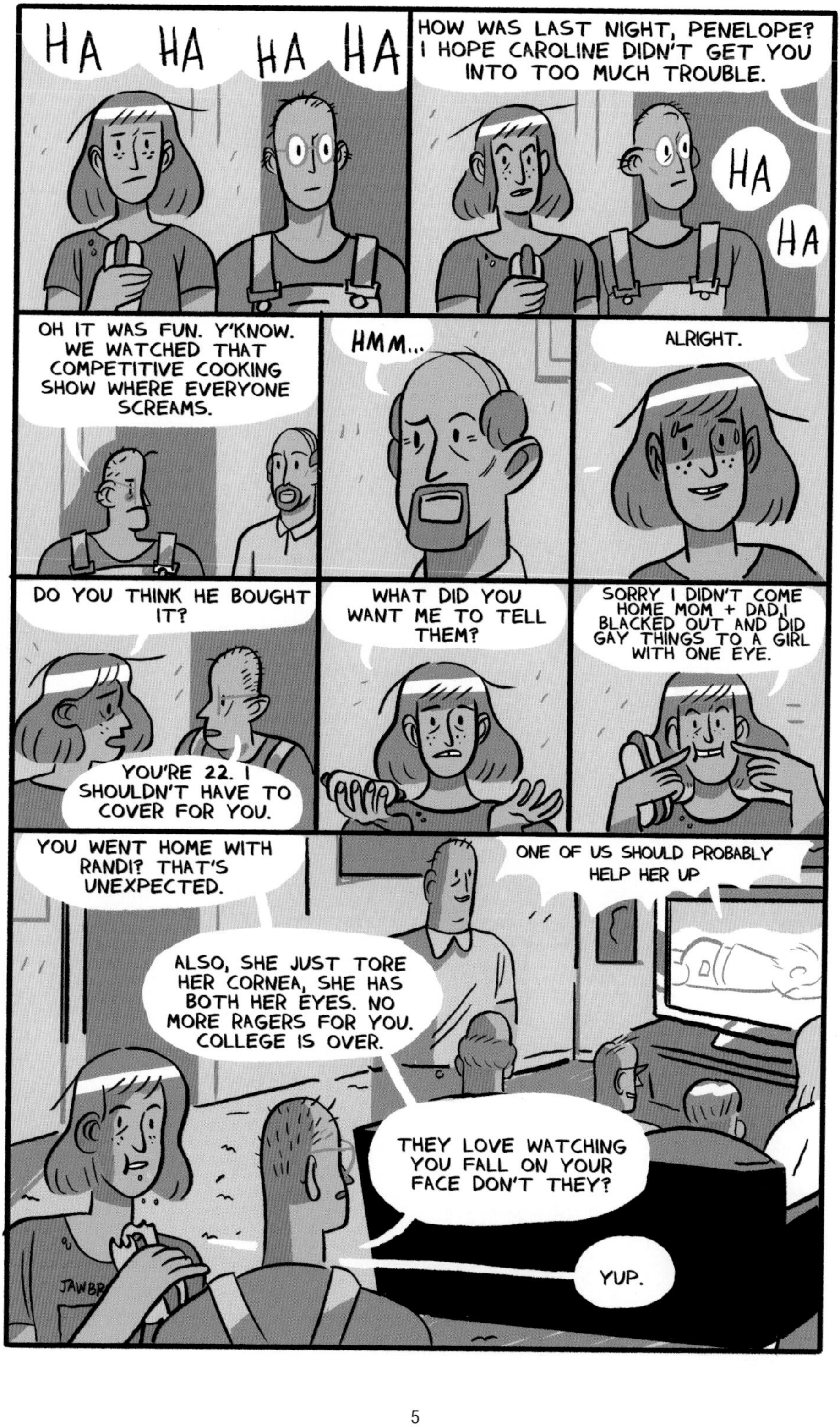
HA HA HA HA
HOW WAS LAST NIGHT, PENELOPE? I HOPE CAROLINE DIDN'T GET YOU INTO TOO MUCH TROUBLE.
HA
HA
OH IT WAS FUN. Y'KNOW. WE WATCHED THAT COMPETITIVE COOKING SHOW WHERE EVERYONE SCREAMS.
HMM...
ALRIGHT.
DO YOU THINK HE BOUGHT IT?
YOU'RE 22. I SHOULDN'T HAVE TO COVER FOR YOU.
WHAT DID YOU WANT ME TO TELL THEM?
SORRY I DIDN'T COME HOME MOM + DAD, I BLACKED OUT AND DID GAY THINGS TO A GIRL WITH ONE EYE.
YOU WENT HOME WITH RANDI? THAT'S UNEXPECTED.
ALSO, SHE JUST TORE HER CORNEA, SHE HAS BOTH HER EYES. NO MORE RAGERS FOR YOU. COLLEGE IS OVER.
ONE OF US SHOULD PROBABLY HELP HER UP
THEY LOVE WATCHING YOU FALL ON YOUR FACE DON'T THEY?
YUP.

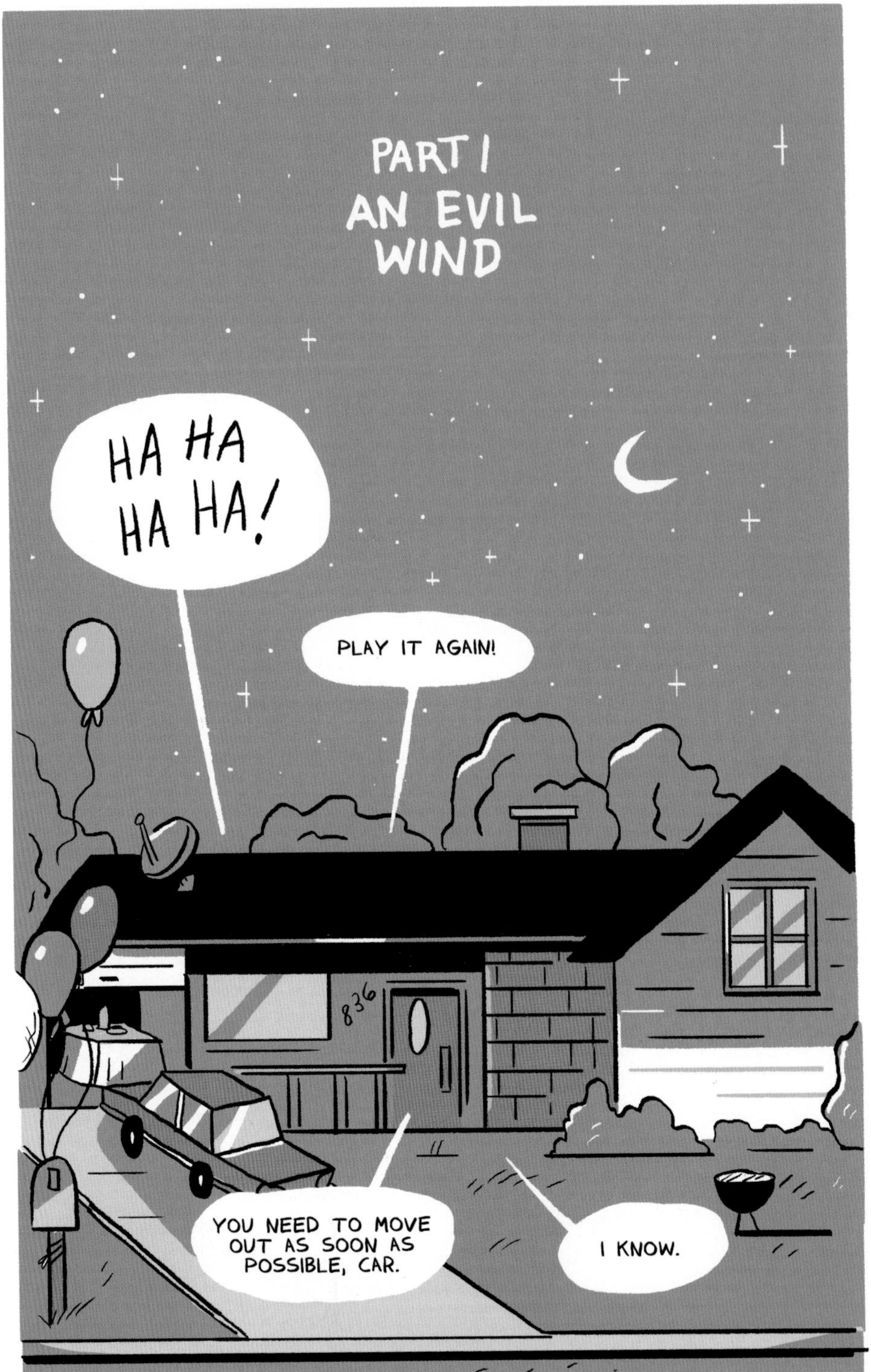
PART I
AN EVIL
WIND
HA HA
HA HA!
PLAY IT AGAIN!
836
YOU NEED TO MOVE OUT AS SOON AS POSSIBLE, CAR.
I KNOW.

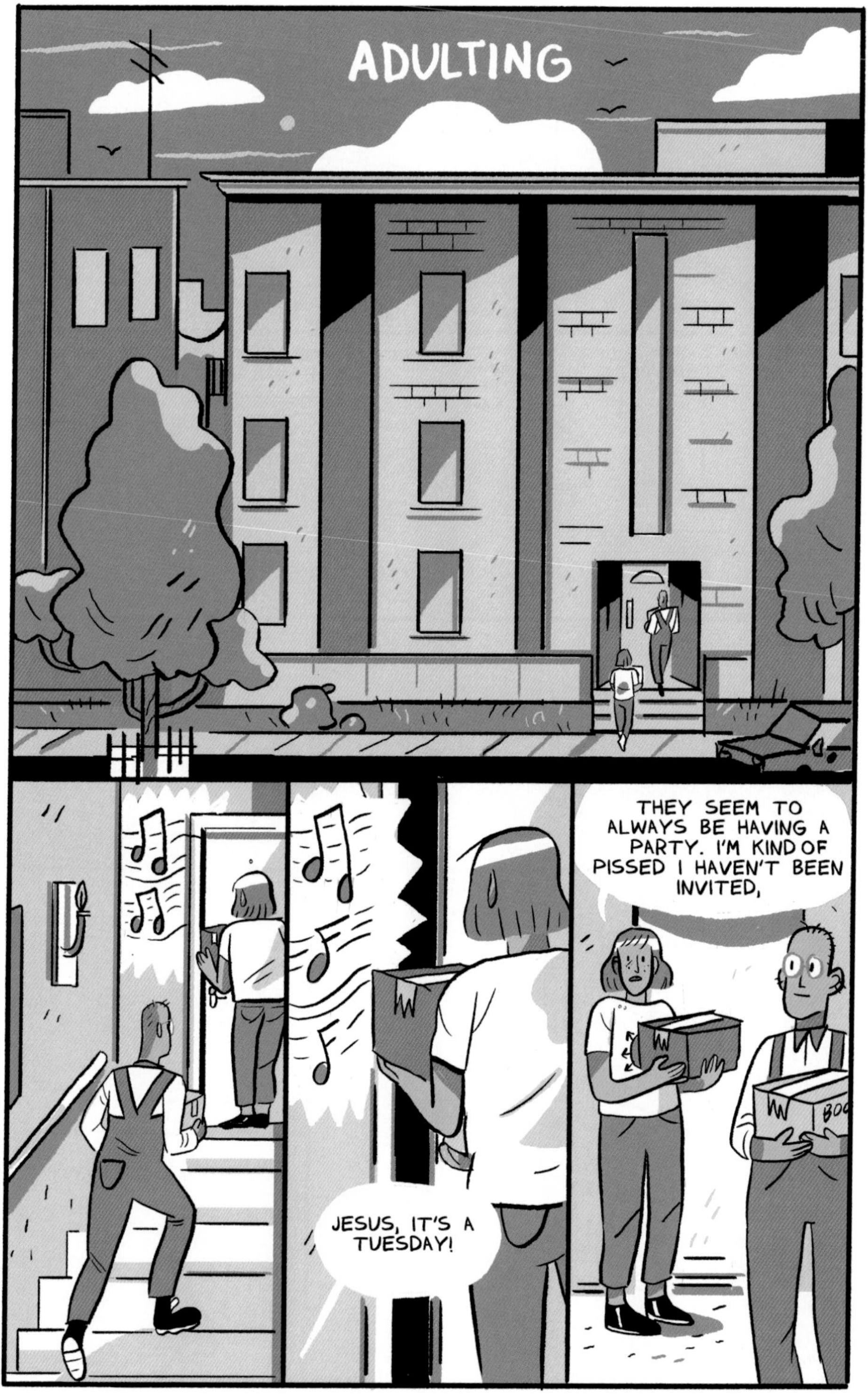
ADULTING
JESUS, IT'S A TUESDAY!
THEY SEEM TO ALWAYS BE HAVING A PARTY. I'M KIND OF PISSED I HAVEN'T BEEN INVITED,

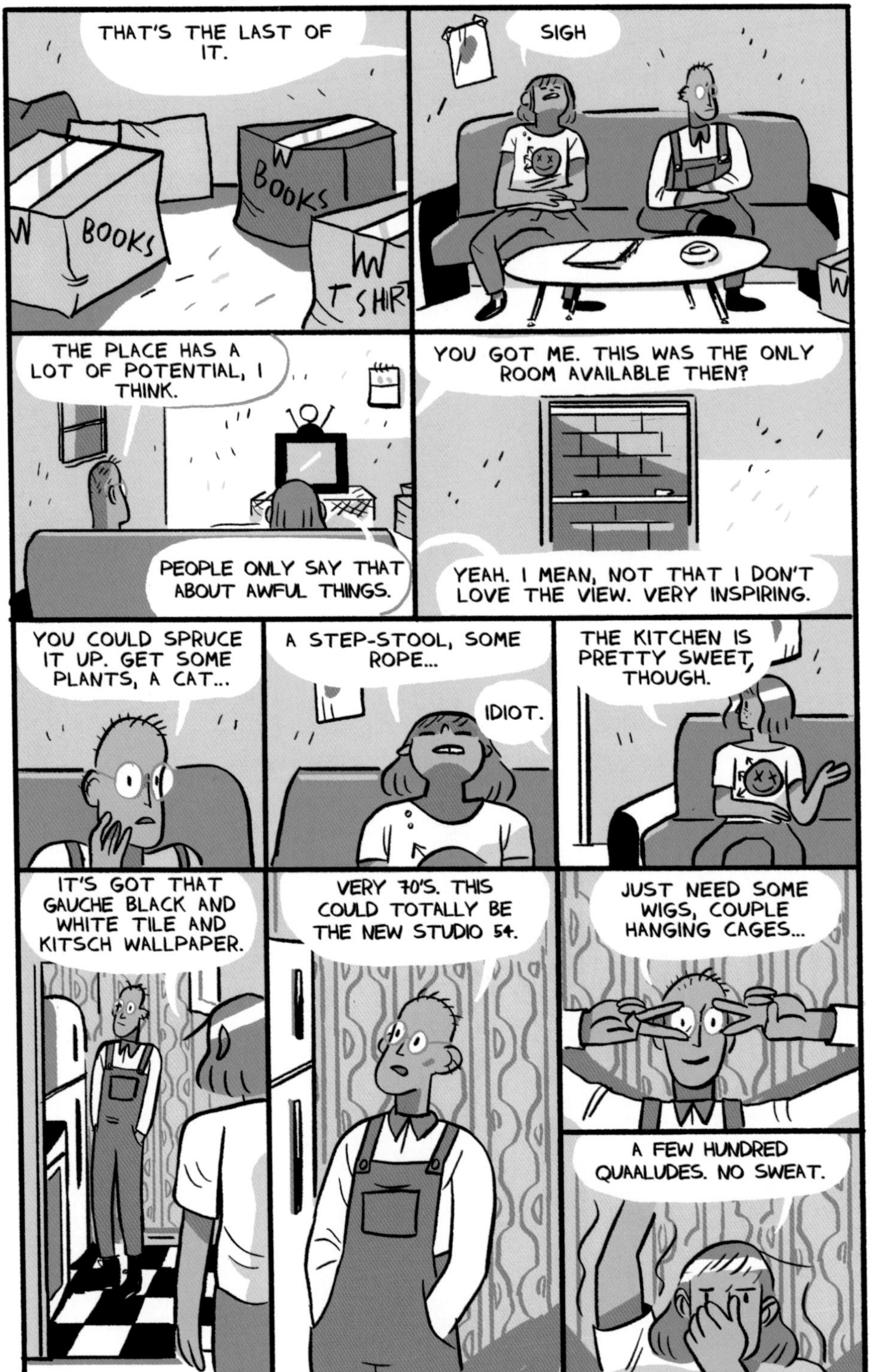
THAT'S THE LAST OF IT.
BOOKS
BOOKS
T SHIR
SIGH
THE PLACE HAS A LOT OF POTENTIAL, I THINK.
PEOPLE ONLY SAY THAT ABOUT AWFUL THINGS.
YOU GOT ME. THIS WAS THE ONLY ROOM AVAILABLE THEN?
YEAH. I MEAN, NOT THAT I DON'T LOVE THE VIEW. VERY INSPIRING.
YOU COULD SPRUCE IT UP. GET SOME PLANTS, A CAT...
A STEP-STOOL, SOME ROPE...
IDIOT.
THE KITCHEN IS PRETTY SWEET, THOUGH.
IT'S GOT THAT GAUCHE BLACK AND WHITE TILE AND KITSCH WALLPAPER.
VERY 70'S. THIS COULD TOTALLY BE THE NEW STUDIO 54.
JUST NEED SOME WIGS, COUPLE HANGING CAGES...
A FEW HUNDRED QUAALUDES. NO SWEAT.

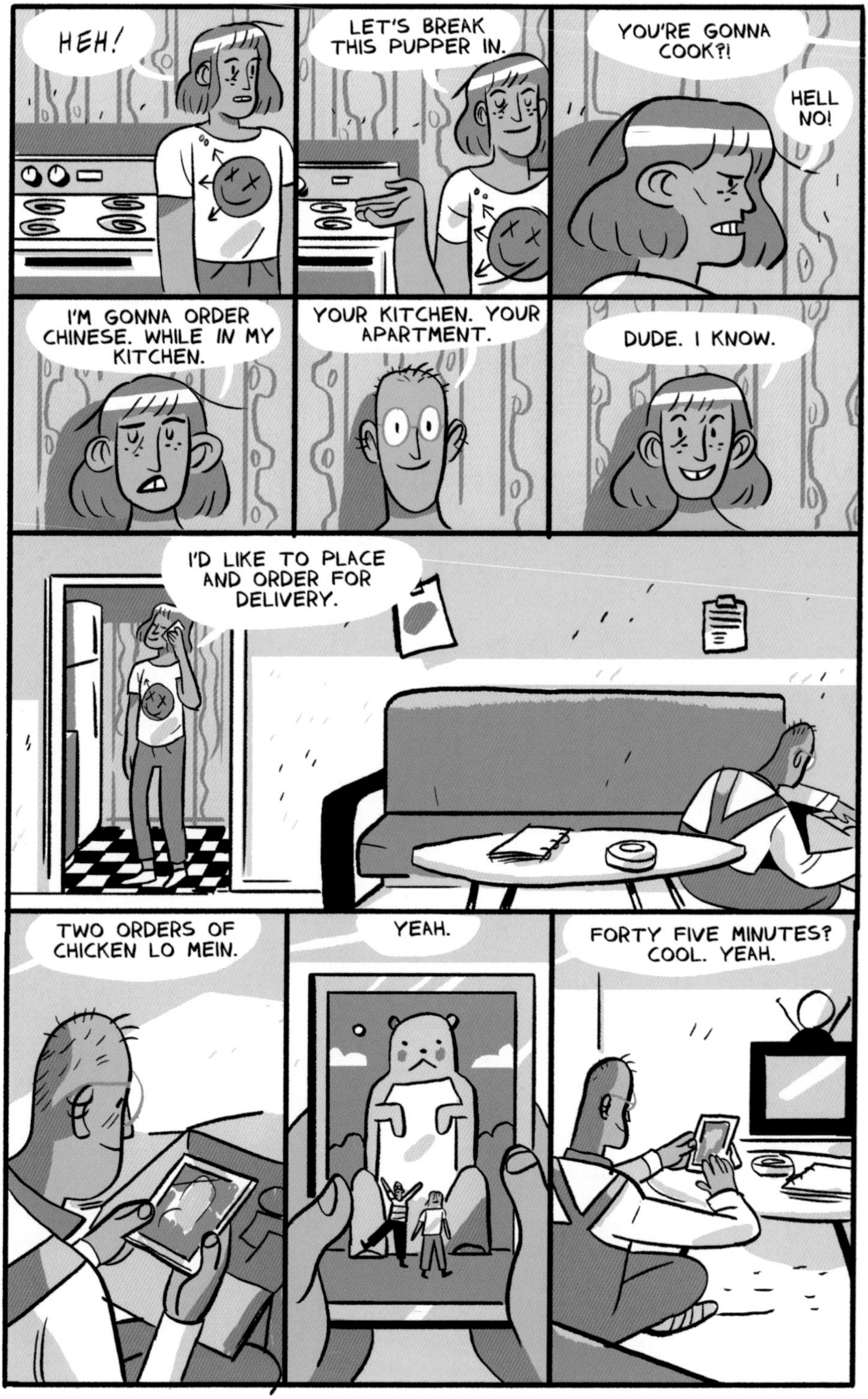
HEH!
LET'S BREAK THIS PUPPER IN.
YOU'RE GONNA COOK?!
HELL NO!
I'M GONNA ORDER CHINESE. WHILE IN MY KITCHEN.
YOUR KITCHEN. YOUR APARTMENT.
DUDE. I KNOW.
I'D LIKE TO PLACE AND ORDER FOR DELIVERY.
TWO ORDERS OF CHICKEN LO MEIN.
YEAH.
FORTY FIVE MINUTES? COOL. YEAH.

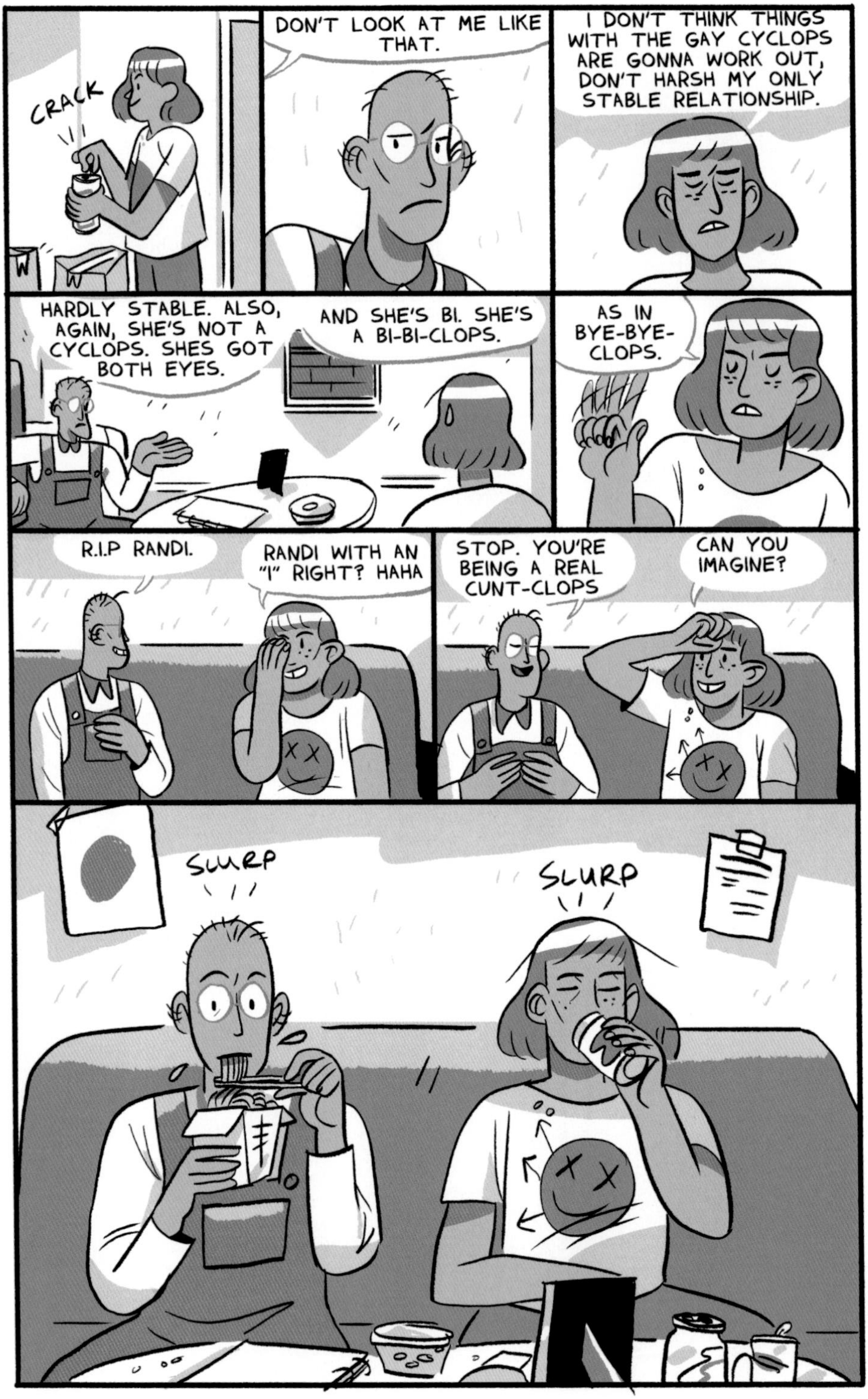
CRACK
DON'T LOOK AT ME LIKE THAT.
I DON'T THINK THINGS WITH THE GAY CYCLOPS ARE GONNA WORK OUT, DON'T HARSH MY ONLY STABLE RELATIONSHIP.
HARDLY STABLE. ALSO, AGAIN, SHE'S NOT A CYCLOPS. SHES GOT BOTH EYES.
AND SHE'S BI. SHE'S A BI-BI-CLOPS.
AS IN BYE-BYE-CLOPS.
R.I.P RANDI.
RANDI WITH AN "I" RIGHT? HAHA
STOP. YOU'RE BEING A REAL CUNT-CLOPS
CAN YOU IMAGINE?
SLURP
SLURP

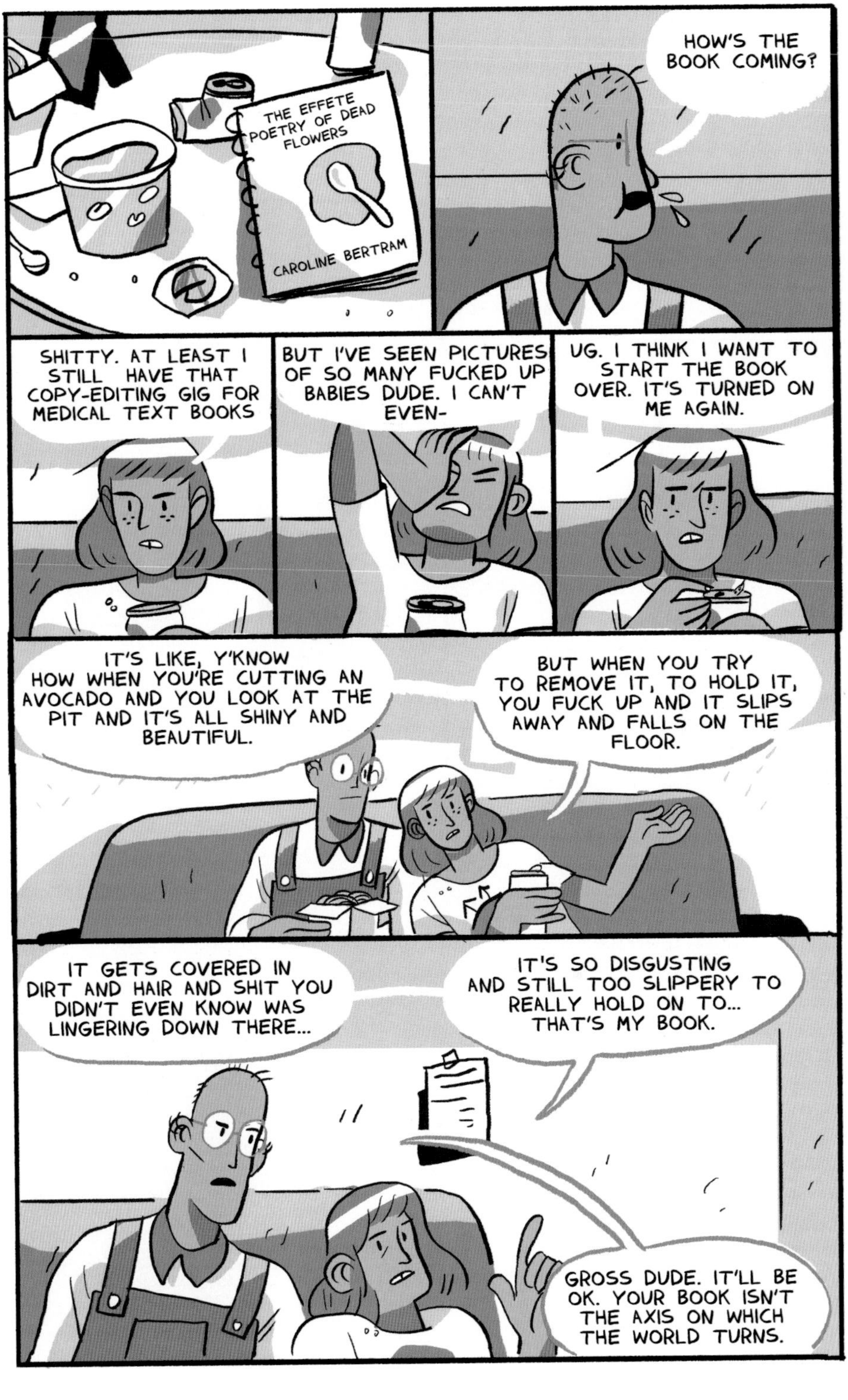
THE EFFETE POETRY OF DEAD FLOWERS
CAROLINE BERTRAM
HOW'S THE BOOK COMING?
SHITTY. AT LEAST I STILL HAVE THAT COPY-EDITING GIG FOR MEDICAL TEXT BOOKS
BUT I'VE SEEN PICTURES OF SO MANY FUCKED UP BABIES DUDE. I CAN'T EVEN-
UG. I THINK I WANT TO START THE BOOK OVER. IT'S TURNED ON ME AGAIN.
IT'S LIKE, Y'KNOW HOW WHEN YOU'RE CUTTING AN AVOCADO AND YOU LOOK AT THE PIT AND IT'S ALL SHINY AND BEAUTIFUL.
BUT WHEN YOU TRY TO REMOVE IT, TO HOLD IT, YOU FUCK UP AND IT SLIPS AWAY AND FALLS ON THE FLOOR.
IT GETS COVERED IN DIRT AND HAIR AND SHIT YOU DIDN'T EVEN KNOW WAS LINGERING DOWN THERE...
IT'S SO DISGUSTING AND STILL TOO SLIPPERY TO REALLY HOLD ON TO... THAT'S MY BOOK.
GROSS DUDE. IT'LL BE OK. YOUR BOOK ISN'T THE AXIS ON WHICH THE WORLD TURNS.

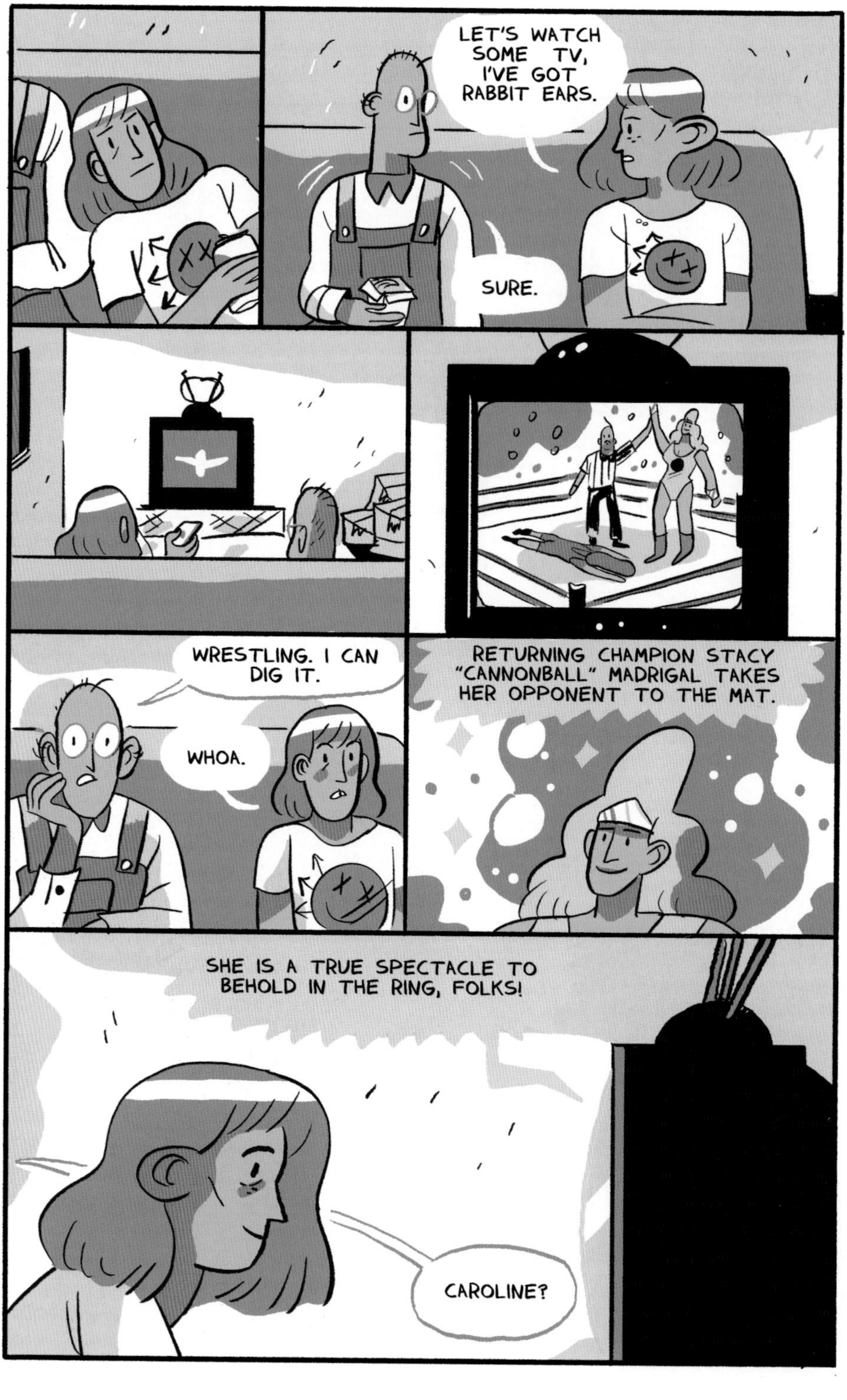
LET'S WATCH SOME TV, I'VE GOT RABBIT EARS.
SURE.
WRESTLING. I CAN DIG IT.
WHOA.
RETURNING CHAMPION STACY "CANNONBALL" MADRIGAL TAKES HER OPPONENT TO THE MAT.
SHE IS A TRUE SPECTACLE TO BEHOLD IN THE RING, FOLKS!
CAROLINE?

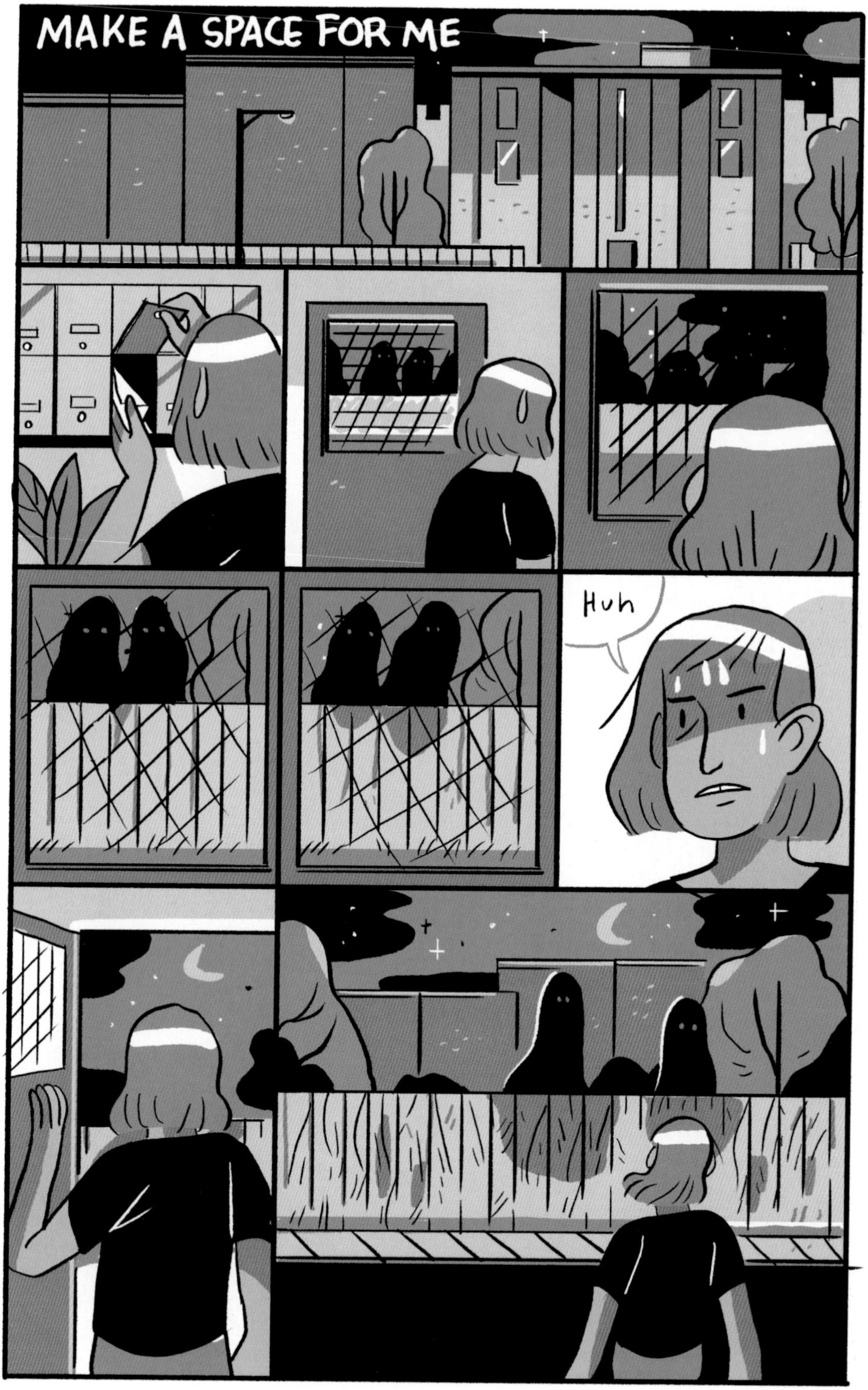
MAKE A SPACE FOR ME
Huh

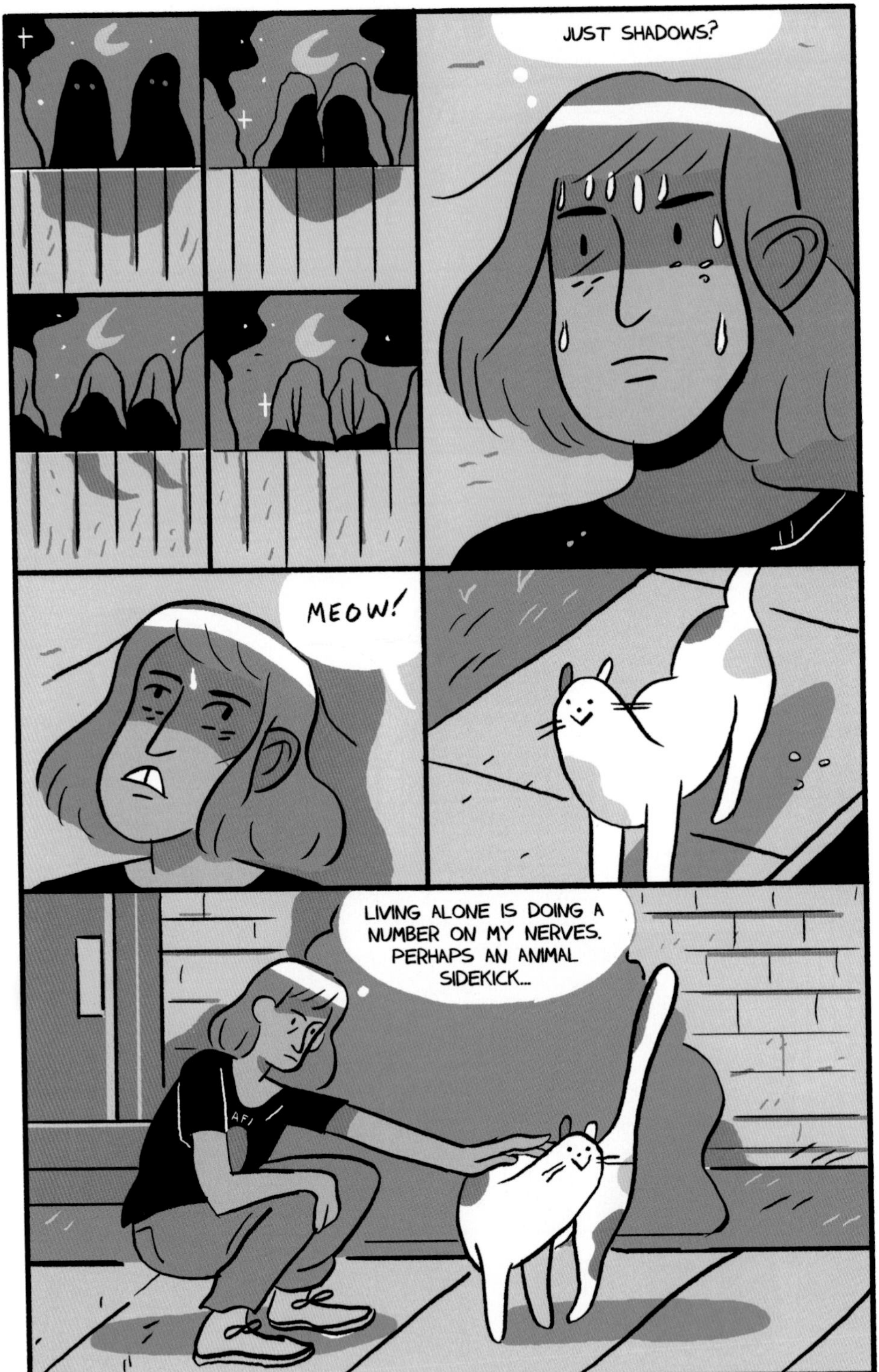
JUST SHADOWS?
MEOW!
LIVING ALONE IS DOING A NUMBER ON MY NERVES. PERHAPS AN ANIMAL SIDEKICK...

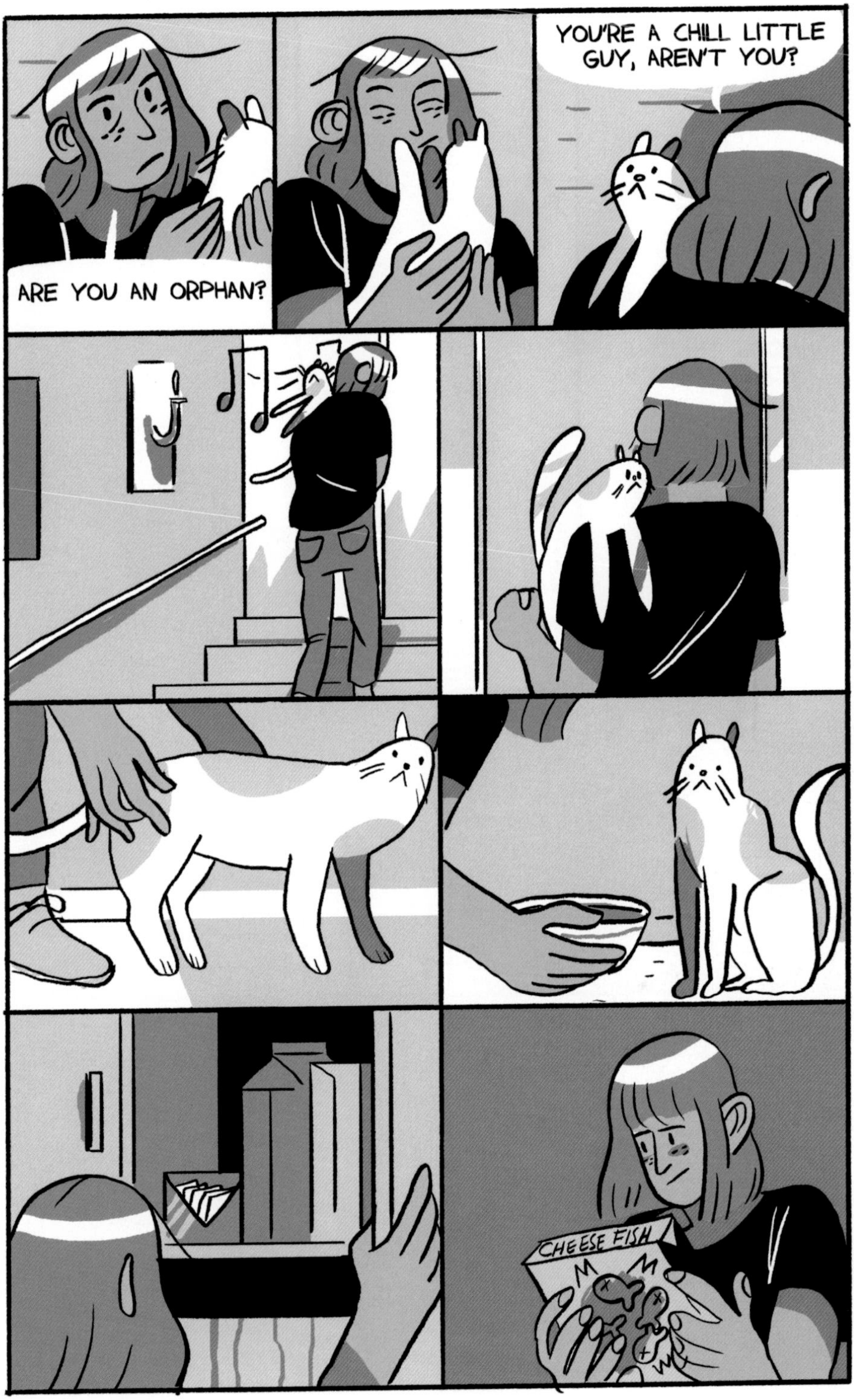
ARE YOU AN ORPHAN?
YOU'RE A CHILL LITTLE GUY, AREN'T YOU?
CHEESE FISH

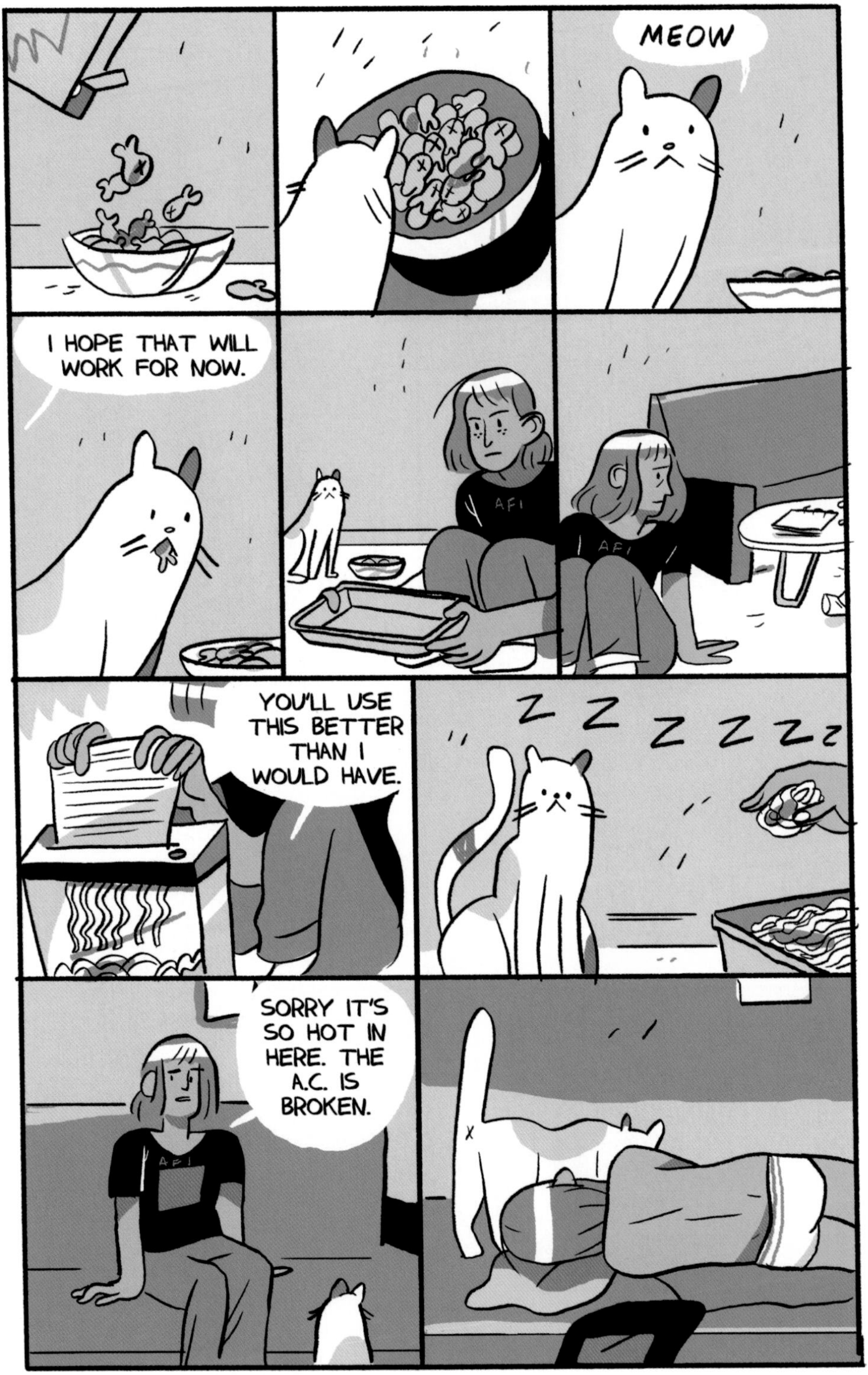
MEOW
I HOPE THAT WILL WORK FOR NOW.
YOU'LL USE THIS BETTER THAN I WOULD HAVE.
Z Z Z Z Z Z
SORRY IT'S SO HOT IN HERE. THE A.C. IS BROKEN.

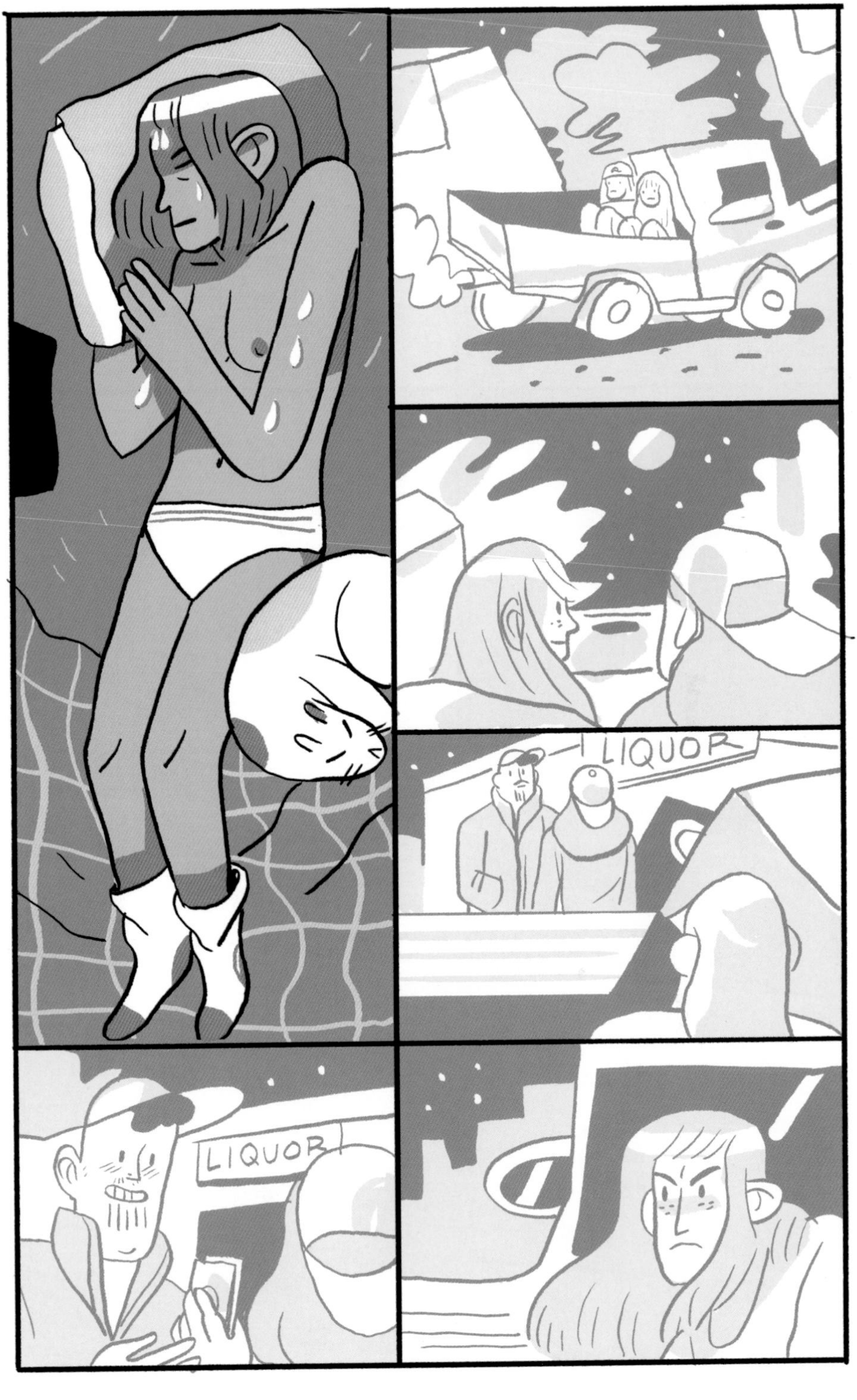
LIQUOR
LIQUOR

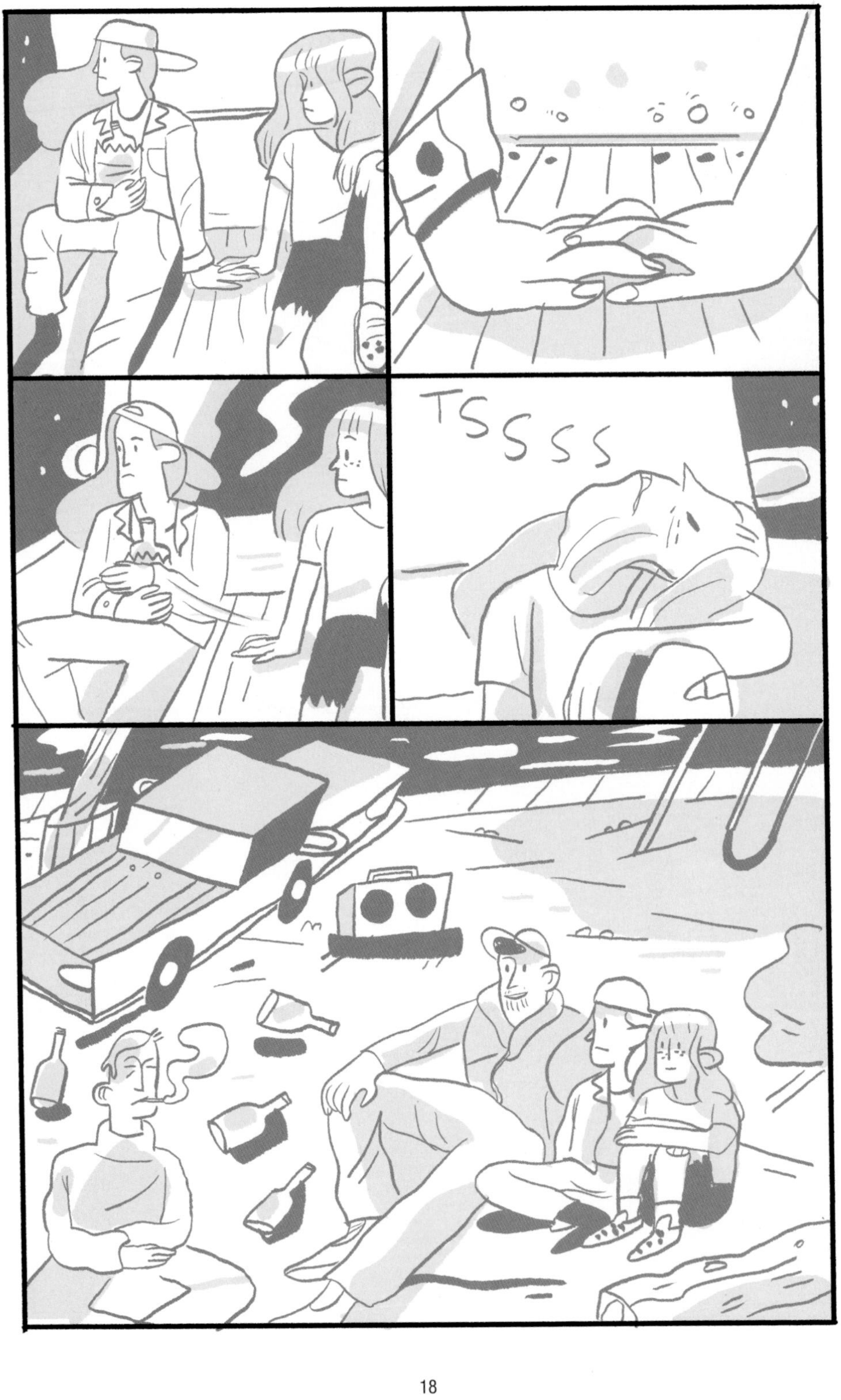
TSSSS

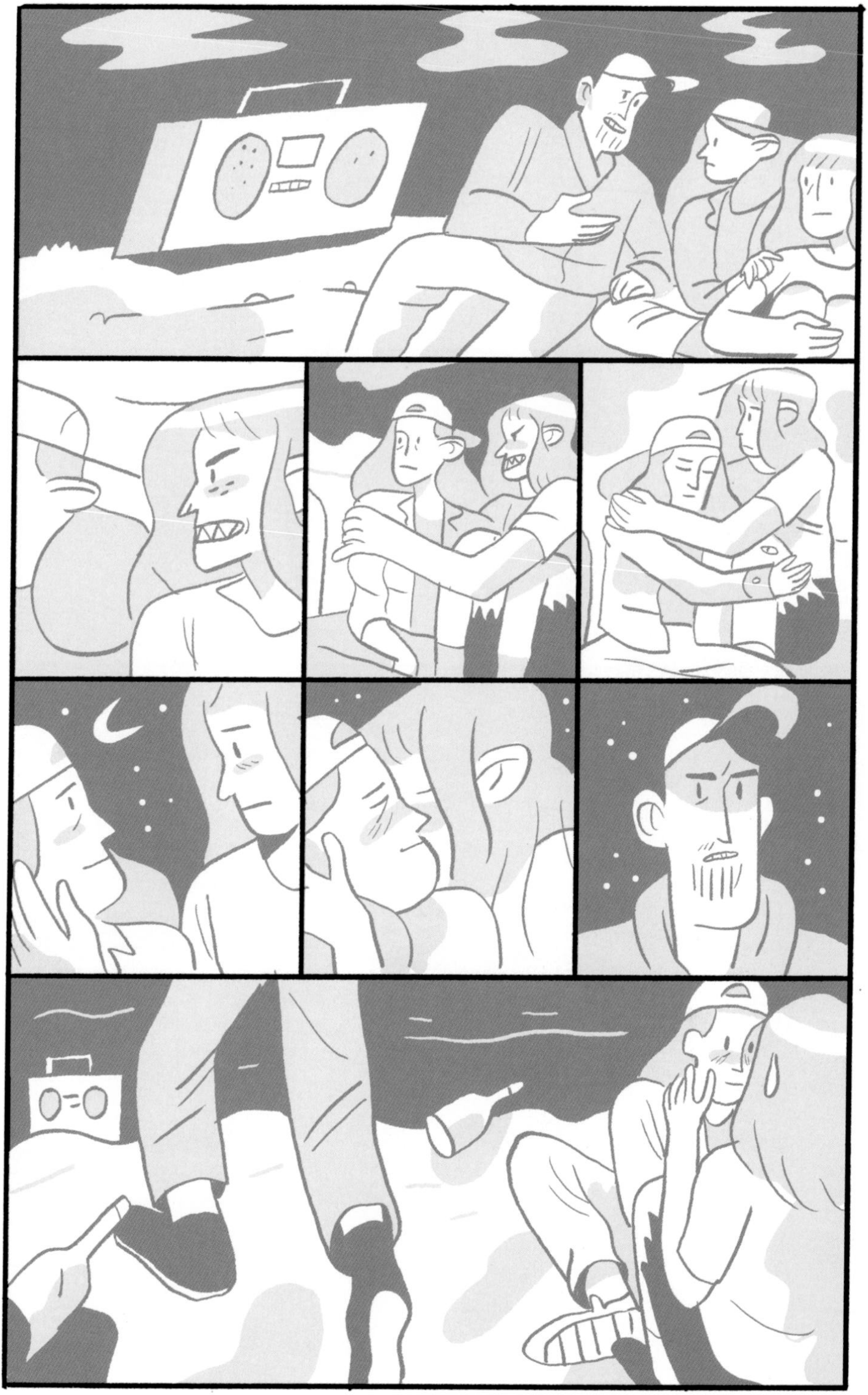

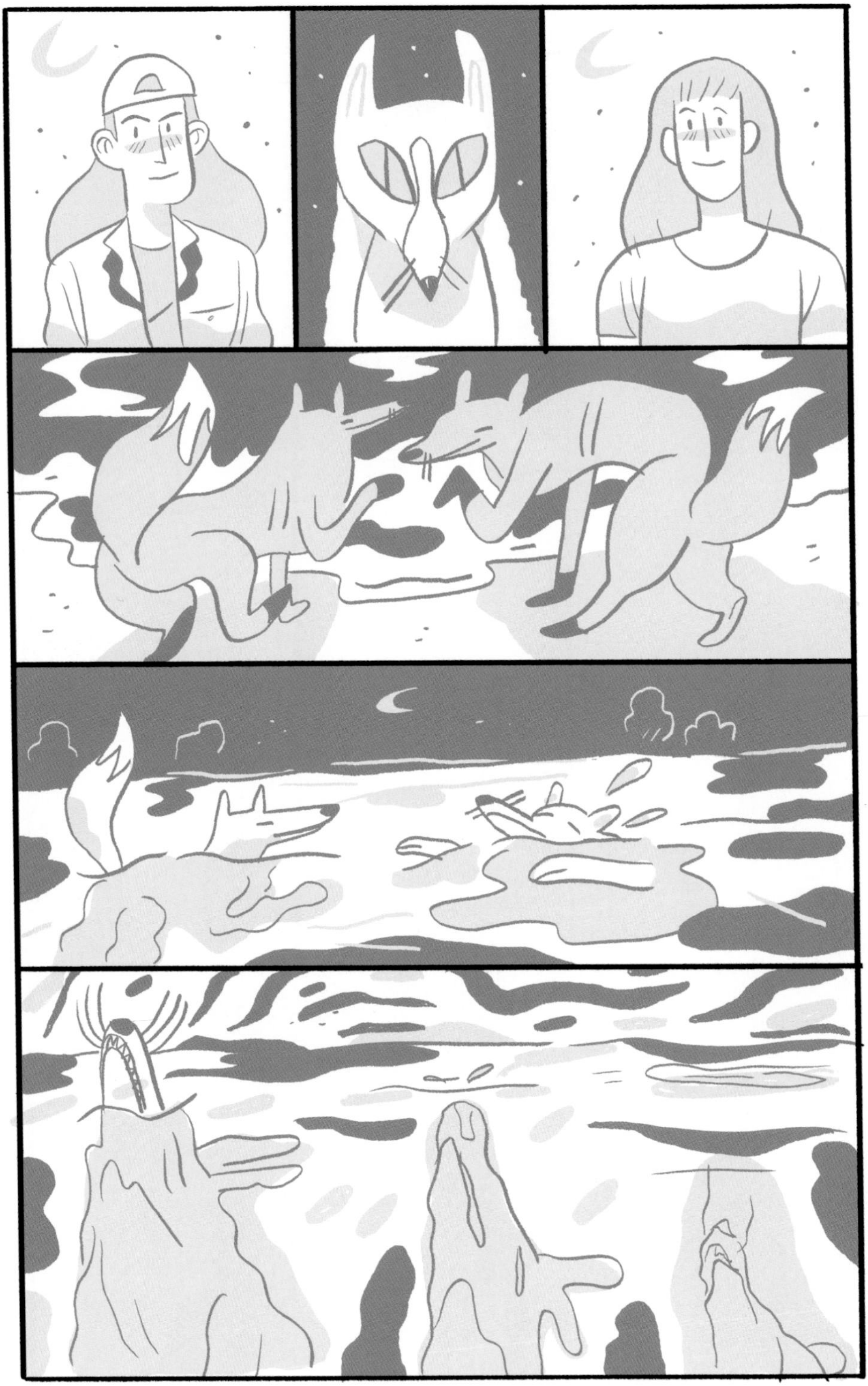

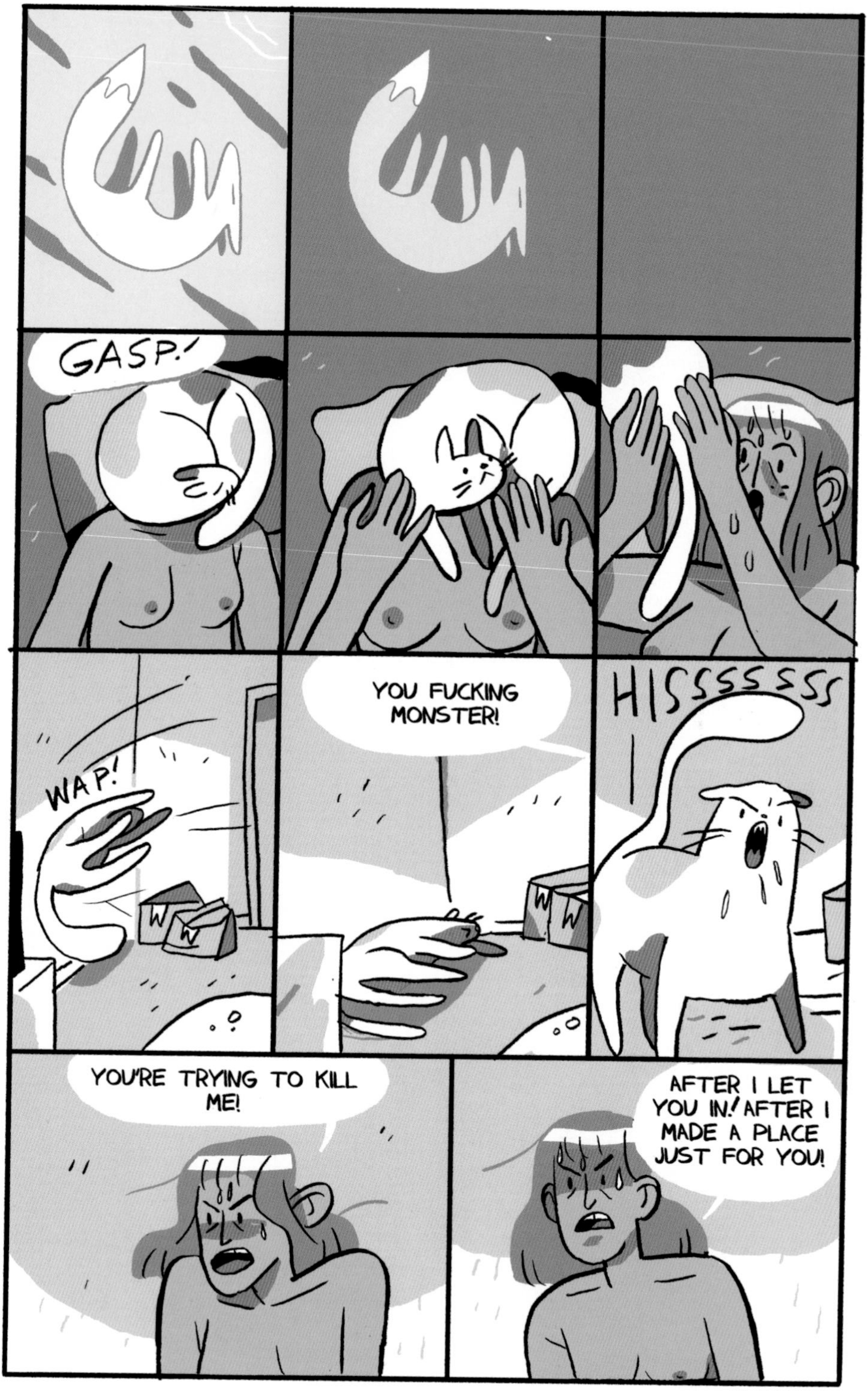
GASP!
WAP!
YOU FUCKING MONSTER!
HISSSSSSS
YOU'RE TRYING TO KILL ME!
AFTER I LET YOU IN! AFTER I MADE A PLACE JUST FOR YOU!

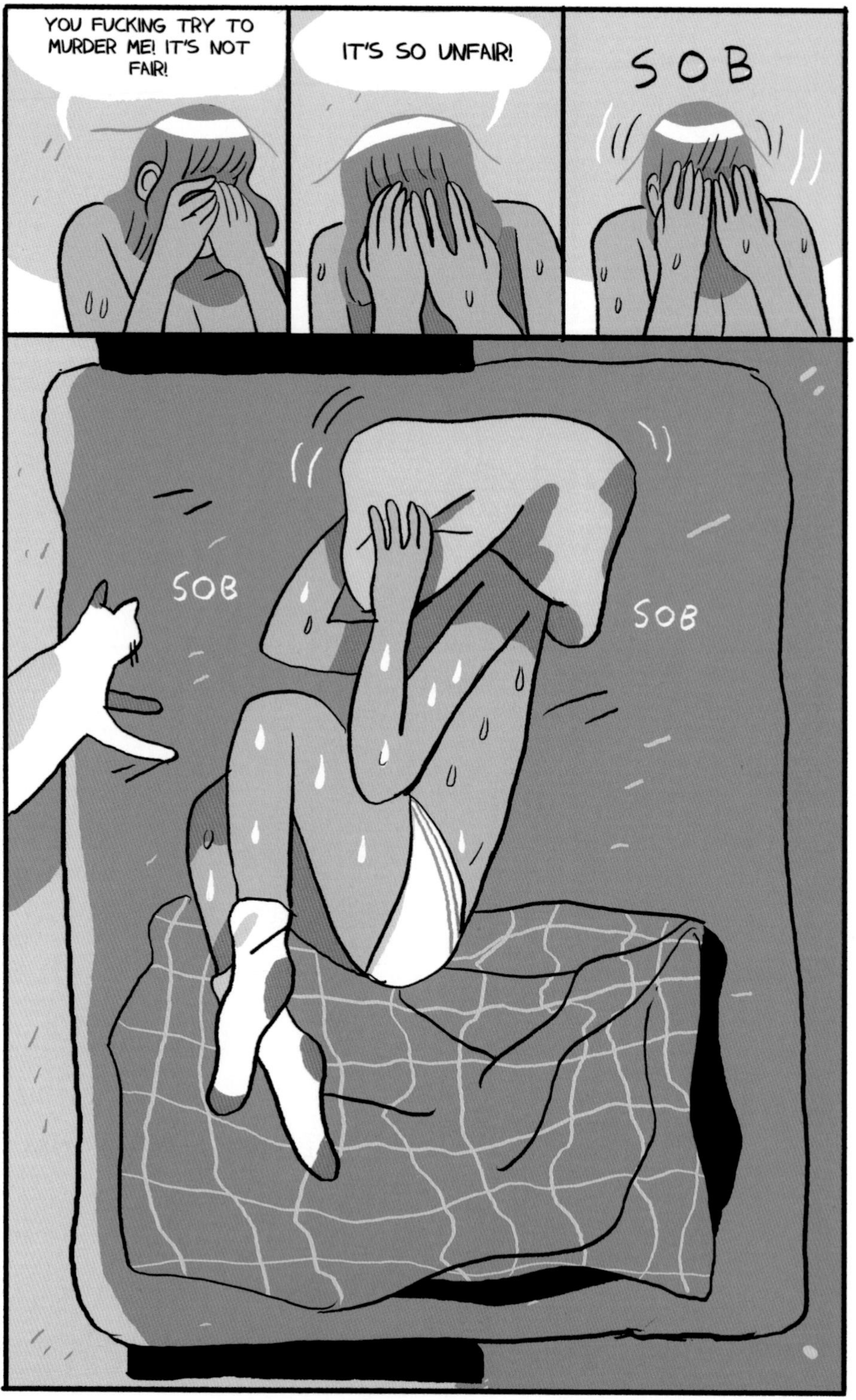
YOU FUCKING TRY TO MURDER ME! IT'S NOT FAIR!
IT'S SO UNFAIR!
SOB
SOB
SOB

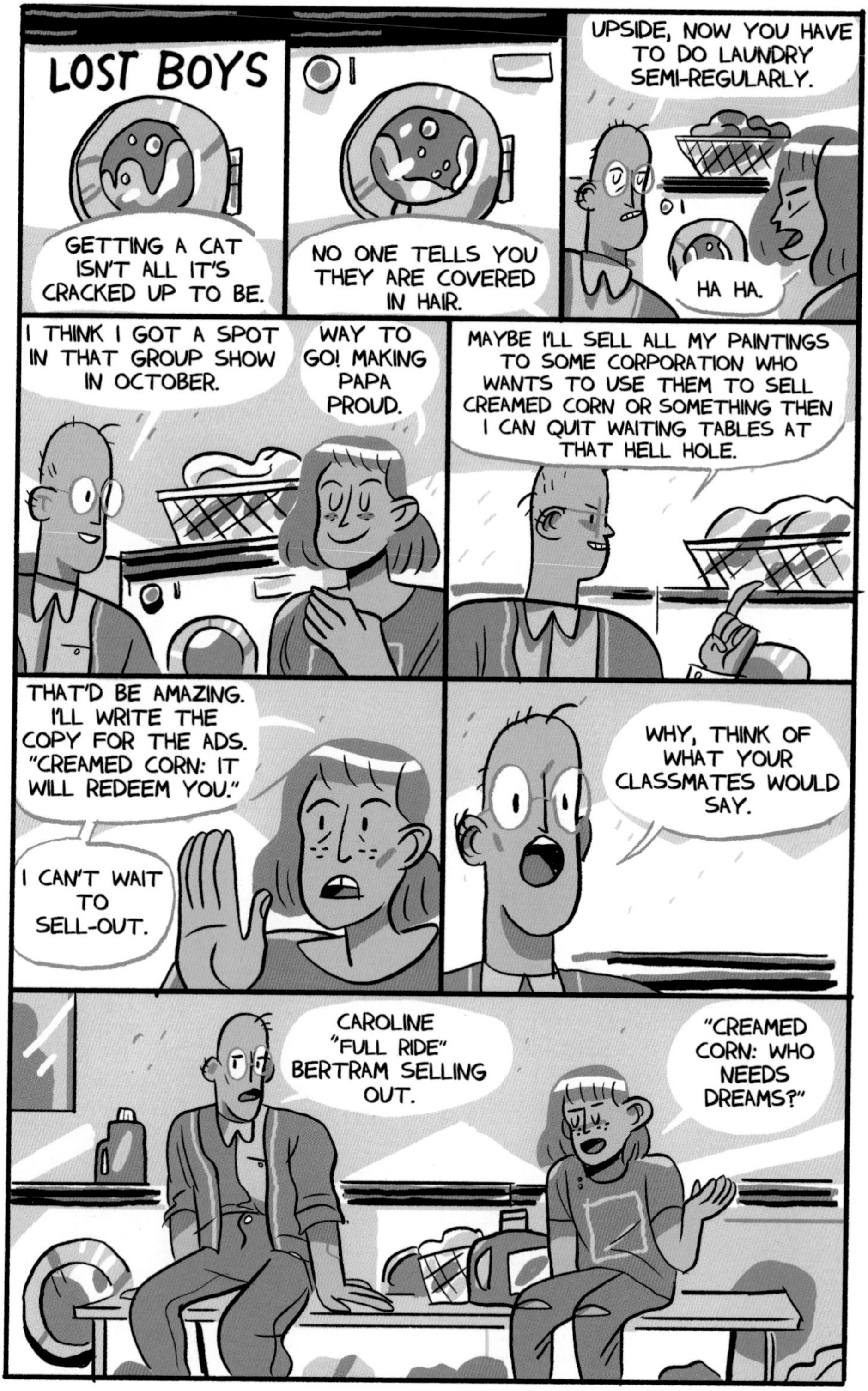
LOST BOYS
GETTING A CAT ISN'T ALL IT'S CRACKED UP TO BE.
NO ONE TELLS YOU THEY ARE COVERED IN HAIR.
UPSIDE, NOW YOU HAVE TO DO LAUNDRY SEMI-REGULARLY.
HA HA.
I THINK I GOT A SPOT IN THAT GROUP SHOW IN OCTOBER.
WAY TO GO! MAKING PAPA PROUD.
MAYBE I'LL SELL ALL MY PAINTINGS TO SOME CORPORATION WHO WANTS TO USE THEM TO SELL CREAMED CORN OR SOMETHING THEN I CAN QUIT WAITING TABLES AT THAT HELL HOLE.
THAT'D BE AMAZING. I'LL WRITE THE COPY FOR THE ADS. "CREAMED CORN: IT WILL REDEEM YOU."
I CAN'T WAIT TO SELL-OUT.
WHY, THINK OF WHAT YOUR CLASSMATES WOULD SAY.
CAROLINE "FULL RIDE" BERTRAM SELLING OUT.
"CREAMED CORN: WHO NEEDS DREAMS?"

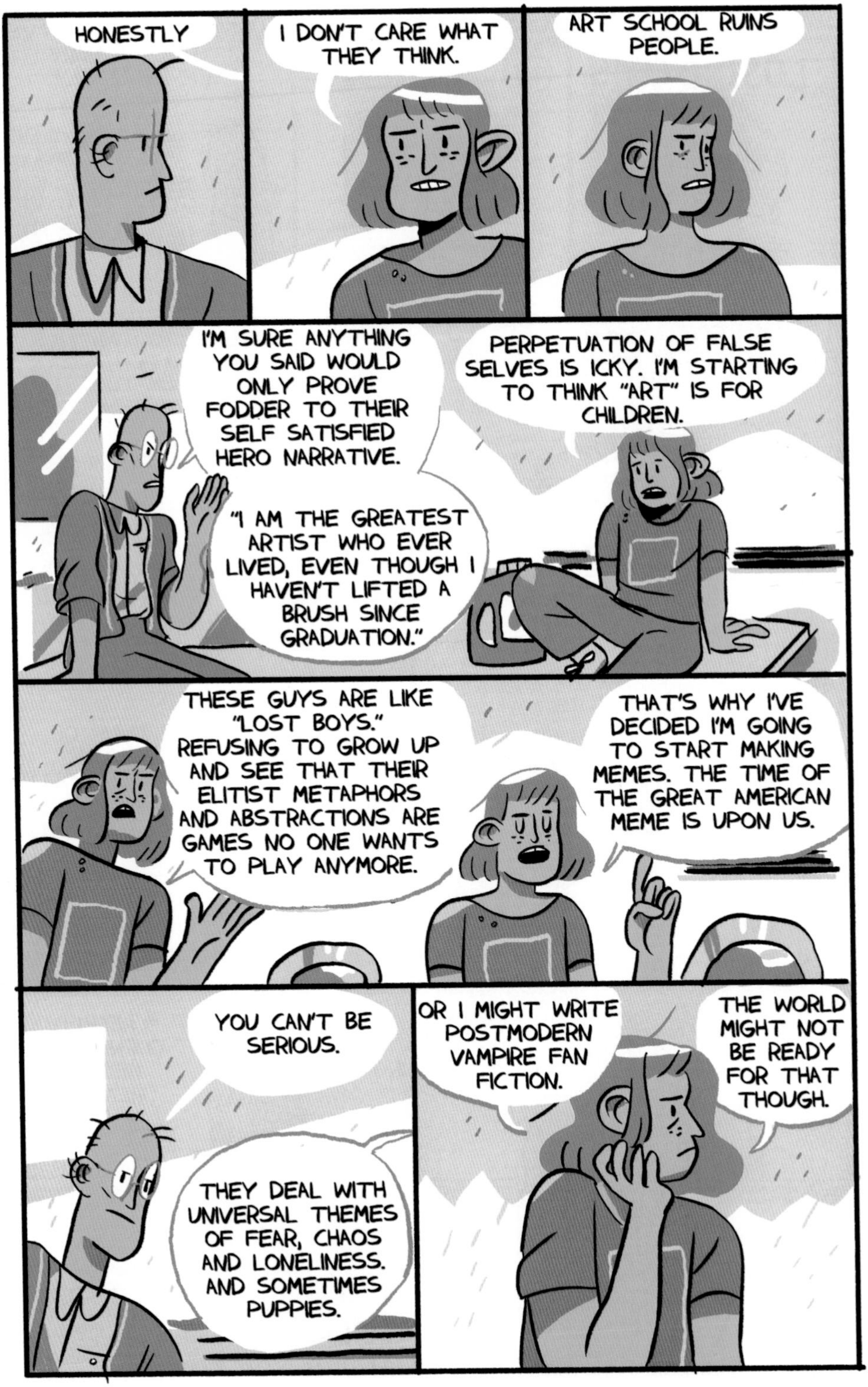
HONESTLY
I DON'T CARE WHAT THEY THINK.
ART SCHOOL RUINS PEOPLE.
I'M SURE ANYTHING YOU SAID WOULD ONLY PROVE FODDER TO THEIR SELF SATISFIED HERO NARRATIVE.
"I AM THE GREATEST ARTIST WHO EVER LIVED, EVEN THOUGH I HAVEN'T LIFTED A BRUSH SINCE GRADUATION."
PERPETUATION OF FALSE SELVES IS ICKY. I'M STARTING TO THINK "ART" IS FOR CHILDREN.
THESE GUYS ARE LIKE "LOST BOYS." REFUSING TO GROW UP AND SEE THAT THEIR ELITIST METAPHORS AND ABSTRACTIONS ARE GAMES NO ONE WANTS TO PLAY ANYMORE.
THAT'S WHY I'VE DECIDED I'M GOING TO START MAKING MEMES. THE TIME OF THE GREAT AMERICAN MEME IS UPON US.
YOU CAN'T BE SERIOUS.
THEY DEAL WITH UNIVERSAL THEMES OF FEAR, CHAOS AND LONELINESS. AND SOMETIMES PUPPIES.
OR I MIGHT WRITE POSTMODERN VAMPIRE FAN FICTION.
THE WORLD MIGHT NOT BE READY FOR THAT THOUGH.

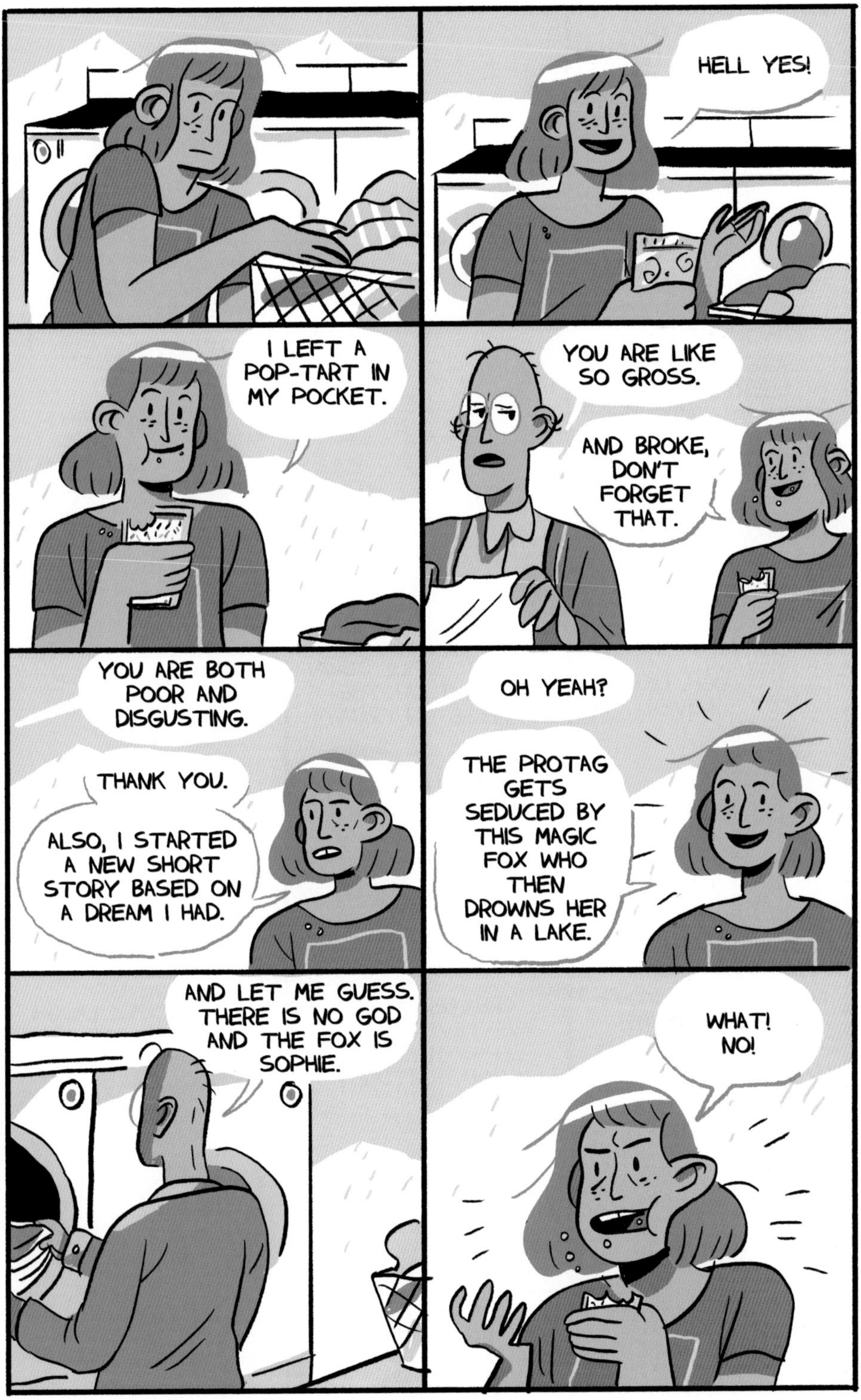
HELL YES!
I LEFT A POP-TART IN MY POCKET.
YOU ARE LIKE SO GROSS.
AND BROKE, DON'T FORGET THAT.
YOU ARE BOTH POOR AND DISGUSTING.
THANK YOU.
ALSO, I STARTED A NEW SHORT STORY BASED ON A DREAM I HAD.
OH YEAH?
THE PROTAG GETS SEDUCED BY THIS MAGIC FOX WHO THEN DROWNS HER IN A LAKE.
AND LET ME GUESS. THERE IS NO GOD AND THE FOX IS SOPHIE.
WHAT! NO!

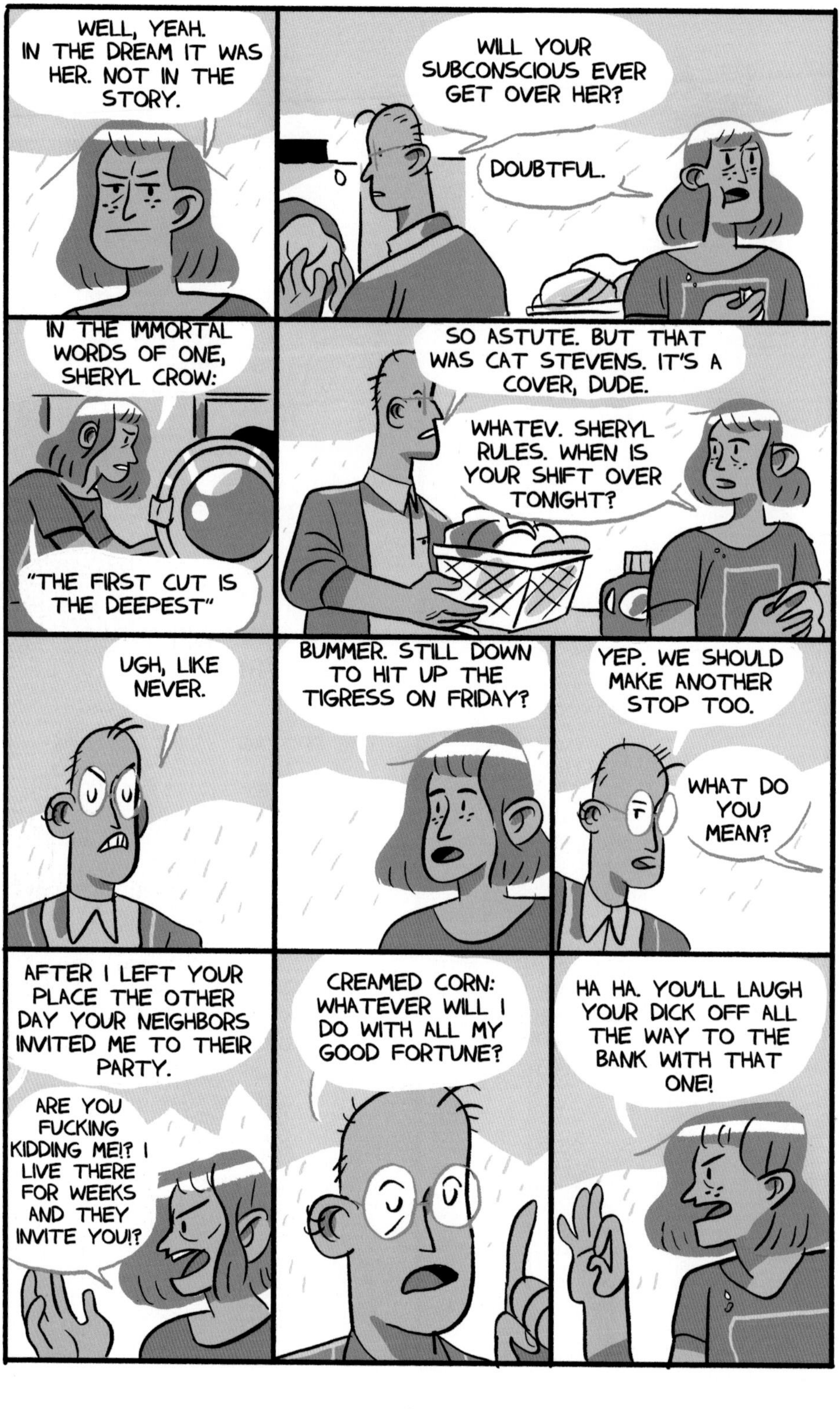
WELL, YEAH. IN THE DREAM IT WAS HER. NOT IN THE STORY.
WILL YOUR SUBCONSCIOUS EVER GET OVER HER?
DOUBTFUL.
IN THE IMMORTAL WORDS OF ONE, SHERYL CROW:
"THE FIRST CUT IS THE DEEPEST"
SO ASTUTE. BUT THAT WAS CAT STEVENS. IT'S A COVER, DUDE.
WHATEV. SHERYL RULES. WHEN IS YOUR SHIFT OVER TONIGHT?
UGH, LIKE NEVER.
BUMMER. STILL DOWN TO HIT UP THE TIGRESS ON FRIDAY?
YEP. WE SHOULD MAKE ANOTHER STOP TOO.
WHAT DO YOU MEAN?
AFTER I LEFT YOUR PLACE THE OTHER DAY YOUR NEIGHBORS INVITED ME TO THEIR PARTY.
ARE YOU FUCKING KIDDING ME!? I LIVE THERE FOR WEEKS AND THEY INVITE YOU!?
CREAMED CORN: WHATEVER WILL I DO WITH ALL MY GOOD FORTUNE?
HA HA. YOU'LL LAUGH YOUR DICK OFF ALL THE WAY TO THE BANK WITH THAT ONE!

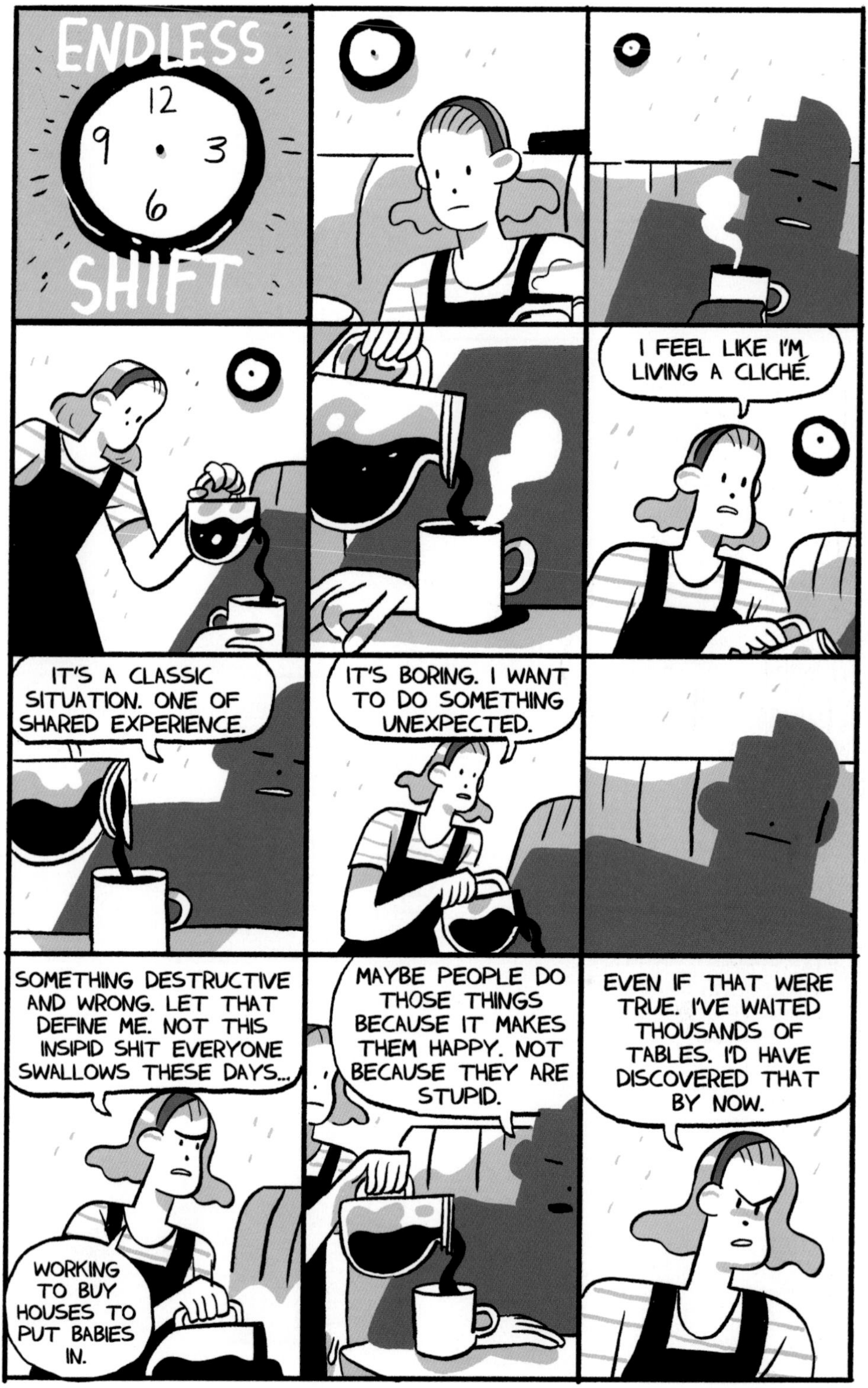
ENDLESS
12
9
3
6
SHIFT
I FEEL LIKE I'M LIVING A CLICHÉ.
IT'S A CLASSIC SITUATION. ONE OF SHARED EXPERIENCE.
IT'S BORING. I WANT TO DO SOMETHING UNEXPECTED.
SOMETHING DESTRUCTIVE AND WRONG. LET THAT DEFINE ME. NOT THIS INSIPID SHIT EVERYONE SWALLOWS THESE DAYS...
WORKING TO BUY HOUSES TO PUT BABIES IN.
MAYBE PEOPLE DO THOSE THINGS BECAUSE IT MAKES THEM HAPPY. NOT BECAUSE THEY ARE STUPID.
EVEN IF THAT WERE TRUE. I'VE WAITED THOUSANDS OF TABLES. I'D HAVE DISCOVERED THAT BY NOW.

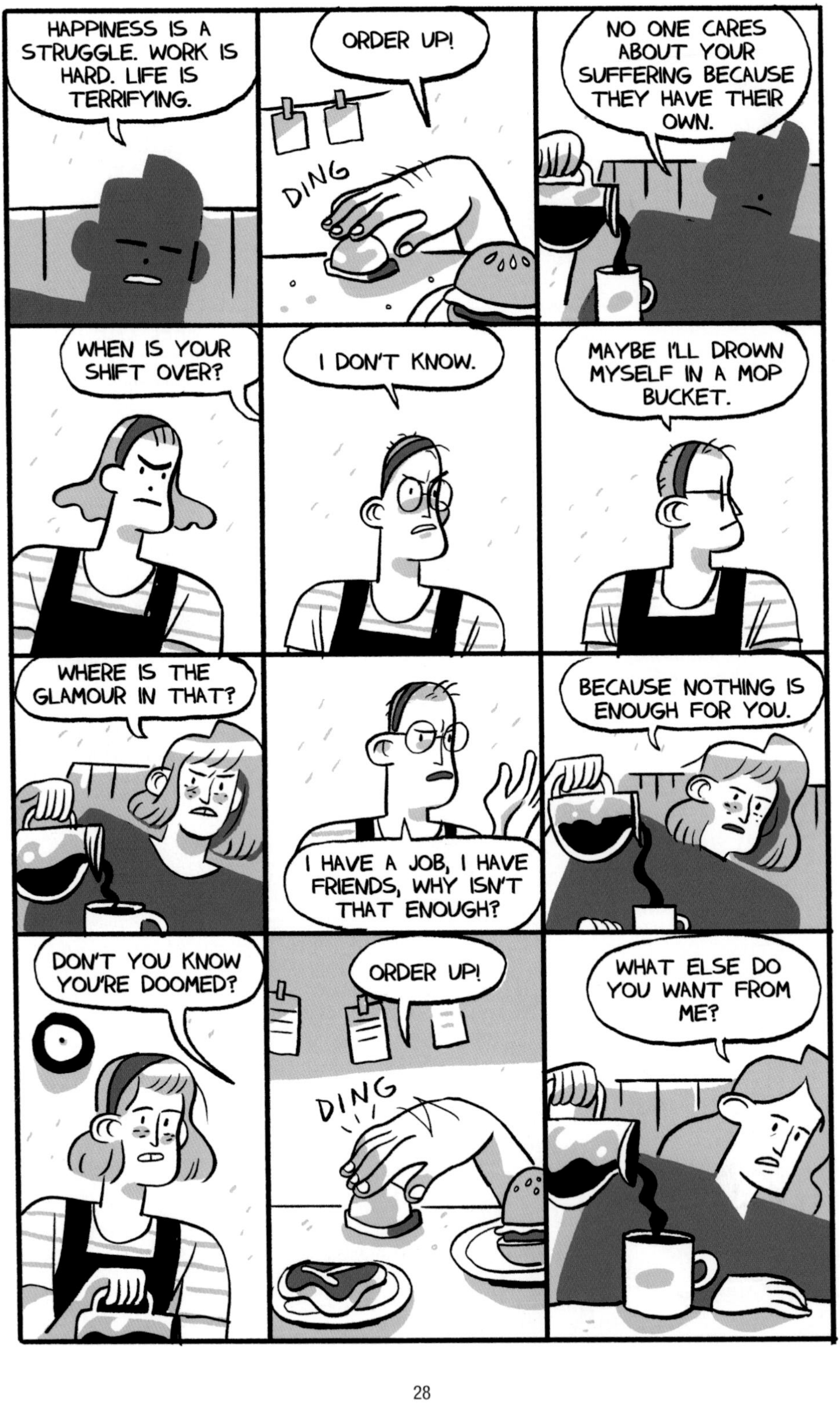
HAPPINESS IS A STRUGGLE. WORK IS HARD. LIFE IS TERRIFYING.
ORDER UP!
DING
NO ONE CARES ABOUT YOUR SUFFERING BECAUSE THEY HAVE THEIR OWN.
WHEN IS YOUR SHIFT OVER?
I DON'T KNOW.
MAYBE I'LL DROWN MYSELF IN A MOP BUCKET.
WHERE IS THE GLAMOUR IN THAT?
I HAVE A JOB, I HAVE FRIENDS, WHY ISN'T THAT ENOUGH?
BECAUSE NOTHING IS ENOUGH FOR YOU.
DON'T YOU KNOW YOU'RE DOOMED?
ORDER UP!
DING
WHAT ELSE DO YOU WANT FROM ME?

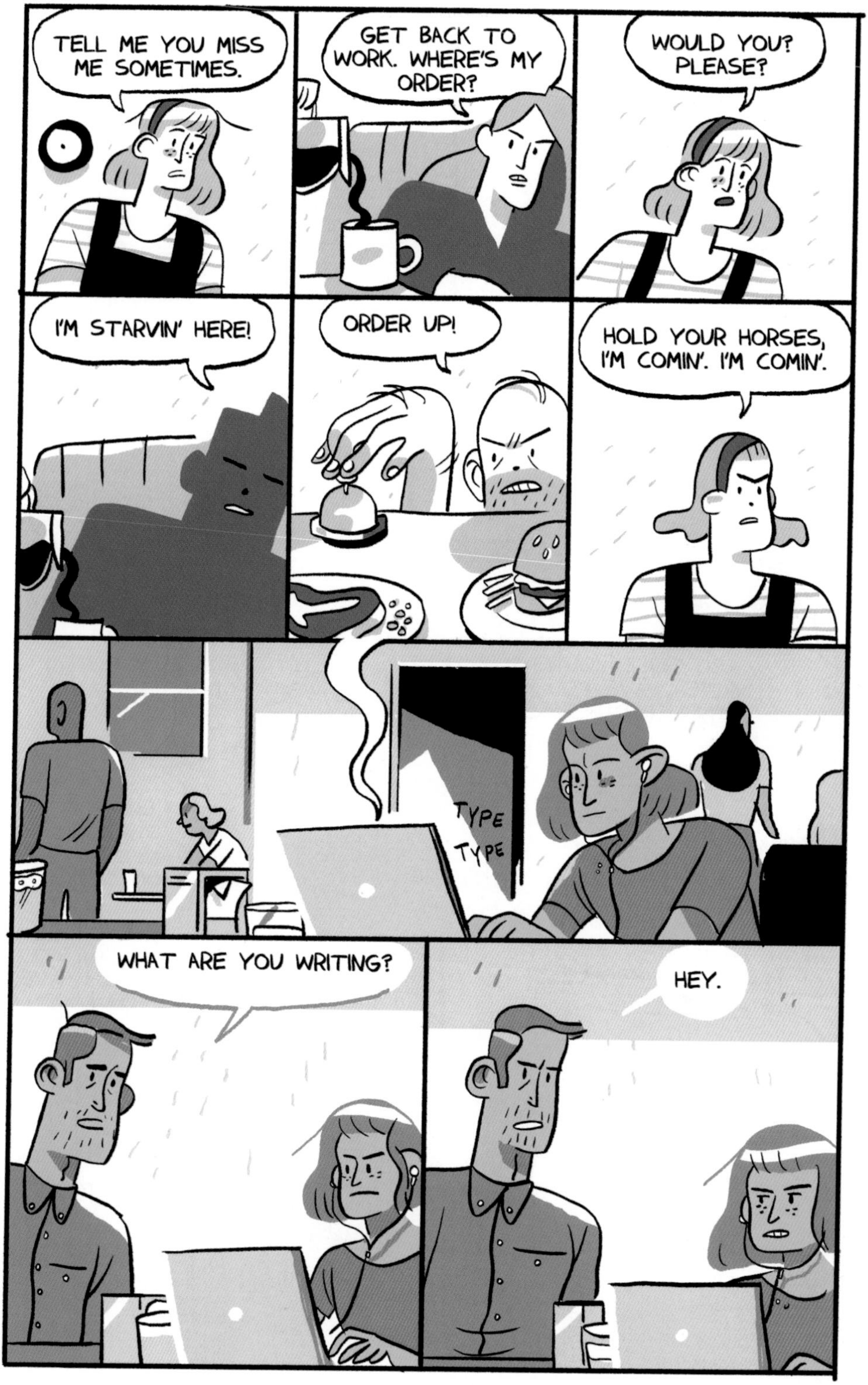
TELL ME YOU MISS ME SOMETIMES.
GET BACK TO WORK. WHERE'S MY ORDER?
WOULD YOU? PLEASE?
I'M STARVIN' HERE!
ORDER UP!
HOLD YOUR HORSES, I'M COMIN'. I'M COMIN'.
TYPE TYPE
WHAT ARE YOU WRITING?
HEY.

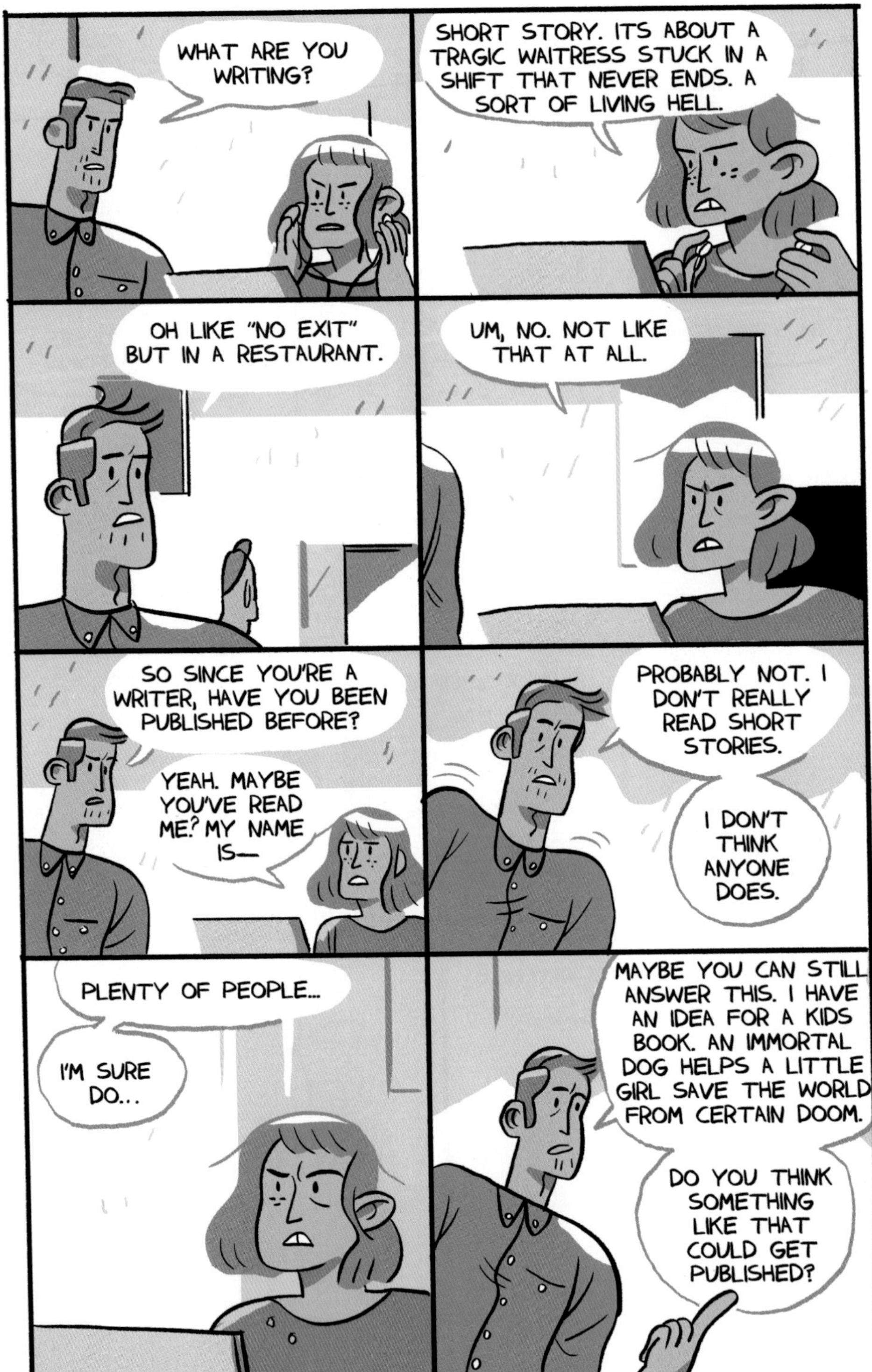
WHAT ARE YOU WRITING?
SHORT STORY. ITS ABOUT A TRAGIC WAITRESS STUCK IN A SHIFT THAT NEVER ENDS. A SORT OF LIVING HELL.
OH LIKE "NO EXIT" BUT IN A RESTAURANT.
UM, NO. NOT LIKE THAT AT ALL.
SO SINCE YOU'RE A WRITER, HAVE YOU BEEN PUBLISHED BEFORE?
YEAH. MAYBE YOU'VE READ ME? MY NAME IS—
PROBABLY NOT. I DON'T REALLY READ SHORT STORIES.
I DON'T THINK ANYONE DOES.
PLENTY OF PEOPLE...
I'M SURE DO...
MAYBE YOU CAN STILL ANSWER THIS. I HAVE AN IDEA FOR A KIDS BOOK. AN IMMORTAL DOG HELPS A LITTLE GIRL SAVE THE WORLD FROM CERTAIN DOOM.
DO YOU THINK SOMETHING LIKE THAT COULD GET PUBLISHED?

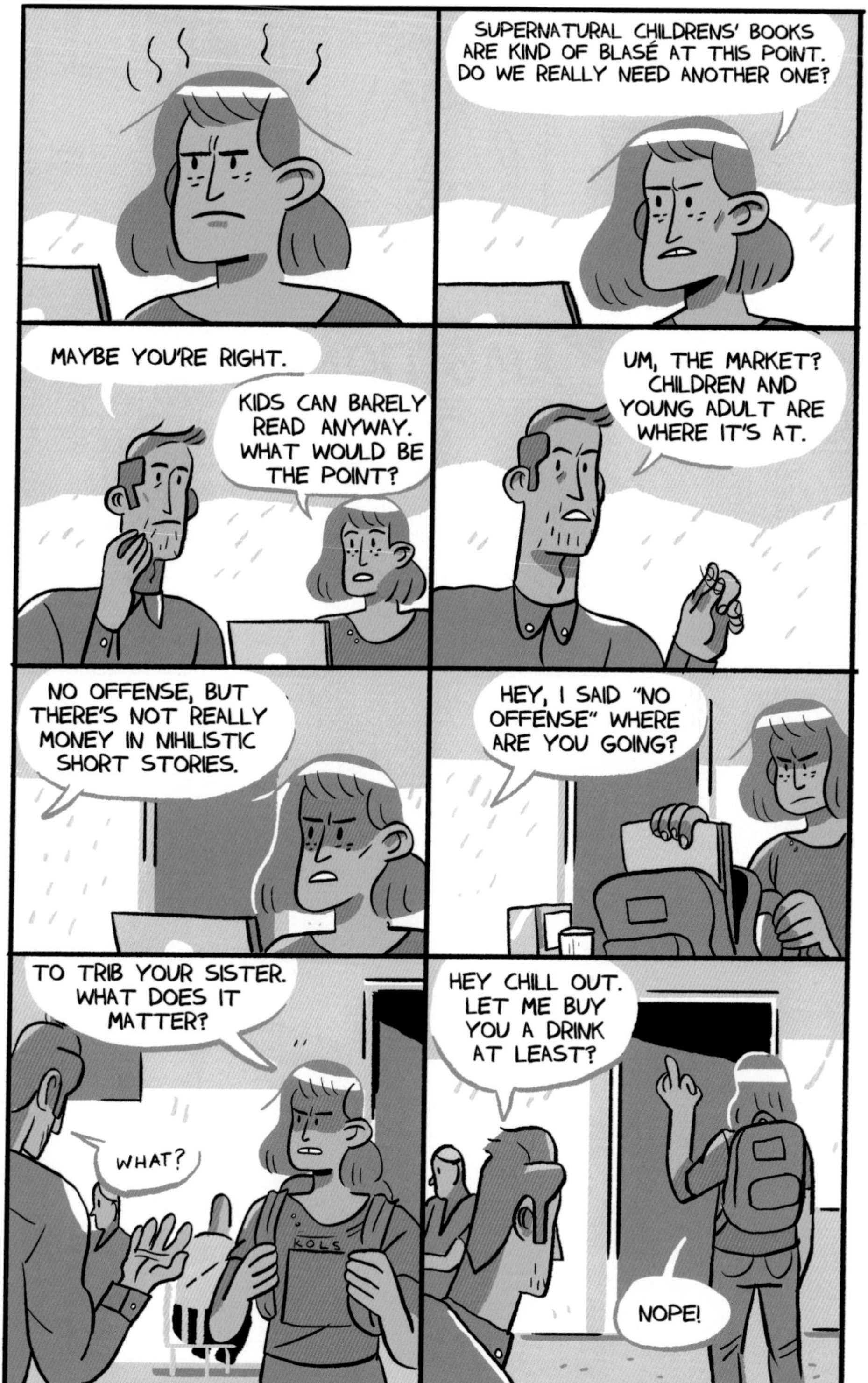
SUPERNATURAL CHILDRENS' BOOKS ARE KIND OF BLASÉ AT THIS POINT. DO WE REALLY NEED ANOTHER ONE?
MAYBE YOU'RE RIGHT.
KIDS CAN BARELY READ ANYWAY. WHAT WOULD BE THE POINT?
UM, THE MARKET? CHILDREN AND YOUNG ADULT ARE WHERE IT'S AT.
NO OFFENSE, BUT THERE'S NOT REALLY MONEY IN NIHILISTIC SHORT STORIES.
HEY, I SAID "NO OFFENSE" WHERE ARE YOU GOING?
TO TRIB YOUR SISTER. WHAT DOES IT MATTER?
WHAT?
KOLS
HEY CHILL OUT. LET ME BUY YOU A DRINK AT LEAST?
NOPE!

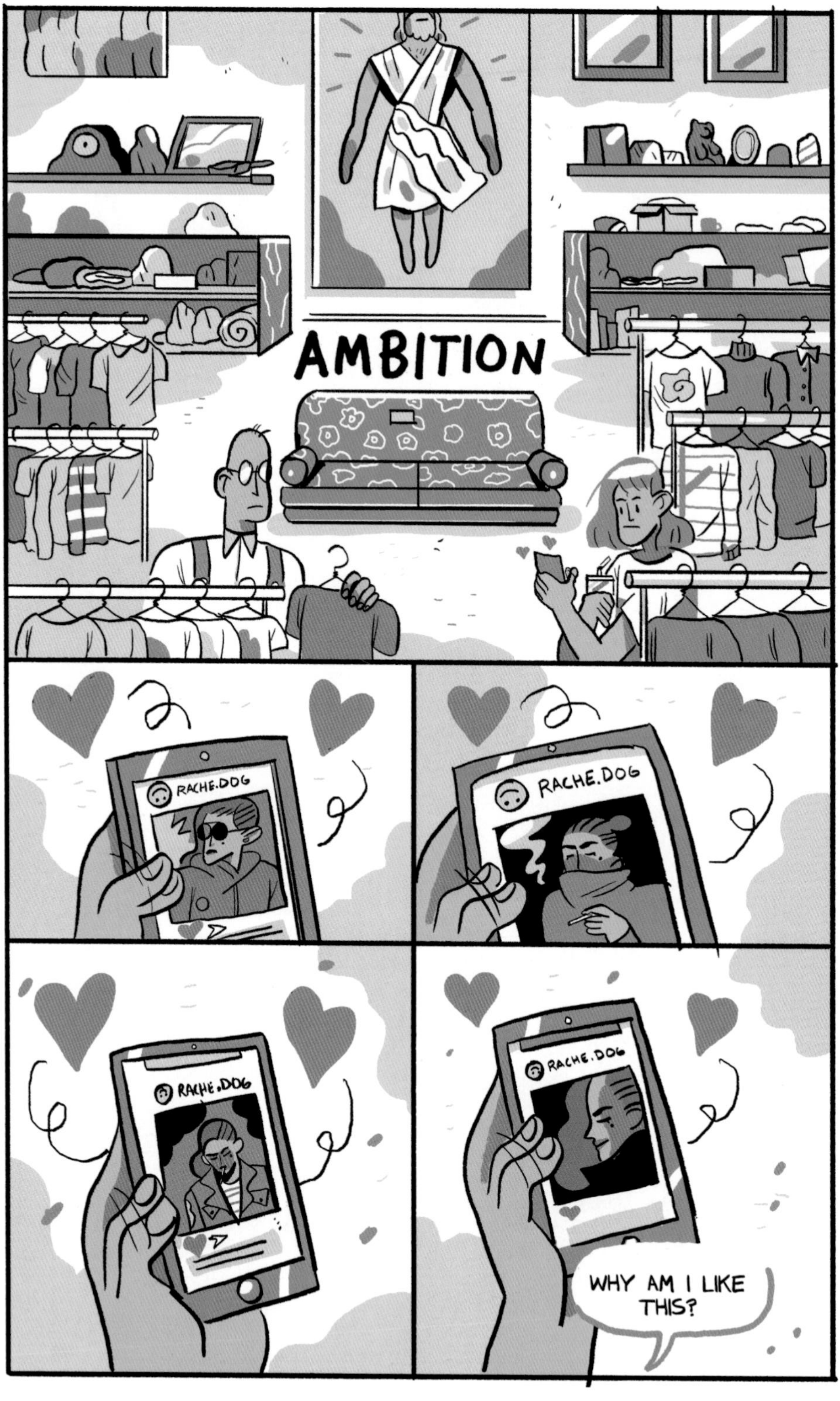
AMBITION
RACHE.DOG
RACHE.DOG
RACHE.DOG
RACHE.DOG
WHY AM I LIKE THIS?

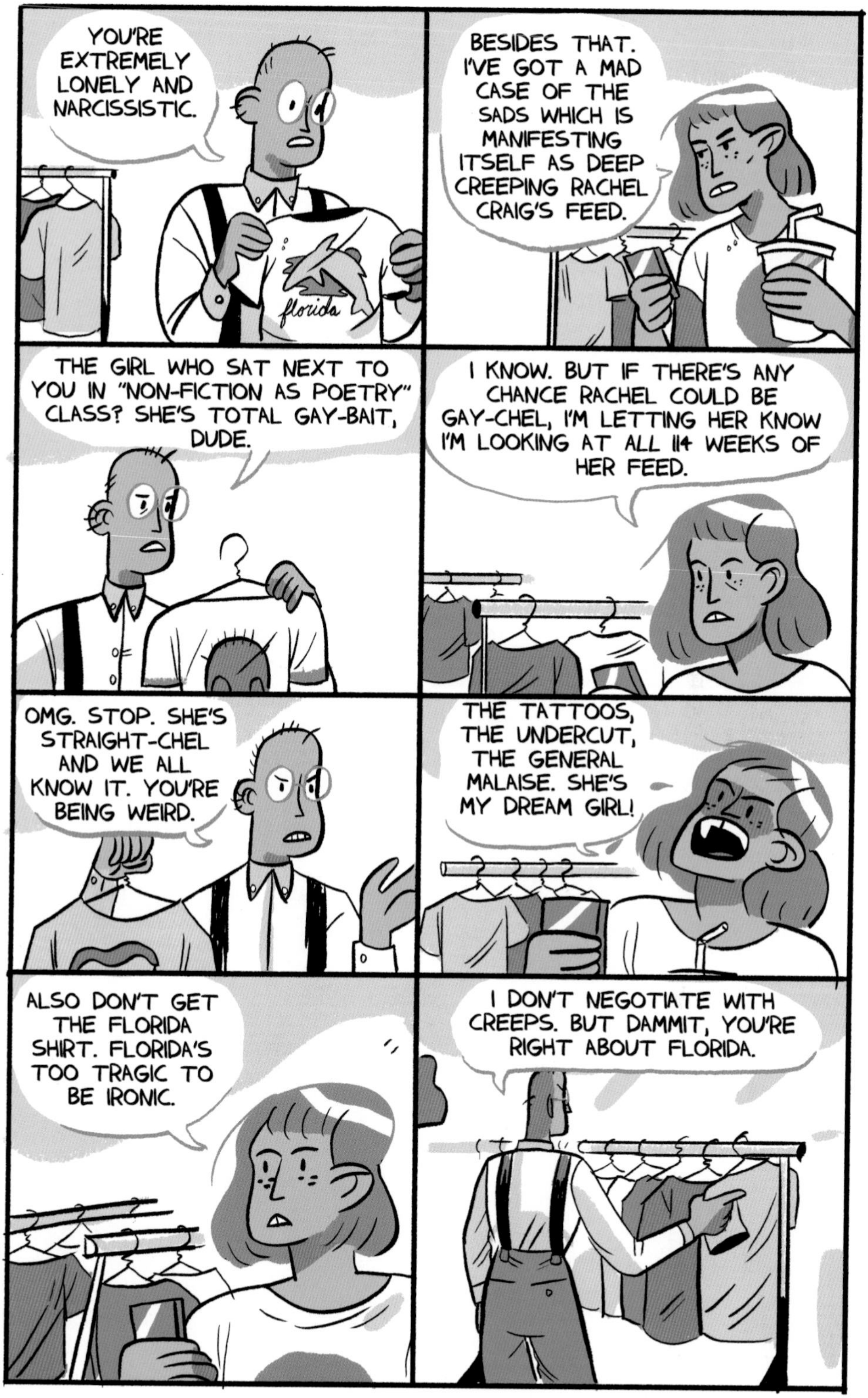
YOU'RE EXTREMELY LONELY AND NARCISSISTIC.
BESIDES THAT. I'VE GOT A MAD CASE OF THE SADS WHICH IS MANIFESTING ITSELF AS DEEP CREEPING RACHEL CRAIG'S FEED.
florida
THE GIRL WHO SAT NEXT TO YOU IN "NON-FICTION AS POETRY" CLASS? SHE'S TOTAL GAY-BAIT, DUDE.
I KNOW. BUT IF THERE'S ANY CHANCE RACHEL COULD BE GAY-CHEL, I'M LETTING HER KNOW I'M LOOKING AT ALL 114 WEEKS OF HER FEED.
OMG. STOP. SHE'S STRAIGHT-CHEL AND WE ALL KNOW IT. YOU'RE BEING WEIRD.
THE TATTOOS, THE UNDERCUT, THE GENERAL MALAISE. SHE'S MY DREAM GIRL!
ALSO DON'T GET THE FLORIDA SHIRT. FLORIDA'S TOO TRAGIC TO BE IRONIC.
I DON'T NEGOTIATE WITH CREEPS. BUT DAMMIT, YOU'RE RIGHT ABOUT FLORIDA.

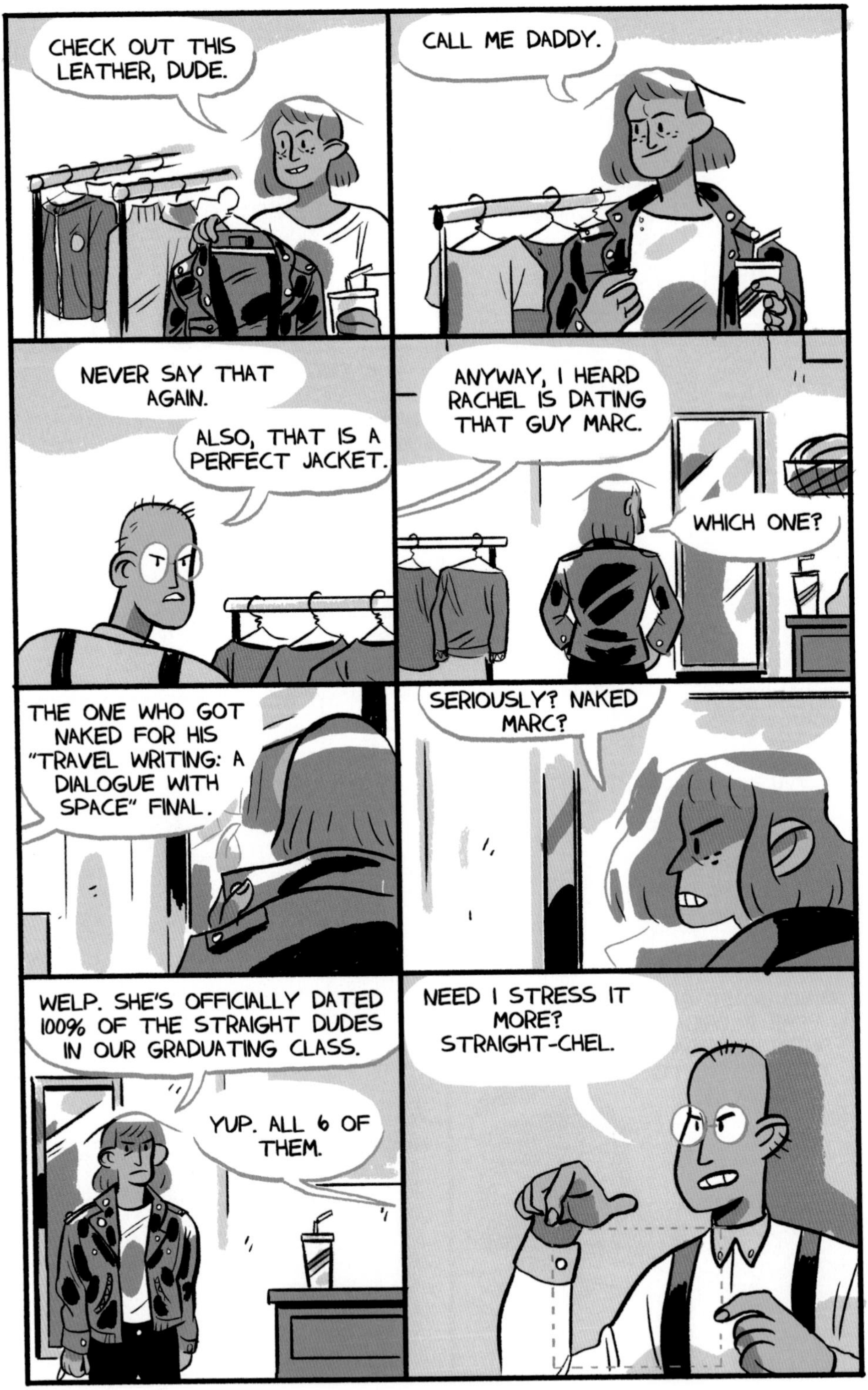
CHECK OUT THIS LEATHER, DUDE.
CALL ME DADDY.
NEVER SAY THAT AGAIN.
ALSO, THAT IS A PERFECT JACKET.
ANYWAY, I HEARD RACHEL IS DATING THAT GUY MARC.
WHICH ONE?
THE ONE WHO GOT NAKED FOR HIS "TRAVEL WRITING: A DIALOGUE WITH SPACE" FINAL.
SERIOUSLY? NAKED MARC?
WELP. SHE'S OFFICIALLY DATED 100% OF THE STRAIGHT DUDES IN OUR GRADUATING CLASS.
YUP. ALL 6 OF THEM.
NEED I STRESS IT MORE? STRAIGHT-CHEL.

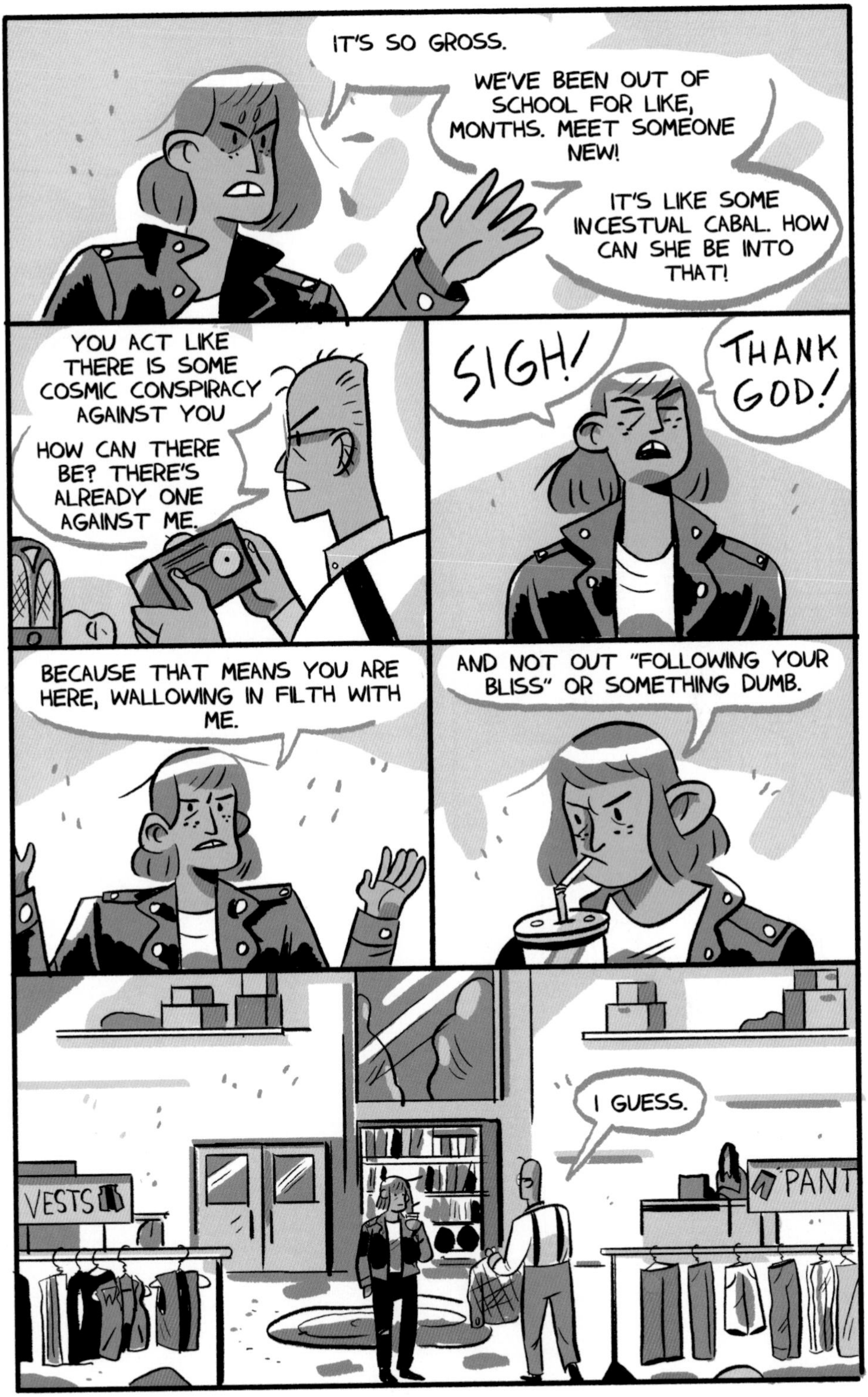
IT'S SO GROSS.
WE'VE BEEN OUT OF SCHOOL FOR LIKE, MONTHS. MEET SOMEONE NEW!
IT'S LIKE SOME INCESTUAL CABAL. HOW CAN SHE BE INTO THAT!
YOU ACT LIKE THERE IS SOME COSMIC CONSPIRACY AGAINST YOU
HOW CAN THERE BE? THERE'S ALREADY ONE AGAINST ME.
SIGH!
THANK GOD!
BECAUSE THAT MEANS YOU ARE HERE, WALLOWING IN FILTH WITH ME.
AND NOT OUT "FOLLOWING YOUR BLISS" OR SOMETHING DUMB.
VESTS
I GUESS.
PANT

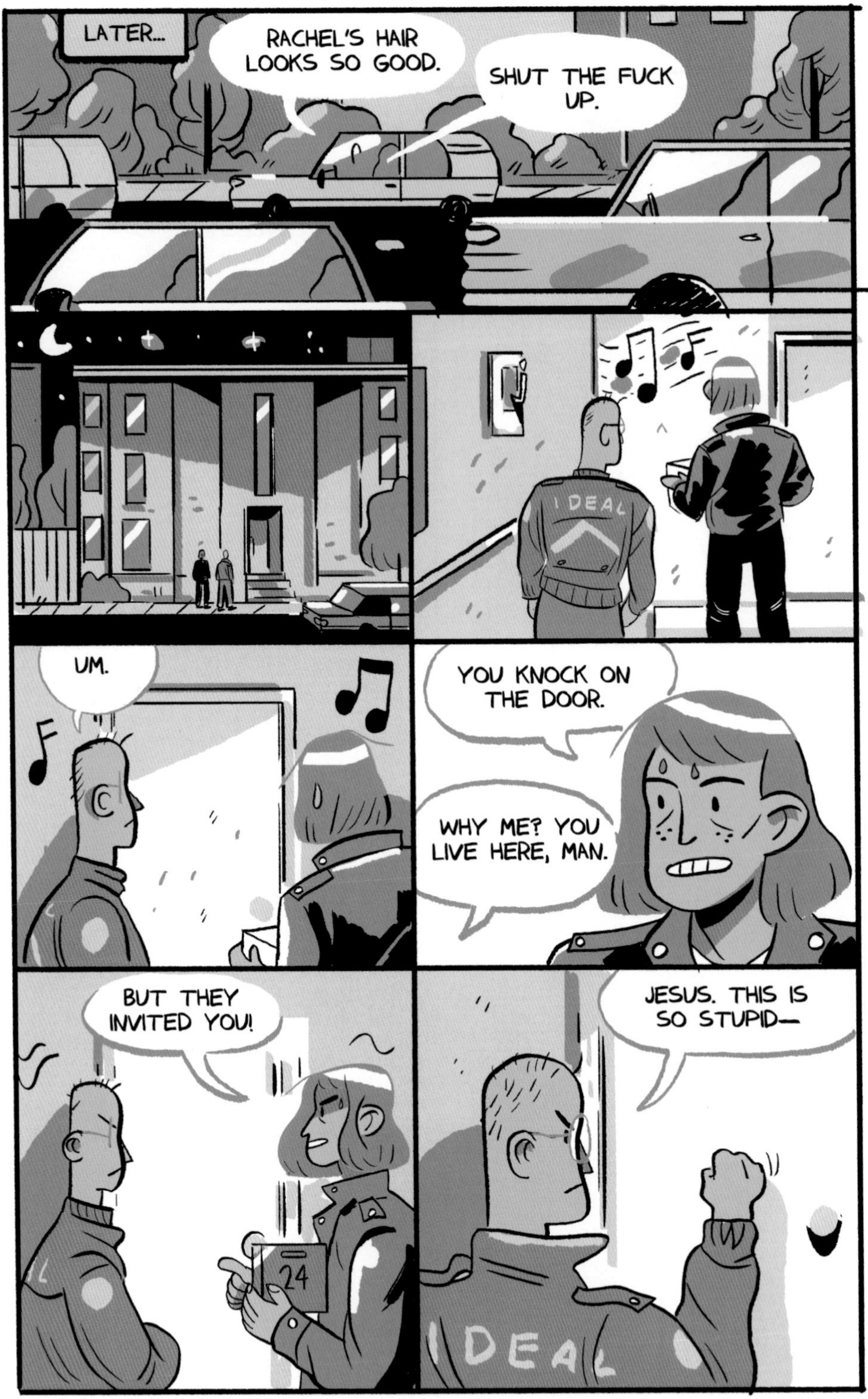
LATER...
RACHEL'S HAIR LOOKS SO GOOD.
SHUT THE FUCK UP.
IDEAL
UM.
YOU KNOCK ON THE DOOR.
WHY ME? YOU LIVE HERE, MAN.
BUT THEY INVITED YOU!
24
JESUS. THIS IS SO STUPID—
IDEAL

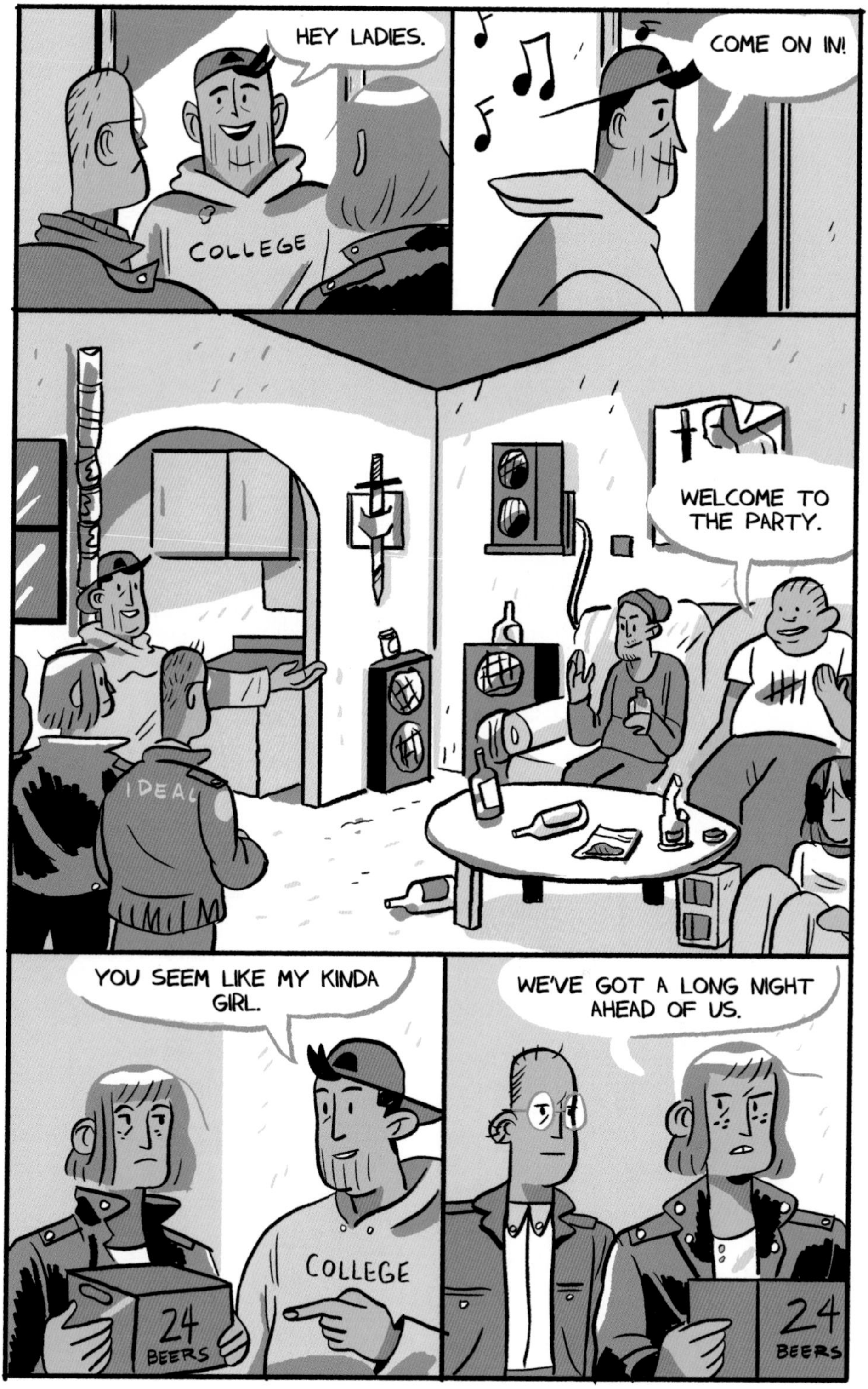
HEY LADIES.
COLLEGE
COME ON IN!
WELCOME TO THE PARTY.
IDEAL
YOU SEEM LIKE MY KINDA GIRL.
COLLEGE
24 BEERS
WE'VE GOT A LONG NIGHT AHEAD OF US.
24 BEERS

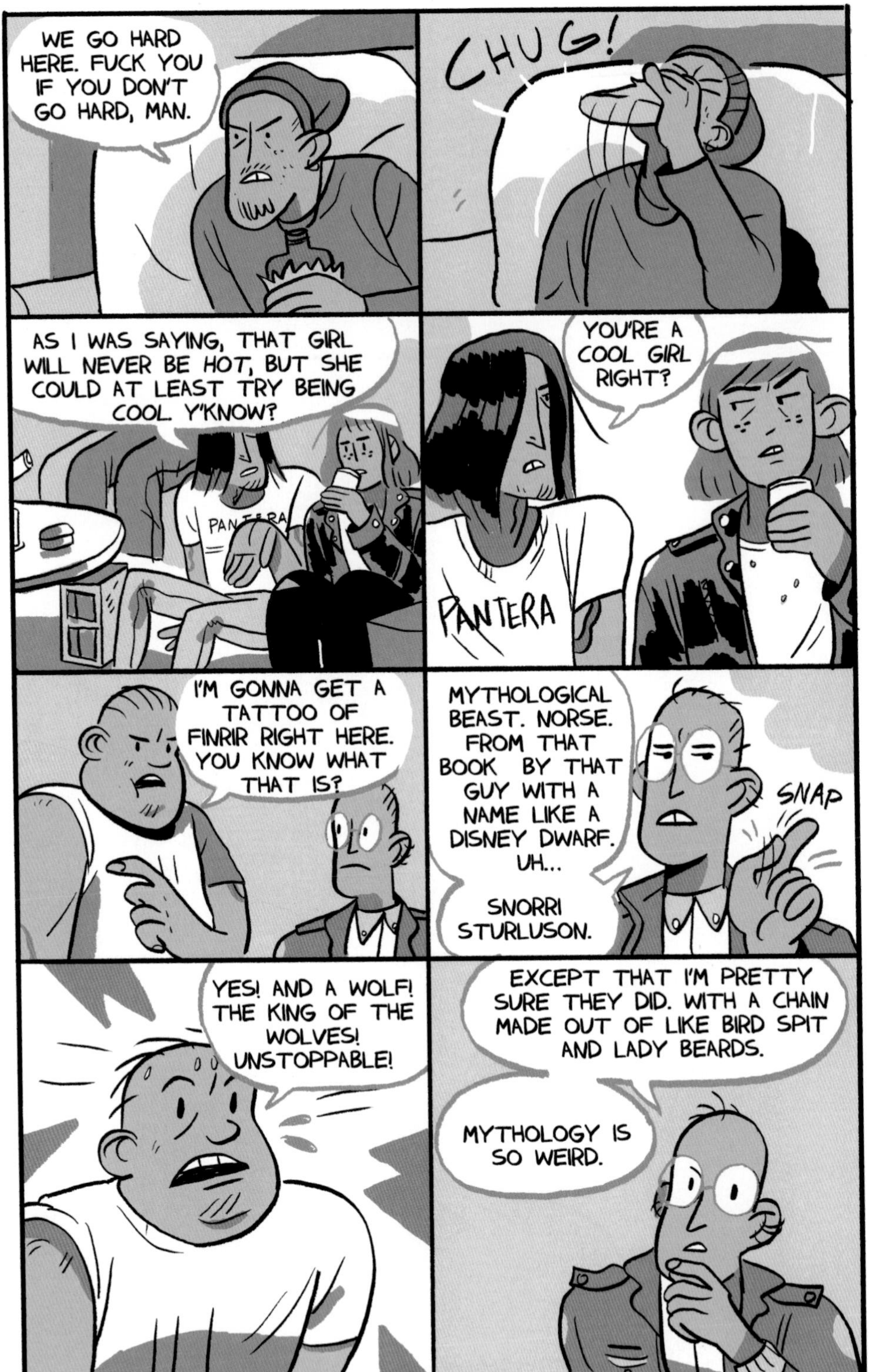
WE GO HARD HERE. FUCK YOU IF YOU DON'T GO HARD, MAN.
CHUG!
AS I WAS SAYING, THAT GIRL WILL NEVER BE HOT, BUT SHE COULD AT LEAST TRY BEING COOL. Y'KNOW?
PANTERA
YOU'RE A COOL GIRL RIGHT?
PANTERA
I'M GONNA GET A TATTOO OF FINRIR RIGHT HERE. YOU KNOW WHAT THAT IS?
MYTHOLOGICAL BEAST. NORSE. FROM THAT BOOK BY THAT GUY WITH A NAME LIKE A DISNEY DWARF. UH...
SNORRI STURLUSON.
SNAP
YES! AND A WOLF! THE KING OF THE WOLVES! UNSTOPPABLE!
EXCEPT THAT I'M PRETTY SURE THEY DID. WITH A CHAIN MADE OUT OF LIKE BIRD SPIT AND LADY BEARDS.
MYTHOLOGY IS SO WEIRD.

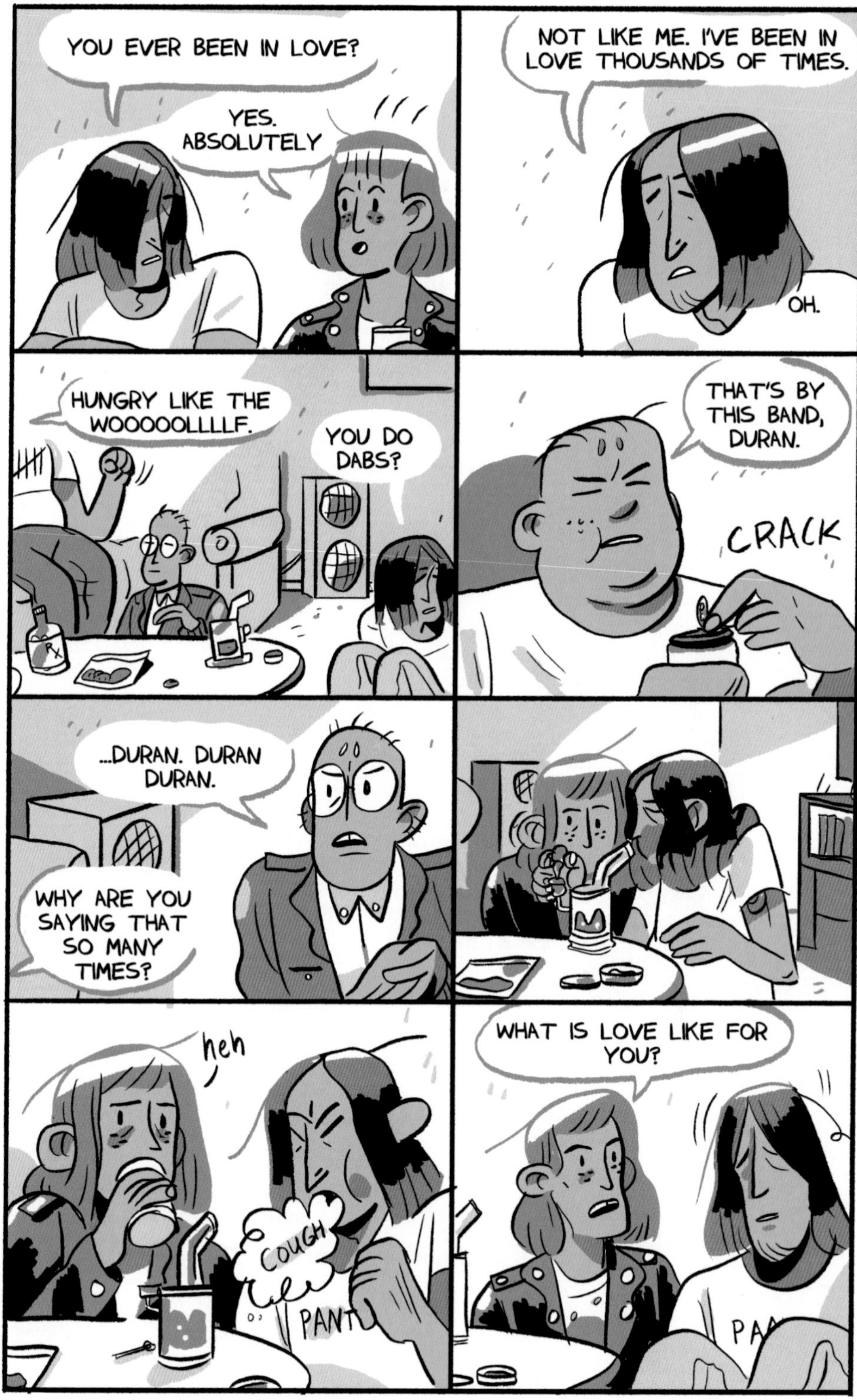
YOU EVER BEEN IN LOVE?
YES. ABSOLUTELY
NOT LIKE ME. I'VE BEEN IN LOVE THOUSANDS OF TIMES.
OH.
HUNGRY LIKE THE WOOOOOLLLLLF.
YOU DO DABS?
THAT'S BY THIS BAND, DURAN.
CRACK
...DURAN. DURAN DURAN.
WHY ARE YOU SAYING THAT SO MANY TIMES?
heh
COUGH
PANT
WHAT IS LOVE LIKE FOR YOU?
PA

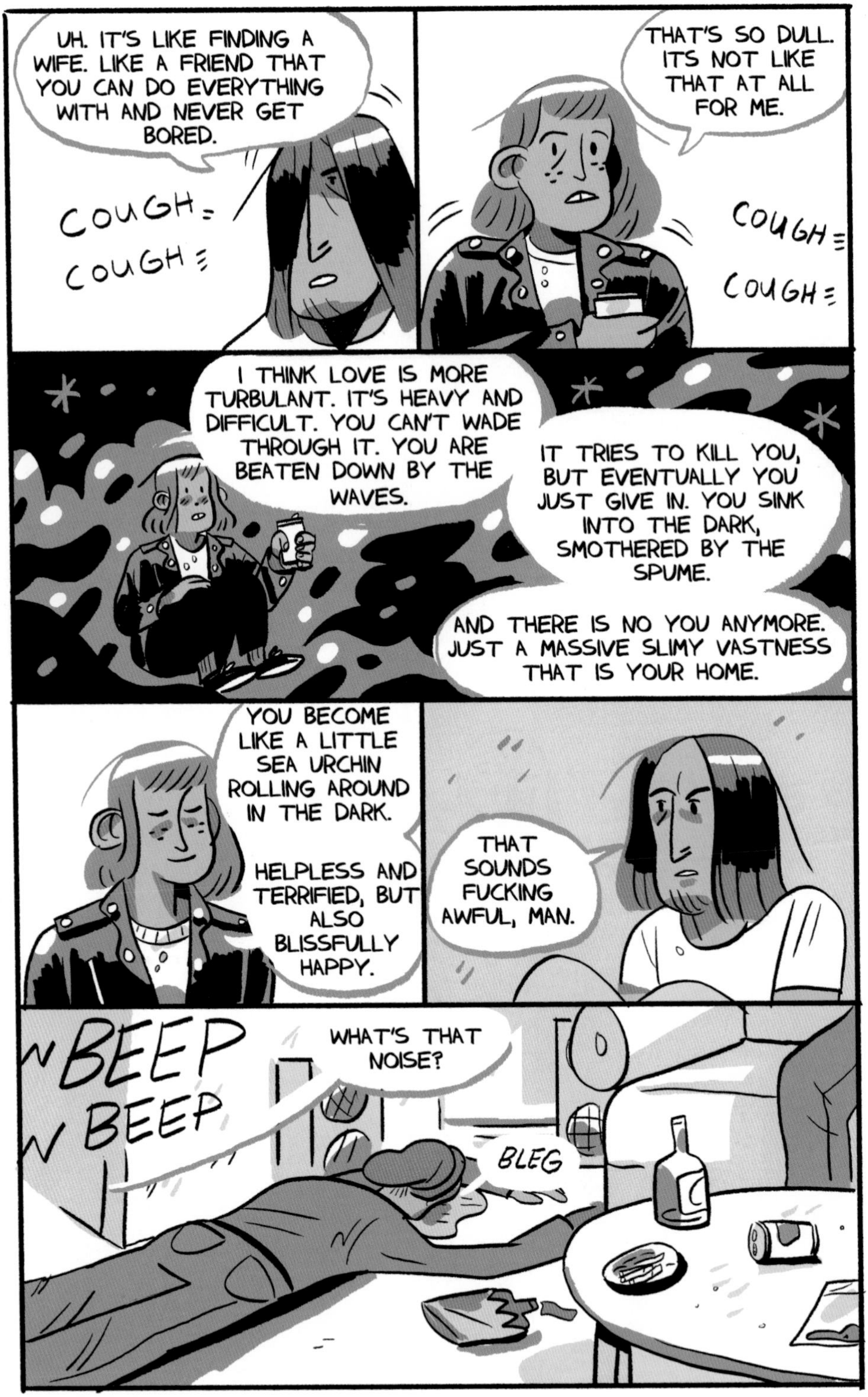
UH. IT'S LIKE FINDING A WIFE. LIKE A FRIEND THAT YOU CAN DO EVERYTHING WITH AND NEVER GET BORED.
COUGH
COUGH
THAT'S SO DULL. ITS NOT LIKE THAT AT ALL FOR ME.
COUGH
COUGH
I THINK LOVE IS MORE TURBULANT. IT'S HEAVY AND DIFFICULT. YOU CAN'T WADE THROUGH IT. YOU ARE BEATEN DOWN BY THE WAVES.
IT TRIES TO KILL YOU, BUT EVENTUALLY YOU JUST GIVE IN. YOU SINK INTO THE DARK, SMOTHERED BY THE SPUME.
AND THERE IS NO YOU ANYMORE. JUST A MASSIVE SLIMY VASTNESS THAT IS YOUR HOME.
YOU BECOME LIKE A LITTLE SEA URCHIN ROLLING AROUND IN THE DARK.
HELPLESS AND TERRIFIED, BUT ALSO BLISSFULLY HAPPY.
THAT SOUNDS FUCKING AWFUL, MAN.
BEEP
BEEP
WHAT'S THAT NOISE?
BLEG

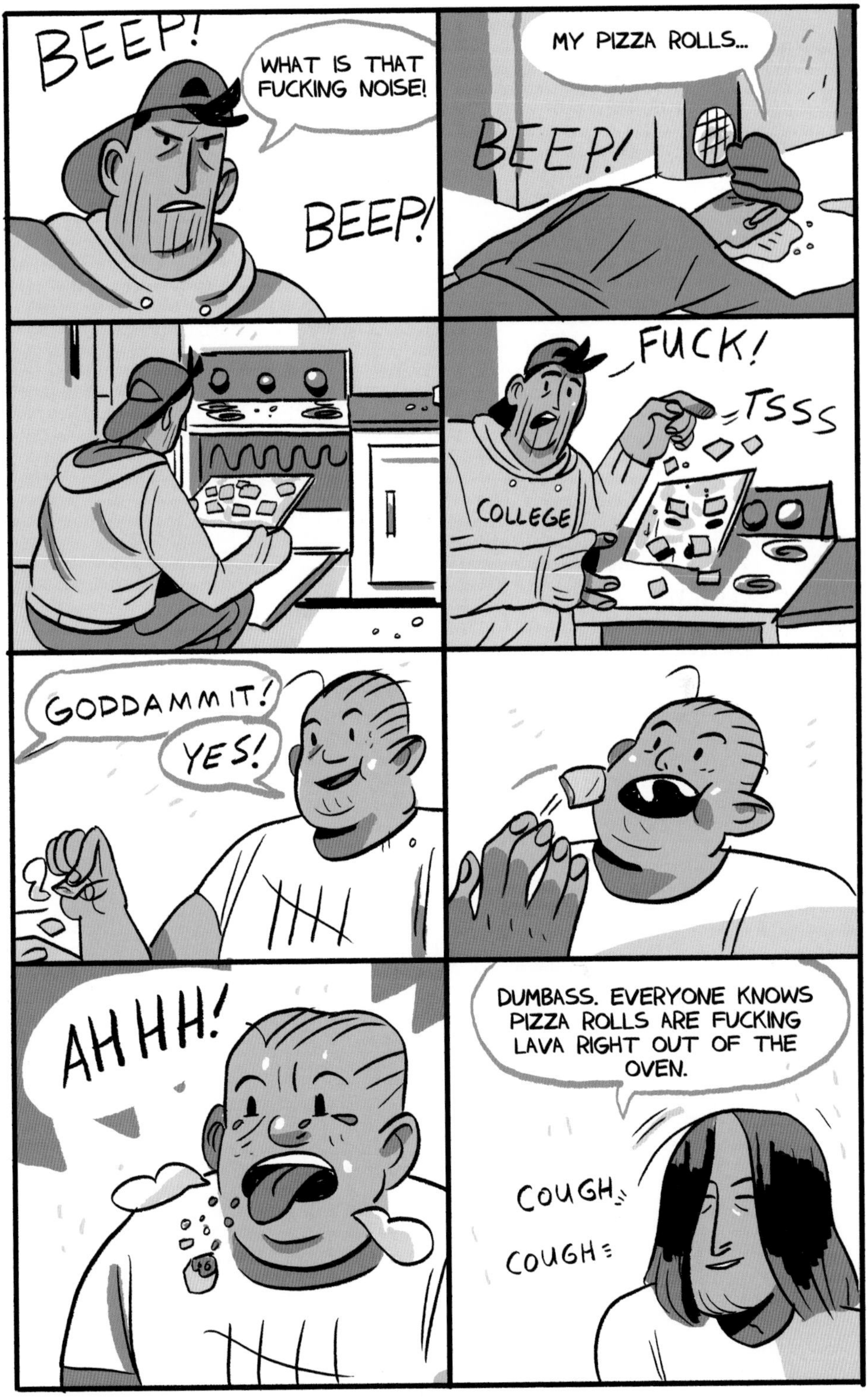
BEEP!
WHAT IS THAT FUCKING NOISE!
BEEP!
MY PIZZA ROLLS...
BEEP!
FUCK!
TSSS
COLLEGE
GODDAMMIT!
YES!
AHHH!
DUMBASS. EVERYONE KNOWS PIZZA ROLLS ARE FUCKING LAVA RIGHT OUT OF THE OVEN.
COUGH
COUGH

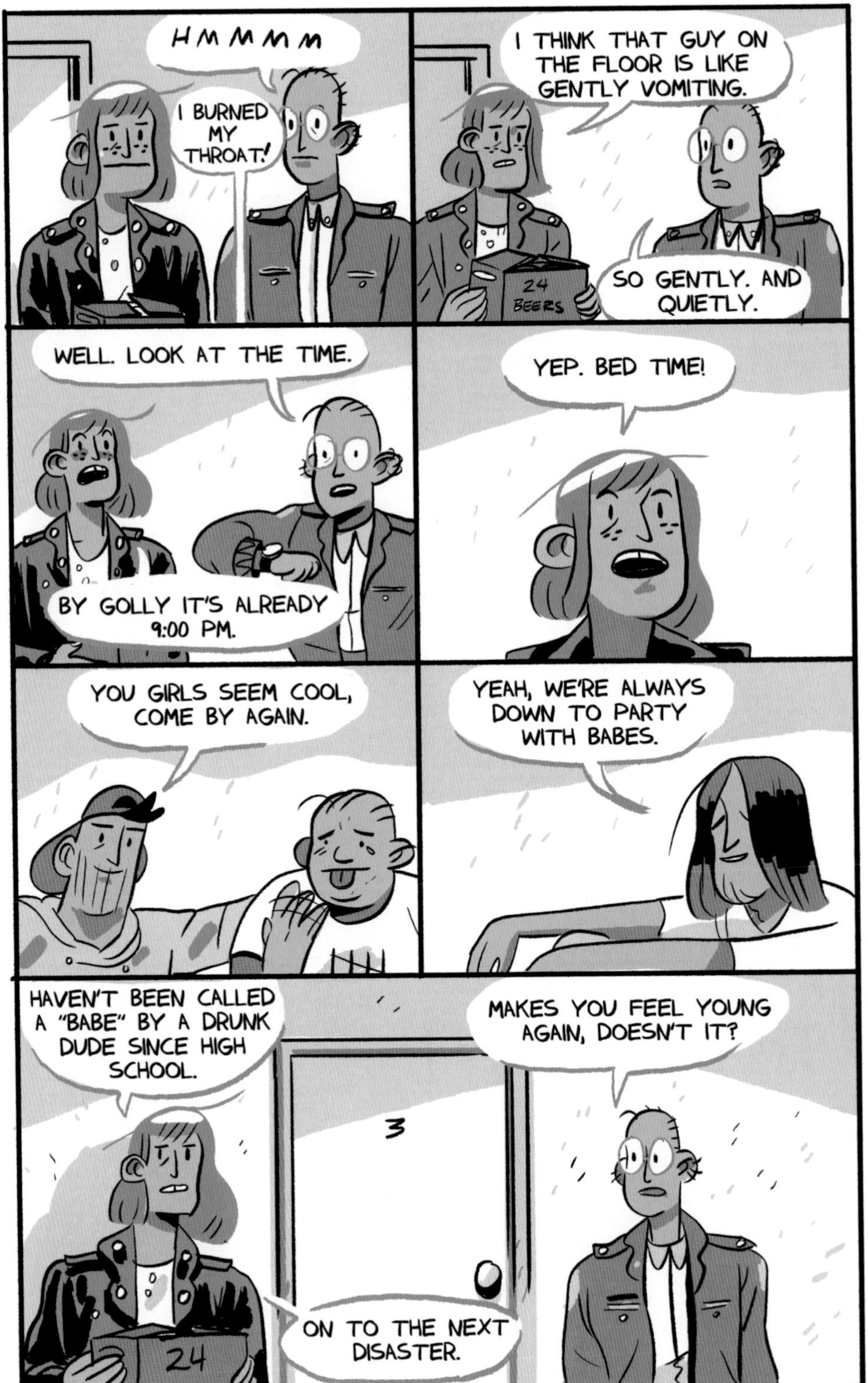
HMMMM
I BURNED MY THROAT!
I THINK THAT GUY ON THE FLOOR IS LIKE GENTLY VOMITING.
24 BEERS
SO GENTLY. AND QUIETLY.
WELL. LOOK AT THE TIME.
BY GOLLY IT'S ALREADY 9:00 PM.
YEP. BED TIME!
YOU GIRLS SEEM COOL, COME BY AGAIN.
YEAH, WE'RE ALWAYS DOWN TO PARTY WITH BABES.
HAVEN'T BEEN CALLED A "BABE" BY A DRUNK DUDE SINCE HIGH SCHOOL.
MAKES YOU FEEL YOUNG AGAIN, DOESN'T IT?
3
ON TO THE NEXT DISASTER.
24

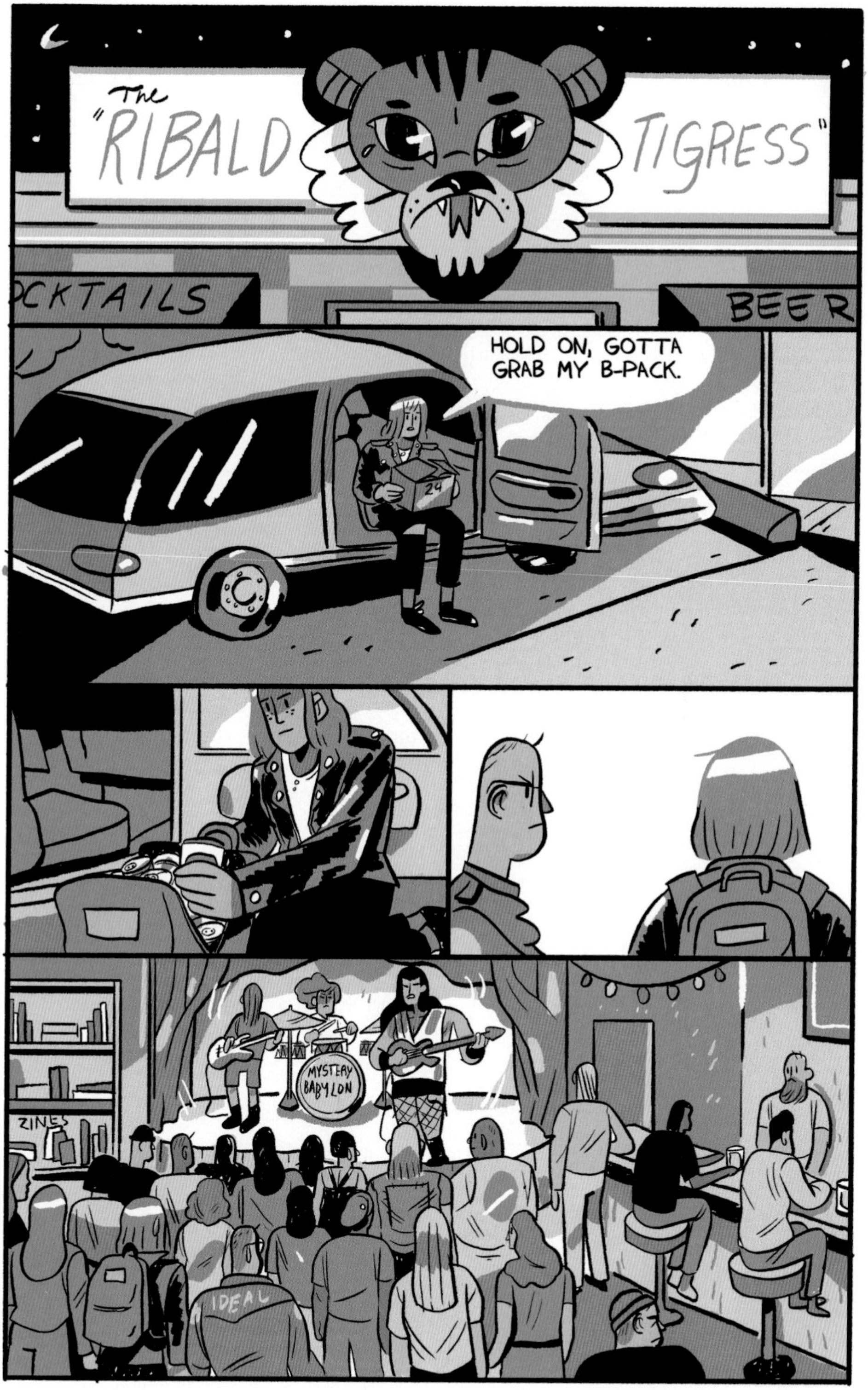
The "RIBALD TIGRESS"
CKTAILS
BEER
HOLD ON, GOTTA GRAB MY B-PACK.
24
MYSTERY BABYLON
ZINES
IDEAL

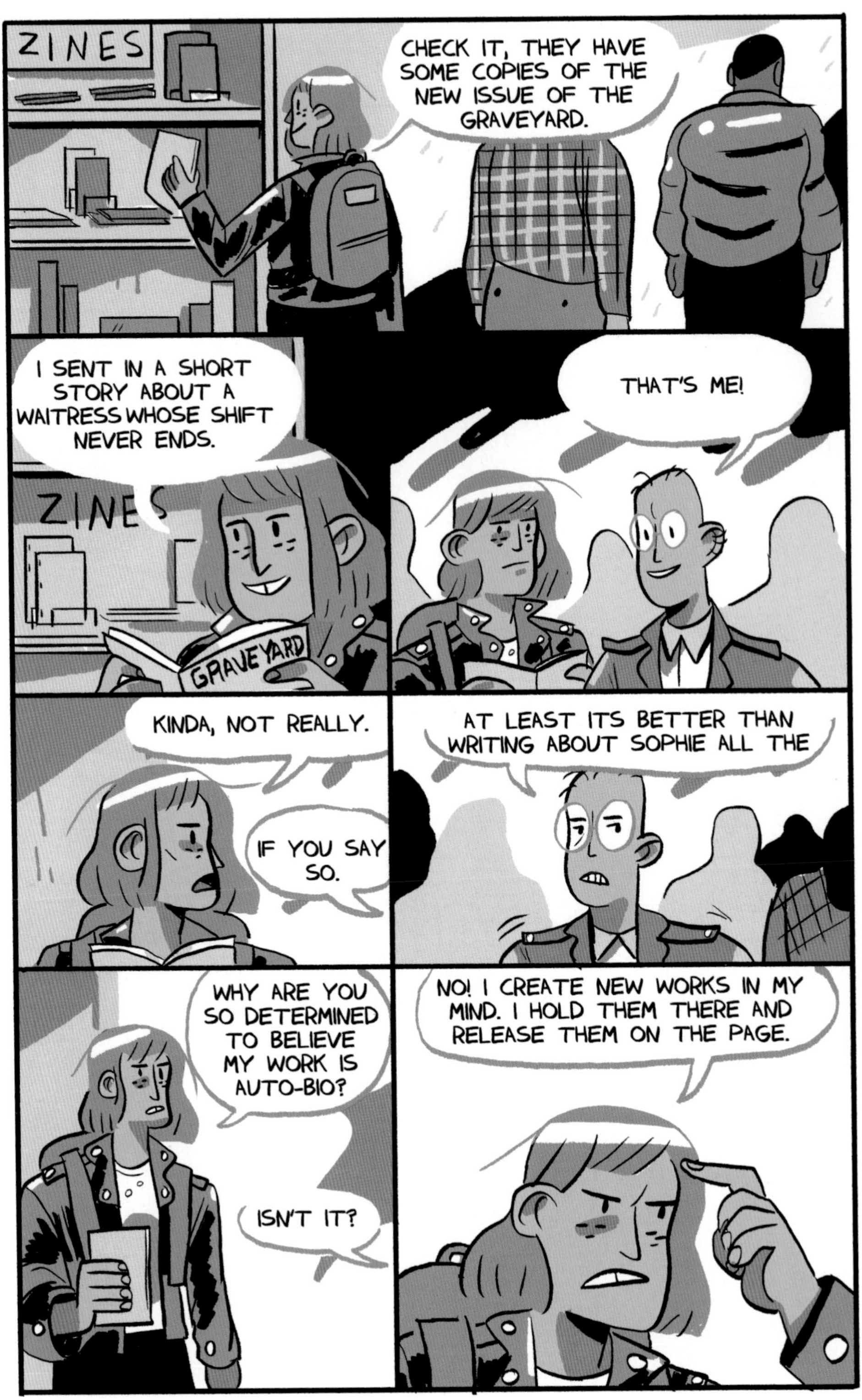
ZINES
CHECK IT, THEY HAVE SOME COPIES OF THE NEW ISSUE OF THE GRAVEYARD.
I SENT IN A SHORT STORY ABOUT A WAITRESS WHOSE SHIFT NEVER ENDS.
ZINES
GRAVEYARD
THAT'S ME!
KINDA, NOT REALLY.
IF YOU SAY SO.
AT LEAST ITS BETTER THAN WRITING ABOUT SOPHIE ALL THE
WHY ARE YOU SO DETERMINED TO BELIEVE MY WORK IS AUTO-BIO?
ISN'T IT?
NO! I CREATE NEW WORKS IN MY MIND. I HOLD THEM THERE AND RELEASE THEM ON THE PAGE.

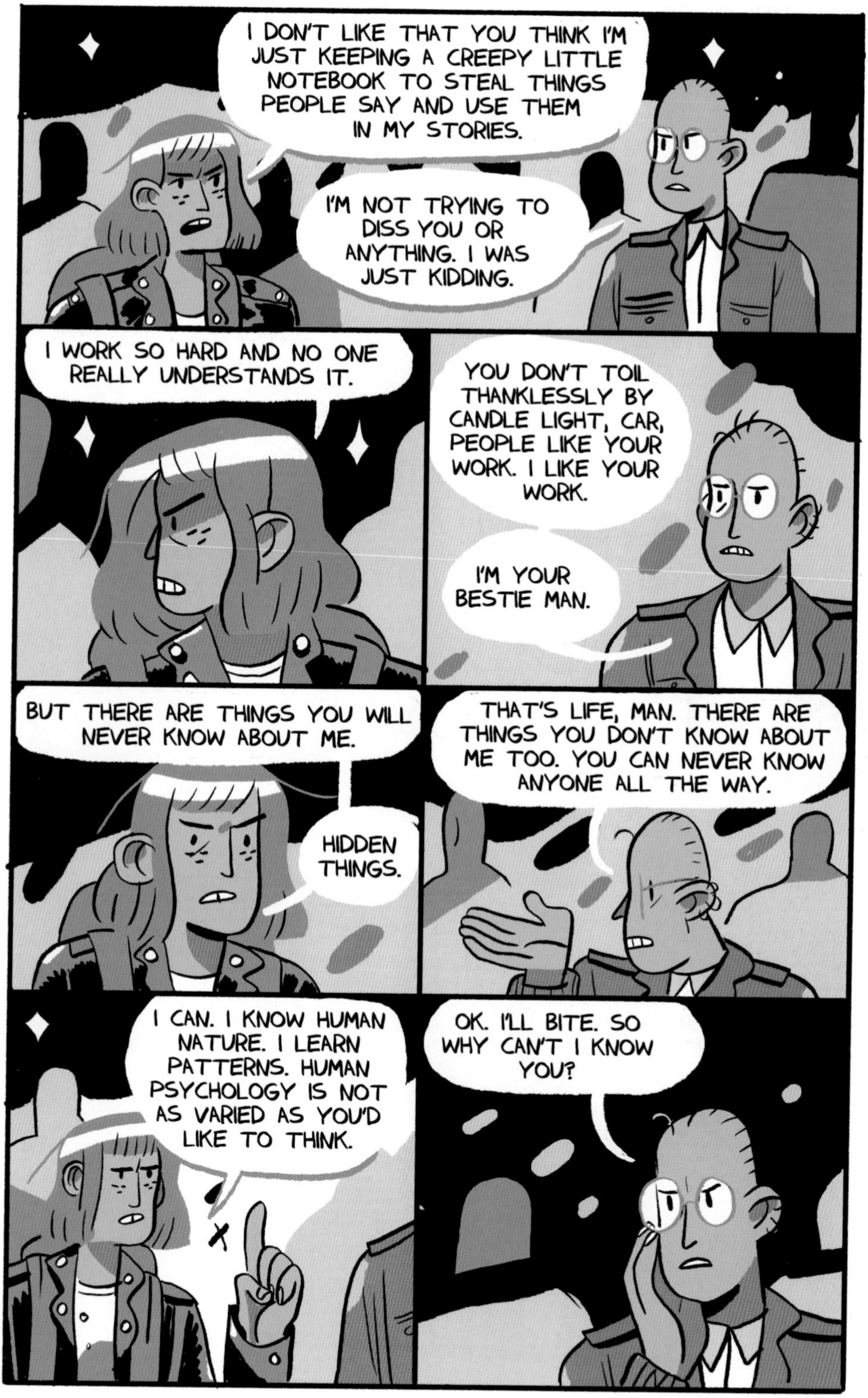
I DON'T LIKE THAT YOU THINK I'M JUST KEEPING A CREEPY LITTLE NOTEBOOK TO STEAL THINGS PEOPLE SAY AND USE THEM IN MY STORIES.
I'M NOT TRYING TO DISS YOU OR ANYTHING. I WAS JUST KIDDING.
I WORK SO HARD AND NO ONE REALLY UNDERSTANDS IT.
YOU DON'T TOIL THANKLESSLY BY CANDLE LIGHT, CAR, PEOPLE LIKE YOUR WORK. I LIKE YOUR WORK.
I'M YOUR BESTIE MAN.
BUT THERE ARE THINGS YOU WILL NEVER KNOW ABOUT ME.
HIDDEN THINGS.
THAT'S LIFE, MAN. THERE ARE THINGS YOU DON'T KNOW ABOUT ME TOO. YOU CAN NEVER KNOW ANYONE ALL THE WAY.
I CAN. I KNOW HUMAN NATURE. I LEARN PATTERNS. HUMAN PSYCHOLOGY IS NOT AS VARIED AS YOU'D LIKE TO THINK.
OK. I'LL BITE. SO WHY CAN'T I KNOW YOU?

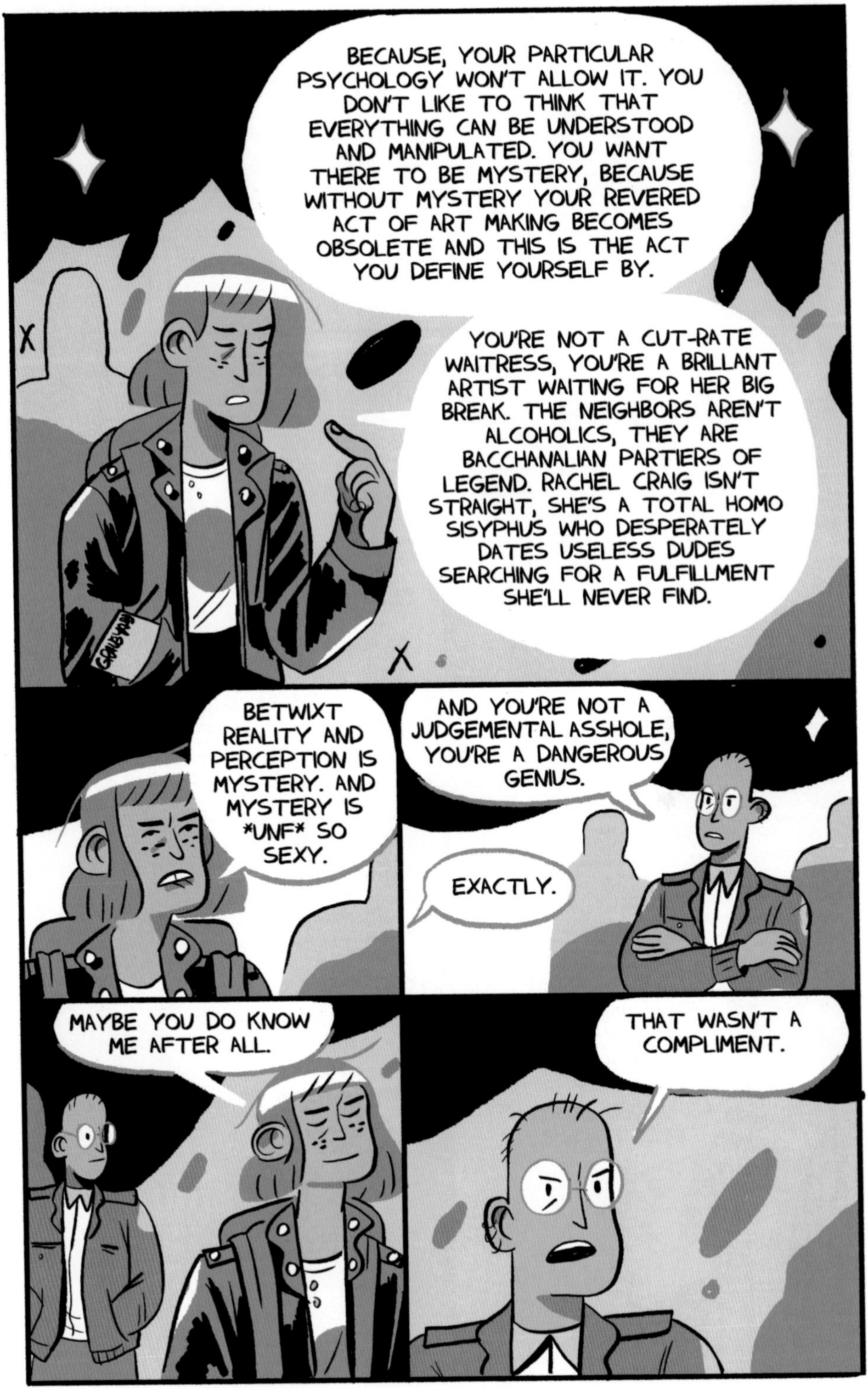
BECAUSE, YOUR PARTICULAR PSYCHOLOGY WON'T ALLOW IT. YOU DON'T LIKE TO THINK THAT EVERYTHING CAN BE UNDERSTOOD AND MANIPULATED. YOU WANT THERE TO BE MYSTERY, BECAUSE WITHOUT MYSTERY YOUR REVERED ACT OF ART MAKING BECOMES OBSOLETE AND THIS IS THE ACT YOU DEFINE YOURSELF BY.
YOU'RE NOT A CUT-RATE WAITRESS, YOU'RE A BRILLANT ARTIST WAITING FOR HER BIG BREAK. THE NEIGHBORS AREN'T ALCOHOLICS, THEY ARE BACCHANALIAN PARTIERS OF LEGEND. RACHEL CRAIG ISN'T STRAIGHT, SHE'S A TOTAL HOMO SISYPHUS WHO DESPERATELY DATES USELESS DUDES SEARCHING FOR A FULFILLMENT SHE'LL NEVER FIND.
BETWIXT REALITY AND PERCEPTION IS MYSTERY. AND MYSTERY IS *UNF* SO SEXY.
AND YOU'RE NOT A JUDGEMENTAL ASSHOLE, YOU'RE A DANGEROUS GENIUS.
EXACTLY.
MAYBE YOU DO KNOW ME AFTER ALL.
THAT WASN'T A COMPLIMENT.

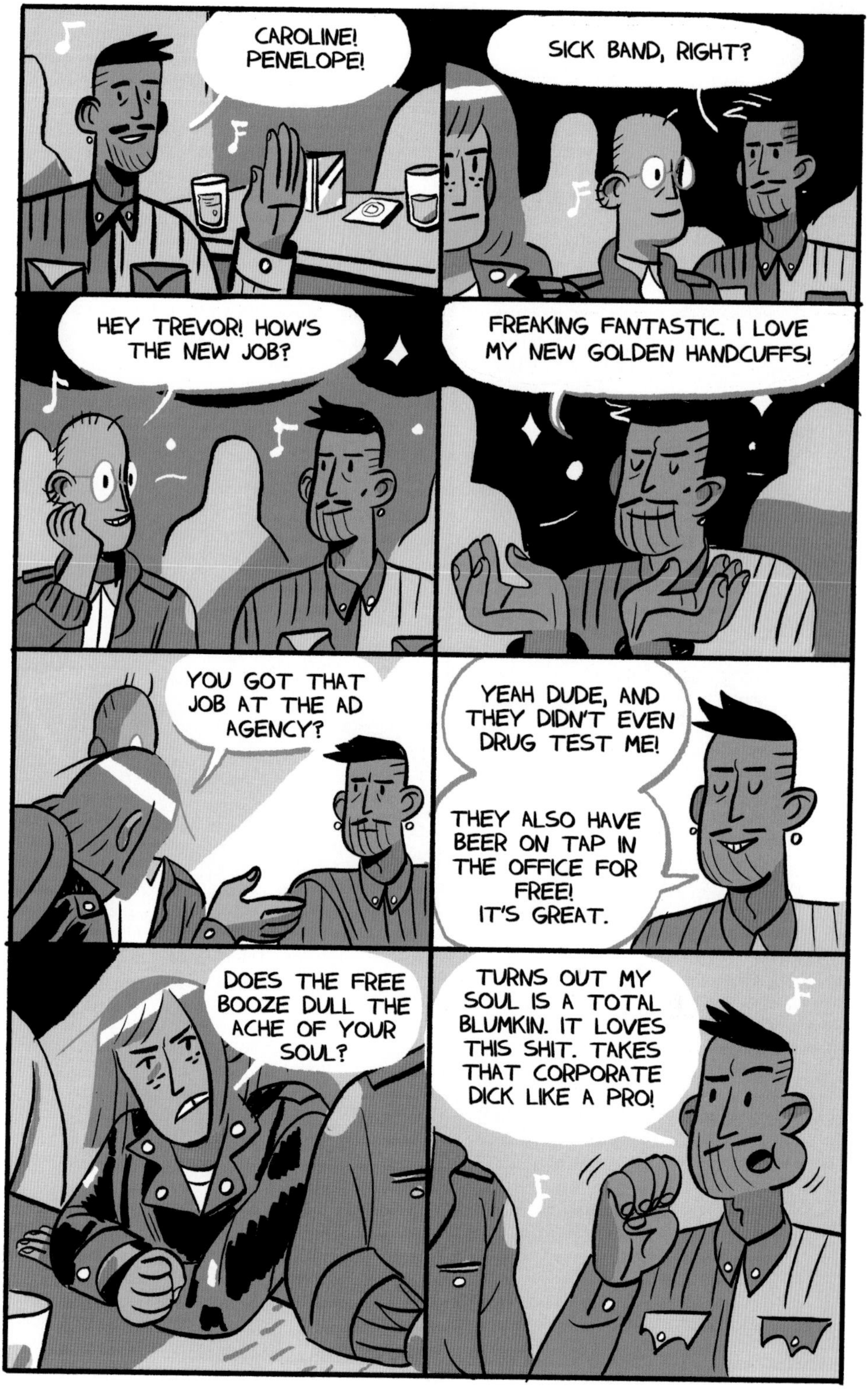
CAROLINE! PENELOPE!
SICK BAND, RIGHT?
HEY TREVOR! HOW'S THE NEW JOB?
FREAKING FANTASTIC. I LOVE MY NEW GOLDEN HANDCUFFS!
YOU GOT THAT JOB AT THE AD AGENCY?
YEAH DUDE, AND THEY DIDN'T EVEN DRUG TEST ME!
THEY ALSO HAVE BEER ON TAP IN THE OFFICE FOR FREE! IT'S GREAT.
DOES THE FREE BOOZE DULL THE ACHE OF YOUR SOUL?
TURNS OUT MY SOUL IS A TOTAL BLUMKIN. IT LOVES THIS SHIT. TAKES THAT CORPORATE DICK LIKE A PRO!

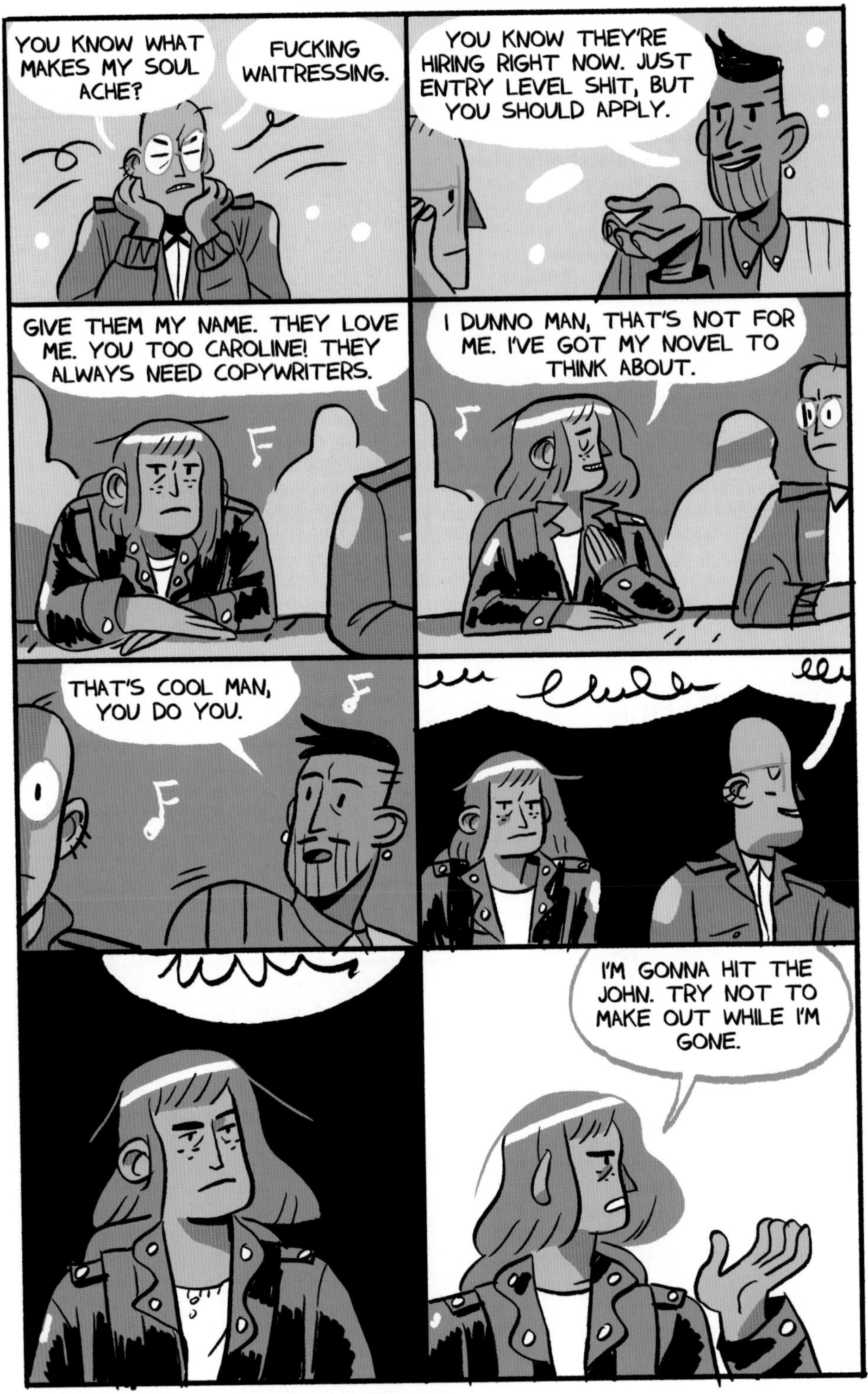
YOU KNOW WHAT MAKES MY SOUL ACHE?
FUCKING WAITRESSING.
YOU KNOW THEY'RE HIRING RIGHT NOW. JUST ENTRY LEVEL SHIT, BUT YOU SHOULD APPLY.
GIVE THEM MY NAME. THEY LOVE ME. YOU TOO CAROLINE! THEY ALWAYS NEED COPYWRITERS.
I DUNNO MAN, THAT'S NOT FOR ME. I'VE GOT MY NOVEL TO THINK ABOUT.
THAT'S COOL MAN, YOU DO YOU.
I'M GONNA HIT THE JOHN. TRY NOT TO MAKE OUT WHILE I'M GONE.

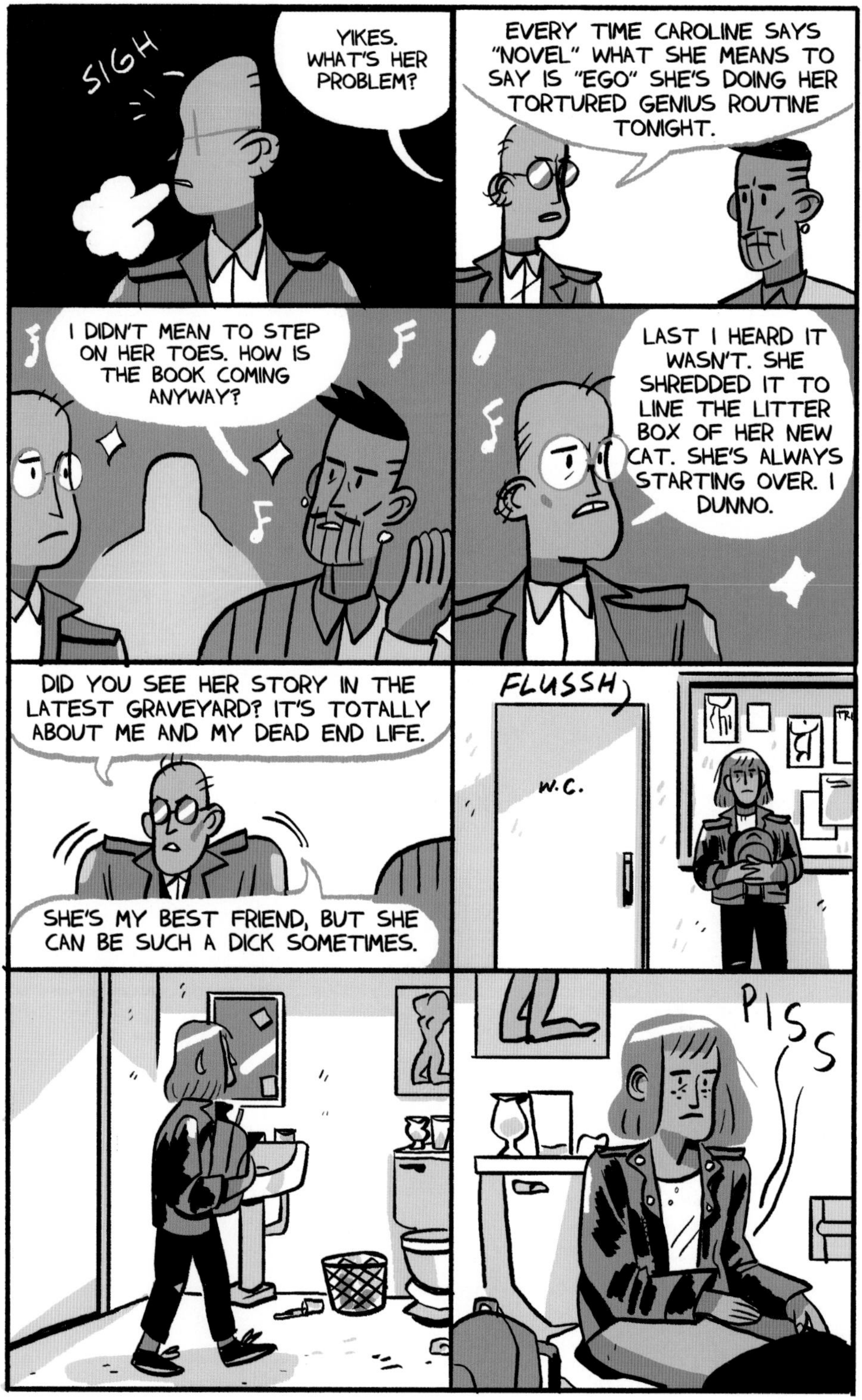
SIGH
YIKES. WHAT'S HER PROBLEM?
EVERY TIME CAROLINE SAYS "NOVEL" WHAT SHE MEANS TO SAY IS "EGO" SHE'S DOING HER TORTURED GENIUS ROUTINE TONIGHT.
I DIDN'T MEAN TO STEP ON HER TOES. HOW IS THE BOOK COMING ANYWAY?
LAST I HEARD IT WASN'T. SHE SHREDDED IT TO LINE THE LITTER BOX OF HER NEW CAT. SHE'S ALWAYS STARTING OVER. I DUNNO.
DID YOU SEE HER STORY IN THE LATEST GRAVEYARD? IT'S TOTALLY ABOUT ME AND MY DEAD END LIFE.
SHE'S MY BEST FRIEND, BUT SHE CAN BE SUCH A DICK SOMETIMES.
FLUSSH
W.C.
PISS

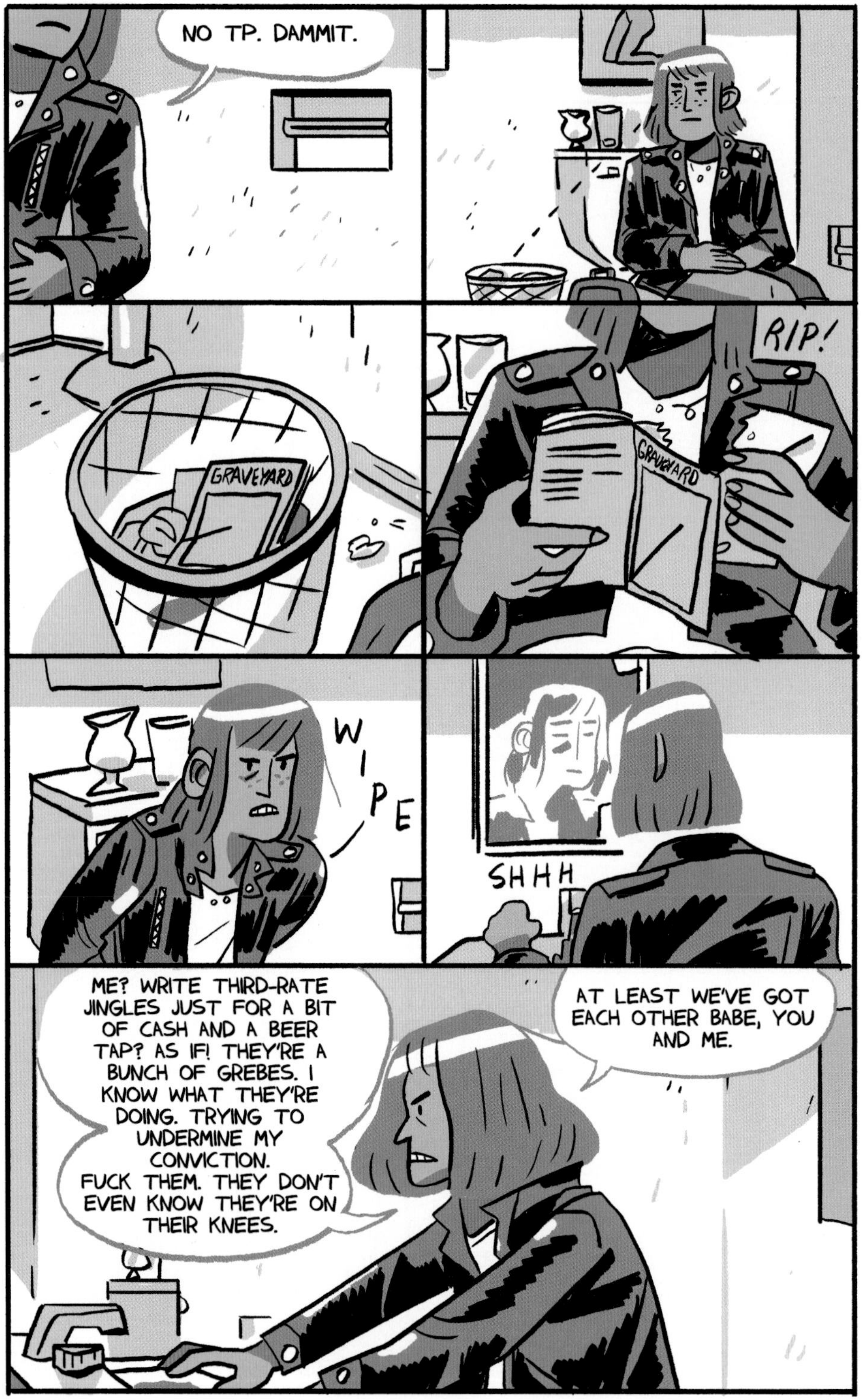

NO TP. DAMMIT.
RIP!
GRAVEYARD
GRAVEYARD
WIPE
SHHH
ME? WRITE THIRD-RATE JINGLES JUST FOR A BIT OF CASH AND A BEER TAP? AS IF! THEY'RE A BUNCH OF GREBES. I KNOW WHAT THEY'RE DOING. TRYING TO UNDERMINE MY CONVICTION. FUCK THEM. THEY DON'T EVEN KNOW THEY'RE ON THEIR KNEES.
AT LEAST WE'VE GOT EACH OTHER BABE, YOU AND ME.

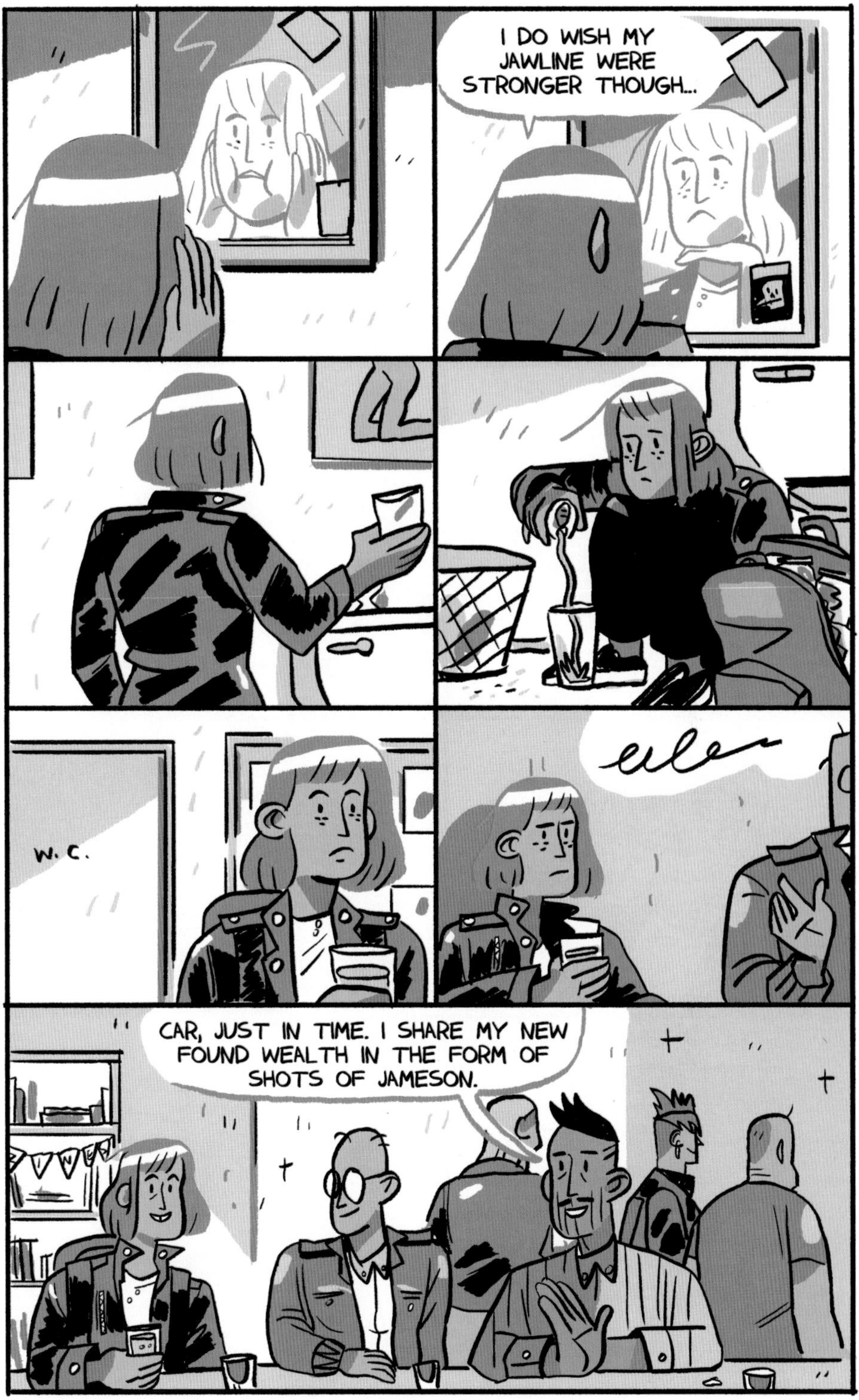
I DO WISH MY JAWLINE WERE STRONGER THOUGH...
W.C.
CAR, JUST IN TIME. I SHARE MY NEW FOUND WEALTH IN THE FORM OF SHOTS OF JAMESON.

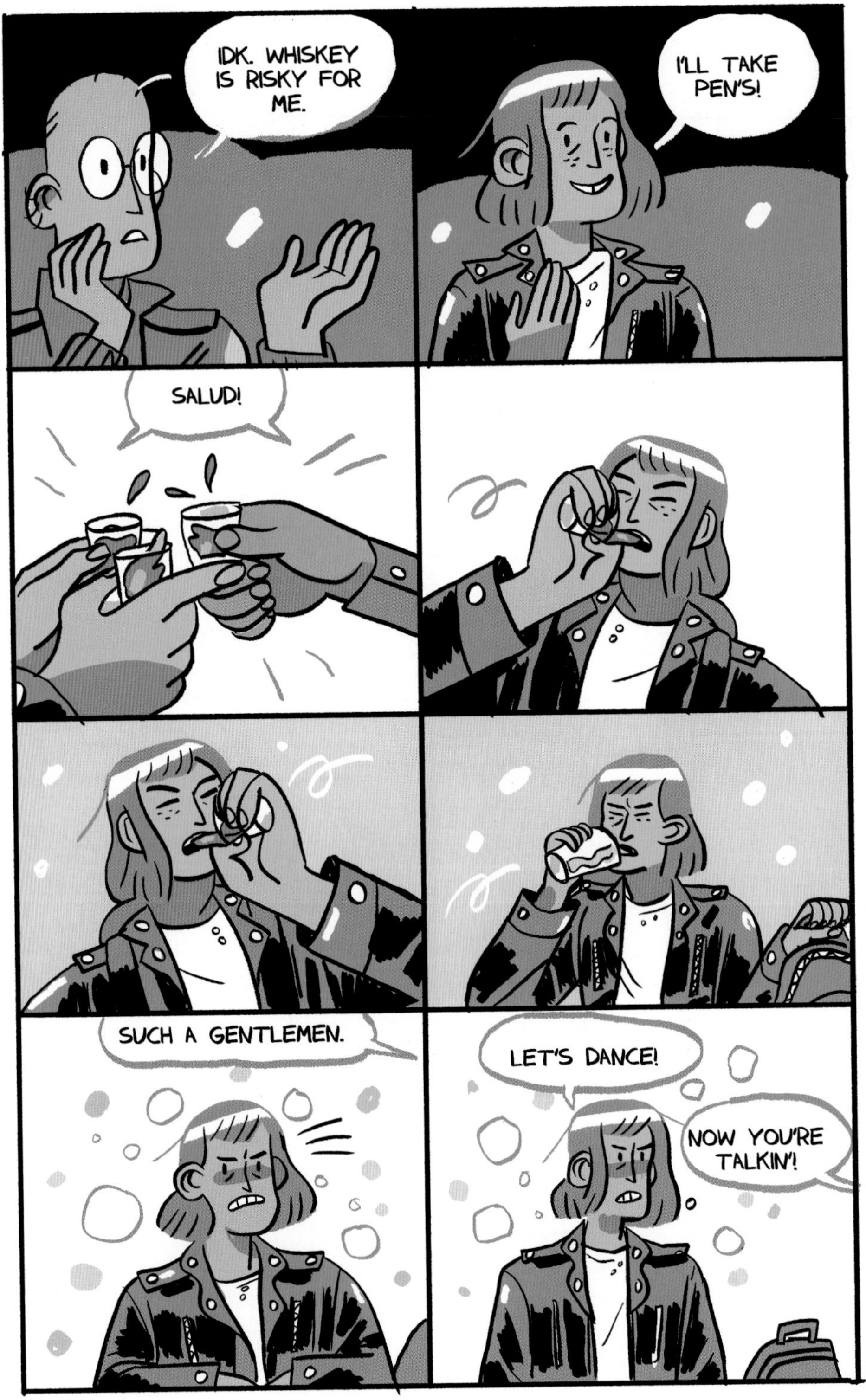
IDK. WHISKEY IS RISKY FOR ME.
I'LL TAKE PEN'S!
SALUD!
SUCH A GENTLEMEN.
LET'S DANCE!
NOW YOU'RE TALKIN'!

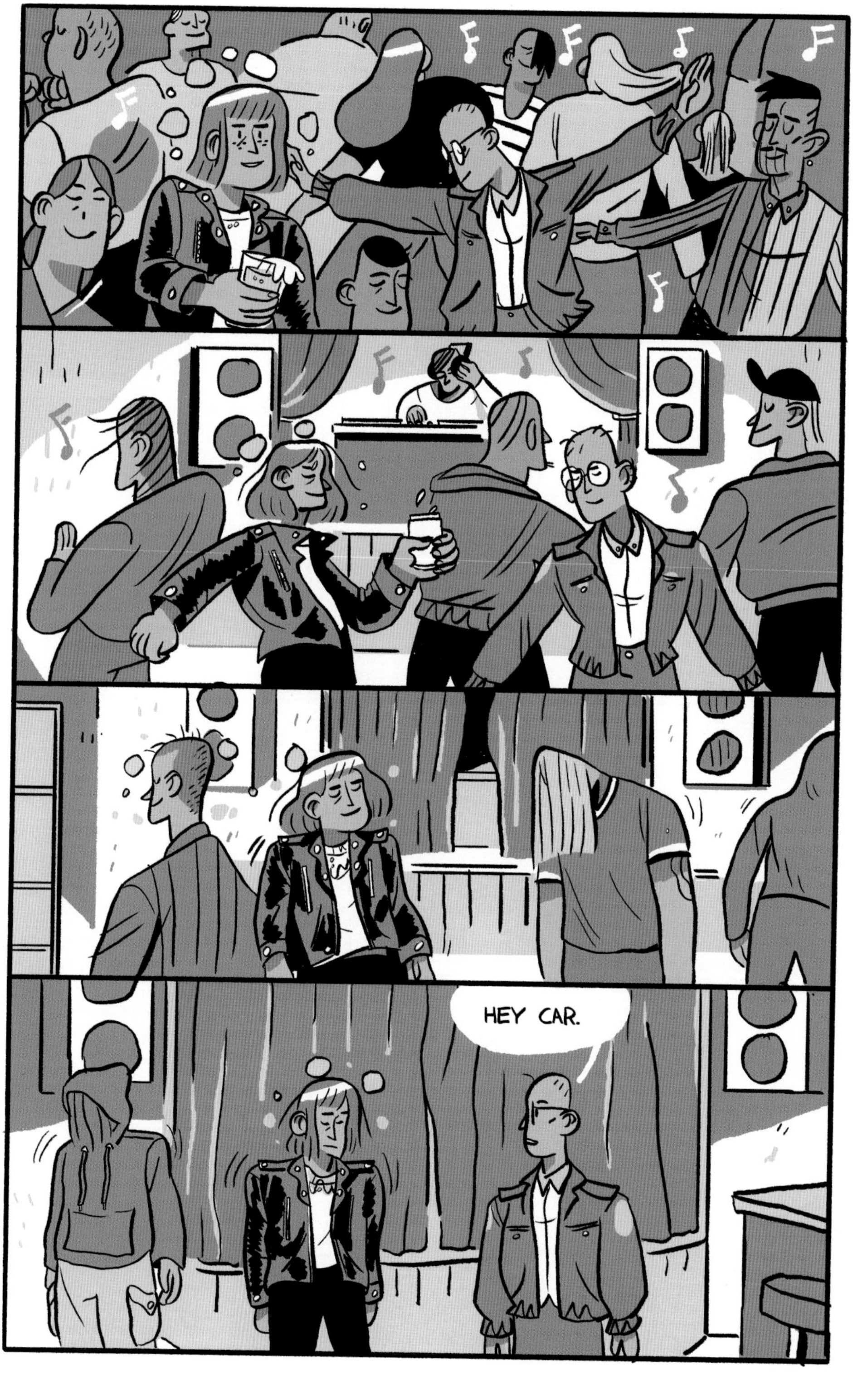
HEY CAR.

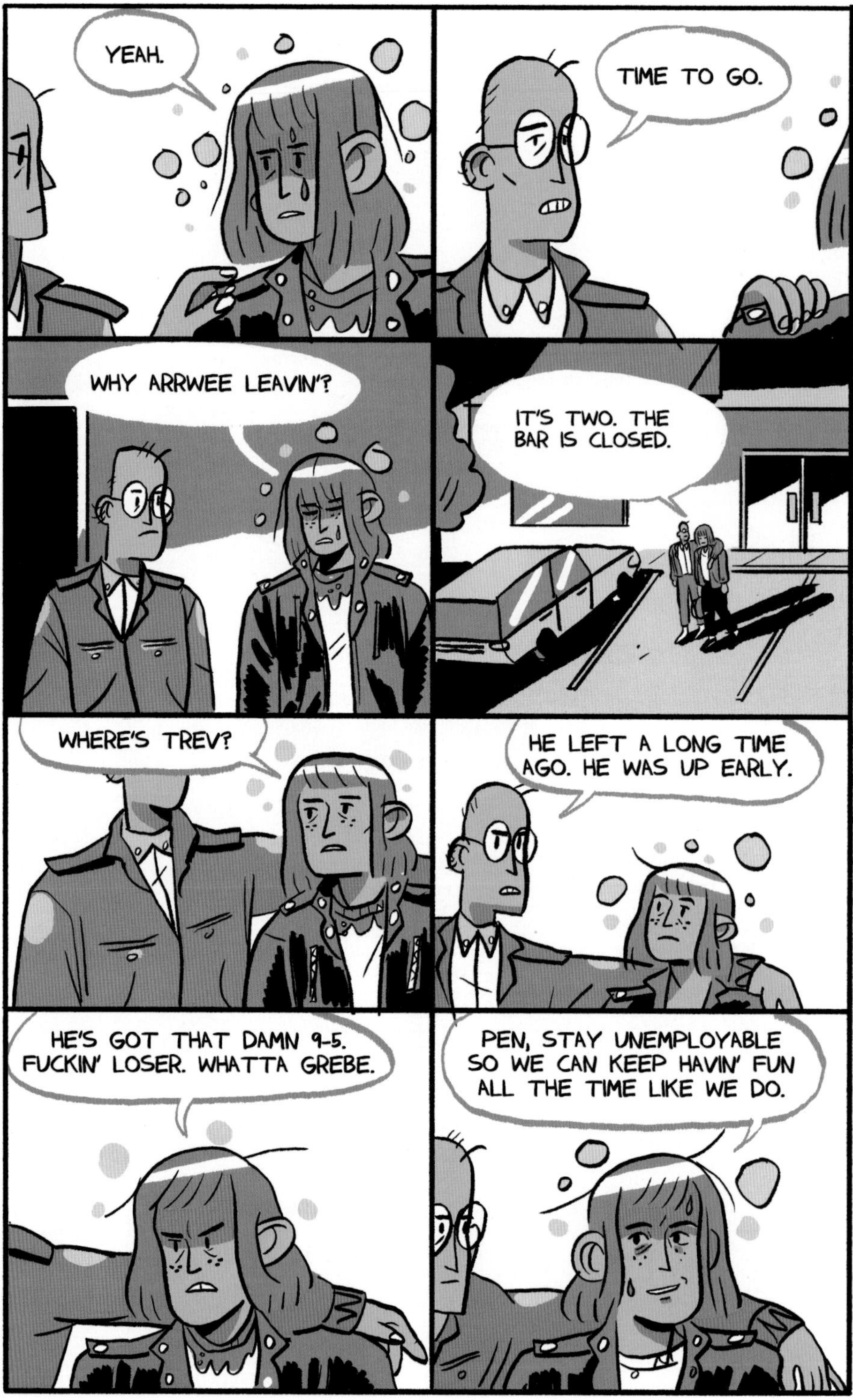
YEAH.
TIME TO GO.
WHY ARRWEE LEAVIN'?
IT'S TWO. THE BAR IS CLOSED.
WHERE'S TREV?
HE LEFT A LONG TIME AGO. HE WAS UP EARLY.
HE'S GOT THAT DAMN 9-5. FUCKIN' LOSER. WHATTA GREBE.
PEN, STAY UNEMPLOYABLE SO WE CAN KEEP HAVIN' FUN ALL THE TIME LIKE WE DO.

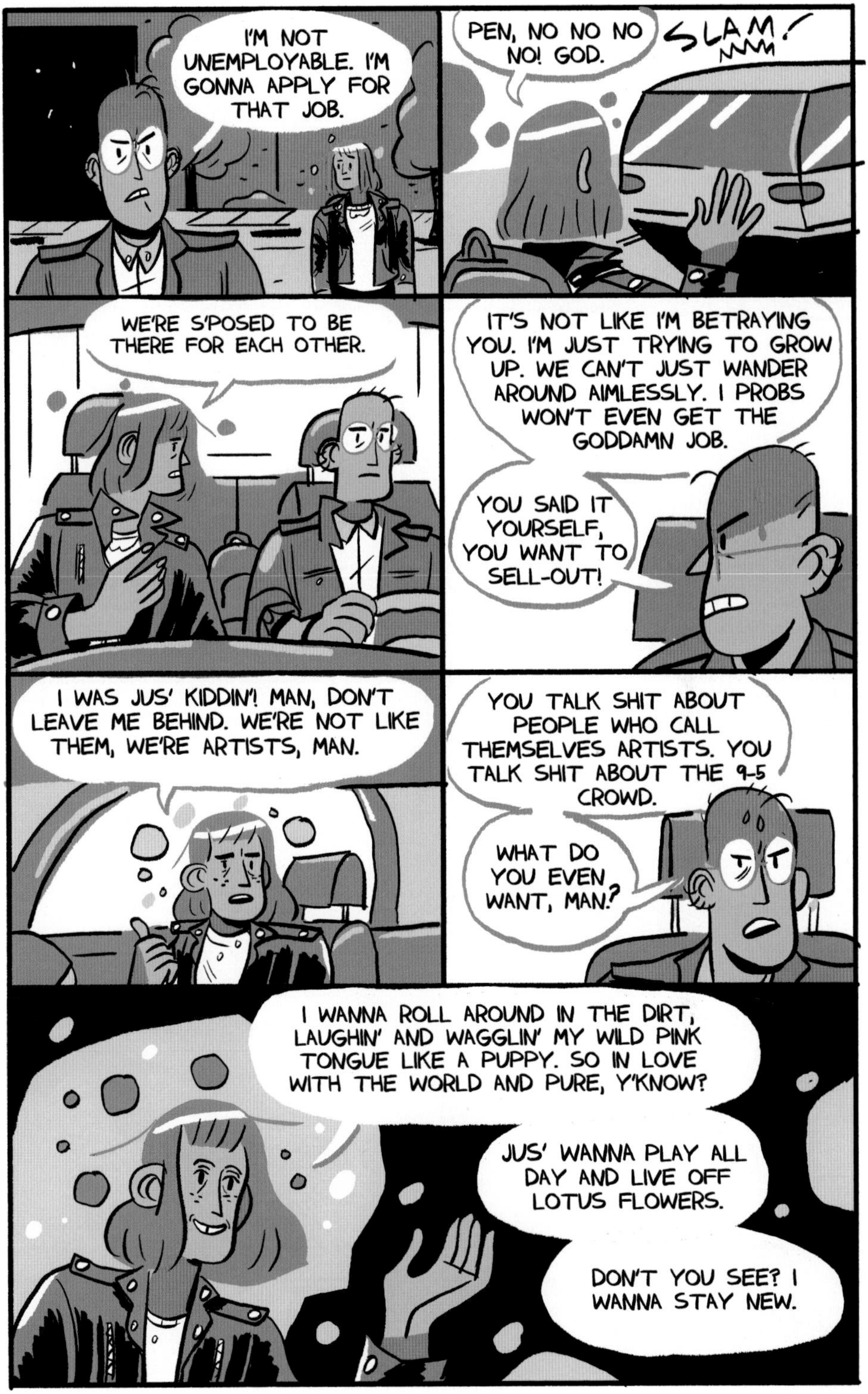
I'M NOT UNEMPLOYABLE. I'M GONNA APPLY FOR THAT JOB.
PEN, NO NO NO NO! GOD.
SLAM!
WE'RE S'POSED TO BE THERE FOR EACH OTHER.
IT'S NOT LIKE I'M BETRAYING YOU. I'M JUST TRYING TO GROW UP. WE CAN'T JUST WANDER AROUND AIMLESSLY. I PROBS WON'T EVEN GET THE GODDAMN JOB.
YOU SAID IT YOURSELF, YOU WANT TO SELL-OUT!
I WAS JUS' KIDDIN'! MAN, DON'T LEAVE ME BEHIND. WE'RE NOT LIKE THEM, WE'RE ARTISTS, MAN.
YOU TALK SHIT ABOUT PEOPLE WHO CALL THEMSELVES ARTISTS. YOU TALK SHIT ABOUT THE 9-5 CROWD.
WHAT DO YOU EVEN WANT, MAN?
I WANNA ROLL AROUND IN THE DIRT, LAUGHIN' AND WAGGLIN' MY WILD PINK TONGUE LIKE A PUPPY. SO IN LOVE WITH THE WORLD AND PURE, Y'KNOW?
JUS' WANNA PLAY ALL DAY AND LIVE OFF LOTUS FLOWERS.
DON'T YOU SEE? I WANNA STAY NEW.

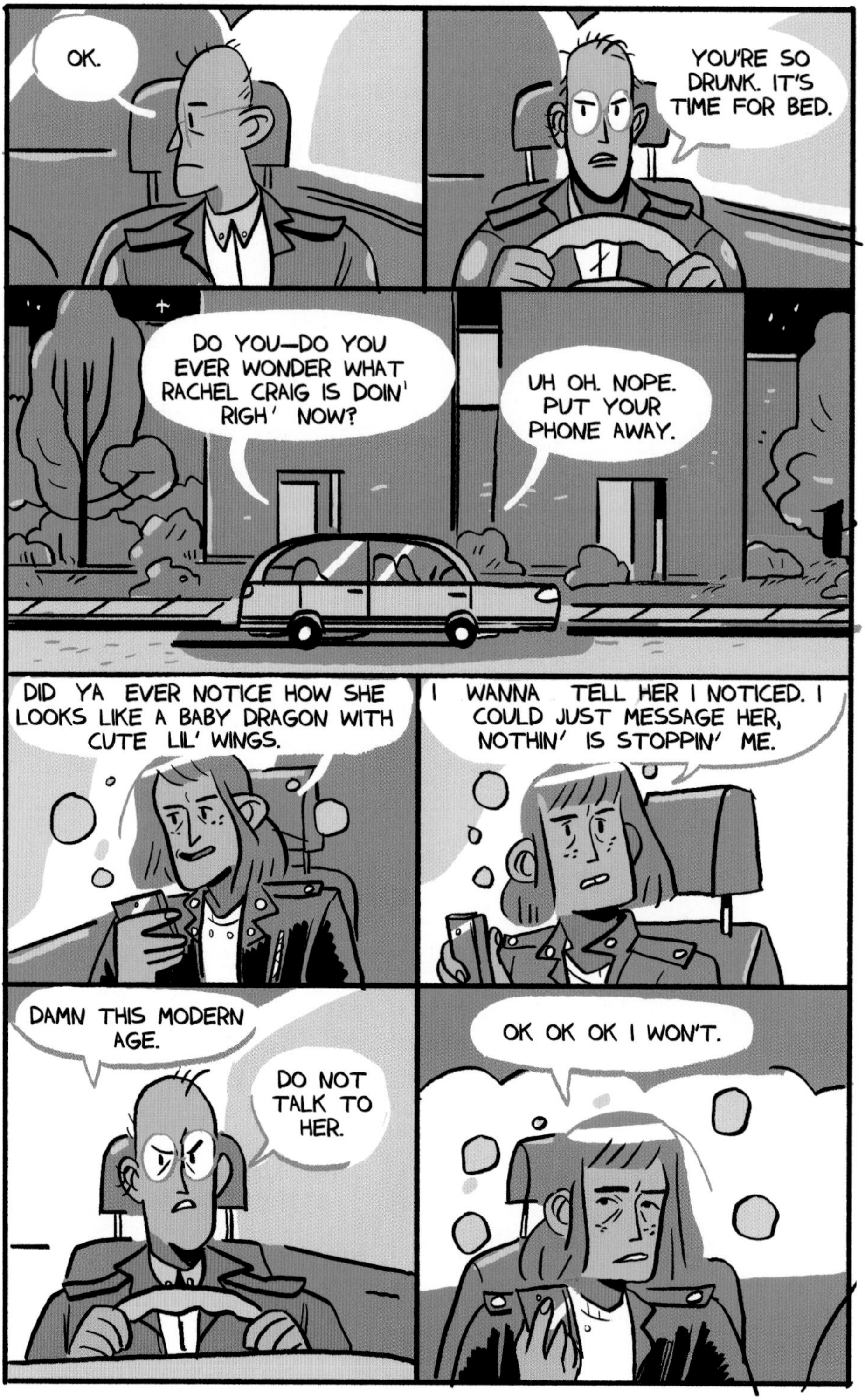
OK.
YOU'RE SO DRUNK. IT'S TIME FOR BED.
DO YOU—DO YOU EVER WONDER WHAT RACHEL CRAIG IS DOIN' RIGH' NOW?
UH OH. NOPE. PUT YOUR PHONE AWAY.
DID YA EVER NOTICE HOW SHE LOOKS LIKE A BABY DRAGON WITH CUTE LIL' WINGS.
I WANNA TELL HER I NOTICED. I COULD JUST MESSAGE HER, NOTHIN' IS STOPPIN' ME.
DAMN THIS MODERN AGE.
DO NOT TALK TO HER.
OK OK OK I WON'T.

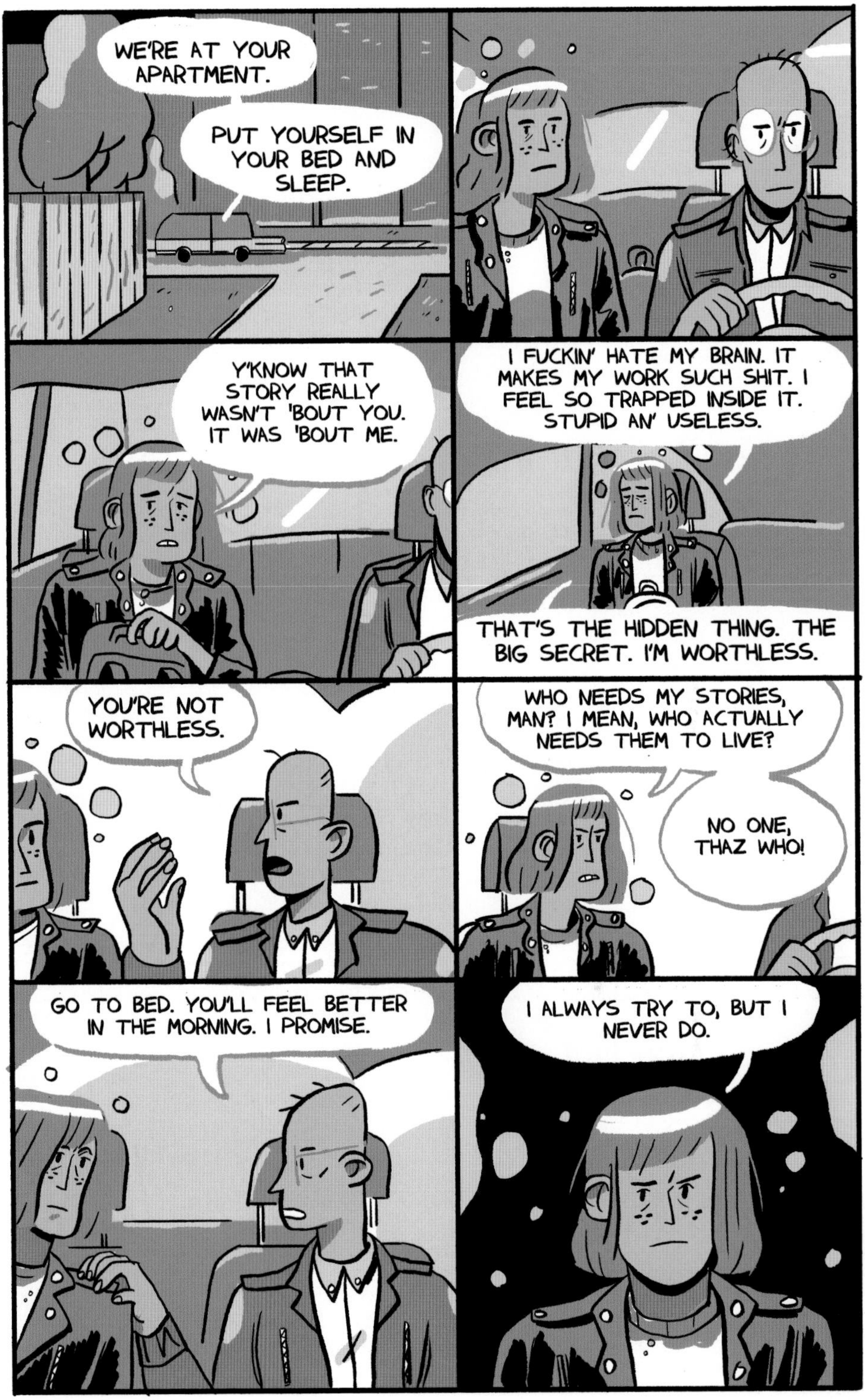
WE'RE AT YOUR APARTMENT.
PUT YOURSELF IN YOUR BED AND SLEEP.
Y'KNOW THAT STORY REALLY WASN'T 'BOUT YOU. IT WAS 'BOUT ME.
I FUCKIN' HATE MY BRAIN. IT MAKES MY WORK SUCH SHIT. I FEEL SO TRAPPED INSIDE IT. STUPID AN' USELESS.
THAT'S THE HIDDEN THING. THE BIG SECRET. I'M WORTHLESS.
YOU'RE NOT WORTHLESS.
WHO NEEDS MY STORIES, MAN? I MEAN, WHO ACTUALLY NEEDS THEM TO LIVE?
NO ONE, THAZ WHO!
GO TO BED. YOU'LL FEEL BETTER IN THE MORNING. I PROMISE.
I ALWAYS TRY TO, BUT I NEVER DO.

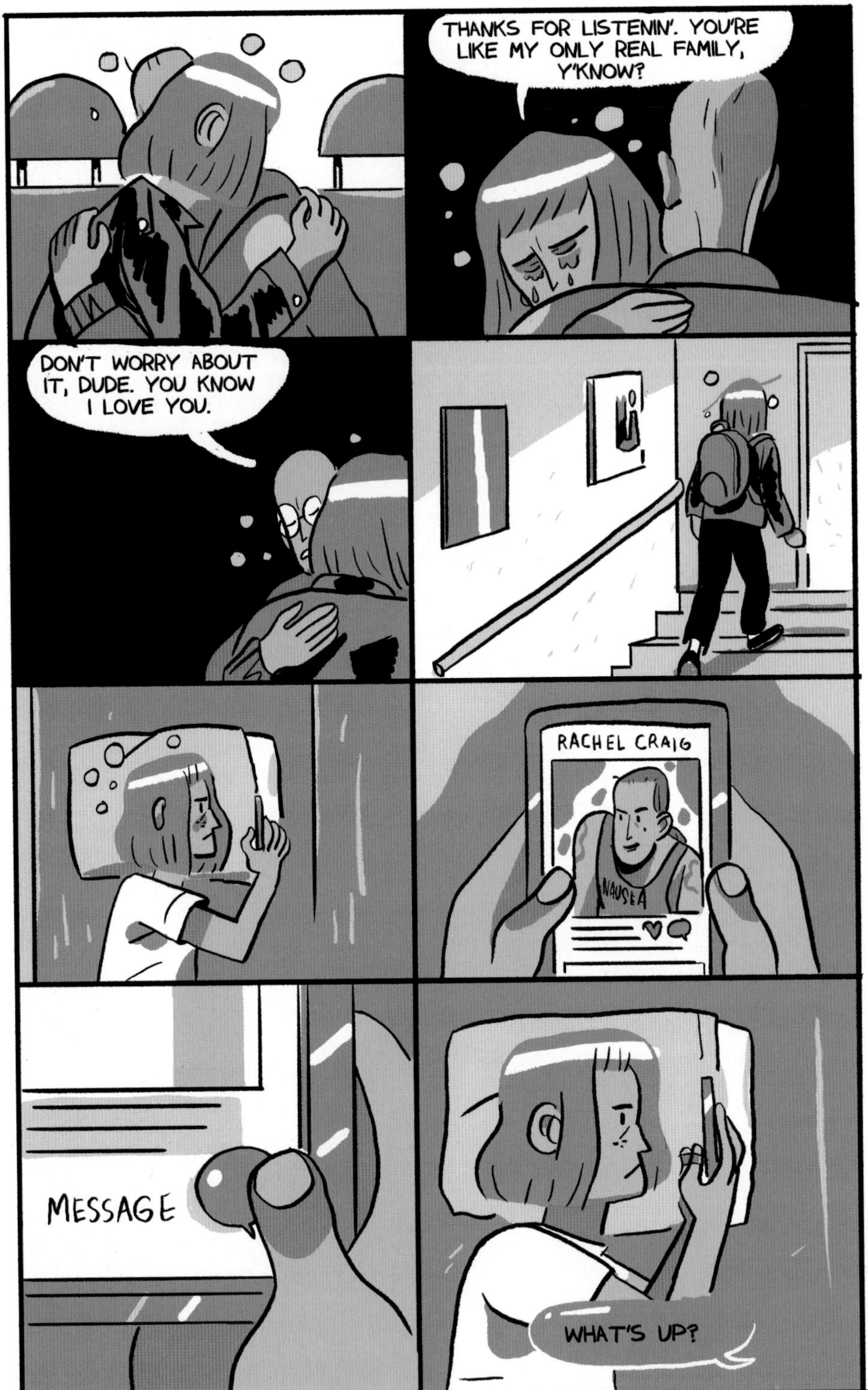
THANKS FOR LISTENIN'. YOU'RE LIKE MY ONLY REAL FAMILY, Y'KNOW?
DON'T WORRY ABOUT IT, DUDE. YOU KNOW I LOVE YOU.
RACHEL CRAIG
NAUSEA
MESSAGE
WHAT'S UP?

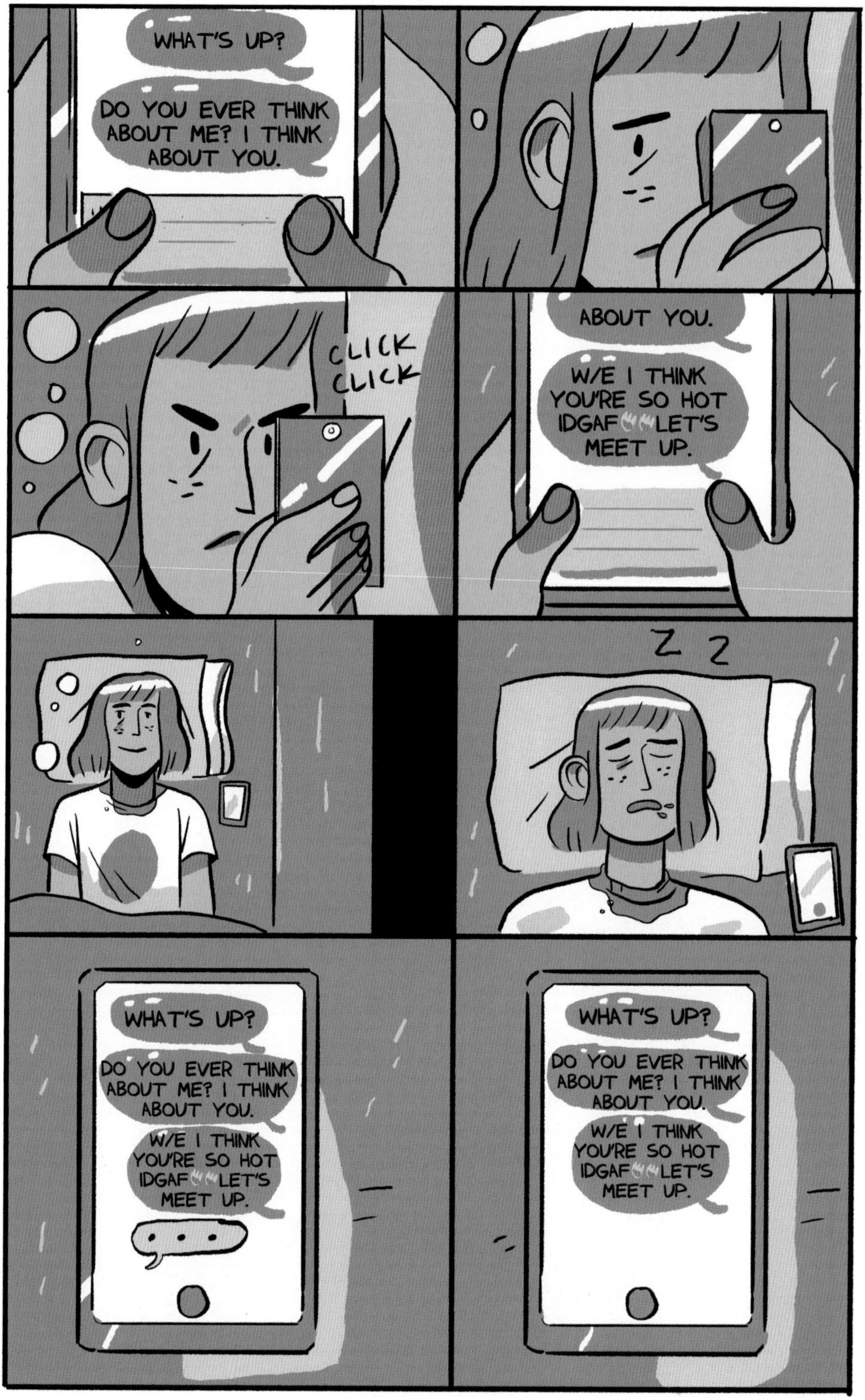
WHAT'S UP?
DO YOU EVER THINK ABOUT ME? I THINK ABOUT YOU.
CLICK CLICK
ABOUT YOU.
W/E I THINK YOU'RE SO HOT IDGAF LET'S MEET UP.
Z Z
WHAT'S UP?
DO YOU EVER THINK ABOUT ME? I THINK ABOUT YOU.
W/E I THINK YOU'RE SO HOT IDGAF LET'S MEET UP.
• • •
WHAT'S UP?
DO YOU EVER THINK ABOUT ME? I THINK ABOUT YOU.
W/E I THINK YOU'RE SO HOT IDGAF LET'S MEET UP.

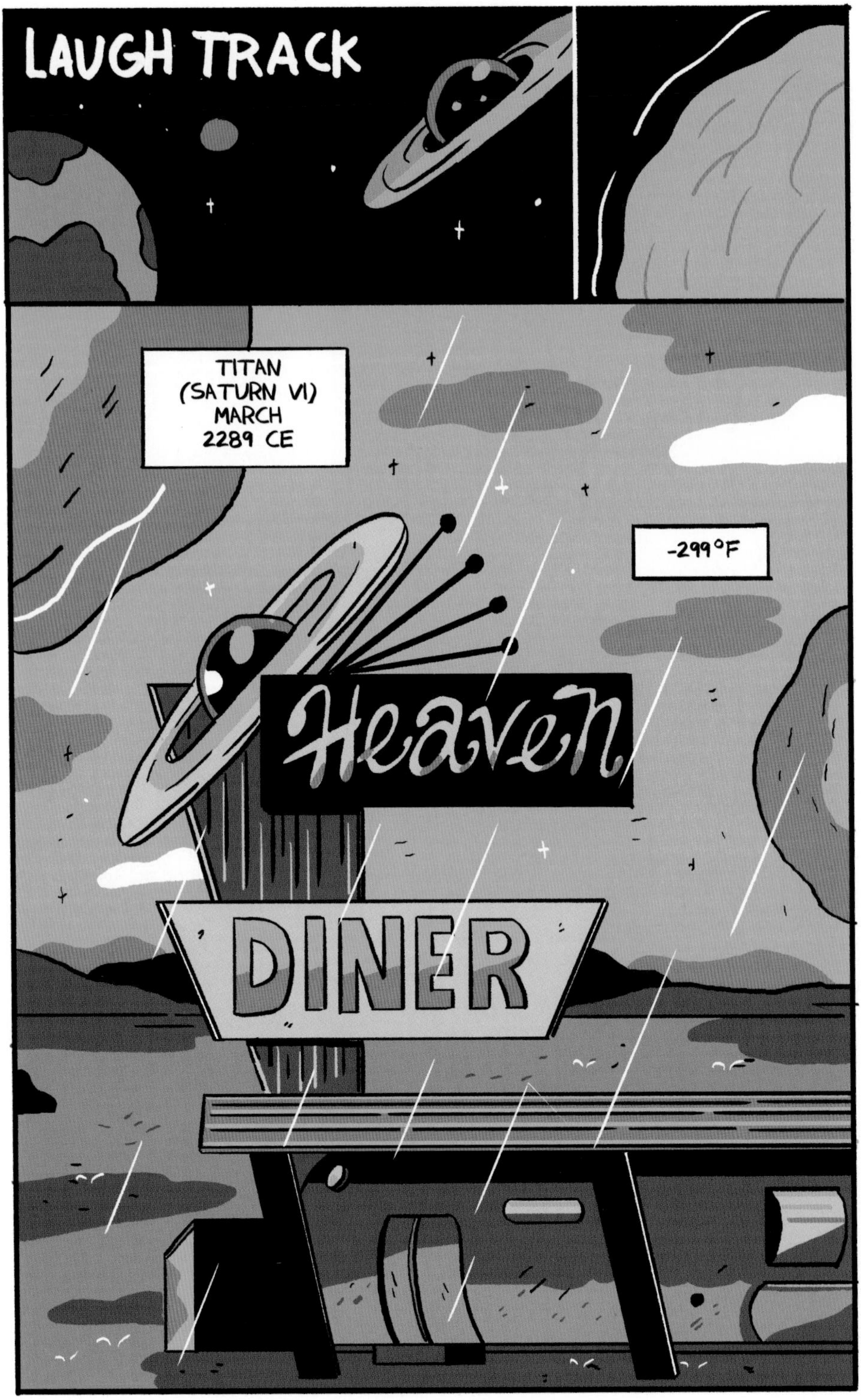
LAUGH TRACK
TITAN
(SATURN VI)
MARCH
2289 CE
-299°F
Heaven
DINER

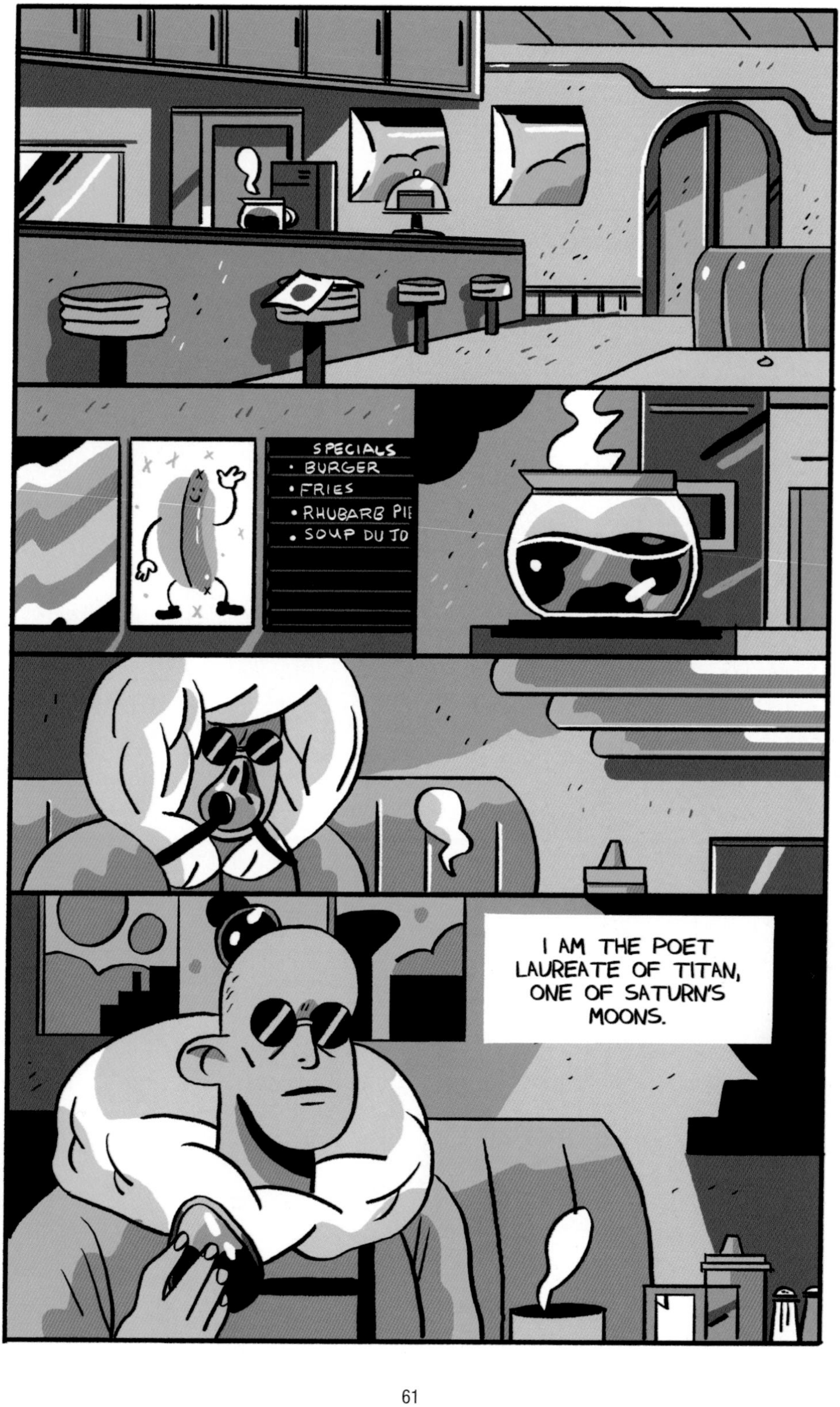
SPECIALS
• BURGER
• FRIES
• RHUBARB PIE
• SOUP DU JO
I AM THE POET LAUREATE OF TITAN, ONE OF SATURN'S MOONS.

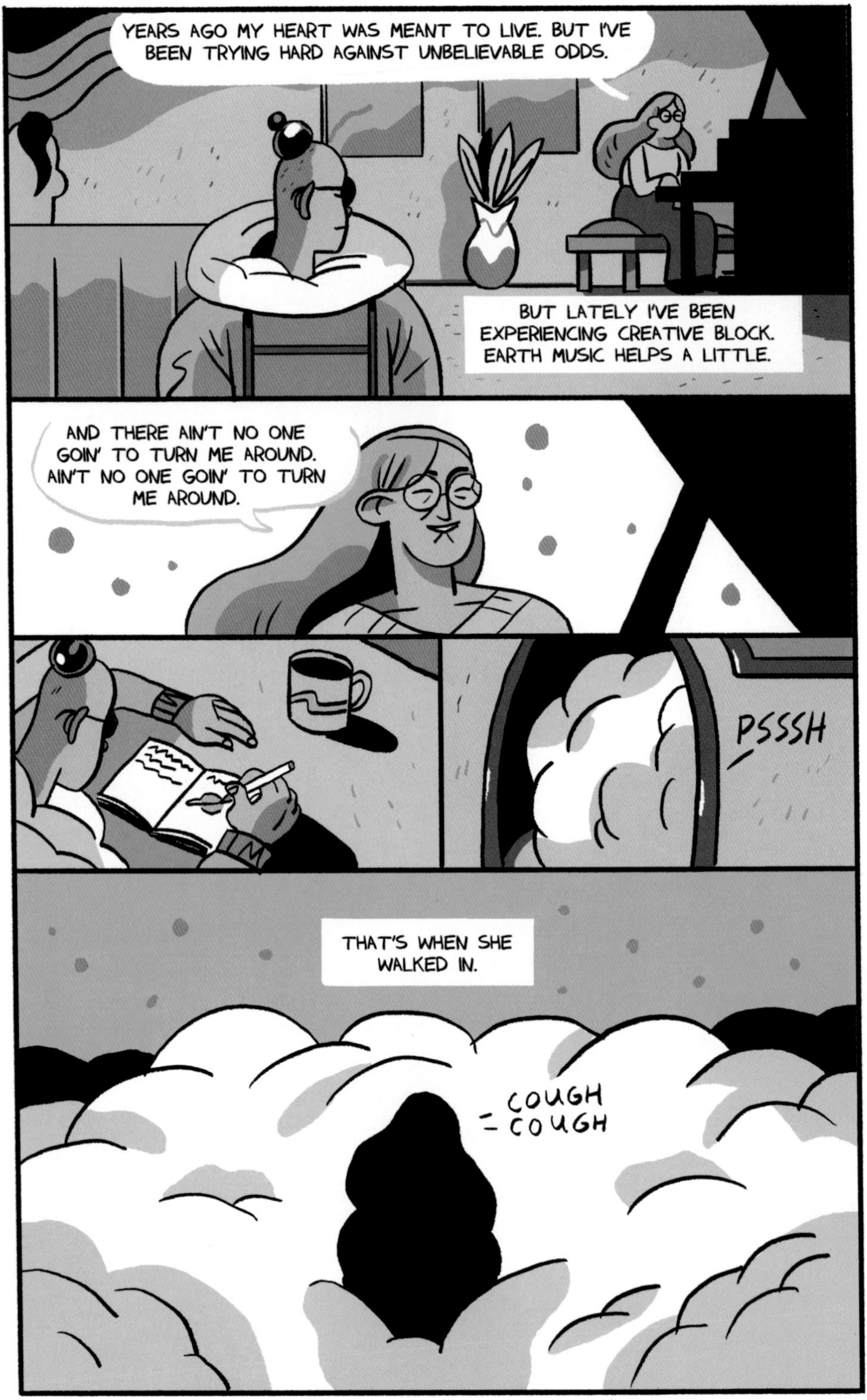
YEARS AGO MY HEART WAS MEANT TO LIVE. BUT I'VE BEEN TRYING HARD AGAINST UNBELIEVABLE ODDS.
BUT LATELY I'VE BEEN EXPERIENCING CREATIVE BLOCK. EARTH MUSIC HELPS A LITTLE.
AND THERE AIN'T NO ONE GOIN' TO TURN ME AROUND. AIN'T NO ONE GOIN' TO TURN ME AROUND.
PSSSH
THAT'S WHEN SHE WALKED IN.
COUGH
COUGH

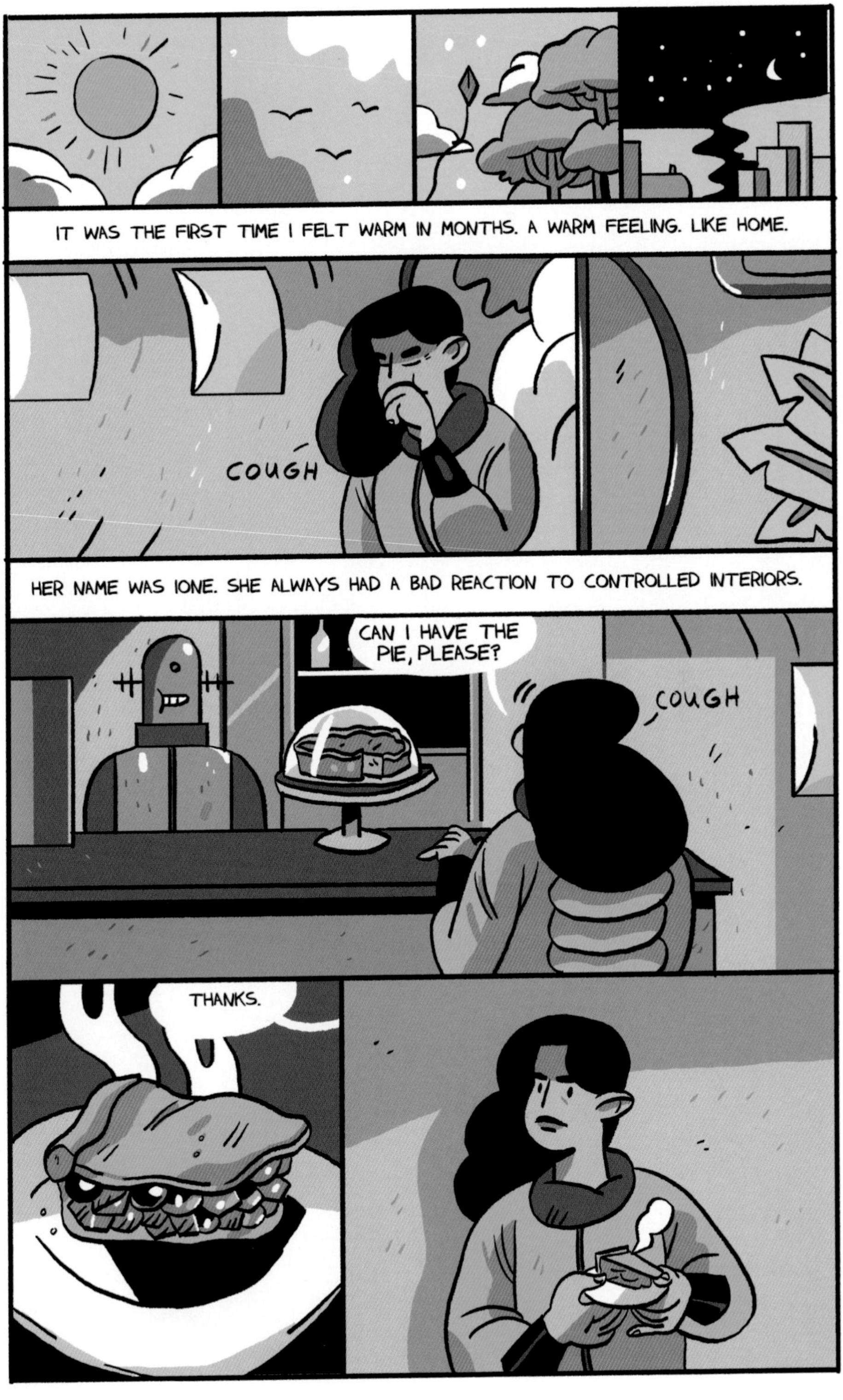
IT WAS THE FIRST TIME I FELT WARM IN MONTHS. A WARM FEELING. LIKE HOME.
COUGH
HER NAME WAS IONE. SHE ALWAYS HAD A BAD REACTION TO CONTROLLED INTERIORS.
CAN I HAVE THE PIE, PLEASE?
COUGH
THANKS.

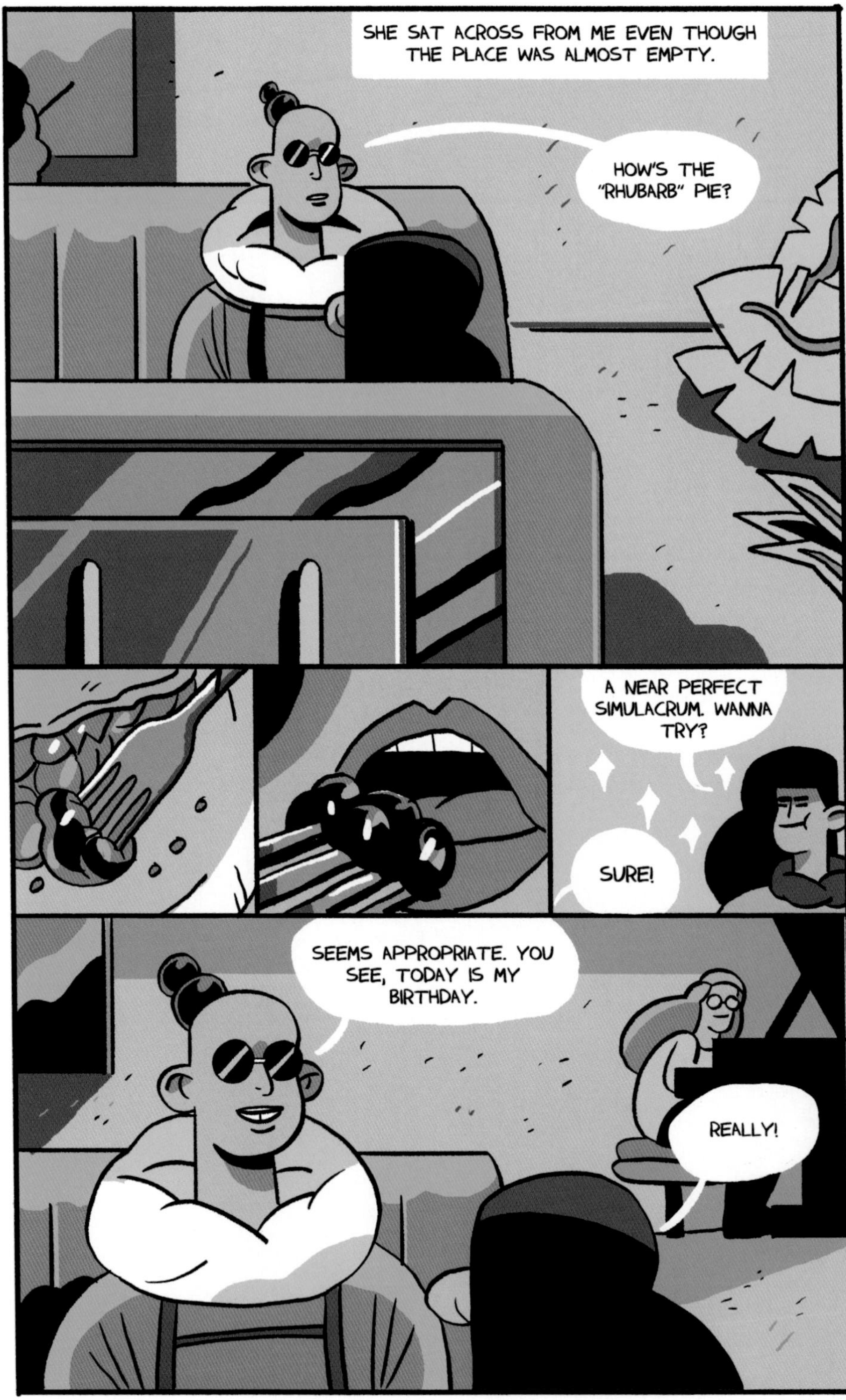
SHE SAT ACROSS FROM ME EVEN THOUGH THE PLACE WAS ALMOST EMPTY.
HOW'S THE "RHUBARB" PIE?
A NEAR PERFECT SIMULACRUM. WANNA TRY?
SURE!
SEEMS APPROPRIATE. YOU SEE, TODAY IS MY BIRTHDAY.
REALLY!

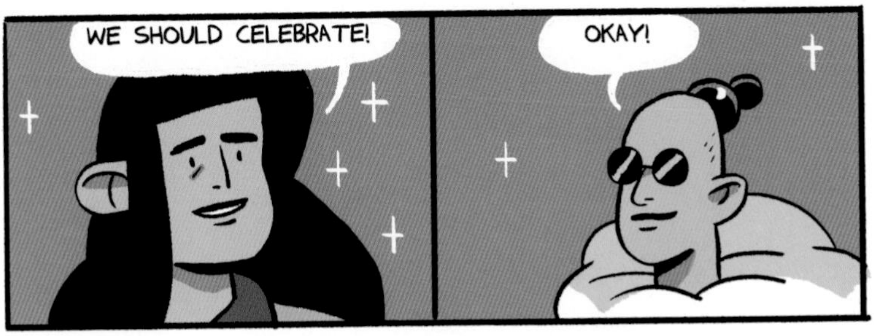
WE SHOULD CELEBRATE!
OKAY!

BUT THE TITAN DAYS ARE 16 EARTH DAYS LONG. WE CELEBRATED MY BIRTHDAY FOR THE NEXT TWO WEEKS.

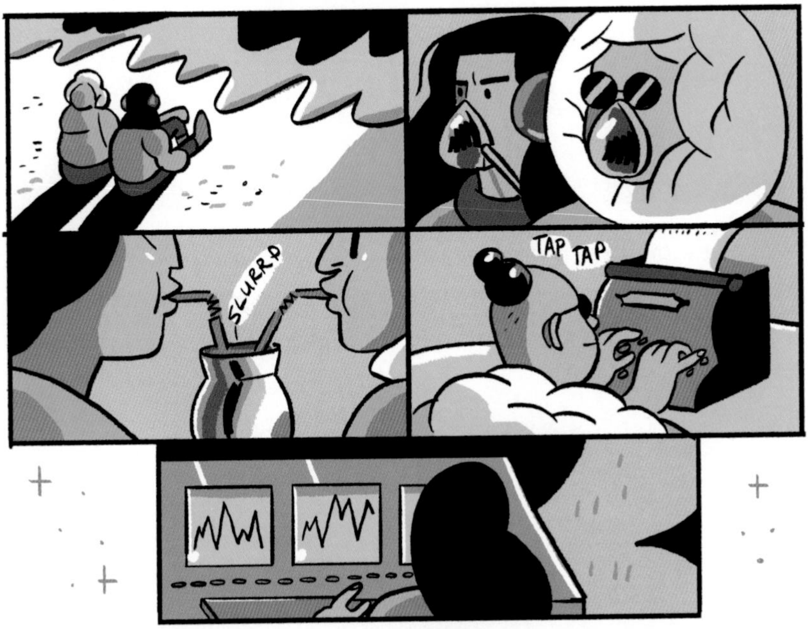
SLURRP
TAP TAP

MY CREATIVE BLOCK WAS GONE. THE WORDS FELL FROM MY FINGERS EFFORTLESSLY. IONE'S WORK WAS NOT GOING AS WELL.

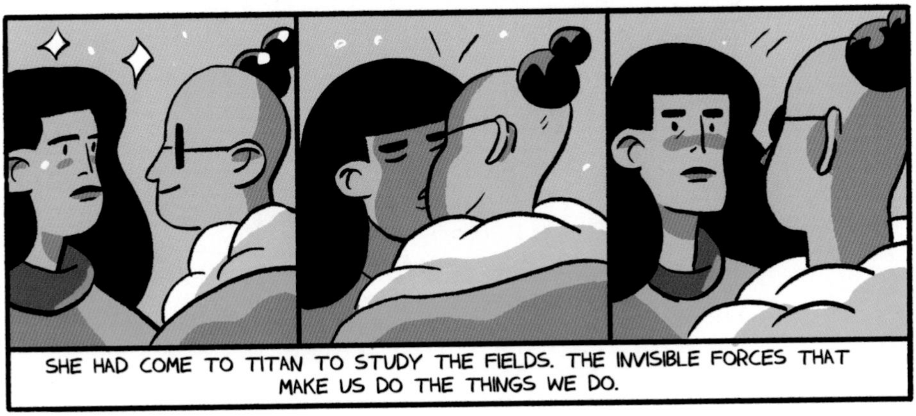
SHE HAD COME TO TITAN TO STUDY THE FIELDS. THE INVISIBLE FORCES THAT MAKE US DO THE THINGS WE DO.

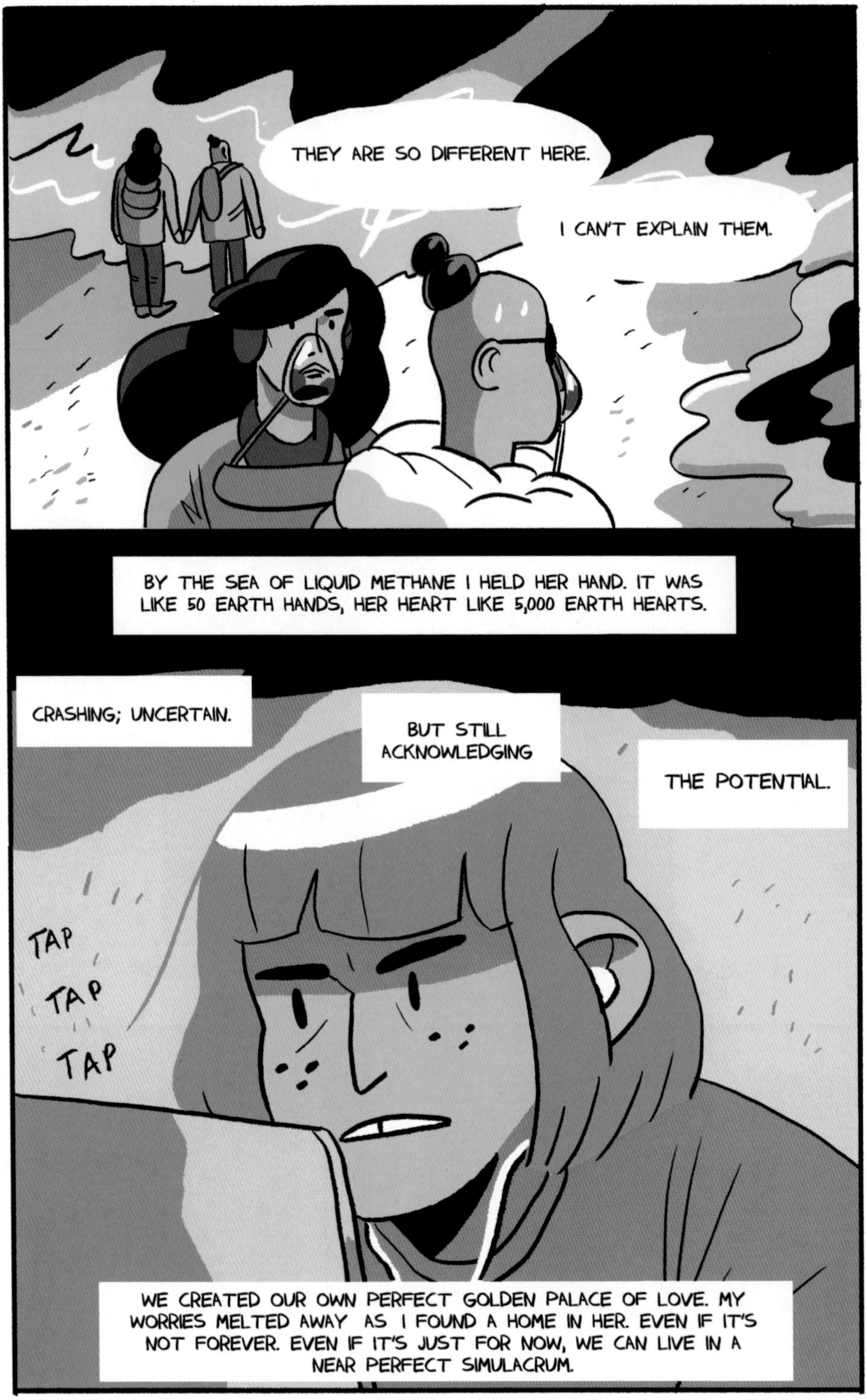
THEY ARE SO DIFFERENT HERE.
I CAN'T EXPLAIN THEM.
BY THE SEA OF LIQUID METHANE I HELD HER HAND. IT WAS LIKE 50 EARTH HANDS, HER HEART LIKE 5,000 EARTH HEARTS.
CRASHING; UNCERTAIN.
BUT STILL ACKNOWLEDGING
THE POTENTIAL.
TAP
TAP
TAP
WE CREATED OUR OWN PERFECT GOLDEN PALACE OF LOVE. MY WORRIES MELTED AWAY AS I FOUND A HOME IN HER. EVEN IF IT'S NOT FOREVER. EVEN IF IT'S JUST FOR NOW, WE CAN LIVE IN A NEAR PERFECT SIMULACRUM.

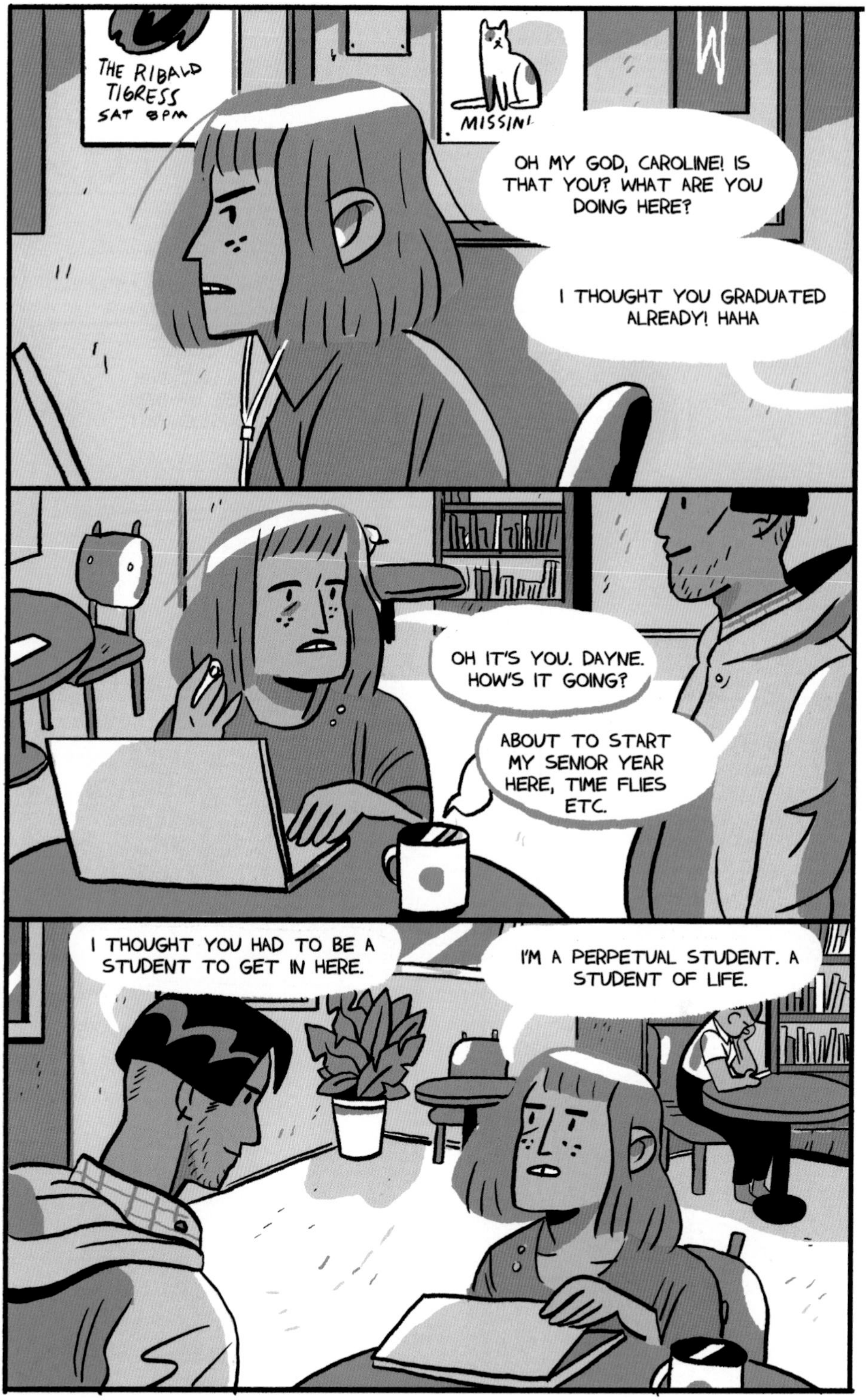
THE RIBALD TIGRESS SAT 8PM
MISSIN
OH MY GOD, CAROLINE! IS THAT YOU? WHAT ARE YOU DOING HERE?
I THOUGHT YOU GRADUATED ALREADY! HAHA
OH IT'S YOU. DAYNE. HOW'S IT GOING?
ABOUT TO START MY SENIOR YEAR HERE, TIME FLIES ETC.
I THOUGHT YOU HAD TO BE A STUDENT TO GET IN HERE.
I'M A PERPETUAL STUDENT. A STUDENT OF LIFE.

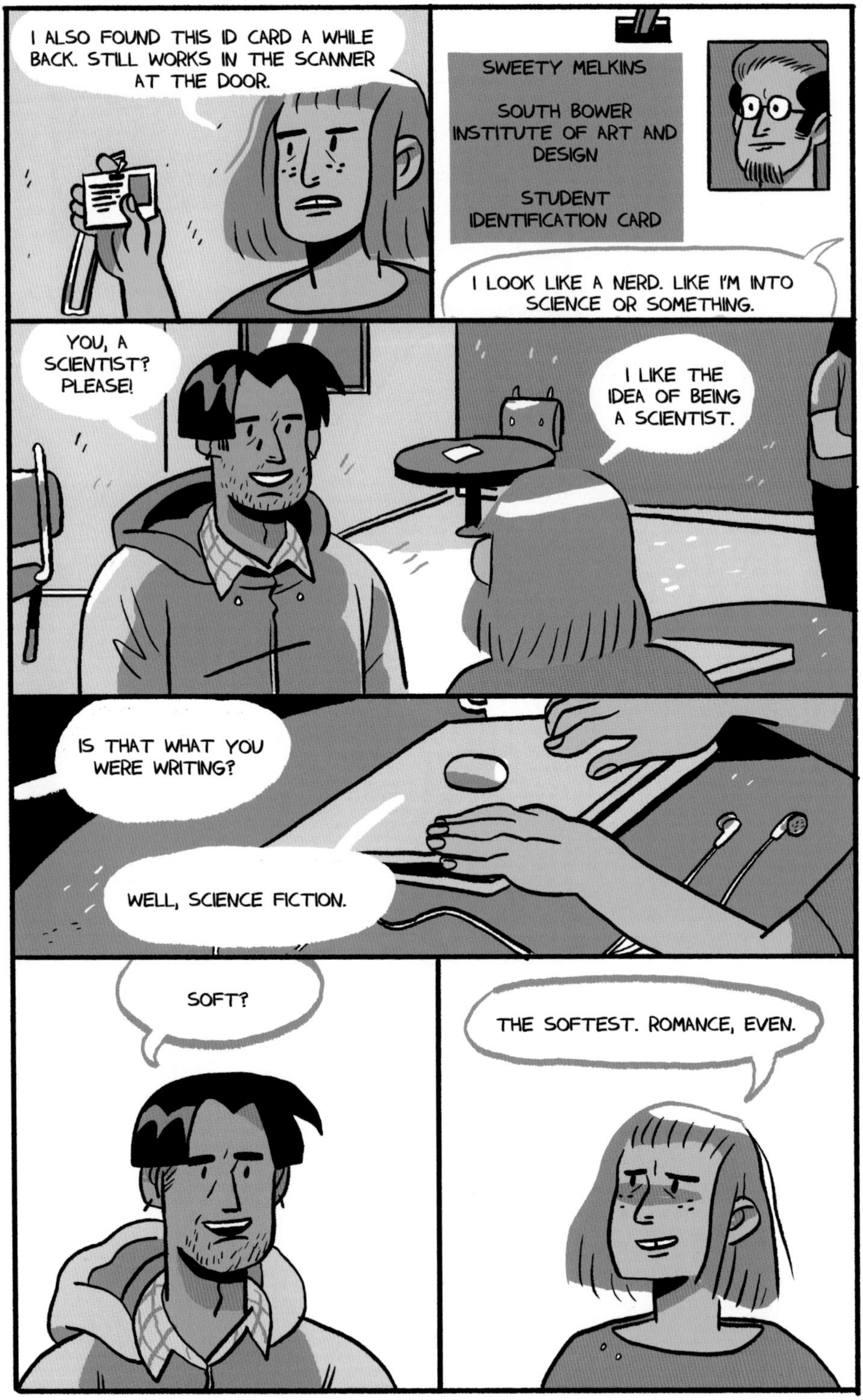
I ALSO FOUND THIS ID CARD A WHILE BACK. STILL WORKS IN THE SCANNER AT THE DOOR.
SWEETY MELKINS
SOUTH BOWER INSTITUTE OF ART AND DESIGN
STUDENT IDENTIFICATION CARD
I LOOK LIKE A NERD. LIKE I'M INTO SCIENCE OR SOMETHING.
YOU, A SCIENTIST? PLEASE!
I LIKE THE IDEA OF BEING A SCIENTIST.
IS THAT WHAT YOU WERE WRITING?
WELL, SCIENCE FICTION.
SOFT?
THE SOFTEST. ROMANCE, EVEN.

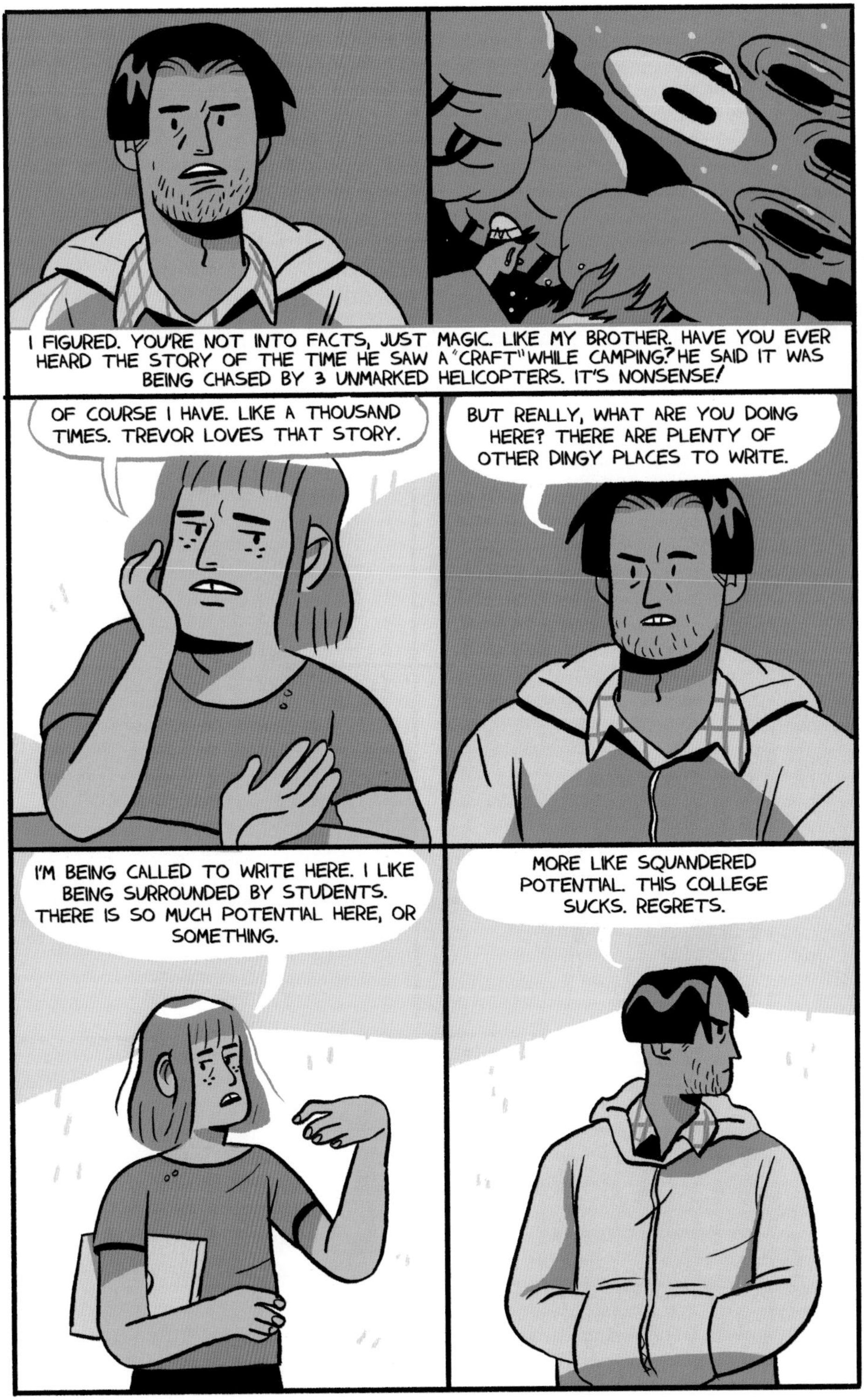
I FIGURED. YOU'RE NOT INTO FACTS, JUST MAGIC. LIKE MY BROTHER. HAVE YOU EVER HEARD THE STORY OF THE TIME HE SAW A "CRAFT" WHILE CAMPING? HE SAID IT WAS BEING CHASED BY 3 UNMARKED HELICOPTERS. IT'S NONSENSE!
OF COURSE I HAVE. LIKE A THOUSAND TIMES. TREVOR LOVES THAT STORY.
BUT REALLY, WHAT ARE YOU DOING HERE? THERE ARE PLENTY OF OTHER DINGY PLACES TO WRITE.
I'M BEING CALLED TO WRITE HERE. I LIKE BEING SURROUNDED BY STUDENTS. THERE IS SO MUCH POTENTIAL HERE, OR SOMETHING.
MORE LIKE SQUANDERED POTENTIAL. THIS COLLEGE SUCKS. REGRETS.

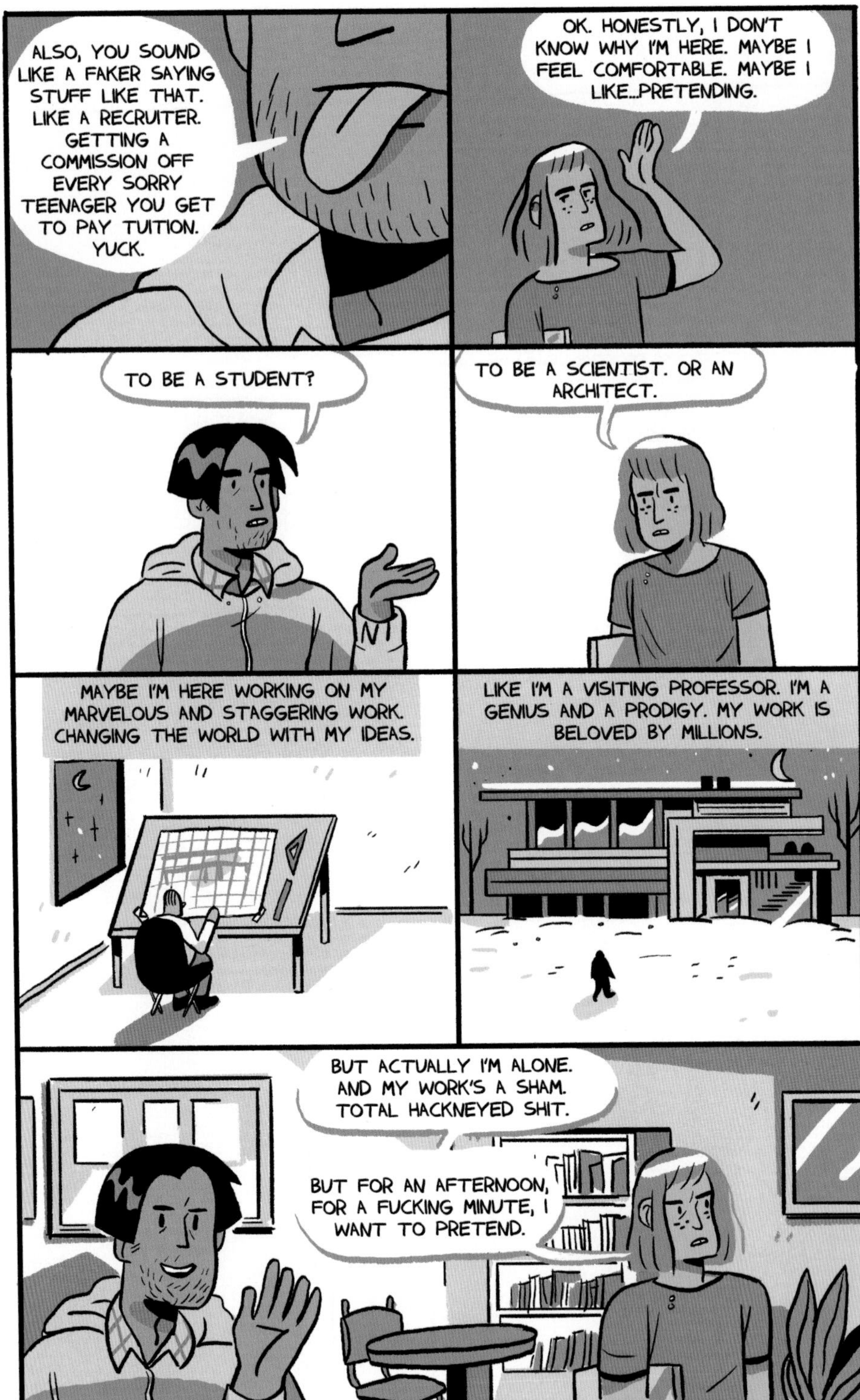
ALSO, YOU SOUND LIKE A FAKER SAYING STUFF LIKE THAT. LIKE A RECRUITER. GETTING A COMMISSION OFF EVERY SORRY TEENAGER YOU GET TO PAY TUITION. YUCK.
OK. HONESTLY, I DON'T KNOW WHY I'M HERE. MAYBE I FEEL COMFORTABLE. MAYBE I LIKE...PRETENDING.
TO BE A STUDENT?
TO BE A SCIENTIST. OR AN ARCHITECT.
MAYBE I'M HERE WORKING ON MY MARVELOUS AND STAGGERING WORK. CHANGING THE WORLD WITH MY IDEAS.
LIKE I'M A VISITING PROFESSOR. I'M A GENIUS AND A PRODIGY. MY WORK IS BELOVED BY MILLIONS.
BUT ACTUALLY I'M ALONE. AND MY WORK'S A SHAM. TOTAL HACKNEYED SHIT.
BUT FOR AN AFTERNOON, FOR A FUCKING MINUTE, I WANT TO PRETEND.

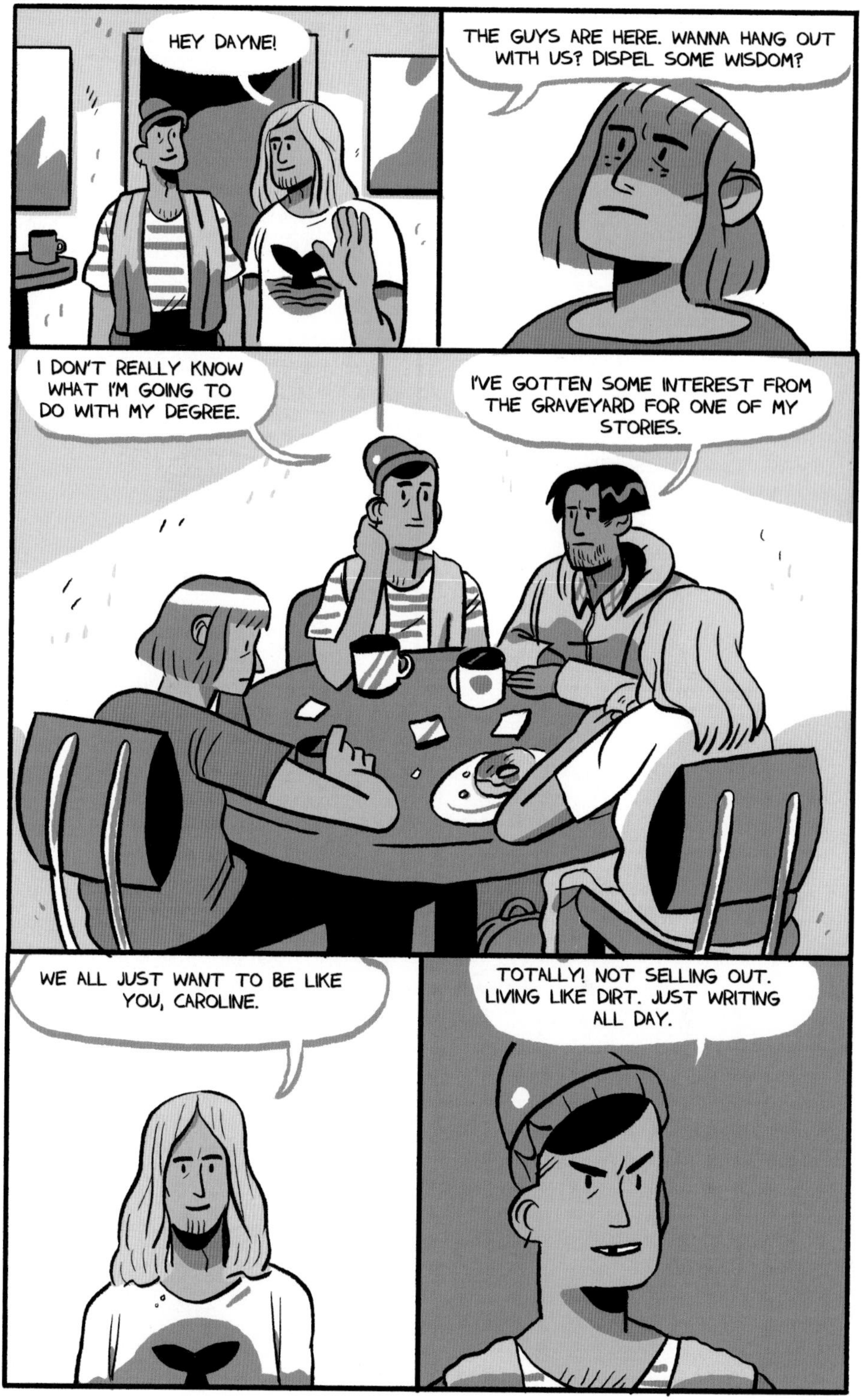
HEY DAYNE!
THE GUYS ARE HERE. WANNA HANG OUT WITH US? DISPEL SOME WISDOM?
I DON'T REALLY KNOW WHAT I'M GOING TO DO WITH MY DEGREE.
I'VE GOTTEN SOME INTEREST FROM THE GRAVEYARD FOR ONE OF MY STORIES.
WE ALL JUST WANT TO BE LIKE YOU, CAROLINE.
TOTALLY! NOT SELLING OUT. LIVING LIKE DIRT. JUST WRITING ALL DAY.

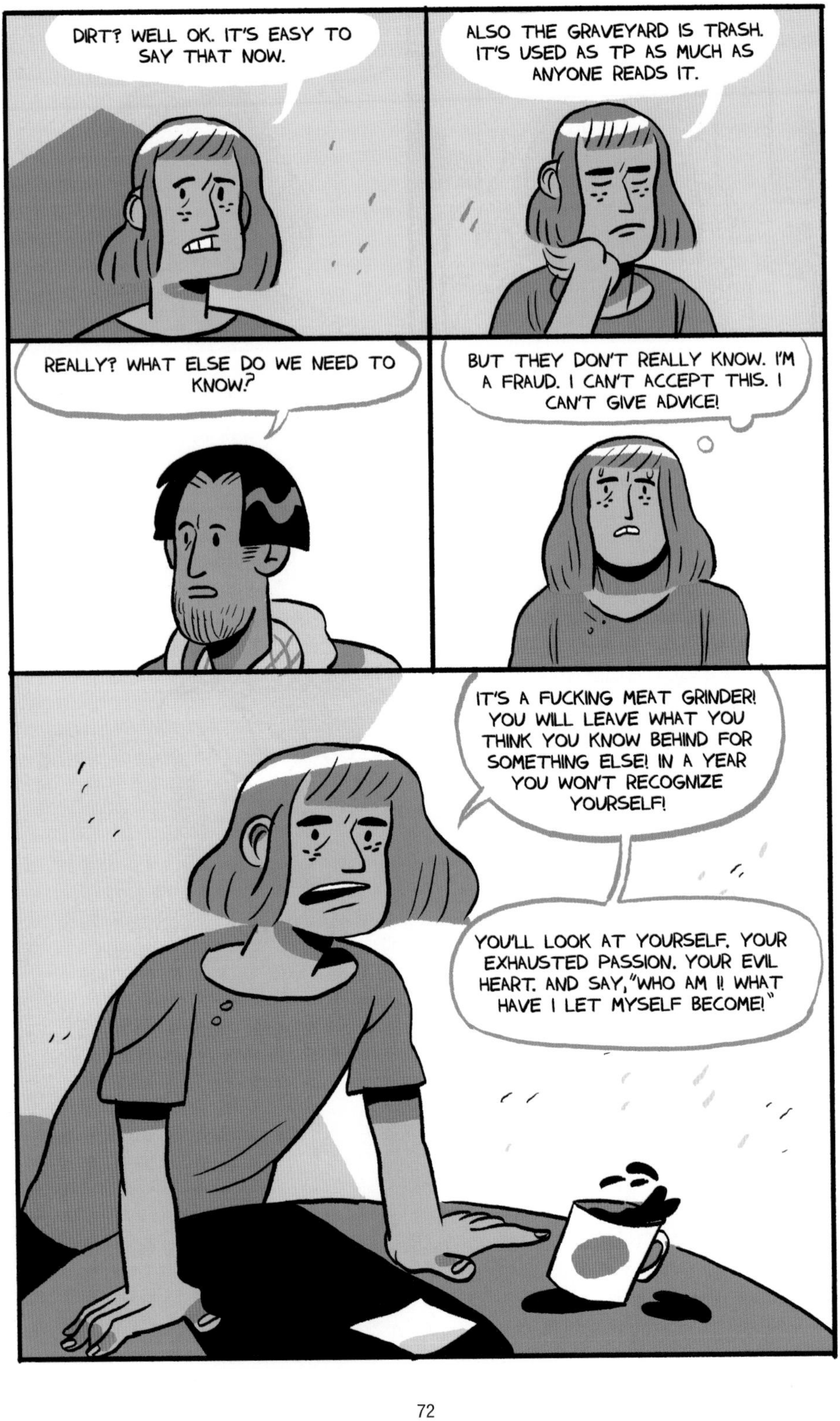
DIRT? WELL OK. IT'S EASY TO SAY THAT NOW.
ALSO THE GRAVEYARD IS TRASH. IT'S USED AS TP AS MUCH AS ANYONE READS IT.
REALLY? WHAT ELSE DO WE NEED TO KNOW?
BUT THEY DON'T REALLY KNOW. I'M A FRAUD. I CAN'T ACCEPT THIS. I CAN'T GIVE ADVICE!
IT'S A FUCKING MEAT GRINDER! YOU WILL LEAVE WHAT YOU THINK YOU KNOW BEHIND FOR SOMETHING ELSE! IN A YEAR YOU WON'T RECOGNIZE YOURSELF!
YOU'LL LOOK AT YOURSELF. YOUR EXHAUSTED PASSION. YOUR EVIL HEART. AND SAY, "WHO AM I! WHAT HAVE I LET MYSELF BECOME!"

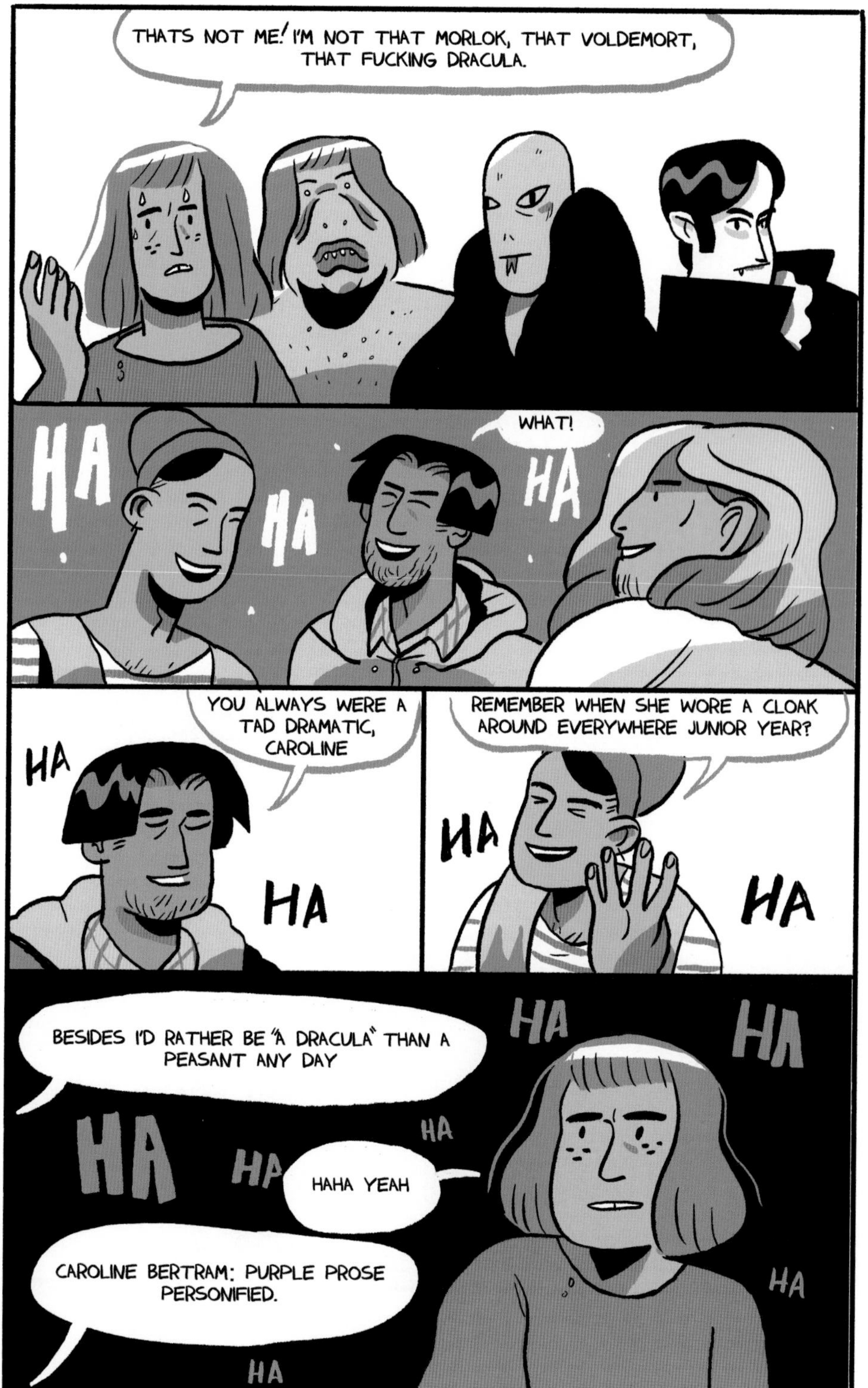
THATS NOT ME! I'M NOT THAT MORLOK, THAT VOLDEMORT, THAT FUCKING DRACULA.
HA
HA
WHAT!
HA
HA
YOU ALWAYS WERE A TAD DRAMATIC, CAROLINE
HA
REMEMBER WHEN SHE WORE A CLOAK AROUND EVERYWHERE JUNIOR YEAR?
HA
HA
BESIDES I'D RATHER BE "A DRACULA" THAN A PEASANT ANY DAY
HA
HA
HA
HA
HA
HAHA YEAH
CAROLINE BERTRAM: PURPLE PROSE PERSONIFIED.
HA
HA

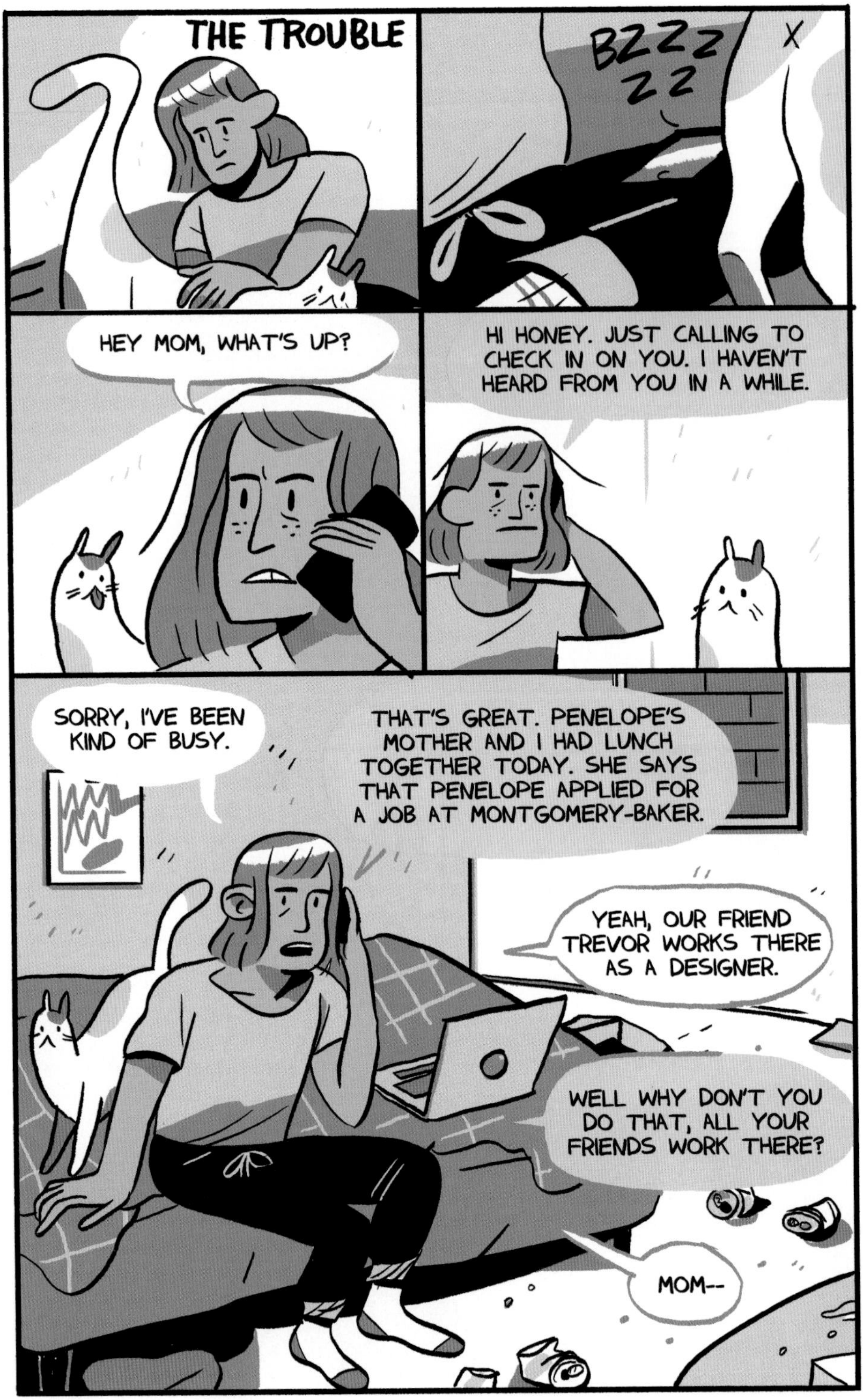
THE TROUBLE
BZZZZ ZZ
HEY MOM, WHAT'S UP?
HI HONEY. JUST CALLING TO CHECK IN ON YOU. I HAVEN'T HEARD FROM YOU IN A WHILE.
SORRY, I'VE BEEN KIND OF BUSY.
THAT'S GREAT. PENELOPE'S MOTHER AND I HAD LUNCH TOGETHER TODAY. SHE SAYS THAT PENELOPE APPLIED FOR A JOB AT MONTGOMERY-BAKER.
YEAH, OUR FRIEND TREVOR WORKS THERE AS A DESIGNER.
WELL WHY DON'T YOU DO THAT, ALL YOUR FRIENDS WORK THERE?
MOM--

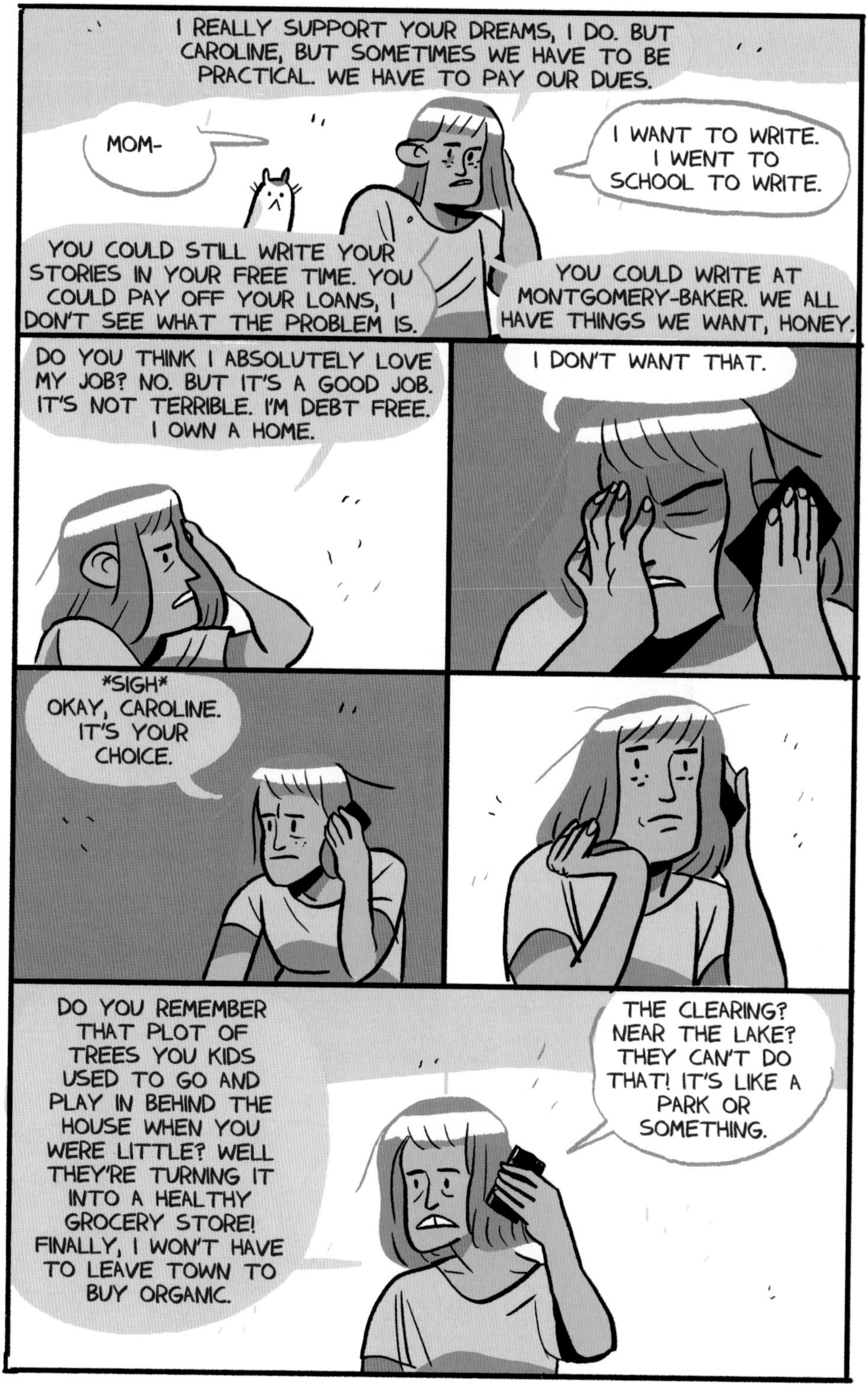
I REALLY SUPPORT YOUR DREAMS, I DO. BUT CAROLINE, BUT SOMETIMES WE HAVE TO BE PRACTICAL. WE HAVE TO PAY OUR DUES.
MOM-
I WANT TO WRITE. I WENT TO SCHOOL TO WRITE.
YOU COULD STILL WRITE YOUR STORIES IN YOUR FREE TIME. YOU COULD PAY OFF YOUR LOANS, I DON'T SEE WHAT THE PROBLEM IS.
YOU COULD WRITE AT MONTGOMERY-BAKER. WE ALL HAVE THINGS WE WANT, HONEY.
DO YOU THINK I ABSOLUTELY LOVE MY JOB? NO. BUT IT'S A GOOD JOB. IT'S NOT TERRIBLE. I'M DEBT FREE. I OWN A HOME.
I DON'T WANT THAT.
*SIGH* OKAY, CAROLINE. IT'S YOUR CHOICE.
DO YOU REMEMBER THAT PLOT OF TREES YOU KIDS USED TO GO AND PLAY IN BEHIND THE HOUSE WHEN YOU WERE LITTLE? WELL THEY'RE TURNING IT INTO A HEALTHY GROCERY STORE! FINALLY, I WON'T HAVE TO LEAVE TOWN TO BUY ORGANIC.
THE CLEARING? NEAR THE LAKE? THEY CAN'T DO THAT! IT'S LIKE A PARK OR SOMETHING.

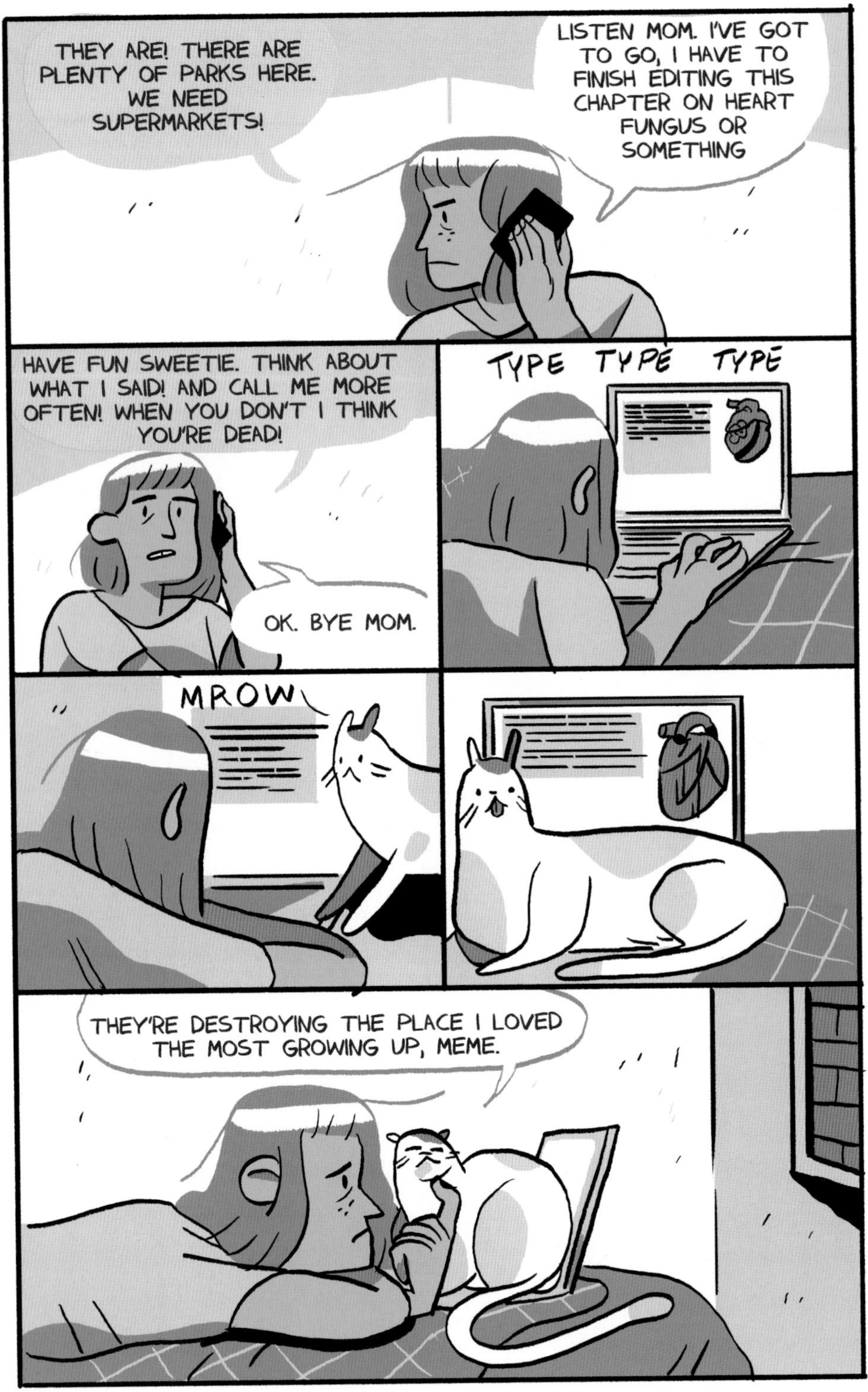
THEY ARE! THERE ARE PLENTY OF PARKS HERE. WE NEED SUPERMARKETS!
LISTEN MOM. I'VE GOT TO GO, I HAVE TO FINISH EDITING THIS CHAPTER ON HEART FUNGUS OR SOMETHING
HAVE FUN SWEETIE. THINK ABOUT WHAT I SAID! AND CALL ME MORE OFTEN! WHEN YOU DON'T I THINK YOU'RE DEAD!
OK. BYE MOM.
TYPE TYPE TYPE
MROW
THEY'RE DESTROYING THE PLACE I LOVED THE MOST GROWING UP, MEME.

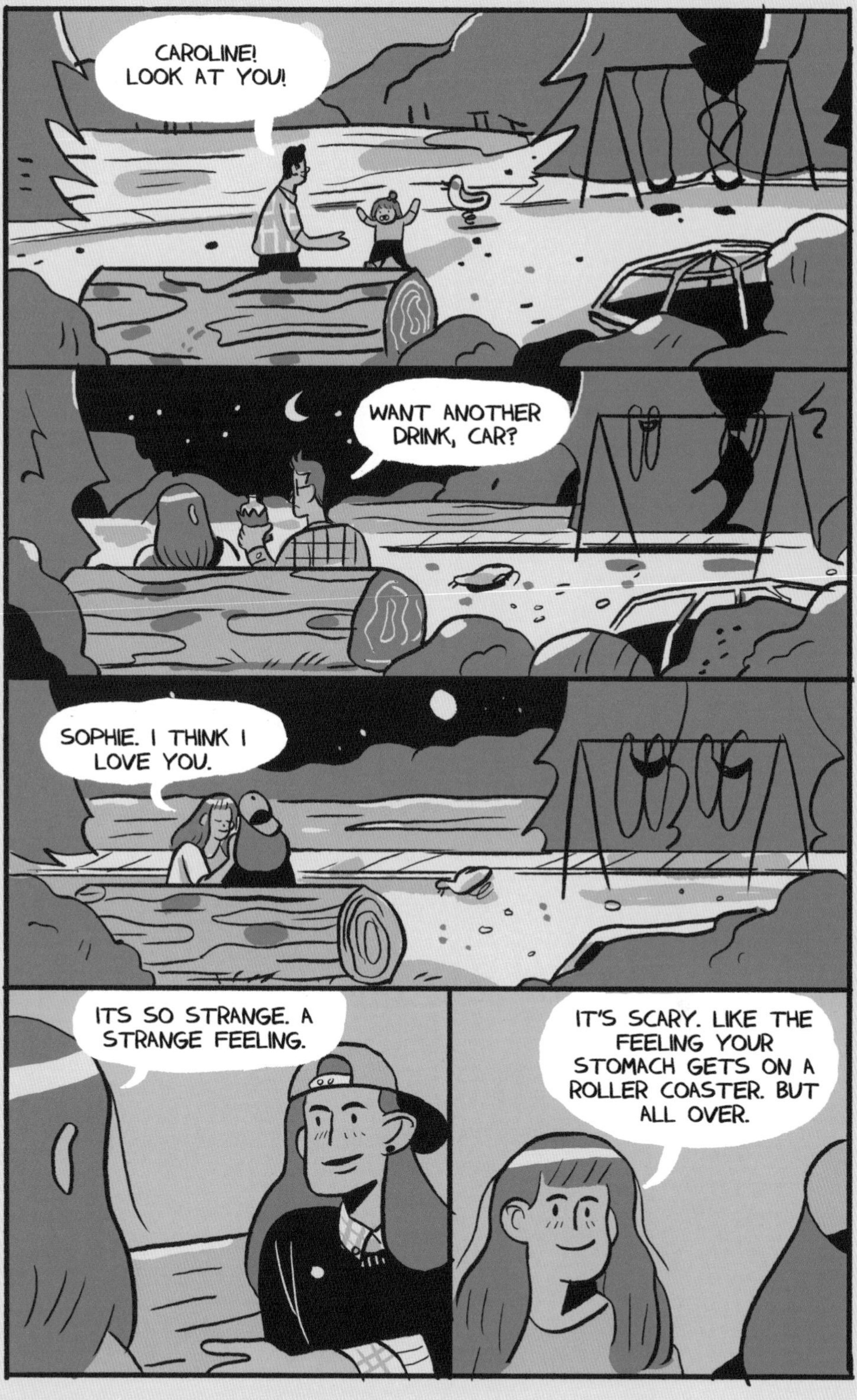
CAROLINE! LOOK AT YOU!
WANT ANOTHER DRINK, CAR?
SOPHIE. I THINK I LOVE YOU.
ITS SO STRANGE. A STRANGE FEELING.
IT'S SCARY. LIKE THE FEELING YOUR STOMACH GETS ON A ROLLER COASTER. BUT ALL OVER.

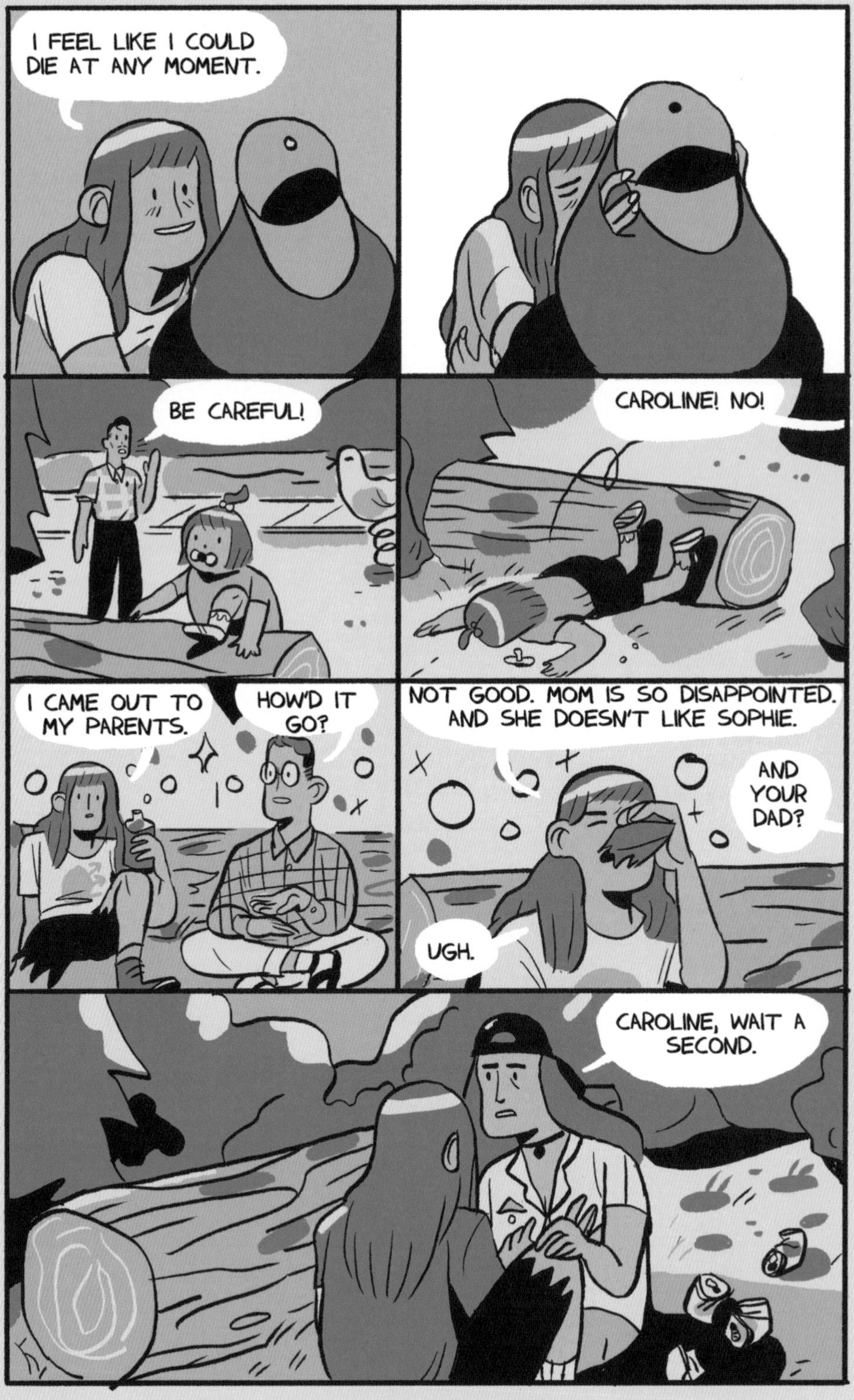

I FEEL LIKE I COULD DIE AT ANY MOMENT.
BE CAREFUL!
CAROLINE! NO!
I CAME OUT TO MY PARENTS.
HOW'D IT GO?
NOT GOOD. MOM IS SO DISAPPOINTED. AND SHE DOESN'T LIKE SOPHIE.
AND YOUR DAD?
UGH.
CAROLINE, WAIT A SECOND.

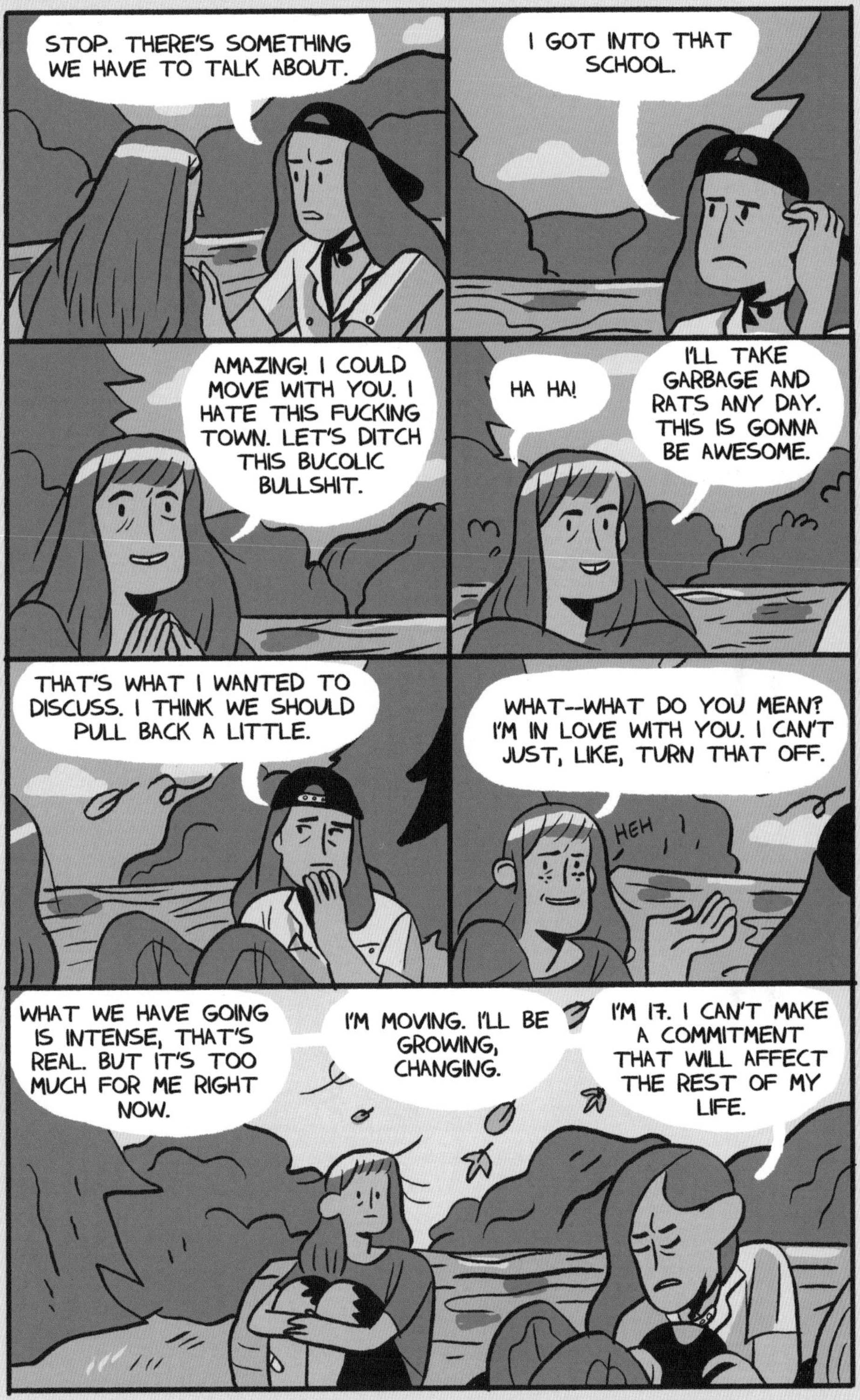
STOP. THERE'S SOMETHING WE HAVE TO TALK ABOUT.
I GOT INTO THAT SCHOOL.
AMAZING! I COULD MOVE WITH YOU. I HATE THIS FUCKING TOWN. LET'S DITCH THIS BUCOLIC BULLSHIT.
HA HA!
I'LL TAKE GARBAGE AND RATS ANY DAY. THIS IS GONNA BE AWESOME.
THAT'S WHAT I WANTED TO DISCUSS. I THINK WE SHOULD PULL BACK A LITTLE.
WHAT--WHAT DO YOU MEAN? I'M IN LOVE WITH YOU. I CAN'T JUST, LIKE, TURN THAT OFF.
HEH
WHAT WE HAVE GOING IS INTENSE, THAT'S REAL. BUT IT'S TOO MUCH FOR ME RIGHT NOW.
I'M MOVING. I'LL BE GROWING, CHANGING.
I'M 17. I CAN'T MAKE A COMMITMENT THAT WILL AFFECT THE REST OF MY LIFE.

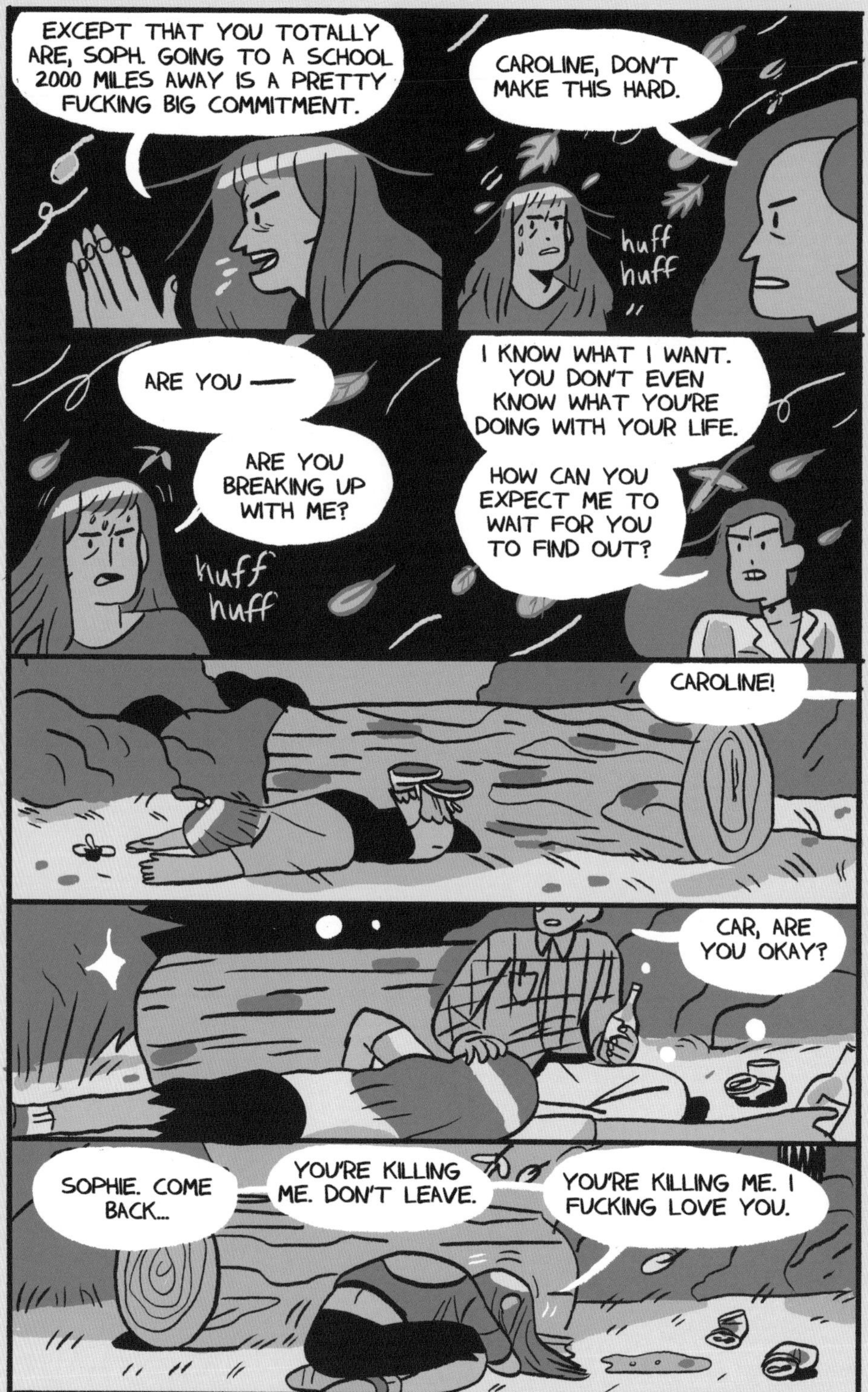
EXCEPT THAT YOU TOTALLY ARE, SOPH. GOING TO A SCHOOL 2000 MILES AWAY IS A PRETTY FUCKING BIG COMMITMENT.
CAROLINE, DON'T MAKE THIS HARD.
huff huff
ARE YOU —
ARE YOU BREAKING UP WITH ME?
huff huff
I KNOW WHAT I WANT. YOU DON'T EVEN KNOW WHAT YOU'RE DOING WITH YOUR LIFE.
HOW CAN YOU EXPECT ME TO WAIT FOR YOU TO FIND OUT?
CAROLINE!
CAR, ARE YOU OKAY?
SOPHIE. COME BACK...
YOU'RE KILLING ME. DON'T LEAVE.
YOU'RE KILLING ME. I FUCKING LOVE YOU.

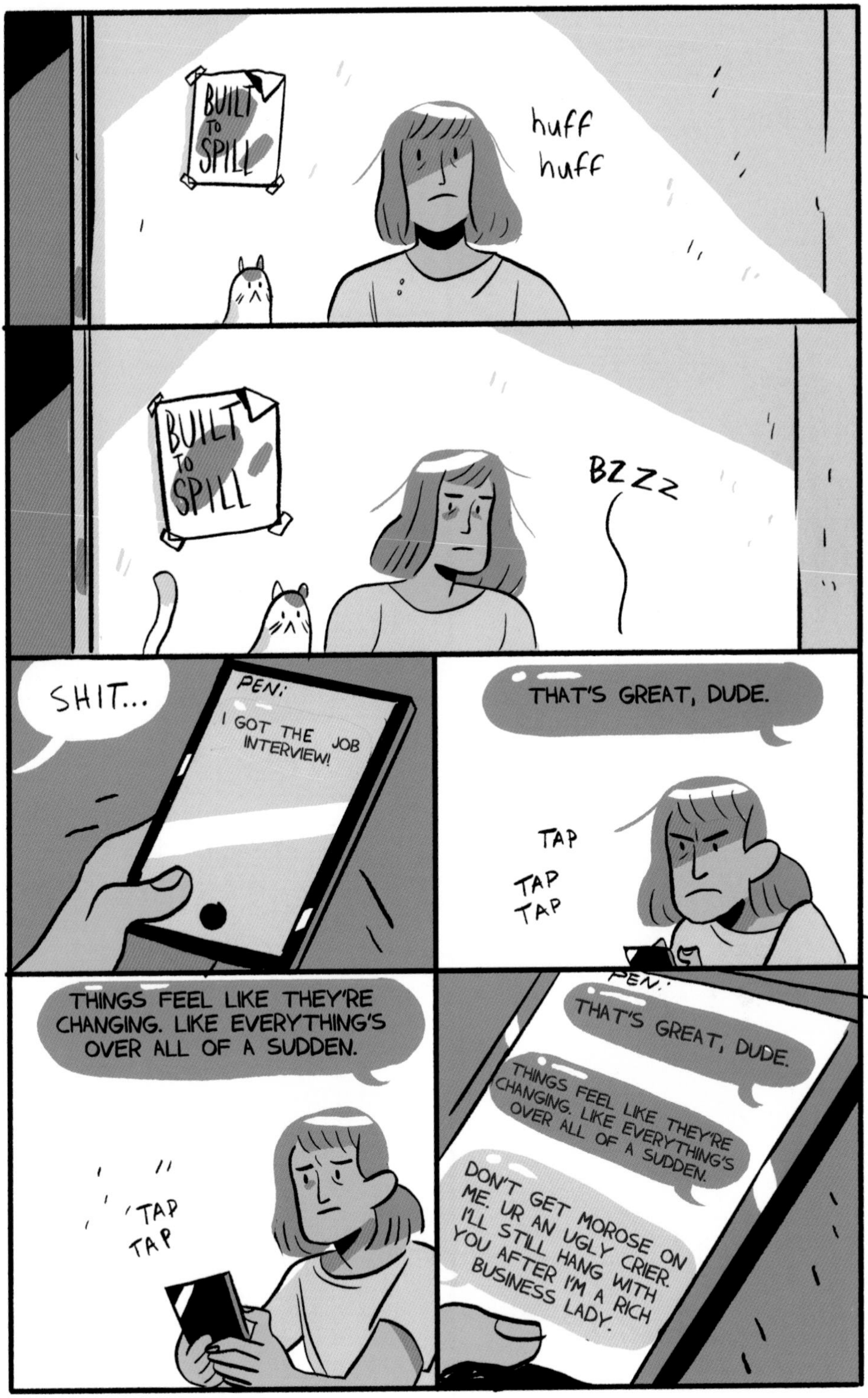
BUILT TO SPILL
huff
huff
BUILT TO SPILL
BZZZ
SHIT...
PEN:
I GOT THE JOB INTERVIEW!
THAT'S GREAT, DUDE.
TAP
TAP
TAP
THINGS FEEL LIKE THEY'RE CHANGING. LIKE EVERYTHING'S OVER ALL OF A SUDDEN.
TAP
TAP
PEN:
THAT'S GREAT, DUDE.
THINGS FEEL LIKE THEY'RE CHANGING. LIKE EVERYTHING'S OVER ALL OF A SUDDEN.
DON'T GET MOROSE ON ME. UR AN UGLY CRIER. I'LL STILL HANG WITH YOU AFTER I'M A RICH BUSINESS LADY.

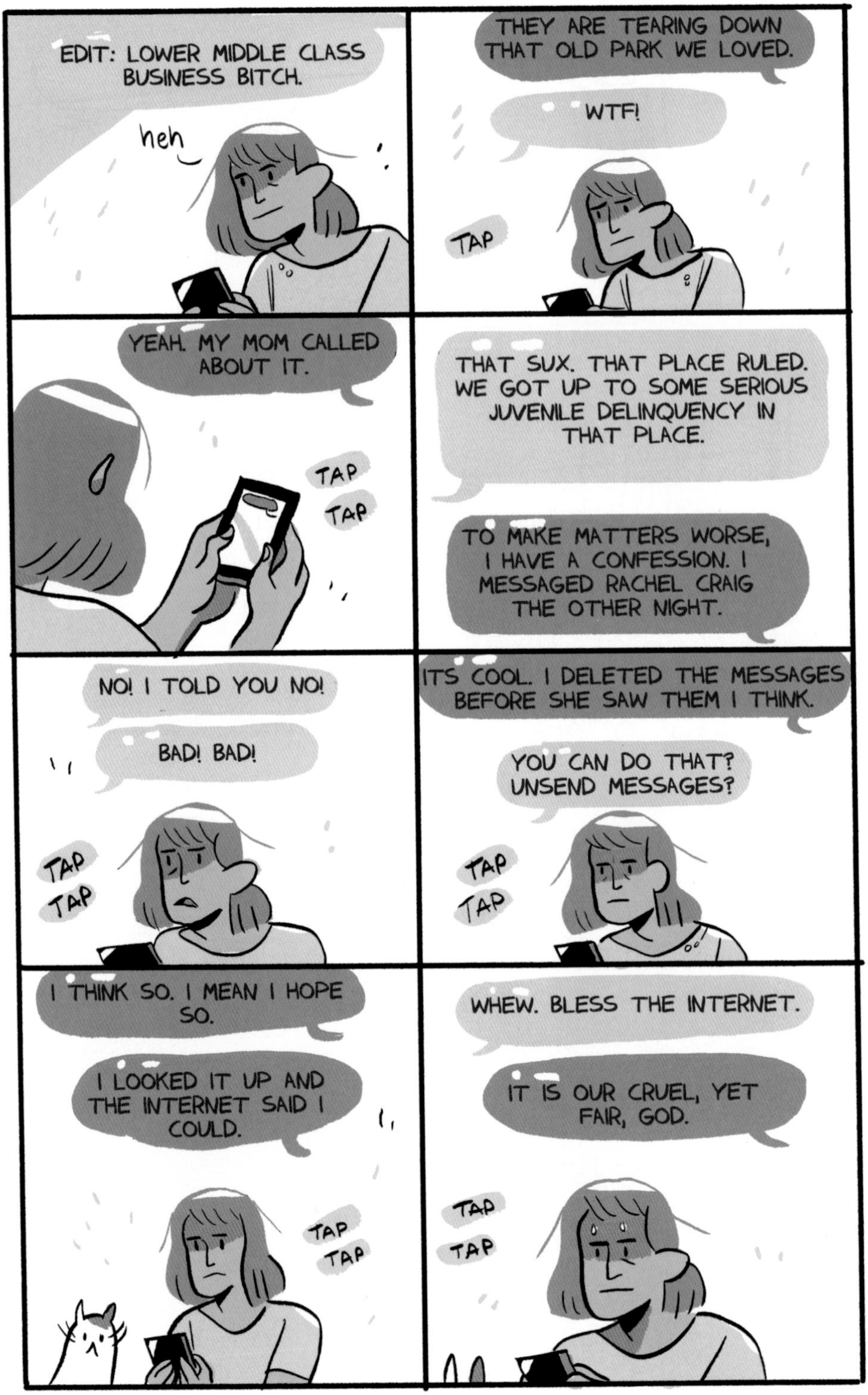
EDIT: LOWER MIDDLE CLASS BUSINESS BITCH.
heh
THEY ARE TEARING DOWN THAT OLD PARK WE LOVED.
WTF!
TAP
YEAH. MY MOM CALLED ABOUT IT.
TAP
TAP
THAT SUX. THAT PLACE RULED. WE GOT UP TO SOME SERIOUS JUVENILE DELINQUENCY IN THAT PLACE.
TO MAKE MATTERS WORSE, I HAVE A CONFESSION. I MESSAGED RACHEL CRAIG THE OTHER NIGHT.
NO! I TOLD YOU NO!
BAD! BAD!
TAP
TAP
ITS COOL. I DELETED THE MESSAGES BEFORE SHE SAW THEM I THINK.
YOU CAN DO THAT? UNSEND MESSAGES?
TAP
TAP
I THINK SO. I MEAN I HOPE SO.
I LOOKED IT UP AND THE INTERNET SAID I COULD.
TAP
TAP
WHEW. BLESS THE INTERNET.
IT IS OUR CRUEL, YET FAIR, GOD.
TAP
TAP

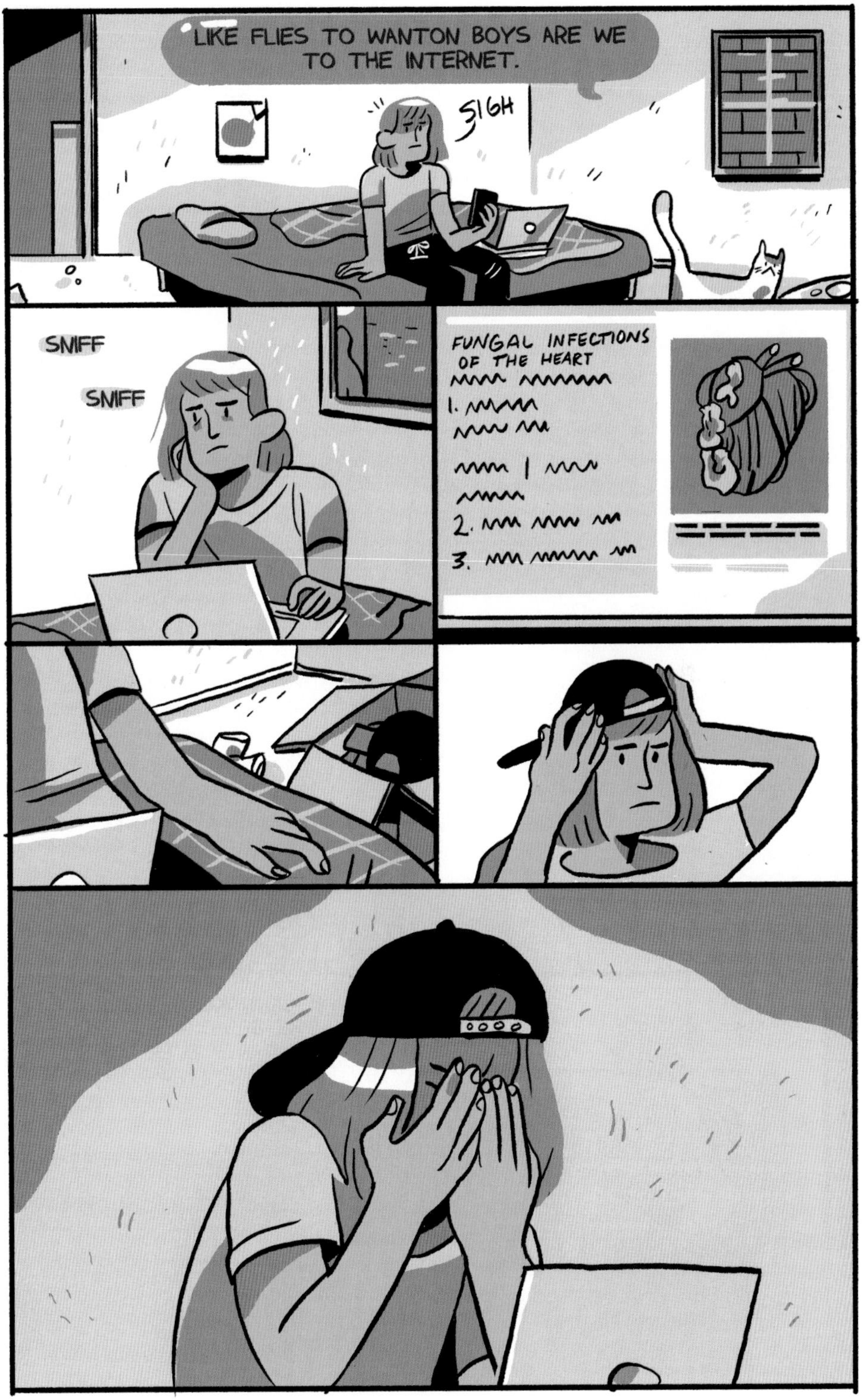
LIKE FLIES TO WANTON BOYS ARE WE TO THE INTERNET.
SIGH
SNIFF
SNIFF
FUNGAL INFECTIONS OF THE HEART
1.
2.
3.

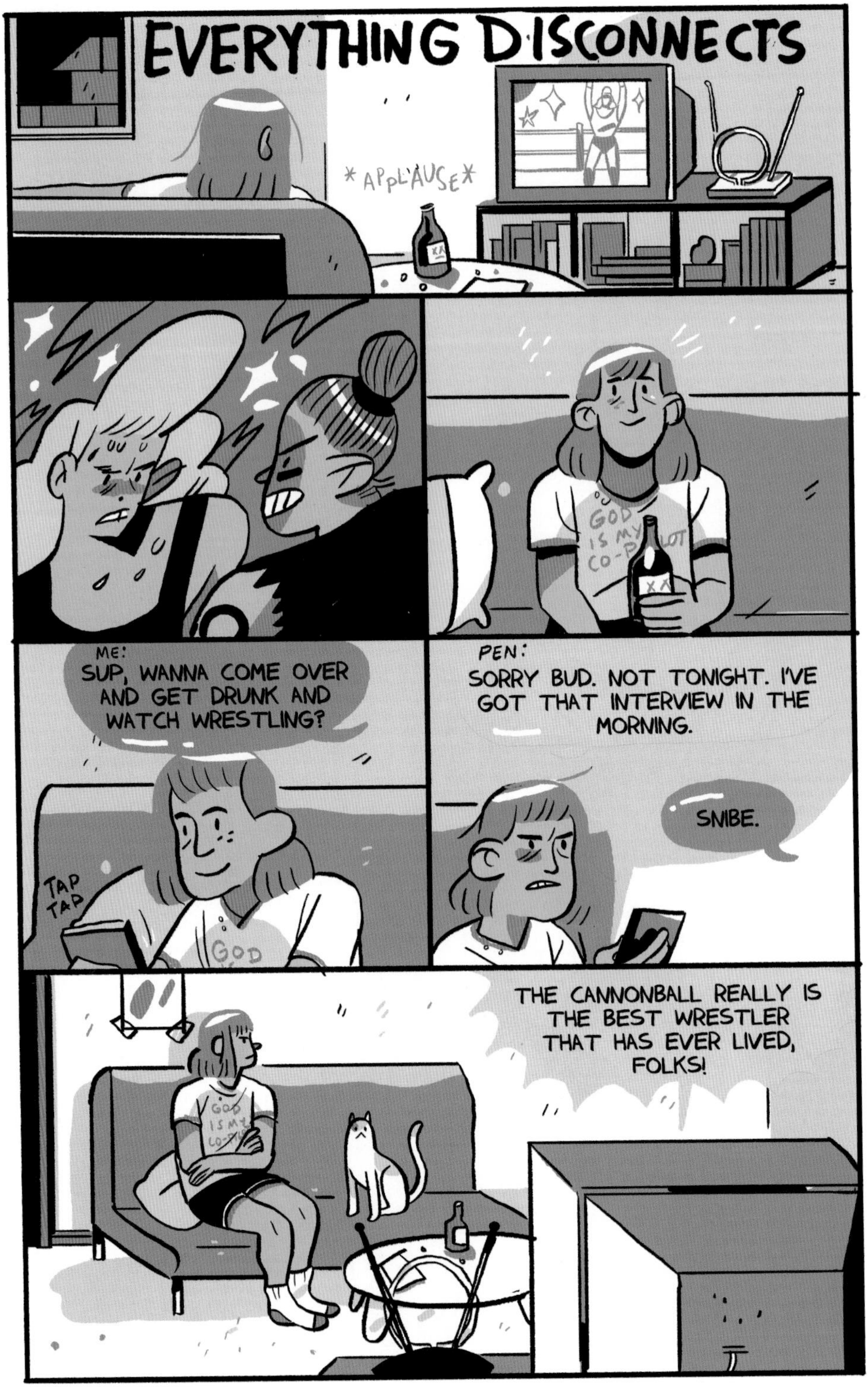
EVERYTHING DISCONNECTS
*APPLAUSE*
GOD IS MY CO-PILOT
ME:
SUP, WANNA COME OVER AND GET DRUNK AND WATCH WRESTLING?
TAP TAP
PEN:
SORRY BUD. NOT TONIGHT. I'VE GOT THAT INTERVIEW IN THE MORNING.
SNIBE.
THE CANNONBALL REALLY IS THE BEST WRESTLER THAT HAS EVER LIVED, FOLKS!

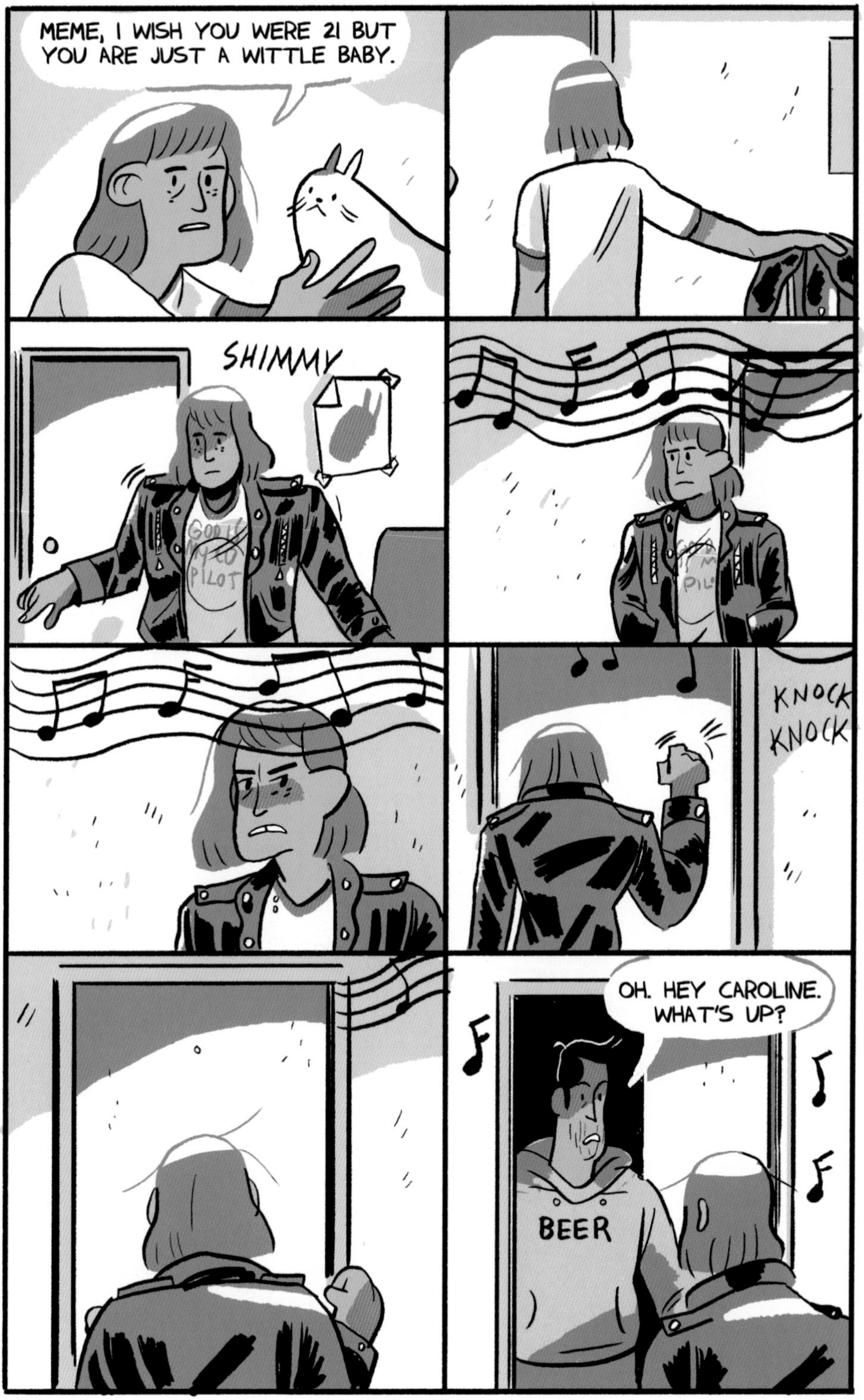
MEME, I WISH YOU WERE 21 BUT YOU ARE JUST A WITTLE BABY.
SHIMMY
KNOCK KNOCK
OH. HEY CAROLINE. WHAT'S UP?
BEER

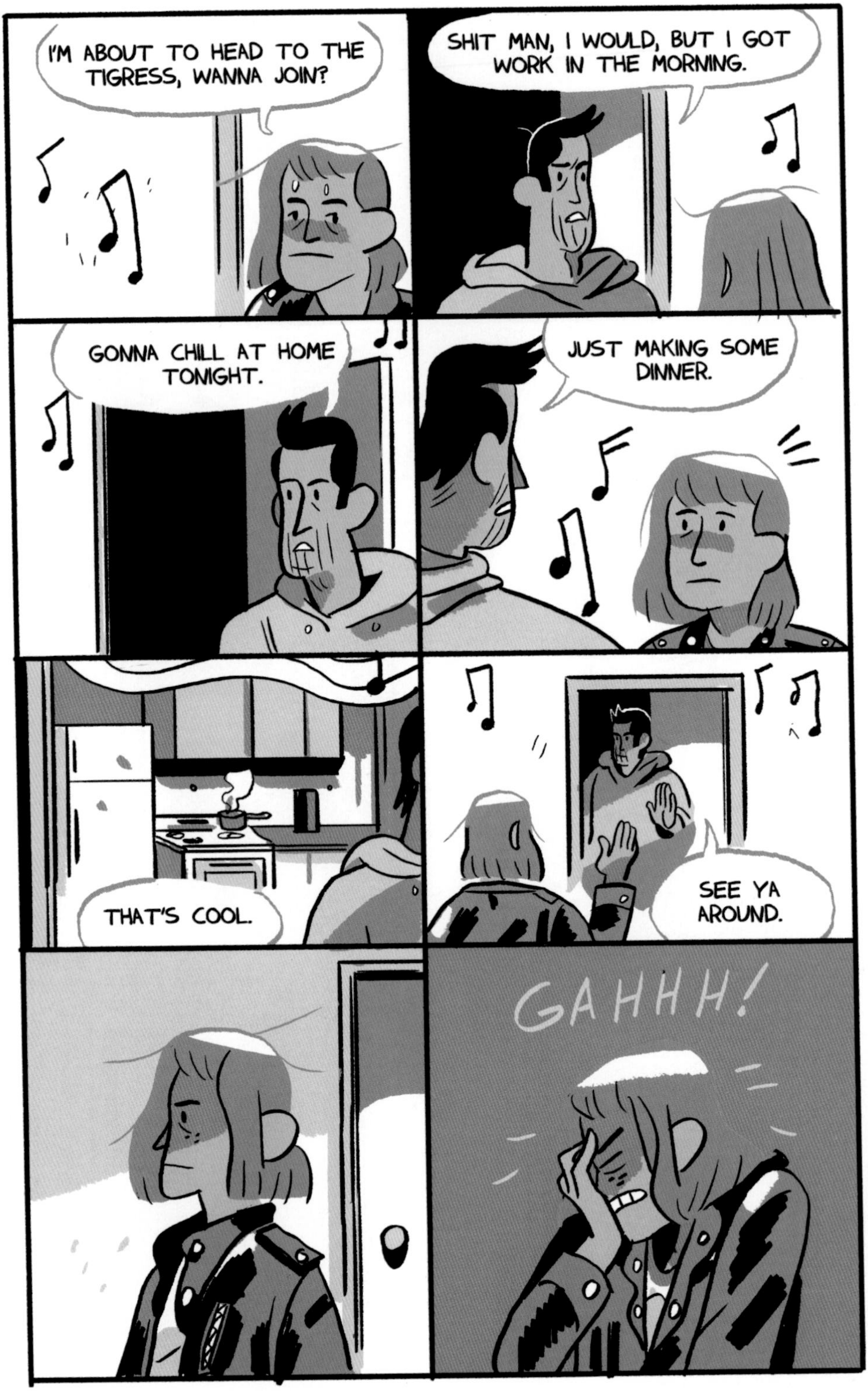
I'M ABOUT TO HEAD TO THE TIGRESS, WANNA JOIN?
SHIT MAN, I WOULD, BUT I GOT WORK IN THE MORNING.
GONNA CHILL AT HOME TONIGHT.
JUST MAKING SOME DINNER.
THAT'S COOL.
SEE YA AROUND.
GAHHH!

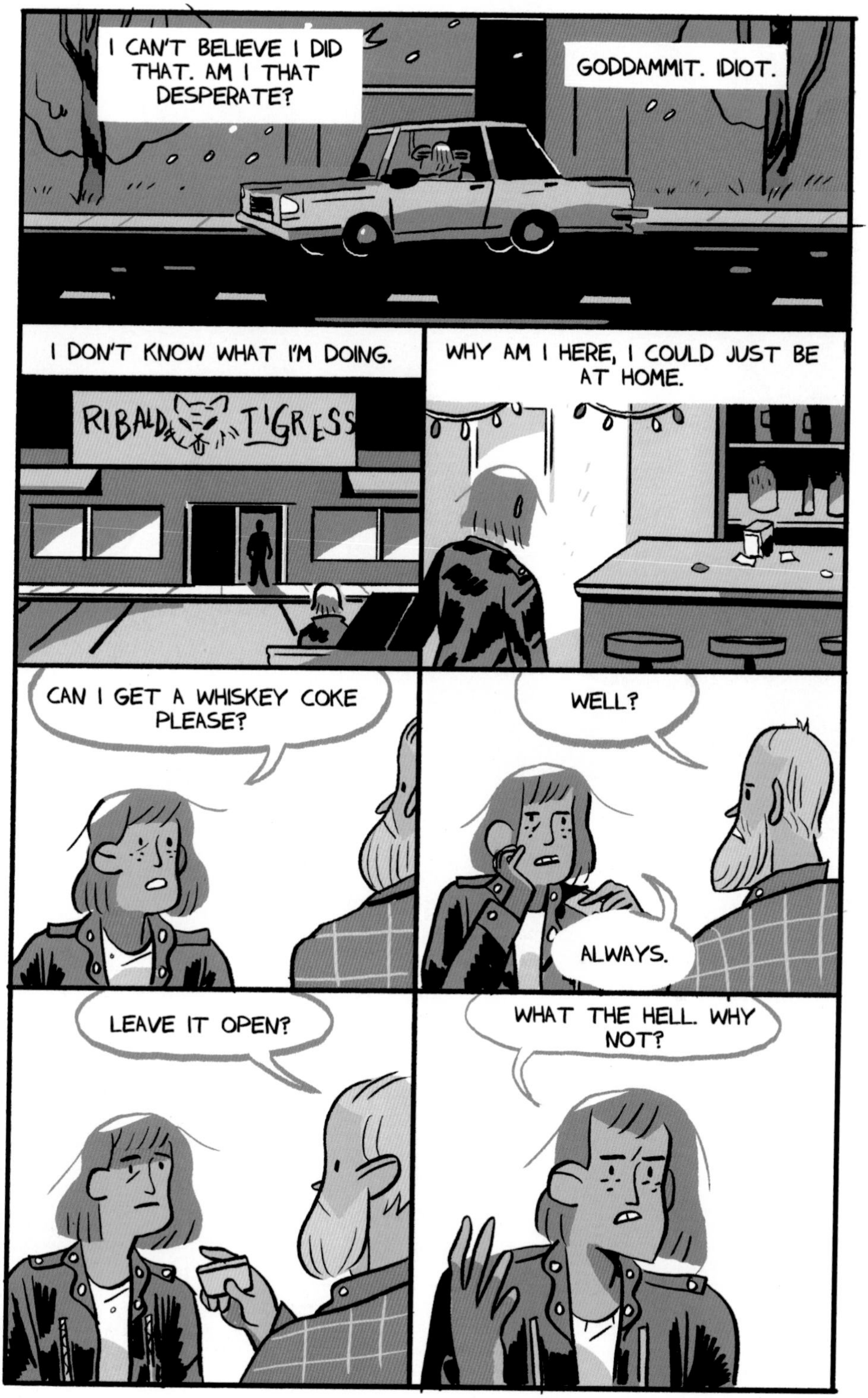
I CAN'T BELIEVE I DID THAT. AM I THAT DESPERATE?
GODDAMMIT. IDIOT.
I DON'T KNOW WHAT I'M DOING.
RIBALD TIGRESS
WHY AM I HERE, I COULD JUST BE AT HOME.
CAN I GET A WHISKEY COKE PLEASE?
WELL?
ALWAYS.
LEAVE IT OPEN?
WHAT THE HELL. WHY NOT?

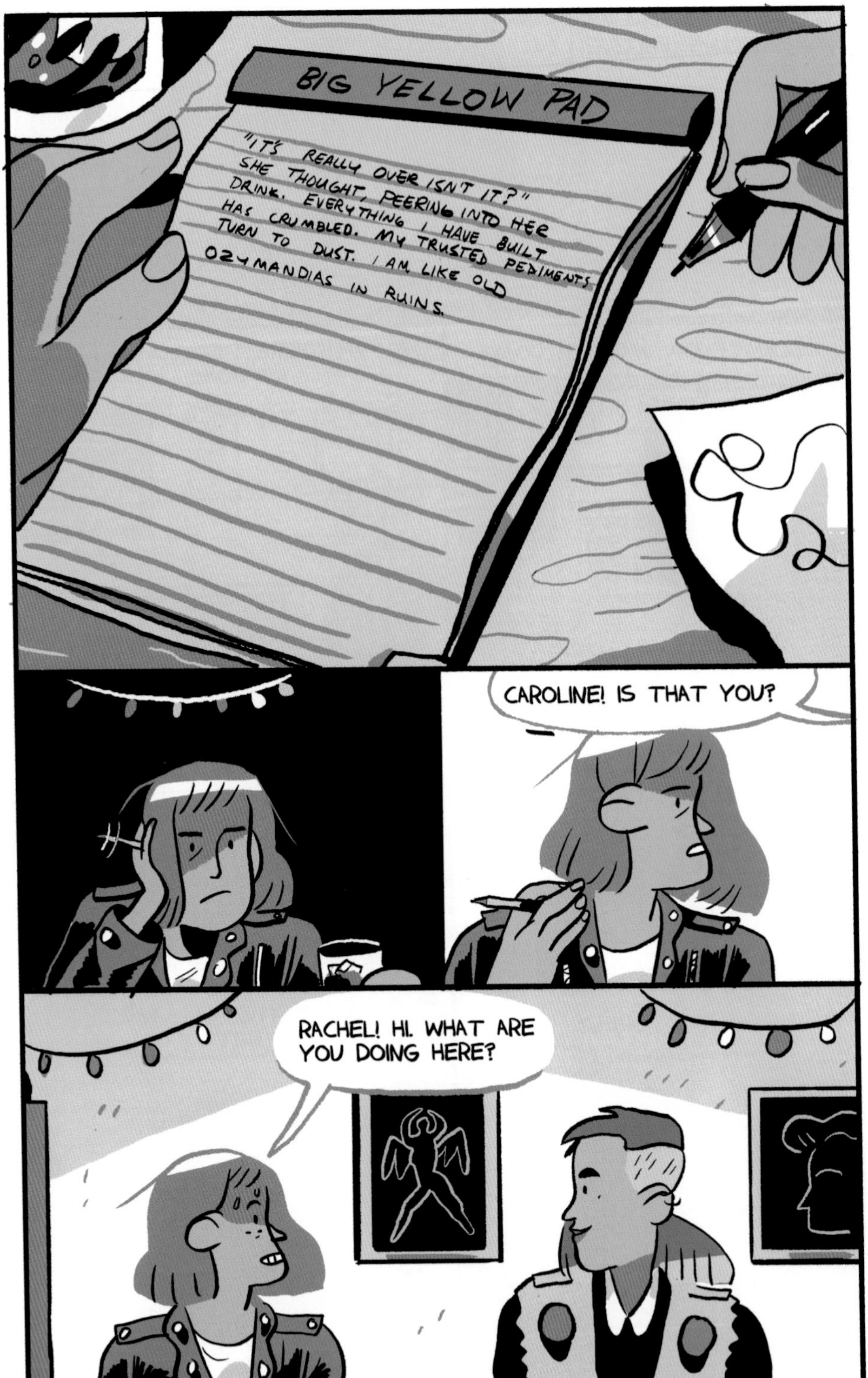
BIG YELLOW PAD
"IT'S REALLY OVER ISN'T IT?" SHE THOUGHT, PEERING INTO HER DRINK. EVERYTHING I HAVE BUILT HAS CRUMBLED. MY TRUSTED PEDIMENTS TURN TO DUST. I AM LIKE OLD OZYMANDIAS IN RUINS.
CAROLINE! IS THAT YOU?
RACHEL! HI. WHAT ARE YOU DOING HERE?

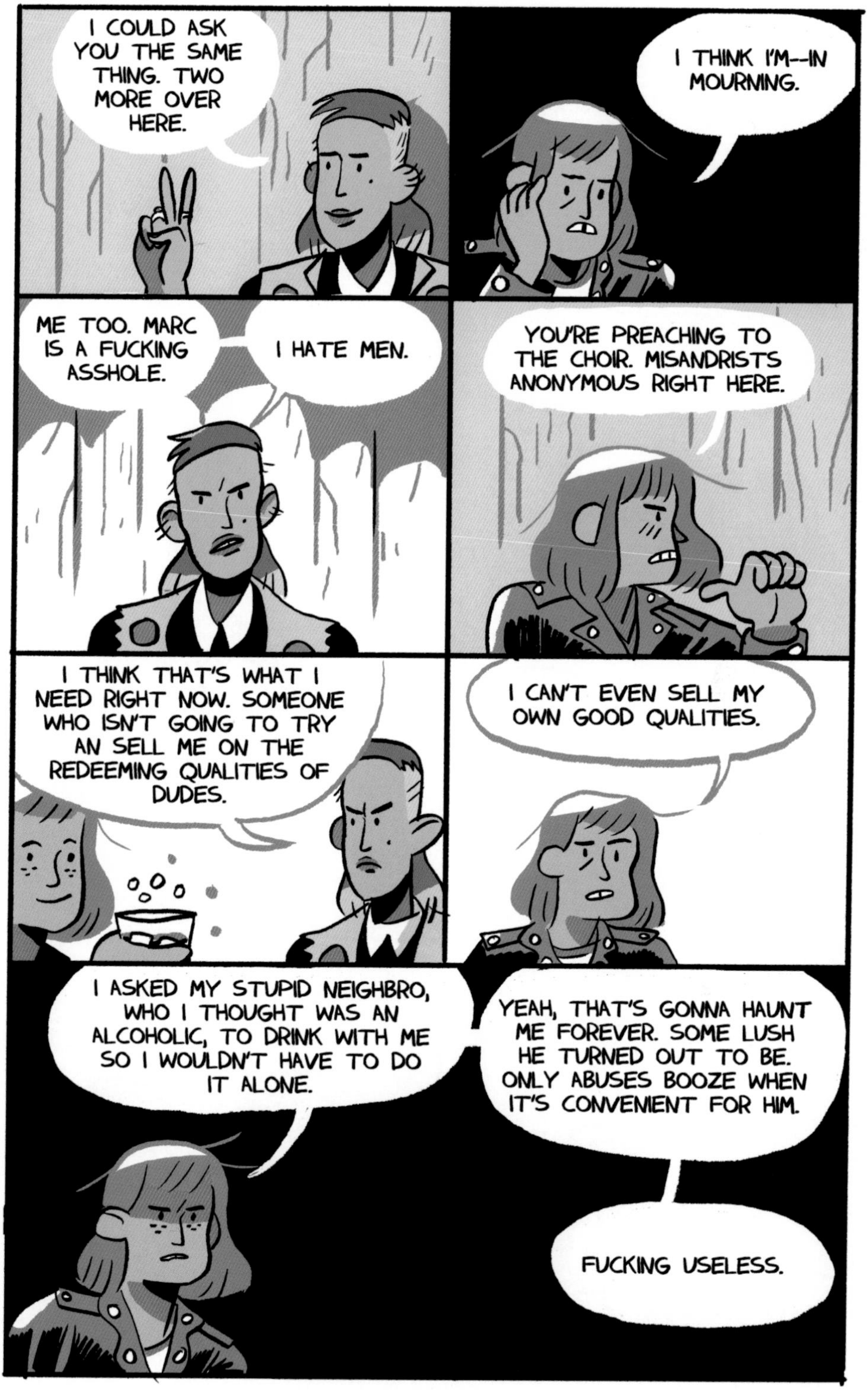
I COULD ASK YOU THE SAME THING. TWO MORE OVER HERE.
I THINK I'M--IN MOURNING.
ME TOO. MARC IS A FUCKING ASSHOLE.
I HATE MEN.
YOU'RE PREACHING TO THE CHOIR. MISANDRISTS ANONYMOUS RIGHT HERE.
I THINK THAT'S WHAT I NEED RIGHT NOW. SOMEONE WHO ISN'T GOING TO TRY AN SELL ME ON THE REDEEMING QUALITIES OF DUDES.
I CAN'T EVEN SELL MY OWN GOOD QUALITIES.
I ASKED MY STUPID NEIGHBRO, WHO I THOUGHT WAS AN ALCOHOLIC, TO DRINK WITH ME SO I WOULDN'T HAVE TO DO IT ALONE.
YEAH, THAT'S GONNA HAUNT ME FOREVER. SOME LUSH HE TURNED OUT TO BE. ONLY ABUSES BOOZE WHEN IT'S CONVENIENT FOR HIM.
FUCKING USELESS.

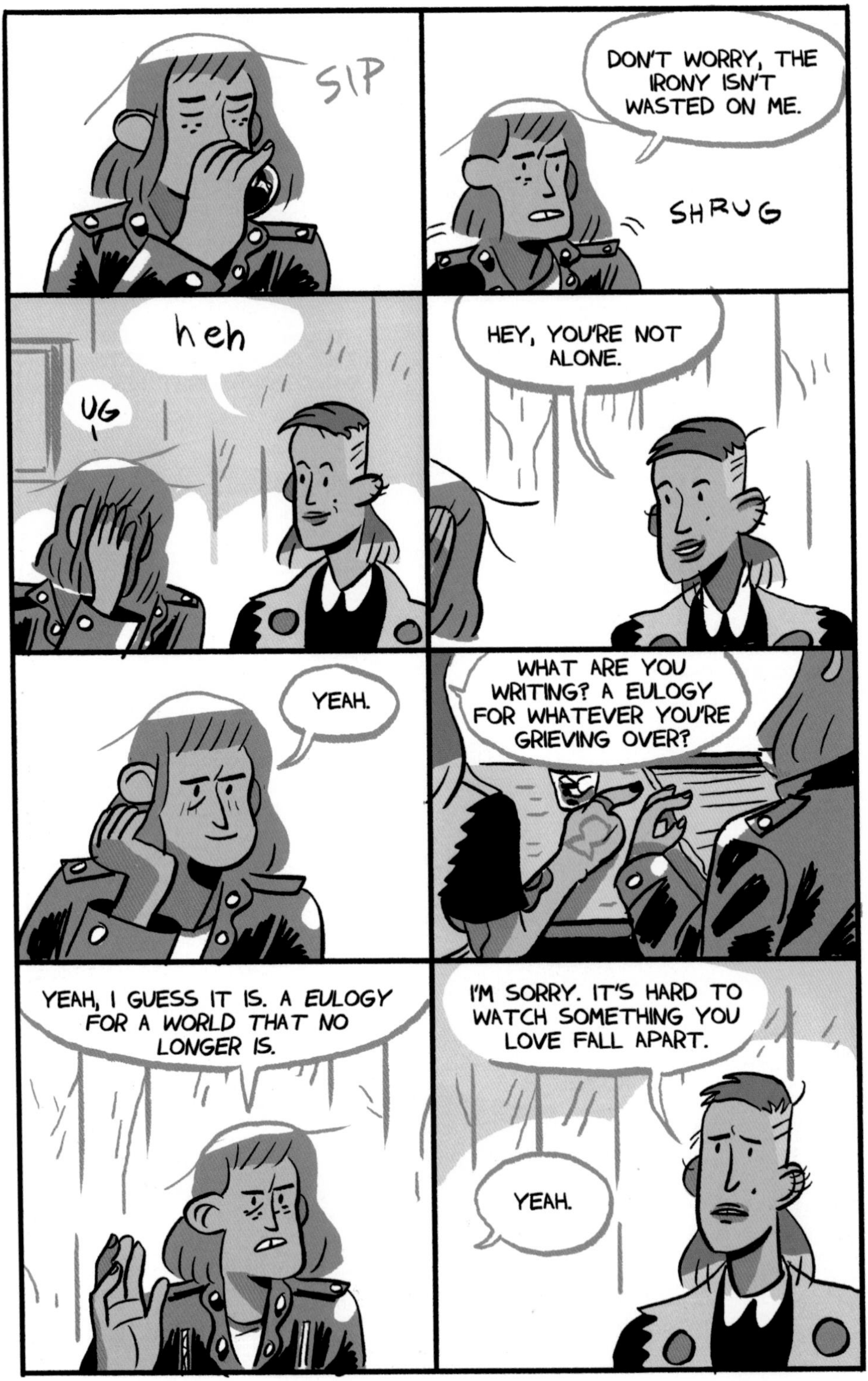
SIP
DON'T WORRY, THE IRONY ISN'T WASTED ON ME.
SHRUG
heh
UG
HEY, YOU'RE NOT ALONE.
YEAH.
WHAT ARE YOU WRITING? A EULOGY FOR WHATEVER YOU'RE GRIEVING OVER?
YEAH, I GUESS IT IS. A EULOGY FOR A WORLD THAT NO LONGER IS.
I'M SORRY. IT'S HARD TO WATCH SOMETHING YOU LOVE FALL APART.
YEAH.

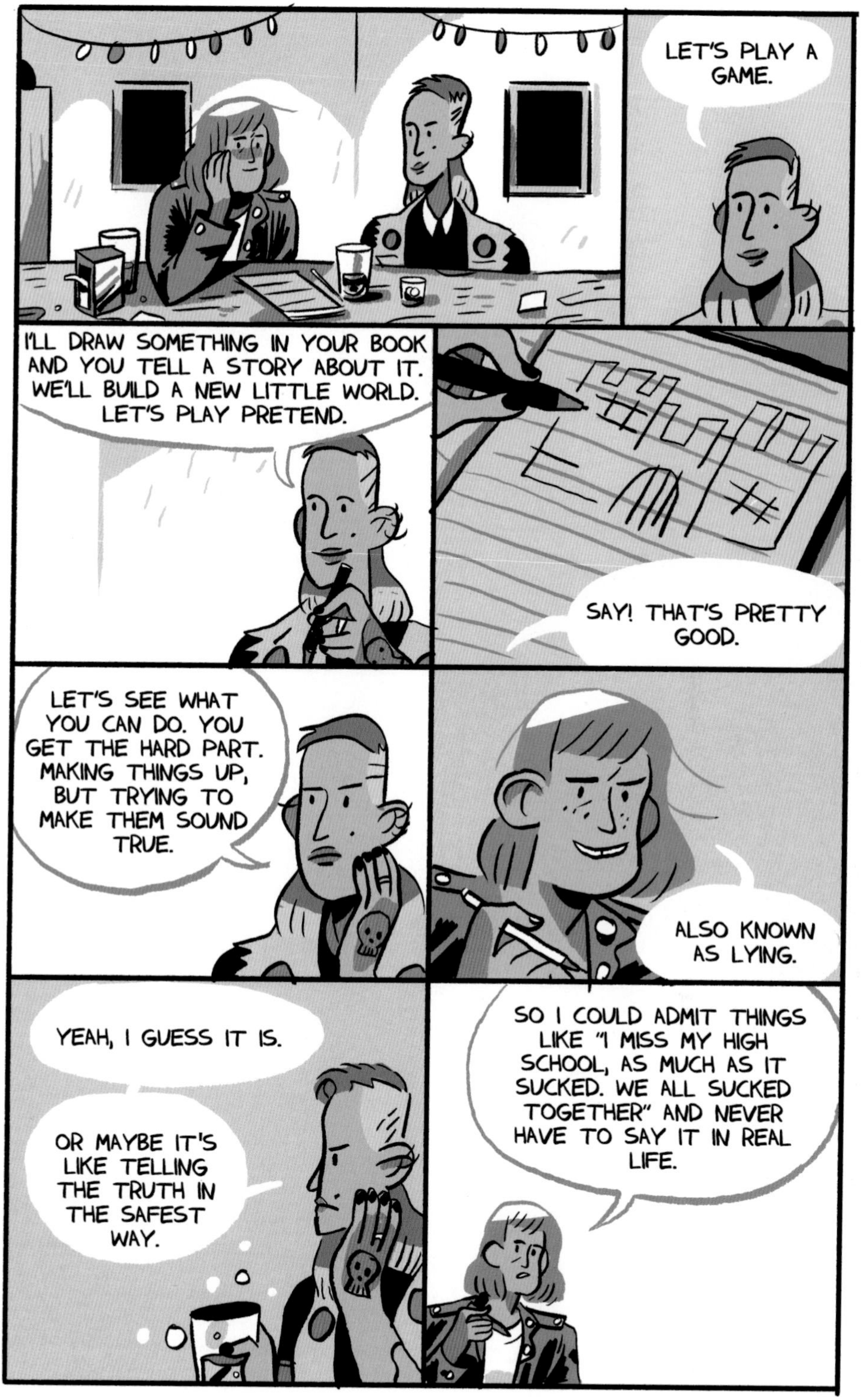

LET'S PLAY A GAME.
I'LL DRAW SOMETHING IN YOUR BOOK AND YOU TELL A STORY ABOUT IT. WE'LL BUILD A NEW LITTLE WORLD. LET'S PLAY PRETEND.
SAY! THAT'S PRETTY GOOD.
LET'S SEE WHAT YOU CAN DO. YOU GET THE HARD PART. MAKING THINGS UP, BUT TRYING TO MAKE THEM SOUND TRUE.
ALSO KNOWN AS LYING.
YEAH, I GUESS IT IS.
OR MAYBE IT'S LIKE TELLING THE TRUTH IN THE SAFEST WAY.
SO I COULD ADMIT THINGS LIKE "I MISS MY HIGH SCHOOL, AS MUCH AS IT SUCKED. WE ALL SUCKED TOGETHER" AND NEVER HAVE TO SAY IT IN REAL LIFE.

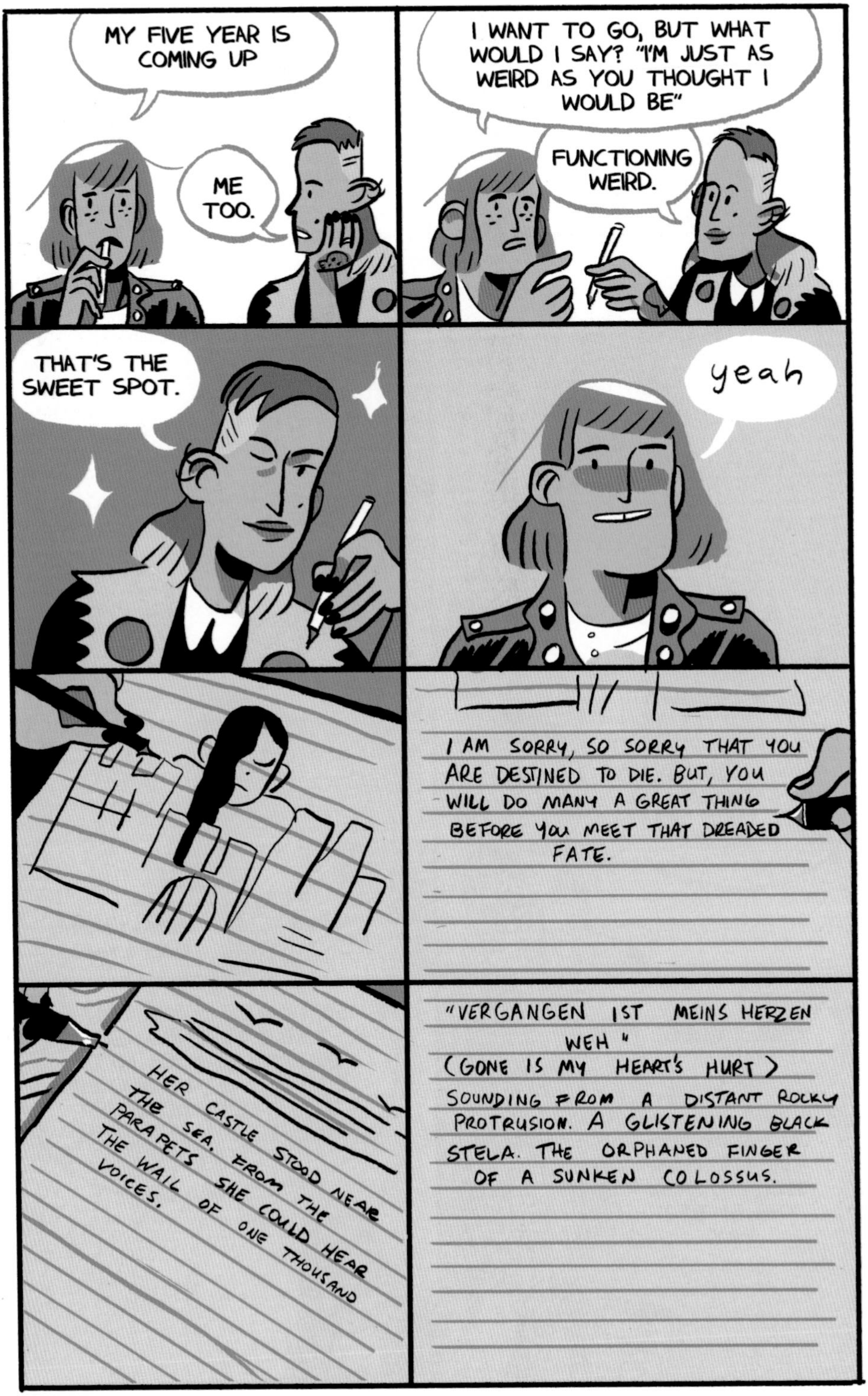

MY FIVE YEAR IS COMING UP
ME TOO.
I WANT TO GO, BUT WHAT WOULD I SAY? "I'M JUST AS WEIRD AS YOU THOUGHT I WOULD BE"
FUNCTIONING WEIRD.
THAT'S THE SWEET SPOT.
yeah
I AM SORRY, SO SORRY THAT YOU ARE DESTINED TO DIE. BUT, YOU WILL DO MANY A GREAT THING BEFORE YOU MEET THAT DREADED FATE.
HER CASTLE STOOD NEAR THE SEA. FROM THE PARAPETS SHE COULD HEAR THE WAIL OF ONE THOUSAND VOICES.
"VERGANGEN IST MEINS HERZEN WEH"
(GONE IS MY HEART'S HURT)
SOUNDING FROM A DISTANT ROCKY PROTRUSION. A GLISTENING BLACK STELA. THE ORPHANED FINGER OF A SUNKEN COLOSSUS.

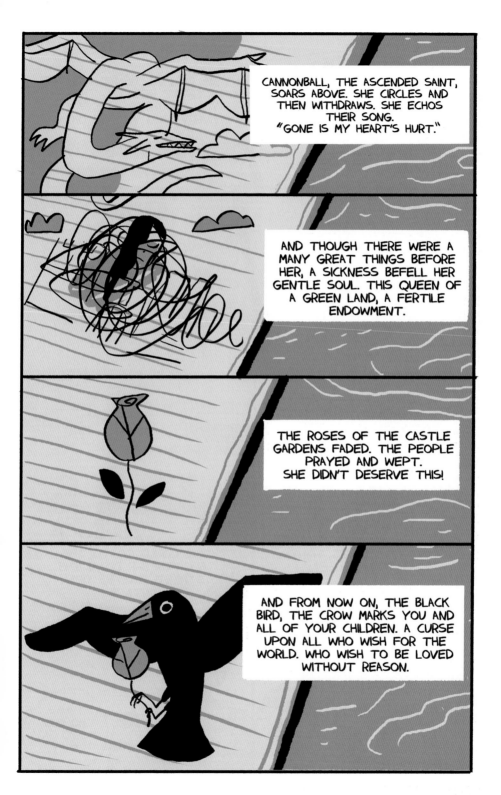

CANNONBALL, THE ASCENDED SAINT, SOARS ABOVE. SHE CIRCLES AND THEN WITHDRAWS. SHE ECHOS THEIR SONG.
"GONE IS MY HEART'S HURT."

AND THOUGH THERE WERE A MANY GREAT THINGS BEFORE HER, A SICKNESS BEFELL HER GENTLE SOUL. THIS QUEEN OF A GREEN LAND, A FERTILE ENDOWMENT.

THE ROSES OF THE CASTLE GARDENS FADED. THE PEOPLE PRAYED AND WEPT.
SHE DIDN'T DESERVE THIS!

AND FROM NOW ON, THE BLACK BIRD, THE CROW MARKS YOU AND ALL OF YOUR CHILDREN. A CURSE UPON ALL WHO WISH FOR THE WORLD. WHO WISH TO BE LOVED WITHOUT REASON.

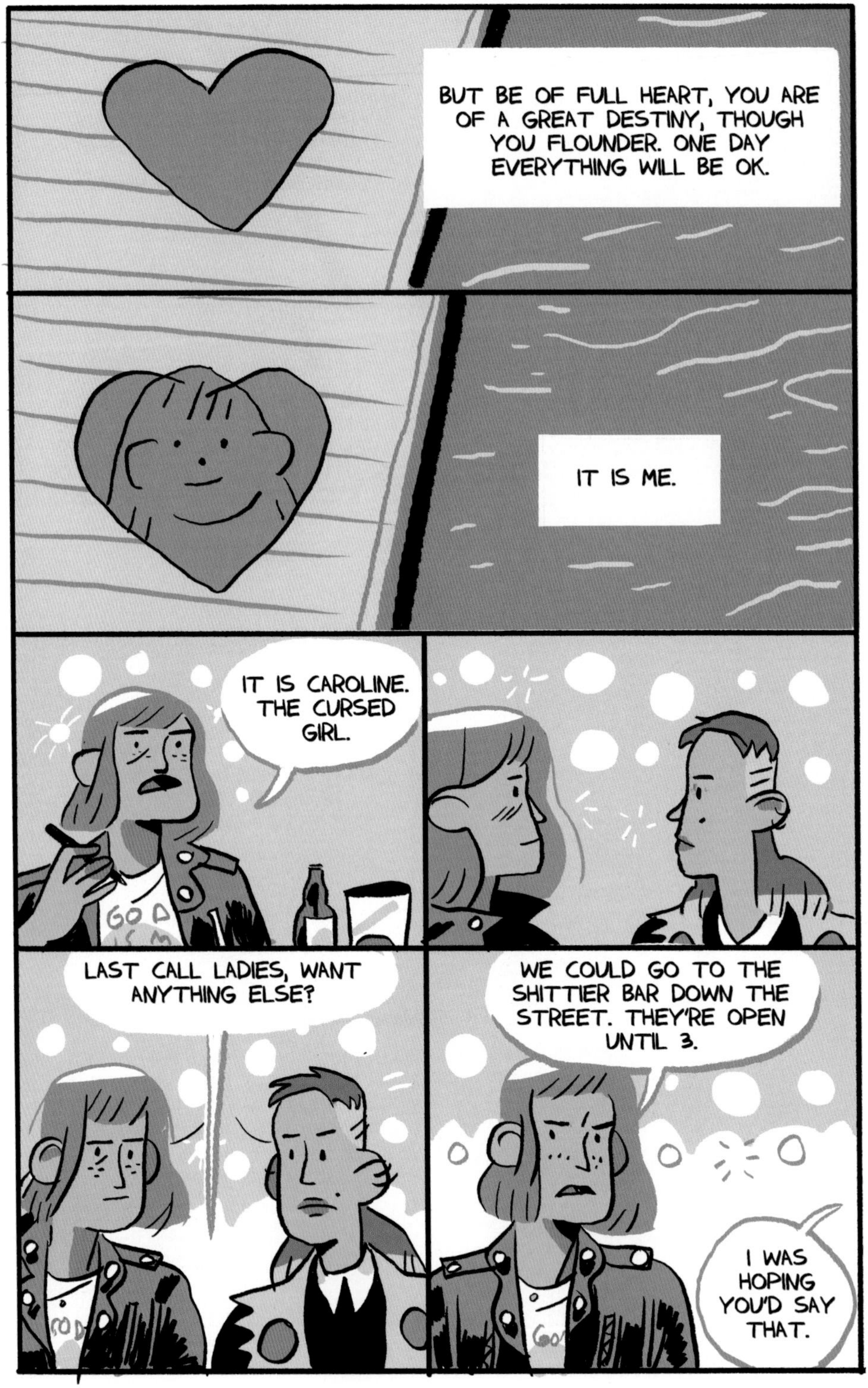
BUT BE OF FULL HEART, YOU ARE OF A GREAT DESTINY, THOUGH YOU FLOUNDER. ONE DAY EVERYTHING WILL BE OK.
IT IS ME.
IT IS CAROLINE. THE CURSED GIRL.
LAST CALL LADIES, WANT ANYTHING ELSE?
WE COULD GO TO THE SHITTIER BAR DOWN THE STREET. THEY'RE OPEN UNTIL 3.
I WAS HOPING YOU'D SAY THAT.

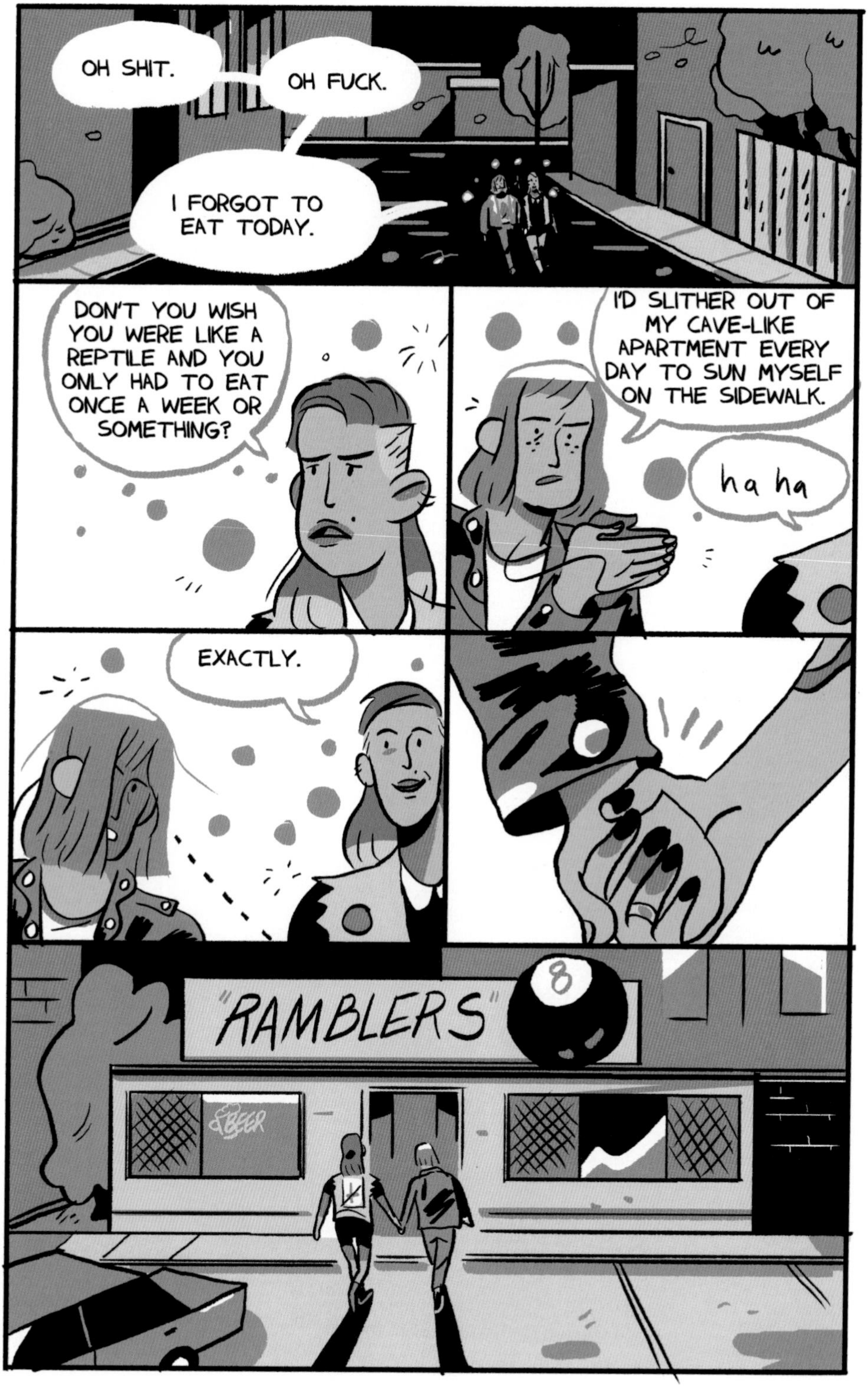
OH SHIT.
OH FUCK.
I FORGOT TO EAT TODAY.
DON'T YOU WISH YOU WERE LIKE A REPTILE AND YOU ONLY HAD TO EAT ONCE A WEEK OR SOMETHING?
I'D SLITHER OUT OF MY CAVE-LIKE APARTMENT EVERY DAY TO SUN MYSELF ON THE SIDEWALK.
ha ha
EXACTLY.
"RAMBLERS"
8
BEER

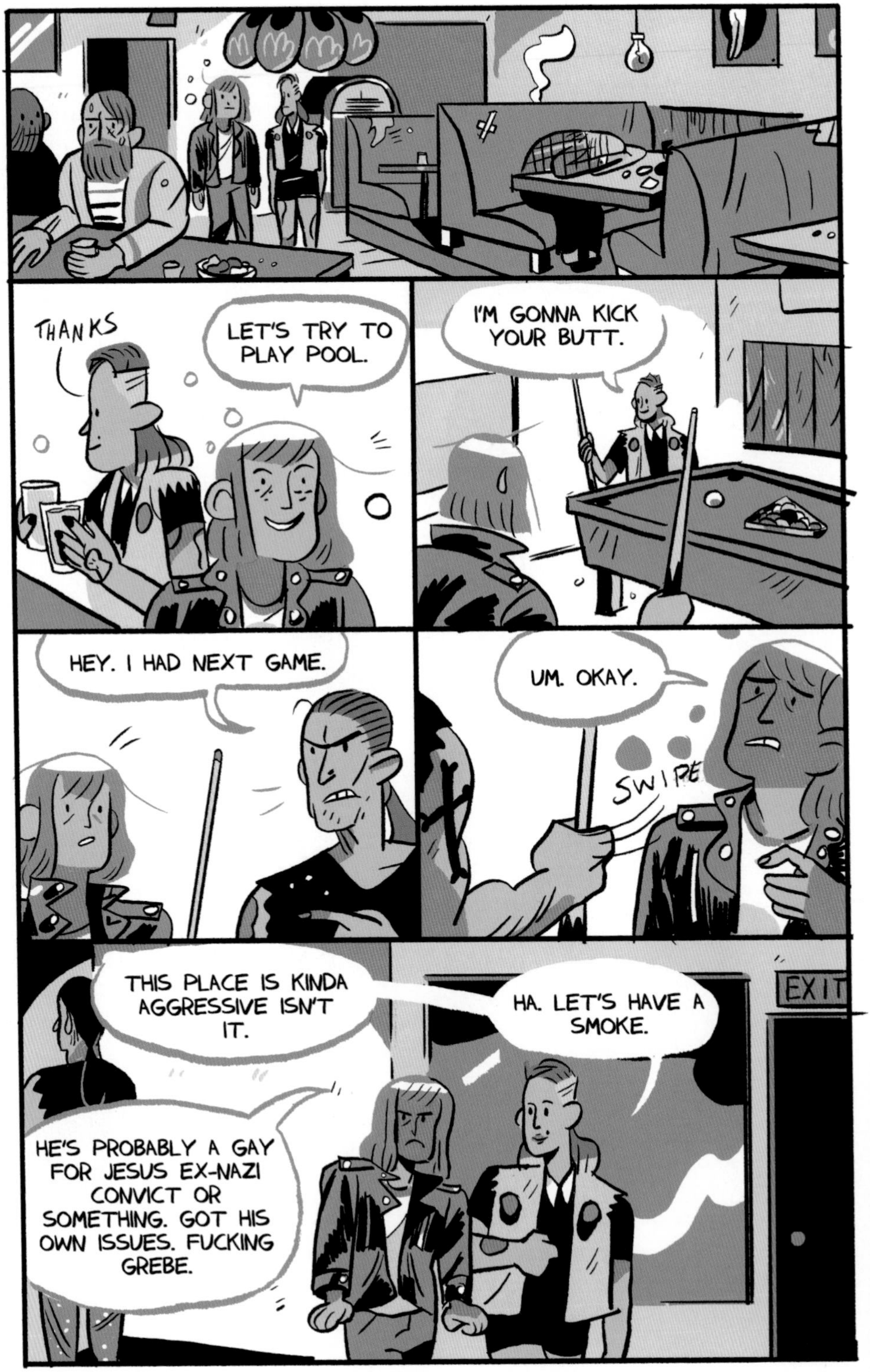
THANKS
LET'S TRY TO PLAY POOL.
I'M GONNA KICK YOUR BUTT.
HEY. I HAD NEXT GAME.
UM. OKAY.
SWIPE
THIS PLACE IS KINDA AGGRESSIVE ISN'T IT.
HA. LET'S HAVE A SMOKE.
EXIT
HE'S PROBABLY A GAY FOR JESUS EX-NAZI CONVICT OR SOMETHING. GOT HIS OWN ISSUES. FUCKING GREBE.

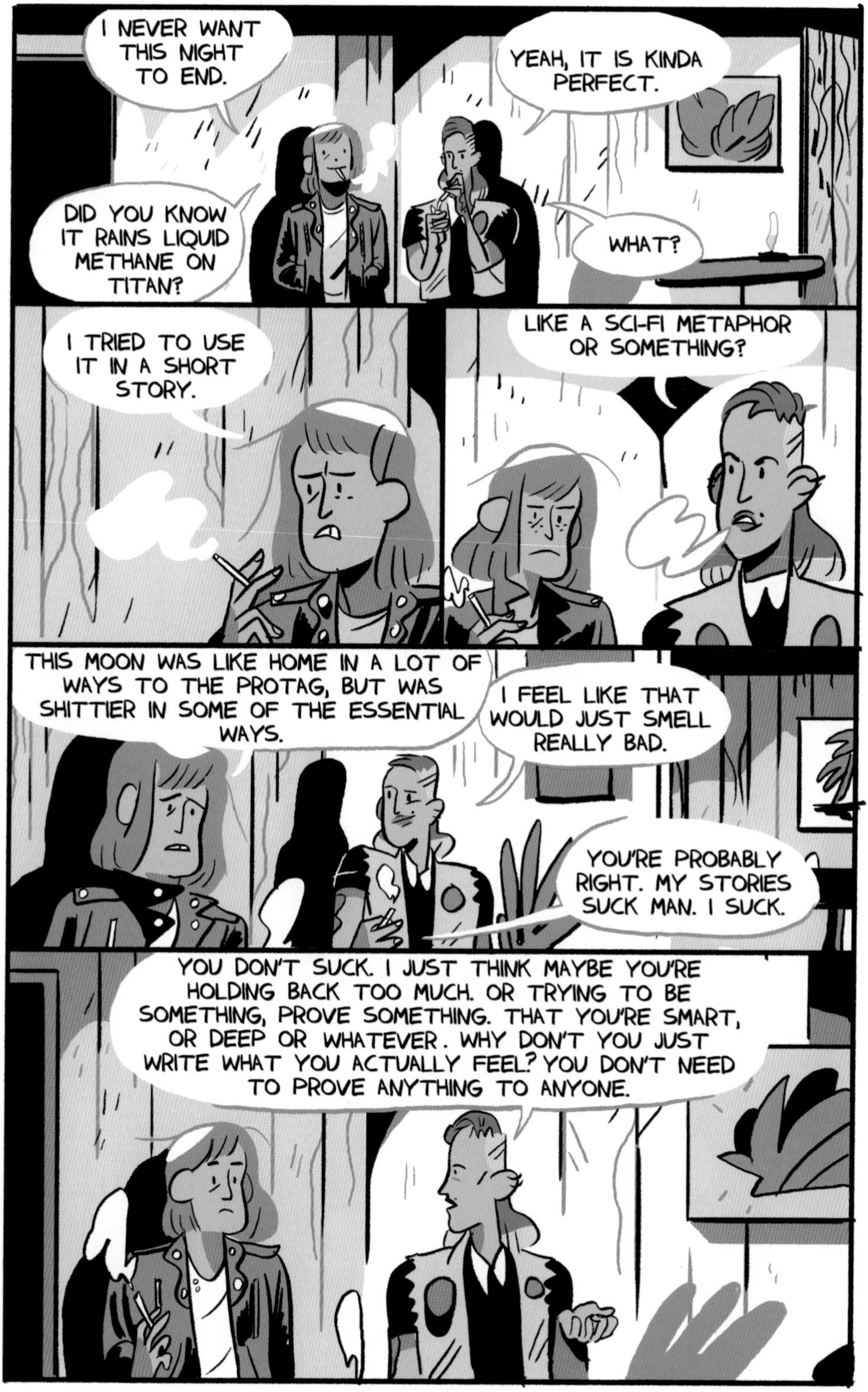
I NEVER WANT THIS NIGHT TO END.
YEAH, IT IS KINDA PERFECT.
DID YOU KNOW IT RAINS LIQUID METHANE ON TITAN?
WHAT?
I TRIED TO USE IT IN A SHORT STORY.
LIKE A SCI-FI METAPHOR OR SOMETHING?
THIS MOON WAS LIKE HOME IN A LOT OF WAYS TO THE PROTAG, BUT WAS SHITTIER IN SOME OF THE ESSENTIAL WAYS.
I FEEL LIKE THAT WOULD JUST SMELL REALLY BAD.
YOU'RE PROBABLY RIGHT. MY STORIES SUCK MAN. I SUCK.
YOU DON'T SUCK. I JUST THINK MAYBE YOU'RE HOLDING BACK TOO MUCH. OR TRYING TO BE SOMETHING, PROVE SOMETHING. THAT YOU'RE SMART, OR DEEP OR WHATEVER. WHY DON'T YOU JUST WRITE WHAT YOU ACTUALLY FEEL? YOU DON'T NEED TO PROVE ANYTHING TO ANYONE.

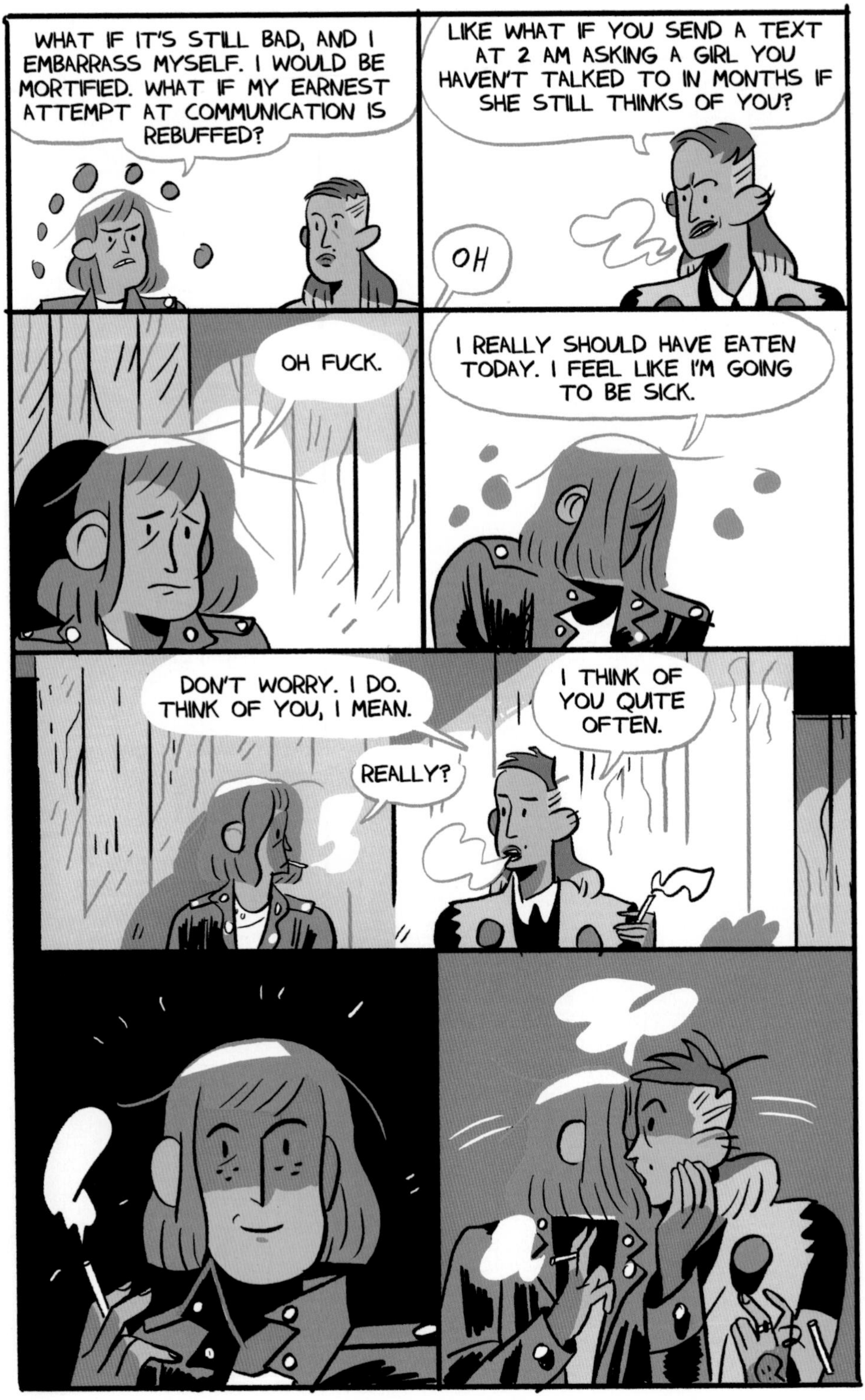
WHAT IF IT'S STILL BAD, AND I EMBARRASS MYSELF. I WOULD BE MORTIFIED. WHAT IF MY EARNEST ATTEMPT AT COMMUNICATION IS REBUFFED?
LIKE WHAT IF YOU SEND A TEXT AT 2 AM ASKING A GIRL YOU HAVEN'T TALKED TO IN MONTHS IF SHE STILL THINKS OF YOU?
OH
OH FUCK.
I REALLY SHOULD HAVE EATEN TODAY. I FEEL LIKE I'M GOING TO BE SICK.
DON'T WORRY. I DO. THINK OF YOU, I MEAN.
REALLY?
I THINK OF YOU QUITE OFTEN.

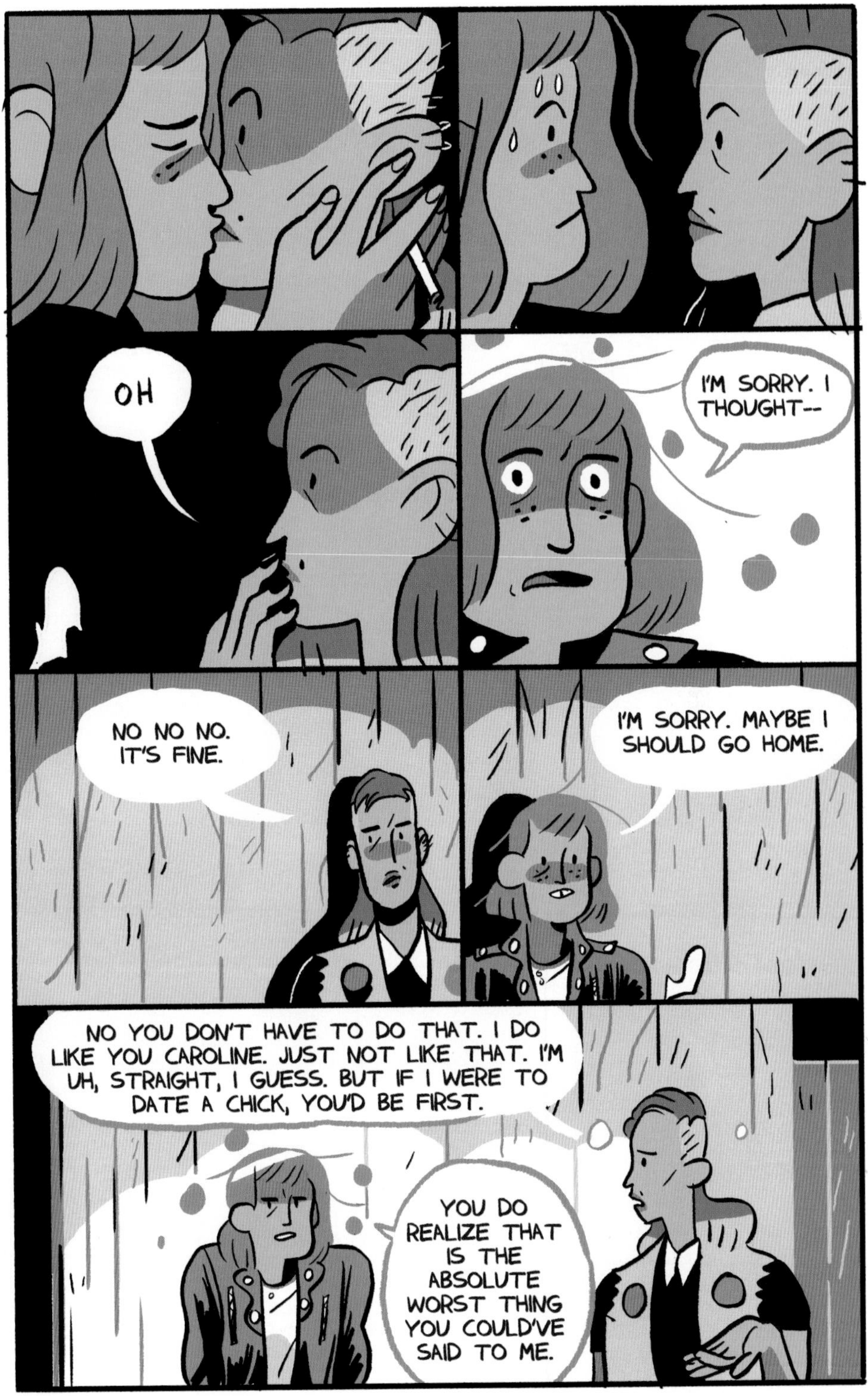
OH
I'M SORRY. I THOUGHT--
NO NO NO. IT'S FINE.
I'M SORRY. MAYBE I SHOULD GO HOME.
NO YOU DON'T HAVE TO DO THAT. I DO LIKE YOU CAROLINE. JUST NOT LIKE THAT. I'M UH, STRAIGHT, I GUESS. BUT IF I WERE TO DATE A CHICK, YOU'D BE FIRST.
YOU DO REALIZE THAT IS THE ABSOLUTE WORST THING YOU COULD'VE SAID TO ME.

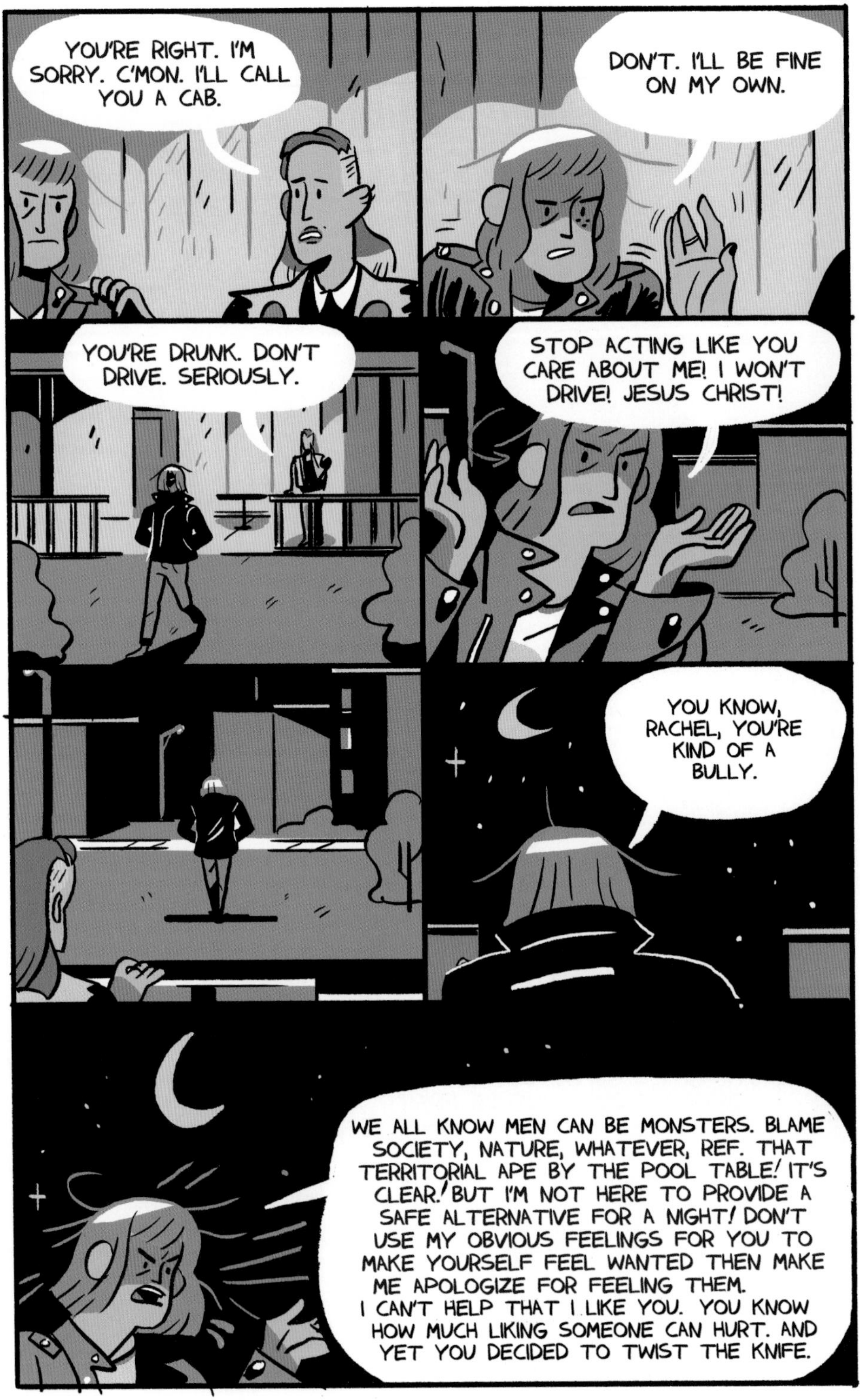
YOU'RE RIGHT. I'M SORRY. C'MON. I'LL CALL YOU A CAB.
DON'T. I'LL BE FINE ON MY OWN.
YOU'RE DRUNK. DON'T DRIVE. SERIOUSLY.
STOP ACTING LIKE YOU CARE ABOUT ME! I WON'T DRIVE! JESUS CHRIST!
YOU KNOW, RACHEL, YOU'RE KIND OF A BULLY.
WE ALL KNOW MEN CAN BE MONSTERS. BLAME SOCIETY, NATURE, WHATEVER, REF. THAT TERRITORIAL APE BY THE POOL TABLE! IT'S CLEAR! BUT I'M NOT HERE TO PROVIDE A SAFE ALTERNATIVE FOR A NIGHT! DON'T USE MY OBVIOUS FEELINGS FOR YOU TO MAKE YOURSELF FEEL WANTED THEN MAKE ME APOLOGIZE FOR FEELING THEM.
I CAN'T HELP THAT I LIKE YOU. YOU KNOW HOW MUCH LIKING SOMEONE CAN HURT. AND YET YOU DECIDED TO TWIST THE KNIFE.

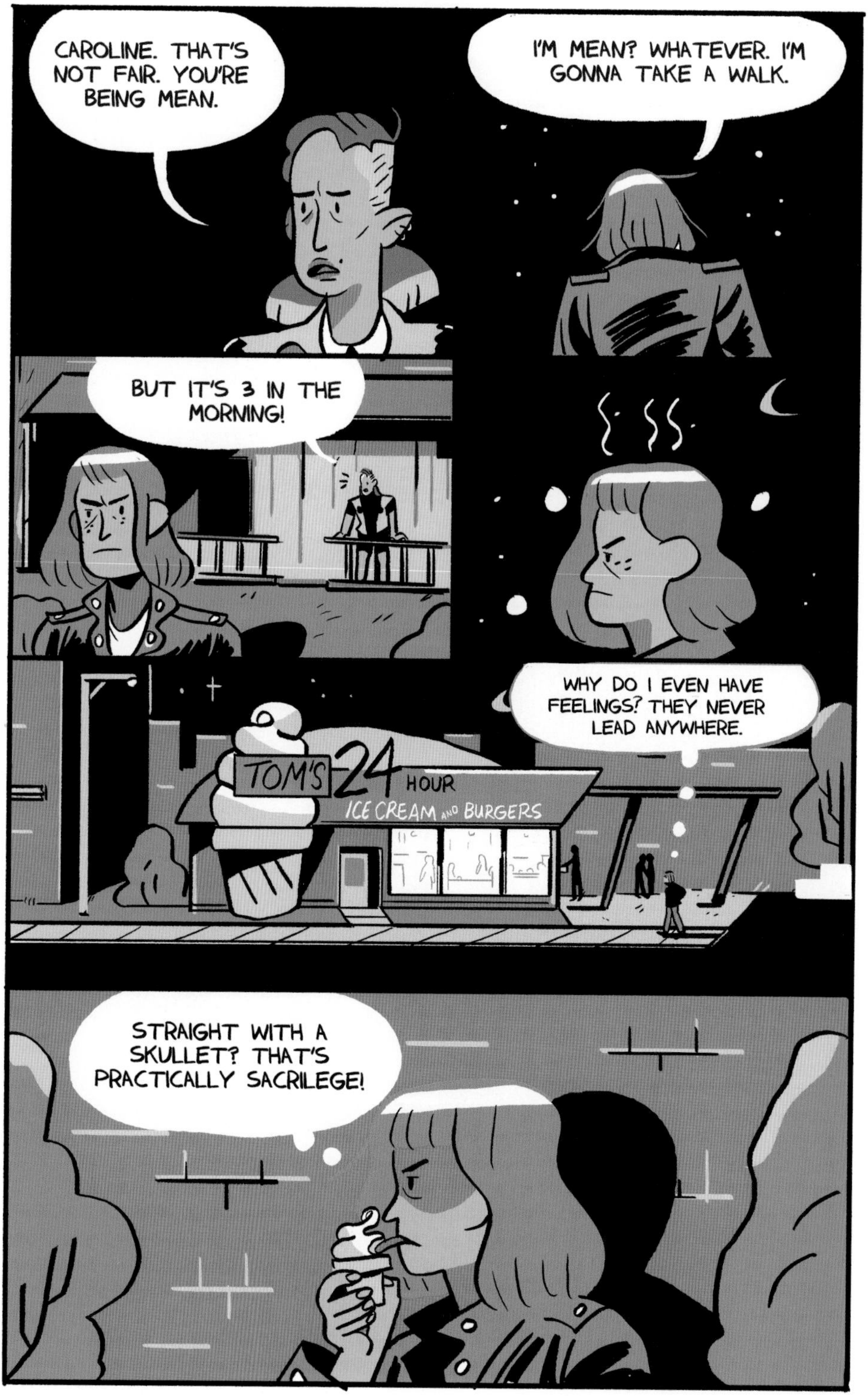
CAROLINE. THAT'S NOT FAIR. YOU'RE BEING MEAN.
I'M MEAN? WHATEVER. I'M GONNA TAKE A WALK.
BUT IT'S 3 IN THE MORNING!
TOM'S 24 HOUR ICE CREAM AND BURGERS
WHY DO I EVEN HAVE FEELINGS? THEY NEVER LEAD ANYWHERE.
STRAIGHT WITH A SKULLET? THAT'S PRACTICALLY SACRILEGE!

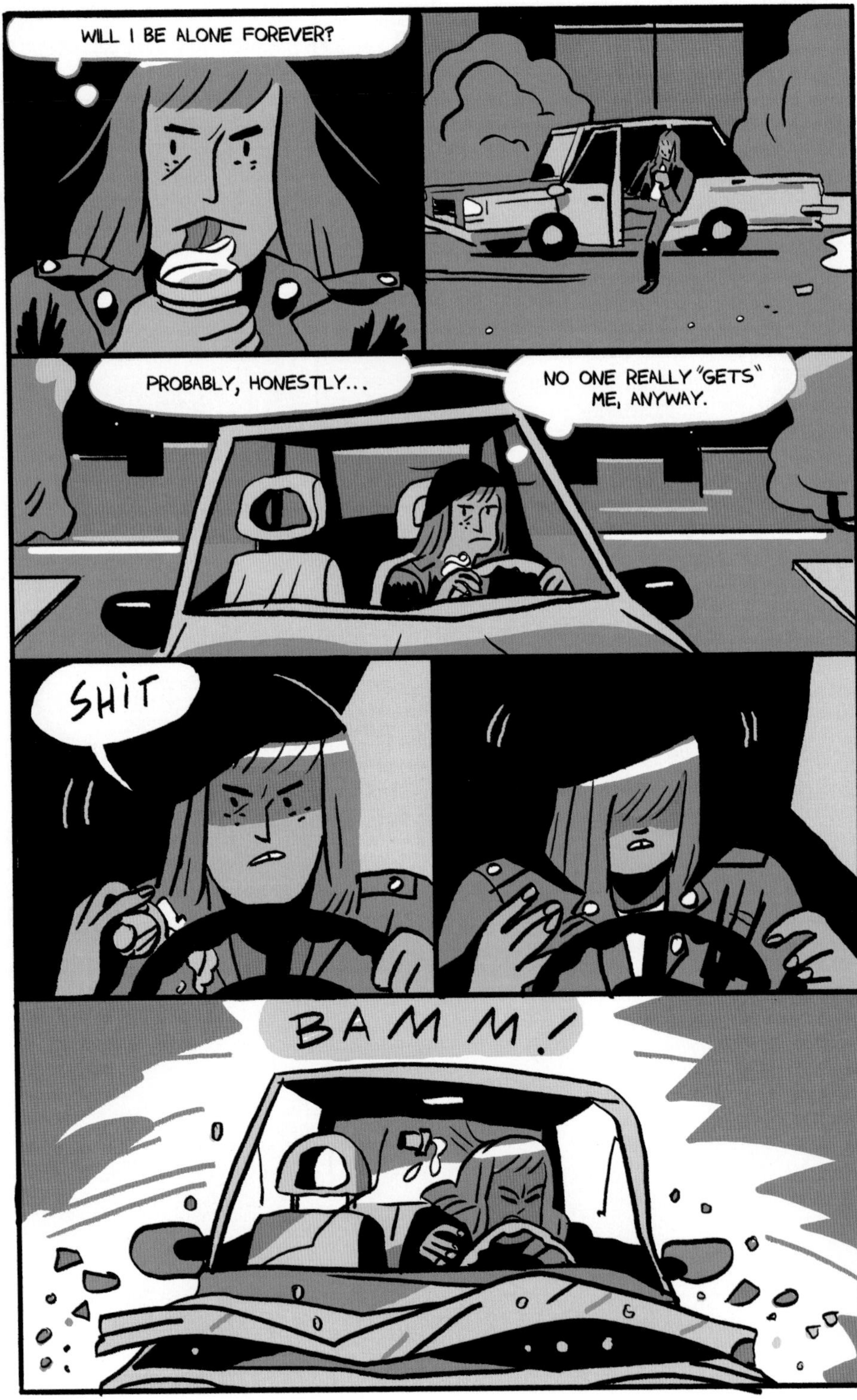
WILL I BE ALONE FOREVER?
PROBABLY, HONESTLY...
NO ONE REALLY "GETS" ME, ANYWAY.
SHIT
BAMM!

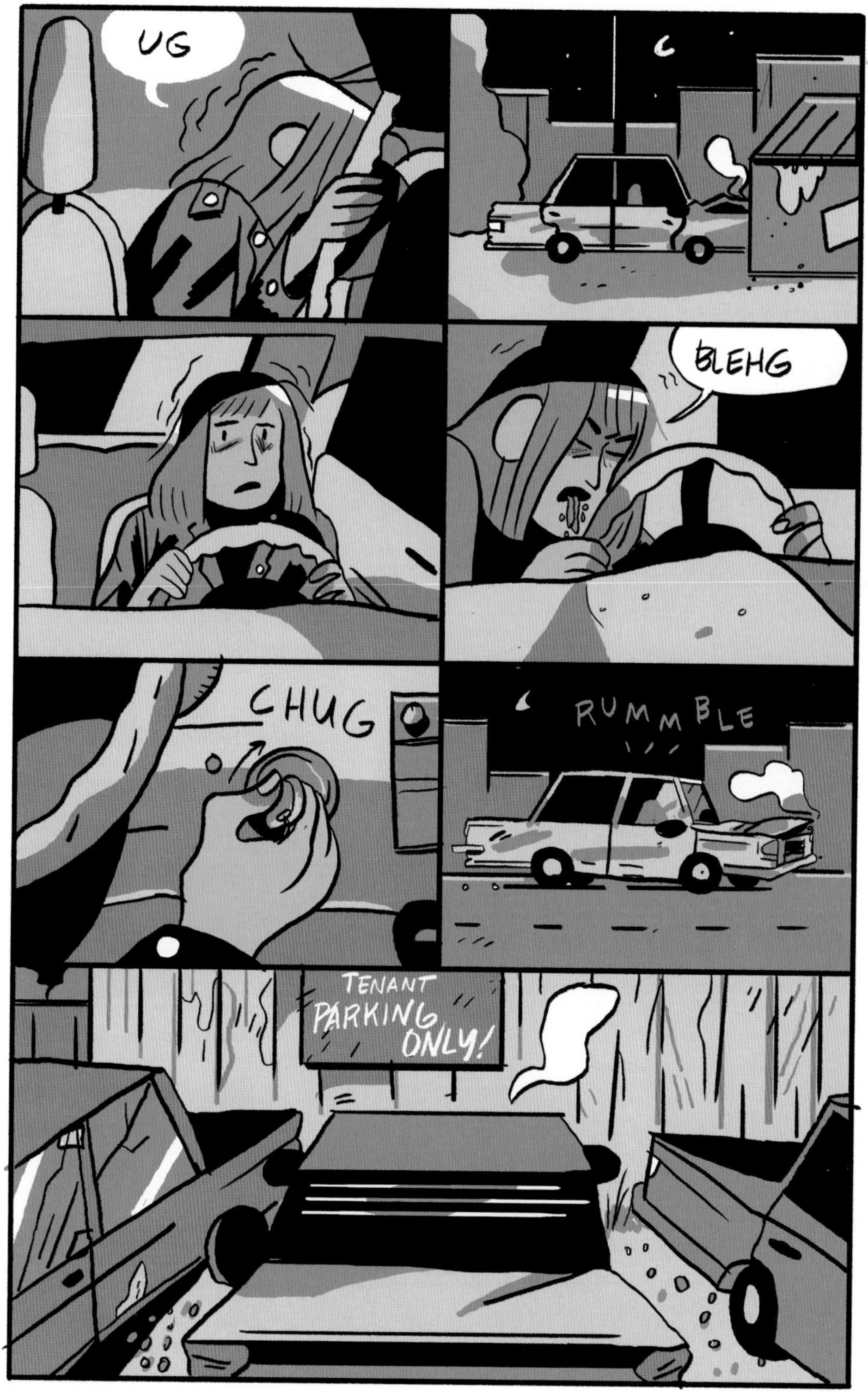

UG
BLEHG
CHUG
RUMMBLE
TENANT PARKING ONLY!

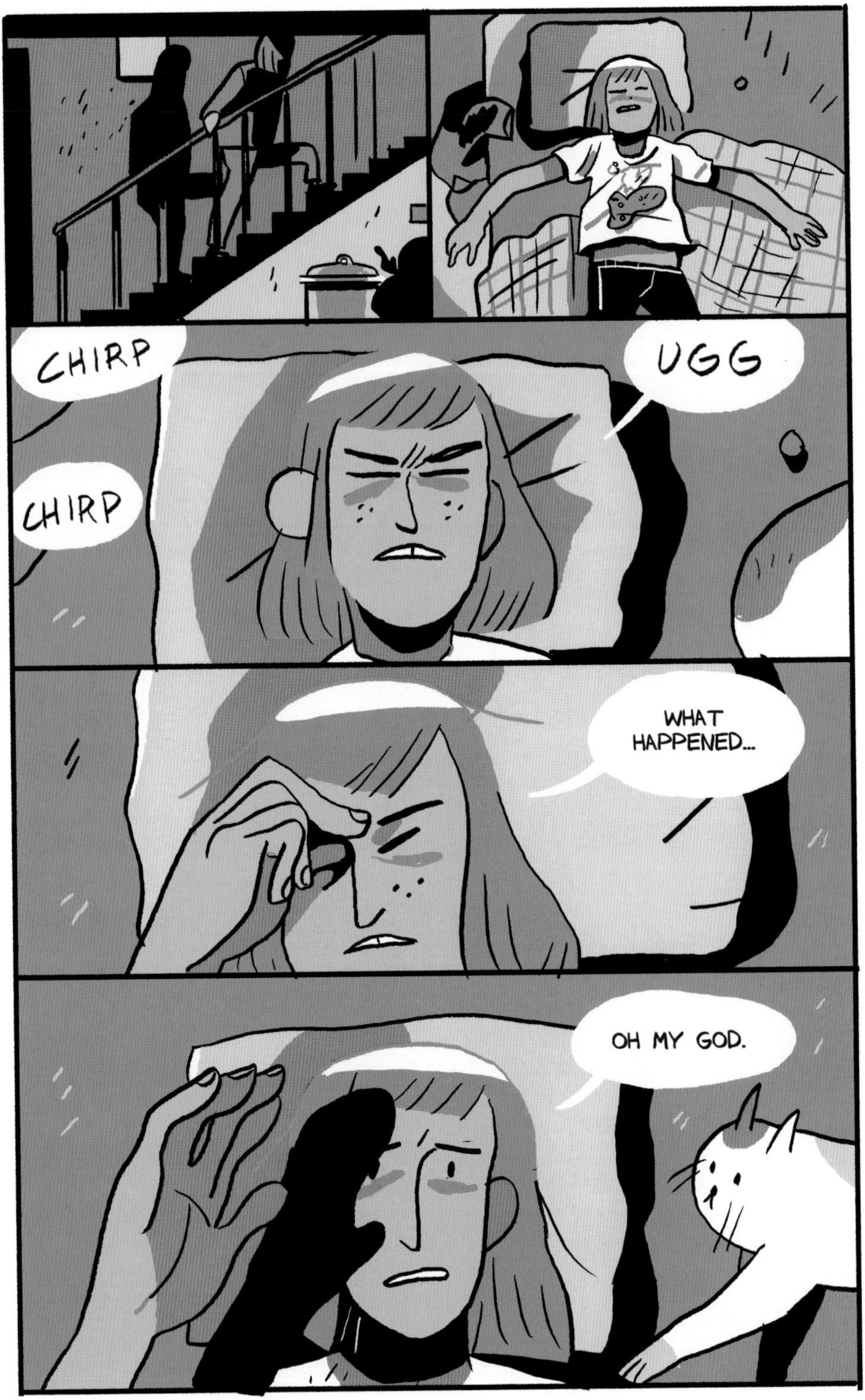
CHIRP
CHIRP
UGG
WHAT HAPPENED...
OH MY GOD.

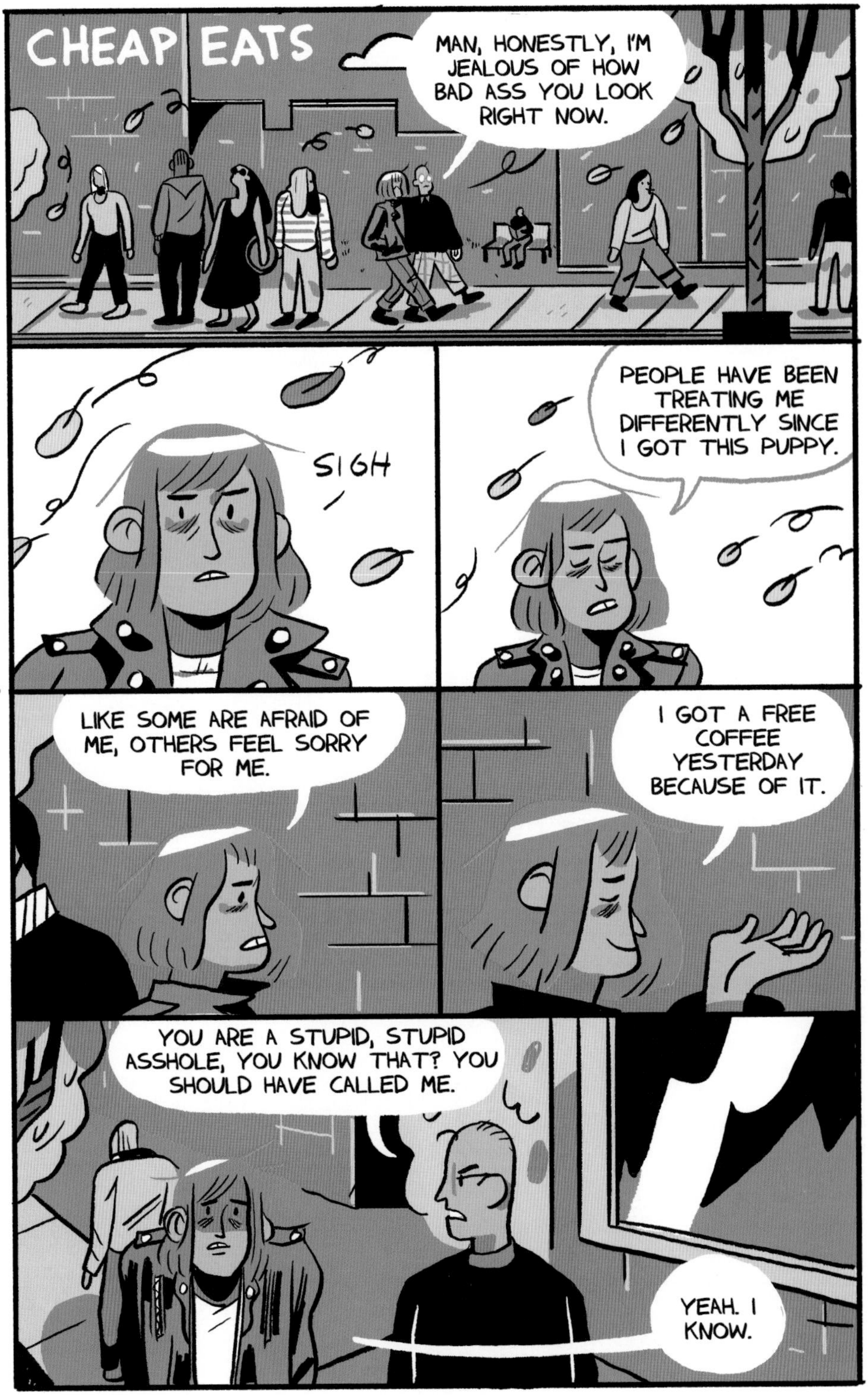
CHEAP EATS
MAN, HONESTLY, I'M JEALOUS OF HOW BAD ASS YOU LOOK RIGHT NOW.
SIGH
PEOPLE HAVE BEEN TREATING ME DIFFERENTLY SINCE I GOT THIS PUPPY.
LIKE SOME ARE AFRAID OF ME, OTHERS FEEL SORRY FOR ME.
I GOT A FREE COFFEE YESTERDAY BECAUSE OF IT.
YOU ARE A STUPID, STUPID ASSHOLE, YOU KNOW THAT? YOU SHOULD HAVE CALLED ME.
YEAH. I KNOW.

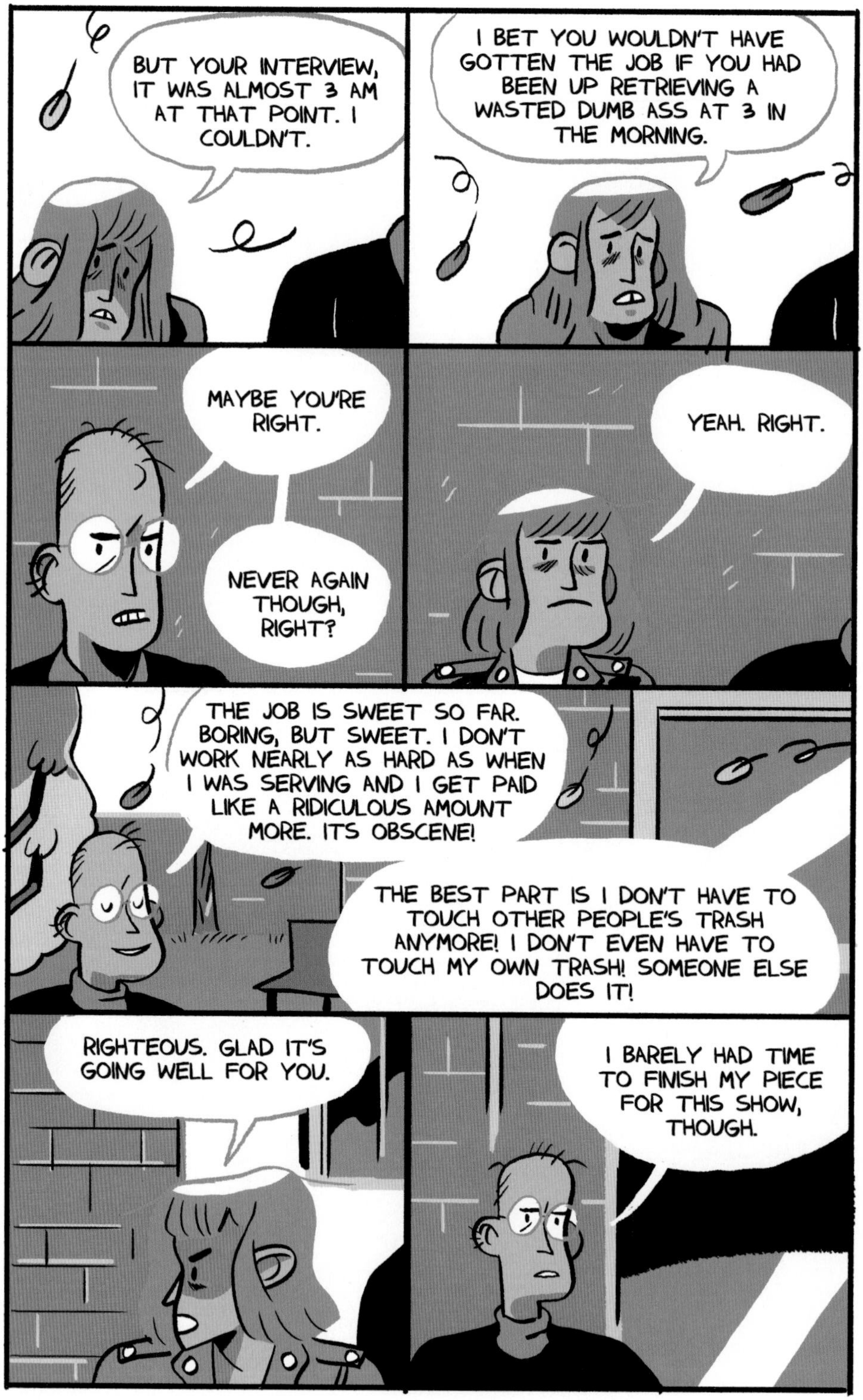
BUT YOUR INTERVIEW, IT WAS ALMOST 3 AM AT THAT POINT. I COULDN'T.
I BET YOU WOULDN'T HAVE GOTTEN THE JOB IF YOU HAD BEEN UP RETRIEVING A WASTED DUMB ASS AT 3 IN THE MORNING.
MAYBE YOU'RE RIGHT.
NEVER AGAIN THOUGH, RIGHT?
YEAH. RIGHT.
THE JOB IS SWEET SO FAR. BORING, BUT SWEET. I DON'T WORK NEARLY AS HARD AS WHEN I WAS SERVING AND I GET PAID LIKE A RIDICULOUS AMOUNT MORE. ITS OBSCENE!
THE BEST PART IS I DON'T HAVE TO TOUCH OTHER PEOPLE'S TRASH ANYMORE! I DON'T EVEN HAVE TO TOUCH MY OWN TRASH! SOMEONE ELSE DOES IT!
RIGHTEOUS. GLAD IT'S GOING WELL FOR YOU.
I BARELY HAD TIME TO FINISH MY PIECE FOR THIS SHOW, THOUGH.

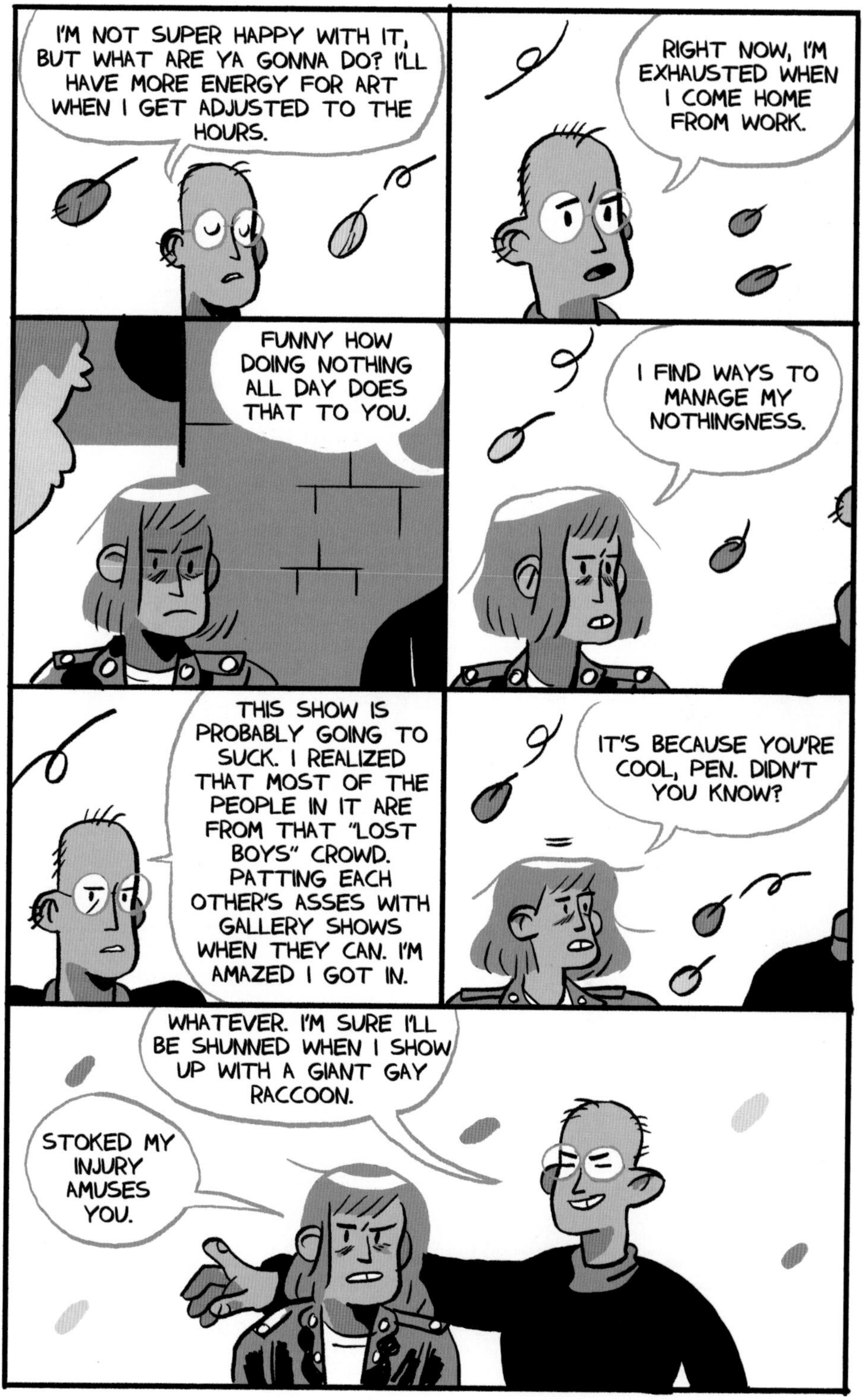
I'M NOT SUPER HAPPY WITH IT, BUT WHAT ARE YA GONNA DO? I'LL HAVE MORE ENERGY FOR ART WHEN I GET ADJUSTED TO THE HOURS.
RIGHT NOW, I'M EXHAUSTED WHEN I COME HOME FROM WORK.
FUNNY HOW DOING NOTHING ALL DAY DOES THAT TO YOU.
I FIND WAYS TO MANAGE MY NOTHINGNESS.
THIS SHOW IS PROBABLY GOING TO SUCK. I REALIZED THAT MOST OF THE PEOPLE IN IT ARE FROM THAT "LOST BOYS" CROWD. PATTING EACH OTHER'S ASSES WITH GALLERY SHOWS WHEN THEY CAN. I'M AMAZED I GOT IN.
IT'S BECAUSE YOU'RE COOL, PEN. DIDN'T YOU KNOW?
WHATEVER. I'M SURE I'LL BE SHUNNED WHEN I SHOW UP WITH A GIANT GAY RACCOON.
STOKED MY INJURY AMUSES YOU.

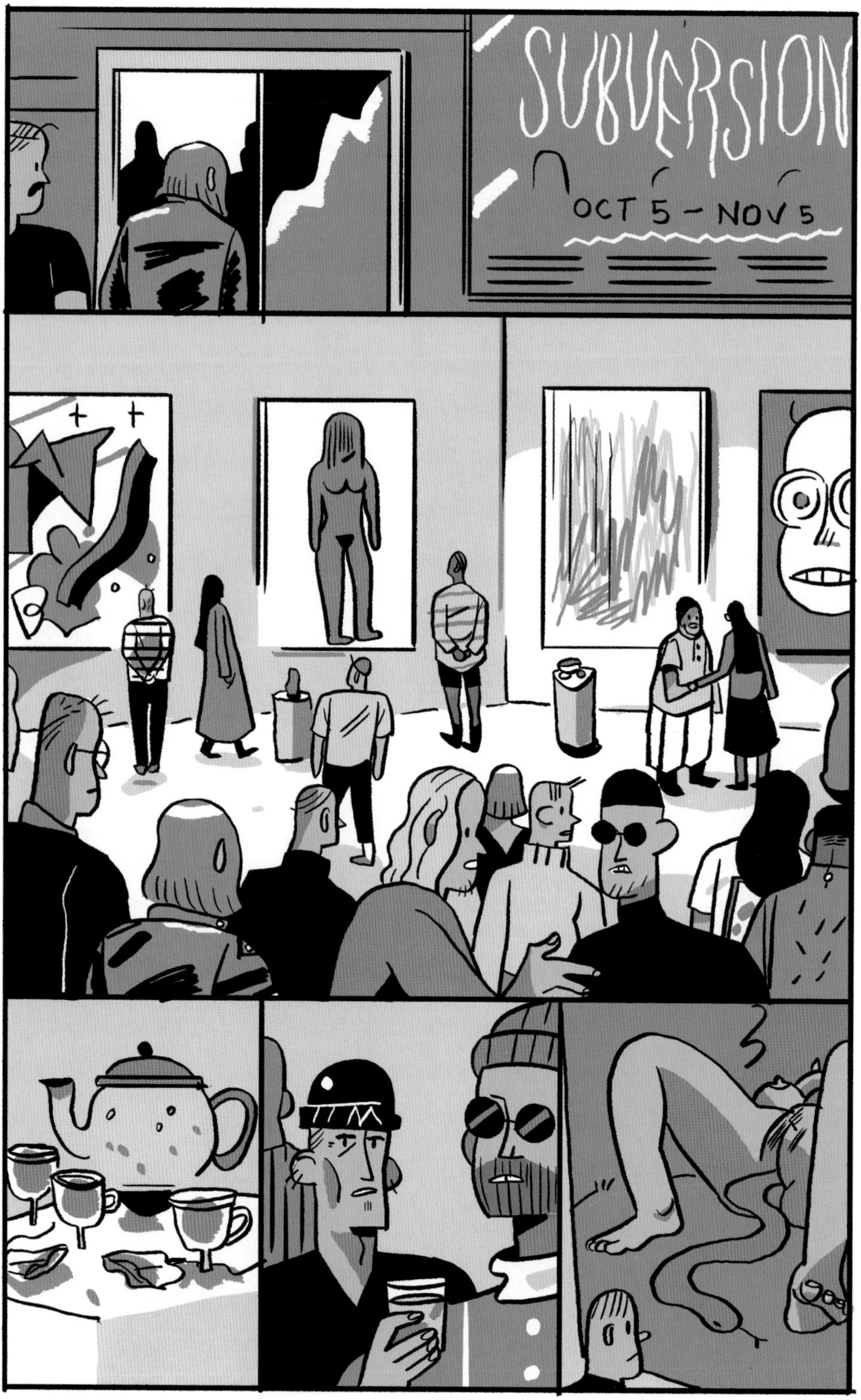
SUBVERSION
OCT 5 – NOV 5

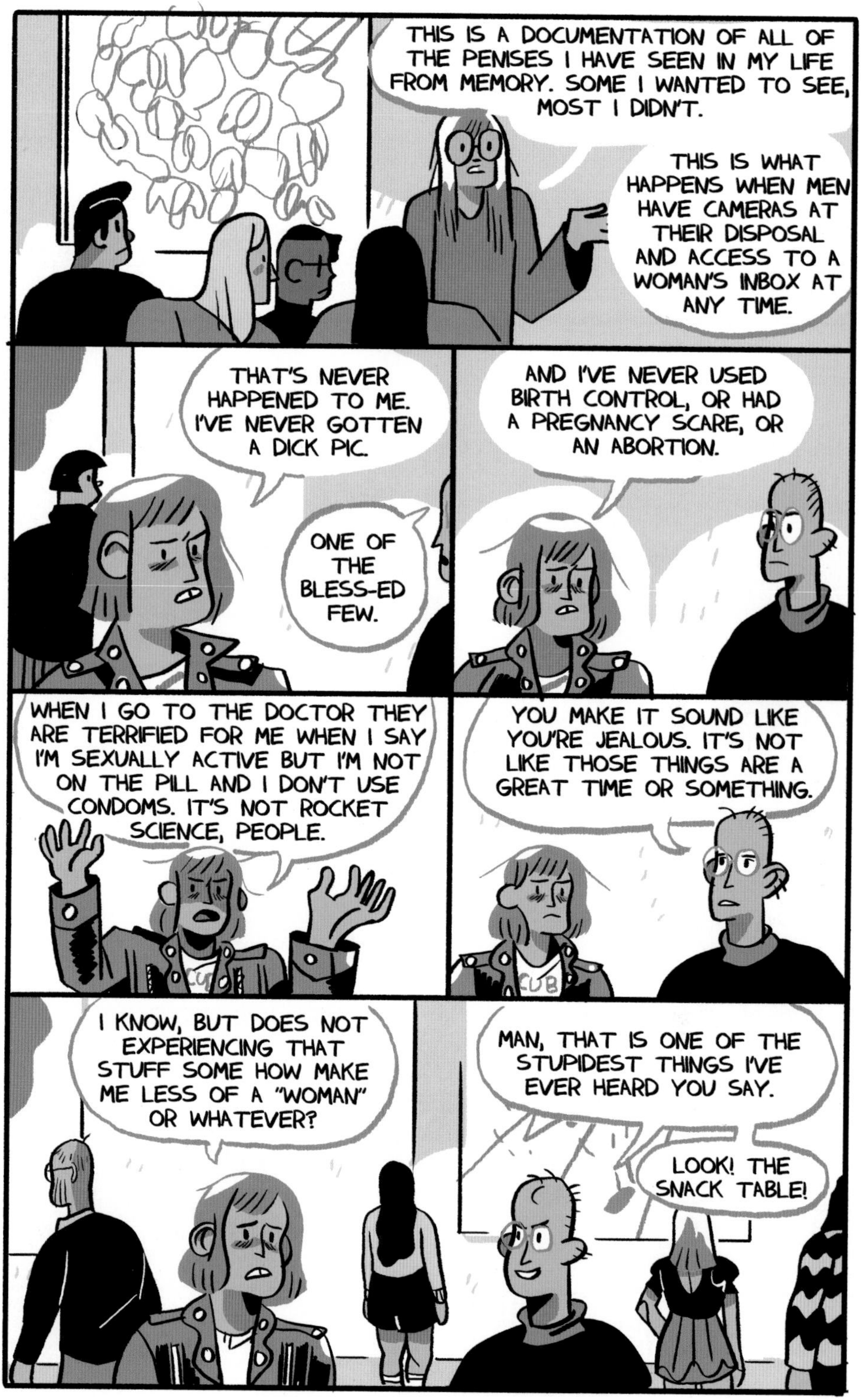
THIS IS A DOCUMENTATION OF ALL OF THE PENISES I HAVE SEEN IN MY LIFE FROM MEMORY. SOME I WANTED TO SEE, MOST I DIDN'T.
THIS IS WHAT HAPPENS WHEN MEN HAVE CAMERAS AT THEIR DISPOSAL AND ACCESS TO A WOMAN'S INBOX AT ANY TIME.
THAT'S NEVER HAPPENED TO ME. I'VE NEVER GOTTEN A DICK PIC.
ONE OF THE BLESS-ED FEW.
AND I'VE NEVER USED BIRTH CONTROL, OR HAD A PREGNANCY SCARE, OR AN ABORTION.
WHEN I GO TO THE DOCTOR THEY ARE TERRIFIED FOR ME WHEN I SAY I'M SEXUALLY ACTIVE BUT I'M NOT ON THE PILL AND I DON'T USE CONDOMS. IT'S NOT ROCKET SCIENCE, PEOPLE.
YOU MAKE IT SOUND LIKE YOU'RE JEALOUS. IT'S NOT LIKE THOSE THINGS ARE A GREAT TIME OR SOMETHING.
I KNOW, BUT DOES NOT EXPERIENCING THAT STUFF SOME HOW MAKE ME LESS OF A "WOMAN" OR WHATEVER?
MAN, THAT IS ONE OF THE STUPIDEST THINGS I'VE EVER HEARD YOU SAY.
LOOK! THE SNACK TABLE!

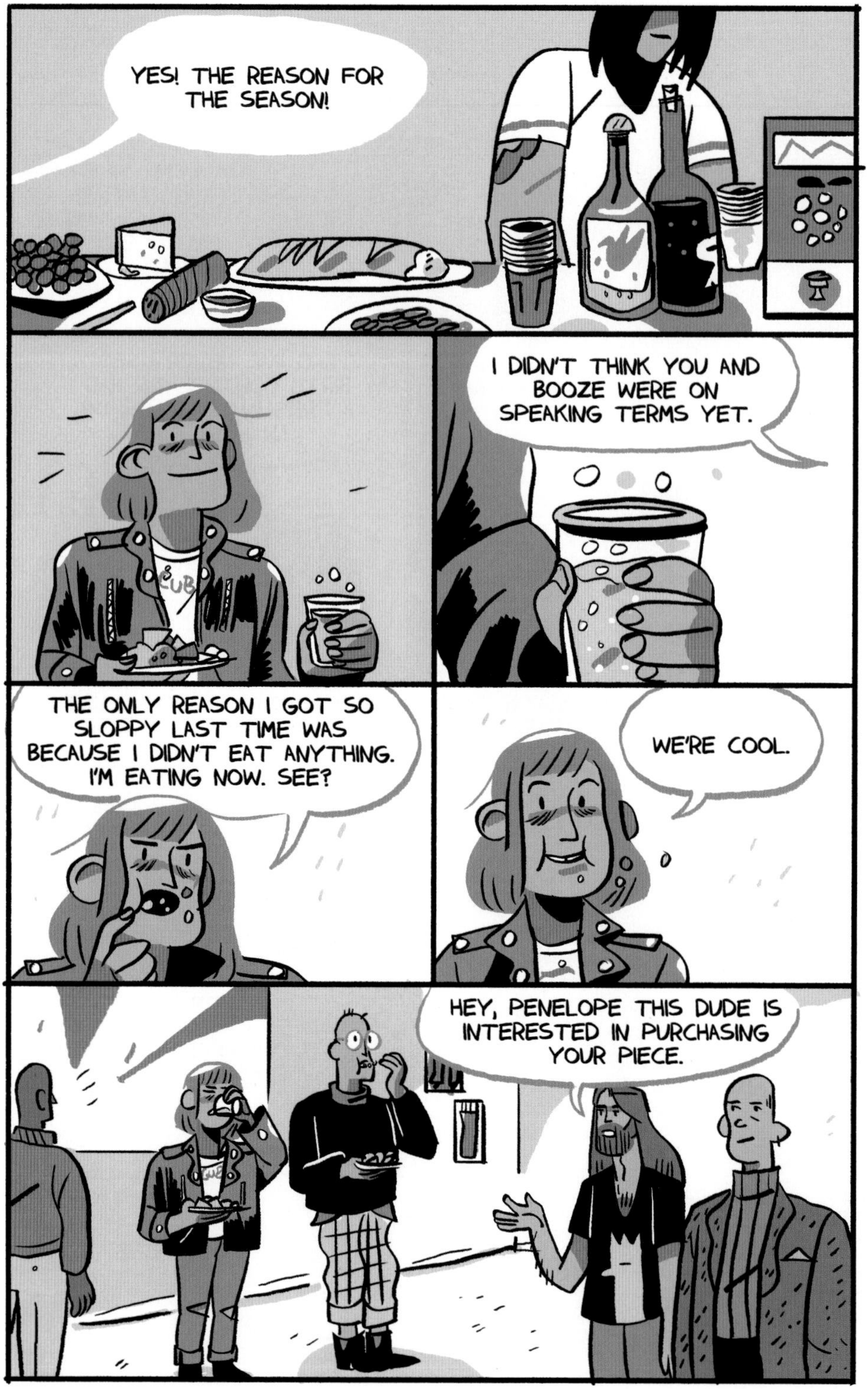
YES! THE REASON FOR THE SEASON!
I DIDN'T THINK YOU AND BOOZE WERE ON SPEAKING TERMS YET.
THE ONLY REASON I GOT SO SLOPPY LAST TIME WAS BECAUSE I DIDN'T EAT ANYTHING. I'M EATING NOW. SEE?
WE'RE COOL.
HEY, PENELOPE THIS DUDE IS INTERESTED IN PURCHASING YOUR PIECE.

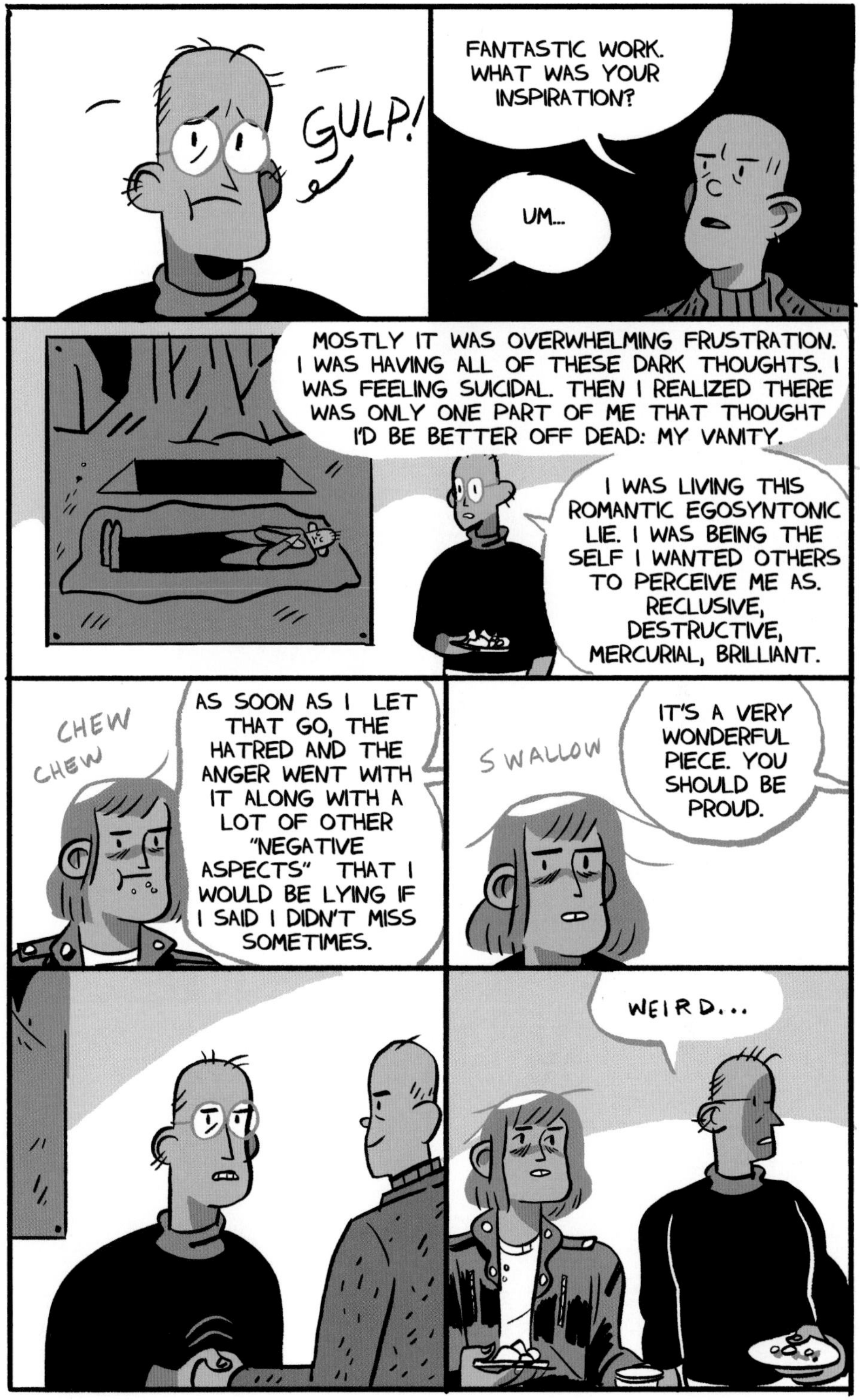
GULP!
FANTASTIC WORK. WHAT WAS YOUR INSPIRATION?
UM...
MOSTLY IT WAS OVERWHELMING FRUSTRATION. I WAS HAVING ALL OF THESE DARK THOUGHTS. I WAS FEELING SUICIDAL. THEN I REALIZED THERE WAS ONLY ONE PART OF ME THAT THOUGHT I'D BE BETTER OFF DEAD: MY VANITY.
I WAS LIVING THIS ROMANTIC EGOSYNTONIC LIE. I WAS BEING THE SELF I WANTED OTHERS TO PERCEIVE ME AS. RECLUSIVE, DESTRUCTIVE, MERCURIAL, BRILLIANT.
CHEW CHEW
AS SOON AS I LET THAT GO, THE HATRED AND THE ANGER WENT WITH IT ALONG WITH A LOT OF OTHER "NEGATIVE ASPECTS" THAT I WOULD BE LYING IF I SAID I DIDN'T MISS SOMETIMES.
SWALLOW
IT'S A VERY WONDERFUL PIECE. YOU SHOULD BE PROUD.
WEIRD...

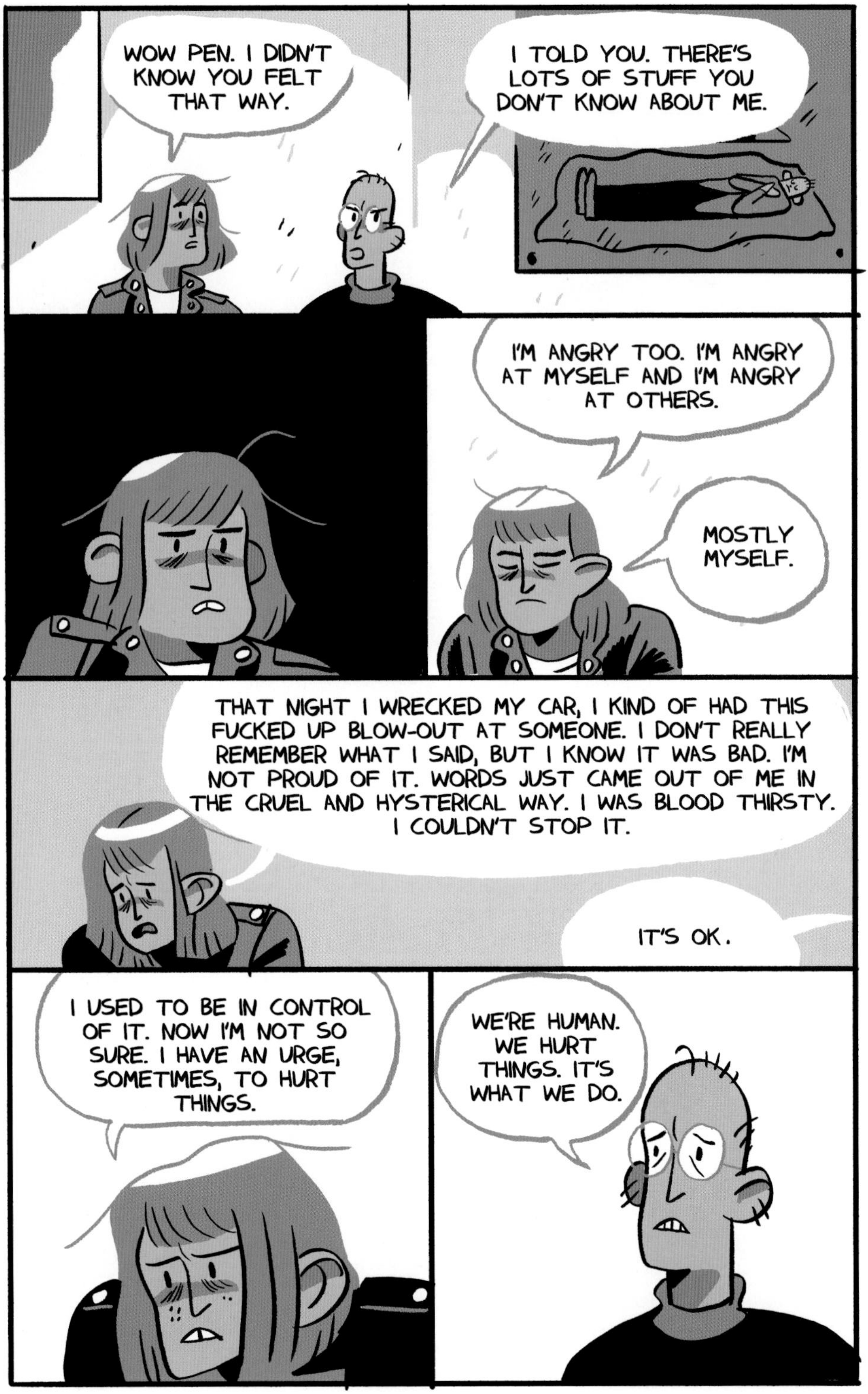
WOW PEN. I DIDN'T KNOW YOU FELT THAT WAY.
I TOLD YOU. THERE'S LOTS OF STUFF YOU DON'T KNOW ABOUT ME.
I'M ANGRY TOO. I'M ANGRY AT MYSELF AND I'M ANGRY AT OTHERS.
MOSTLY MYSELF.
THAT NIGHT I WRECKED MY CAR, I KIND OF HAD THIS FUCKED UP BLOW-OUT AT SOMEONE. I DON'T REALLY REMEMBER WHAT I SAID, BUT I KNOW IT WAS BAD. I'M NOT PROUD OF IT. WORDS JUST CAME OUT OF ME IN THE CRUEL AND HYSTERICAL WAY. I WAS BLOOD THIRSTY. I COULDN'T STOP IT.
IT'S OK.
I USED TO BE IN CONTROL OF IT. NOW I'M NOT SO SURE. I HAVE AN URGE, SOMETIMES, TO HURT THINGS.
WE'RE HUMAN. WE HURT THINGS. IT'S WHAT WE DO.

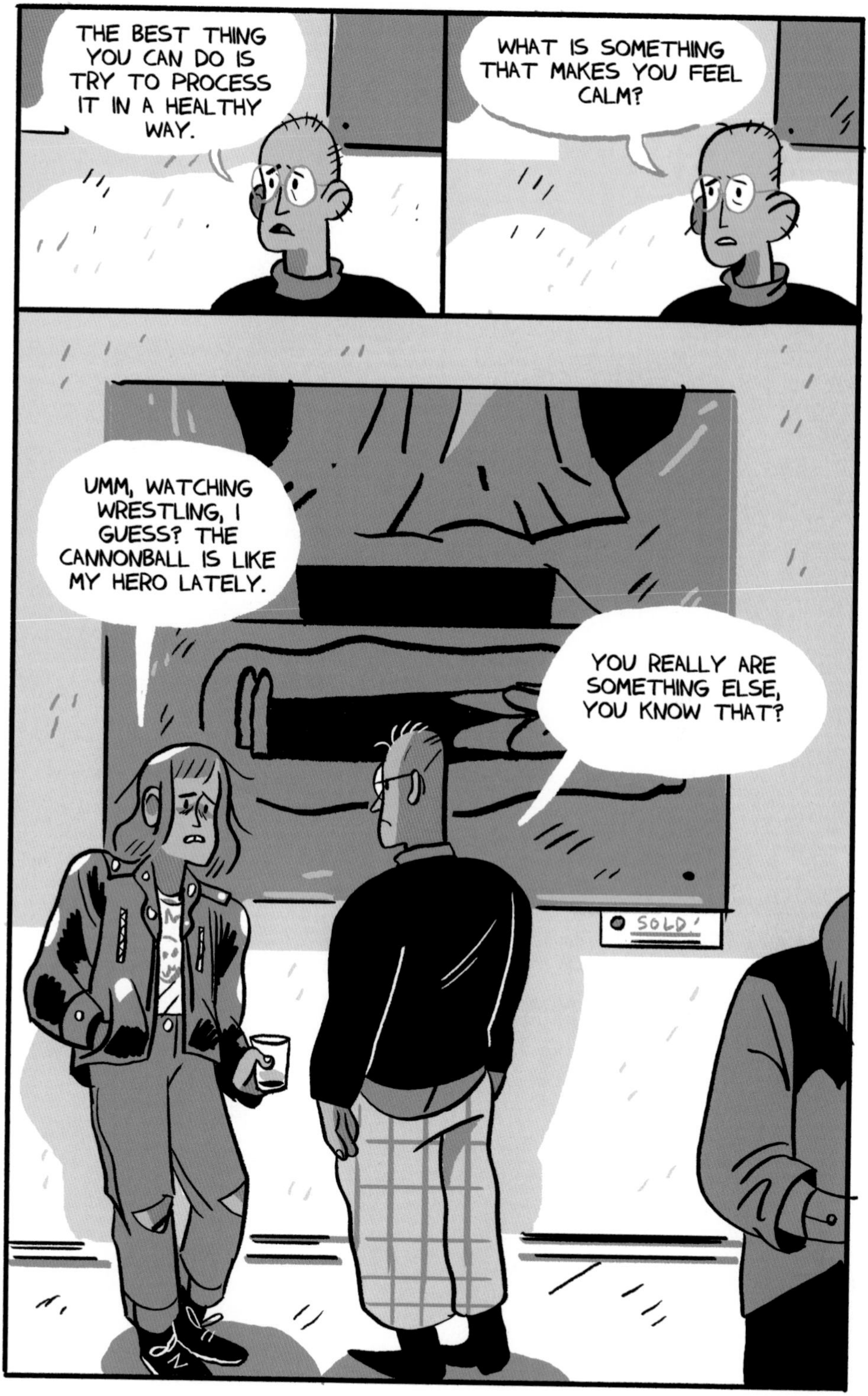
THE BEST THING YOU CAN DO IS TRY TO PROCESS IT IN A HEALTHY WAY.
WHAT IS SOMETHING THAT MAKES YOU FEEL CALM?
UMM, WATCHING WRESTLING, I GUESS? THE CANNONBALL IS LIKE MY HERO LATELY.
YOU REALLY ARE SOMETHING ELSE, YOU KNOW THAT?
SOLD!

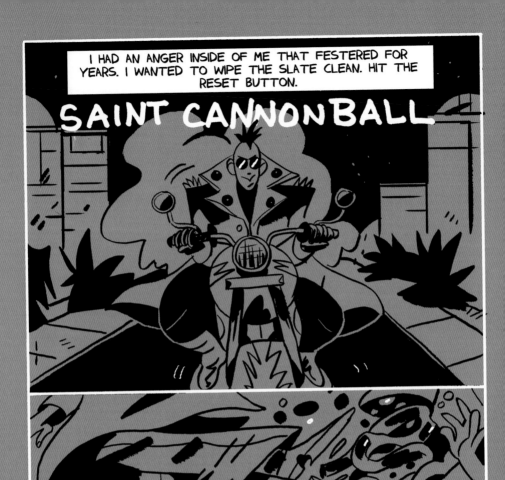

I HAD AN ANGER INSIDE OF ME THAT FESTERED FOR YEARS. I WANTED TO WIPE THE SLATE CLEAN. HIT THE RESET BUTTON.

# SAINT CANNONBALL

I ALSO RECENTLY FOUND MYSELF WITH THE ABILITY TO KICK THE GUTS OUT OF ANYTHING, SO THAT HELPED A LOT.

CRASH!

THE END BEGINS TODAY!

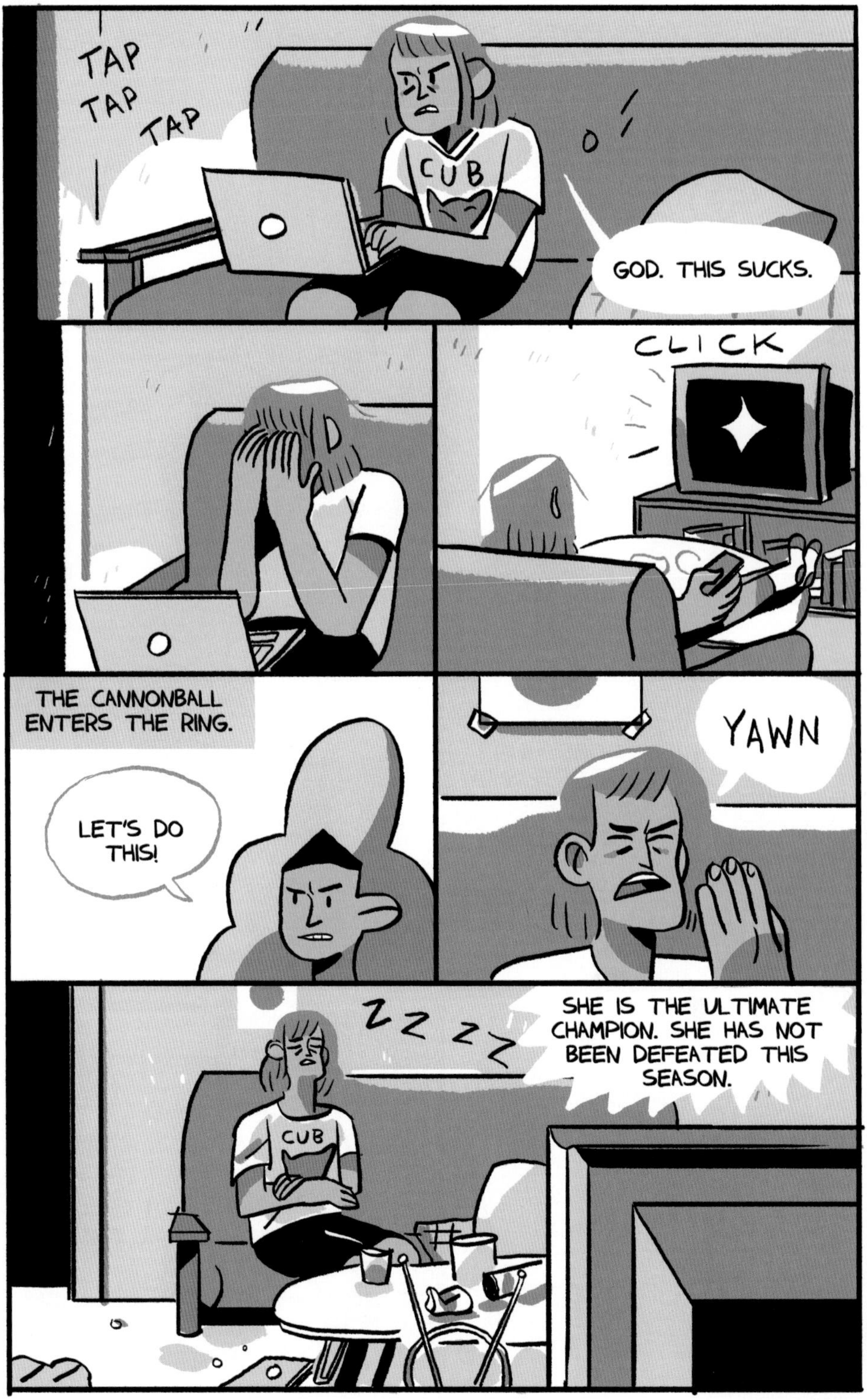

TAP
TAP
TAP
GOD. THIS SUCKS.
CLICK
THE CANNONBALL ENTERS THE RING.
LET'S DO THIS!
YAWN
Z Z Z Z
SHE IS THE ULTIMATE CHAMPION. SHE HAS NOT BEEN DEFEATED THIS SEASON.

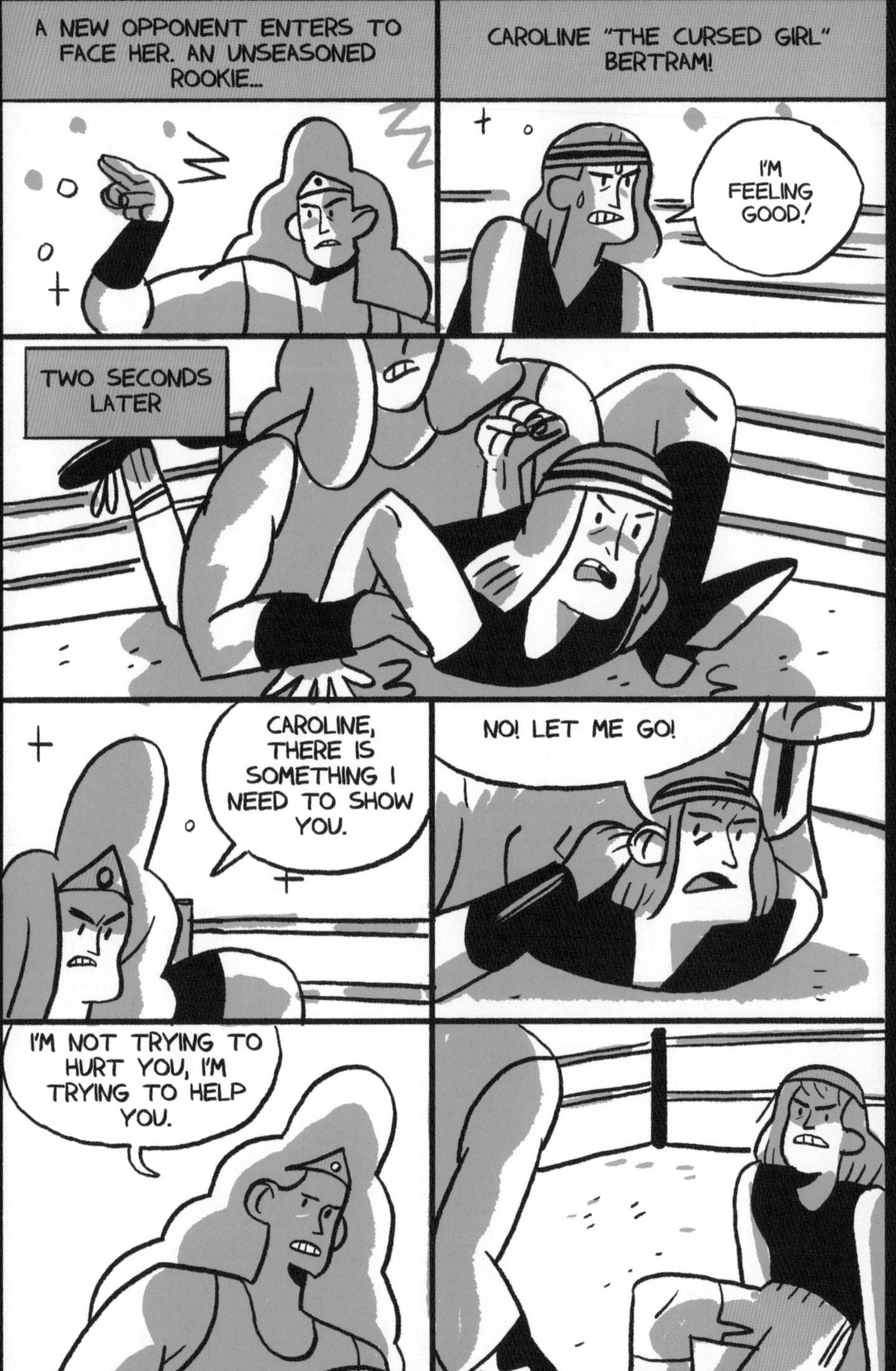
A NEW OPPONENT ENTERS TO FACE HER. AN UNSEASONED ROOKIE...
CAROLINE "THE CURSED GIRL" BERTRAM!
I'M FEELING GOOD!
TWO SECONDS LATER
CAROLINE, THERE IS SOMETHING I NEED TO SHOW YOU.
NO! LET ME GO!
I'M NOT TRYING TO HURT YOU, I'M TRYING TO HELP YOU.

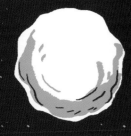

HUH?

WHAT IS THAT, CANNONBALL?

oh...

THE CREPUSCULE. IT'S THE END, REALLY.

IT'S THE SIGN OF A CHANGE. THE ADVENT OF A NEW KIND OF SADNESS.

COME WITH ME. I'LL SHOW YOU.

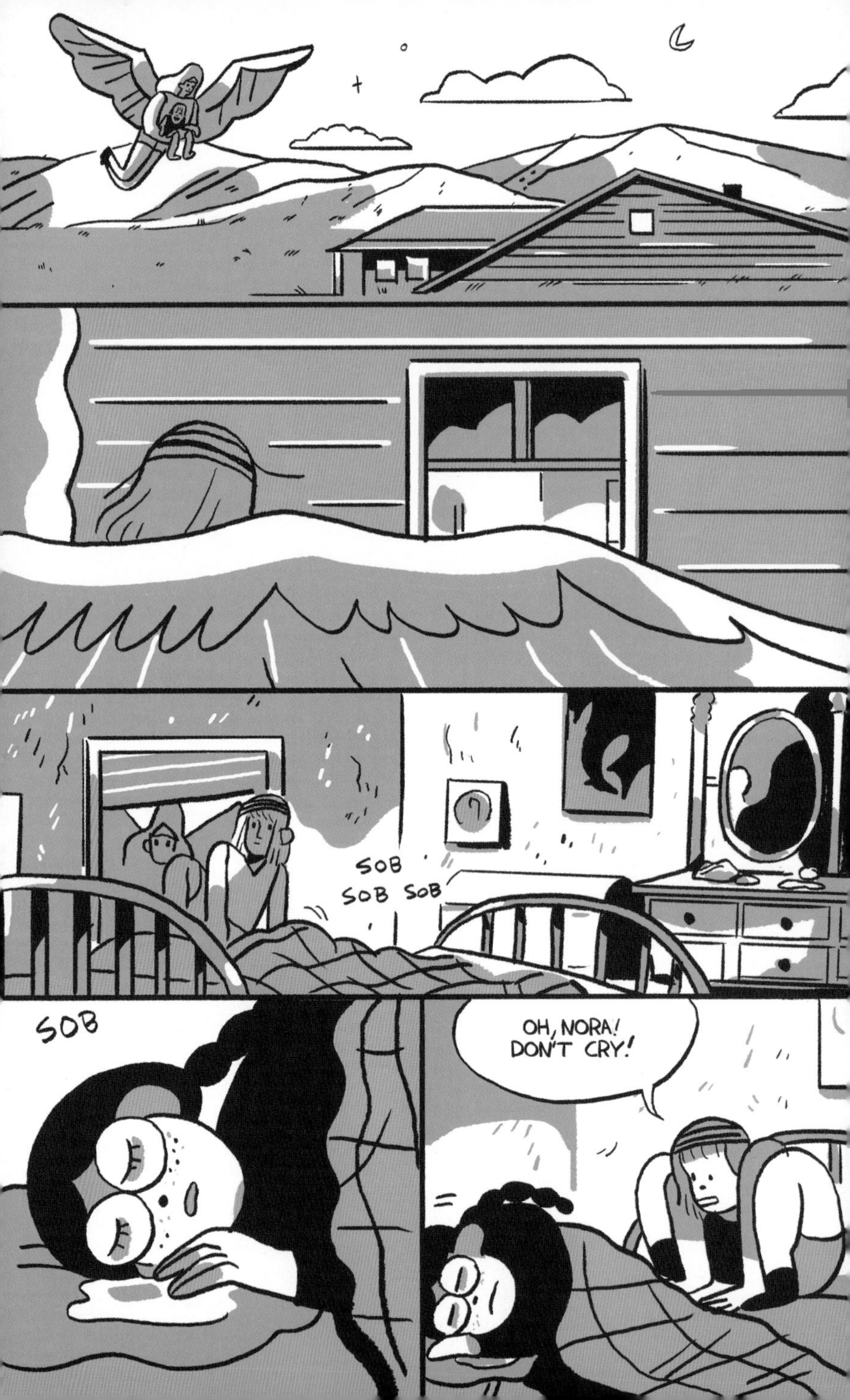
SOB
SOB SOB
SOB
OH, NORA! DON'T CRY!

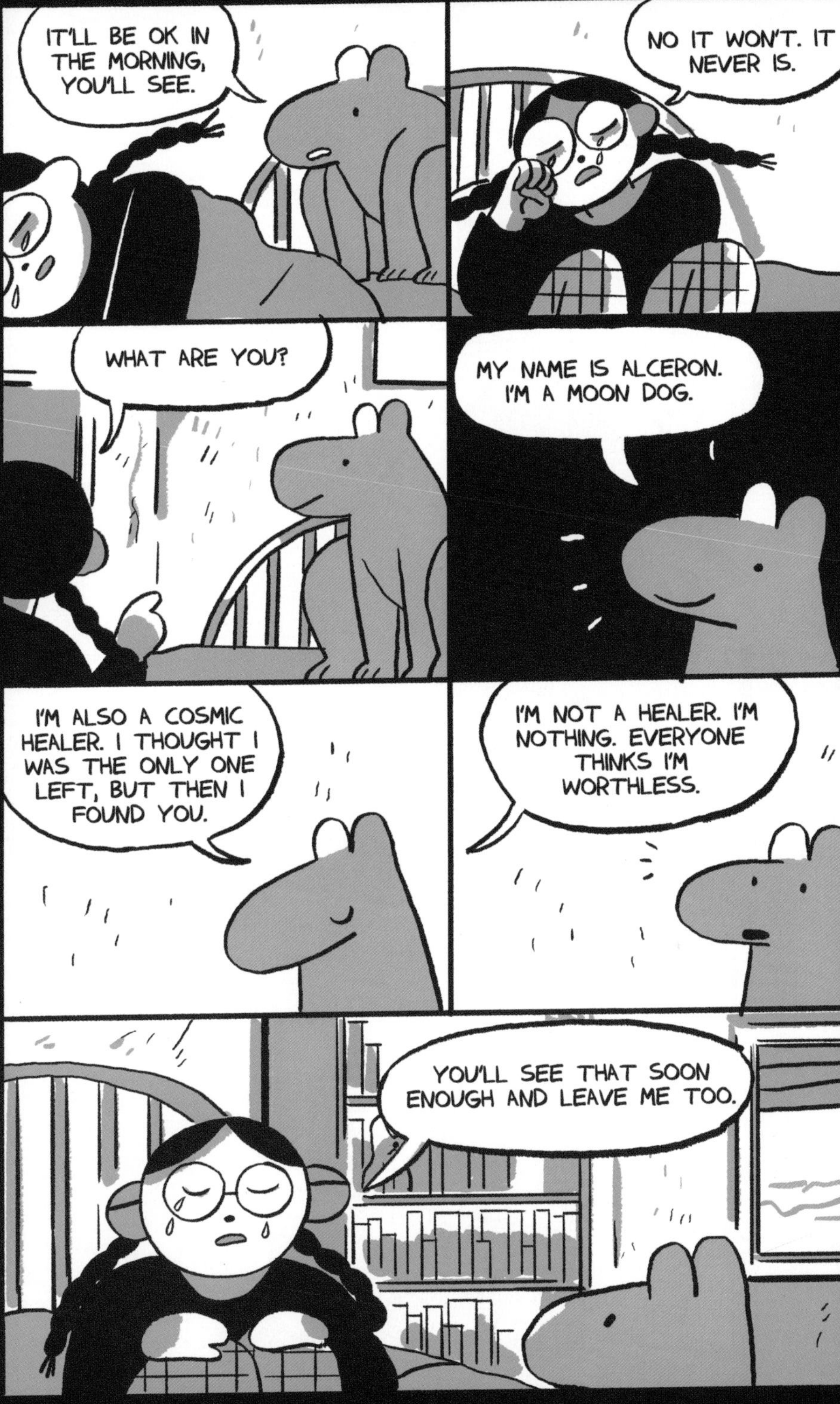
IT'LL BE OK IN THE MORNING, YOU'LL SEE.
NO IT WON'T. IT NEVER IS.
WHAT ARE YOU?
MY NAME IS ALCERON. I'M A MOON DOG.
I'M ALSO A COSMIC HEALER. I THOUGHT I WAS THE ONLY ONE LEFT, BUT THEN I FOUND YOU.
I'M NOT A HEALER. I'M NOTHING. EVERYONE THINKS I'M WORTHLESS.
YOU'LL SEE THAT SOON ENOUGH AND LEAVE ME TOO.

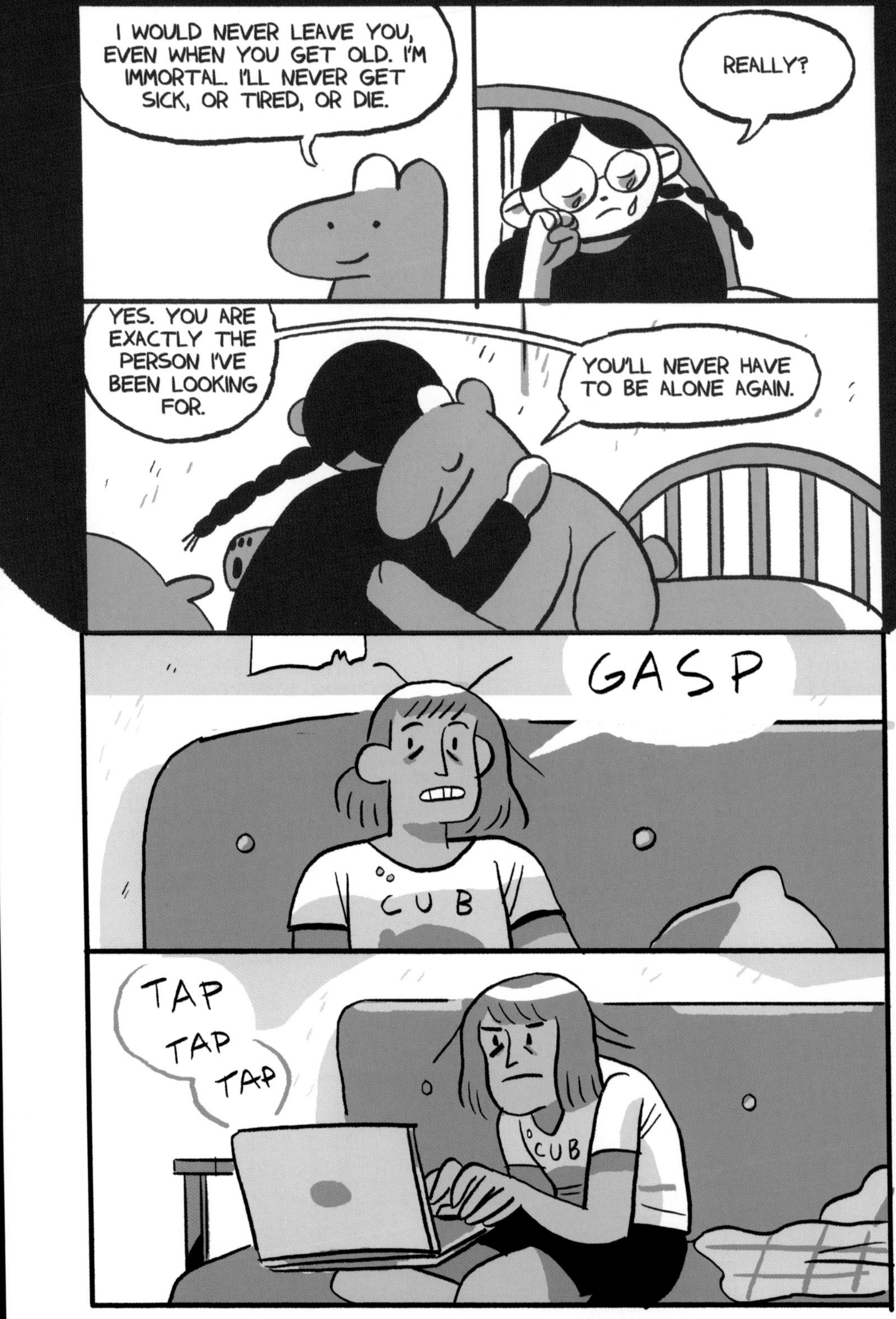
I WOULD NEVER LEAVE YOU, EVEN WHEN YOU GET OLD. I'M IMMORTAL. I'LL NEVER GET SICK, OR TIRED, OR DIE.
REALLY?
YES. YOU ARE EXACTLY THE PERSON I'VE BEEN LOOKING FOR.
YOU'LL NEVER HAVE TO BE ALONE AGAIN.
GASP
TAP
TAP
TAP
CUB
CUB

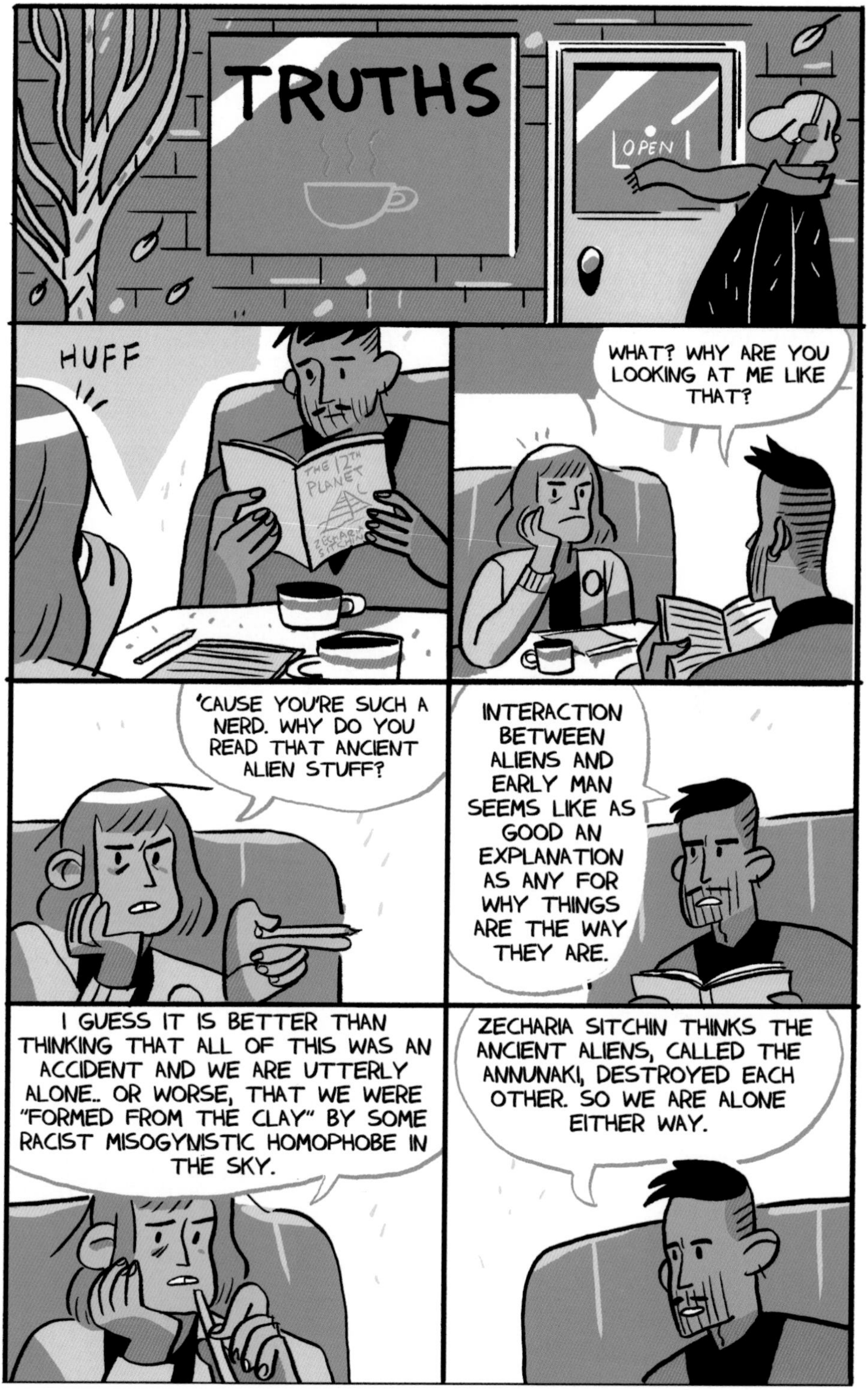
TRUTHS
OPEN
HUFF
THE 12TH PLANET
ZECHARIA SITCHIN
WHAT? WHY ARE YOU LOOKING AT ME LIKE THAT?
'CAUSE YOU'RE SUCH A NERD. WHY DO YOU READ THAT ANCIENT ALIEN STUFF?
INTERACTION BETWEEN ALIENS AND EARLY MAN SEEMS LIKE AS GOOD AN EXPLANATION AS ANY FOR WHY THINGS ARE THE WAY THEY ARE.
I GUESS IT IS BETTER THAN THINKING THAT ALL OF THIS WAS AN ACCIDENT AND WE ARE UTTERLY ALONE.. OR WORSE, THAT WE WERE "FORMED FROM THE CLAY" BY SOME RACIST MISOGYNISTIC HOMOPHOBE IN THE SKY.
ZECHARIA SITCHIN THINKS THE ANCIENT ALIENS, CALLED THE ANNUNAKI, DESTROYED EACH OTHER. SO WE ARE ALONE EITHER WAY.

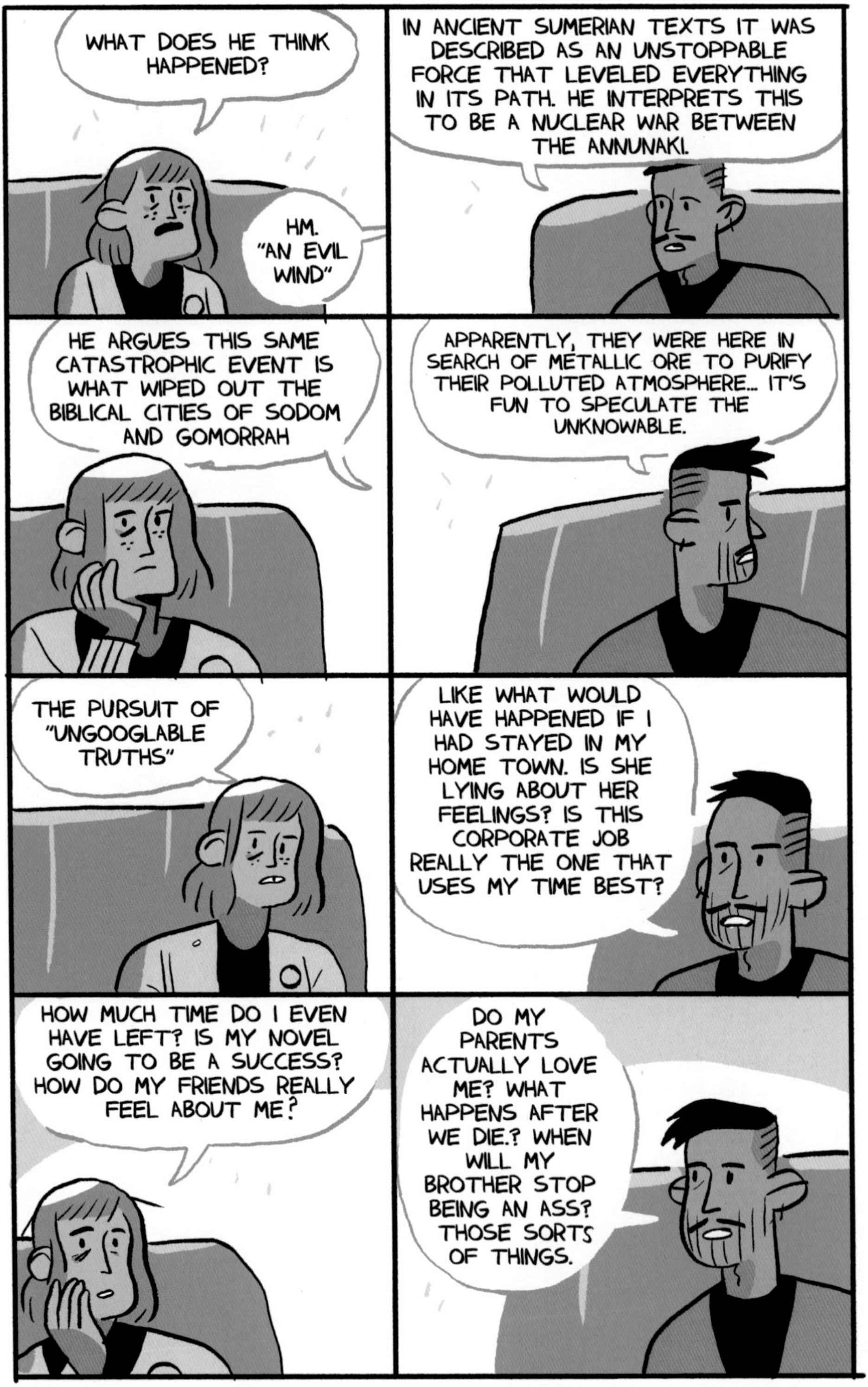
WHAT DOES HE THINK HAPPENED?
HM. "AN EVIL WIND"
IN ANCIENT SUMERIAN TEXTS IT WAS DESCRIBED AS AN UNSTOPPABLE FORCE THAT LEVELED EVERYTHING IN ITS PATH. HE INTERPRETS THIS TO BE A NUCLEAR WAR BETWEEN THE ANNUNAKI.
HE ARGUES THIS SAME CATASTROPHIC EVENT IS WHAT WIPED OUT THE BIBLICAL CITIES OF SODOM AND GOMORRAH
APPARENTLY, THEY WERE HERE IN SEARCH OF METALLIC ORE TO PURIFY THEIR POLLUTED ATMOSPHERE... IT'S FUN TO SPECULATE THE UNKNOWABLE.
THE PURSUIT OF "UNGOOGLABLE TRUTHS"
LIKE WHAT WOULD HAVE HAPPENED IF I HAD STAYED IN MY HOME TOWN. IS SHE LYING ABOUT HER FEELINGS? IS THIS CORPORATE JOB REALLY THE ONE THAT USES MY TIME BEST?
HOW MUCH TIME DO I EVEN HAVE LEFT? IS MY NOVEL GOING TO BE A SUCCESS? HOW DO MY FRIENDS REALLY FEEL ABOUT ME?
DO MY PARENTS ACTUALLY LOVE ME? WHAT HAPPENS AFTER WE DIE.? WHEN WILL MY BROTHER STOP BEING AN ASS? THOSE SORTS OF THINGS.

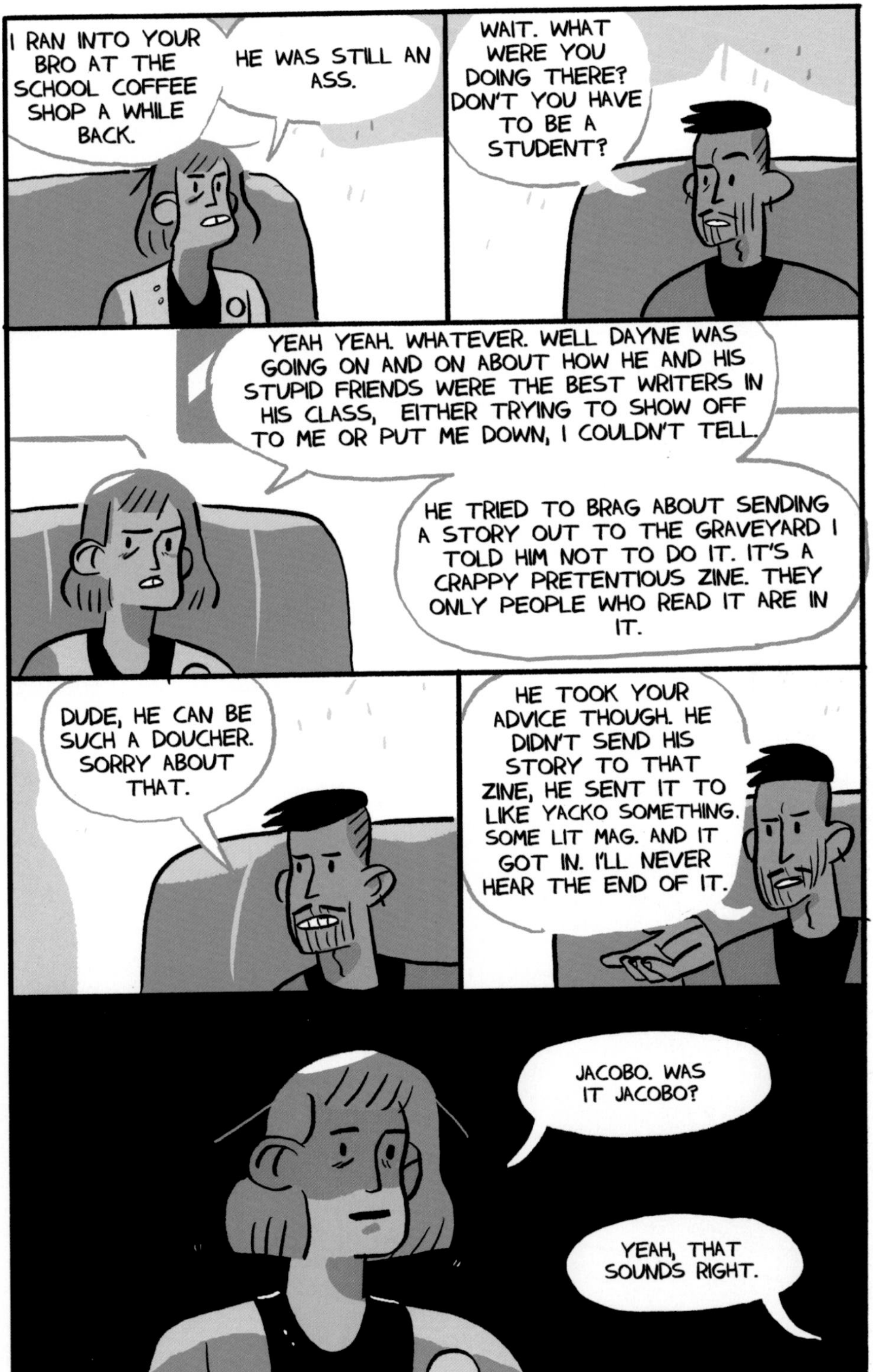
I RAN INTO YOUR BRO AT THE SCHOOL COFFEE SHOP A WHILE BACK.
HE WAS STILL AN ASS.
WAIT. WHAT WERE YOU DOING THERE? DON'T YOU HAVE TO BE A STUDENT?
YEAH YEAH. WHATEVER. WELL DAYNE WAS GOING ON AND ON ABOUT HOW HE AND HIS STUPID FRIENDS WERE THE BEST WRITERS IN HIS CLASS, EITHER TRYING TO SHOW OFF TO ME OR PUT ME DOWN, I COULDN'T TELL.
HE TRIED TO BRAG ABOUT SENDING A STORY OUT TO THE GRAVEYARD I TOLD HIM NOT TO DO IT. IT'S A CRAPPY PRETENTIOUS ZINE. THEY ONLY PEOPLE WHO READ IT ARE IN IT.
DUDE, HE CAN BE SUCH A DOUCHER. SORRY ABOUT THAT.
HE TOOK YOUR ADVICE THOUGH. HE DIDN'T SEND HIS STORY TO THAT ZINE, HE SENT IT TO LIKE YACKO SOMETHING. SOME LIT MAG. AND IT GOT IN. I'LL NEVER HEAR THE END OF IT.
JACOBO. WAS IT JACOBO?
YEAH, THAT SOUNDS RIGHT.

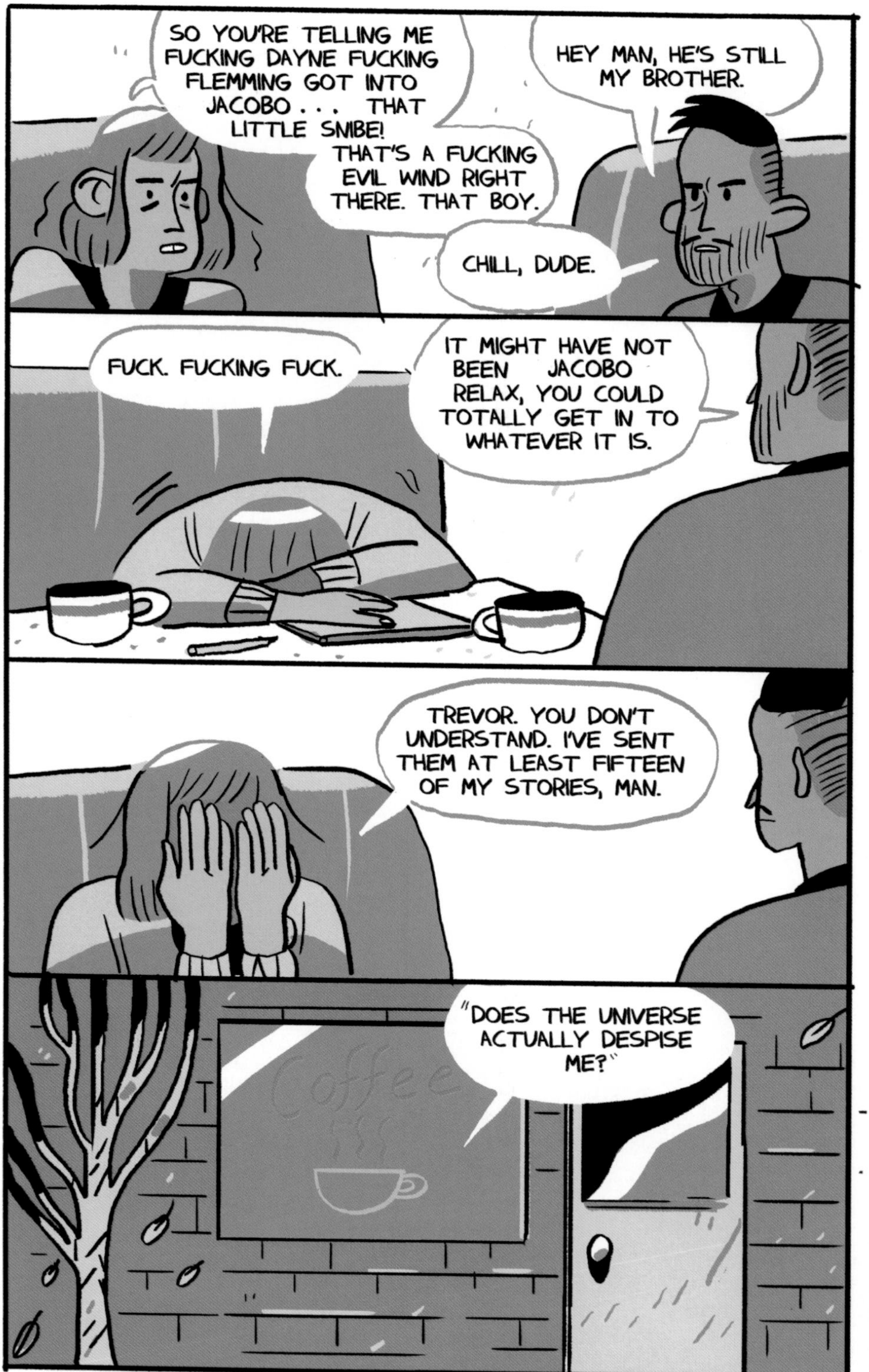
SO YOU'RE TELLING ME FUCKING DAYNE FUCKING FLEMMING GOT INTO JACOBO . . . THAT LITTLE SNIBE!
THAT'S A FUCKING EVIL WIND RIGHT THERE. THAT BOY.
HEY MAN, HE'S STILL MY BROTHER.
CHILL, DUDE.
FUCK. FUCKING FUCK.
IT MIGHT HAVE NOT BEEN JACOBO RELAX, YOU COULD TOTALLY GET IN TO WHATEVER IT IS.
TREVOR. YOU DON'T UNDERSTAND. I'VE SENT THEM AT LEAST FIFTEEN OF MY STORIES, MAN.
Coffee
"DOES THE UNIVERSE ACTUALLY DESPISE ME?"

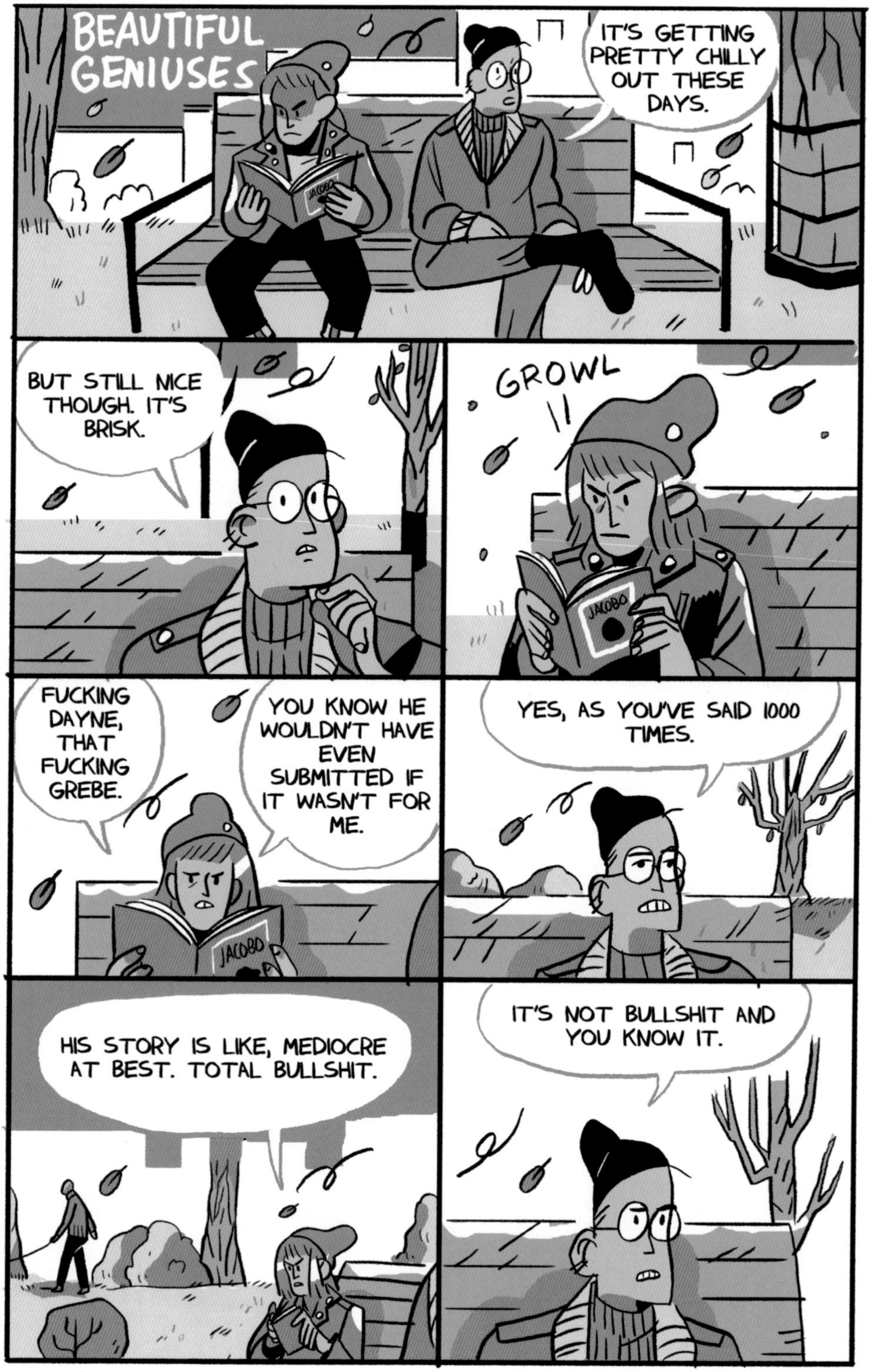
BEAUTIFUL GENIUSES
IT'S GETTING PRETTY CHILLY OUT THESE DAYS.
JACOBO
BUT STILL NICE THOUGH. IT'S BRISK.
GROWL
JACOBO
FUCKING DAYNE, THAT FUCKING GREBE.
YOU KNOW HE WOULDN'T HAVE EVEN SUBMITTED IF IT WASN'T FOR ME.
JACOBO
YES, AS YOU'VE SAID 1000 TIMES.
HIS STORY IS LIKE, MEDIOCRE AT BEST. TOTAL BULLSHIT.
IT'S NOT BULLSHIT AND YOU KNOW IT.

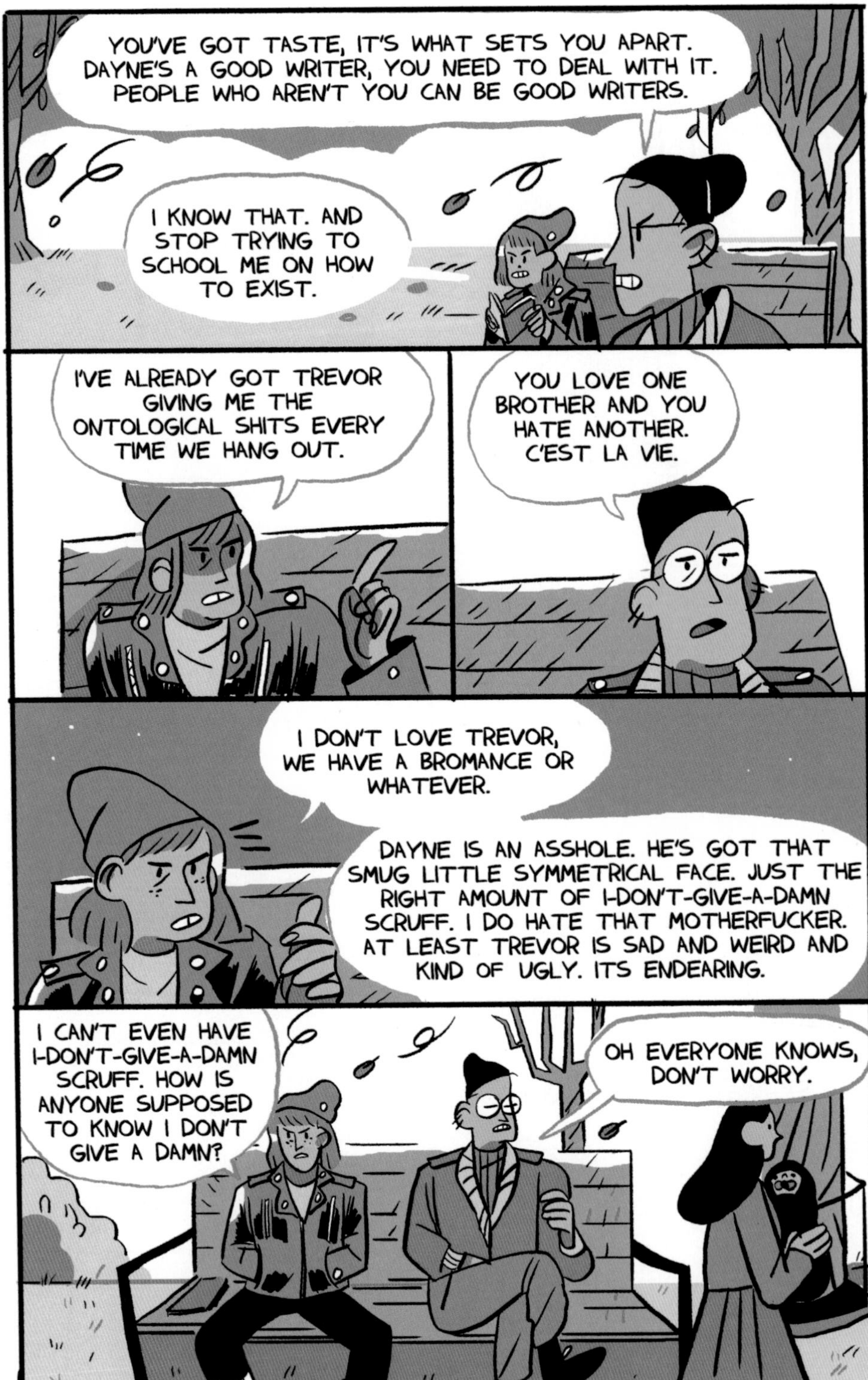
YOU'VE GOT TASTE, IT'S WHAT SETS YOU APART. DAYNE'S A GOOD WRITER, YOU NEED TO DEAL WITH IT. PEOPLE WHO AREN'T YOU CAN BE GOOD WRITERS.
I KNOW THAT. AND STOP TRYING TO SCHOOL ME ON HOW TO EXIST.
I'VE ALREADY GOT TREVOR GIVING ME THE ONTOLOGICAL SHITS EVERY TIME WE HANG OUT.
YOU LOVE ONE BROTHER AND YOU HATE ANOTHER. C'EST LA VIE.
I DON'T LOVE TREVOR, WE HAVE A BROMANCE OR WHATEVER.
DAYNE IS AN ASSHOLE. HE'S GOT THAT SMUG LITTLE SYMMETRICAL FACE. JUST THE RIGHT AMOUNT OF I-DON'T-GIVE-A-DAMN SCRUFF. I DO HATE THAT MOTHERFUCKER. AT LEAST TREVOR IS SAD AND WEIRD AND KIND OF UGLY. ITS ENDEARING.
I CAN'T EVEN HAVE I-DON'T-GIVE-A-DAMN SCRUFF. HOW IS ANYONE SUPPOSED TO KNOW I DON'T GIVE A DAMN?
OH EVERYONE KNOWS, DON'T WORRY.

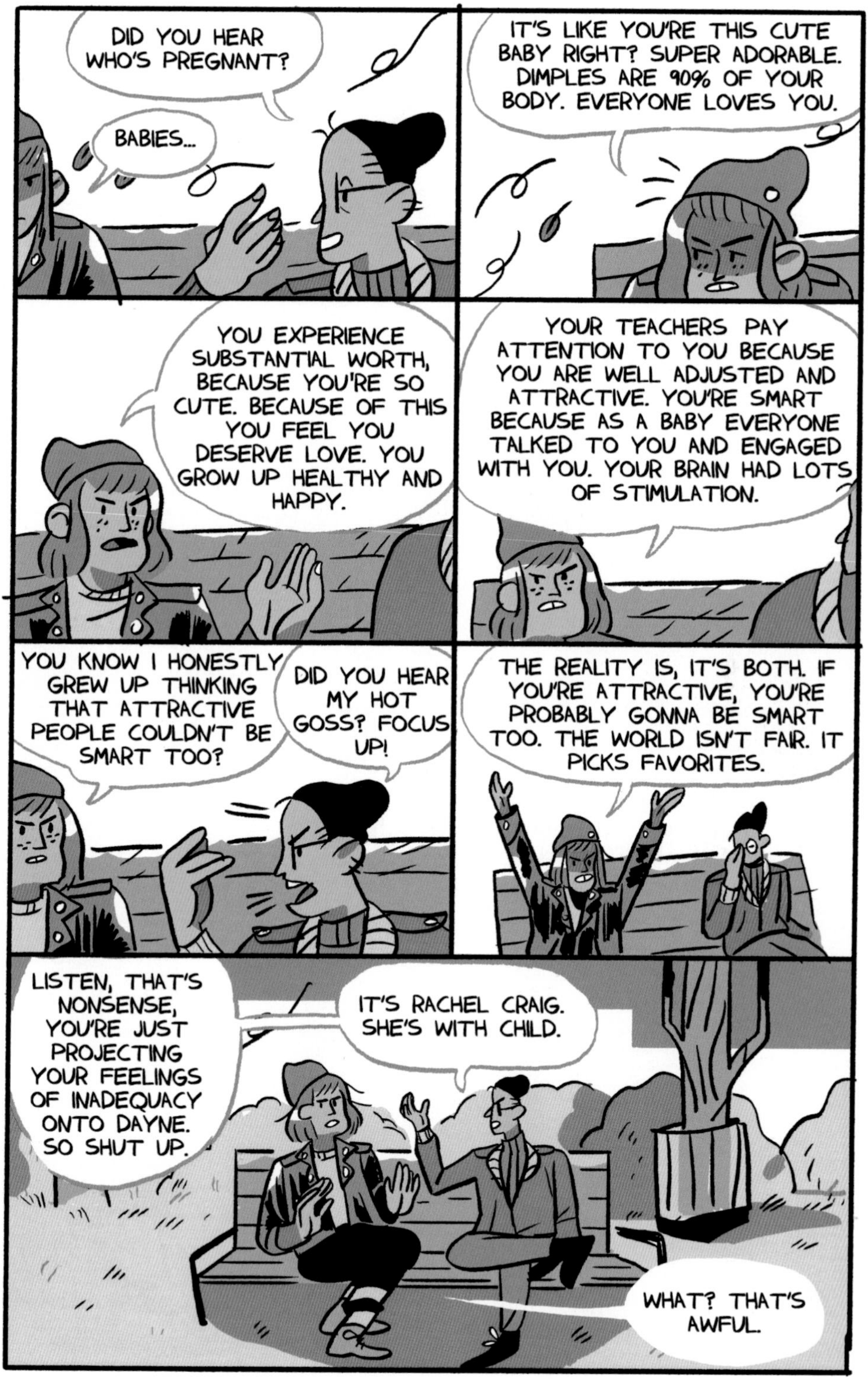
DID YOU HEAR WHO'S PREGNANT?
BABIES...
IT'S LIKE YOU'RE THIS CUTE BABY RIGHT? SUPER ADORABLE. DIMPLES ARE 90% OF YOUR BODY. EVERYONE LOVES YOU.
YOU EXPERIENCE SUBSTANTIAL WORTH, BECAUSE YOU'RE SO CUTE. BECAUSE OF THIS YOU FEEL YOU DESERVE LOVE. YOU GROW UP HEALTHY AND HAPPY.
YOUR TEACHERS PAY ATTENTION TO YOU BECAUSE YOU ARE WELL ADJUSTED AND ATTRACTIVE. YOU'RE SMART BECAUSE AS A BABY EVERYONE TALKED TO YOU AND ENGAGED WITH YOU. YOUR BRAIN HAD LOTS OF STIMULATION.
YOU KNOW I HONESTLY GREW UP THINKING THAT ATTRACTIVE PEOPLE COULDN'T BE SMART TOO?
DID YOU HEAR MY HOT GOSS? FOCUS UP!
THE REALITY IS, IT'S BOTH. IF YOU'RE ATTRACTIVE, YOU'RE PROBABLY GONNA BE SMART TOO. THE WORLD ISN'T FAIR. IT PICKS FAVORITES.
LISTEN, THAT'S NONSENSE, YOU'RE JUST PROJECTING YOUR FEELINGS OF INADEQUACY ONTO DAYNE. SO SHUT UP.
IT'S RACHEL CRAIG. SHE'S WITH CHILD.
WHAT? THAT'S AWFUL.

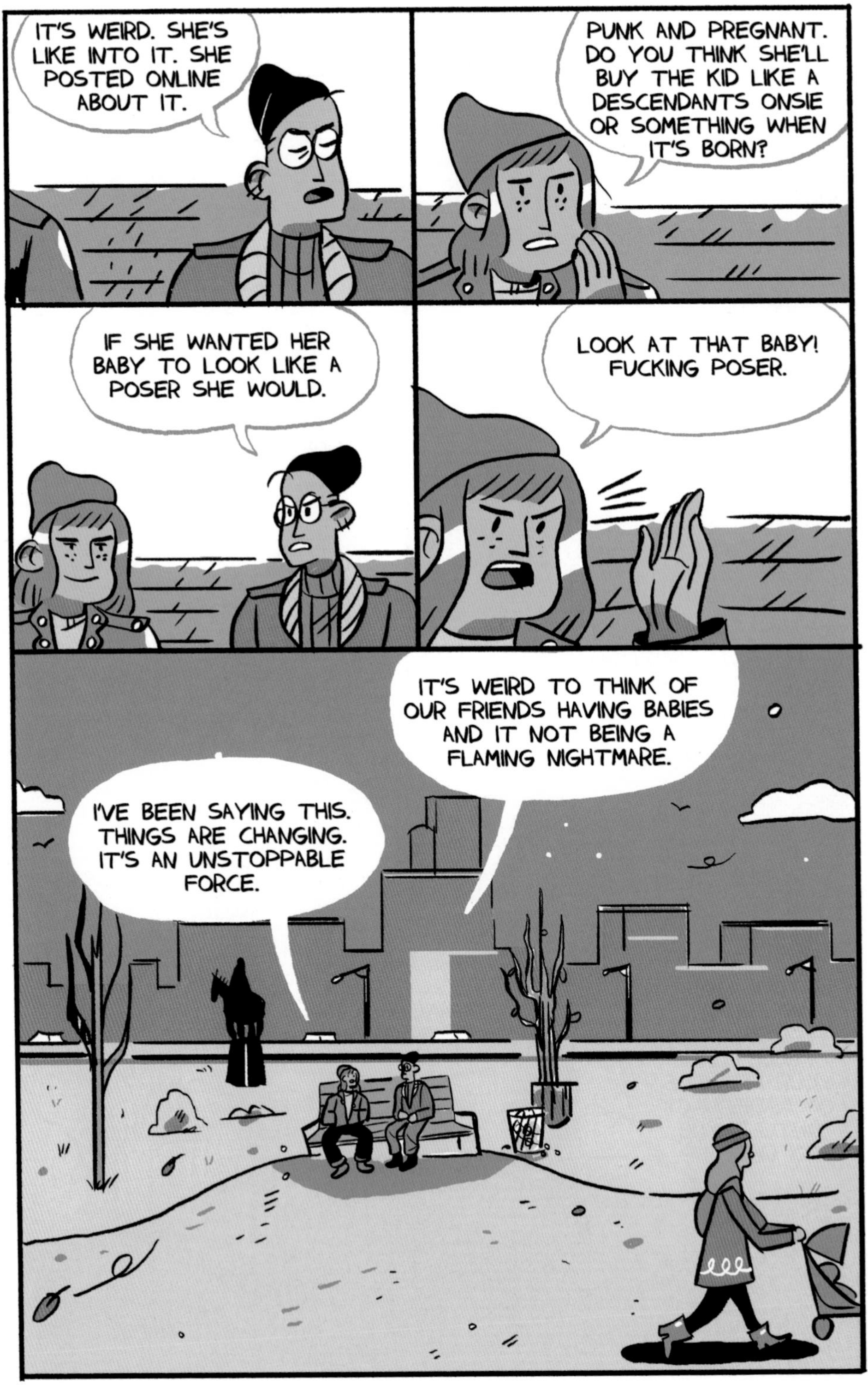
IT'S WEIRD. SHE'S LIKE INTO IT. SHE POSTED ONLINE ABOUT IT.
PUNK AND PREGNANT. DO YOU THINK SHE'LL BUY THE KID LIKE A DESCENDANTS ONSIE OR SOMETHING WHEN IT'S BORN?
IF SHE WANTED HER BABY TO LOOK LIKE A POSER SHE WOULD.
LOOK AT THAT BABY! FUCKING POSER.
I'VE BEEN SAYING THIS. THINGS ARE CHANGING. IT'S AN UNSTOPPABLE FORCE.
IT'S WEIRD TO THINK OF OUR FRIENDS HAVING BABIES AND IT NOT BEING A FLAMING NIGHTMARE.

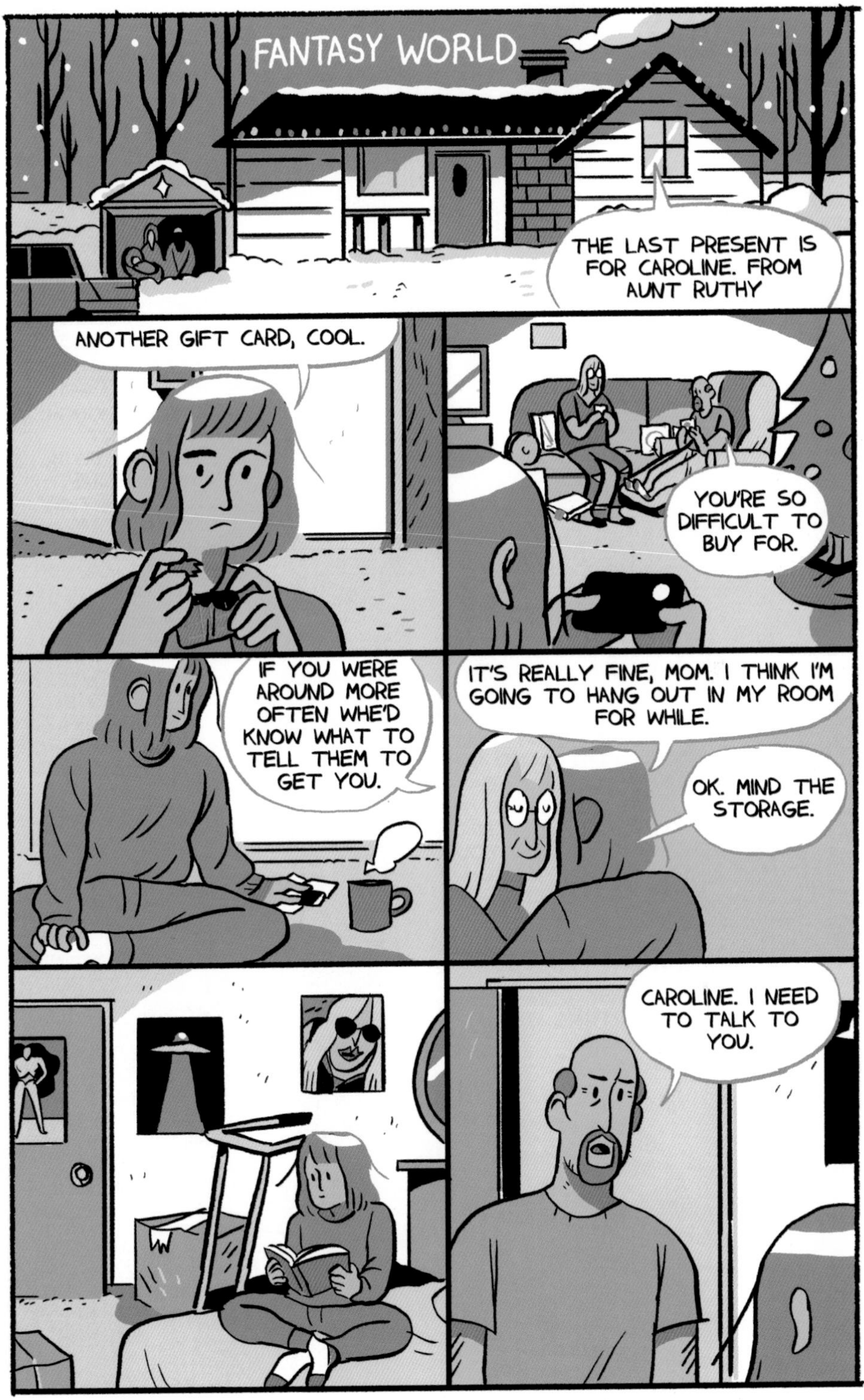
FANTASY WORLD
THE LAST PRESENT IS FOR CAROLINE. FROM AUNT RUTHY
ANOTHER GIFT CARD, COOL.
YOU'RE SO DIFFICULT TO BUY FOR.
IF YOU WERE AROUND MORE OFTEN WHE'D KNOW WHAT TO TELL THEM TO GET YOU.
IT'S REALLY FINE, MOM. I THINK I'M GOING TO HANG OUT IN MY ROOM FOR WHILE.
OK. MIND THE STORAGE.
CAROLINE. I NEED TO TALK TO YOU.

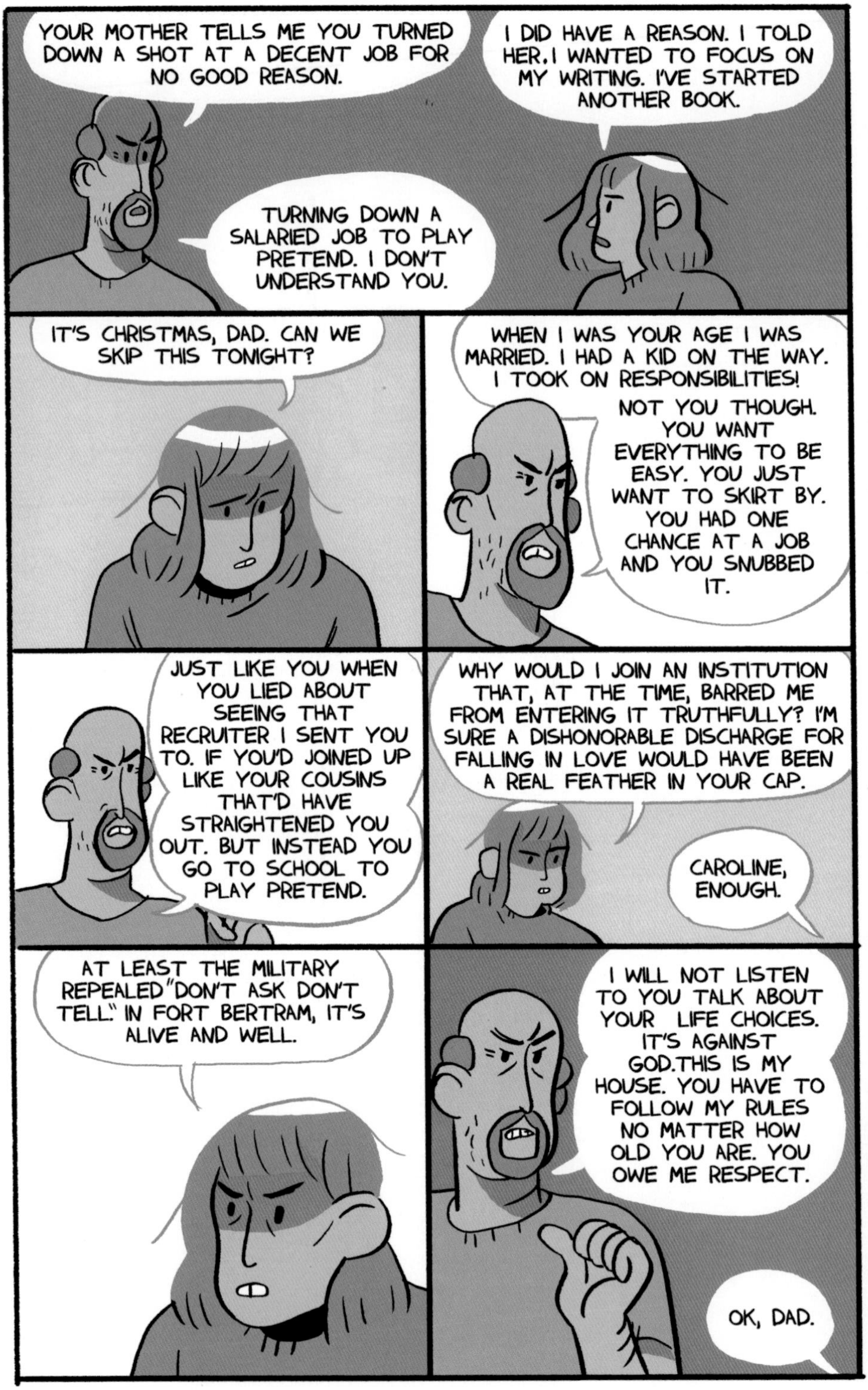
YOUR MOTHER TELLS ME YOU TURNED DOWN A SHOT AT A DECENT JOB FOR NO GOOD REASON.
I DID HAVE A REASON. I TOLD HER. I WANTED TO FOCUS ON MY WRITING. I'VE STARTED ANOTHER BOOK.
TURNING DOWN A SALARIED JOB TO PLAY PRETEND. I DON'T UNDERSTAND YOU.
IT'S CHRISTMAS, DAD. CAN WE SKIP THIS TONIGHT?
WHEN I WAS YOUR AGE I WAS MARRIED. I HAD A KID ON THE WAY. I TOOK ON RESPONSIBILITIES!
NOT YOU THOUGH. YOU WANT EVERYTHING TO BE EASY. YOU JUST WANT TO SKIRT BY. YOU HAD ONE CHANCE AT A JOB AND YOU SNUBBED IT.
JUST LIKE YOU WHEN YOU LIED ABOUT SEEING THAT RECRUITER I SENT YOU TO. IF YOU'D JOINED UP LIKE YOUR COUSINS THAT'D HAVE STRAIGHTENED YOU OUT. BUT INSTEAD YOU GO TO SCHOOL TO PLAY PRETEND.
WHY WOULD I JOIN AN INSTITUTION THAT, AT THE TIME, BARRED ME FROM ENTERING IT TRUTHFULLY? I'M SURE A DISHONORABLE DISCHARGE FOR FALLING IN LOVE WOULD HAVE BEEN A REAL FEATHER IN YOUR CAP.
CAROLINE, ENOUGH.
AT LEAST THE MILITARY REPEALED "DON'T ASK DON'T TELL." IN FORT BERTRAM, IT'S ALIVE AND WELL.
I WILL NOT LISTEN TO YOU TALK ABOUT YOUR LIFE CHOICES. IT'S AGAINST GOD. THIS IS MY HOUSE. YOU HAVE TO FOLLOW MY RULES NO MATTER HOW OLD YOU ARE. YOU OWE ME RESPECT.
OK, DAD.

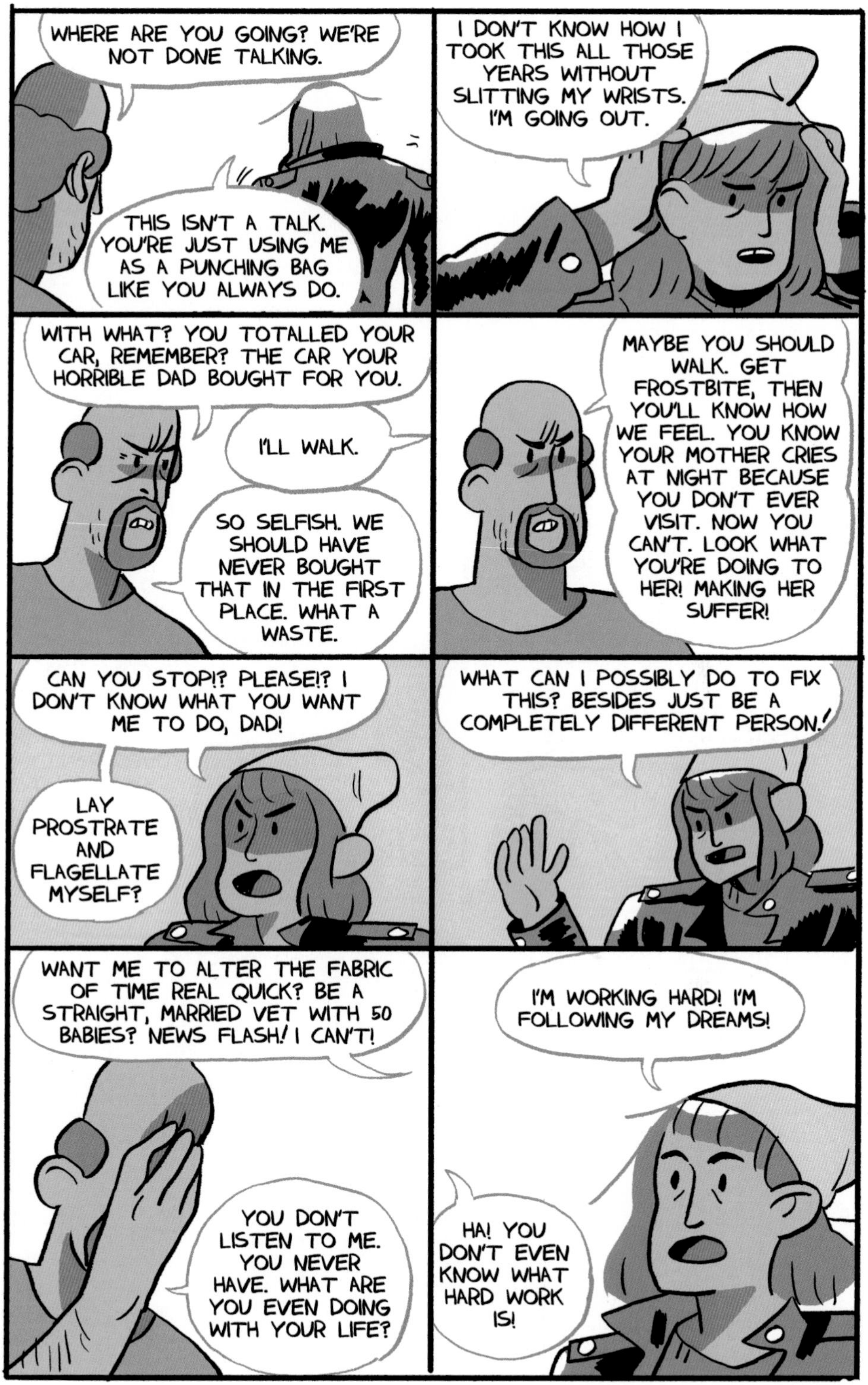
WHERE ARE YOU GOING? WE'RE NOT DONE TALKING.
THIS ISN'T A TALK. YOU'RE JUST USING ME AS A PUNCHING BAG LIKE YOU ALWAYS DO.
I DON'T KNOW HOW I TOOK THIS ALL THOSE YEARS WITHOUT SLITTING MY WRISTS. I'M GOING OUT.
WITH WHAT? YOU TOTALLED YOUR CAR, REMEMBER? THE CAR YOUR HORRIBLE DAD BOUGHT FOR YOU.
I'LL WALK.
SO SELFISH. WE SHOULD HAVE NEVER BOUGHT THAT IN THE FIRST PLACE. WHAT A WASTE.
MAYBE YOU SHOULD WALK. GET FROSTBITE, THEN YOU'LL KNOW HOW WE FEEL. YOU KNOW YOUR MOTHER CRIES AT NIGHT BECAUSE YOU DON'T EVER VISIT. NOW YOU CAN'T. LOOK WHAT YOU'RE DOING TO HER! MAKING HER SUFFER!
CAN YOU STOP!? PLEASE!? I DON'T KNOW WHAT YOU WANT ME TO DO, DAD!
LAY PROSTRATE AND FLAGELLATE MYSELF?
WHAT CAN I POSSIBLY DO TO FIX THIS? BESIDES JUST BE A COMPLETELY DIFFERENT PERSON!
WANT ME TO ALTER THE FABRIC OF TIME REAL QUICK? BE A STRAIGHT, MARRIED VET WITH 50 BABIES? NEWS FLASH! I CAN'T!
YOU DON'T LISTEN TO ME. YOU NEVER HAVE. WHAT ARE YOU EVEN DOING WITH YOUR LIFE?
I'M WORKING HARD! I'M FOLLOWING MY DREAMS!
HA! YOU DON'T EVEN KNOW WHAT HARD WORK IS!

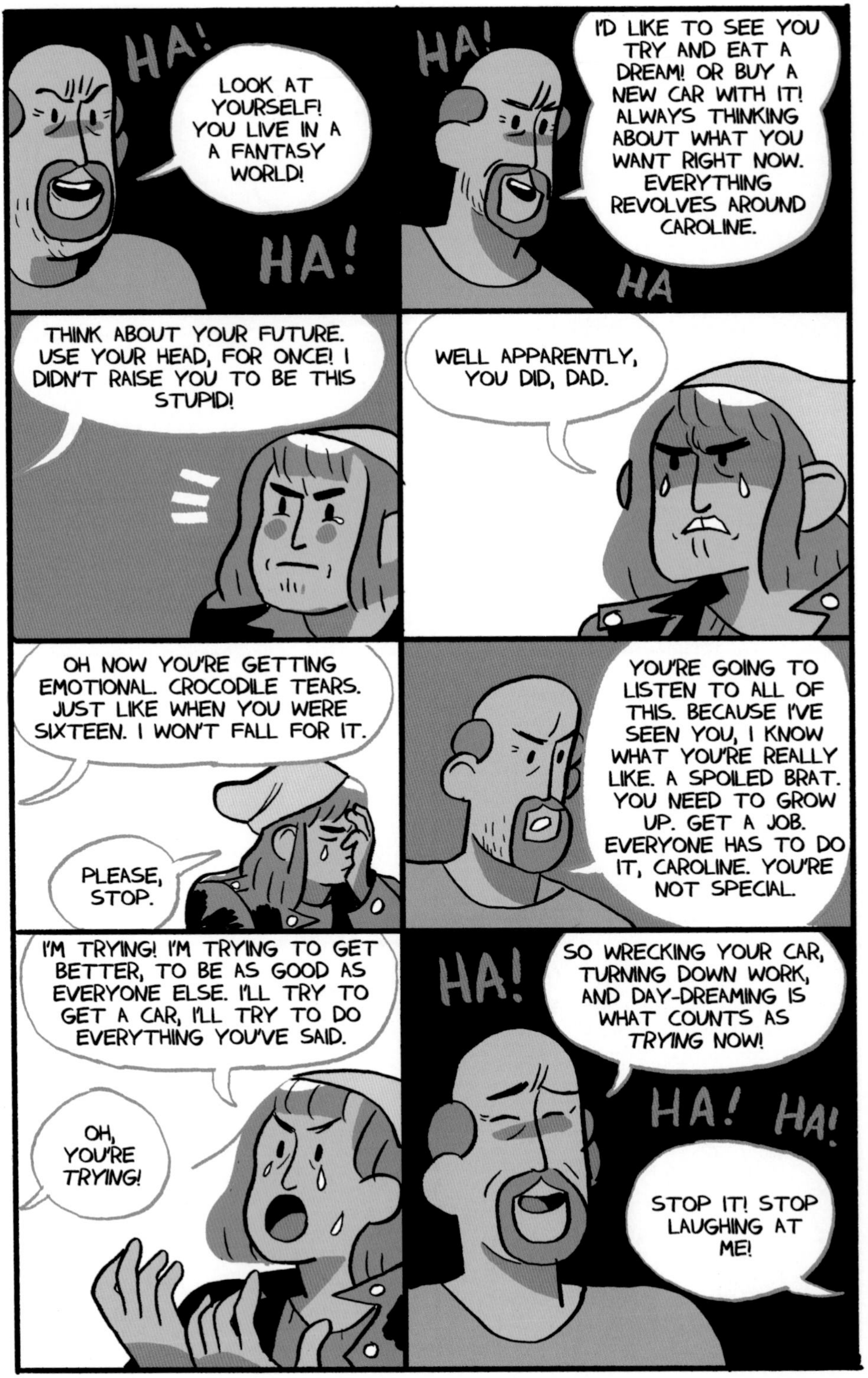
HA!
LOOK AT YOURSELF! YOU LIVE IN A A FANTASY WORLD!
HA!
HA!
I'D LIKE TO SEE YOU TRY AND EAT A DREAM! OR BUY A NEW CAR WITH IT! ALWAYS THINKING ABOUT WHAT YOU WANT RIGHT NOW. EVERYTHING REVOLVES AROUND CAROLINE.
HA
THINK ABOUT YOUR FUTURE. USE YOUR HEAD, FOR ONCE! I DIDN'T RAISE YOU TO BE THIS STUPID!
WELL APPARENTLY, YOU DID, DAD.
OH NOW YOU'RE GETTING EMOTIONAL. CROCODILE TEARS. JUST LIKE WHEN YOU WERE SIXTEEN. I WON'T FALL FOR IT.
PLEASE, STOP.
YOU'RE GOING TO LISTEN TO ALL OF THIS. BECAUSE I'VE SEEN YOU, I KNOW WHAT YOU'RE REALLY LIKE. A SPOILED BRAT. YOU NEED TO GROW UP. GET A JOB. EVERYONE HAS TO DO IT, CAROLINE. YOU'RE NOT SPECIAL.
I'M TRYING! I'M TRYING TO GET BETTER, TO BE AS GOOD AS EVERYONE ELSE. I'LL TRY TO GET A CAR, I'LL TRY TO DO EVERYTHING YOU'VE SAID.
OH, YOU'RE *TRYING*!
HA!
SO WRECKING YOUR CAR, TURNING DOWN WORK, AND DAY-DREAMING IS WHAT COUNTS AS *TRYING* NOW!
HA! HA!
STOP IT! STOP LAUGHING AT ME!

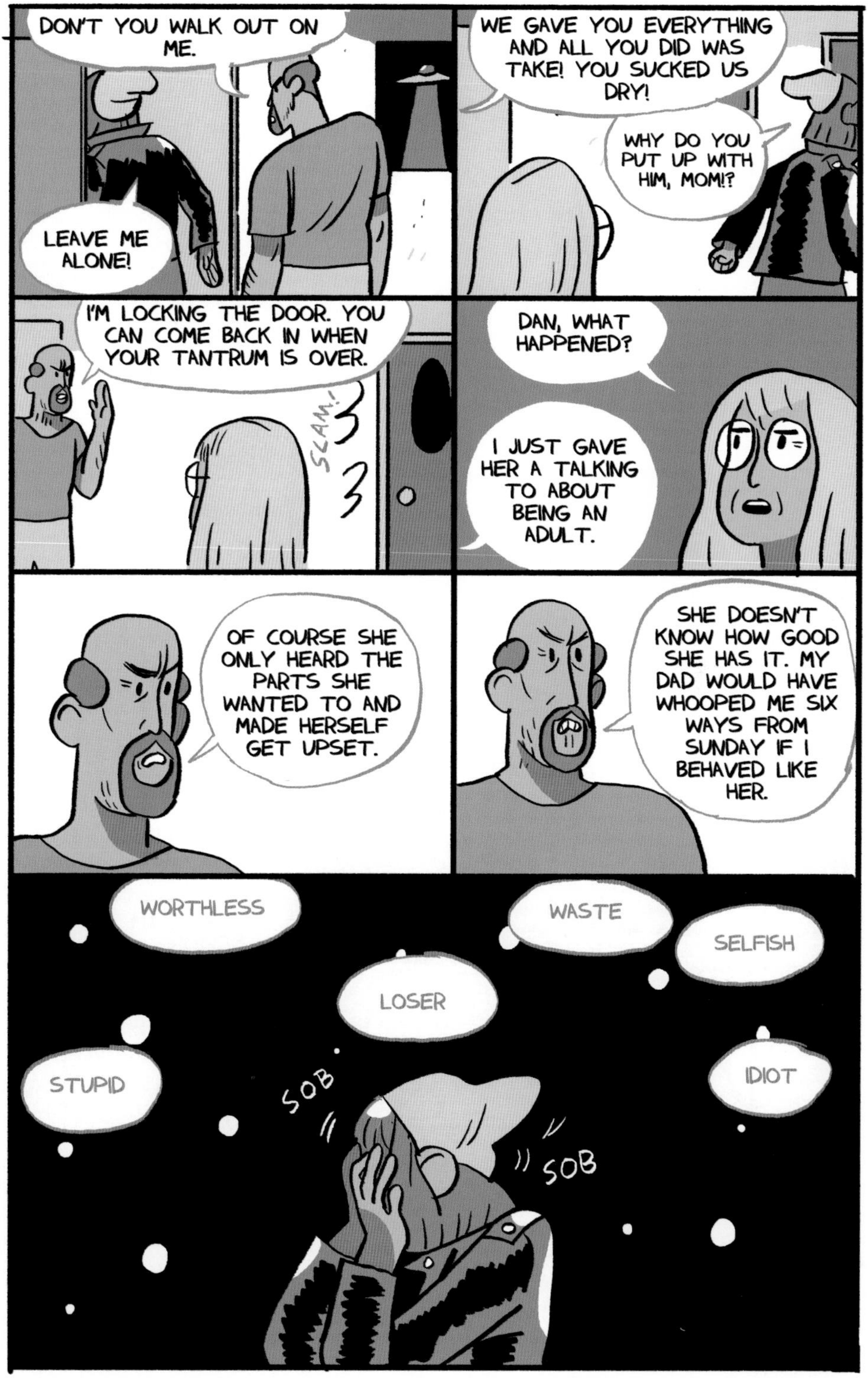
DON'T YOU WALK OUT ON ME.
LEAVE ME ALONE!
WE GAVE YOU EVERYTHING AND ALL YOU DID WAS TAKE! YOU SUCKED US DRY!
WHY DO YOU PUT UP WITH HIM, MOM!?
I'M LOCKING THE DOOR. YOU CAN COME BACK IN WHEN YOUR TANTRUM IS OVER.
SLAM!
DAN, WHAT HAPPENED?
I JUST GAVE HER A TALKING TO ABOUT BEING AN ADULT.
OF COURSE SHE ONLY HEARD THE PARTS SHE WANTED TO AND MADE HERSELF GET UPSET.
SHE DOESN'T KNOW HOW GOOD SHE HAS IT. MY DAD WOULD HAVE WHOOPED ME SIX WAYS FROM SUNDAY IF I BEHAVED LIKE HER.
WORTHLESS
WASTE
SELFISH
LOSER
STUPID
IDIOT
SOB
SOB

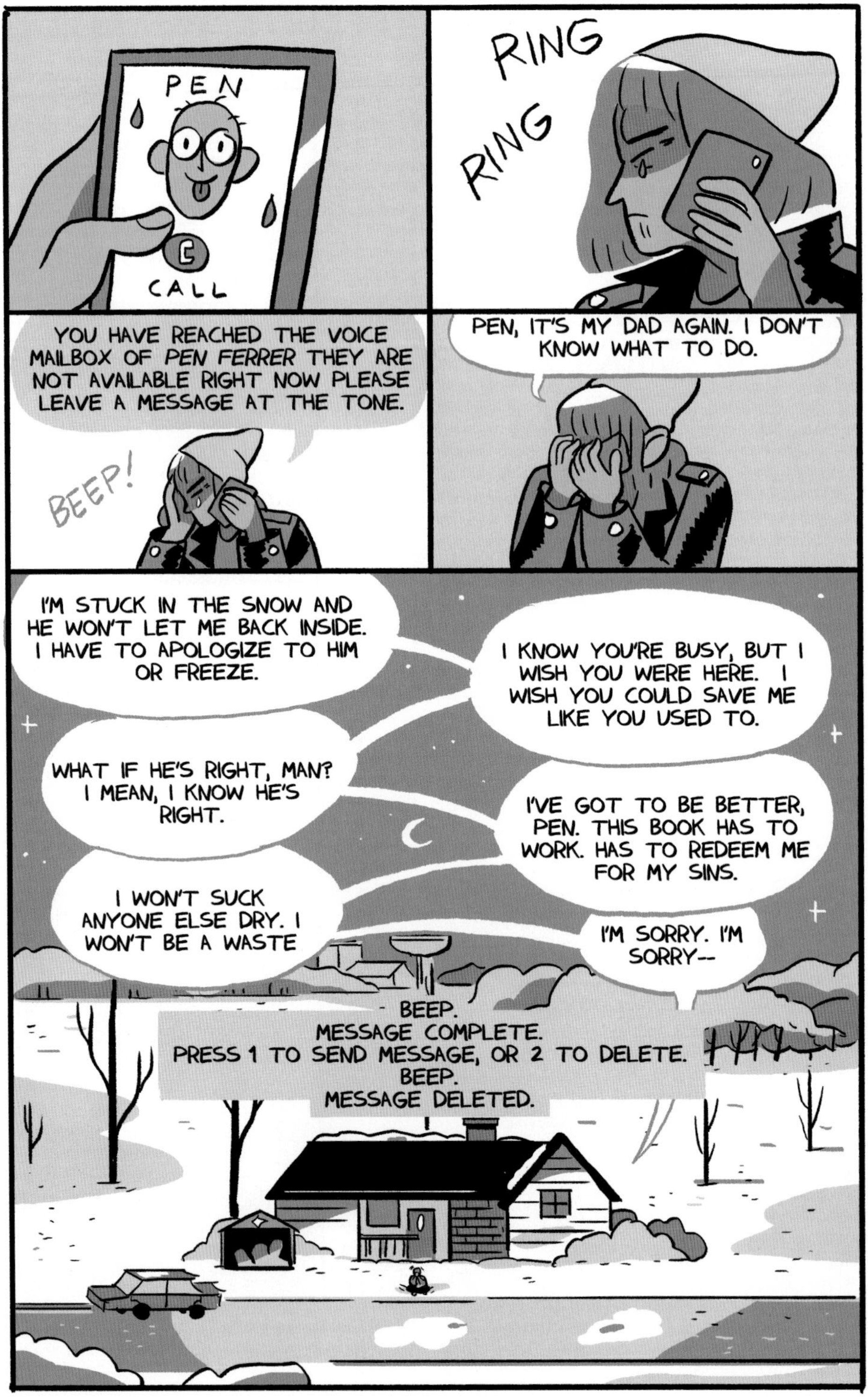
PEN
CALL
RING
RING
YOU HAVE REACHED THE VOICE MAILBOX OF *PEN FERRER* THEY ARE NOT AVAILABLE RIGHT NOW PLEASE LEAVE A MESSAGE AT THE TONE.
BEEP!
PEN, IT'S MY DAD AGAIN. I DON'T KNOW WHAT TO DO.
I'M STUCK IN THE SNOW AND HE WON'T LET ME BACK INSIDE. I HAVE TO APOLOGIZE TO HIM OR FREEZE.
I KNOW YOU'RE BUSY, BUT I WISH YOU WERE HERE. I WISH YOU COULD SAVE ME LIKE YOU USED TO.
WHAT IF HE'S RIGHT, MAN? I MEAN, I KNOW HE'S RIGHT.
I'VE GOT TO BE BETTER, PEN. THIS BOOK HAS TO WORK. HAS TO REDEEM ME FOR MY SINS.
I WON'T SUCK ANYONE ELSE DRY. I WON'T BE A WASTE
I'M SORRY. I'M SORRY--
BEEP.
MESSAGE COMPLETE.
PRESS 1 TO SEND MESSAGE, OR 2 TO DELETE.
BEEP.
MESSAGE DELETED.

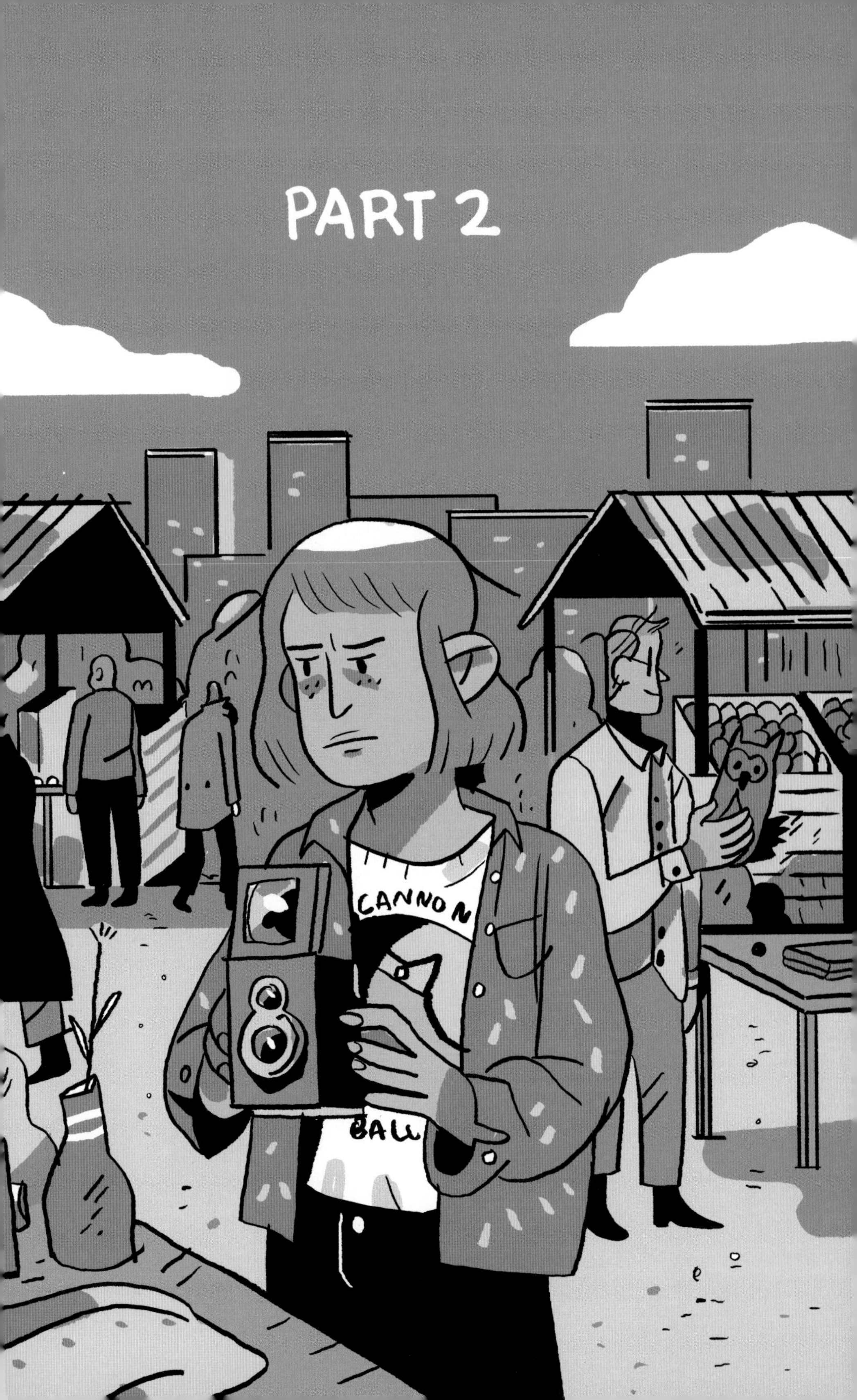
PART 2
CANNON
BALL

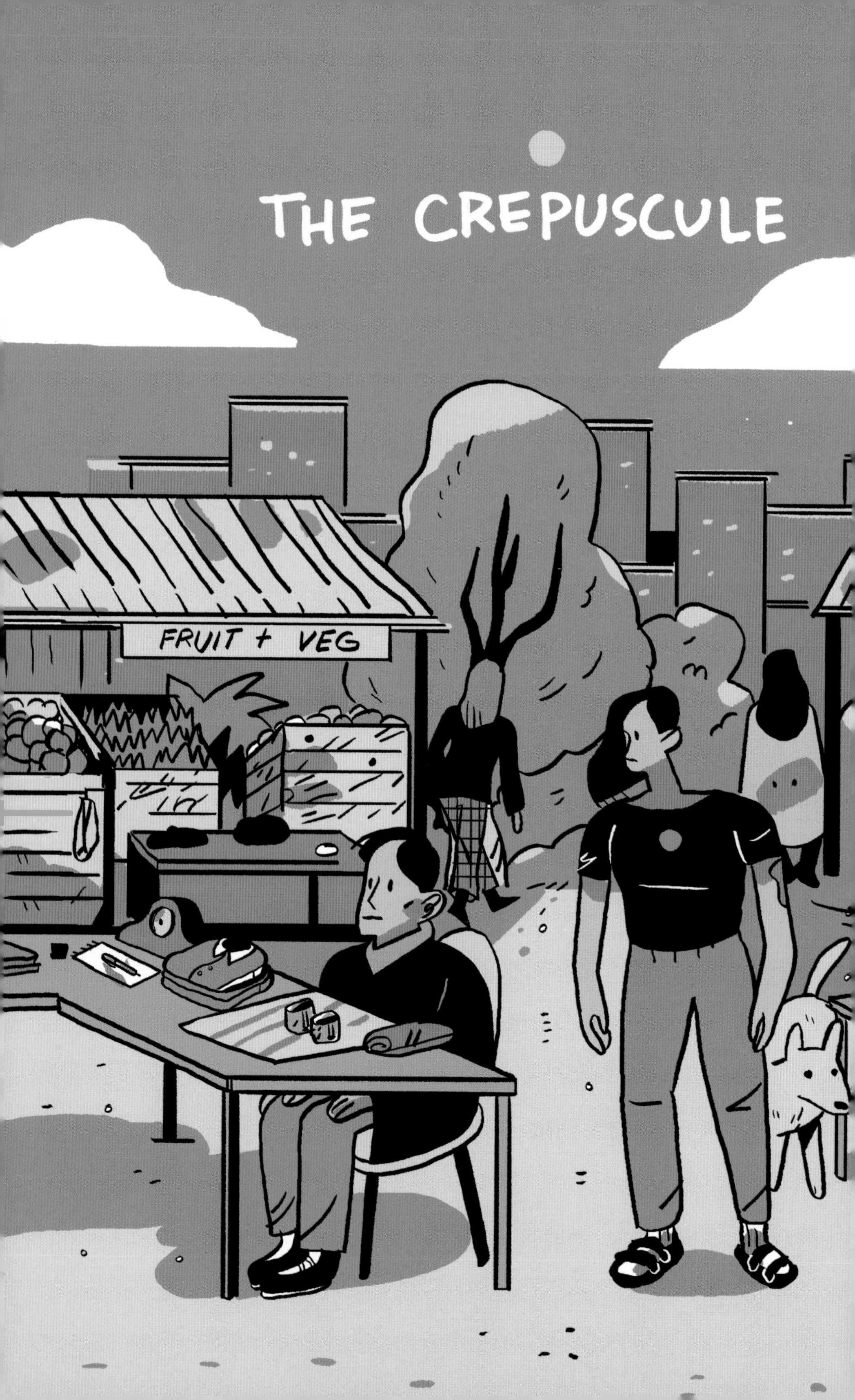
THE CREPUSCULE
FRUIT + VEG

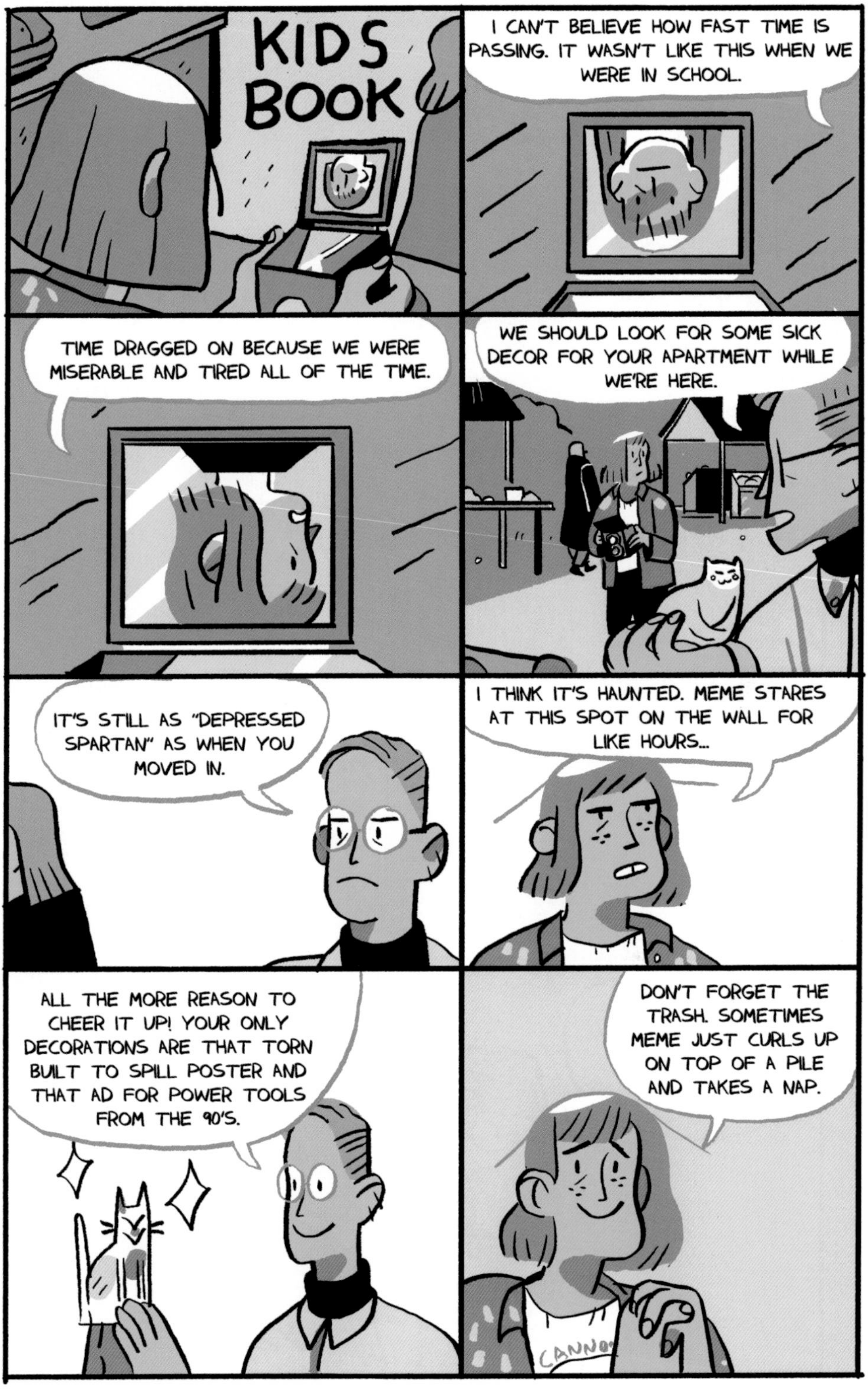
KIDS BOOK
I CAN'T BELIEVE HOW FAST TIME IS PASSING. IT WASN'T LIKE THIS WHEN WE WERE IN SCHOOL.
TIME DRAGGED ON BECAUSE WE WERE MISERABLE AND TIRED ALL OF THE TIME.
WE SHOULD LOOK FOR SOME SICK DECOR FOR YOUR APARTMENT WHILE WE'RE HERE.
IT'S STILL AS "DEPRESSED SPARTAN" AS WHEN YOU MOVED IN.
I THINK IT'S HAUNTED. MEME STARES AT THIS SPOT ON THE WALL FOR LIKE HOURS...
ALL THE MORE REASON TO CHEER IT UP! YOUR ONLY DECORATIONS ARE THAT TORN BUILT TO SPILL POSTER AND THAT AD FOR POWER TOOLS FROM THE 90'S.
DON'T FORGET THE TRASH. SOMETIMES MEME JUST CURLS UP ON TOP OF A PILE AND TAKES A NAP.

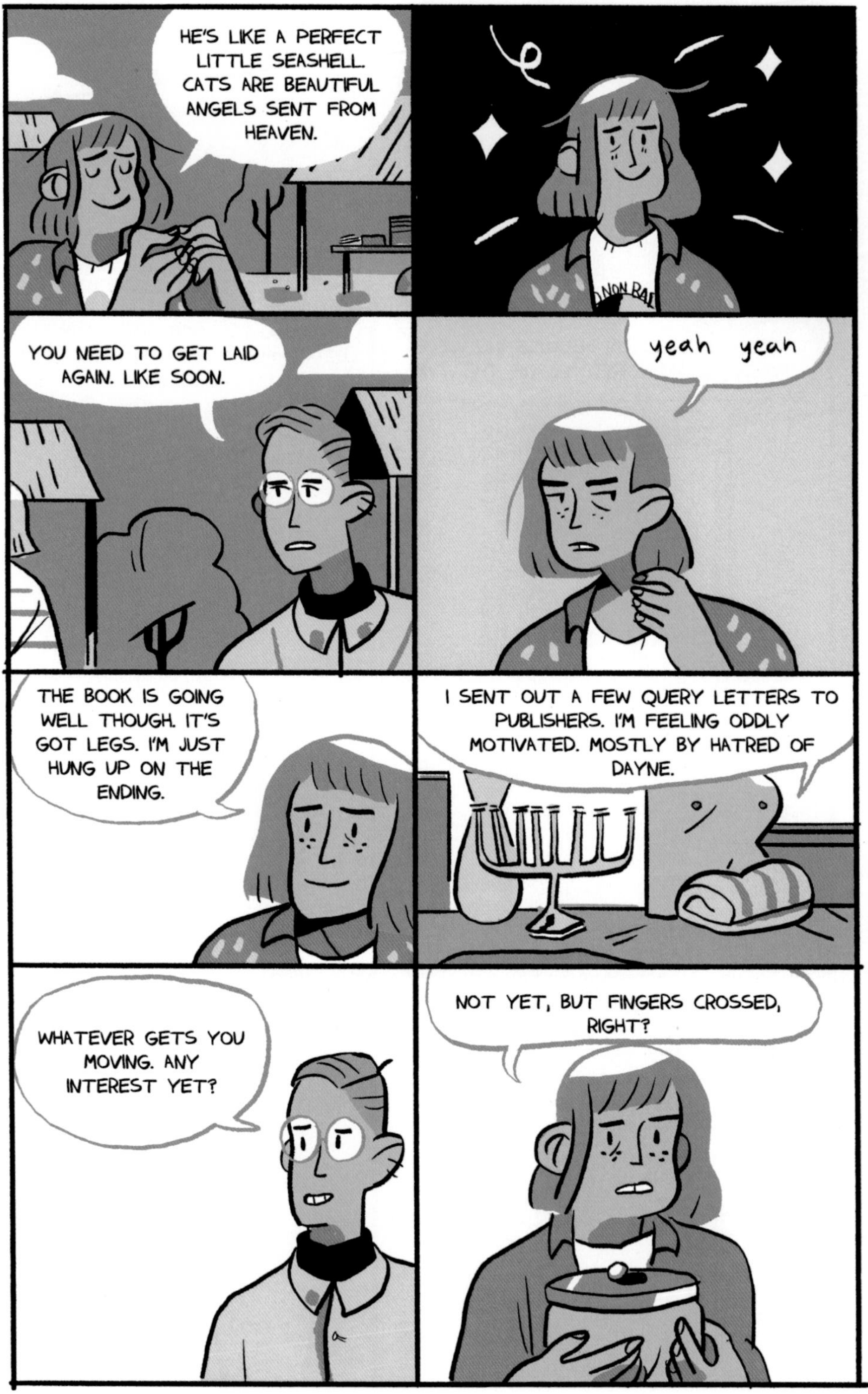
HE'S LIKE A PERFECT LITTLE SEASHELL. CATS ARE BEAUTIFUL ANGELS SENT FROM HEAVEN.
YOU NEED TO GET LAID AGAIN. LIKE SOON.
yeah yeah
THE BOOK IS GOING WELL THOUGH. IT'S GOT LEGS. I'M JUST HUNG UP ON THE ENDING.
I SENT OUT A FEW QUERY LETTERS TO PUBLISHERS. I'M FEELING ODDLY MOTIVATED. MOSTLY BY HATRED OF DAYNE.
WHATEVER GETS YOU MOVING. ANY INTEREST YET?
NOT YET, BUT FINGERS CROSSED, RIGHT?

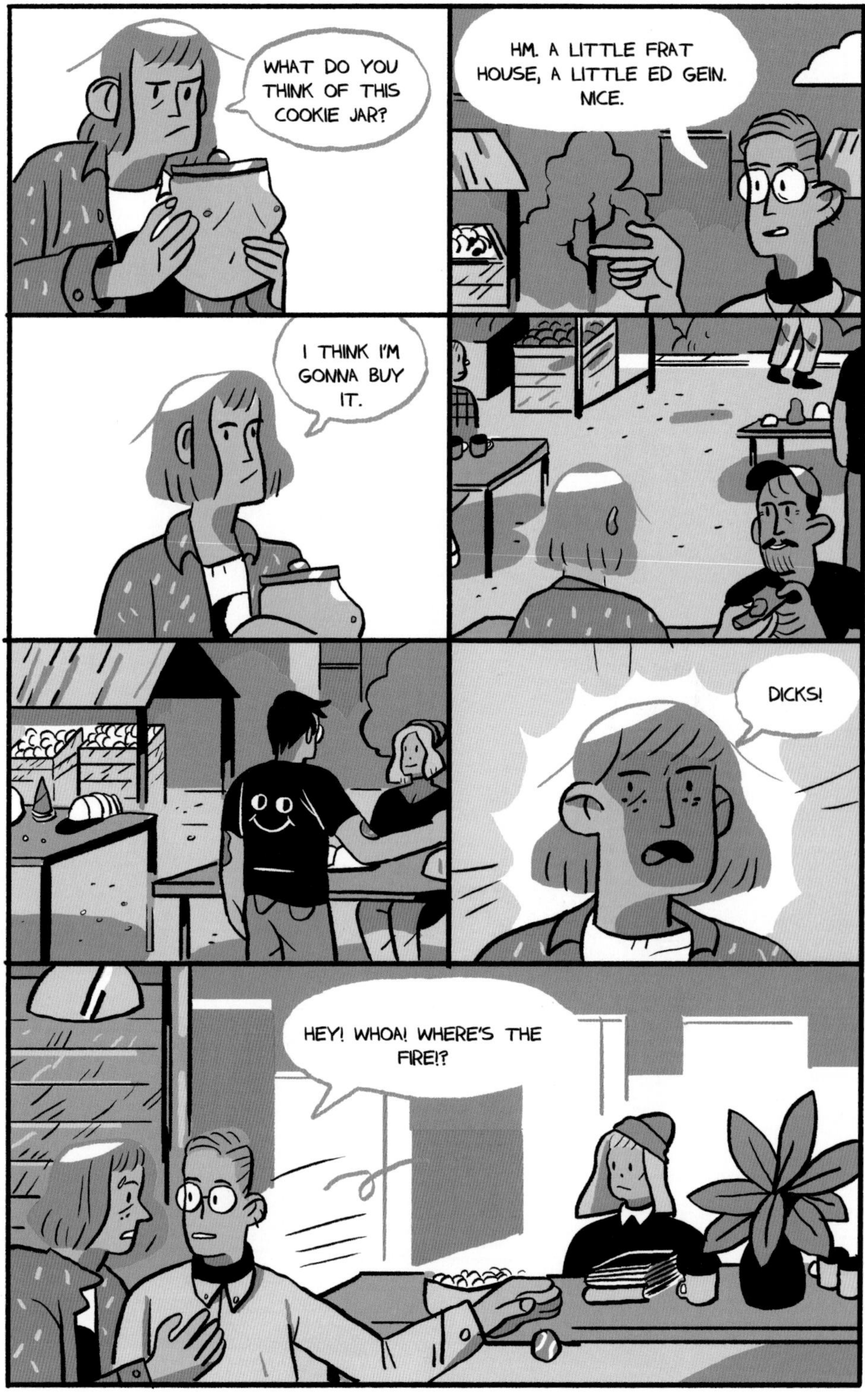
WHAT DO YOU THINK OF THIS COOKIE JAR?
HM. A LITTLE FRAT HOUSE, A LITTLE ED GEIN. NICE.
I THINK I'M GONNA BUY IT.
DICKS!
HEY! WHOA! WHERE'S THE FIRE!?

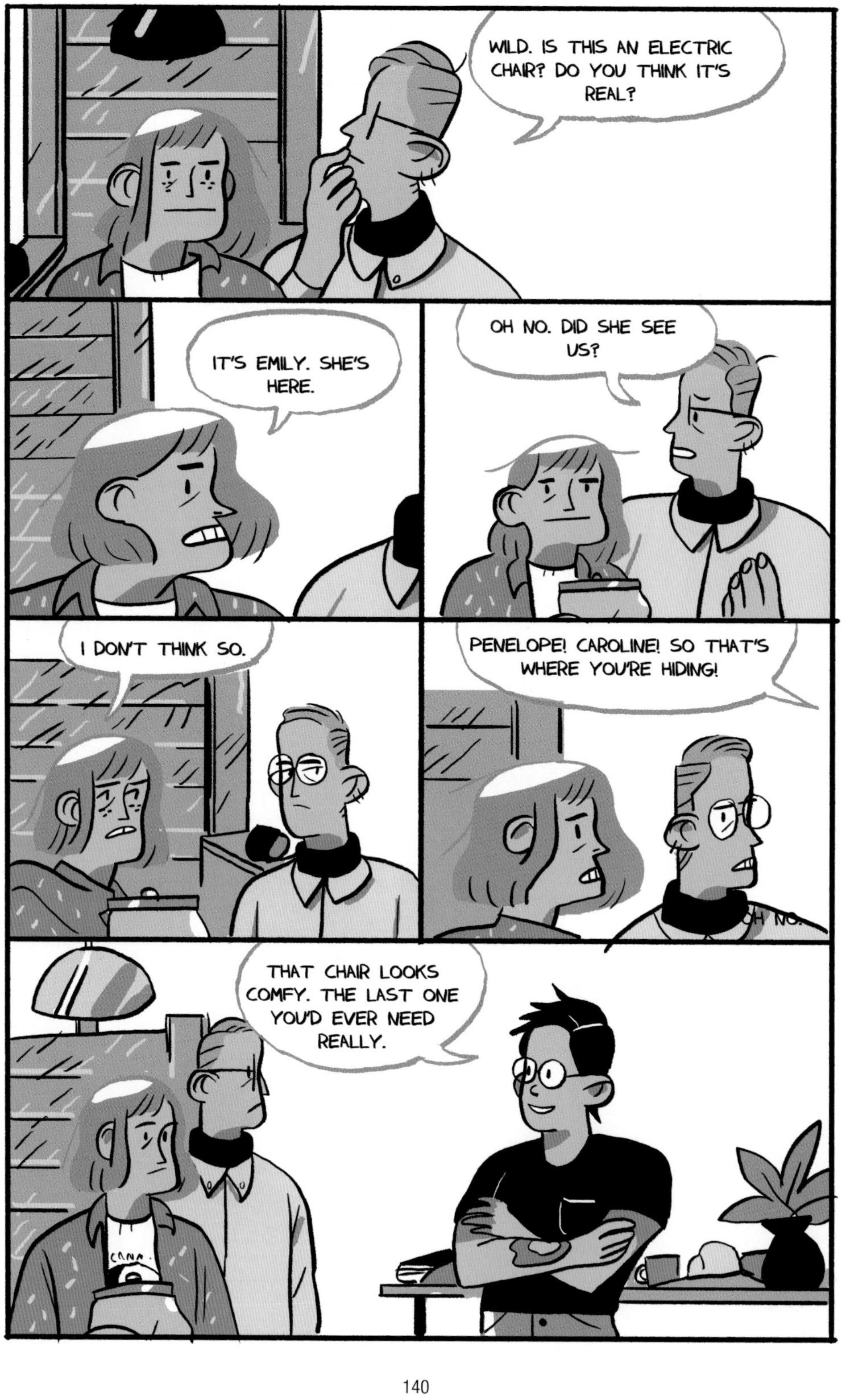
WILD. IS THIS AN ELECTRIC CHAIR? DO YOU THINK IT'S REAL?
IT'S EMILY. SHE'S HERE.
OH NO. DID SHE SEE US?
I DON'T THINK SO.
PENELOPE! CAROLINE! SO THAT'S WHERE YOU'RE HIDING!
OH NO.
THAT CHAIR LOOKS COMFY. THE LAST ONE YOU'D EVER NEED REALLY.

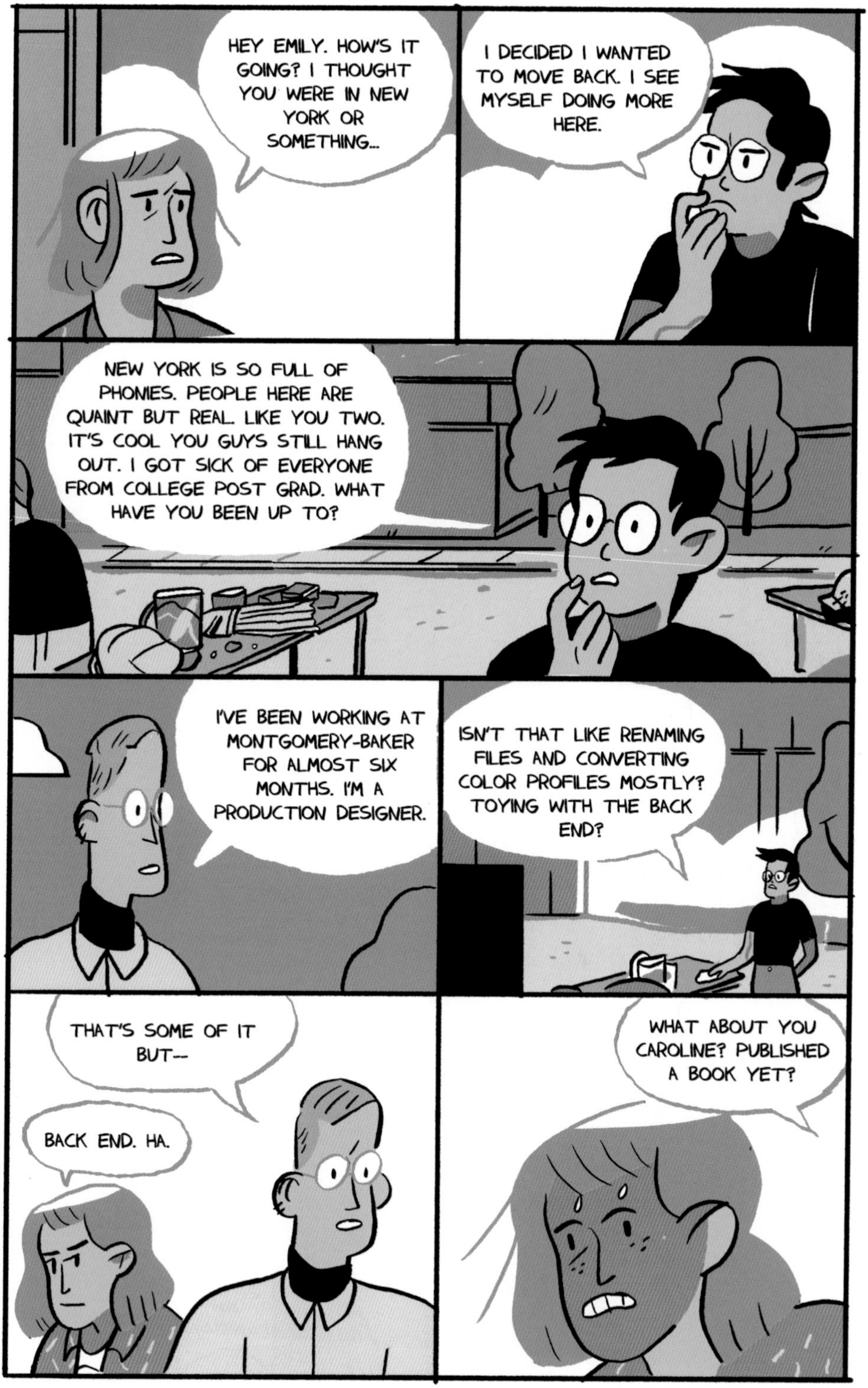
HEY EMILY. HOW'S IT GOING? I THOUGHT YOU WERE IN NEW YORK OR SOMETHING...
I DECIDED I WANTED TO MOVE BACK. I SEE MYSELF DOING MORE HERE.
NEW YORK IS SO FULL OF PHONIES. PEOPLE HERE ARE QUAINT BUT REAL. LIKE YOU TWO. IT'S COOL YOU GUYS STILL HANG OUT. I GOT SICK OF EVERYONE FROM COLLEGE POST GRAD. WHAT HAVE YOU BEEN UP TO?
I'VE BEEN WORKING AT MONTGOMERY-BAKER FOR ALMOST SIX MONTHS. I'M A PRODUCTION DESIGNER.
ISN'T THAT LIKE RENAMING FILES AND CONVERTING COLOR PROFILES MOSTLY? TOYING WITH THE BACK END?
THAT'S SOME OF IT BUT--
BACK END. HA.
WHAT ABOUT YOU CAROLINE? PUBLISHED A BOOK YET?

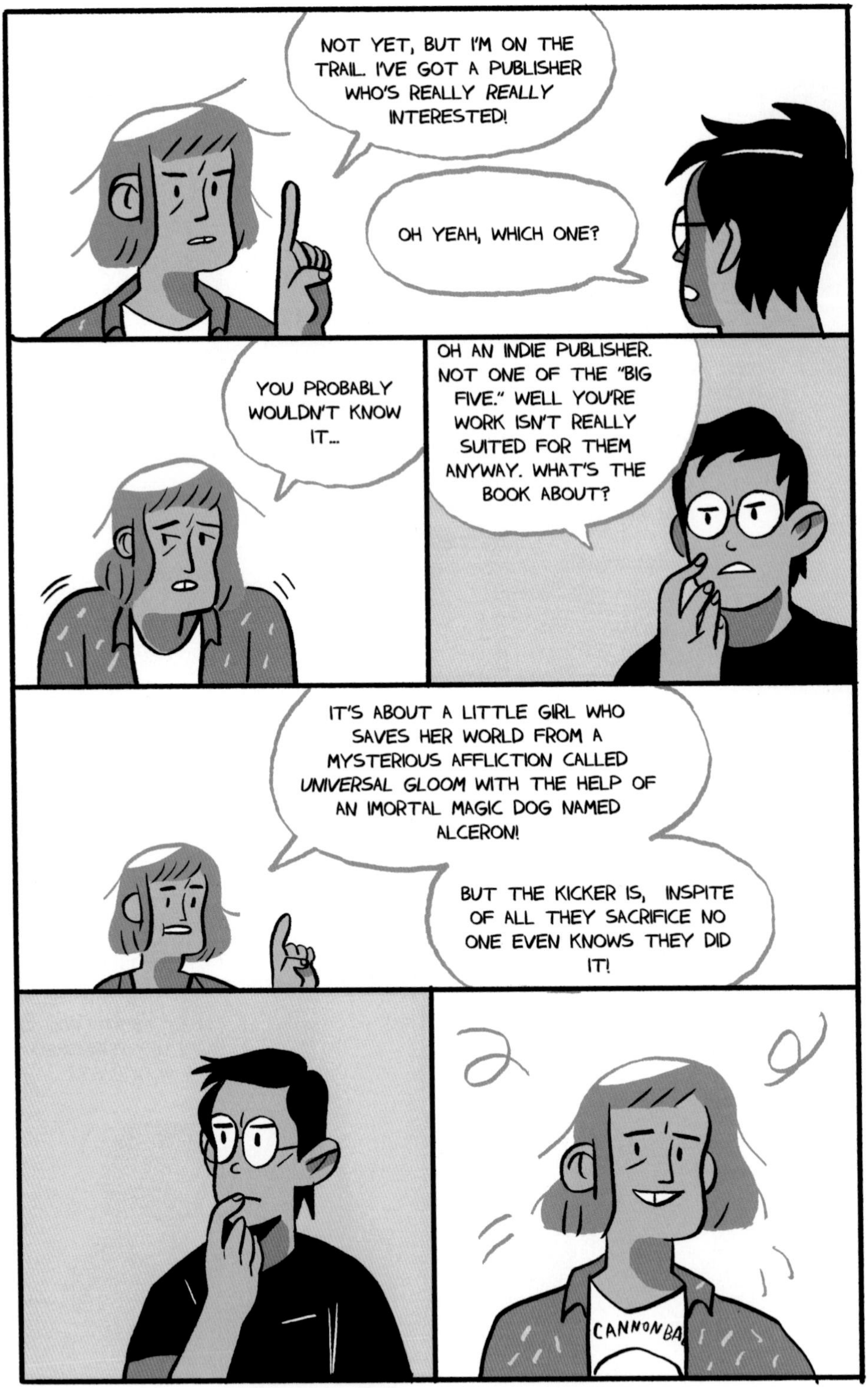
NOT YET, BUT I'M ON THE TRAIL. I'VE GOT A PUBLISHER WHO'S REALLY *REALLY* INTERESTED!
OH YEAH, WHICH ONE?
YOU PROBABLY WOULDN'T KNOW IT...
OH AN INDIE PUBLISHER. NOT ONE OF THE "BIG FIVE." WELL YOU'RE WORK ISN'T REALLY SUITED FOR THEM ANYWAY. WHAT'S THE BOOK ABOUT?
IT'S ABOUT A LITTLE GIRL WHO SAVES HER WORLD FROM A MYSTERIOUS AFFLICTION CALLED *UNIVERSAL GLOOM* WITH THE HELP OF AN IMORTAL MAGIC DOG NAMED ALCERON!
BUT THE KICKER IS, INSPITE OF ALL THEY SACRIFICE NO ONE EVEN KNOWS THEY DID IT!
CANNONBA

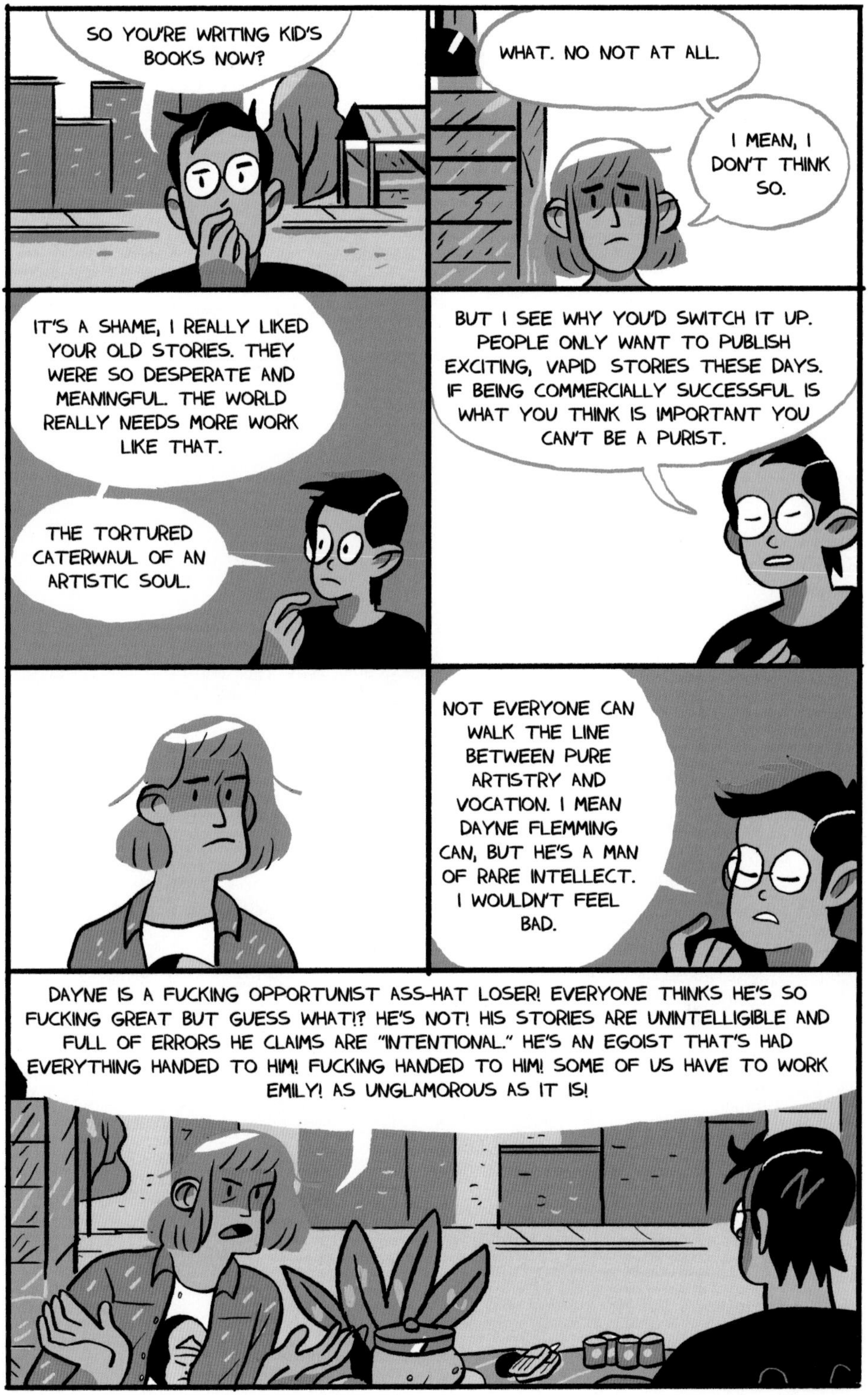
SO YOU'RE WRITING KID'S BOOKS NOW?
WHAT. NO NOT AT ALL.
I MEAN, I DON'T THINK SO.
IT'S A SHAME, I REALLY LIKED YOUR OLD STORIES. THEY WERE SO DESPERATE AND MEANINGFUL. THE WORLD REALLY NEEDS MORE WORK LIKE THAT.
THE TORTURED CATERWAUL OF AN ARTISTIC SOUL.
BUT I SEE WHY YOU'D SWITCH IT UP. PEOPLE ONLY WANT TO PUBLISH EXCITING, VAPID STORIES THESE DAYS. IF BEING COMMERCIALLY SUCCESSFUL IS WHAT YOU THINK IS IMPORTANT YOU CAN'T BE A PURIST.
NOT EVERYONE CAN WALK THE LINE BETWEEN PURE ARTISTRY AND VOCATION. I MEAN DAYNE FLEMMING CAN, BUT HE'S A MAN OF RARE INTELLECT. I WOULDN'T FEEL BAD.
DAYNE IS A FUCKING OPPORTUNIST ASS-HAT LOSER! EVERYONE THINKS HE'S SO FUCKING GREAT BUT GUESS WHAT!? HE'S NOT! HIS STORIES ARE UNINTELLIGIBLE AND FULL OF ERRORS HE CLAIMS ARE "INTENTIONAL." HE'S AN EGOIST THAT'S HAD EVERYTHING HANDED TO HIM! FUCKING HANDED TO HIM! SOME OF US HAVE TO WORK EMILY! AS UNGLAMOROUS AS IT IS!

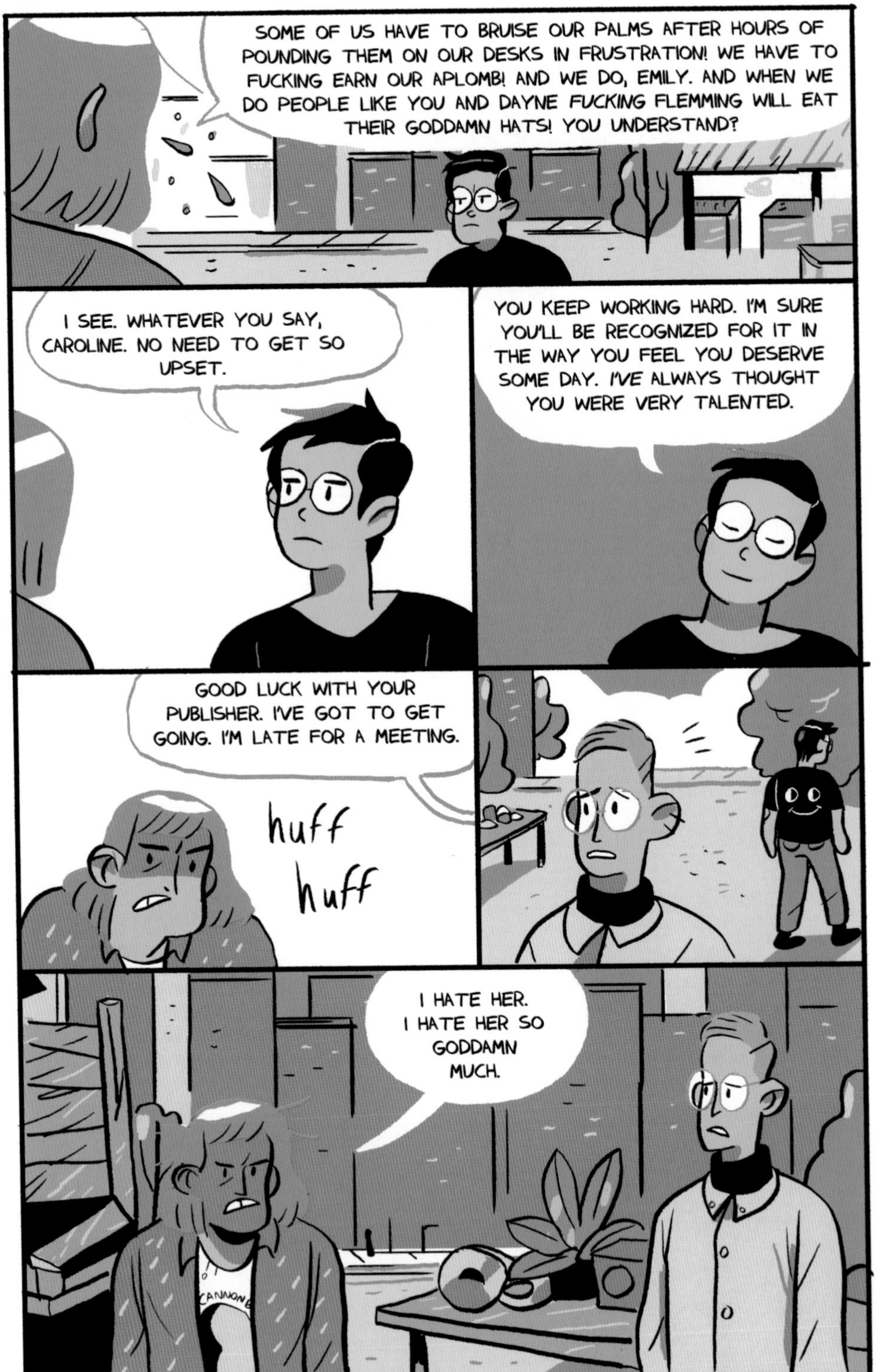
SOME OF US HAVE TO BRUISE OUR PALMS AFTER HOURS OF POUNDING THEM ON OUR DESKS IN FRUSTRATION! WE HAVE TO FUCKING EARN OUR APLOMB! AND WE DO, EMILY. AND WHEN WE DO PEOPLE LIKE YOU AND DAYNE *FUCKING* FLEMMING WILL EAT THEIR GODDAMN HATS! YOU UNDERSTAND?
I SEE. WHATEVER YOU SAY, CAROLINE. NO NEED TO GET SO UPSET.
YOU KEEP WORKING HARD. I'M SURE YOU'LL BE RECOGNIZED FOR IT IN THE WAY YOU FEEL YOU DESERVE SOME DAY. *I'VE* ALWAYS THOUGHT YOU WERE VERY TALENTED.
GOOD LUCK WITH YOUR PUBLISHER. I'VE GOT TO GET GOING. I'M LATE FOR A MEETING.
huff
huff
I HATE HER. I HATE HER SO GODDAMN MUCH.

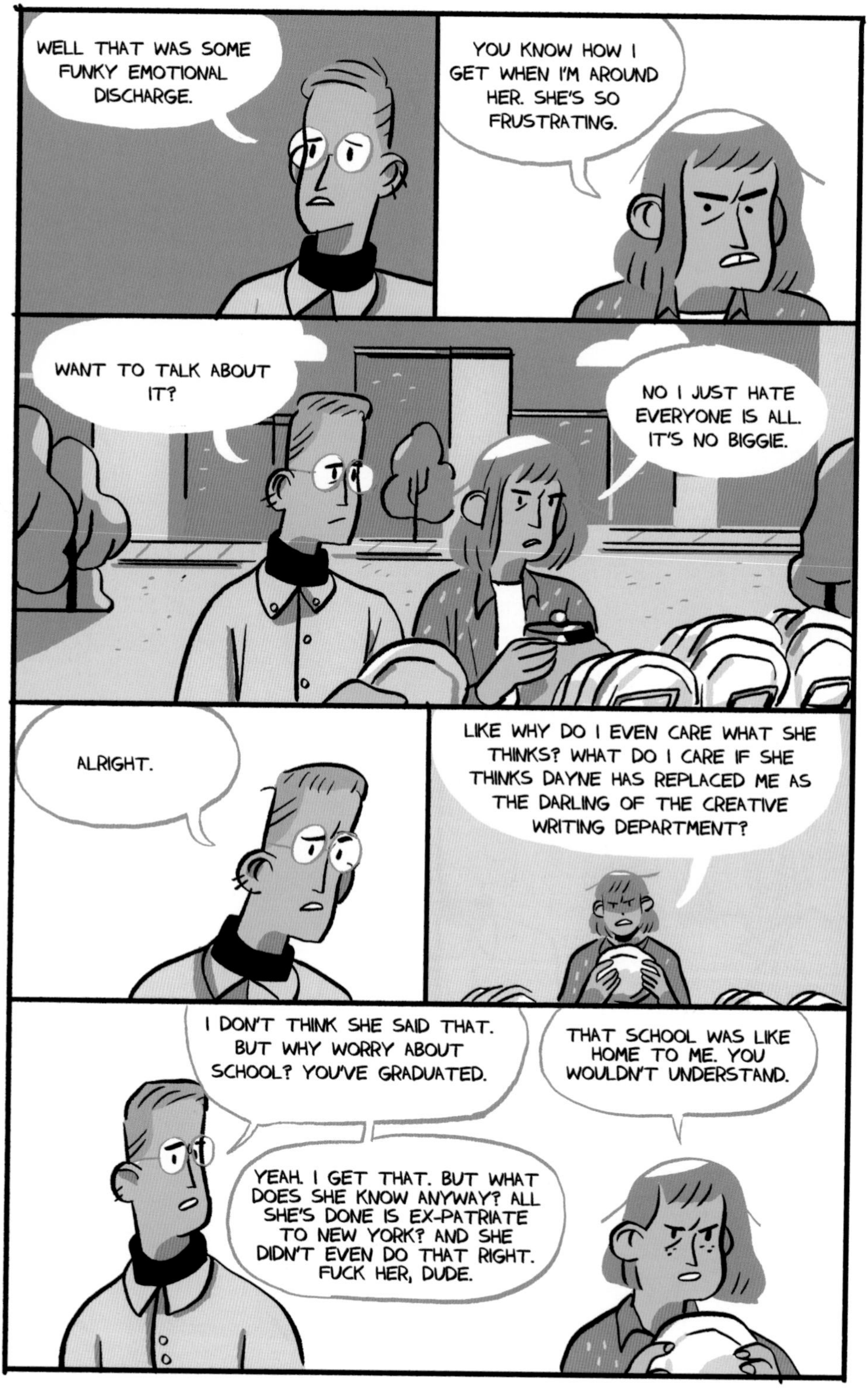
WELL THAT WAS SOME FUNKY EMOTIONAL DISCHARGE.
YOU KNOW HOW I GET WHEN I'M AROUND HER. SHE'S SO FRUSTRATING.
WANT TO TALK ABOUT IT?
NO I JUST HATE EVERYONE IS ALL. IT'S NO BIGGIE.
ALRIGHT.
LIKE WHY DO I EVEN CARE WHAT SHE THINKS? WHAT DO I CARE IF SHE THINKS DAYNE HAS REPLACED ME AS THE DARLING OF THE CREATIVE WRITING DEPARTMENT?
I DON'T THINK SHE SAID THAT. BUT WHY WORRY ABOUT SCHOOL? YOU'VE GRADUATED.
THAT SCHOOL WAS LIKE HOME TO ME. YOU WOULDN'T UNDERSTAND.
YEAH. I GET THAT. BUT WHAT DOES SHE KNOW ANYWAY? ALL SHE'S DONE IS EX-PATRIATE TO NEW YORK? AND SHE DIDN'T EVEN DO THAT RIGHT. FUCK HER, DUDE.

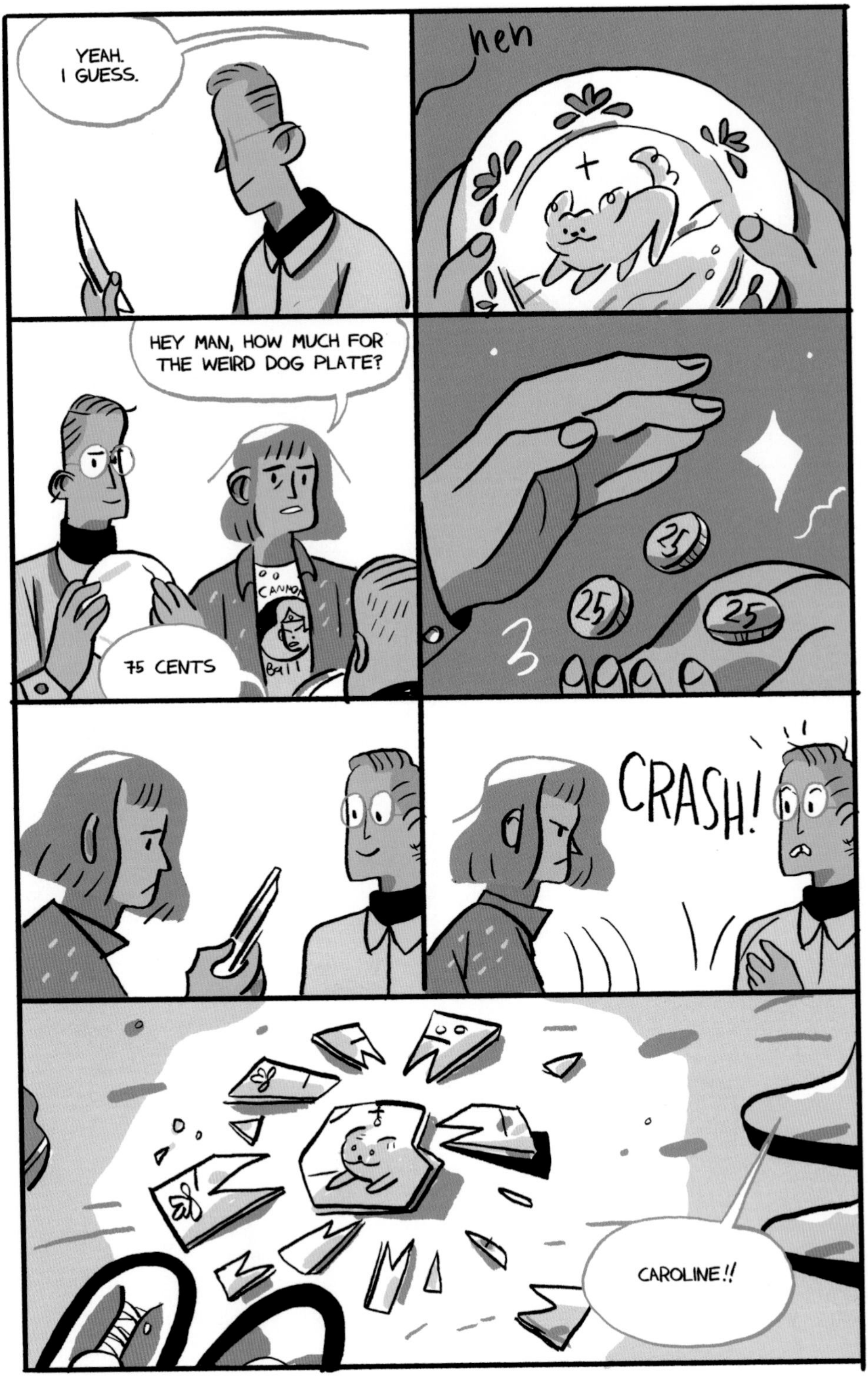
YEAH. I GUESS.
heh
HEY MAN, HOW MUCH FOR THE WEIRD DOG PLATE?
75 CENTS
CRASH!
CAROLINE!!

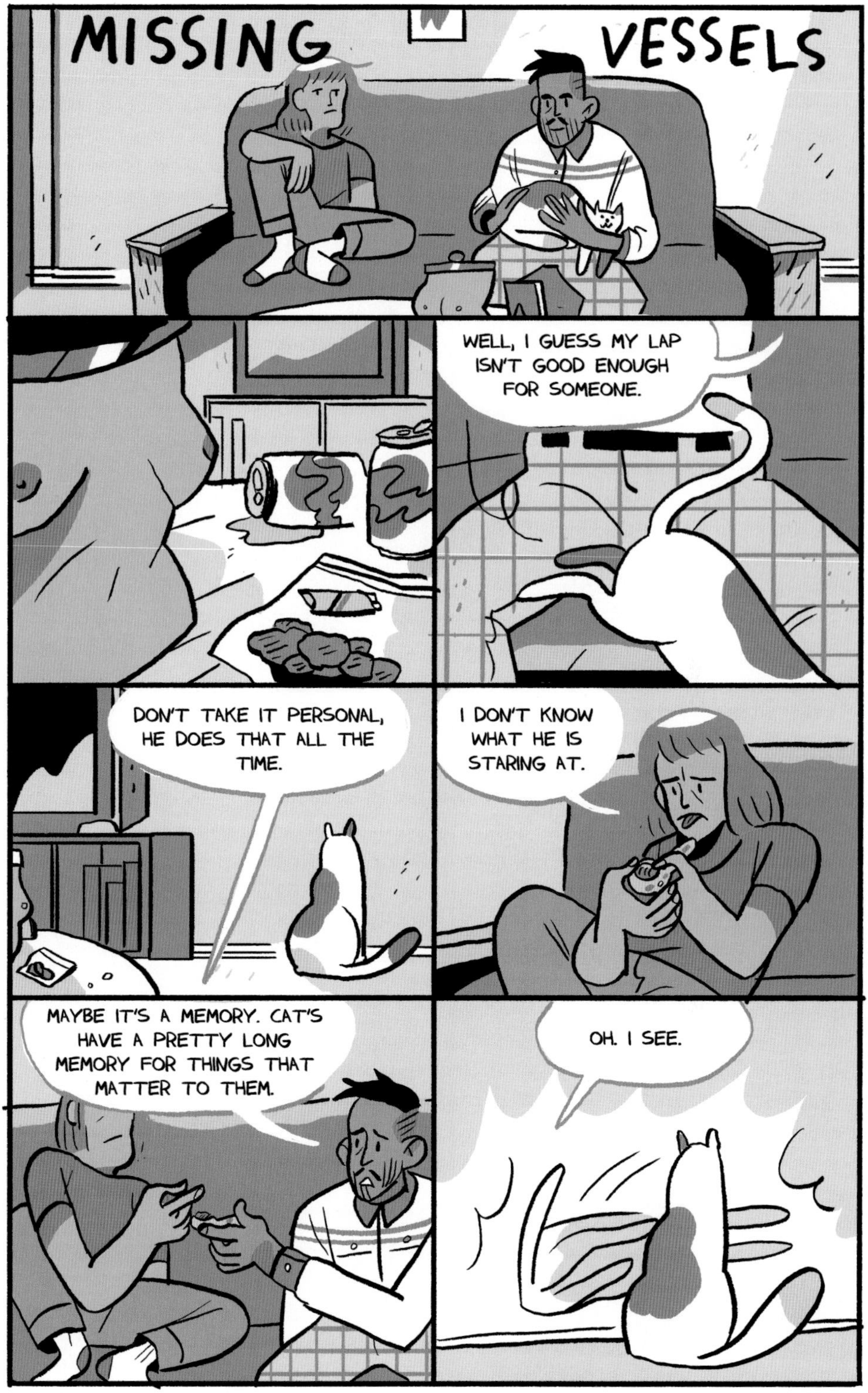
MISSING VESSELS
WELL, I GUESS MY LAP ISN'T GOOD ENOUGH FOR SOMEONE.
DON'T TAKE IT PERSONAL, HE DOES THAT ALL THE TIME.
I DON'T KNOW WHAT HE IS STARING AT.
MAYBE IT'S A MEMORY. CAT'S HAVE A PRETTY LONG MEMORY FOR THINGS THAT MATTER TO THEM.
OH. I SEE.

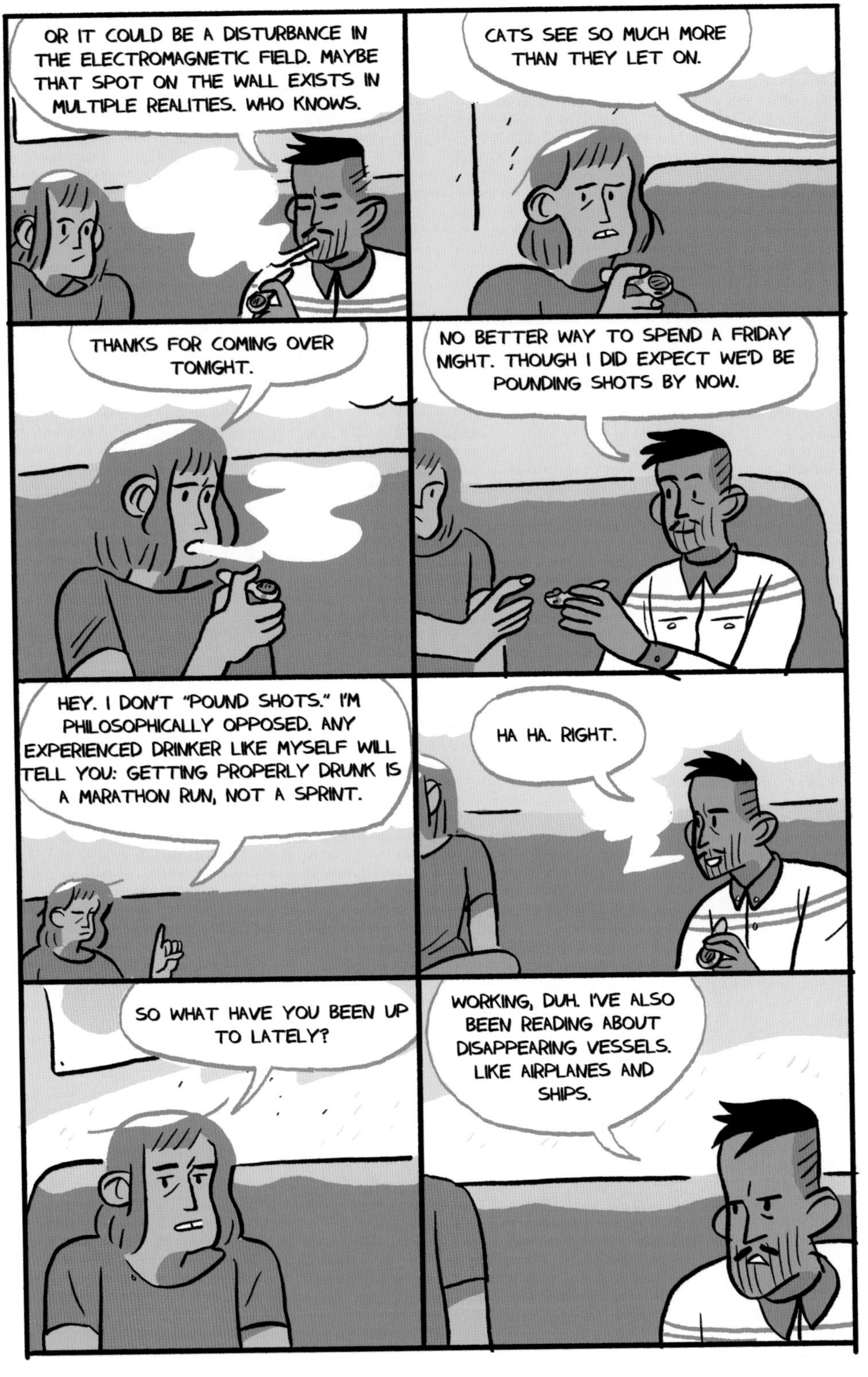
OR IT COULD BE A DISTURBANCE IN THE ELECTROMAGNETIC FIELD. MAYBE THAT SPOT ON THE WALL EXISTS IN MULTIPLE REALITIES. WHO KNOWS.
CATS SEE SO MUCH MORE THAN THEY LET ON.
THANKS FOR COMING OVER TONIGHT.
NO BETTER WAY TO SPEND A FRIDAY NIGHT. THOUGH I DID EXPECT WE'D BE POUNDING SHOTS BY NOW.
HEY. I DON'T "POUND SHOTS." I'M PHILOSOPHICALLY OPPOSED. ANY EXPERIENCED DRINKER LIKE MYSELF WILL TELL YOU: GETTING PROPERLY DRUNK IS A MARATHON RUN, NOT A SPRINT.
HA HA. RIGHT.
SO WHAT HAVE YOU BEEN UP TO LATELY?
WORKING, DUH. I'VE ALSO BEEN READING ABOUT DISAPPEARING VESSELS. LIKE AIRPLANES AND SHIPS.

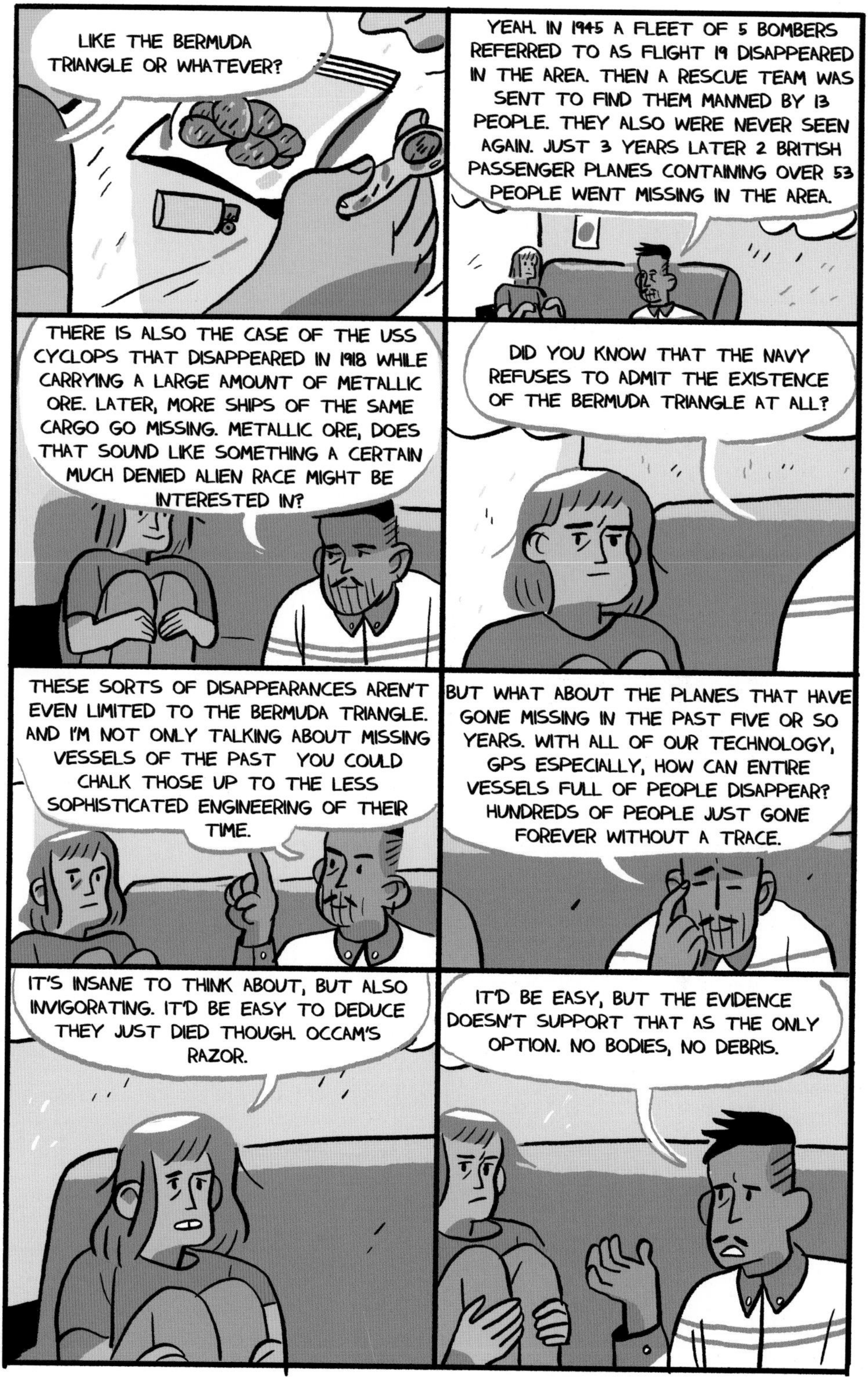
LIKE THE BERMUDA TRIANGLE OR WHATEVER?
YEAH. IN 1945 A FLEET OF 5 BOMBERS REFERRED TO AS FLIGHT 19 DISAPPEARED IN THE AREA. THEN A RESCUE TEAM WAS SENT TO FIND THEM MANNED BY 13 PEOPLE. THEY ALSO WERE NEVER SEEN AGAIN. JUST 3 YEARS LATER 2 BRITISH PASSENGER PLANES CONTAINING OVER 53 PEOPLE WENT MISSING IN THE AREA.
THERE IS ALSO THE CASE OF THE USS CYCLOPS THAT DISAPPEARED IN 1918 WHILE CARRYING A LARGE AMOUNT OF METALLIC ORE. LATER, MORE SHIPS OF THE SAME CARGO GO MISSING. METALLIC ORE, DOES THAT SOUND LIKE SOMETHING A CERTAIN MUCH DENIED ALIEN RACE MIGHT BE INTERESTED IN?
DID YOU KNOW THAT THE NAVY REFUSES TO ADMIT THE EXISTENCE OF THE BERMUDA TRIANGLE AT ALL?
THESE SORTS OF DISAPPEARANCES AREN'T EVEN LIMITED TO THE BERMUDA TRIANGLE. AND I'M NOT ONLY TALKING ABOUT MISSING VESSELS OF THE PAST YOU COULD CHALK THOSE UP TO THE LESS SOPHISTICATED ENGINEERING OF THEIR TIME.
BUT WHAT ABOUT THE PLANES THAT HAVE GONE MISSING IN THE PAST FIVE OR SO YEARS. WITH ALL OF OUR TECHNOLOGY, GPS ESPECIALLY, HOW CAN ENTIRE VESSELS FULL OF PEOPLE DISAPPEAR? HUNDREDS OF PEOPLE JUST GONE FOREVER WITHOUT A TRACE.
IT'S INSANE TO THINK ABOUT, BUT ALSO INVIGORATING. IT'D BE EASY TO DEDUCE THEY JUST DIED THOUGH. OCCAM'S RAZOR.
IT'D BE EASY, BUT THE EVIDENCE DOESN'T SUPPORT THAT AS THE ONLY OPTION. NO BODIES, NO DEBRIS.

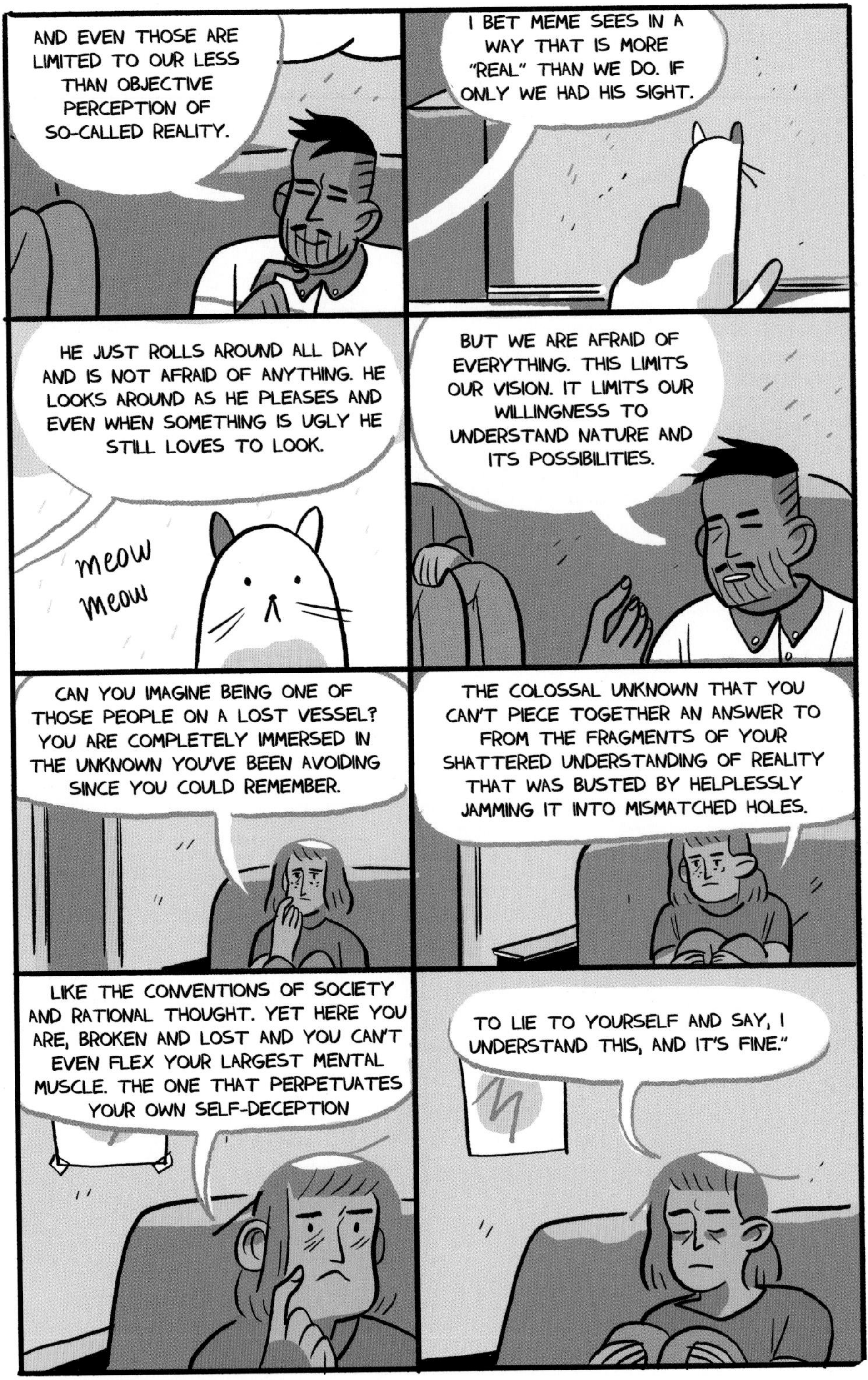
AND EVEN THOSE ARE LIMITED TO OUR LESS THAN OBJECTIVE PERCEPTION OF SO-CALLED REALITY.
I BET MEME SEES IN A WAY THAT IS MORE "REAL" THAN WE DO. IF ONLY WE HAD HIS SIGHT.
HE JUST ROLLS AROUND ALL DAY AND IS NOT AFRAID OF ANYTHING. HE LOOKS AROUND AS HE PLEASES AND EVEN WHEN SOMETHING IS UGLY HE STILL LOVES TO LOOK.
meow meow
BUT WE ARE AFRAID OF EVERYTHING. THIS LIMITS OUR VISION. IT LIMITS OUR WILLINGNESS TO UNDERSTAND NATURE AND ITS POSSIBILITIES.
CAN YOU IMAGINE BEING ONE OF THOSE PEOPLE ON A LOST VESSEL? YOU ARE COMPLETELY IMMERSED IN THE UNKNOWN YOU'VE BEEN AVOIDING SINCE YOU COULD REMEMBER.
THE COLOSSAL UNKNOWN THAT YOU CAN'T PIECE TOGETHER AN ANSWER TO FROM THE FRAGMENTS OF YOUR SHATTERED UNDERSTANDING OF REALITY THAT WAS BUSTED BY HELPLESSLY JAMMING IT INTO MISMATCHED HOLES.
LIKE THE CONVENTIONS OF SOCIETY AND RATIONAL THOUGHT. YET HERE YOU ARE, BROKEN AND LOST AND YOU CAN'T EVEN FLEX YOUR LARGEST MENTAL MUSCLE. THE ONE THAT PERPETUATES YOUR OWN SELF-DECEPTION
TO LIE TO YOURSELF AND SAY, I UNDERSTAND THIS, AND IT'S FINE."

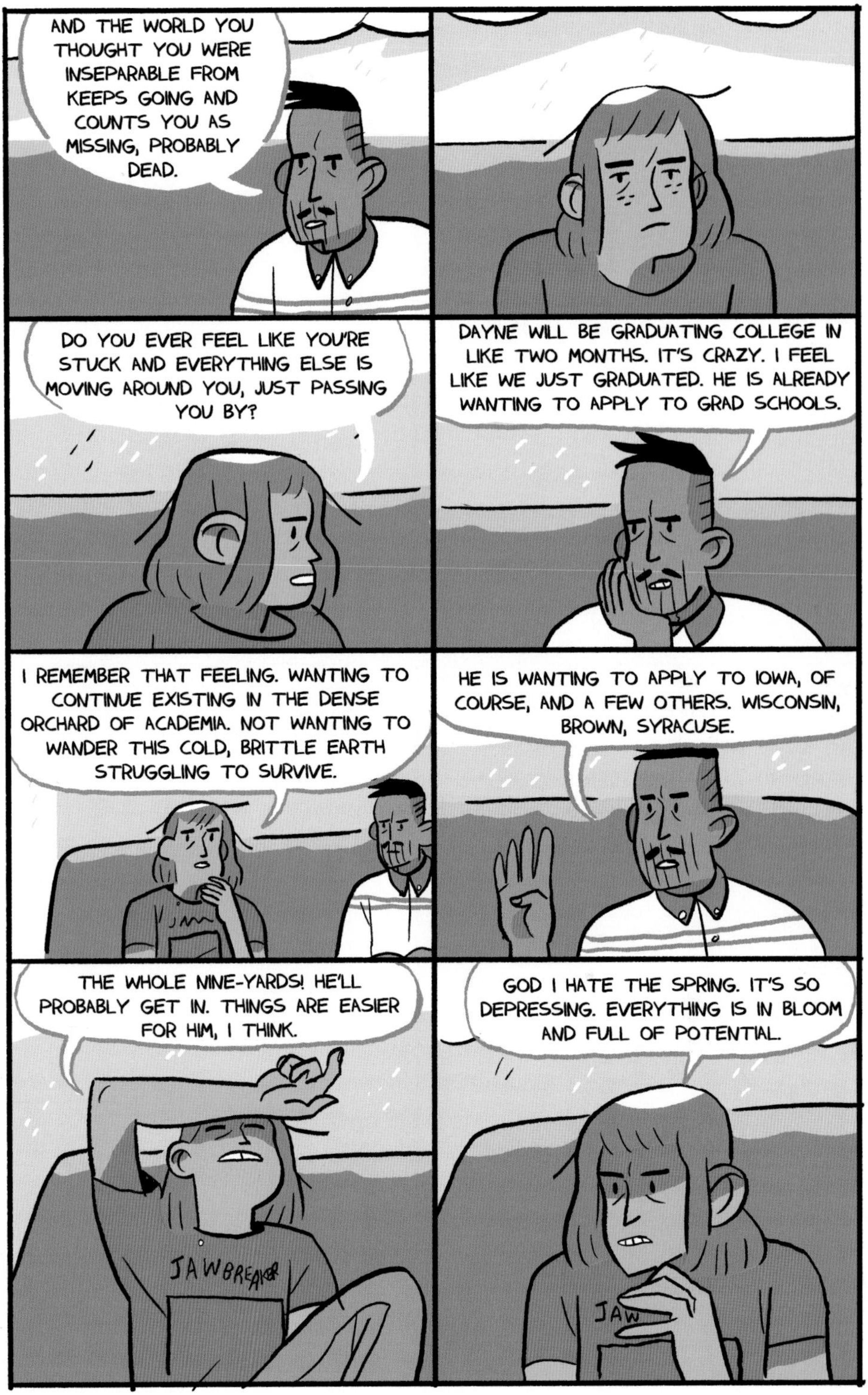
AND THE WORLD YOU THOUGHT YOU WERE INSEPARABLE FROM KEEPS GOING AND COUNTS YOU AS MISSING, PROBABLY DEAD.
DO YOU EVER FEEL LIKE YOU'RE STUCK AND EVERYTHING ELSE IS MOVING AROUND YOU, JUST PASSING YOU BY?
DAYNE WILL BE GRADUATING COLLEGE IN LIKE TWO MONTHS. IT'S CRAZY. I FEEL LIKE WE JUST GRADUATED. HE IS ALREADY WANTING TO APPLY TO GRAD SCHOOLS.
I REMEMBER THAT FEELING. WANTING TO CONTINUE EXISTING IN THE DENSE ORCHARD OF ACADEMIA. NOT WANTING TO WANDER THIS COLD, BRITTLE EARTH STRUGGLING TO SURVIVE.
HE IS WANTING TO APPLY TO IOWA, OF COURSE, AND A FEW OTHERS. WISCONSIN, BROWN, SYRACUSE.
THE WHOLE NINE-YARDS! HE'LL PROBABLY GET IN. THINGS ARE EASIER FOR HIM, I THINK.
JAWBREAKER
GOD I HATE THE SPRING. IT'S SO DEPRESSING. EVERYTHING IS IN BLOOM AND FULL OF POTENTIAL.
JAW

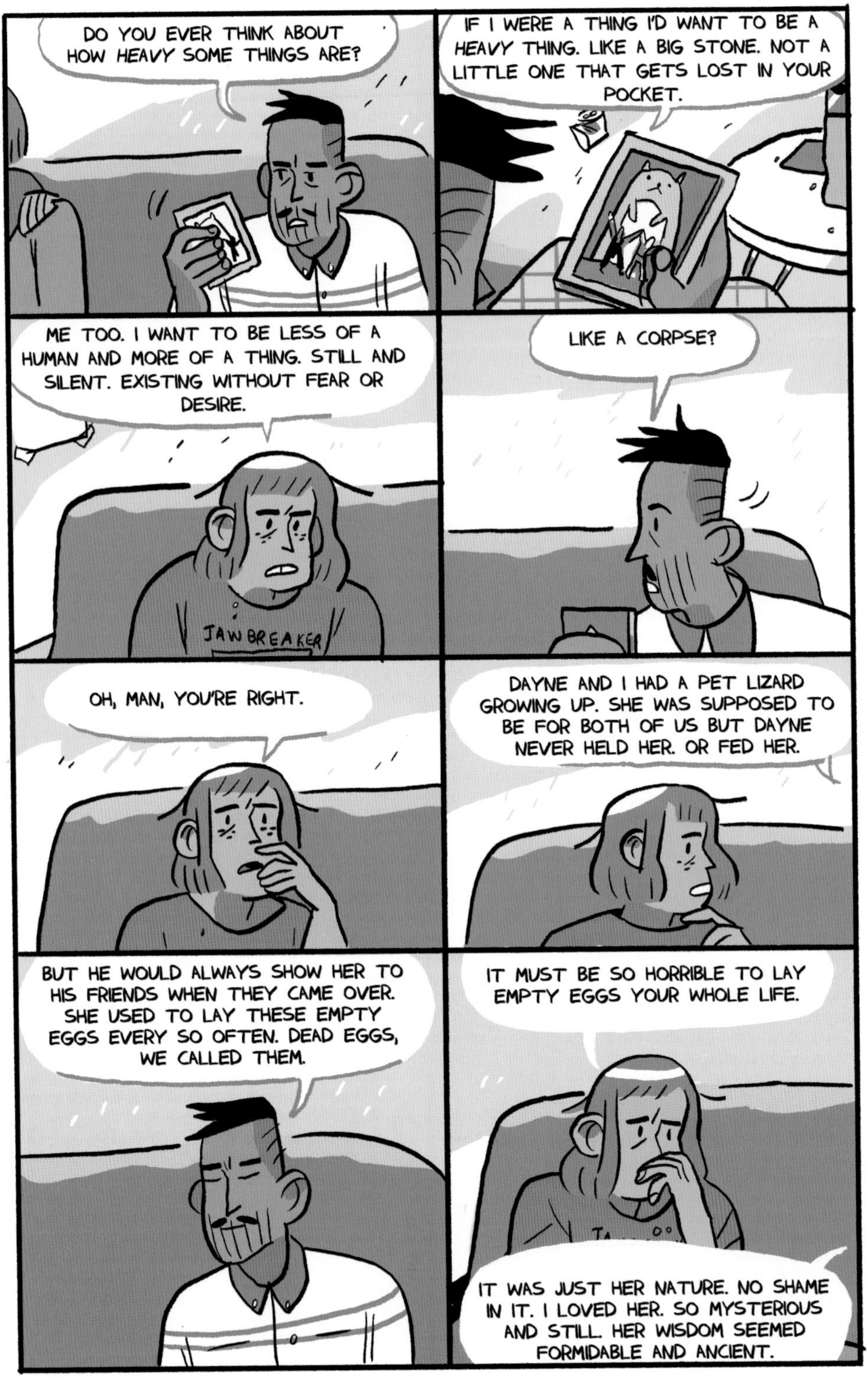
DO YOU EVER THINK ABOUT HOW HEAVY SOME THINGS ARE?
IF I WERE A THING I'D WANT TO BE A HEAVY THING. LIKE A BIG STONE. NOT A LITTLE ONE THAT GETS LOST IN YOUR POCKET.
ME TOO. I WANT TO BE LESS OF A HUMAN AND MORE OF A THING. STILL AND SILENT. EXISTING WITHOUT FEAR OR DESIRE.
JAWBREAKER
LIKE A CORPSE?
OH, MAN, YOU'RE RIGHT.
DAYNE AND I HAD A PET LIZARD GROWING UP. SHE WAS SUPPOSED TO BE FOR BOTH OF US BUT DAYNE NEVER HELD HER. OR FED HER.
BUT HE WOULD ALWAYS SHOW HER TO HIS FRIENDS WHEN THEY CAME OVER. SHE USED TO LAY THESE EMPTY EGGS EVERY SO OFTEN. DEAD EGGS, WE CALLED THEM.
IT MUST BE SO HORRIBLE TO LAY EMPTY EGGS YOUR WHOLE LIFE.
IT WAS JUST HER NATURE. NO SHAME IN IT. I LOVED HER. SO MYSTERIOUS AND STILL. HER WISDOM SEEMED FORMIDABLE AND ANCIENT.

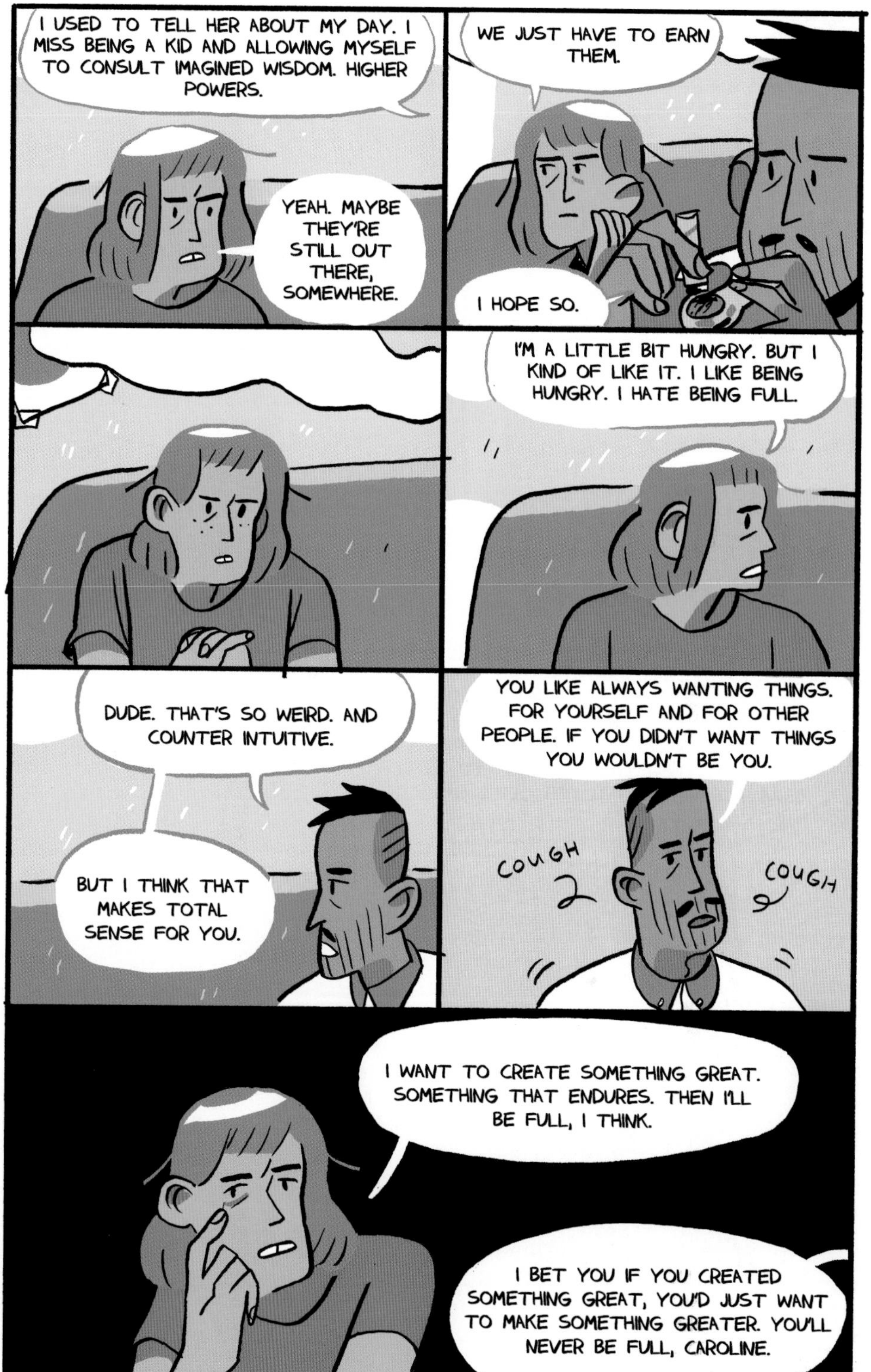
I USED TO TELL HER ABOUT MY DAY. I MISS BEING A KID AND ALLOWING MYSELF TO CONSULT IMAGINED WISDOM. HIGHER POWERS.
YEAH. MAYBE THEY'RE STILL OUT THERE, SOMEWHERE.
WE JUST HAVE TO EARN THEM.
I HOPE SO.
I'M A LITTLE BIT HUNGRY. BUT I KIND OF LIKE IT. I LIKE BEING HUNGRY. I HATE BEING FULL.
DUDE. THAT'S SO WEIRD. AND COUNTER INTUITIVE.
BUT I THINK THAT MAKES TOTAL SENSE FOR YOU.
YOU LIKE ALWAYS WANTING THINGS. FOR YOURSELF AND FOR OTHER PEOPLE. IF YOU DIDN'T WANT THINGS YOU WOULDN'T BE YOU.
COUGH
COUGH
I WANT TO CREATE SOMETHING GREAT. SOMETHING THAT ENDURES. THEN I'LL BE FULL, I THINK.
I BET YOU IF YOU CREATED SOMETHING GREAT, YOU'D JUST WANT TO MAKE SOMETHING GREATER. YOU'LL NEVER BE FULL, CAROLINE.

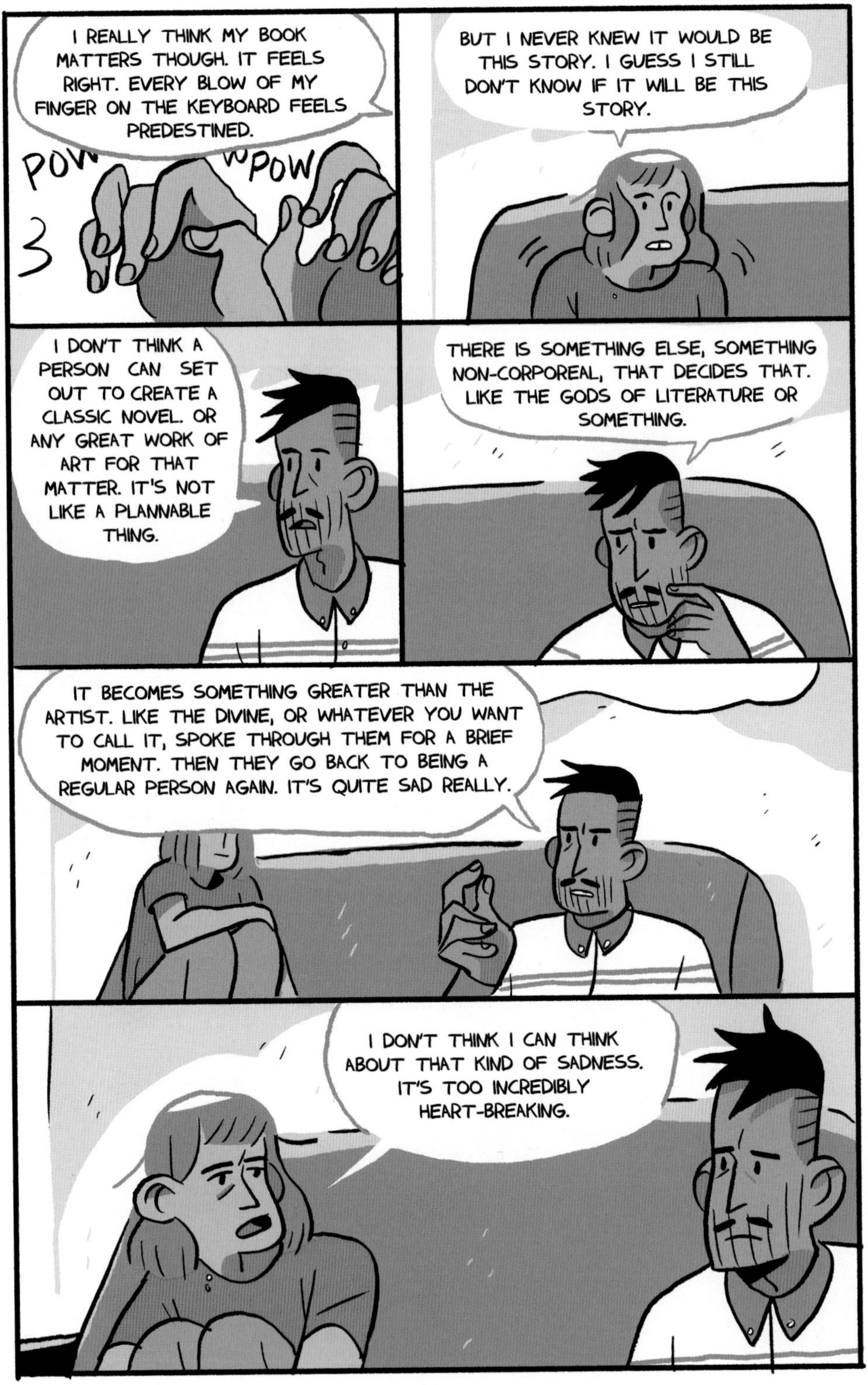
I REALLY THINK MY BOOK MATTERS THOUGH. IT FEELS RIGHT. EVERY BLOW OF MY FINGER ON THE KEYBOARD FEELS PREDESTINED.
POW
POW
BUT I NEVER KNEW IT WOULD BE THIS STORY. I GUESS I STILL DON'T KNOW IF IT WILL BE THIS STORY.
I DON'T THINK A PERSON CAN SET OUT TO CREATE A CLASSIC NOVEL. OR ANY GREAT WORK OF ART FOR THAT MATTER. IT'S NOT LIKE A PLANNABLE THING.
THERE IS SOMETHING ELSE, SOMETHING NON-CORPOREAL, THAT DECIDES THAT. LIKE THE GODS OF LITERATURE OR SOMETHING.
IT BECOMES SOMETHING GREATER THAN THE ARTIST. LIKE THE DIVINE, OR WHATEVER YOU WANT TO CALL IT, SPOKE THROUGH THEM FOR A BRIEF MOMENT. THEN THEY GO BACK TO BEING A REGULAR PERSON AGAIN. IT'S QUITE SAD REALLY.
I DON'T THINK I CAN THINK ABOUT THAT KIND OF SADNESS. IT'S TOO INCREDIBLY HEART-BREAKING.

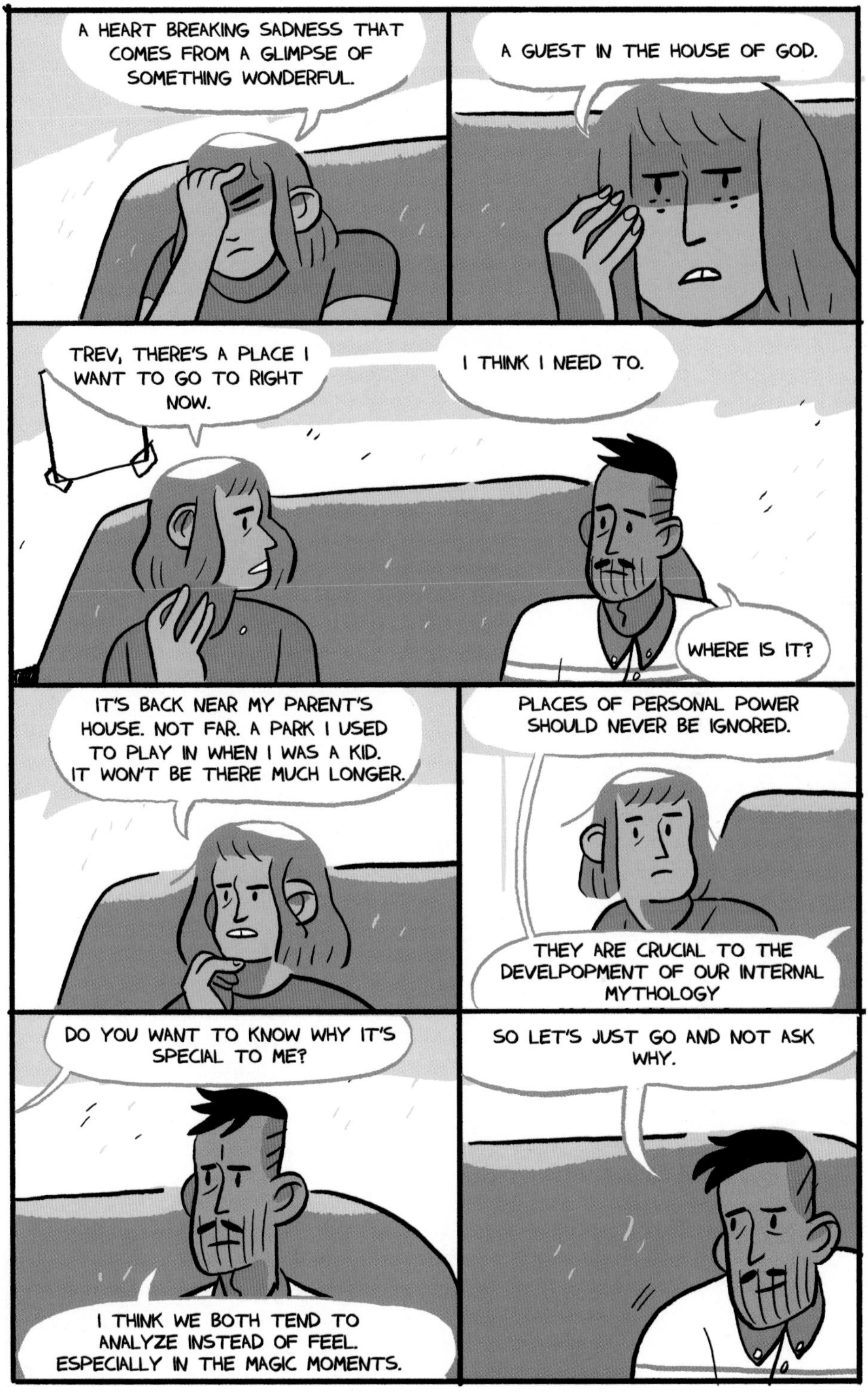
A HEART BREAKING SADNESS THAT COMES FROM A GLIMPSE OF SOMETHING WONDERFUL.
A GUEST IN THE HOUSE OF GOD.
TREV, THERE'S A PLACE I WANT TO GO TO RIGHT NOW.
I THINK I NEED TO.
WHERE IS IT?
IT'S BACK NEAR MY PARENT'S HOUSE. NOT FAR. A PARK I USED TO PLAY IN WHEN I WAS A KID. IT WON'T BE THERE MUCH LONGER.
PLACES OF PERSONAL POWER SHOULD NEVER BE IGNORED.
THEY ARE CRUCIAL TO THE DEVELPOPMENT OF OUR INTERNAL MYTHOLOGY
DO YOU WANT TO KNOW WHY IT'S SPECIAL TO ME?
I THINK WE BOTH TEND TO ANALYZE INSTEAD OF FEEL. ESPECIALLY IN THE MAGIC MOMENTS.
SO LET'S JUST GO AND NOT ASK WHY.

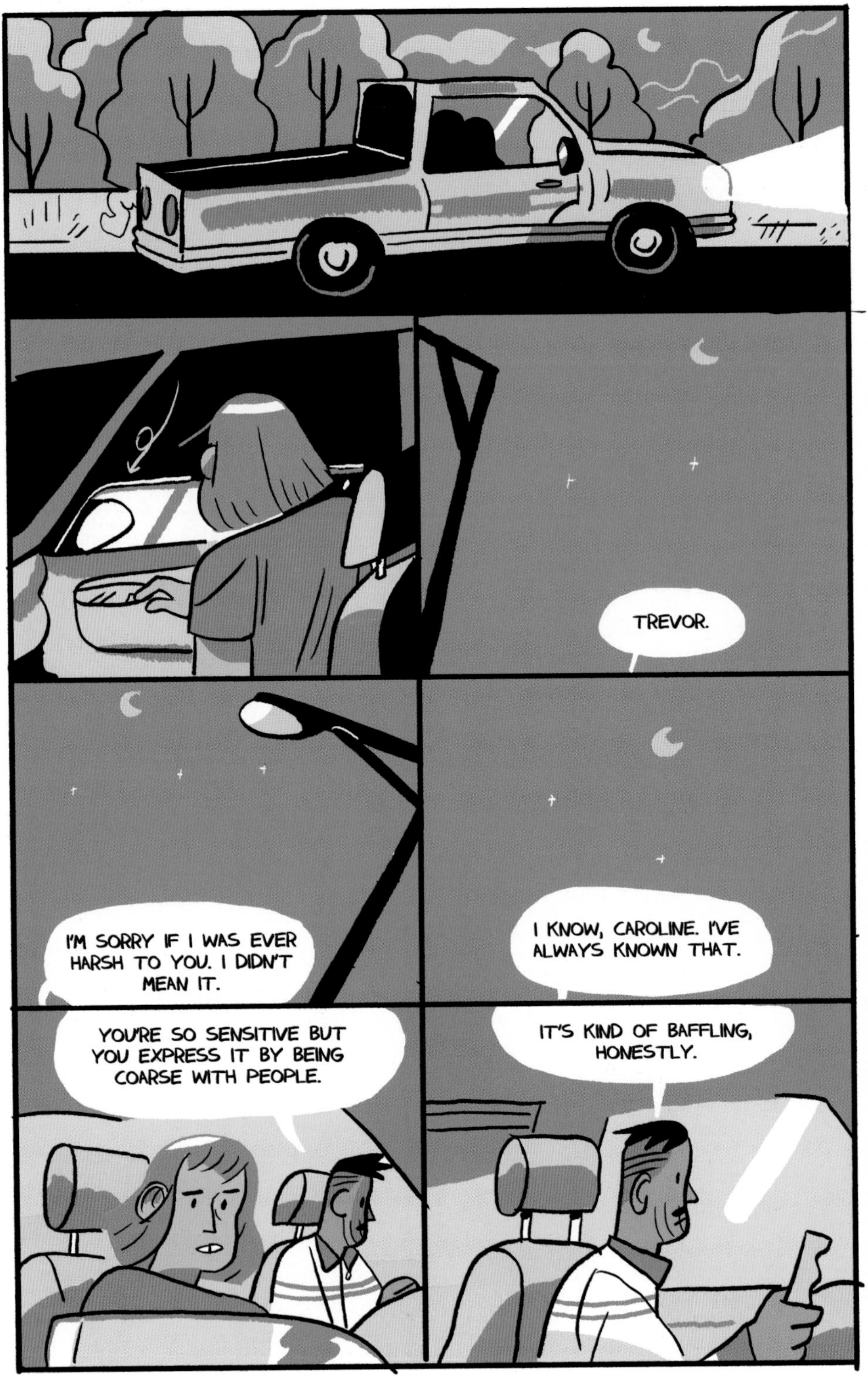
TREVOR.
I'M SORRY IF I WAS EVER HARSH TO YOU. I DIDN'T MEAN IT.
I KNOW, CAROLINE. I'VE ALWAYS KNOWN THAT.
YOU'RE SO SENSITIVE BUT YOU EXPRESS IT BY BEING COARSE WITH PEOPLE.
IT'S KIND OF BAFFLING, HONESTLY.

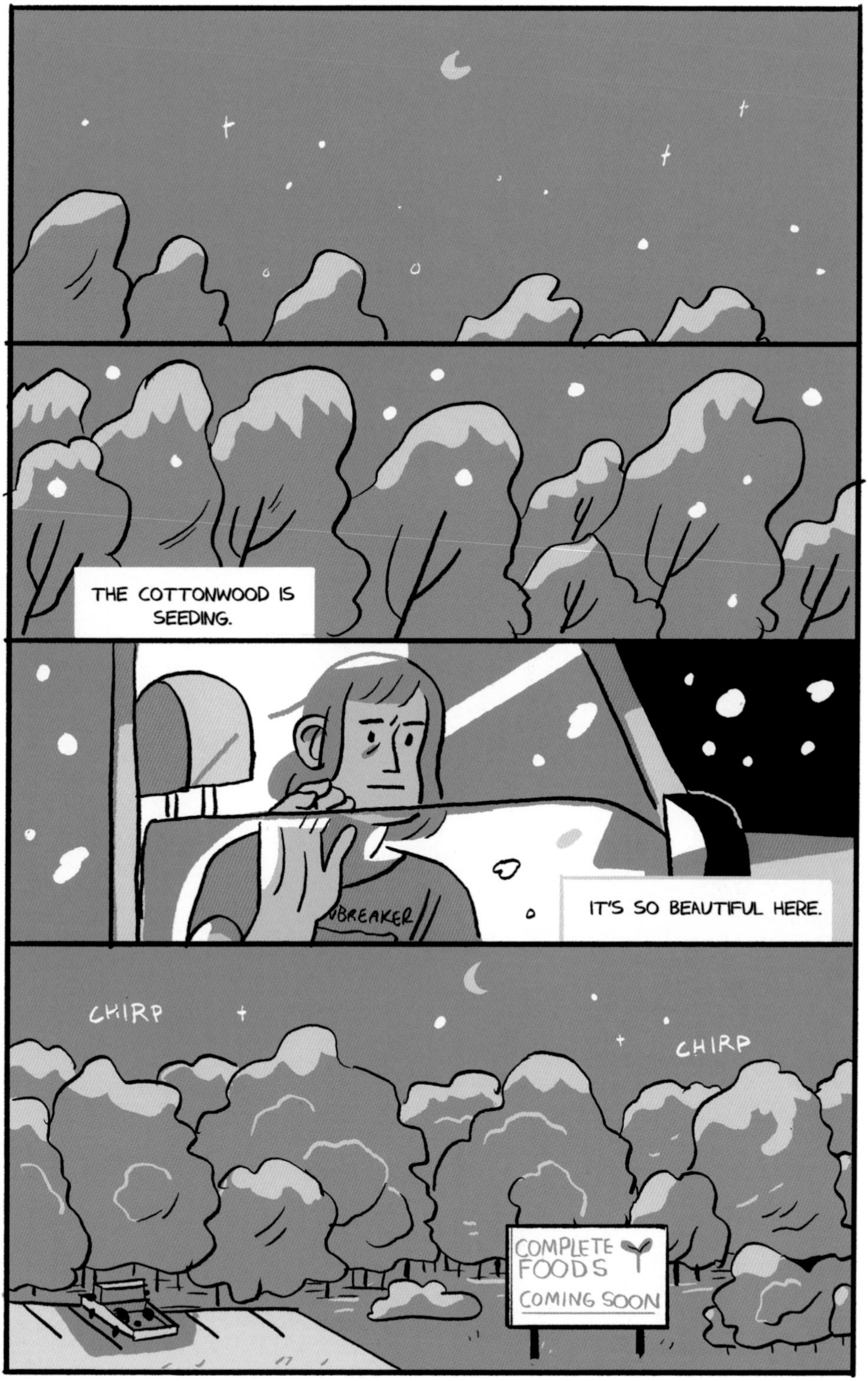
THE COTTONWOOD IS SEEDING.
NBREAKER
IT'S SO BEAUTIFUL HERE.
CHIRP
CHIRP
COMPLETE FOODS
COMING SOON

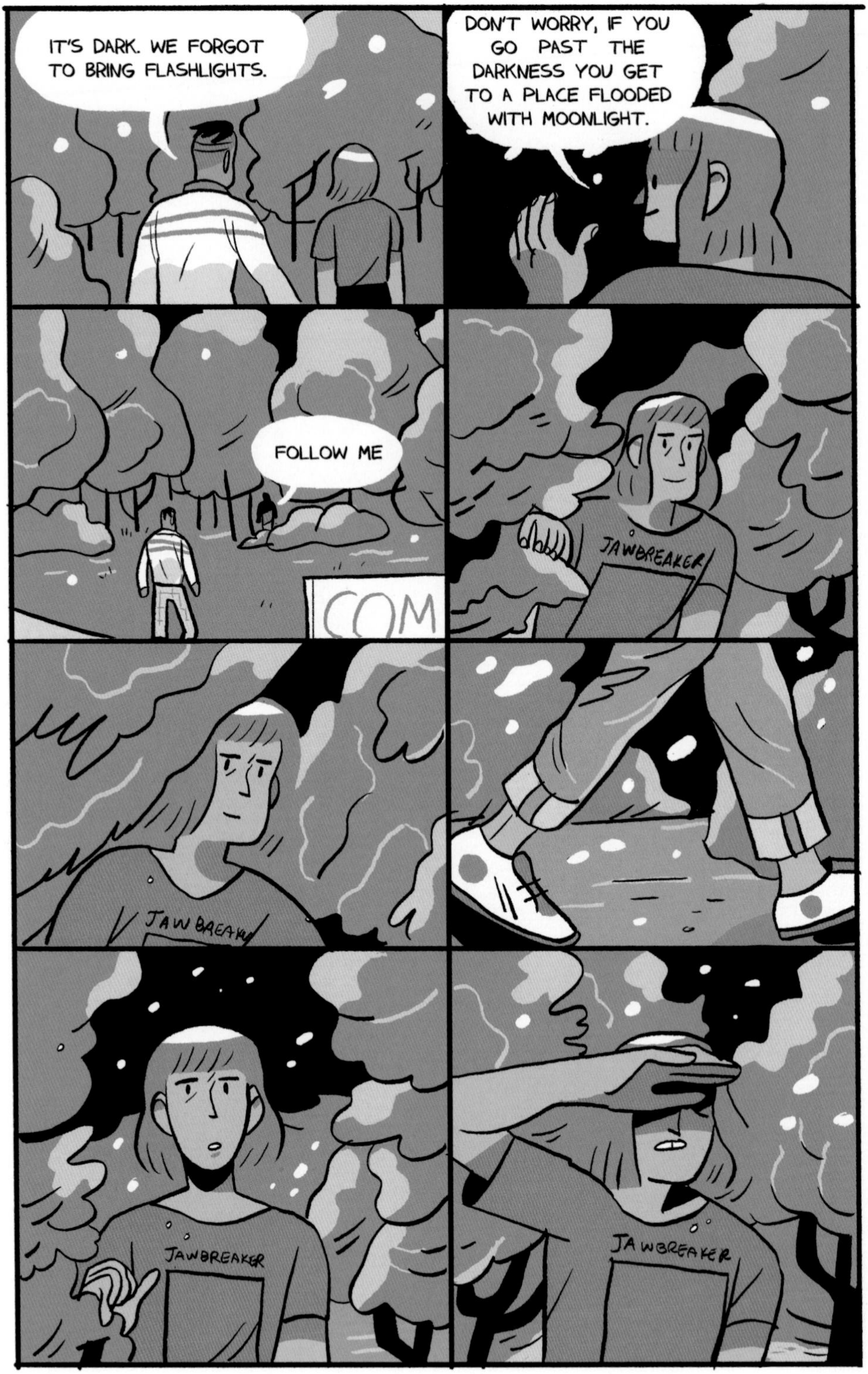
IT'S DARK. WE FORGOT TO BRING FLASHLIGHTS.
DON'T WORRY, IF YOU GO PAST THE DARKNESS YOU GET TO A PLACE FLOODED WITH MOONLIGHT.
FOLLOW ME
COM
JAWBREAKER
JAWBREAKER
JAWBREAKER

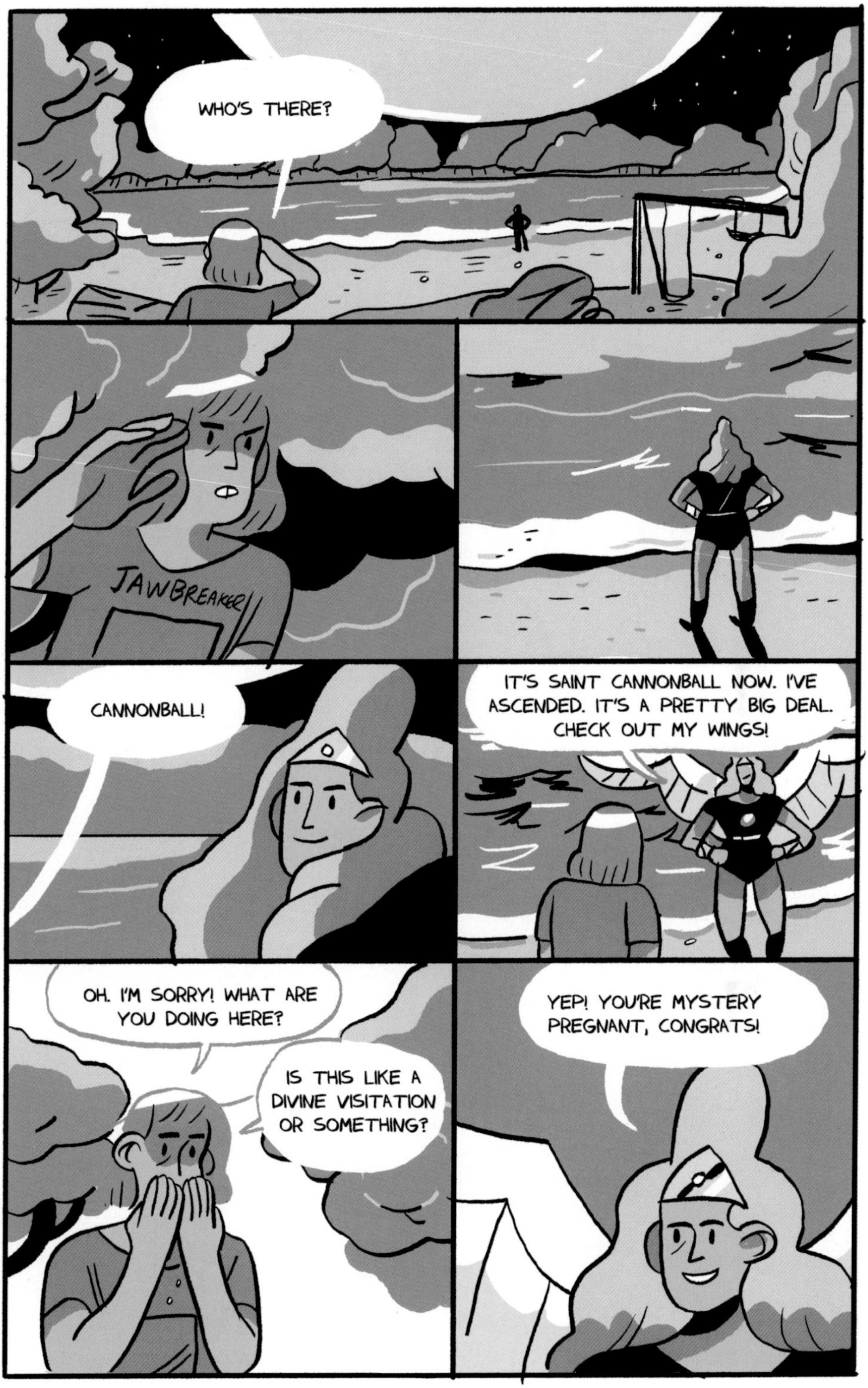
WHO'S THERE?
CANNONBALL!
IT'S SAINT CANNONBALL NOW. I'VE ASCENDED. IT'S A PRETTY BIG DEAL. CHECK OUT MY WINGS!
OH. I'M SORRY! WHAT ARE YOU DOING HERE?
IS THIS LIKE A DIVINE VISITATION OR SOMETHING?
YEP! YOU'RE MYSTERY PREGNANT, CONGRATS!

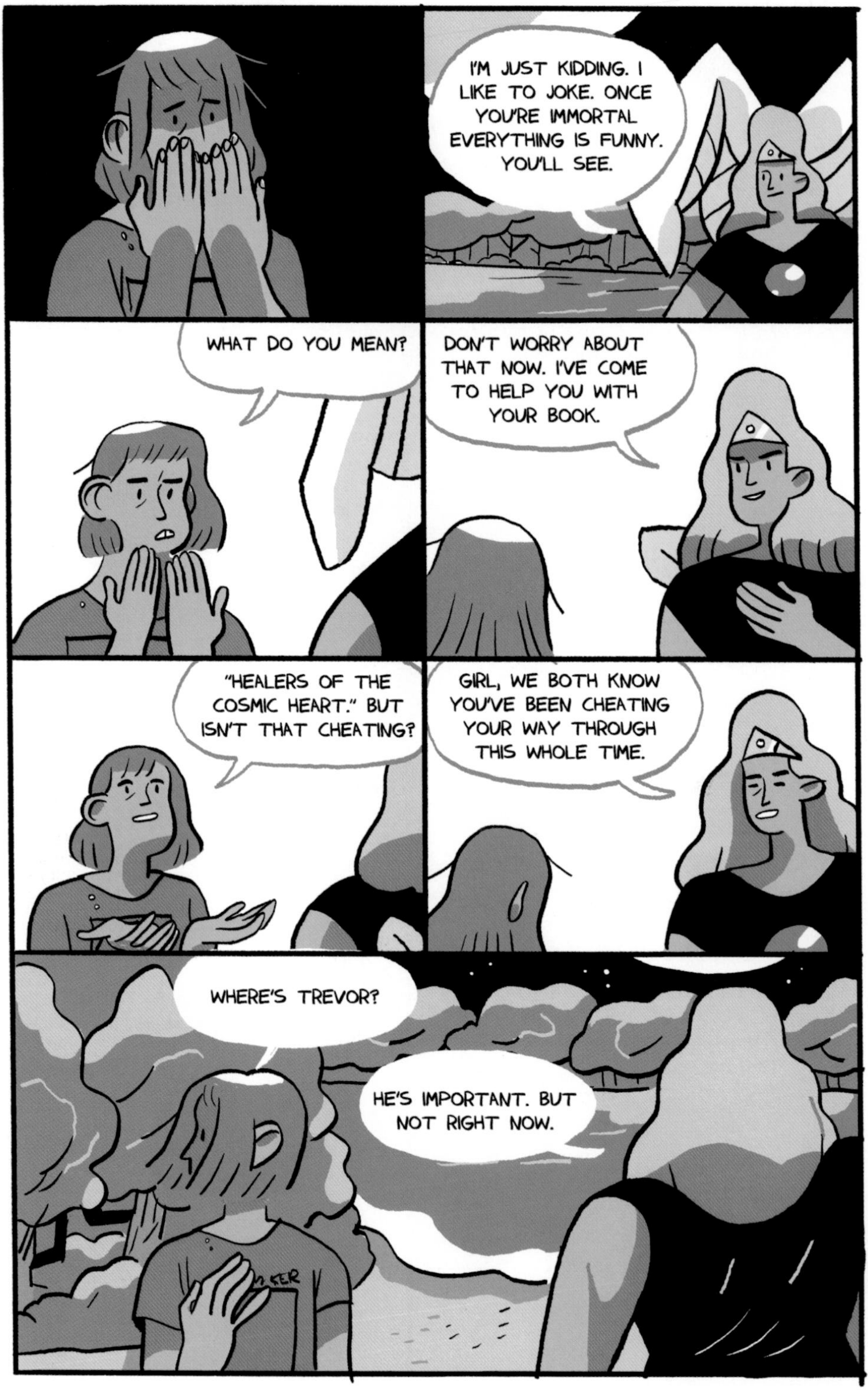
I'M JUST KIDDING. I LIKE TO JOKE. ONCE YOU'RE IMMORTAL EVERYTHING IS FUNNY. YOU'LL SEE.
WHAT DO YOU MEAN?
DON'T WORRY ABOUT THAT NOW. I'VE COME TO HELP YOU WITH YOUR BOOK.
"HEALERS OF THE COSMIC HEART." BUT ISN'T THAT CHEATING?
GIRL, WE BOTH KNOW YOU'VE BEEN CHEATING YOUR WAY THROUGH THIS WHOLE TIME.
WHERE'S TREVOR?
HE'S IMPORTANT. BUT NOT RIGHT NOW.

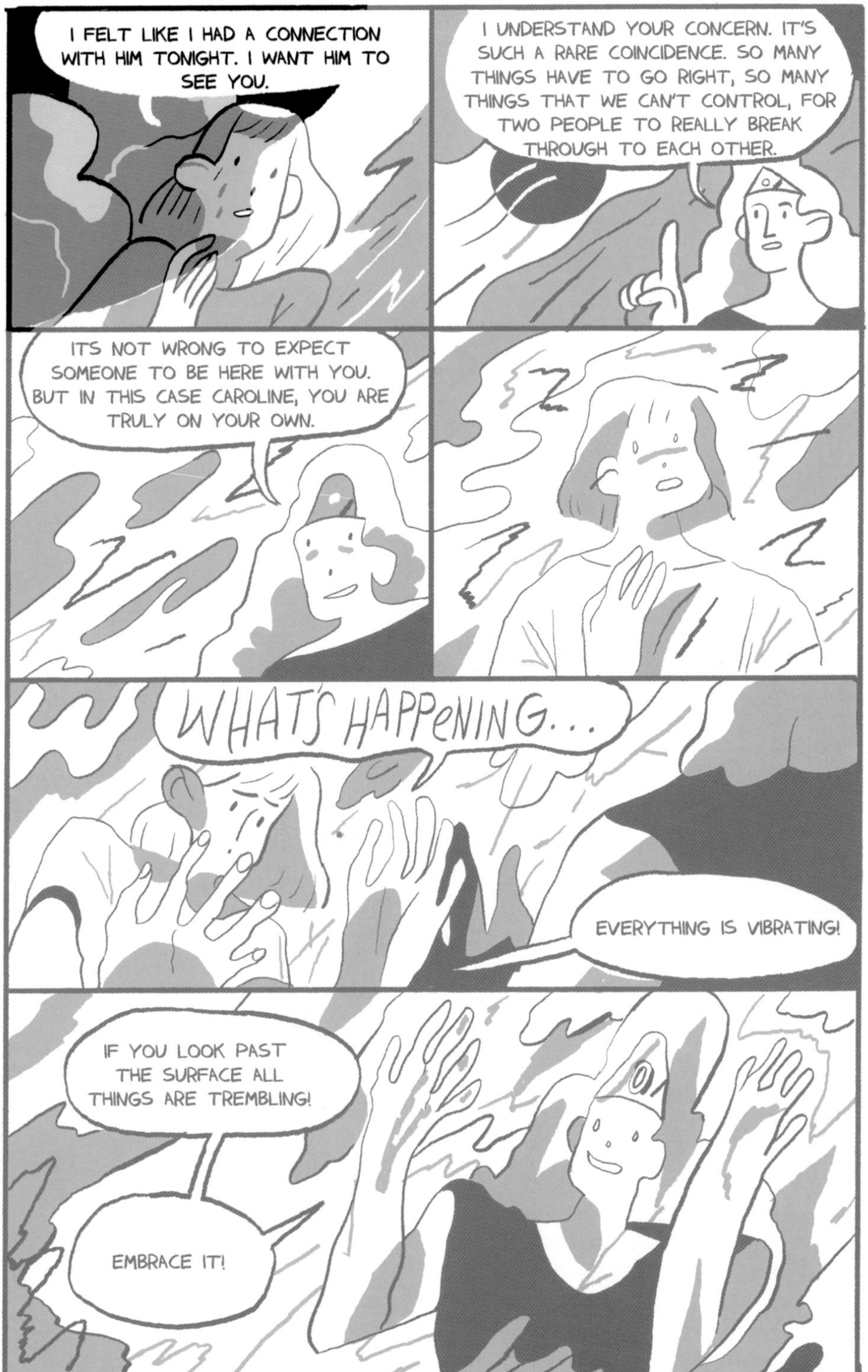

I FELT LIKE I HAD A CONNECTION WITH HIM TONIGHT. I WANT HIM TO SEE YOU.
I UNDERSTAND YOUR CONCERN. IT'S SUCH A RARE COINCIDENCE. SO MANY THINGS HAVE TO GO RIGHT, SO MANY THINGS THAT WE CAN'T CONTROL, FOR TWO PEOPLE TO REALLY BREAK THROUGH TO EACH OTHER.
ITS NOT WRONG TO EXPECT SOMEONE TO BE HERE WITH YOU. BUT IN THIS CASE CAROLINE, YOU ARE TRULY ON YOUR OWN.
WHAT'S HAPPENING...
EVERYTHING IS VIBRATING!
IF YOU LOOK PAST THE SURFACE ALL THINGS ARE TREMBLING!
EMBRACE IT!

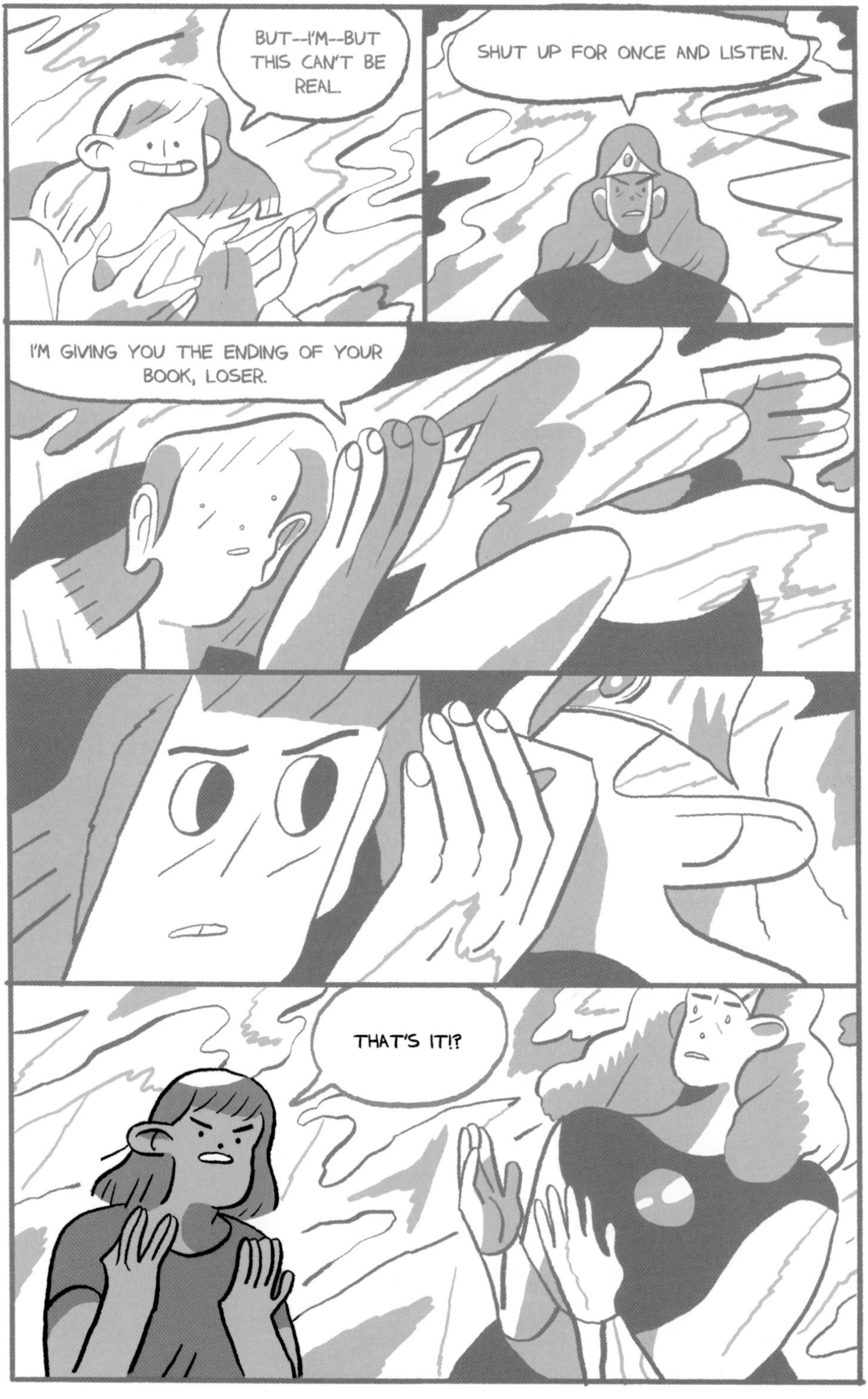
BUT--I'M--BUT THIS CAN'T BE REAL.
SHUT UP FOR ONCE AND LISTEN.
I'M GIVING YOU THE ENDING OF YOUR BOOK, LOSER.
THAT'S IT!?

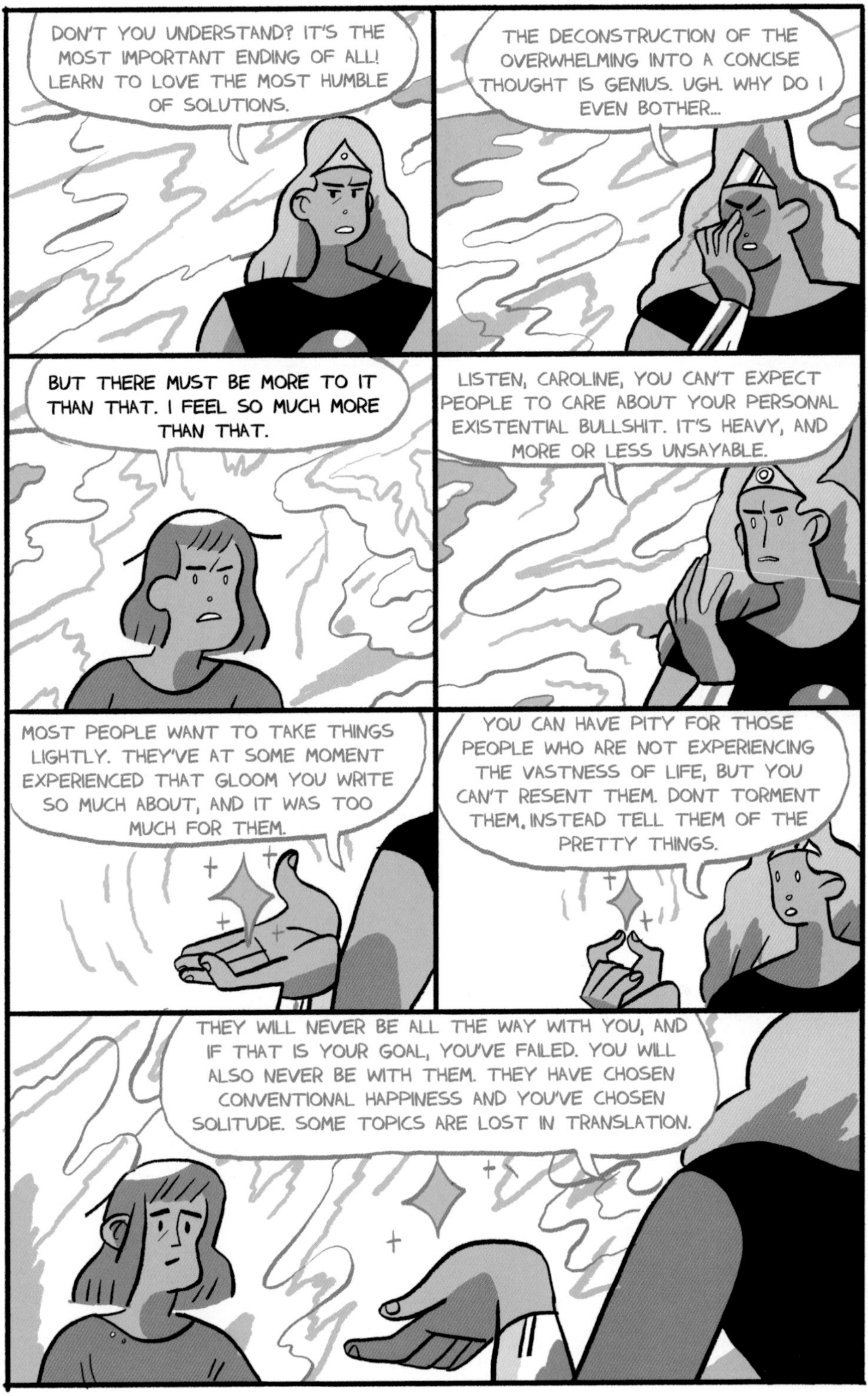
DON'T YOU UNDERSTAND? IT'S THE MOST IMPORTANT ENDING OF ALL! LEARN TO LOVE THE MOST HUMBLE OF SOLUTIONS.
THE DECONSTRUCTION OF THE OVERWHELMING INTO A CONCISE THOUGHT IS GENIUS. UGH. WHY DO I EVEN BOTHER...
BUT THERE MUST BE MORE TO IT THAN THAT. I FEEL SO MUCH MORE THAN THAT.
LISTEN, CAROLINE, YOU CAN'T EXPECT PEOPLE TO CARE ABOUT YOUR PERSONAL EXISTENTIAL BULLSHIT. IT'S HEAVY, AND MORE OR LESS UNSAYABLE.
MOST PEOPLE WANT TO TAKE THINGS LIGHTLY. THEY'VE AT SOME MOMENT EXPERIENCED THAT GLOOM YOU WRITE SO MUCH ABOUT, AND IT WAS TOO MUCH FOR THEM.
YOU CAN HAVE PITY FOR THOSE PEOPLE WHO ARE NOT EXPERIENCING THE VASTNESS OF LIFE, BUT YOU CAN'T RESENT THEM. DONT TORMENT THEM. INSTEAD TELL THEM OF THE PRETTY THINGS.
THEY WILL NEVER BE ALL THE WAY WITH YOU, AND IF THAT IS YOUR GOAL, YOU'VE FAILED. YOU WILL ALSO NEVER BE WITH THEM. THEY HAVE CHOSEN CONVENTIONAL HAPPINESS AND YOU'VE CHOSEN SOLITUDE. SOME TOPICS ARE LOST IN TRANSLATION.

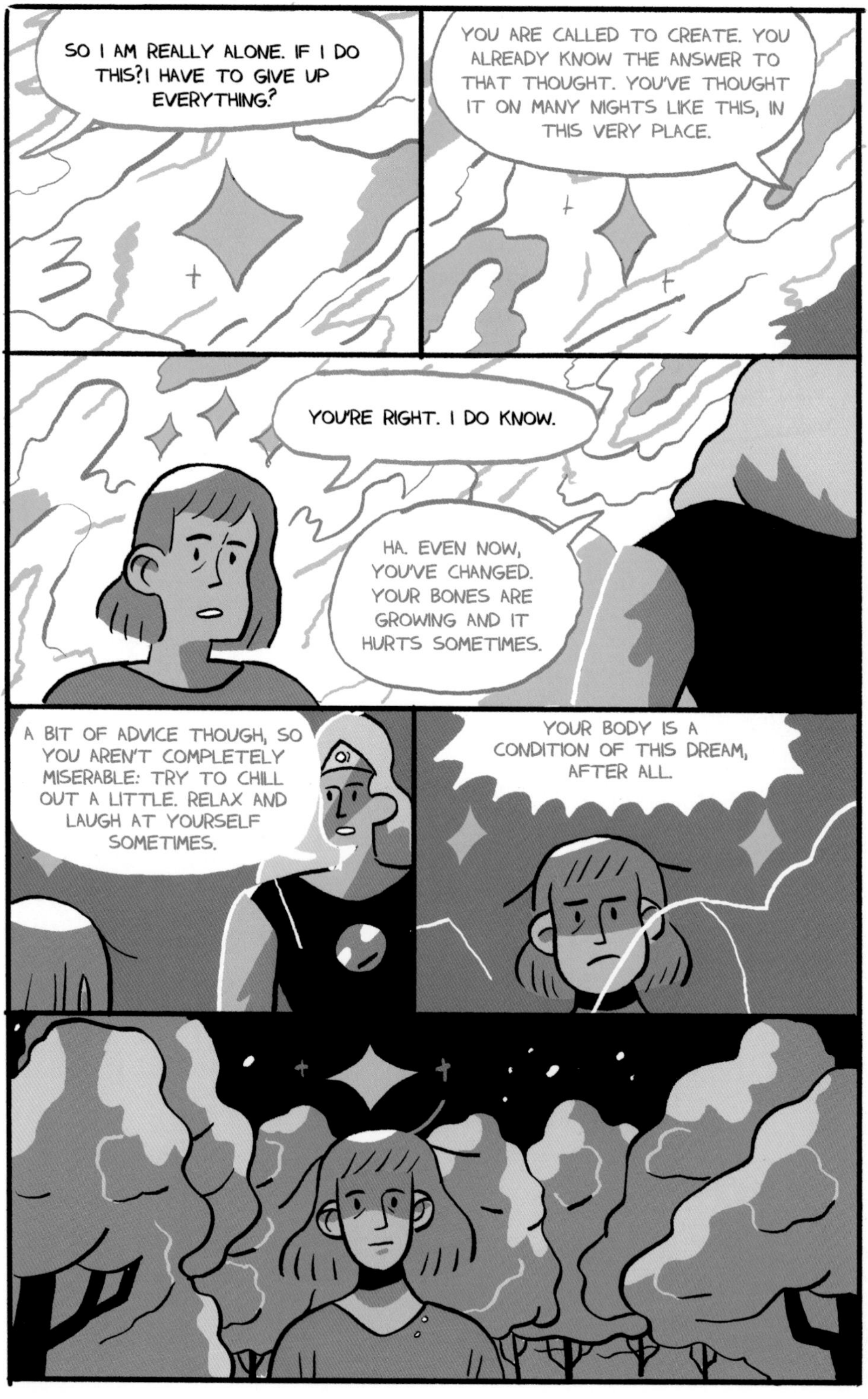
SO I AM REALLY ALONE. IF I DO THIS?I HAVE TO GIVE UP EVERYTHING?
YOU ARE CALLED TO CREATE. YOU ALREADY KNOW THE ANSWER TO THAT THOUGHT. YOU'VE THOUGHT IT ON MANY NIGHTS LIKE THIS, IN THIS VERY PLACE.
YOU'RE RIGHT. I DO KNOW.
HA. EVEN NOW, YOU'VE CHANGED. YOUR BONES ARE GROWING AND IT HURTS SOMETIMES.
A BIT OF ADVICE THOUGH, SO YOU AREN'T COMPLETELY MISERABLE: TRY TO CHILL OUT A LITTLE. RELAX AND LAUGH AT YOURSELF SOMETIMES.
YOUR BODY IS A CONDITION OF THIS DREAM, AFTER ALL.

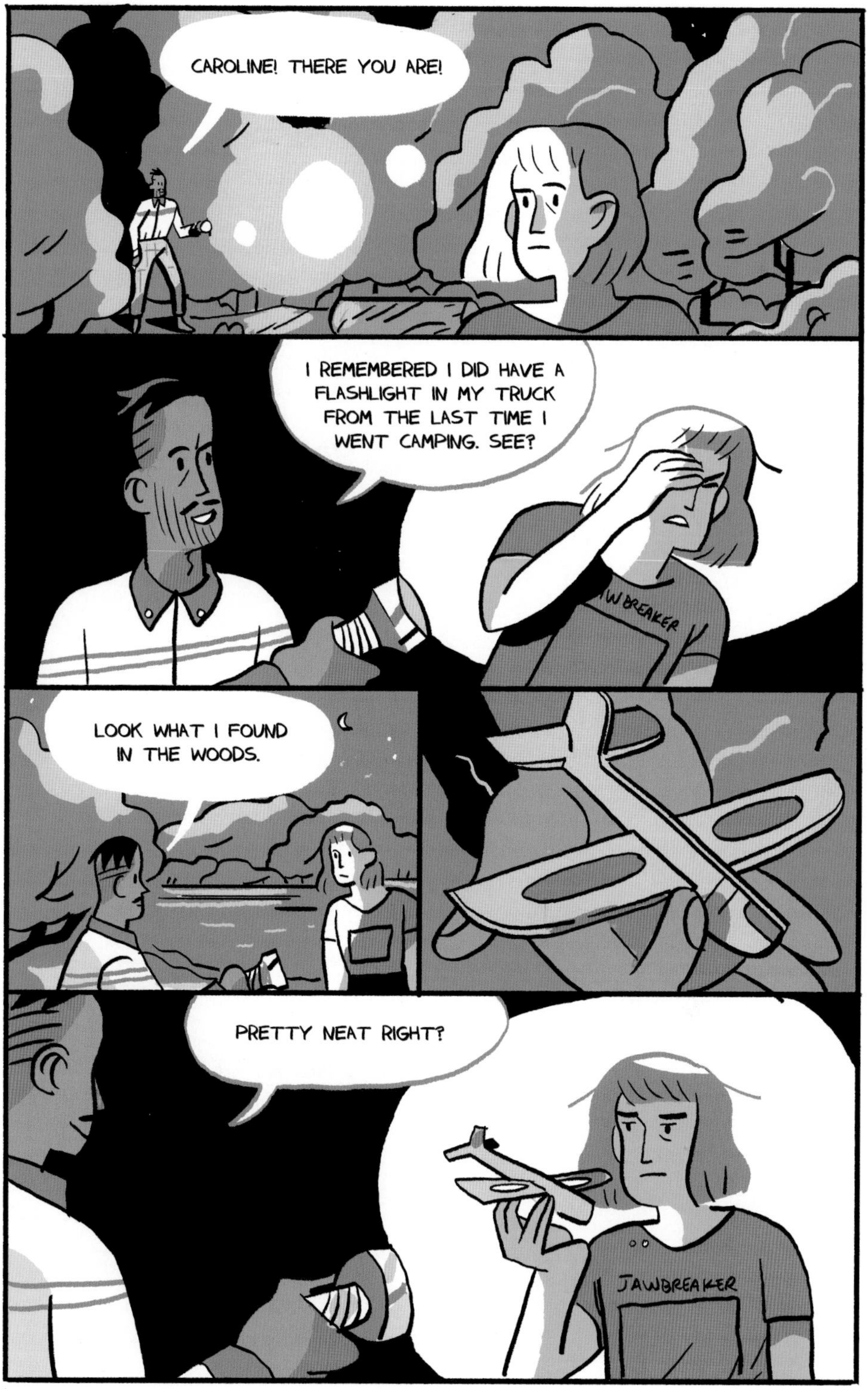
CAROLINE! THERE YOU ARE!
I REMEMBERED I DID HAVE A FLASHLIGHT IN MY TRUCK FROM THE LAST TIME I WENT CAMPING. SEE?
LOOK WHAT I FOUND IN THE WOODS.
PRETTY NEAT RIGHT?
JAWBREAKER

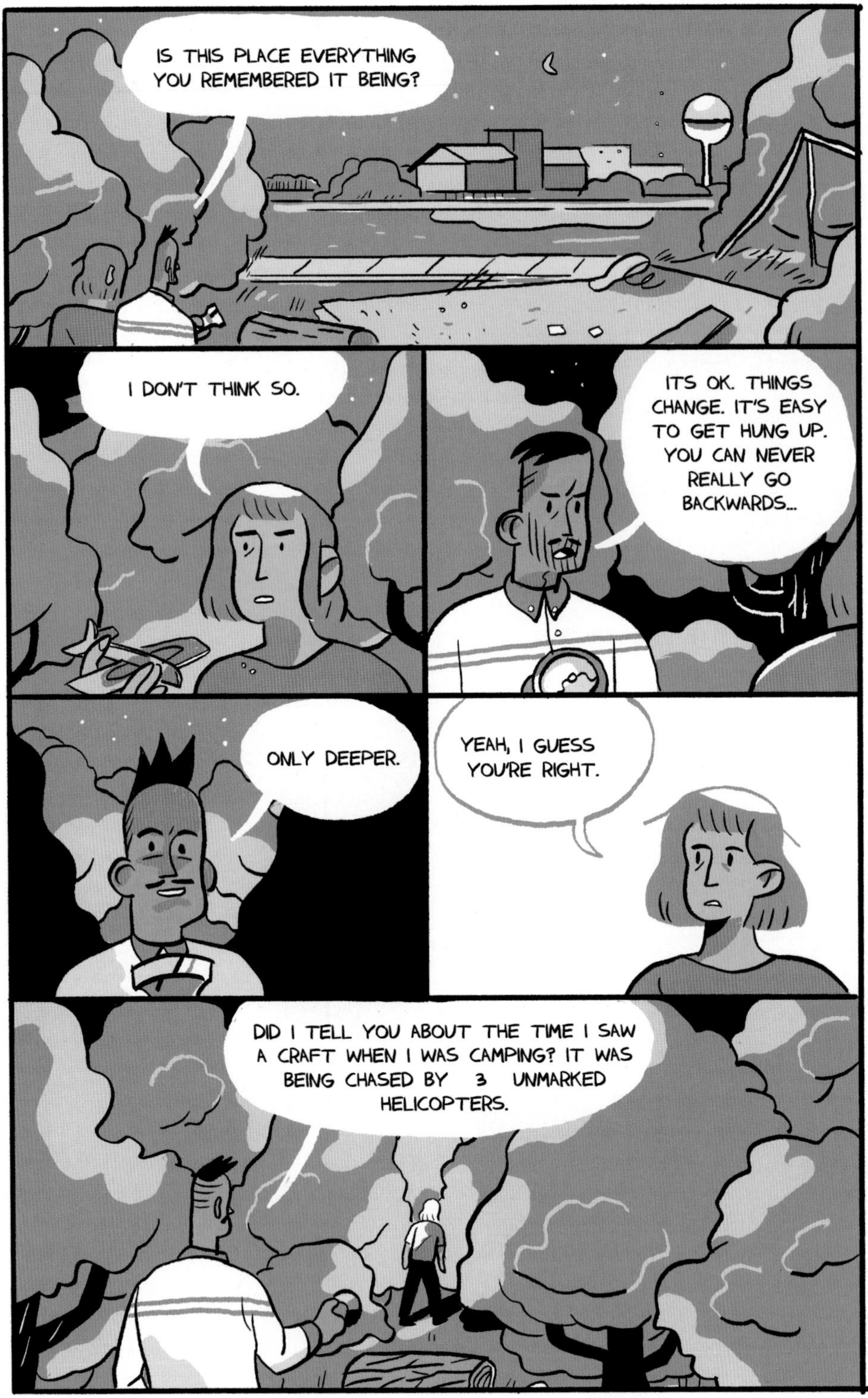
IS THIS PLACE EVERYTHING YOU REMEMBERED IT BEING?
I DON'T THINK SO.
ITS OK. THINGS CHANGE. IT'S EASY TO GET HUNG UP. YOU CAN NEVER REALLY GO BACKWARDS...
ONLY DEEPER.
YEAH, I GUESS YOU'RE RIGHT.
DID I TELL YOU ABOUT THE TIME I SAW A CRAFT WHEN I WAS CAMPING? IT WAS BEING CHASED BY 3 UNMARKED HELICOPTERS.

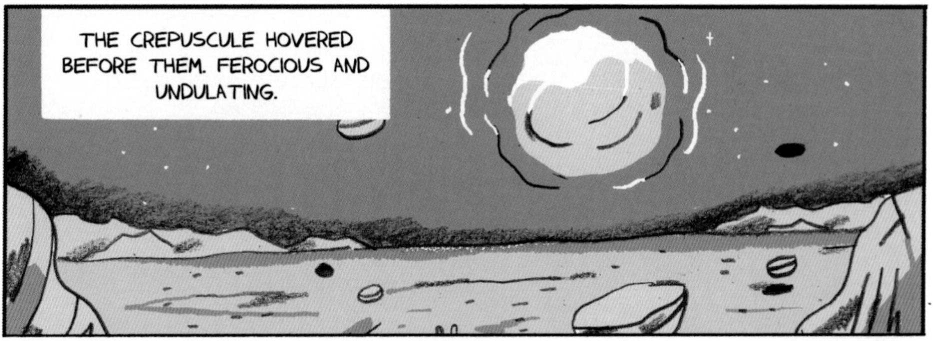
THE CREPUSCULE HOVERED BEFORE THEM. FEROCIOUS AND UNDULATING.

# HEALERS OF THE COSMIC HEART

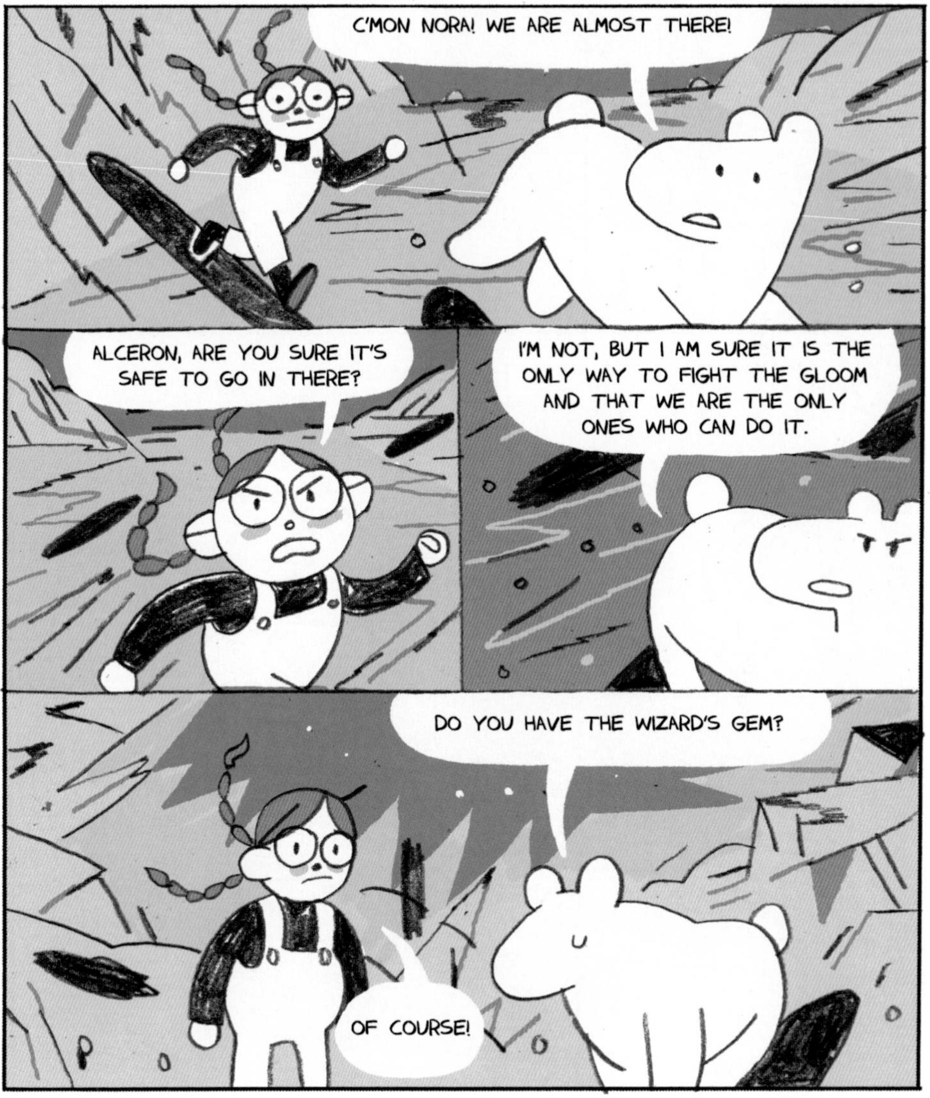
C'MON NORA! WE ARE ALMOST THERE!
ALCERON, ARE YOU SURE IT'S SAFE TO GO IN THERE?
I'M NOT, BUT I AM SURE IT IS THE ONLY WAY TO FIGHT THE GLOOM AND THAT WE ARE THE ONLY ONES WHO CAN DO IT.
DO YOU HAVE THE WIZARD'S GEM?
OF COURSE!

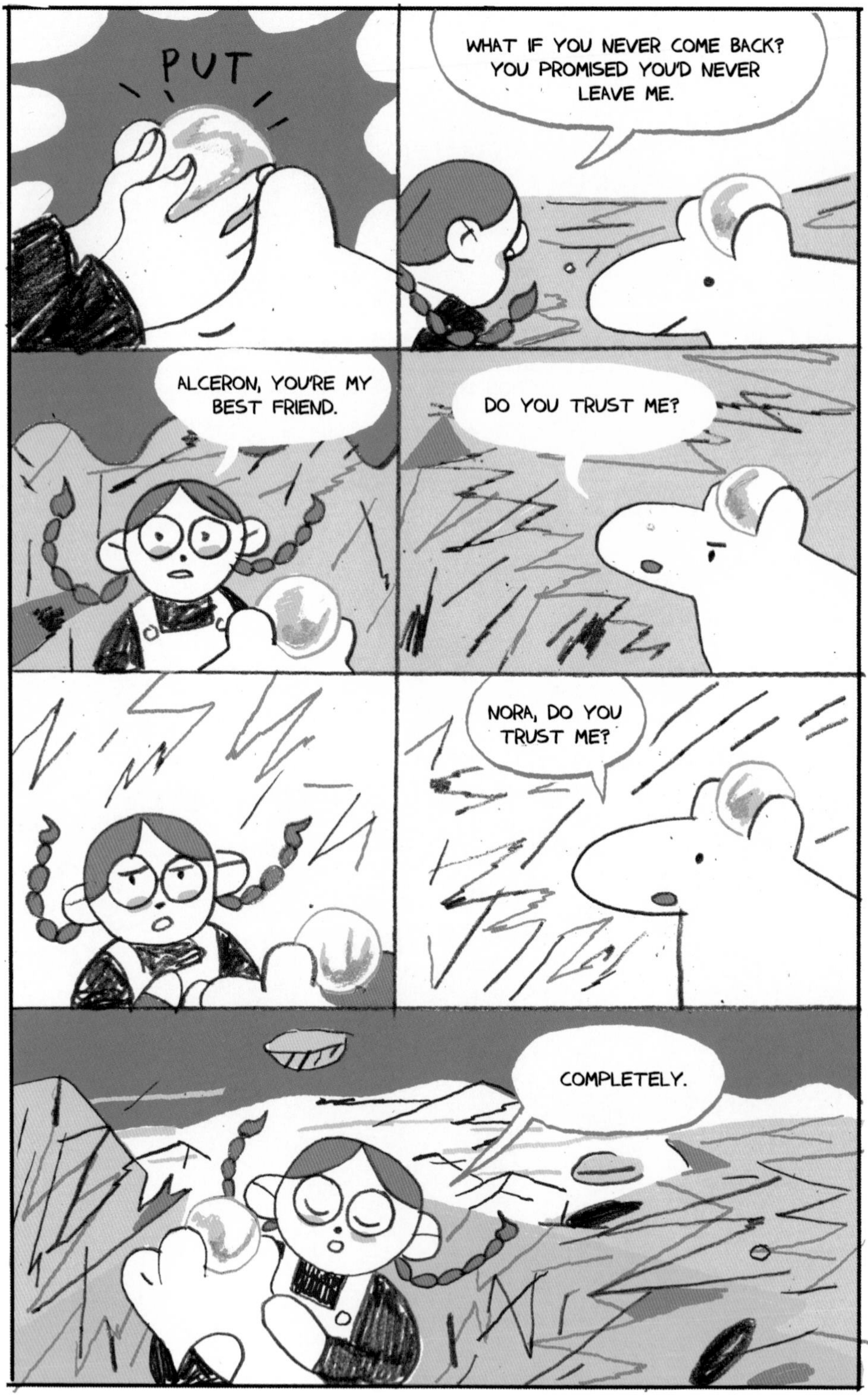
PUT
WHAT IF YOU NEVER COME BACK? YOU PROMISED YOU'D NEVER LEAVE ME.
ALCERON, YOU'RE MY BEST FRIEND.
DO YOU TRUST ME?
NORA, DO YOU TRUST ME?
COMPLETELY.

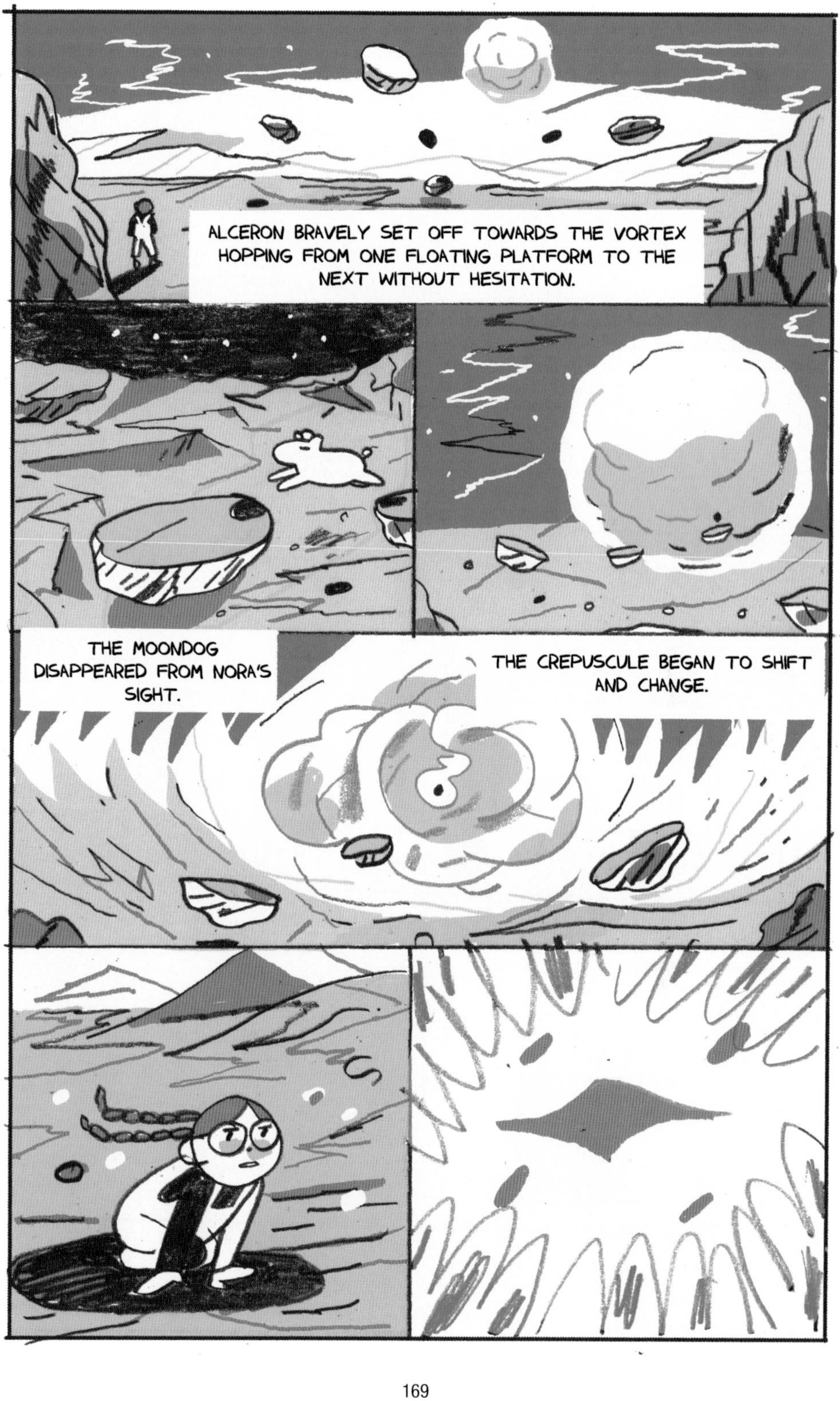
ALCERON BRAVELY SET OFF TOWARDS THE VORTEX HOPPING FROM ONE FLOATING PLATFORM TO THE NEXT WITHOUT HESITATION.
THE MOONDOG DISAPPEARED FROM NORA'S SIGHT.
THE CREPUSCULE BEGAN TO SHIFT AND CHANGE.

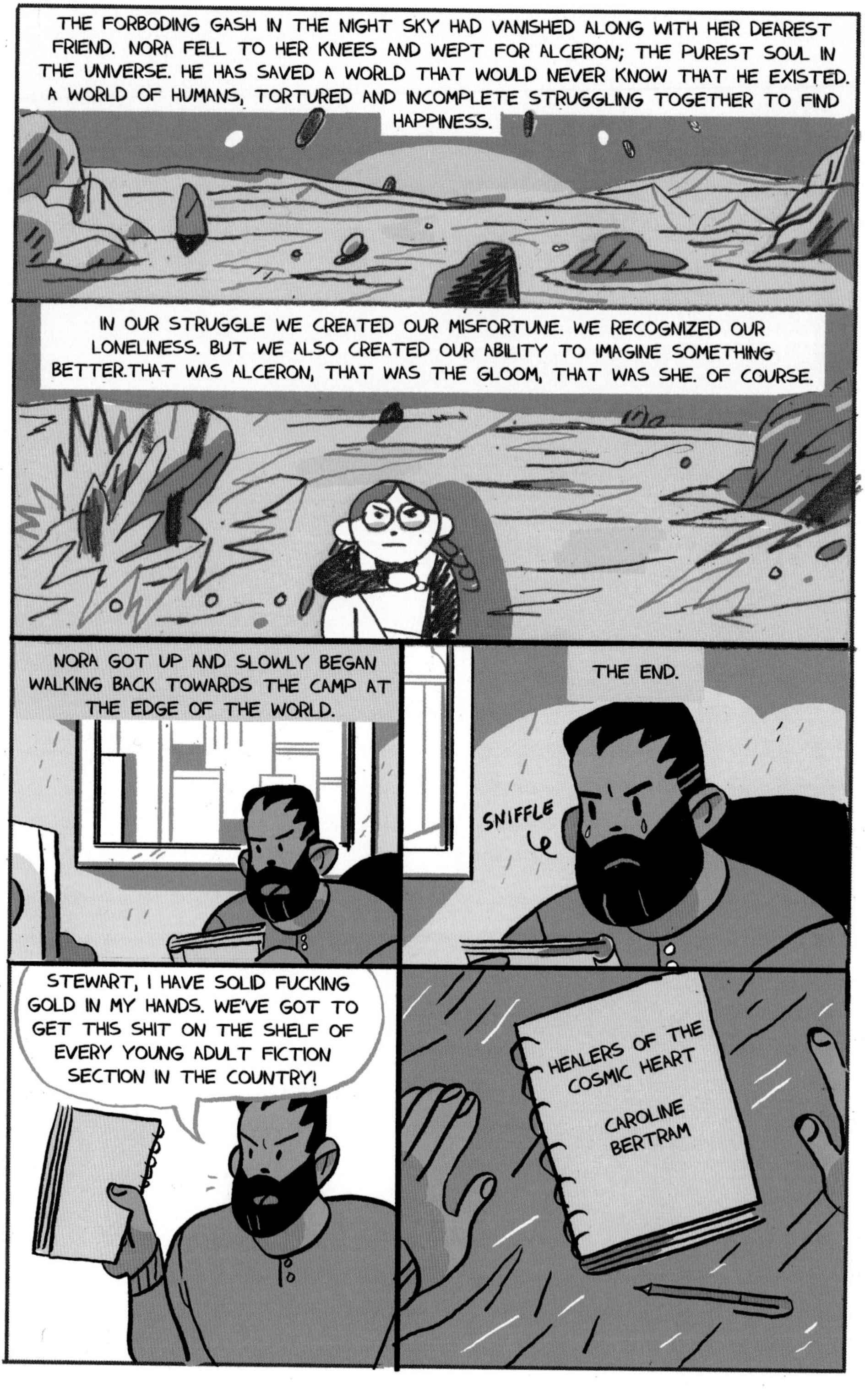
THE FORBODING GASH IN THE NIGHT SKY HAD VANISHED ALONG WITH HER DEAREST FRIEND. NORA FELL TO HER KNEES AND WEPT FOR ALCERON; THE PUREST SOUL IN THE UNIVERSE. HE HAS SAVED A WORLD THAT WOULD NEVER KNOW THAT HE EXISTED. A WORLD OF HUMANS, TORTURED AND INCOMPLETE STRUGGLING TOGETHER TO FIND HAPPINESS.
IN OUR STRUGGLE WE CREATED OUR MISFORTUNE. WE RECOGNIZED OUR LONELINESS. BUT WE ALSO CREATED OUR ABILITY TO IMAGINE SOMETHING BETTER.THAT WAS ALCERON, THAT WAS THE GLOOM, THAT WAS SHE. OF COURSE.
NORA GOT UP AND SLOWLY BEGAN WALKING BACK TOWARDS THE CAMP AT THE EDGE OF THE WORLD.
THE END.
SNIFFLE
STEWART, I HAVE SOLID FUCKING GOLD IN MY HANDS. WE'VE GOT TO GET THIS SHIT ON THE SHELF OF EVERY YOUNG ADULT FICTION SECTION IN THE COUNTRY!
HEALERS OF THE COSMIC HEART
CAROLINE BERTRAM

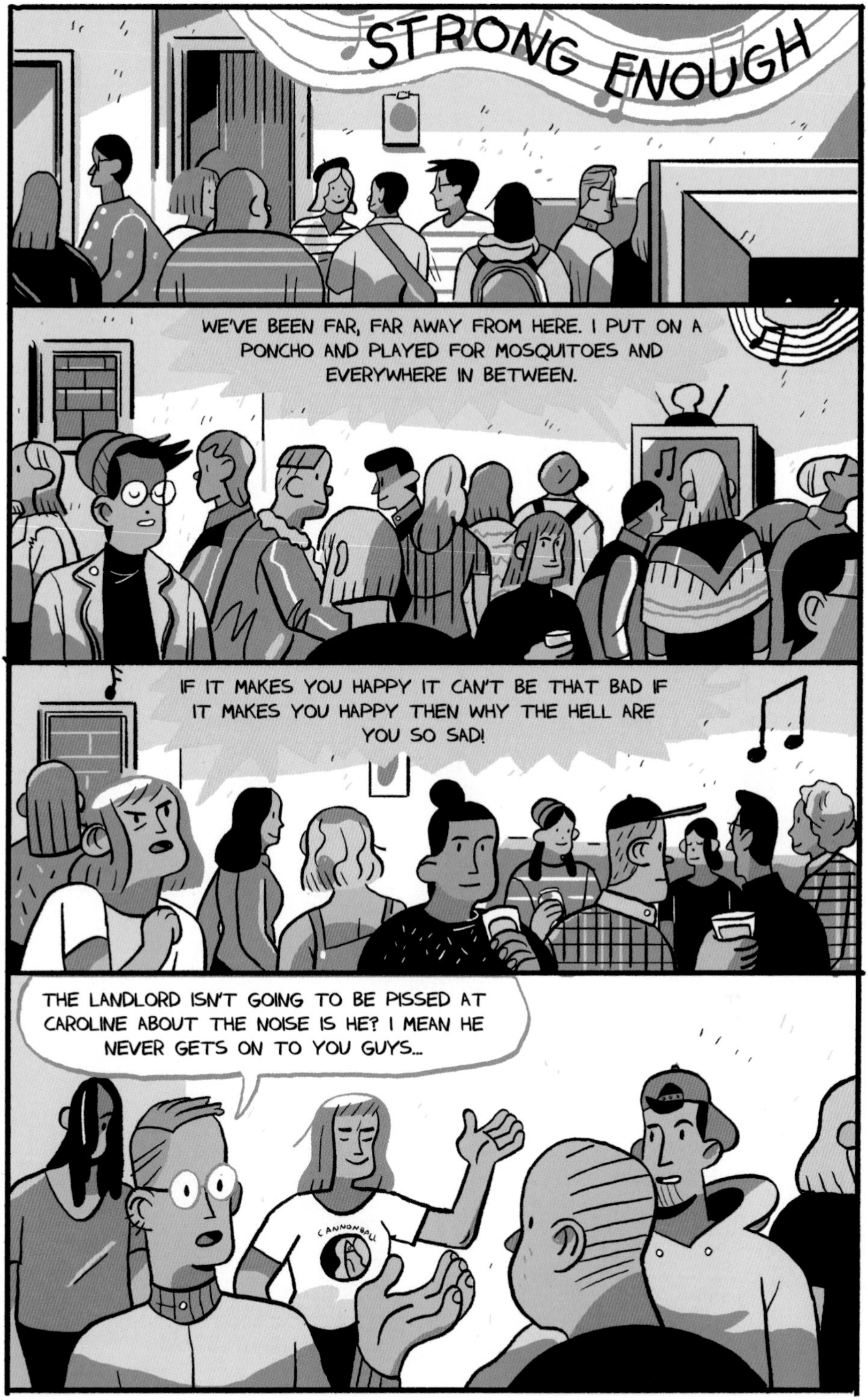
STRONG ENOUGH
WE'VE BEEN FAR, FAR AWAY FROM HERE. I PUT ON A PONCHO AND PLAYED FOR MOSQUITOES AND EVERYWHERE IN BETWEEN.
IF IT MAKES YOU HAPPY IT CAN'T BE THAT BAD IF IT MAKES YOU HAPPY THEN WHY THE HELL ARE YOU SO SAD!
THE LANDLORD ISN'T GOING TO BE PISSED AT CAROLINE ABOUT THE NOISE IS HE? I MEAN HE NEVER GETS ON TO YOU GUYS...
CANNONBALL

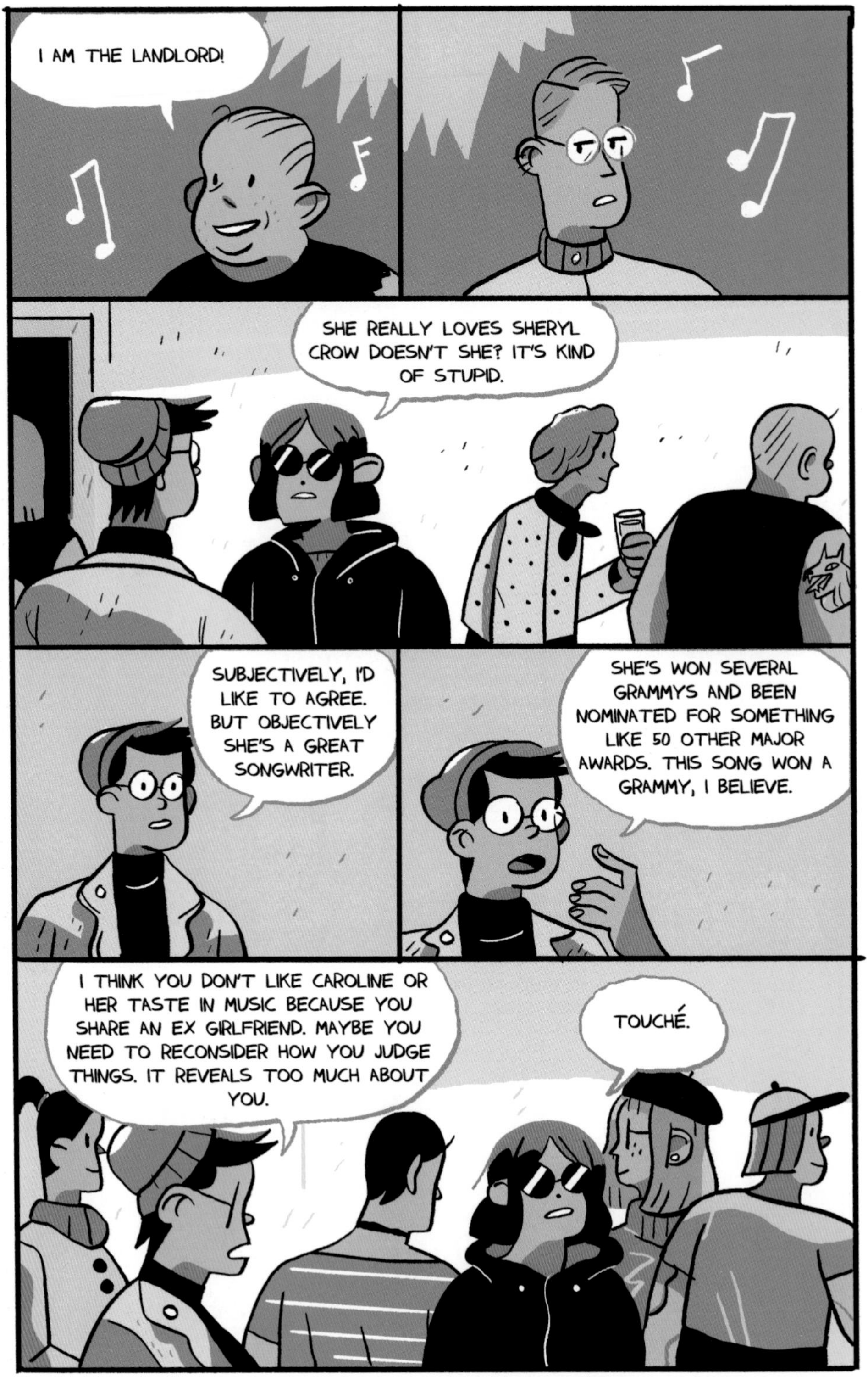
I AM THE LANDLORD!
SHE REALLY LOVES SHERYL CROW DOESN'T SHE? IT'S KIND OF STUPID.
SUBJECTIVELY, I'D LIKE TO AGREE. BUT OBJECTIVELY SHE'S A GREAT SONGWRITER.
SHE'S WON SEVERAL GRAMMYS AND BEEN NOMINATED FOR SOMETHING LIKE 50 OTHER MAJOR AWARDS. THIS SONG WON A GRAMMY, I BELIEVE.
I THINK YOU DON'T LIKE CAROLINE OR HER TASTE IN MUSIC BECAUSE YOU SHARE AN EX GIRLFRIEND. MAYBE YOU NEED TO RECONSIDER HOW YOU JUDGE THINGS. IT REVEALS TOO MUCH ABOUT YOU.
TOUCHÉ.

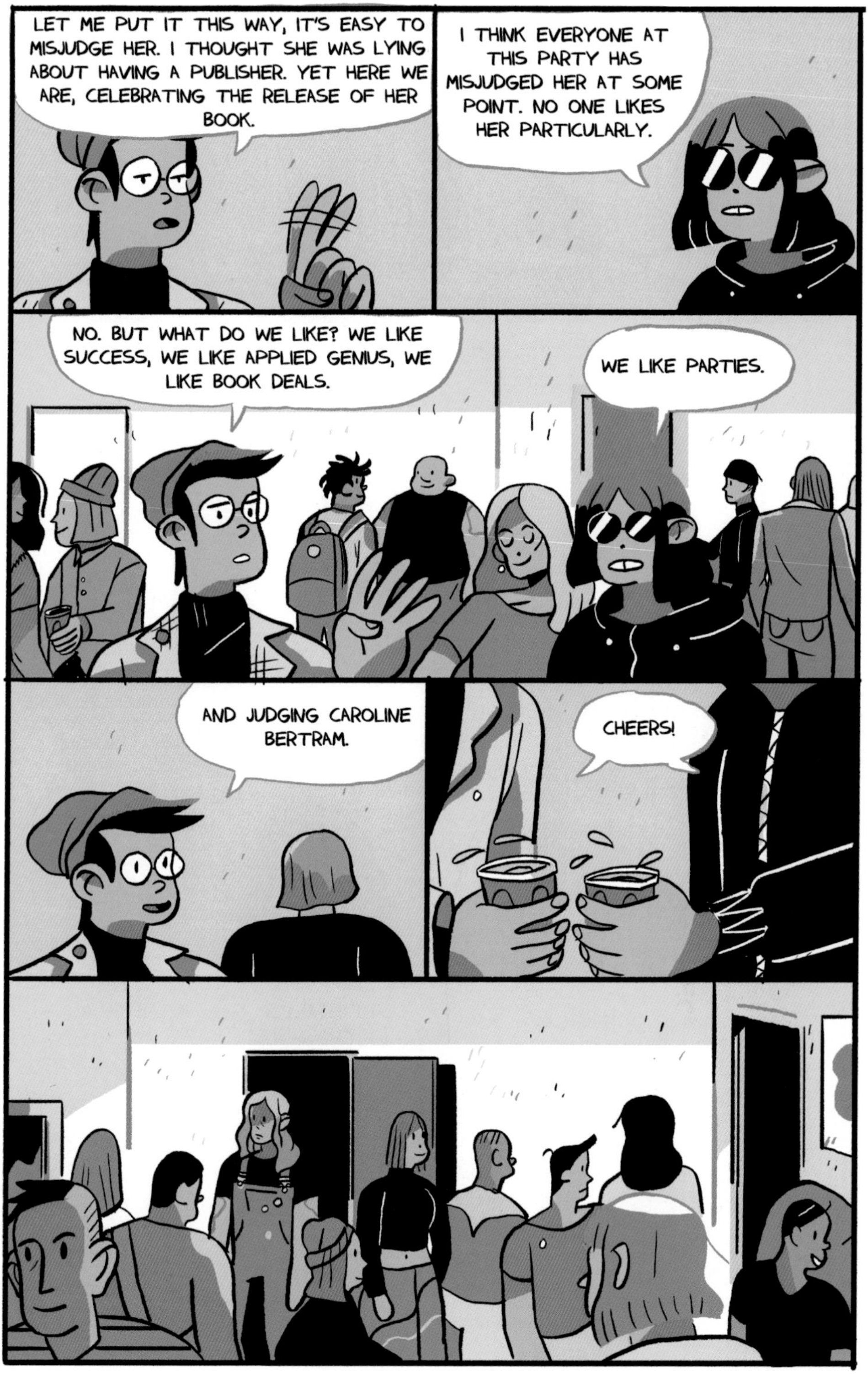

LET ME PUT IT THIS WAY, IT'S EASY TO MISJUDGE HER. I THOUGHT SHE WAS LYING ABOUT HAVING A PUBLISHER. YET HERE WE ARE, CELEBRATING THE RELEASE OF HER BOOK.
I THINK EVERYONE AT THIS PARTY HAS MISJUDGED HER AT SOME POINT. NO ONE LIKES HER PARTICULARLY.
NO. BUT WHAT DO WE LIKE? WE LIKE SUCCESS, WE LIKE APPLIED GENIUS, WE LIKE BOOK DEALS.
WE LIKE PARTIES.
AND JUDGING CAROLINE BERTRAM.
CHEERS!

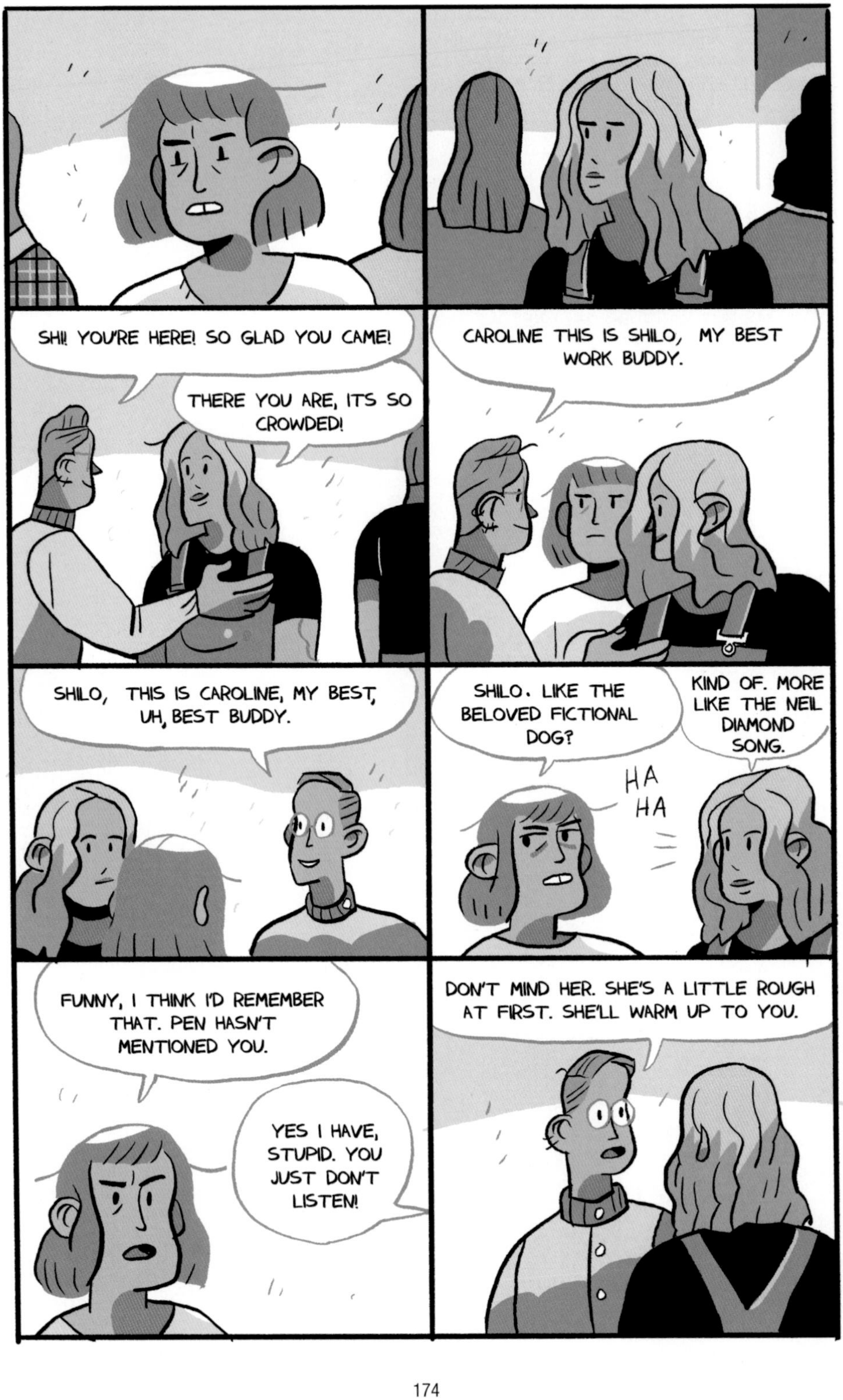
SHI! YOU'RE HERE! SO GLAD YOU CAME!
THERE YOU ARE, ITS SO CROWDED!
CAROLINE THIS IS SHILO, MY BEST WORK BUDDY.
SHILO, THIS IS CAROLINE, MY BEST, UH, BEST BUDDY.
SHILO. LIKE THE BELOVED FICTIONAL DOG?
KIND OF. MORE LIKE THE NEIL DIAMOND SONG.
HA HA
FUNNY, I THINK I'D REMEMBER THAT. PEN HASN'T MENTIONED YOU.
YES I HAVE, STUPID. YOU JUST DON'T LISTEN!
DON'T MIND HER. SHE'S A LITTLE ROUGH AT FIRST. SHE'LL WARM UP TO YOU.

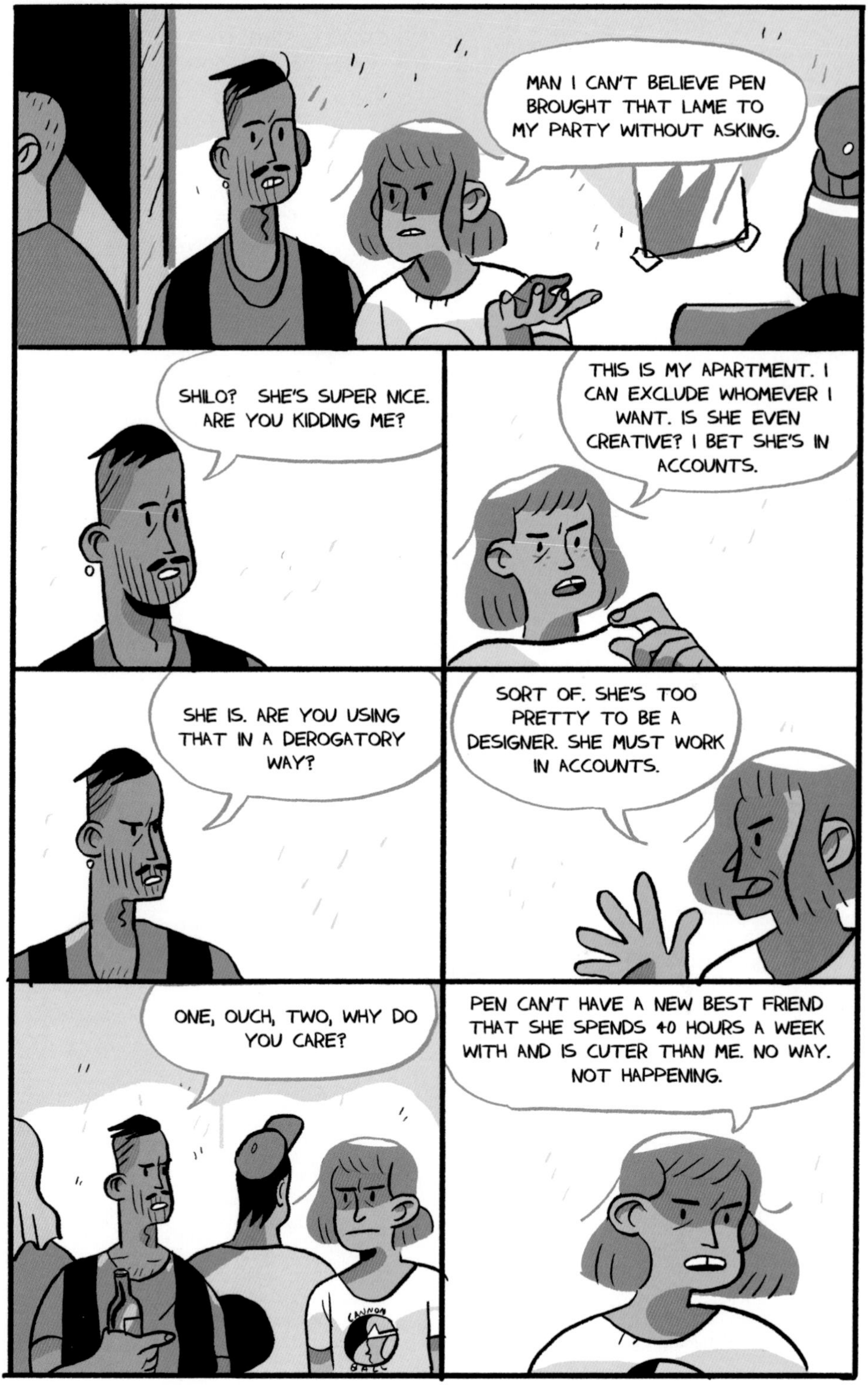
MAN I CAN'T BELIEVE PEN BROUGHT THAT LAME TO MY PARTY WITHOUT ASKING.
SHILO? SHE'S SUPER NICE. ARE YOU KIDDING ME?
THIS IS MY APARTMENT. I CAN EXCLUDE WHOMEVER I WANT. IS SHE EVEN CREATIVE? I BET SHE'S IN ACCOUNTS.
SHE IS. ARE YOU USING THAT IN A DEROGATORY WAY?
SORT OF. SHE'S TOO PRETTY TO BE A DESIGNER. SHE MUST WORK IN ACCOUNTS.
ONE, OUCH, TWO, WHY DO YOU CARE?
PEN CAN'T HAVE A NEW BEST FRIEND THAT SHE SPENDS 40 HOURS A WEEK WITH AND IS CUTER THAN ME. NO WAY. NOT HAPPENING.

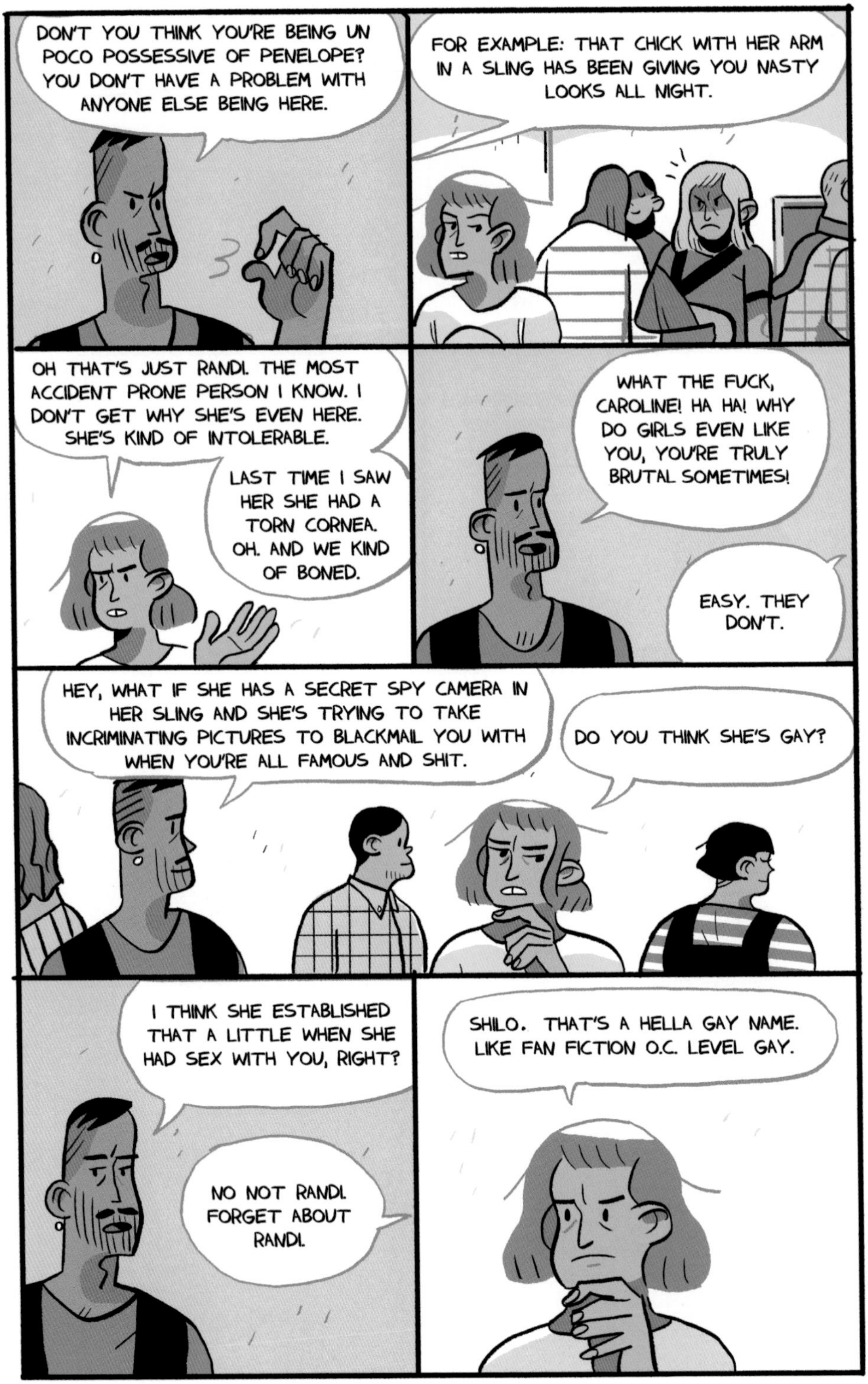
DON'T YOU THINK YOU'RE BEING UN POCO POSSESSIVE OF PENELOPE? YOU DON'T HAVE A PROBLEM WITH ANYONE ELSE BEING HERE.
FOR EXAMPLE: THAT CHICK WITH HER ARM IN A SLING HAS BEEN GIVING YOU NASTY LOOKS ALL NIGHT.
OH THAT'S JUST RANDI. THE MOST ACCIDENT PRONE PERSON I KNOW. I DON'T GET WHY SHE'S EVEN HERE. SHE'S KIND OF INTOLERABLE.
LAST TIME I SAW HER SHE HAD A TORN CORNEA. OH. AND WE KIND OF BONED.
WHAT THE FUCK, CAROLINE! HA HA! WHY DO GIRLS EVEN LIKE YOU, YOU'RE TRULY BRUTAL SOMETIMES!
EASY. THEY DON'T.
HEY, WHAT IF SHE HAS A SECRET SPY CAMERA IN HER SLING AND SHE'S TRYING TO TAKE INCRIMINATING PICTURES TO BLACKMAIL YOU WITH WHEN YOU'RE ALL FAMOUS AND SHIT.
DO YOU THINK SHE'S GAY?
I THINK SHE ESTABLISHED THAT A LITTLE WHEN SHE HAD SEX WITH YOU, RIGHT?
NO NOT RANDI. FORGET ABOUT RANDI.
SHILO. THAT'S A HELLA GAY NAME. LIKE FAN FICTION O.C. LEVEL GAY.

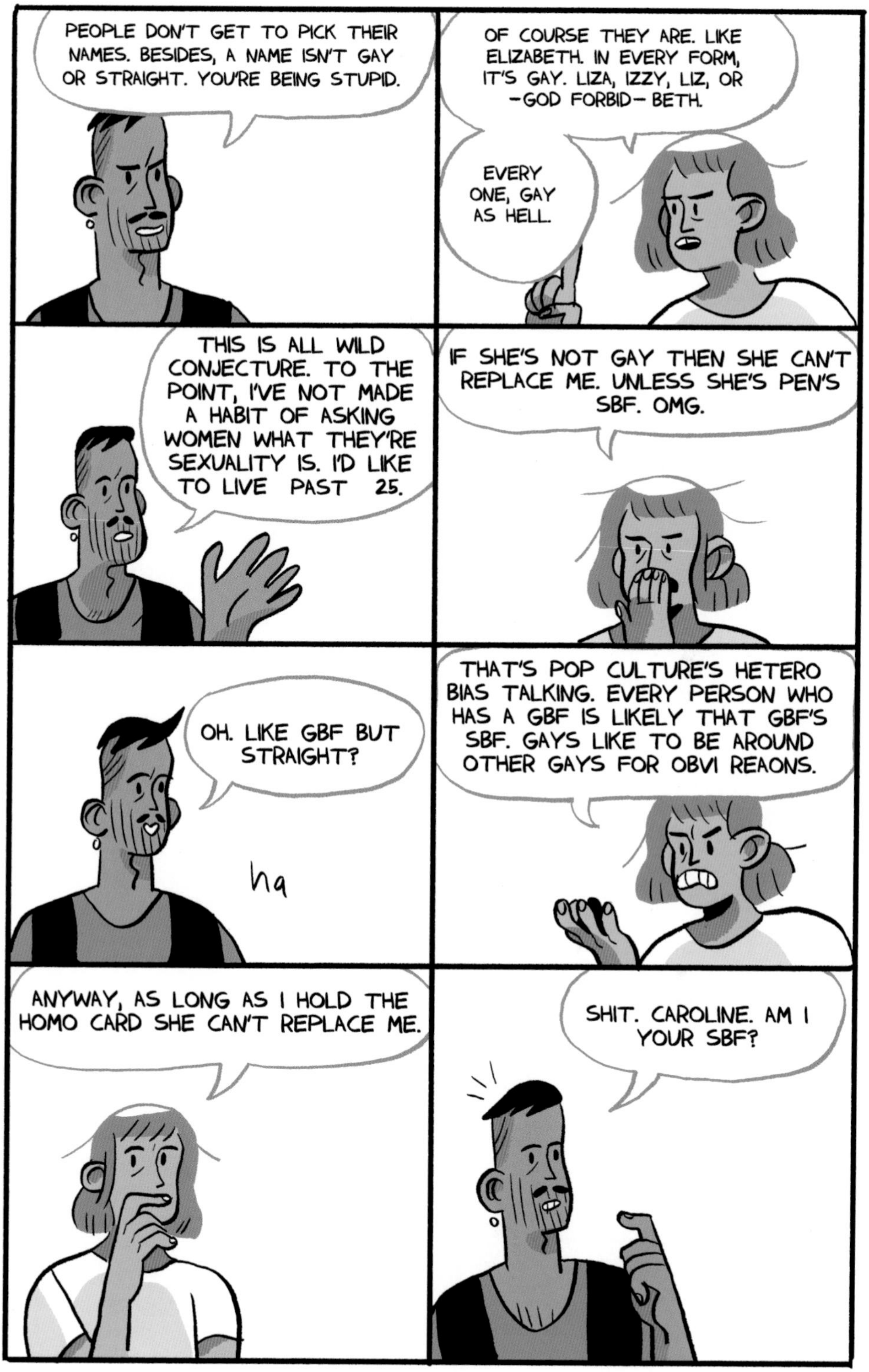
PEOPLE DON'T GET TO PICK THEIR NAMES. BESIDES, A NAME ISN'T GAY OR STRAIGHT. YOU'RE BEING STUPID.
OF COURSE THEY ARE. LIKE ELIZABETH. IN EVERY FORM, IT'S GAY. LIZA, IZZY, LIZ, OR —GOD FORBID— BETH.
EVERY ONE, GAY AS HELL.
THIS IS ALL WILD CONJECTURE. TO THE POINT, I'VE NOT MADE A HABIT OF ASKING WOMEN WHAT THEY'RE SEXUALITY IS. I'D LIKE TO LIVE PAST 25.
IF SHE'S NOT GAY THEN SHE CAN'T REPLACE ME. UNLESS SHE'S PEN'S SBF. OMG.
OH. LIKE GBF BUT STRAIGHT?
ha
THAT'S POP CULTURE'S HETERO BIAS TALKING. EVERY PERSON WHO HAS A GBF IS LIKELY THAT GBF'S SBF. GAYS LIKE TO BE AROUND OTHER GAYS FOR OBVI REAONS.
ANYWAY, AS LONG AS I HOLD THE HOMO CARD SHE CAN'T REPLACE ME.
SHIT. CAROLINE. AM I YOUR SBF?

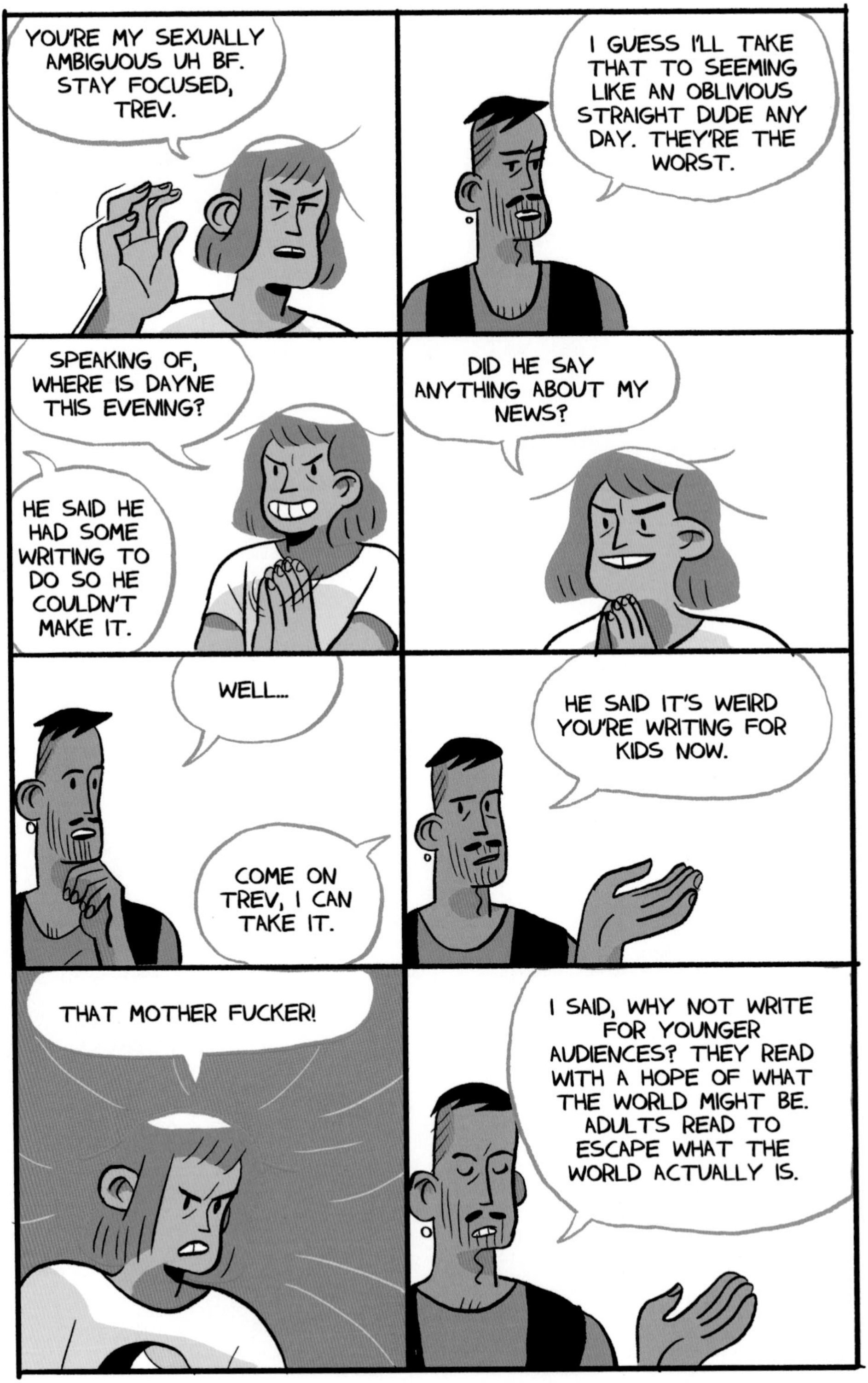
YOU'RE MY SEXUALLY AMBIGUOUS UH BF. STAY FOCUSED, TREV.
I GUESS I'LL TAKE THAT TO SEEMING LIKE AN OBLIVIOUS STRAIGHT DUDE ANY DAY. THEY'RE THE WORST.
SPEAKING OF, WHERE IS DAYNE THIS EVENING?
HE SAID HE HAD SOME WRITING TO DO SO HE COULDN'T MAKE IT.
DID HE SAY ANYTHING ABOUT MY NEWS?
WELL...
COME ON TREV, I CAN TAKE IT.
HE SAID IT'S WEIRD YOU'RE WRITING FOR KIDS NOW.
THAT MOTHER FUCKER!
I SAID, WHY NOT WRITE FOR YOUNGER AUDIENCES? THEY READ WITH A HOPE OF WHAT THE WORLD MIGHT BE. ADULTS READ TO ESCAPE WHAT THE WORLD ACTUALLY IS.

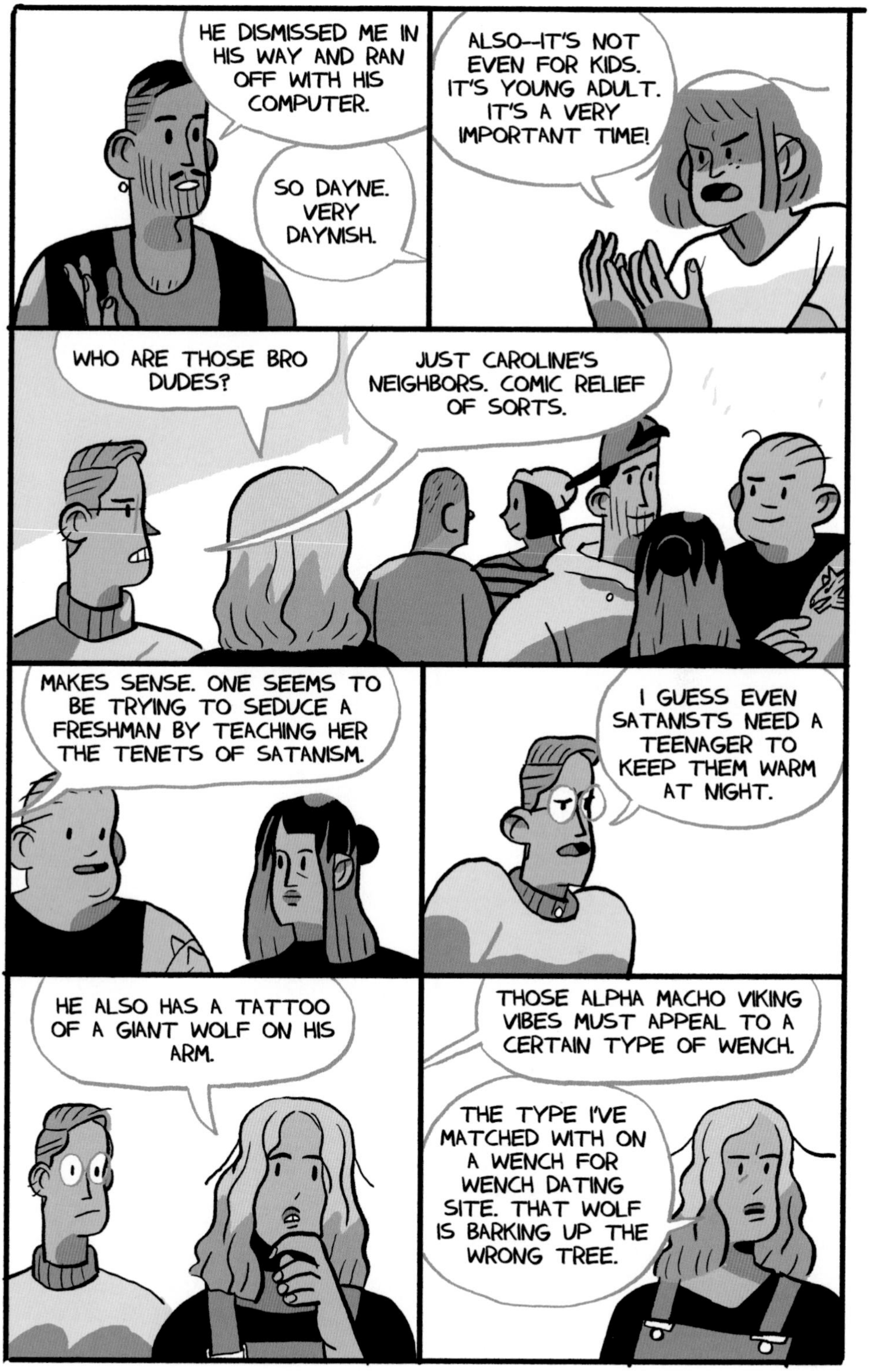
HE DISMISSED ME IN HIS WAY AND RAN OFF WITH HIS COMPUTER.
SO DAYNE. VERY DAYNISH.
ALSO--IT'S NOT EVEN FOR KIDS. IT'S YOUNG ADULT. IT'S A VERY IMPORTANT TIME!
WHO ARE THOSE BRO DUDES?
JUST CAROLINE'S NEIGHBORS. COMIC RELIEF OF SORTS.
MAKES SENSE. ONE SEEMS TO BE TRYING TO SEDUCE A FRESHMAN BY TEACHING HER THE TENETS OF SATANISM.
I GUESS EVEN SATANISTS NEED A TEENAGER TO KEEP THEM WARM AT NIGHT.
HE ALSO HAS A TATTOO OF A GIANT WOLF ON HIS ARM.
THOSE ALPHA MACHO VIKING VIBES MUST APPEAL TO A CERTAIN TYPE OF WENCH.
THE TYPE I'VE MATCHED WITH ON A WENCH FOR WENCH DATING SITE. THAT WOLF IS BARKING UP THE WRONG TREE.

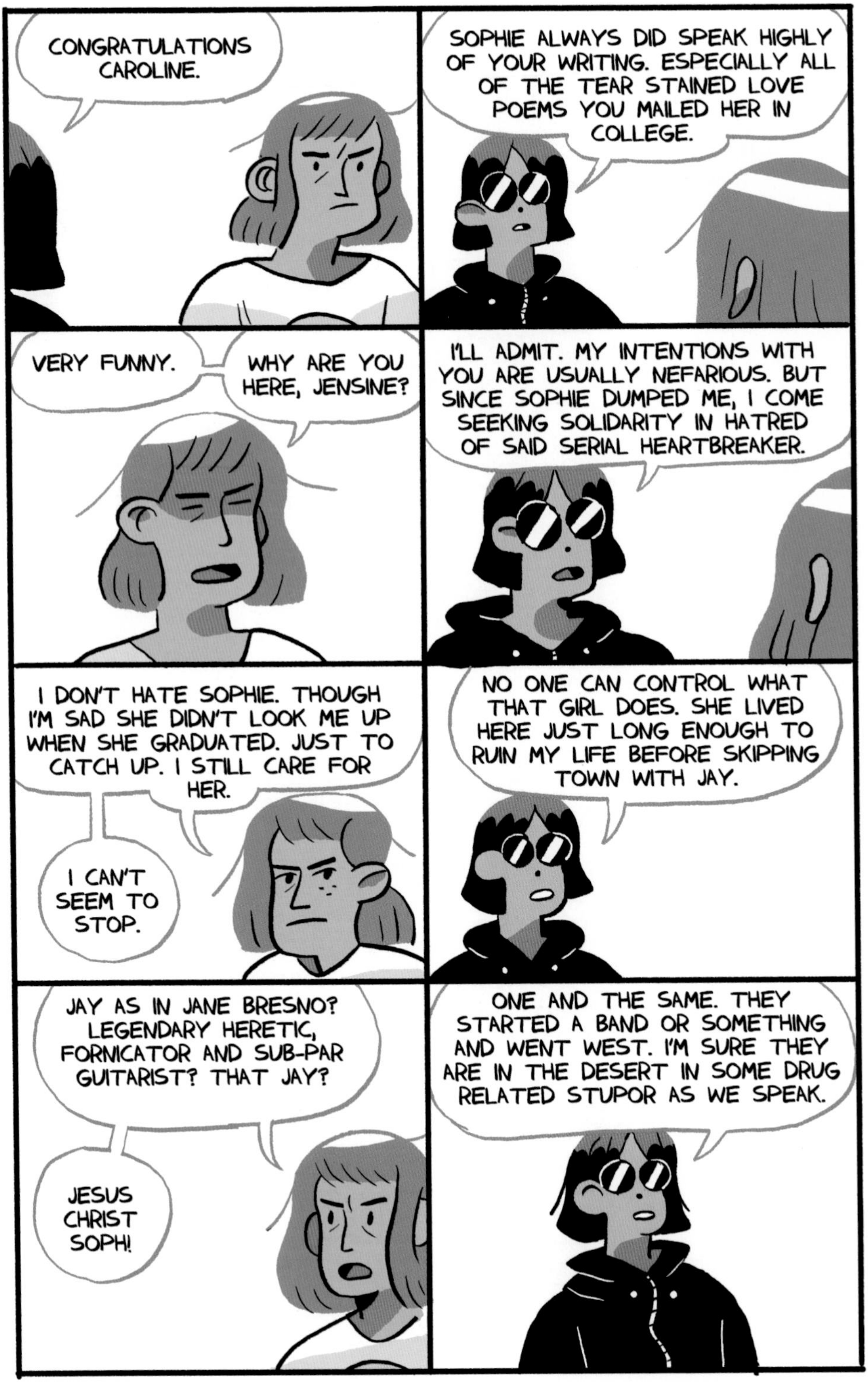
CONGRATULATIONS CAROLINE.
SOPHIE ALWAYS DID SPEAK HIGHLY OF YOUR WRITING. ESPECIALLY ALL OF THE TEAR STAINED LOVE POEMS YOU MAILED HER IN COLLEGE.
VERY FUNNY.
WHY ARE YOU HERE, JENSINE?
I'LL ADMIT. MY INTENTIONS WITH YOU ARE USUALLY NEFARIOUS. BUT SINCE SOPHIE DUMPED ME, I COME SEEKING SOLIDARITY IN HATRED OF SAID SERIAL HEARTBREAKER.
I DON'T HATE SOPHIE. THOUGH I'M SAD SHE DIDN'T LOOK ME UP WHEN SHE GRADUATED. JUST TO CATCH UP. I STILL CARE FOR HER.
I CAN'T SEEM TO STOP.
NO ONE CAN CONTROL WHAT THAT GIRL DOES. SHE LIVED HERE JUST LONG ENOUGH TO RUIN MY LIFE BEFORE SKIPPING TOWN WITH JAY.
JAY AS IN JANE BRESNO? LEGENDARY HERETIC, FORNICATOR AND SUB-PAR GUITARIST? THAT JAY?
JESUS CHRIST SOPH!
ONE AND THE SAME. THEY STARTED A BAND OR SOMETHING AND WENT WEST. I'M SURE THEY ARE IN THE DESERT IN SOME DRUG RELATED STUPOR AS WE SPEAK.

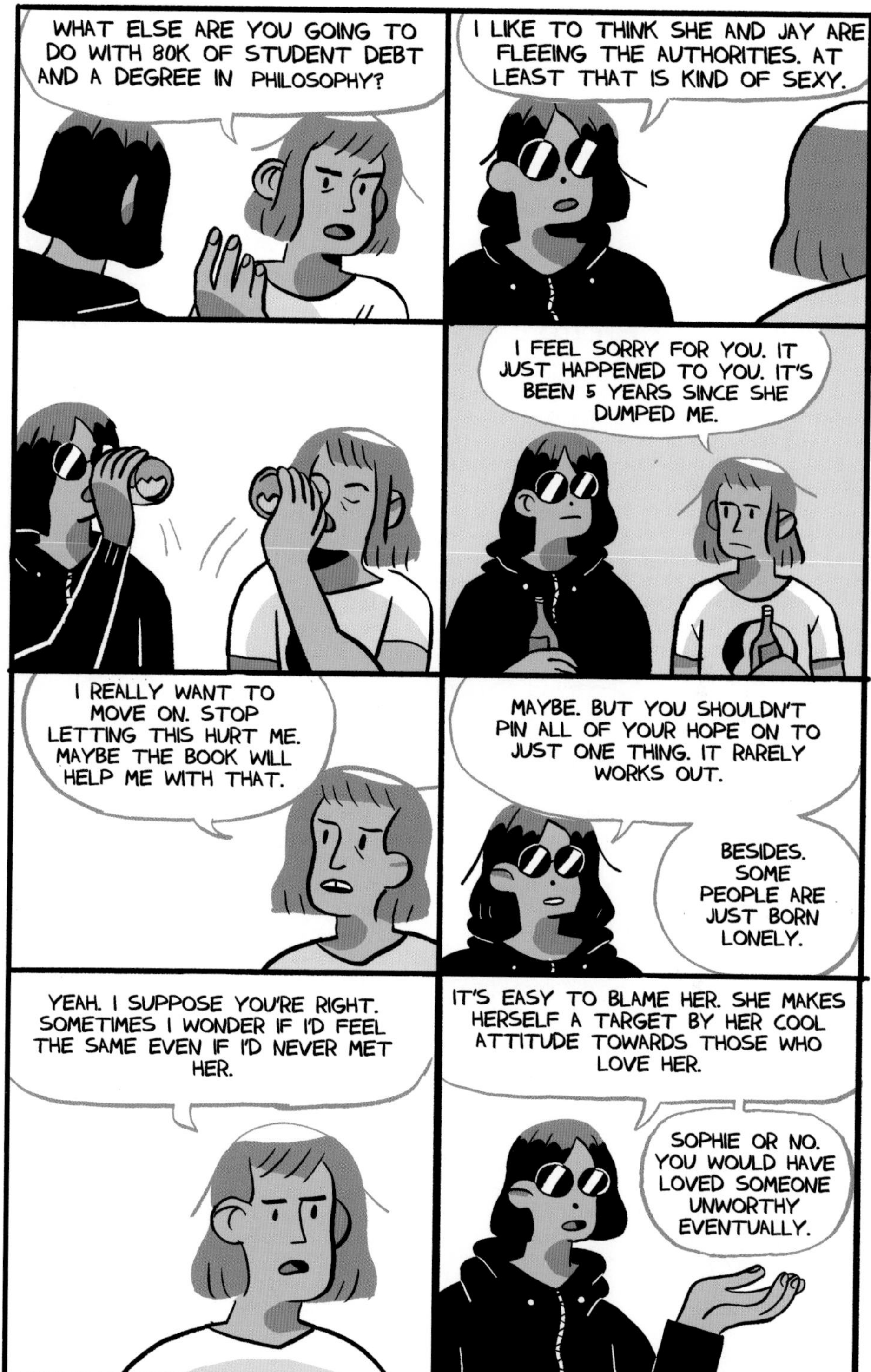
WHAT ELSE ARE YOU GOING TO DO WITH 80K OF STUDENT DEBT AND A DEGREE IN PHILOSOPHY?
I LIKE TO THINK SHE AND JAY ARE FLEEING THE AUTHORITIES. AT LEAST THAT IS KIND OF SEXY.
I FEEL SORRY FOR YOU. IT JUST HAPPENED TO YOU. IT'S BEEN 5 YEARS SINCE SHE DUMPED ME.
I REALLY WANT TO MOVE ON. STOP LETTING THIS HURT ME. MAYBE THE BOOK WILL HELP ME WITH THAT.
MAYBE. BUT YOU SHOULDN'T PIN ALL OF YOUR HOPE ON TO JUST ONE THING. IT RARELY WORKS OUT.
BESIDES. SOME PEOPLE ARE JUST BORN LONELY.
YEAH. I SUPPOSE YOU'RE RIGHT. SOMETIMES I WONDER IF I'D FEEL THE SAME EVEN IF I'D NEVER MET HER.
IT'S EASY TO BLAME HER. SHE MAKES HERSELF A TARGET BY HER COOL ATTITUDE TOWARDS THOSE WHO LOVE HER.
SOPHIE OR NO. YOU WOULD HAVE LOVED SOMEONE UNWORTHY EVENTUALLY.

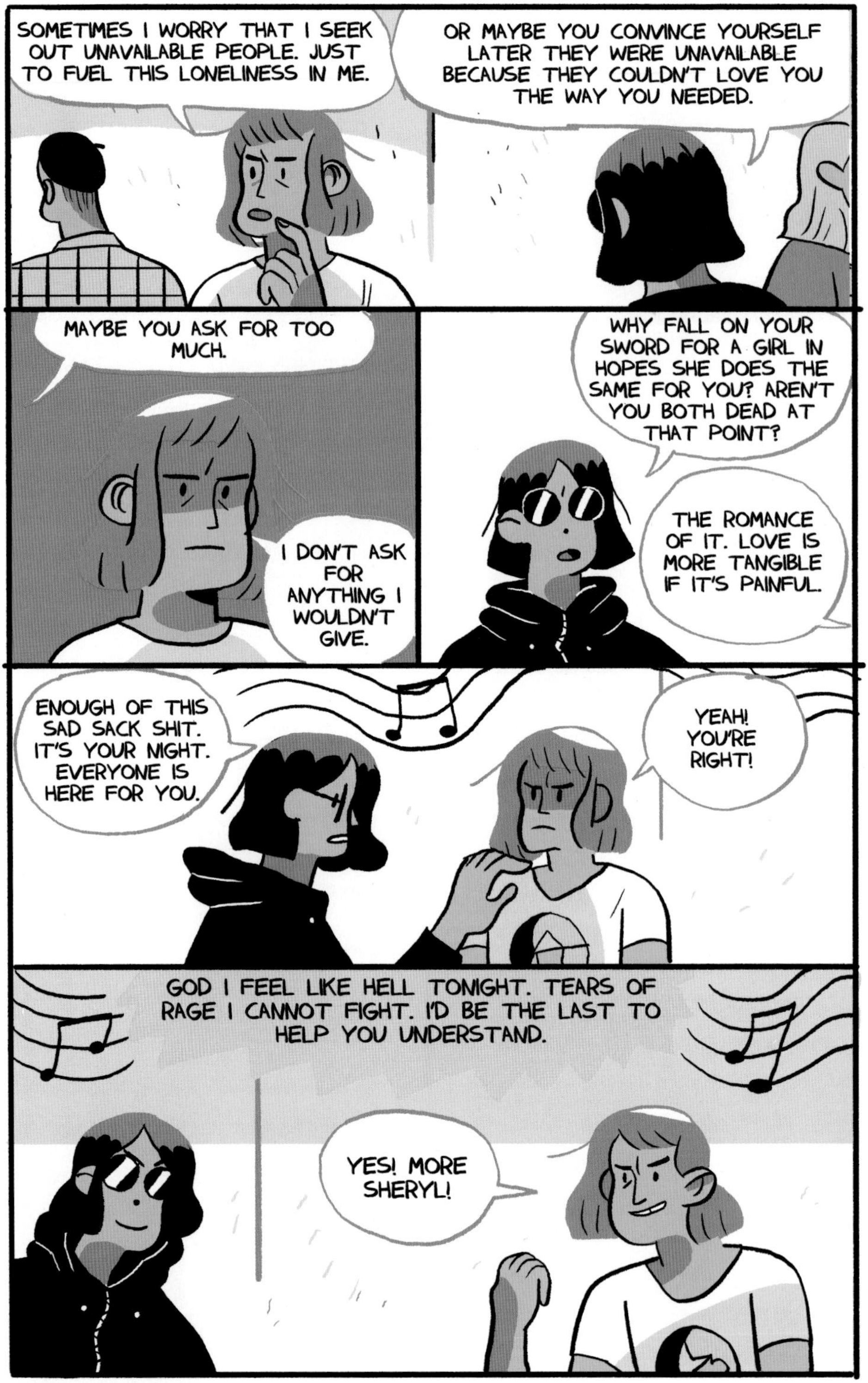
SOMETIMES I WORRY THAT I SEEK OUT UNAVAILABLE PEOPLE. JUST TO FUEL THIS LONELINESS IN ME.
OR MAYBE YOU CONVINCE YOURSELF LATER THEY WERE UNAVAILABLE BECAUSE THEY COULDN'T LOVE YOU THE WAY YOU NEEDED.
MAYBE YOU ASK FOR TOO MUCH.
I DON'T ASK FOR ANYTHING I WOULDN'T GIVE.
WHY FALL ON YOUR SWORD FOR A GIRL IN HOPES SHE DOES THE SAME FOR YOU? AREN'T YOU BOTH DEAD AT THAT POINT?
THE ROMANCE OF IT. LOVE IS MORE TANGIBLE IF IT'S PAINFUL.
ENOUGH OF THIS SAD SACK SHIT. IT'S YOUR NIGHT. EVERYONE IS HERE FOR YOU.
YEAH! YOU'RE RIGHT!
GOD I FEEL LIKE HELL TONIGHT. TEARS OF RAGE I CANNOT FIGHT. I'D BE THE LAST TO HELP YOU UNDERSTAND.
YES! MORE SHERYL!

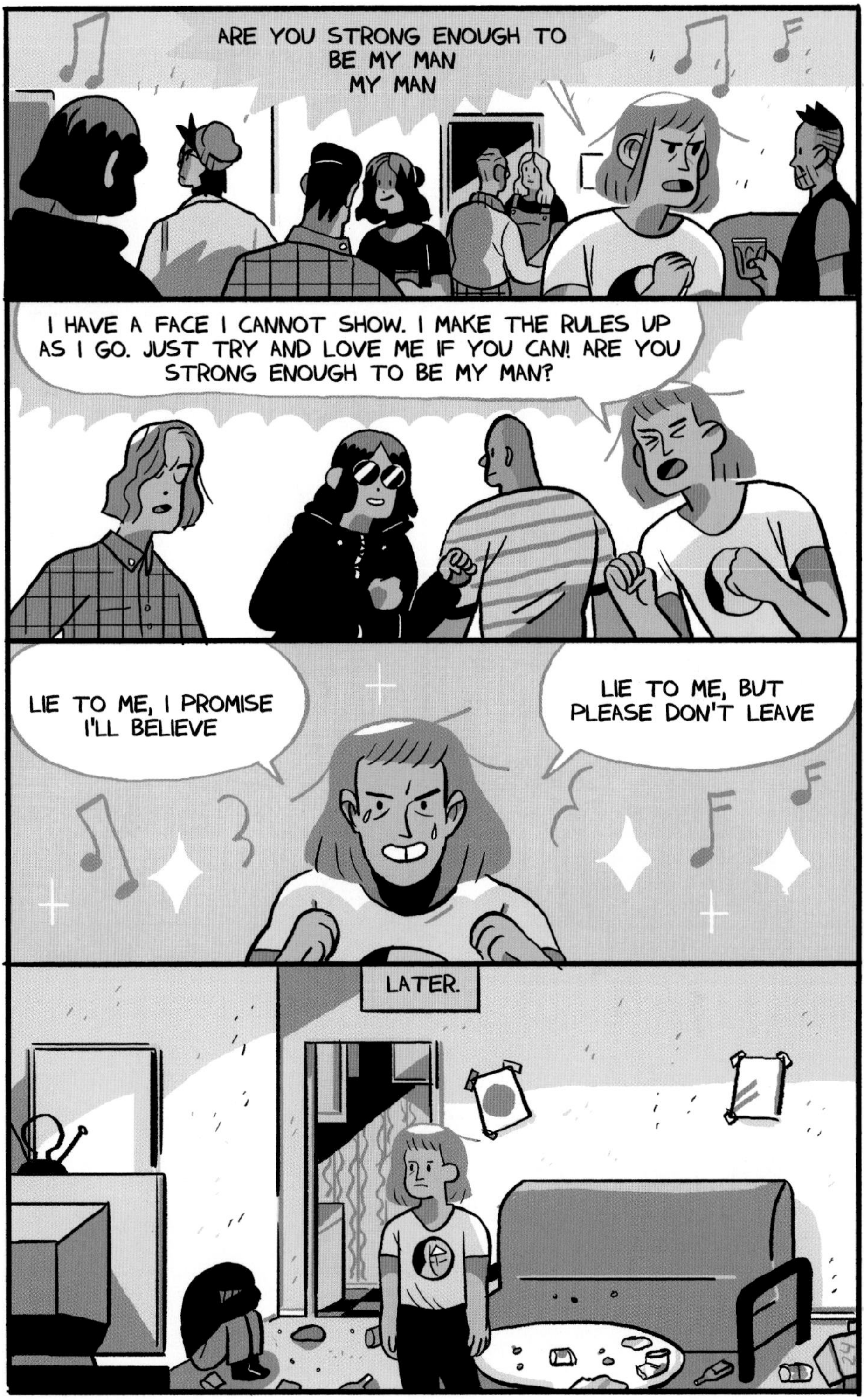
ARE YOU STRONG ENOUGH TO BE MY MAN MY MAN
I HAVE A FACE I CANNOT SHOW. I MAKE THE RULES UP AS I GO. JUST TRY AND LOVE ME IF YOU CAN! ARE YOU STRONG ENOUGH TO BE MY MAN?
LIE TO ME, I PROMISE I'LL BELIEVE
LIE TO ME, BUT PLEASE DON'T LEAVE
LATER.

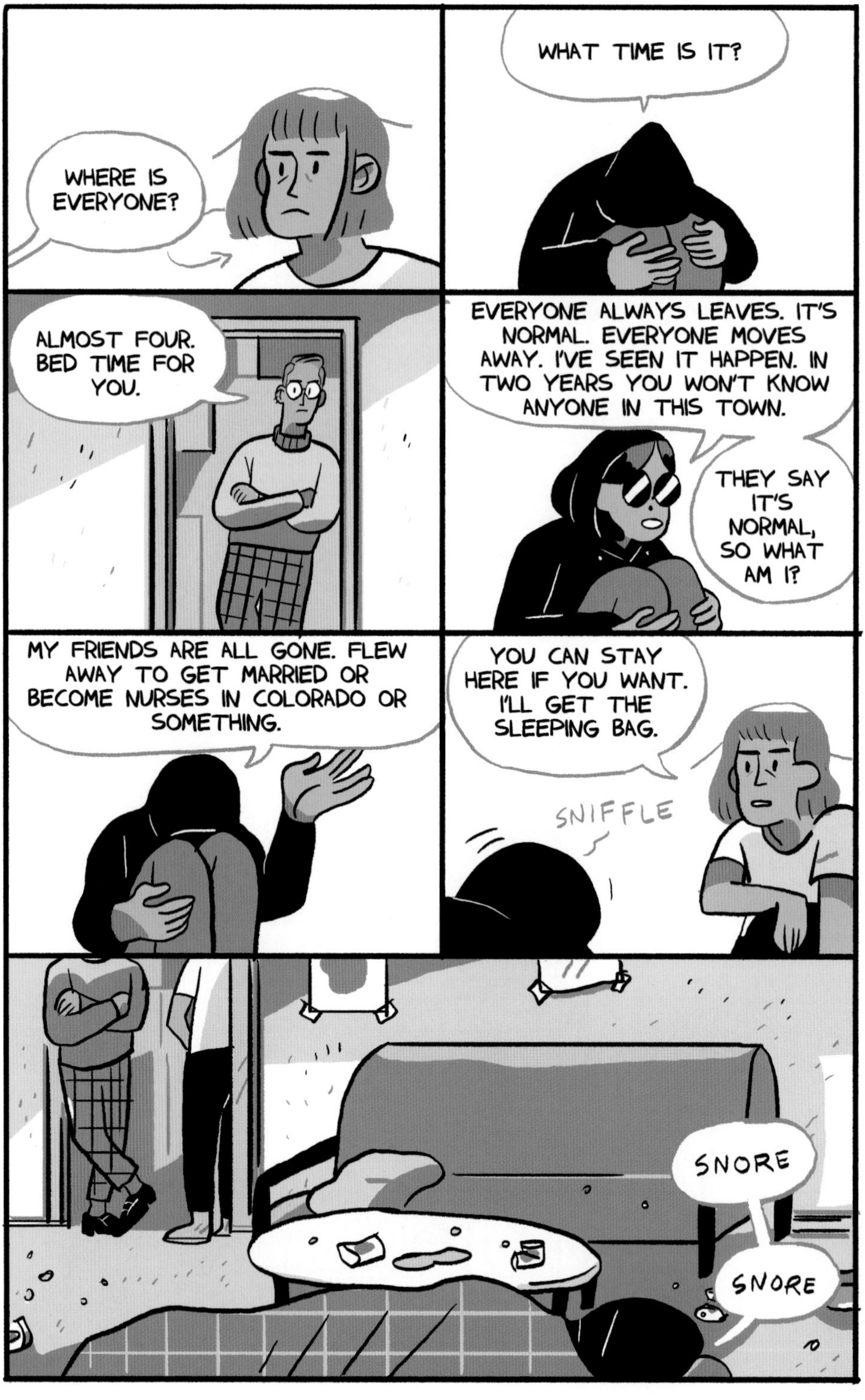
WHERE IS EVERYONE?
WHAT TIME IS IT?
ALMOST FOUR. BED TIME FOR YOU.
EVERYONE ALWAYS LEAVES. IT'S NORMAL. EVERYONE MOVES AWAY. I'VE SEEN IT HAPPEN. IN TWO YEARS YOU WON'T KNOW ANYONE IN THIS TOWN.
THEY SAY IT'S NORMAL, SO WHAT AM I?
MY FRIENDS ARE ALL GONE. FLEW AWAY TO GET MARRIED OR BECOME NURSES IN COLORADO OR SOMETHING.
YOU CAN STAY HERE IF YOU WANT. I'LL GET THE SLEEPING BAG.
SNIFFLE
SNORE
SNORE

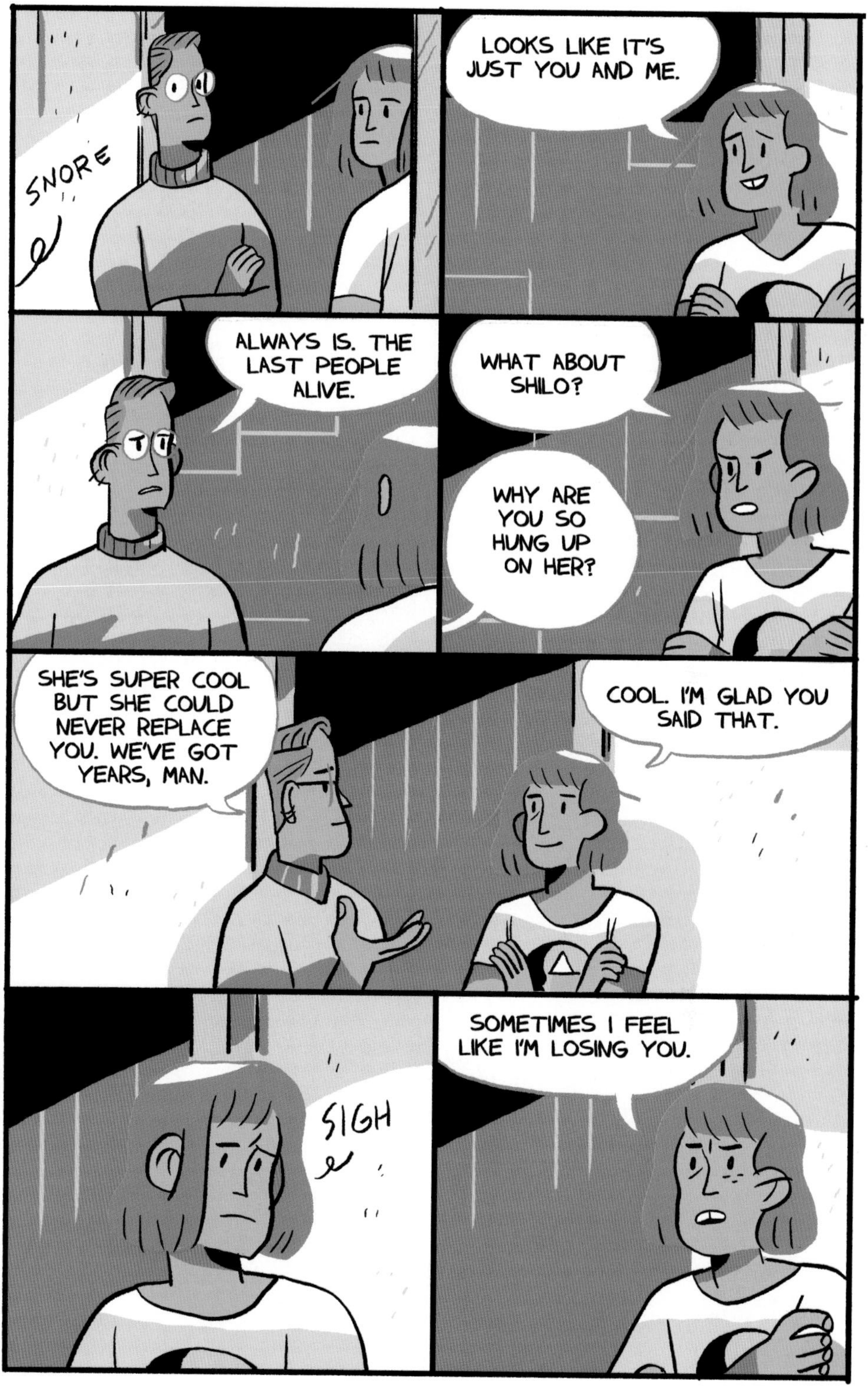
SNORE
LOOKS LIKE IT'S JUST YOU AND ME.
ALWAYS IS. THE LAST PEOPLE ALIVE.
WHAT ABOUT SHILO?
WHY ARE YOU SO HUNG UP ON HER?
SHE'S SUPER COOL BUT SHE COULD NEVER REPLACE YOU. WE'VE GOT YEARS, MAN.
COOL. I'M GLAD YOU SAID THAT.
SIGH
SOMETIMES I FEEL LIKE I'M LOSING YOU.

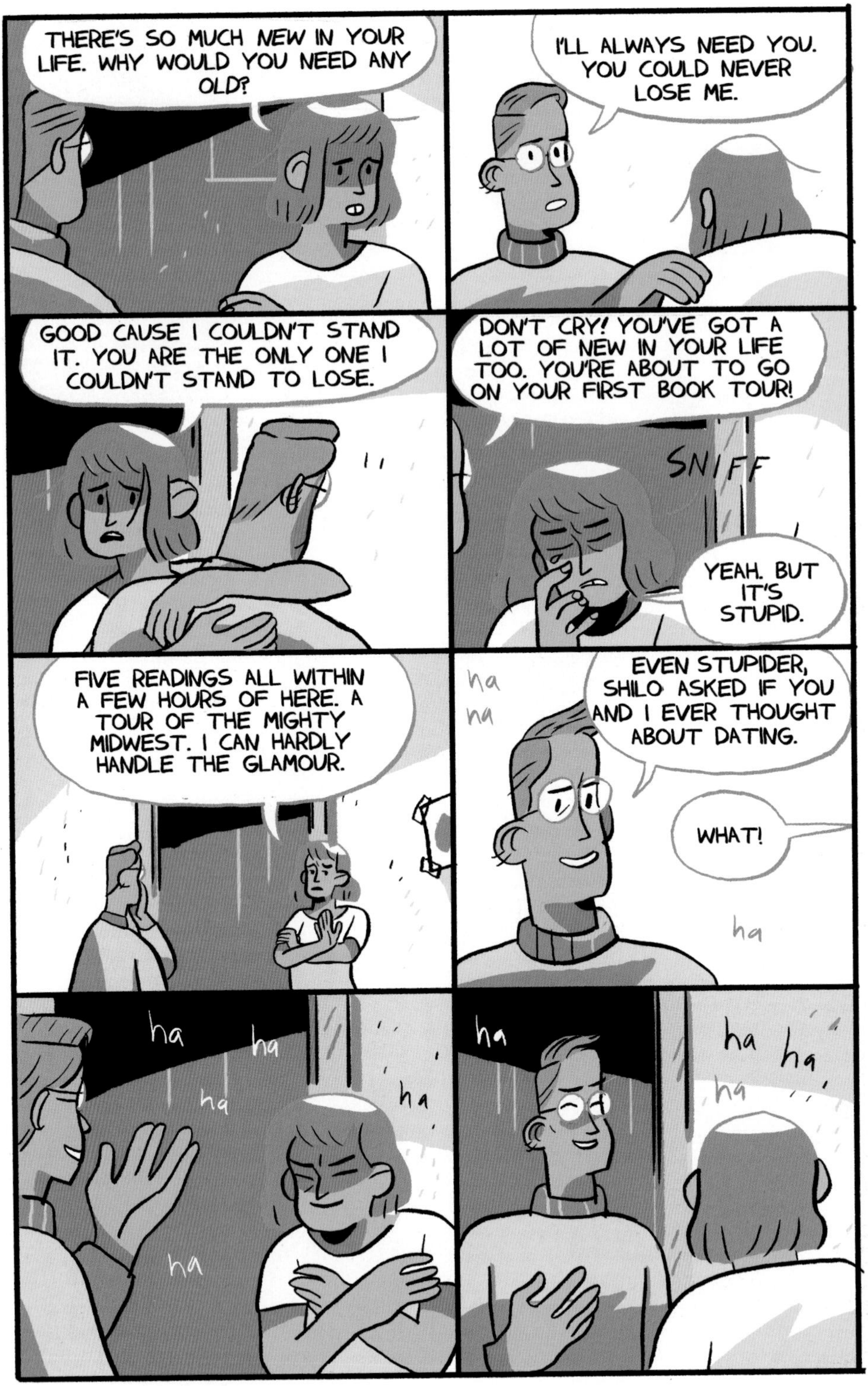
THERE'S SO MUCH NEW IN YOUR LIFE. WHY WOULD YOU NEED ANY OLD?
I'LL ALWAYS NEED YOU. YOU COULD NEVER LOSE ME.
GOOD CAUSE I COULDN'T STAND IT. YOU ARE THE ONLY ONE I COULDN'T STAND TO LOSE.
DON'T CRY! YOU'VE GOT A LOT OF NEW IN YOUR LIFE TOO. YOU'RE ABOUT TO GO ON YOUR FIRST BOOK TOUR!
SNIFF
YEAH. BUT IT'S STUPID.
FIVE READINGS ALL WITHIN A FEW HOURS OF HERE. A TOUR OF THE MIGHTY MIDWEST. I CAN HARDLY HANDLE THE GLAMOUR.
ha
ha
EVEN STUPIDER, SHILO ASKED IF YOU AND I EVER THOUGHT ABOUT DATING.
WHAT!
ha
ha ha ha ha ha
ha ha ha ha

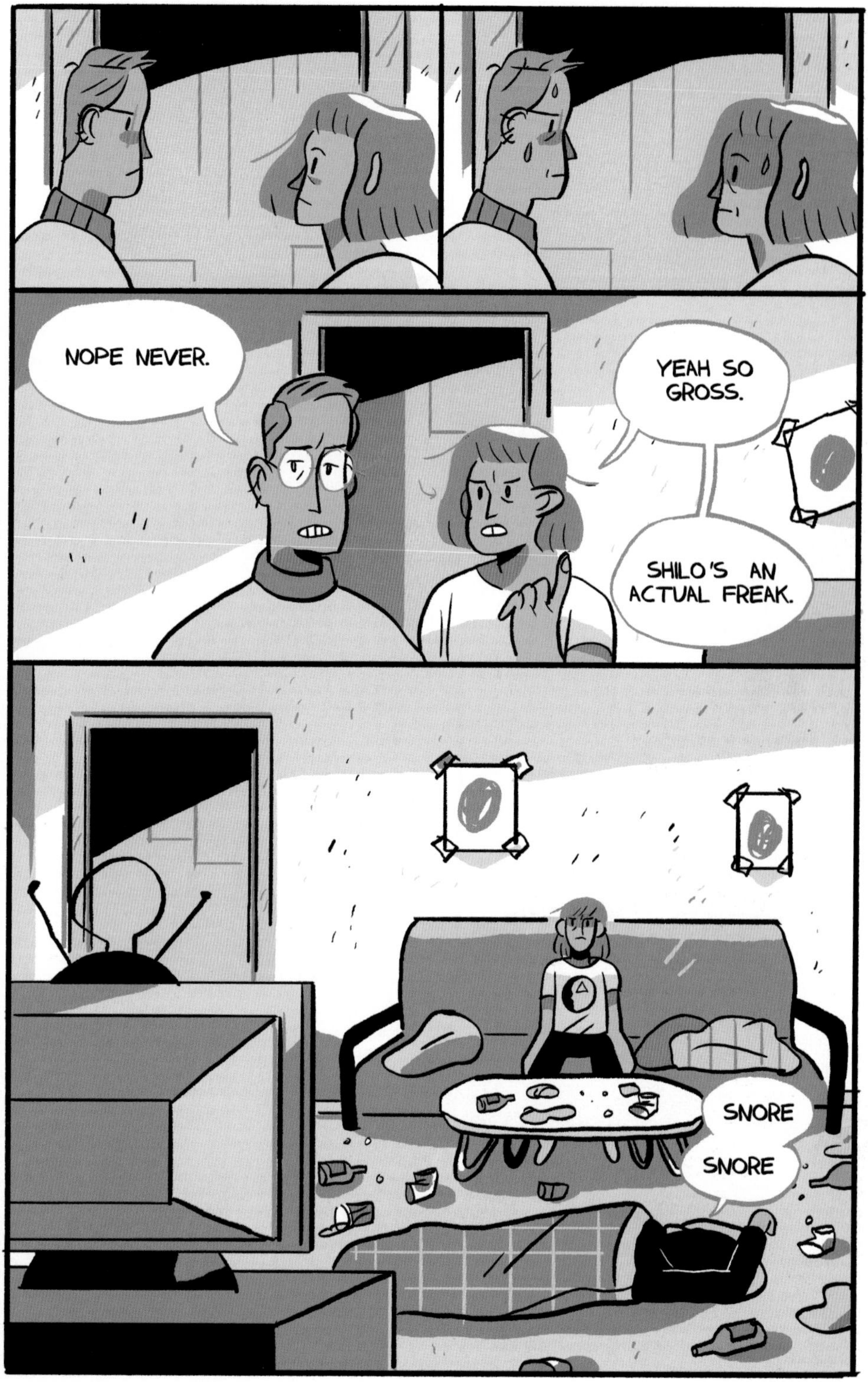
NOPE NEVER.
YEAH SO GROSS.
SHILO'S AN ACTUAL FREAK.
SNORE
SNORE

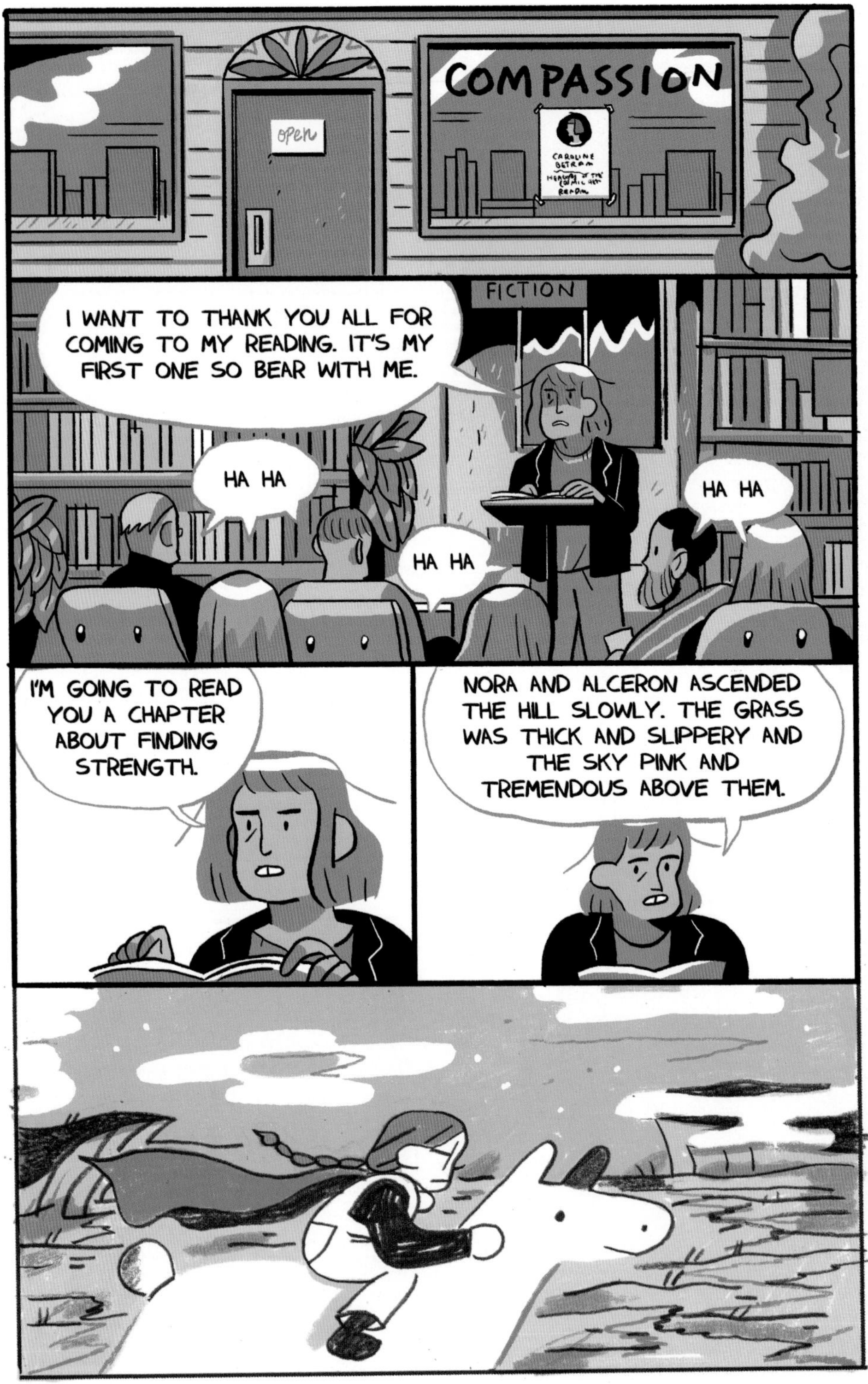
COMPASSION
open
FICTION
I WANT TO THANK YOU ALL FOR COMING TO MY READING. IT'S MY FIRST ONE SO BEAR WITH ME.
HA HA
HA HA
HA HA
I'M GOING TO READ YOU A CHAPTER ABOUT FINDING STRENGTH.
NORA AND ALCERON ASCENDED THE HILL SLOWLY. THE GRASS WAS THICK AND SLIPPERY AND THE SKY PINK AND TREMENDOUS ABOVE THEM.

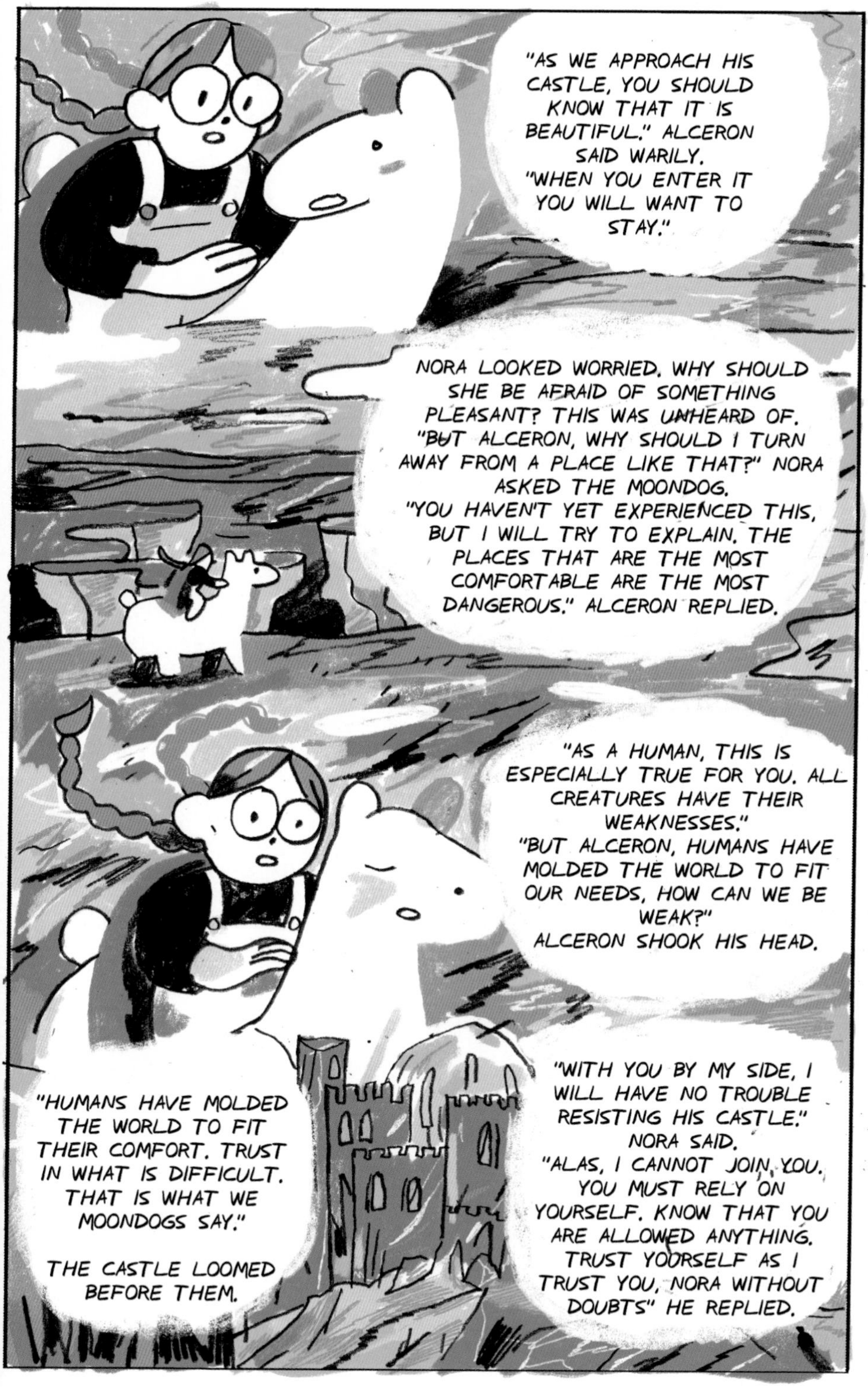
"AS WE APPROACH HIS CASTLE, YOU SHOULD KNOW THAT IT IS BEAUTIFUL." ALCERON SAID WARILY. "WHEN YOU ENTER IT YOU WILL WANT TO STAY."
NORA LOOKED WORRIED. WHY SHOULD SHE BE AFRAID OF SOMETHING PLEASANT? THIS WAS UNHEARD OF. "BUT ALCERON, WHY SHOULD I TURN AWAY FROM A PLACE LIKE THAT?" NORA ASKED THE MOONDOG. "YOU HAVEN'T YET EXPERIENCED THIS, BUT I WILL TRY TO EXPLAIN. THE PLACES THAT ARE THE MOST COMFORTABLE ARE THE MOST DANGEROUS." ALCERON REPLIED.
"AS A HUMAN, THIS IS ESPECIALLY TRUE FOR YOU. ALL CREATURES HAVE THEIR WEAKNESSES." "BUT ALCERON, HUMANS HAVE MOLDED THE WORLD TO FIT OUR NEEDS, HOW CAN WE BE WEAK?" ALCERON SHOOK HIS HEAD.
"HUMANS HAVE MOLDED THE WORLD TO FIT THEIR COMFORT. TRUST IN WHAT IS DIFFICULT. THAT IS WHAT WE MOONDOGS SAY."
THE CASTLE LOOMED BEFORE THEM.
"WITH YOU BY MY SIDE, I WILL HAVE NO TROUBLE RESISTING HIS CASTLE." NORA SAID. "ALAS, I CANNOT JOIN YOU. YOU MUST RELY ON YOURSELF. KNOW THAT YOU ARE ALLOWED ANYTHING. TRUST YOURSELF AS I TRUST YOU, NORA WITHOUT DOUBTS" HE REPLIED.

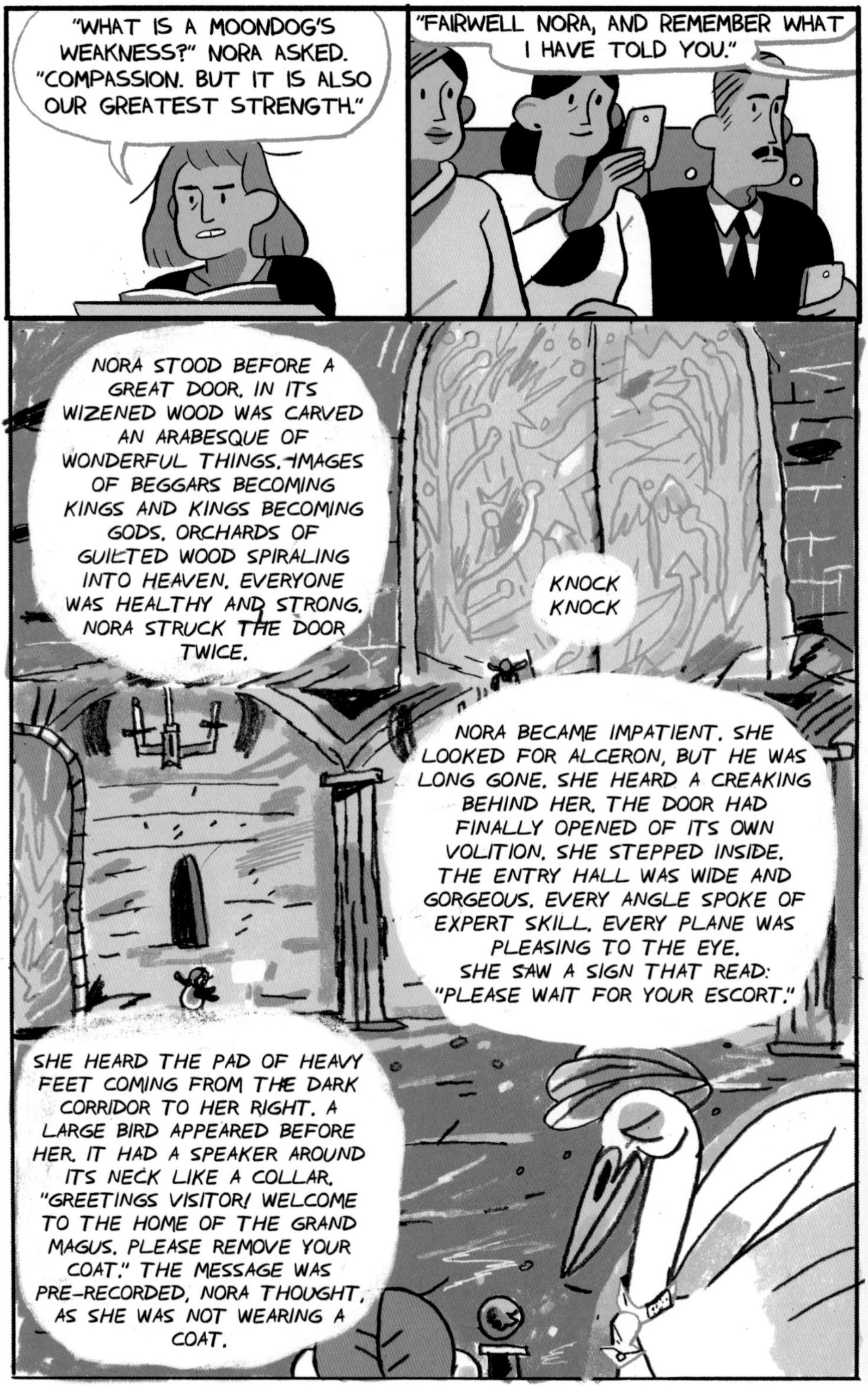
"WHAT IS A MOONDOG'S WEAKNESS?" NORA ASKED. "COMPASSION. BUT IT IS ALSO OUR GREATEST STRENGTH."
"FAIRWELL NORA, AND REMEMBER WHAT I HAVE TOLD YOU."
NORA STOOD BEFORE A GREAT DOOR. IN ITS WIZENED WOOD WAS CARVED AN ARABESQUE OF WONDERFUL THINGS. IMAGES OF BEGGARS BECOMING KINGS AND KINGS BECOMING GODS. ORCHARDS OF GUILTED WOOD SPIRALING INTO HEAVEN. EVERYONE WAS HEALTHY AND STRONG. NORA STRUCK THE DOOR TWICE.
KNOCK KNOCK
NORA BECAME IMPATIENT. SHE LOOKED FOR ALCERON, BUT HE WAS LONG GONE. SHE HEARD A CREAKING BEHIND HER. THE DOOR HAD FINALLY OPENED OF ITS OWN VOLITION. SHE STEPPED INSIDE. THE ENTRY HALL WAS WIDE AND GORGEOUS. EVERY ANGLE SPOKE OF EXPERT SKILL. EVERY PLANE WAS PLEASING TO THE EYE. SHE SAW A SIGN THAT READ: "PLEASE WAIT FOR YOUR ESCORT."
SHE HEARD THE PAD OF HEAVY FEET COMING FROM THE DARK CORRIDOR TO HER RIGHT. A LARGE BIRD APPEARED BEFORE HER. IT HAD A SPEAKER AROUND ITS NECK LIKE A COLLAR. "GREETINGS VISITOR! WELCOME TO THE HOME OF THE GRAND MAGUS. PLEASE REMOVE YOUR COAT." THE MESSAGE WAS PRE-RECORDED, NORA THOUGHT, AS SHE WAS NOT WEARING A COAT.

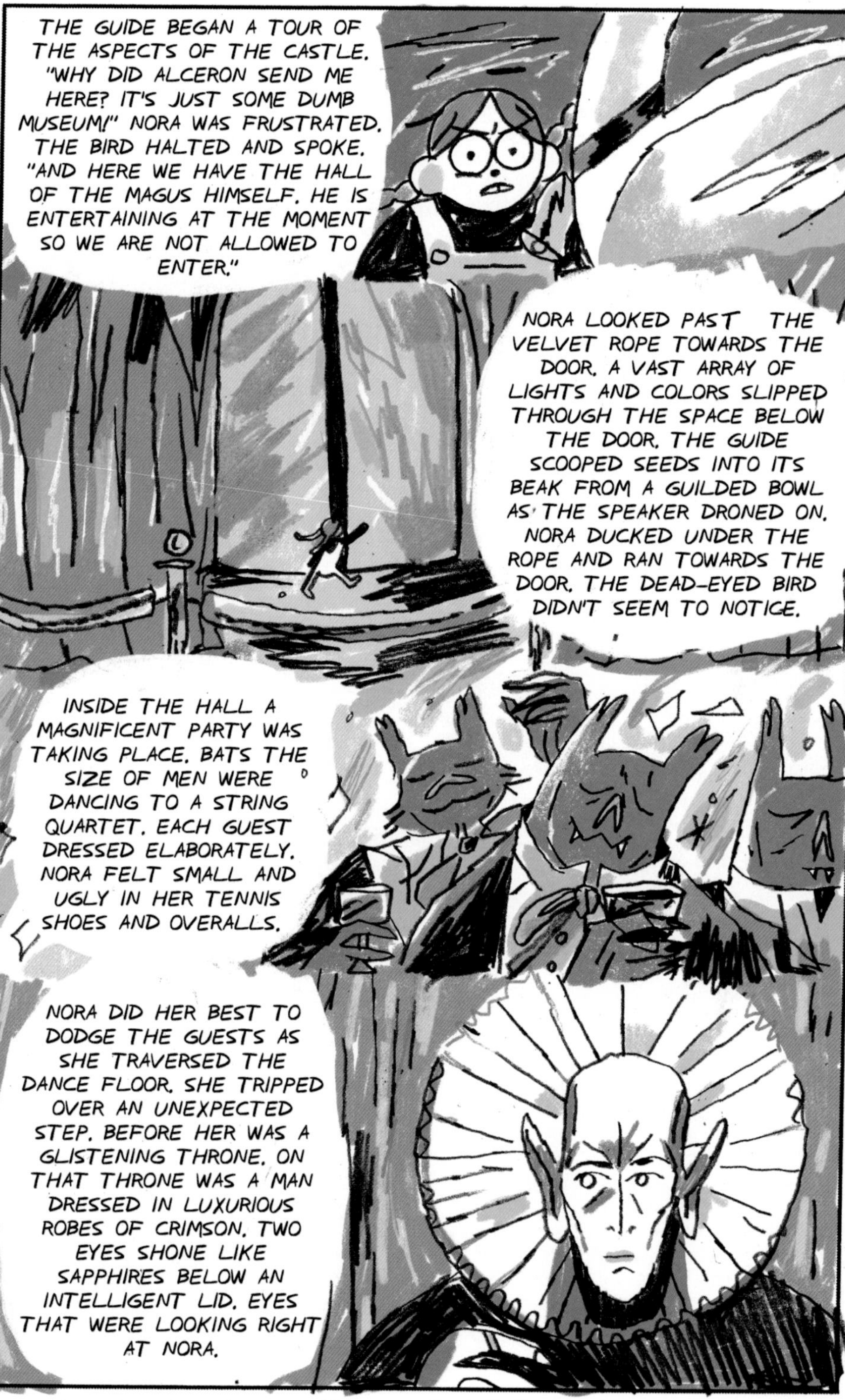
THE GUIDE BEGAN A TOUR OF THE ASPECTS OF THE CASTLE. "WHY DID ALCERON SEND ME HERE? IT'S JUST SOME DUMB MUSEUM!" NORA WAS FRUSTRATED. THE BIRD HALTED AND SPOKE. "AND HERE WE HAVE THE HALL OF THE MAGUS HIMSELF. HE IS ENTERTAINING AT THE MOMENT SO WE ARE NOT ALLOWED TO ENTER."
NORA LOOKED PAST THE VELVET ROPE TOWARDS THE DOOR. A VAST ARRAY OF LIGHTS AND COLORS SLIPPED THROUGH THE SPACE BELOW THE DOOR. THE GUIDE SCOOPED SEEDS INTO ITS BEAK FROM A GUILDED BOWL AS THE SPEAKER DRONED ON. NORA DUCKED UNDER THE ROPE AND RAN TOWARDS THE DOOR. THE DEAD-EYED BIRD DIDN'T SEEM TO NOTICE.
INSIDE THE HALL A MAGNIFICENT PARTY WAS TAKING PLACE. BATS THE SIZE OF MEN WERE DANCING TO A STRING QUARTET. EACH GUEST DRESSED ELABORATELY. NORA FELT SMALL AND UGLY IN HER TENNIS SHOES AND OVERALLS.
NORA DID HER BEST TO DODGE THE GUESTS AS SHE TRAVERSED THE DANCE FLOOR. SHE TRIPPED OVER AN UNEXPECTED STEP. BEFORE HER WAS A GLISTENING THRONE. ON THAT THRONE WAS A MAN DRESSED IN LUXURIOUS ROBES OF CRIMSON. TWO EYES SHONE LIKE SAPPHIRES BELOW AN INTELLIGENT LID. EYES THAT WERE LOOKING RIGHT AT NORA.

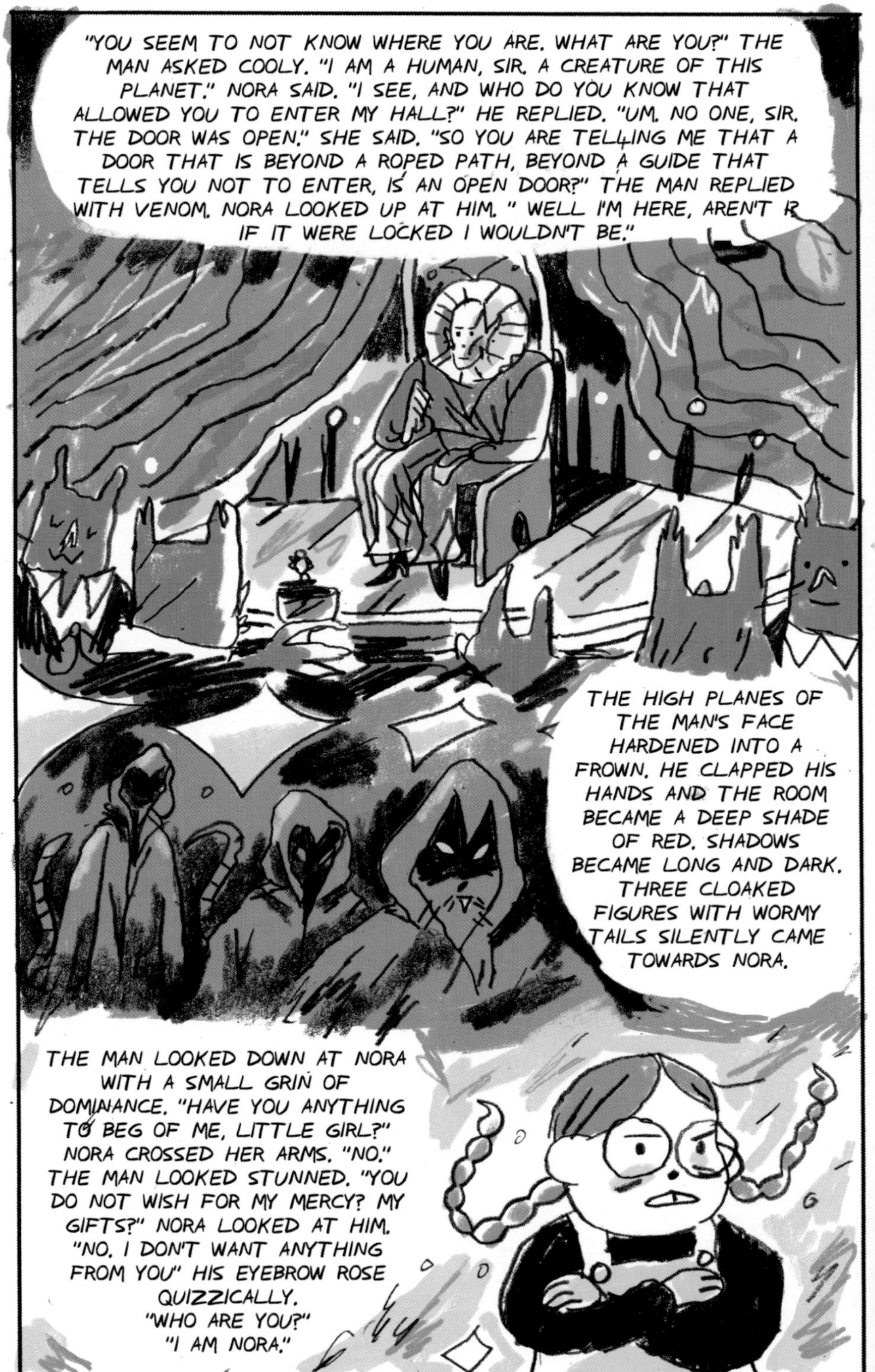
"YOU SEEM TO NOT KNOW WHERE YOU ARE. WHAT ARE YOU?" THE MAN ASKED COOLY. "I AM A HUMAN, SIR. A CREATURE OF THIS PLANET." NORA SAID. "I SEE, AND WHO DO YOU KNOW THAT ALLOWED YOU TO ENTER MY HALL?" HE REPLIED. "UM. NO ONE, SIR. THE DOOR WAS OPEN." SHE SAID. "SO YOU ARE TELLING ME THAT A DOOR THAT IS BEYOND A ROPED PATH, BEYOND A GUIDE THAT TELLS YOU NOT TO ENTER, IS AN OPEN DOOR?" THE MAN REPLIED WITH VENOM. NORA LOOKED UP AT HIM. " WELL I'M HERE, AREN'T I? IF IT WERE LOCKED I WOULDN'T BE."
THE HIGH PLANES OF THE MAN'S FACE HARDENED INTO A FROWN. HE CLAPPED HIS HANDS AND THE ROOM BECAME A DEEP SHADE OF RED. SHADOWS BECAME LONG AND DARK. THREE CLOAKED FIGURES WITH WORMY TAILS SILENTLY CAME TOWARDS NORA.
THE MAN LOOKED DOWN AT NORA WITH A SMALL GRIN OF DOMINANCE. "HAVE YOU ANYTHING TO BEG OF ME, LITTLE GIRL?" NORA CROSSED HER ARMS. "NO." THE MAN LOOKED STUNNED. "YOU DO NOT WISH FOR MY MERCY? MY GIFTS?" NORA LOOKED AT HIM. "NO. I DON'T WANT ANYTHING FROM YOU" HIS EYEBROW ROSE QUIZZICALLY.
"WHO ARE YOU?"
"I AM NORA."

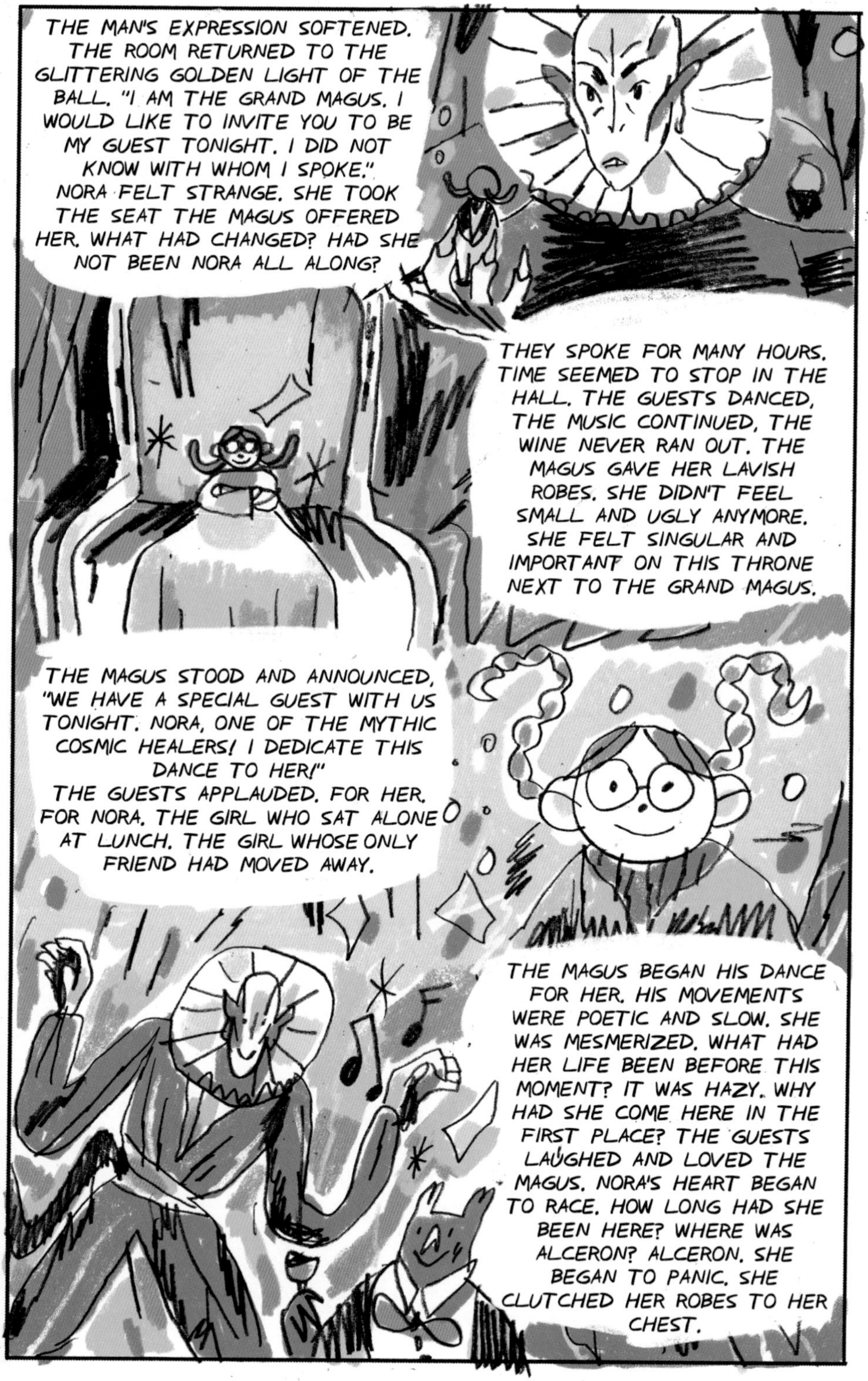
THE MAN'S EXPRESSION SOFTENED. THE ROOM RETURNED TO THE GLITTERING GOLDEN LIGHT OF THE BALL. "I AM THE GRAND MAGUS. I WOULD LIKE TO INVITE YOU TO BE MY GUEST TONIGHT. I DID NOT KNOW WITH WHOM I SPOKE." NORA FELT STRANGE. SHE TOOK THE SEAT THE MAGUS OFFERED HER. WHAT HAD CHANGED? HAD SHE NOT BEEN NORA ALL ALONG?
THEY SPOKE FOR MANY HOURS. TIME SEEMED TO STOP IN THE HALL. THE GUESTS DANCED, THE MUSIC CONTINUED, THE WINE NEVER RAN OUT. THE MAGUS GAVE HER LAVISH ROBES. SHE DIDN'T FEEL SMALL AND UGLY ANYMORE. SHE FELT SINGULAR AND IMPORTANT ON THIS THRONE NEXT TO THE GRAND MAGUS.
THE MAGUS STOOD AND ANNOUNCED, "WE HAVE A SPECIAL GUEST WITH US TONIGHT. NORA, ONE OF THE MYTHIC COSMIC HEALERS! I DEDICATE THIS DANCE TO HER!" THE GUESTS APPLAUDED. FOR HER. FOR NORA. THE GIRL WHO SAT ALONE AT LUNCH. THE GIRL WHOSE ONLY FRIEND HAD MOVED AWAY.
THE MAGUS BEGAN HIS DANCE FOR HER. HIS MOVEMENTS WERE POETIC AND SLOW. SHE WAS MESMERIZED. WHAT HAD HER LIFE BEEN BEFORE THIS MOMENT? IT WAS HAZY. WHY HAD SHE COME HERE IN THE FIRST PLACE? THE GUESTS LAUGHED AND LOVED THE MAGUS. NORA'S HEART BEGAN TO RACE. HOW LONG HAD SHE BEEN HERE? WHERE WAS ALCERON? ALCERON. SHE BEGAN TO PANIC. SHE CLUTCHED HER ROBES TO HER CHEST.

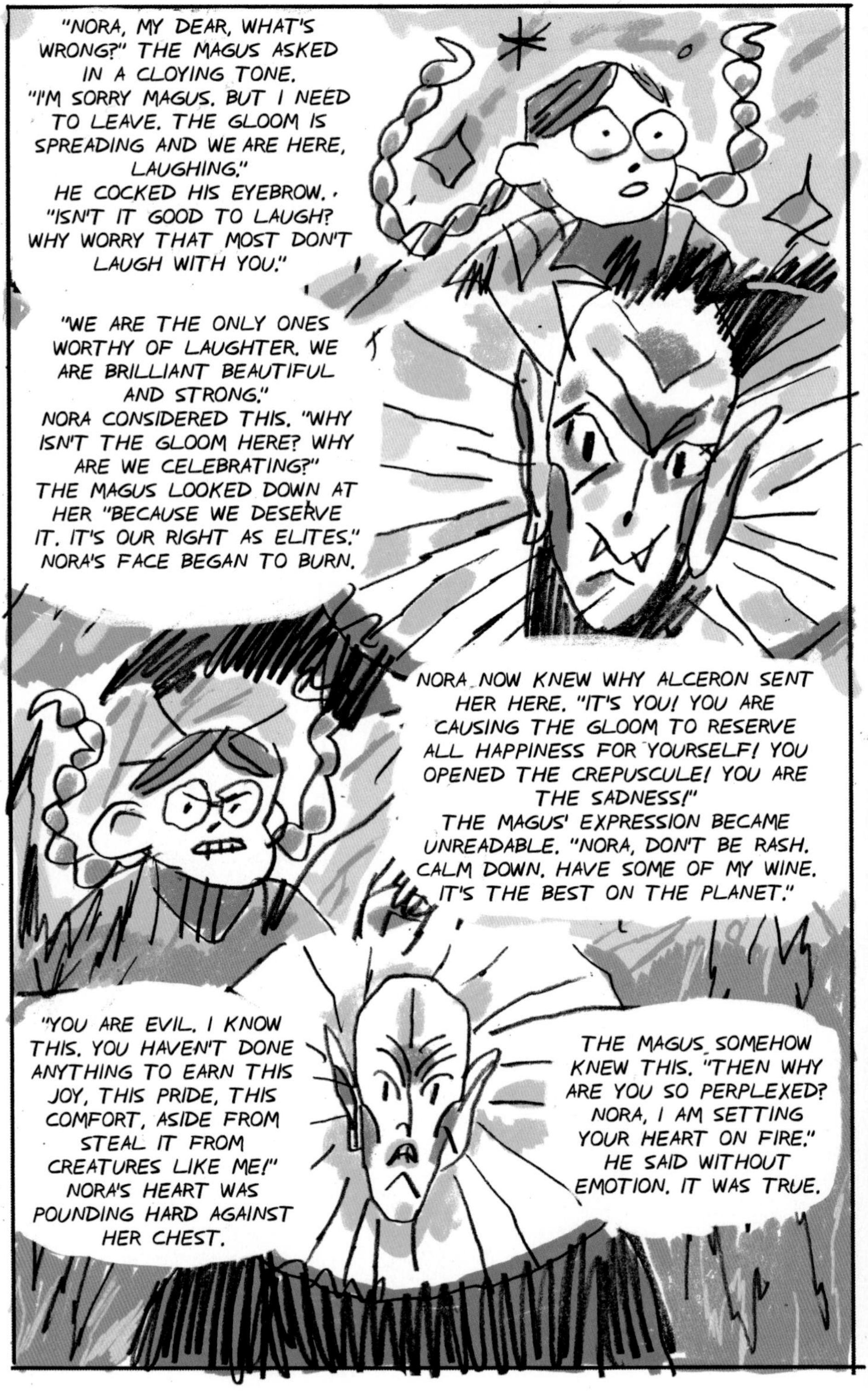
"NORA, MY DEAR, WHAT'S WRONG?" THE MAGUS ASKED IN A CLOYING TONE. "I'M SORRY MAGUS. BUT I NEED TO LEAVE. THE GLOOM IS SPREADING AND WE ARE HERE, LAUGHING." HE COCKED HIS EYEBROW. "ISN'T IT GOOD TO LAUGH? WHY WORRY THAT MOST DON'T LAUGH WITH YOU."
"WE ARE THE ONLY ONES WORTHY OF LAUGHTER. WE ARE BRILLIANT BEAUTIFUL AND STRONG." NORA CONSIDERED THIS. "WHY ISN'T THE GLOOM HERE? WHY ARE WE CELEBRATING?" THE MAGUS LOOKED DOWN AT HER "BECAUSE WE DESERVE IT. IT'S OUR RIGHT AS ELITES." NORA'S FACE BEGAN TO BURN.
NORA NOW KNEW WHY ALCERON SENT HER HERE. "IT'S YOU! YOU ARE CAUSING THE GLOOM TO RESERVE ALL HAPPINESS FOR YOURSELF! YOU OPENED THE CREPUSCULE! YOU ARE THE SADNESS!" THE MAGUS' EXPRESSION BECAME UNREADABLE. "NORA, DON'T BE RASH. CALM DOWN. HAVE SOME OF MY WINE. IT'S THE BEST ON THE PLANET."
"YOU ARE EVIL. I KNOW THIS. YOU HAVEN'T DONE ANYTHING TO EARN THIS JOY, THIS PRIDE, THIS COMFORT, ASIDE FROM STEAL IT FROM CREATURES LIKE ME!" NORA'S HEART WAS POUNDING HARD AGAINST HER CHEST.
THE MAGUS SOMEHOW KNEW THIS. "THEN WHY ARE YOU SO PERPLEXED? NORA, I AM SETTING YOUR HEART ON FIRE." HE SAID WITHOUT EMOTION. IT WAS TRUE.

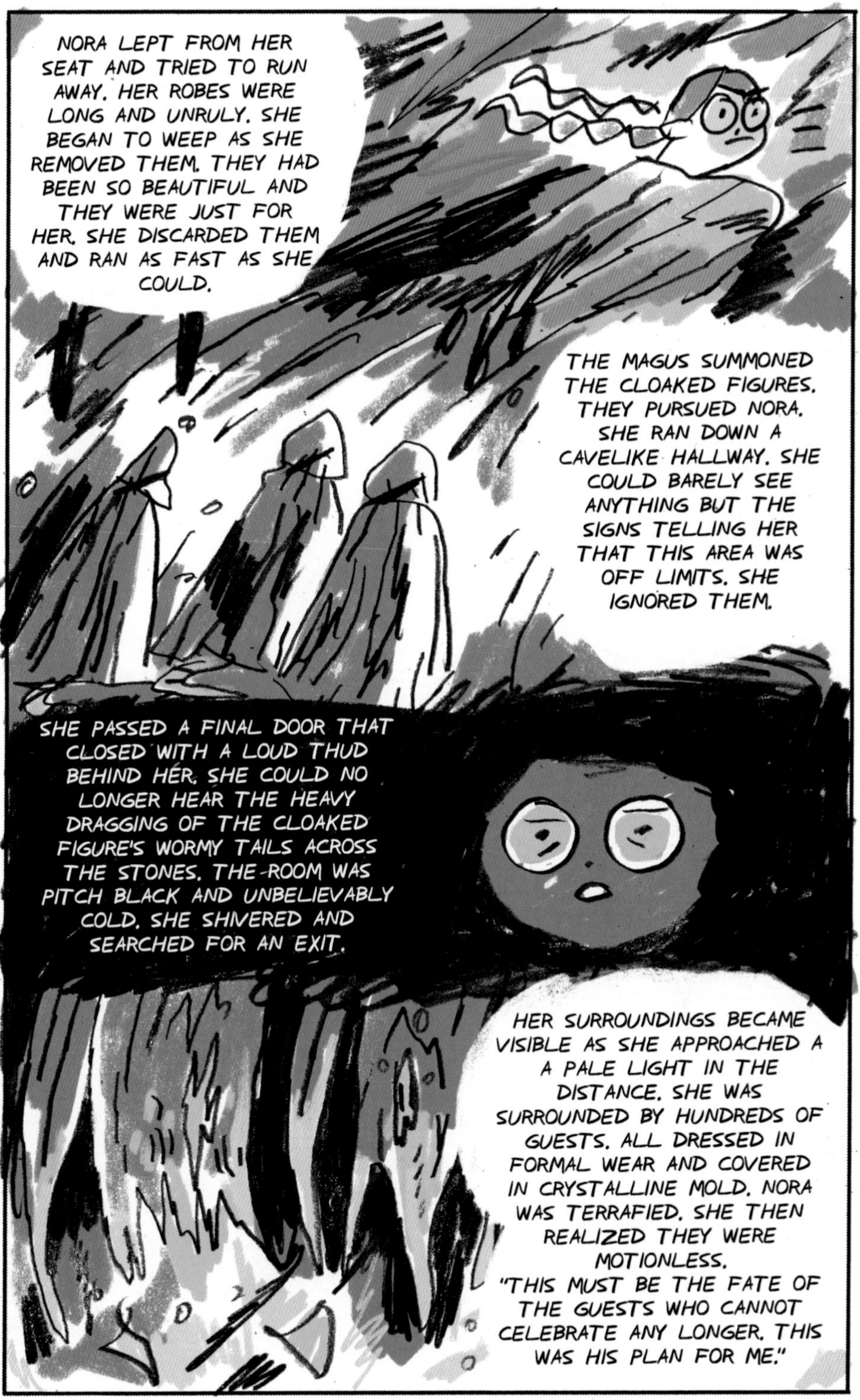
NORA LEPT FROM HER SEAT AND TRIED TO RUN AWAY. HER ROBES WERE LONG AND UNRULY. SHE BEGAN TO WEEP AS SHE REMOVED THEM. THEY HAD BEEN SO BEAUTIFUL AND THEY WERE JUST FOR HER. SHE DISCARDED THEM AND RAN AS FAST AS SHE COULD.
THE MAGUS SUMMONED THE CLOAKED FIGURES. THEY PURSUED NORA. SHE RAN DOWN A CAVELIKE HALLWAY. SHE COULD BARELY SEE ANYTHING BUT THE SIGNS TELLING HER THAT THIS AREA WAS OFF LIMITS. SHE IGNORED THEM.
SHE PASSED A FINAL DOOR THAT CLOSED WITH A LOUD THUD BEHIND HER. SHE COULD NO LONGER HEAR THE HEAVY DRAGGING OF THE CLOAKED FIGURE'S WORMY TAILS ACROSS THE STONES. THE ROOM WAS PITCH BLACK AND UNBELIEVABLY COLD. SHE SHIVERED AND SEARCHED FOR AN EXIT.
HER SURROUNDINGS BECAME VISIBLE AS SHE APPROACHED A A PALE LIGHT IN THE DISTANCE. SHE WAS SURROUNDED BY HUNDREDS OF GUESTS. ALL DRESSED IN FORMAL WEAR AND COVERED IN CRYSTALLINE MOLD. NORA WAS TERRAFIED. SHE THEN REALIZED THEY WERE MOTIONLESS.
"THIS MUST BE THE FATE OF THE GUESTS WHO CANNOT CELEBRATE ANY LONGER. THIS WAS HIS PLAN FOR ME."

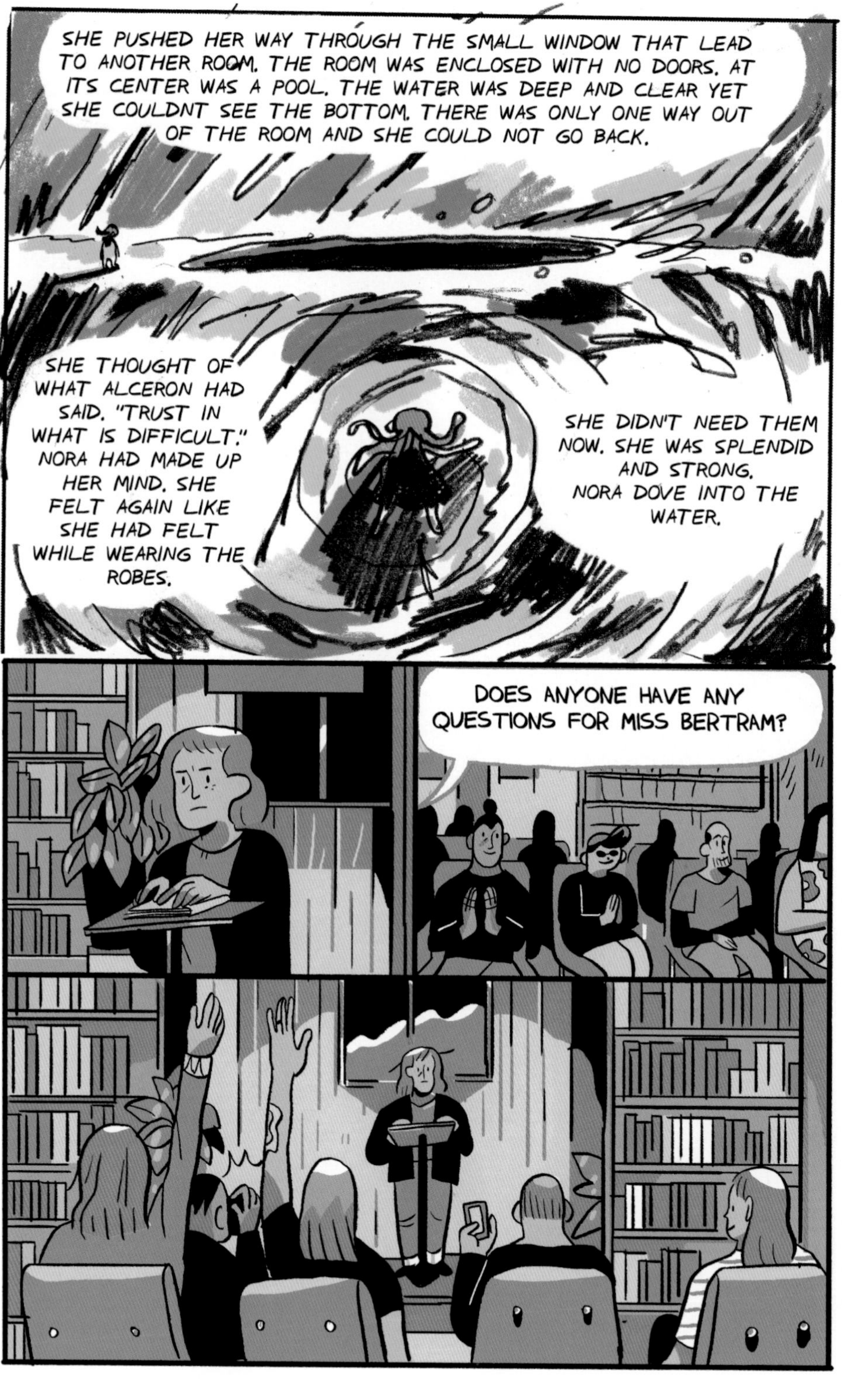
SHE PUSHED HER WAY THROUGH THE SMALL WINDOW THAT LEAD TO ANOTHER ROOM. THE ROOM WAS ENCLOSED WITH NO DOORS. AT ITS CENTER WAS A POOL. THE WATER WAS DEEP AND CLEAR YET SHE COULDNT SEE THE BOTTOM. THERE WAS ONLY ONE WAY OUT OF THE ROOM AND SHE COULD NOT GO BACK.
SHE THOUGHT OF WHAT ALCERON HAD SAID. "TRUST IN WHAT IS DIFFICULT." NORA HAD MADE UP HER MIND. SHE FELT AGAIN LIKE SHE HAD FELT WHILE WEARING THE ROBES.
SHE DIDN'T NEED THEM NOW. SHE WAS SPLENDID AND STRONG. NORA DOVE INTO THE WATER.
DOES ANYONE HAVE ANY QUESTIONS FOR MISS BERTRAM?

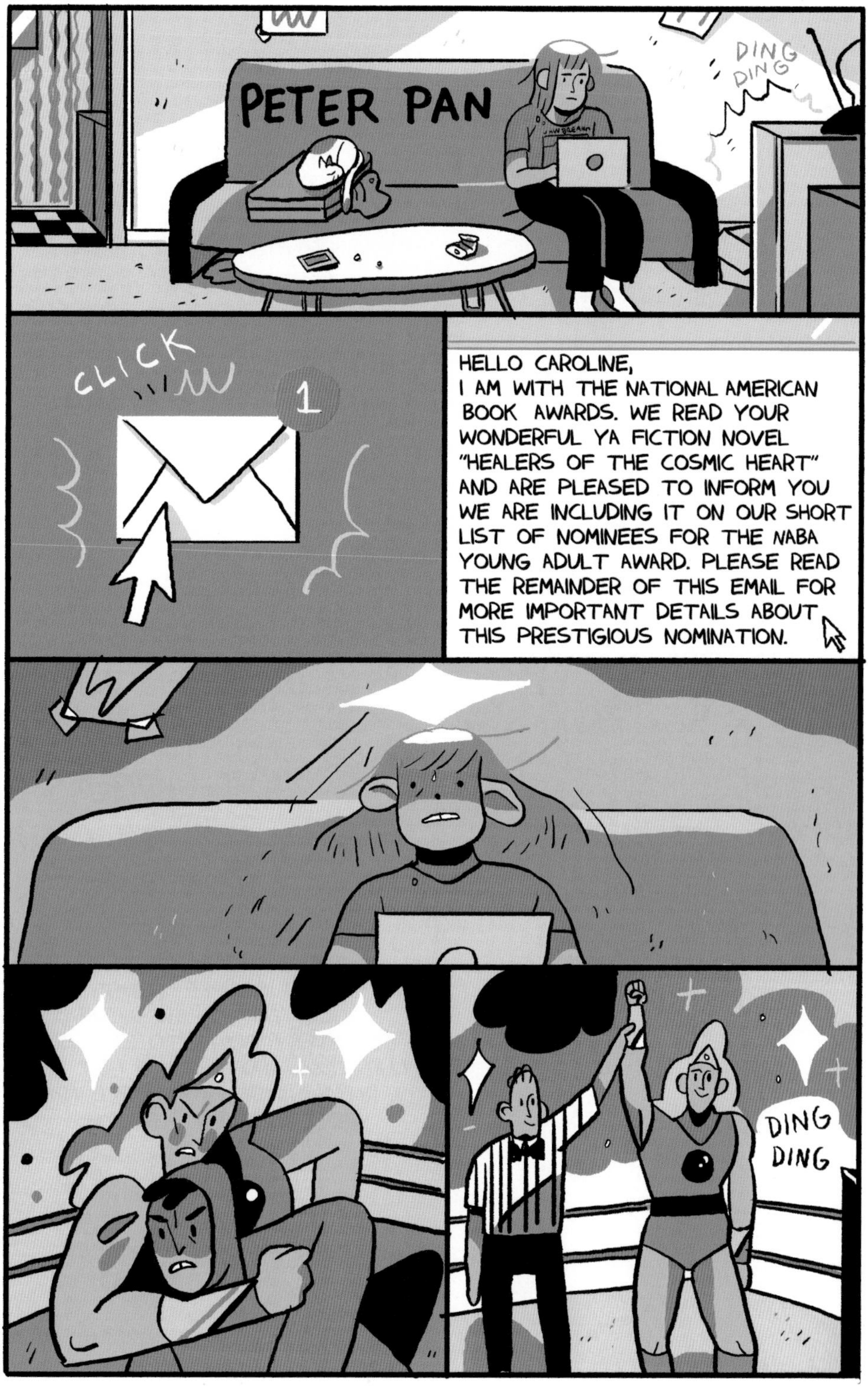
PETER PAN
DING DING
CLICK
1
HELLO CAROLINE,
I AM WITH THE NATIONAL AMERICAN BOOK AWARDS. WE READ YOUR WONDERFUL YA FICTION NOVEL "HEALERS OF THE COSMIC HEART" AND ARE PLEASED TO INFORM YOU WE ARE INCLUDING IT ON OUR SHORT LIST OF NOMINEES FOR THE NABA YOUNG ADULT AWARD. PLEASE READ THE REMAINDER OF THIS EMAIL FOR MORE IMPORTANT DETAILS ABOUT THIS PRESTIGIOUS NOMINATION.
DING DING

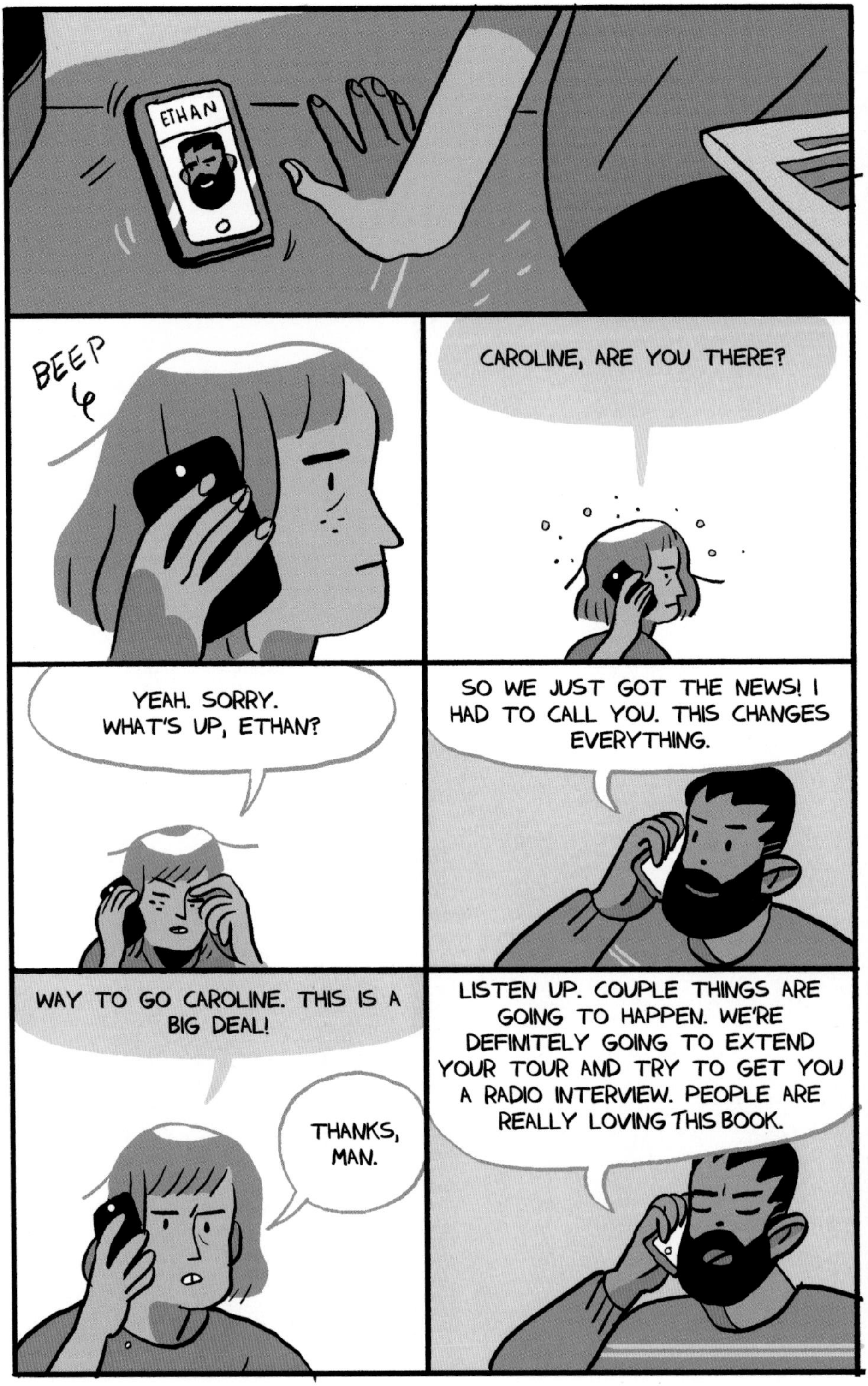
ETHAN
BEEP
CAROLINE, ARE YOU THERE?
YEAH. SORRY. WHAT'S UP, ETHAN?
SO WE JUST GOT THE NEWS! I HAD TO CALL YOU. THIS CHANGES EVERYTHING.
WAY TO GO CAROLINE. THIS IS A BIG DEAL!
THANKS, MAN.
LISTEN UP. COUPLE THINGS ARE GOING TO HAPPEN. WE'RE DEFINITELY GOING TO EXTEND YOUR TOUR AND TRY TO GET YOU A RADIO INTERVIEW. PEOPLE ARE REALLY LOVING THIS BOOK.

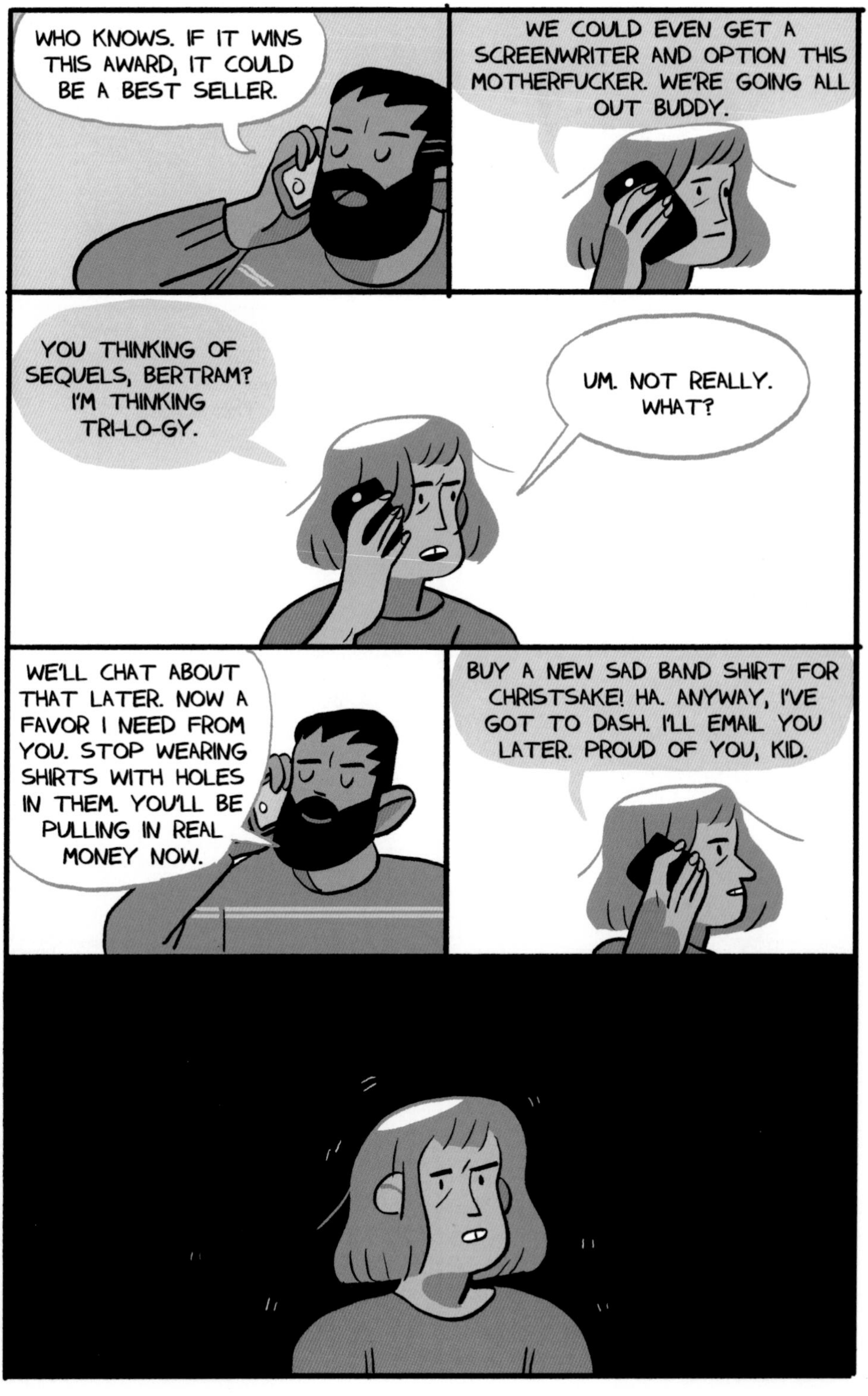
WHO KNOWS. IF IT WINS THIS AWARD, IT COULD BE A BEST SELLER.
WE COULD EVEN GET A SCREENWRITER AND OPTION THIS MOTHERFUCKER. WE'RE GOING ALL OUT BUDDY.
YOU THINKING OF SEQUELS, BERTRAM? I'M THINKING TRI-LO-GY.
UM. NOT REALLY. WHAT?
WE'LL CHAT ABOUT THAT LATER. NOW A FAVOR I NEED FROM YOU. STOP WEARING SHIRTS WITH HOLES IN THEM. YOU'LL BE PULLING IN REAL MONEY NOW.
BUY A NEW SAD BAND SHIRT FOR CHRISTSAKE! HA. ANYWAY, I'VE GOT TO DASH. I'LL EMAIL YOU LATER. PROUD OF YOU, KID.

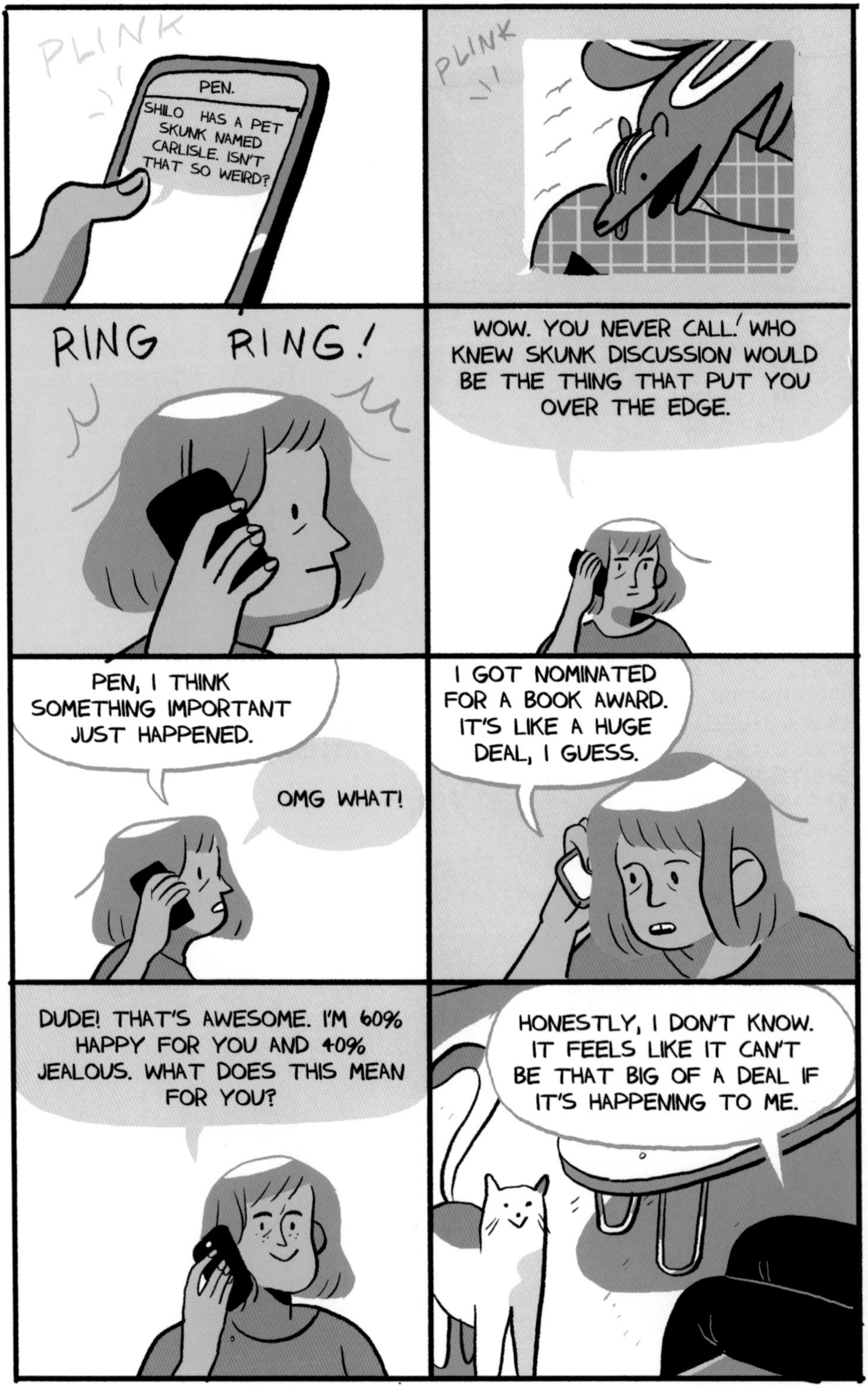
PLINK
PEN.
SHILO HAS A PET SKUNK NAMED CARLISLE. ISN'T THAT SO WEIRD?
PLINK
RING RING!
WOW. YOU NEVER CALL! WHO KNEW SKUNK DISCUSSION WOULD BE THE THING THAT PUT YOU OVER THE EDGE.
PEN, I THINK SOMETHING IMPORTANT JUST HAPPENED.
OMG WHAT!
I GOT NOMINATED FOR A BOOK AWARD. IT'S LIKE A HUGE DEAL, I GUESS.
DUDE! THAT'S AWESOME. I'M 60% HAPPY FOR YOU AND 40% JEALOUS. WHAT DOES THIS MEAN FOR YOU?
HONESTLY, I DON'T KNOW. IT FEELS LIKE IT CAN'T BE THAT BIG OF A DEAL IF IT'S HAPPENING TO ME.

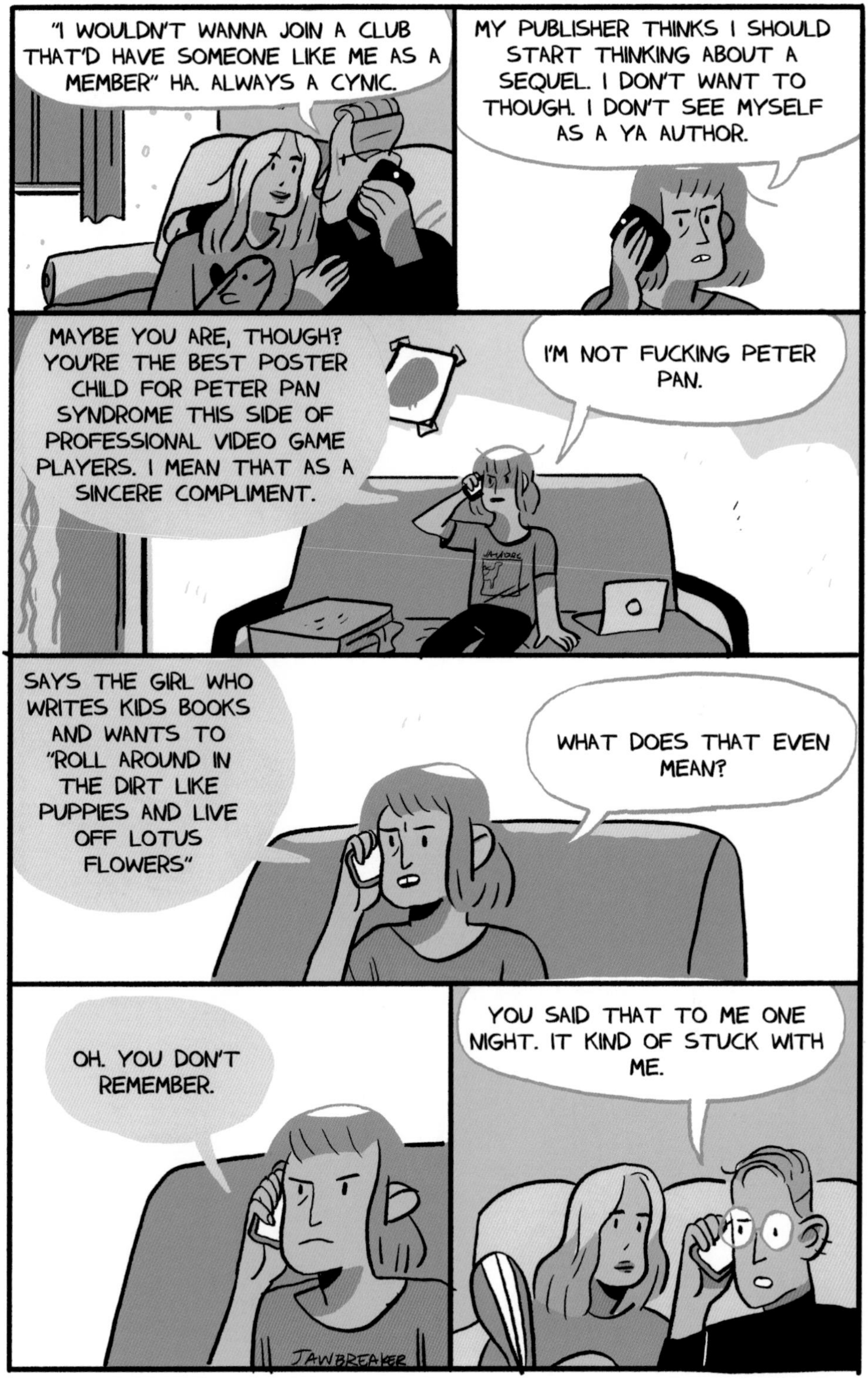
"I WOULDN'T WANNA JOIN A CLUB THAT'D HAVE SOMEONE LIKE ME AS A MEMBER" HA. ALWAYS A CYNIC.
MY PUBLISHER THINKS I SHOULD START THINKING ABOUT A SEQUEL. I DON'T WANT TO THOUGH. I DON'T SEE MYSELF AS A YA AUTHOR.
MAYBE YOU ARE, THOUGH? YOU'RE THE BEST POSTER CHILD FOR PETER PAN SYNDROME THIS SIDE OF PROFESSIONAL VIDEO GAME PLAYERS. I MEAN THAT AS A SINCERE COMPLIMENT.
I'M NOT FUCKING PETER PAN.
SAYS THE GIRL WHO WRITES KIDS BOOKS AND WANTS TO "ROLL AROUND IN THE DIRT LIKE PUPPIES AND LIVE OFF LOTUS FLOWERS"
WHAT DOES THAT EVEN MEAN?
OH. YOU DON'T REMEMBER.
YOU SAID THAT TO ME ONE NIGHT. IT KIND OF STUCK WITH ME.
JAWBREAKER

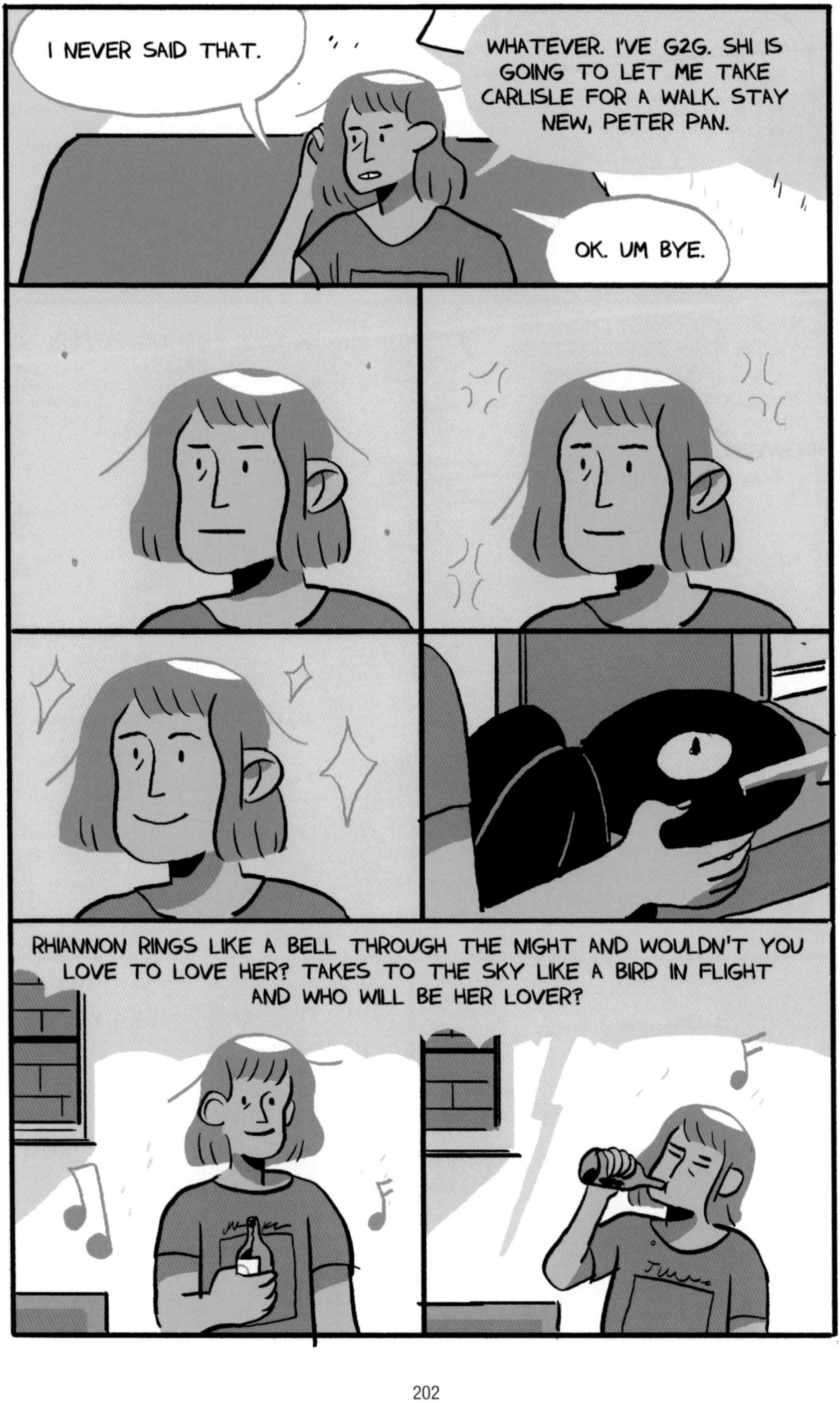
I NEVER SAID THAT.
WHATEVER. I'VE G2G. SHI IS GOING TO LET ME TAKE CARLISLE FOR A WALK. STAY NEW, PETER PAN.
OK. UM BYE.
RHIANNON RINGS LIKE A BELL THROUGH THE NIGHT AND WOULDN'T YOU LOVE TO LOVE HER? TAKES TO THE SKY LIKE A BIRD IN FLIGHT AND WHO WILL BE HER LOVER?

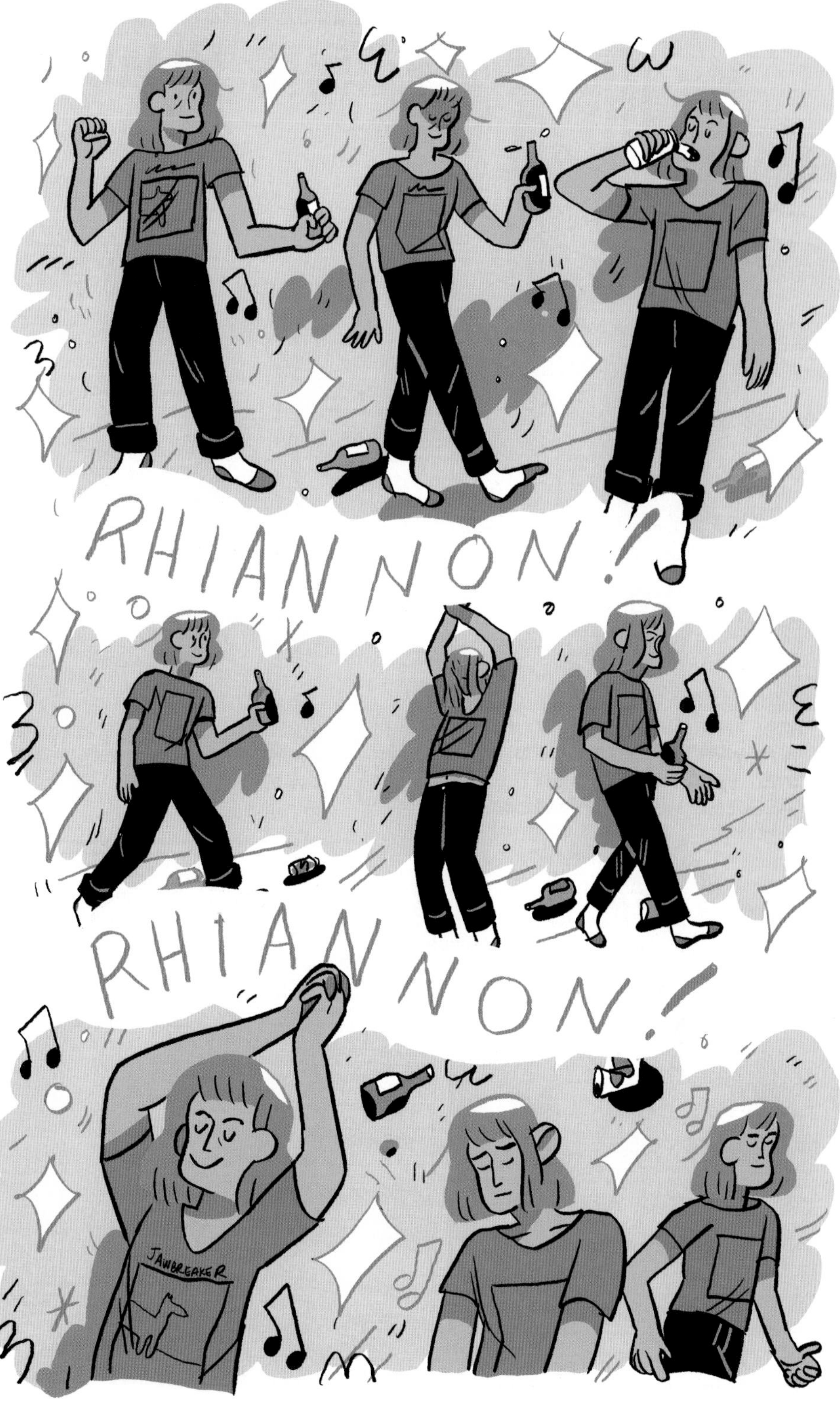
RHIANNON!
RHIANNON!
JAWBREAKER

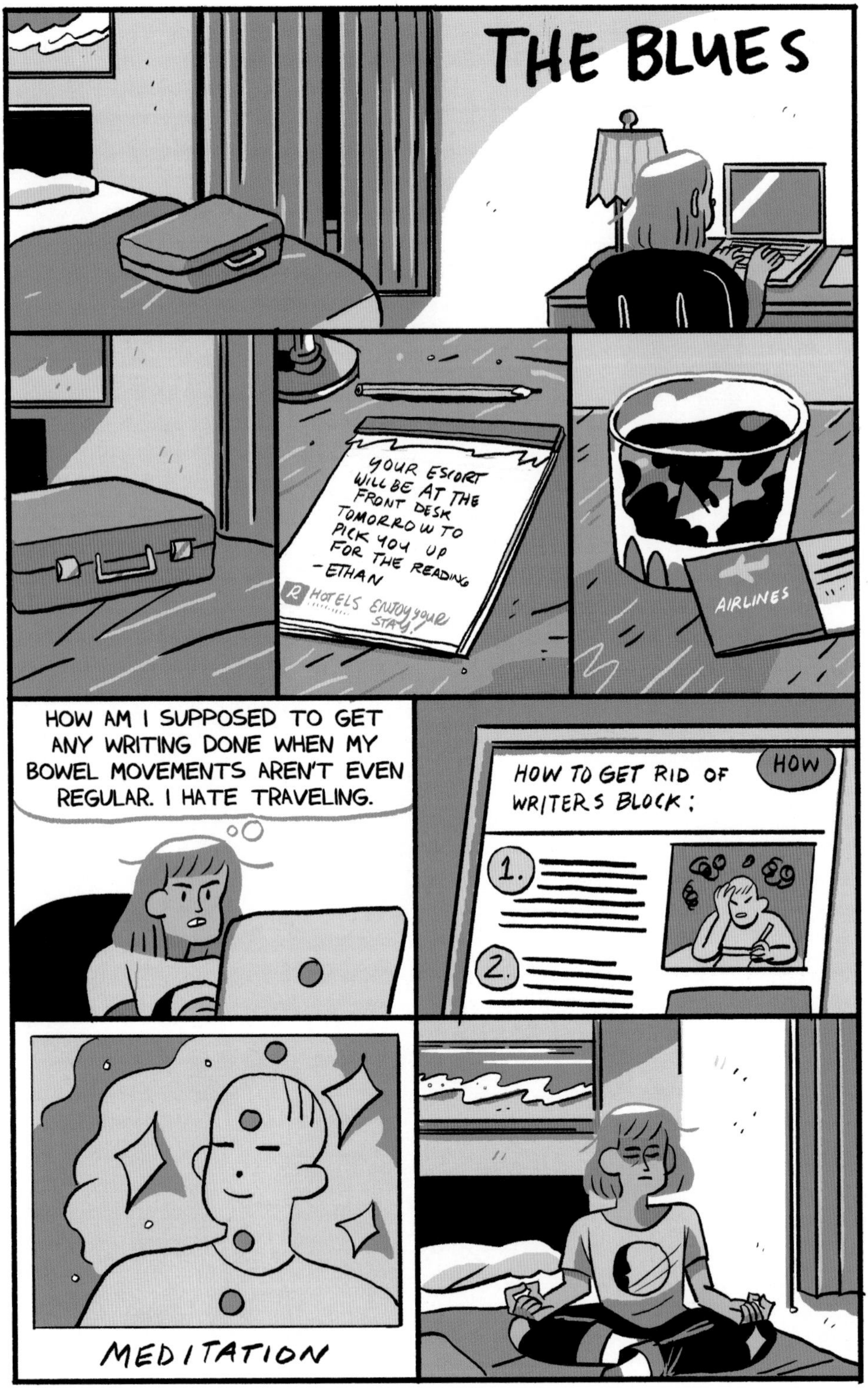
THE BLUES
YOUR ESCORT WILL BE AT THE FRONT DESK TOMORROW TO PICK YOU UP FOR THE READING
-ETHAN
R HOTELS ENJOY YOUR STAY!
AIRLINES
HOW AM I SUPPOSED TO GET ANY WRITING DONE WHEN MY BOWEL MOVEMENTS AREN'T EVEN REGULAR. I HATE TRAVELING.
HOW TO GET RID OF WRITERS BLOCK:
HOW
1.
2.
MEDITATION

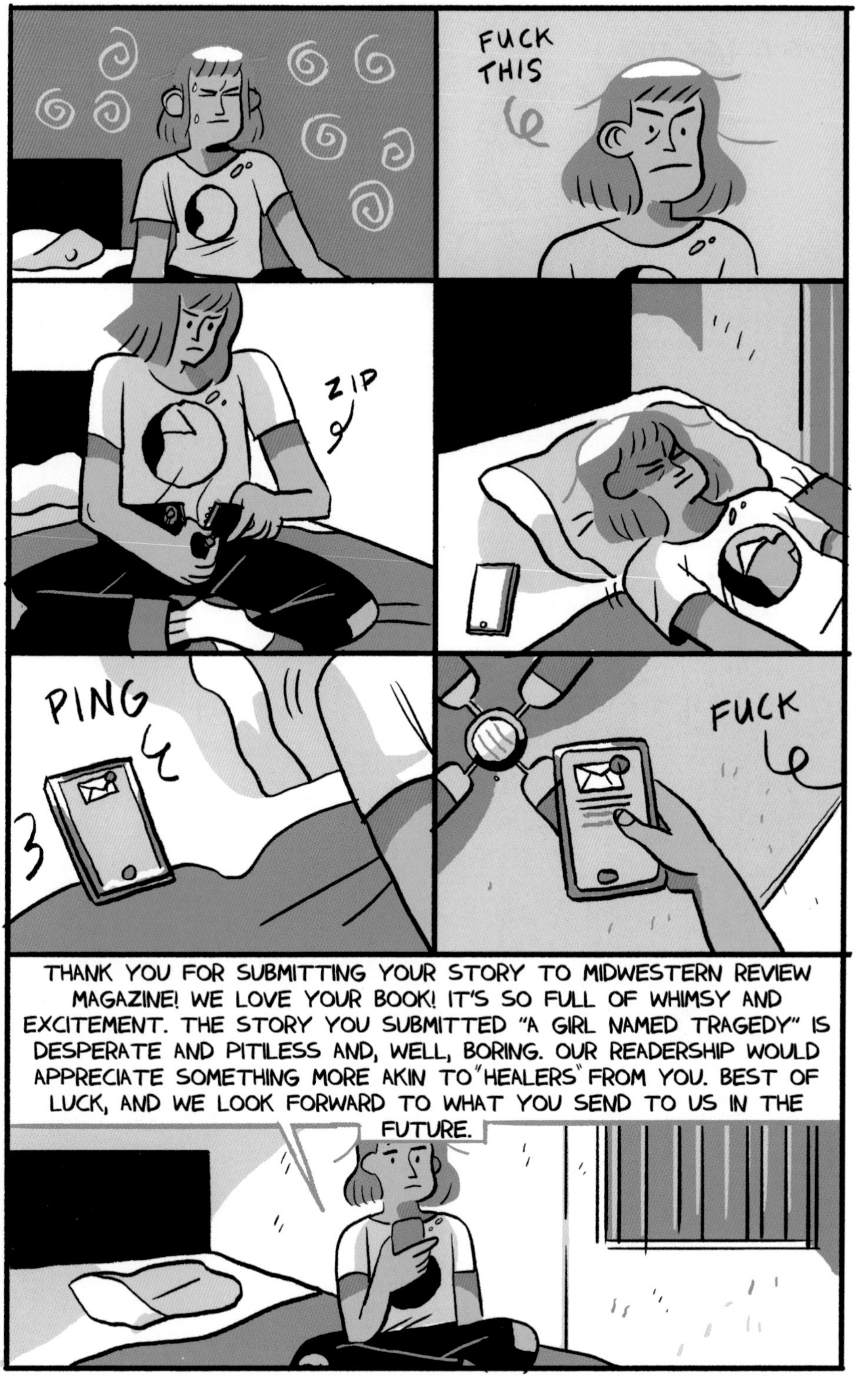
FUCK THIS
ZIP
PING
FUCK
THANK YOU FOR SUBMITTING YOUR STORY TO MIDWESTERN REVIEW MAGAZINE! WE LOVE YOUR BOOK! IT'S SO FULL OF WHIMSY AND EXCITEMENT. THE STORY YOU SUBMITTED "A GIRL NAMED TRAGEDY" IS DESPERATE AND PITILESS AND, WELL, BORING. OUR READERSHIP WOULD APPRECIATE SOMETHING MORE AKIN TO "HEALERS" FROM YOU. BEST OF LUCK, AND WE LOOK FORWARD TO WHAT YOU SEND TO US IN THE FUTURE.

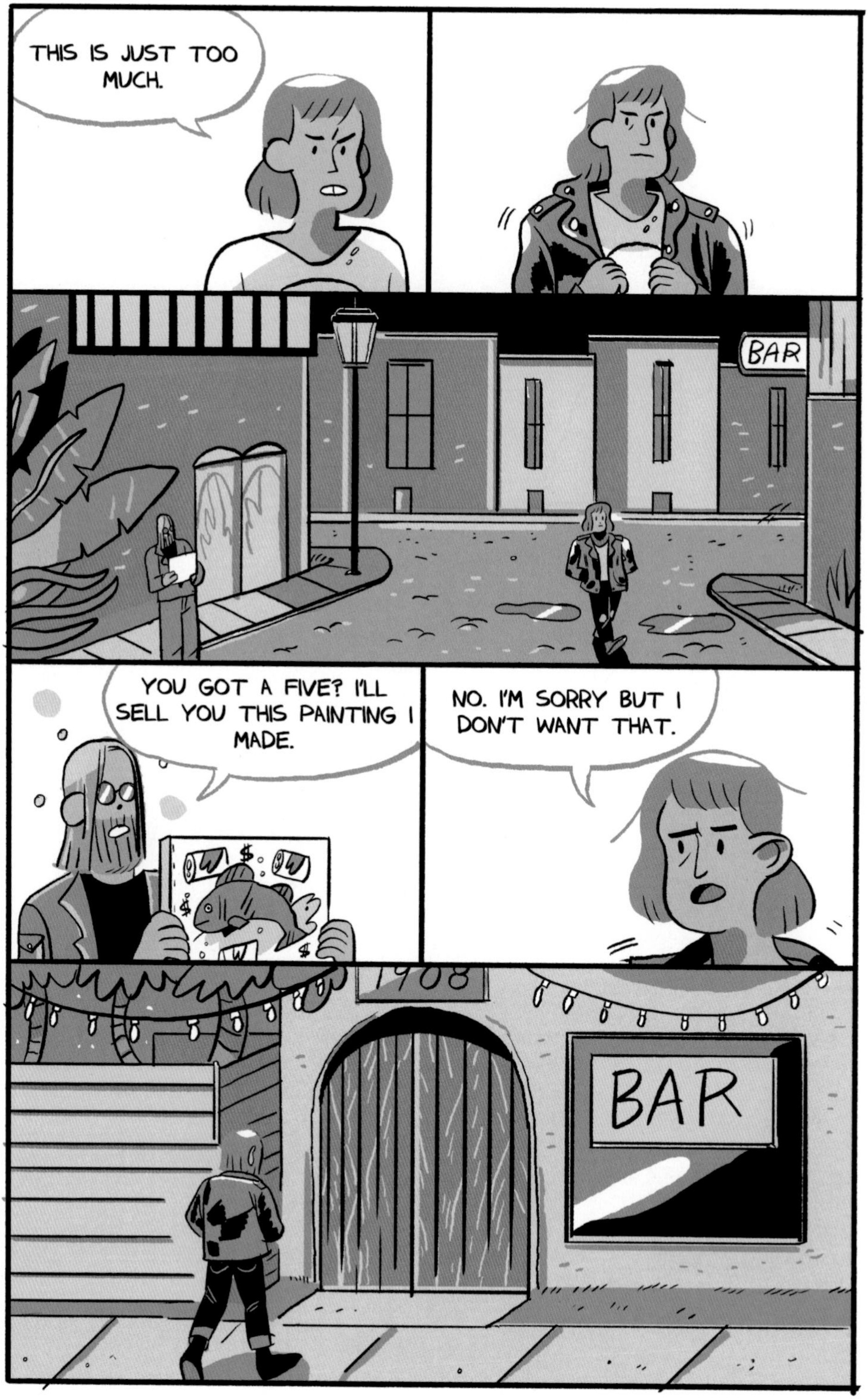
THIS IS JUST TOO MUCH.
BAR
YOU GOT A FIVE? I'LL SELL YOU THIS PAINTING I MADE.
NO. I'M SORRY BUT I DON'T WANT THAT.
1908
BAR

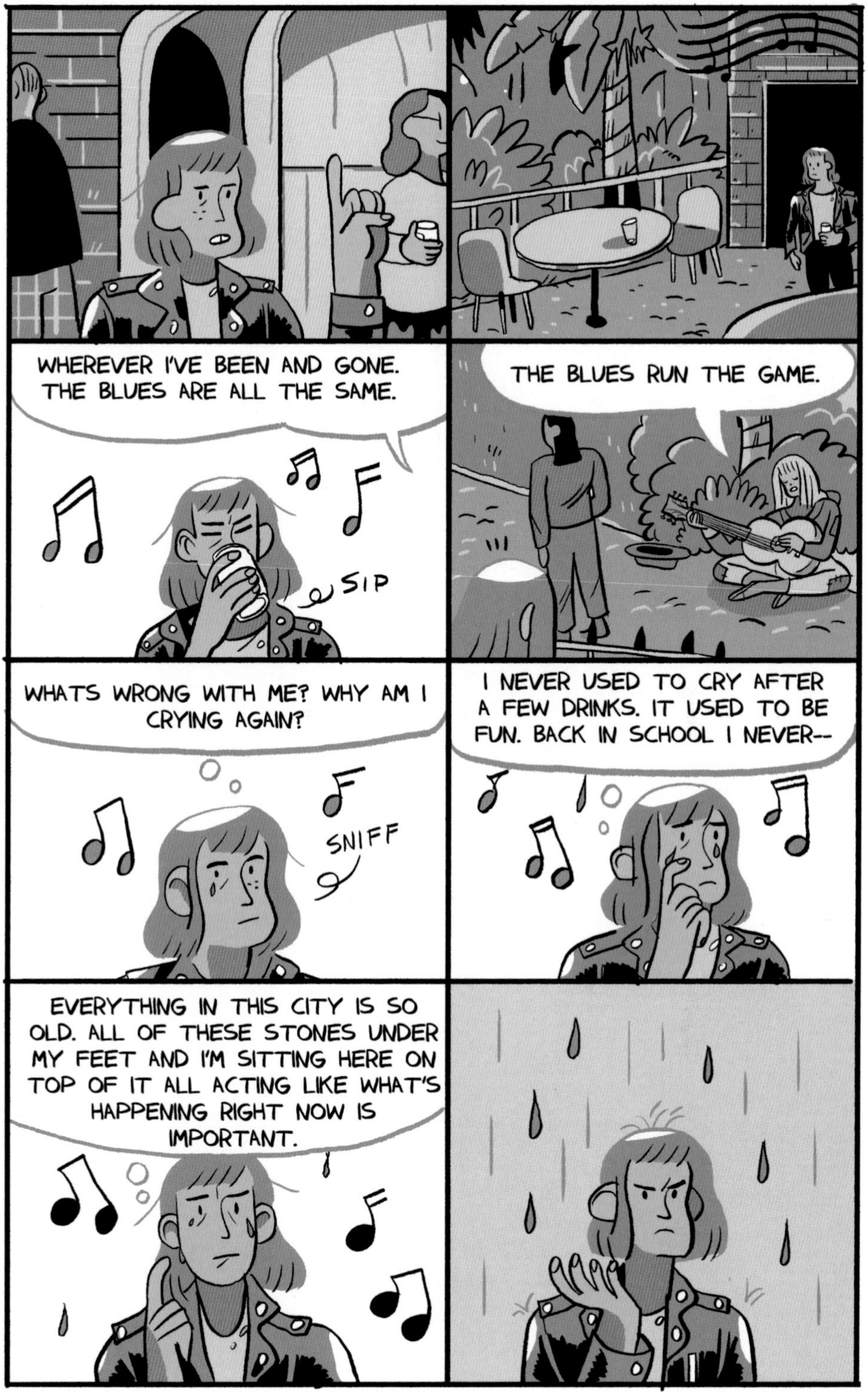
WHEREVER I'VE BEEN AND GONE. THE BLUES ARE ALL THE SAME.
SIP
THE BLUES RUN THE GAME.
WHATS WRONG WITH ME? WHY AM I CRYING AGAIN?
SNIFF
I NEVER USED TO CRY AFTER A FEW DRINKS. IT USED TO BE FUN. BACK IN SCHOOL I NEVER--
EVERYTHING IN THIS CITY IS SO OLD. ALL OF THESE STONES UNDER MY FEET AND I'M SITTING HERE ON TOP OF IT ALL ACTING LIKE WHAT'S HAPPENING RIGHT NOW IS IMPORTANT.

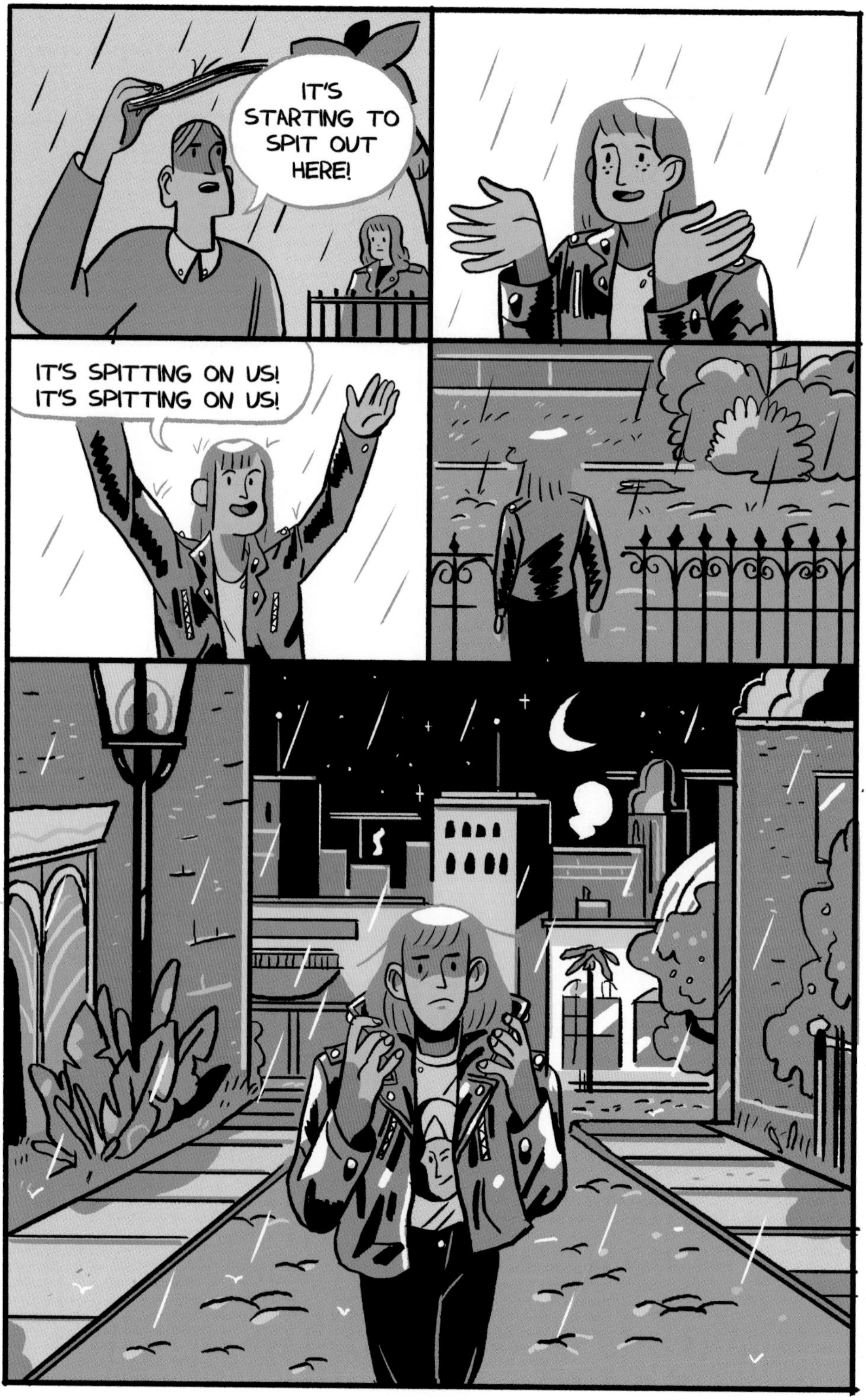
IT'S STARTING TO SPIT OUT HERE!
IT'S SPITTING ON US! IT'S SPITTING ON US!

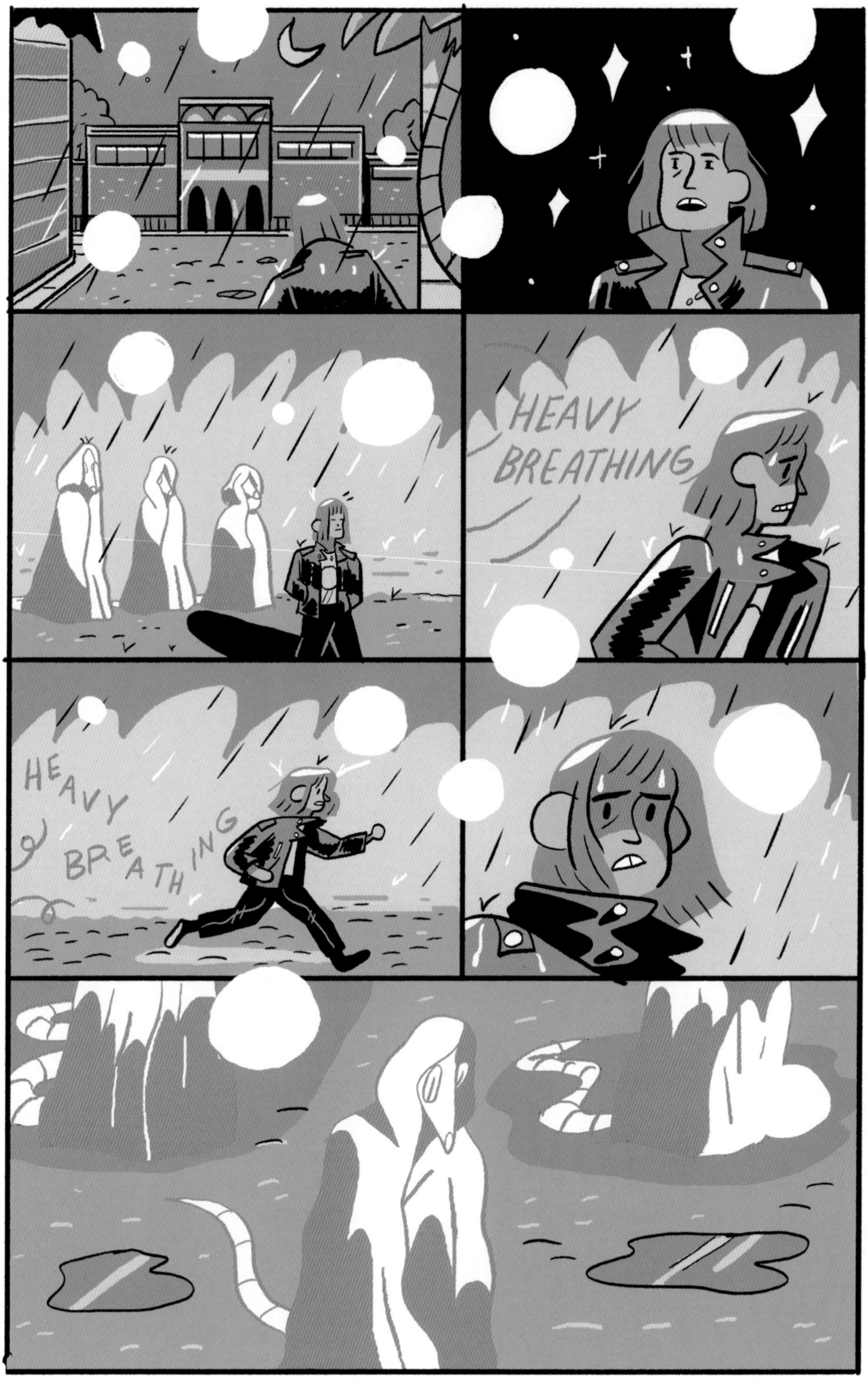
HEAVY BREATHING
HEAVY BREATHING

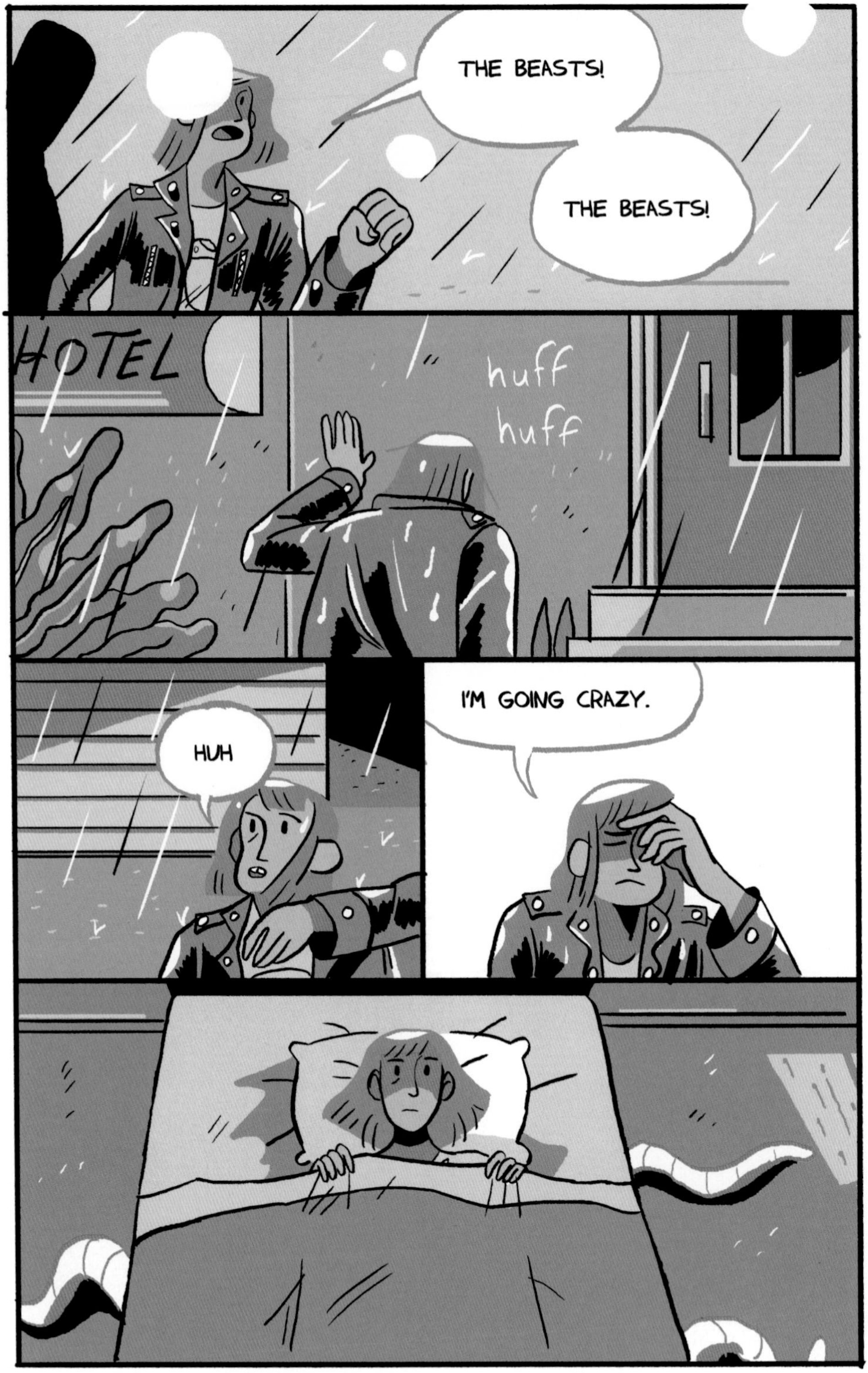
THE BEASTS!
THE BEASTS!
HOTEL
huff
huff
HUH
I'M GOING CRAZY.

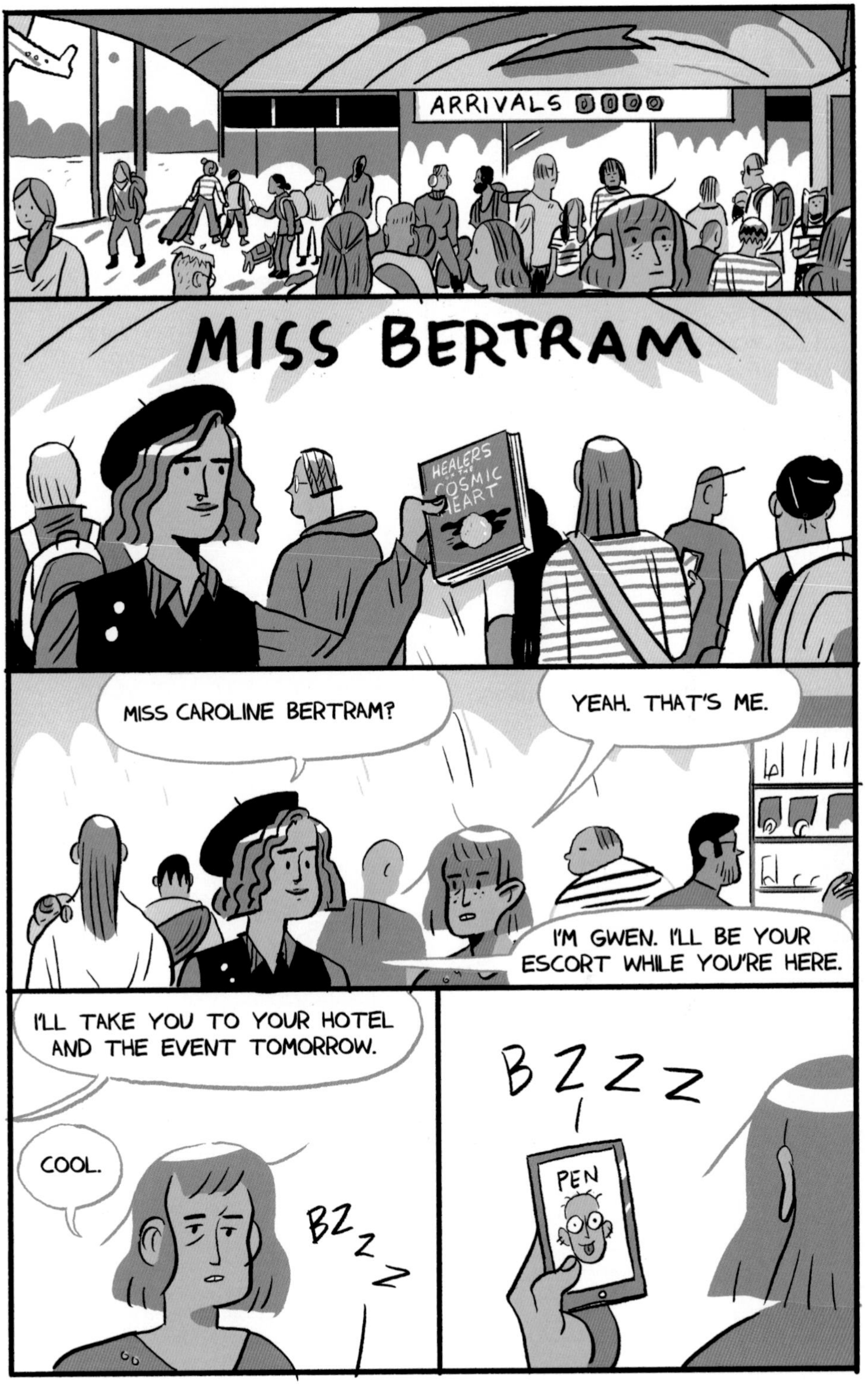

ARRIVALS
MISS BERTRAM
HEALERS OF THE COSMIC HEART
MISS CAROLINE BERTRAM?
YEAH. THAT'S ME.
I'M GWEN. I'LL BE YOUR ESCORT WHILE YOU'RE HERE.
I'LL TAKE YOU TO YOUR HOTEL AND THE EVENT TOMORROW.
COOL.
BZZZ
BZZZ
PEN

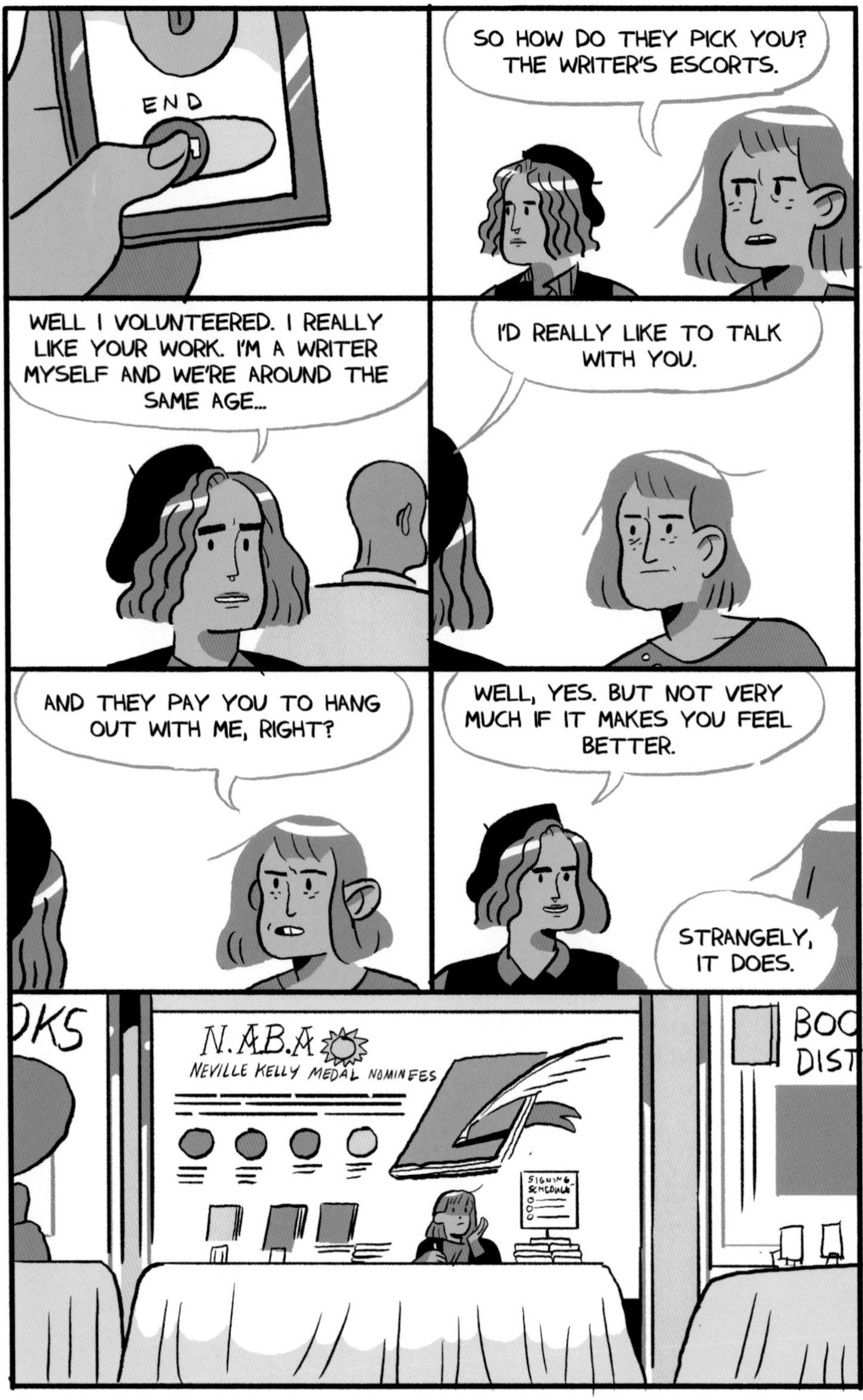
END
SO HOW DO THEY PICK YOU? THE WRITER'S ESCORTS.
WELL I VOLUNTEERED. I REALLY LIKE YOUR WORK. I'M A WRITER MYSELF AND WE'RE AROUND THE SAME AGE...
I'D REALLY LIKE TO TALK WITH YOU.
AND THEY PAY YOU TO HANG OUT WITH ME, RIGHT?
WELL, YES. BUT NOT VERY MUCH IF IT MAKES YOU FEEL BETTER.
STRANGELY, IT DOES.
N.A.B.A
NEVILLE KELLY MEDAL NOMINEES
SIGNING SCHEDULE

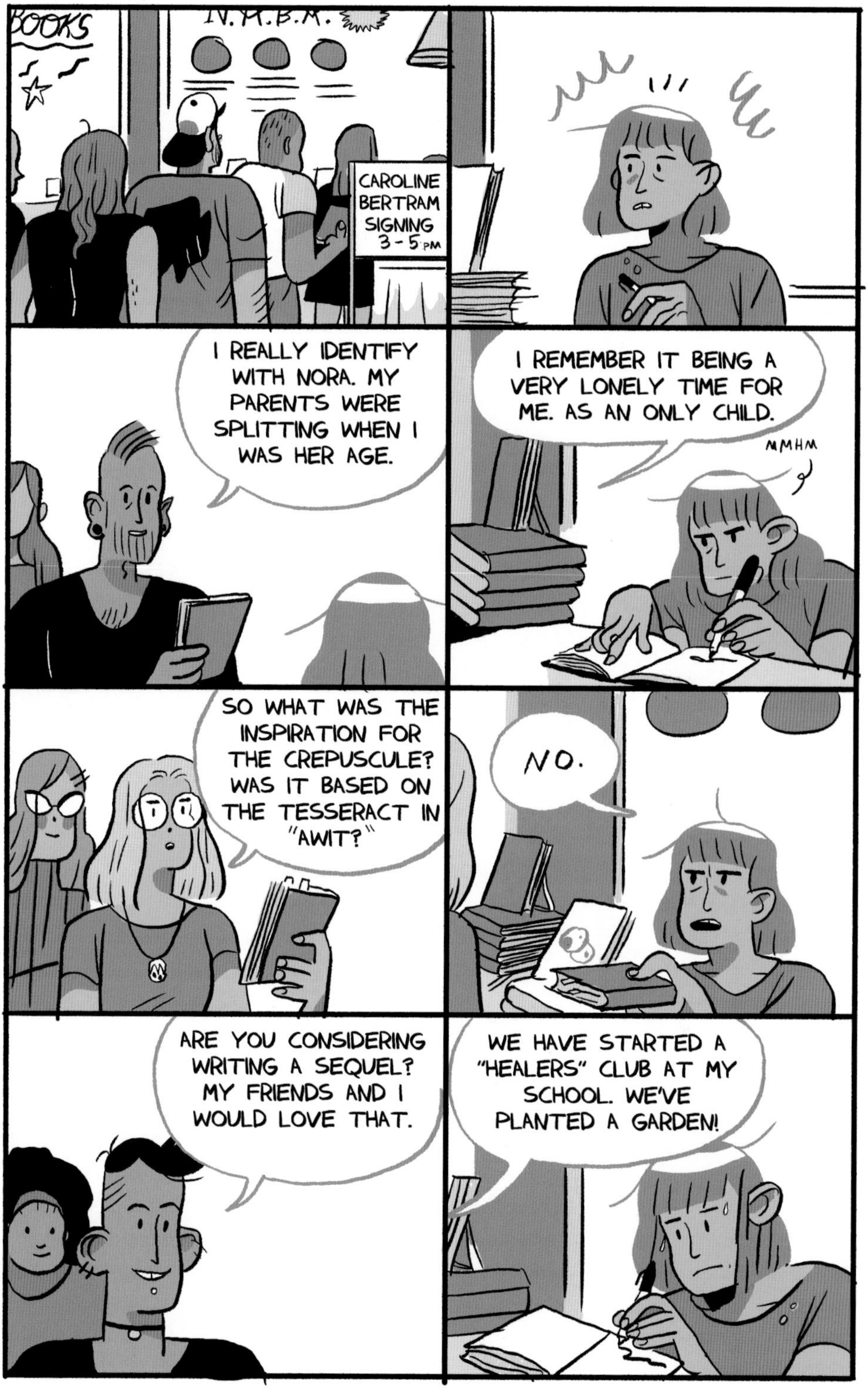
BOOKS
N.Y.B.A.
CAROLINE BERTRAM SIGNING 3-5 PM
I REALLY IDENTIFY WITH NORA. MY PARENTS WERE SPLITTING WHEN I WAS HER AGE.
I REMEMBER IT BEING A VERY LONELY TIME FOR ME. AS AN ONLY CHILD.
MMHM
SO WHAT WAS THE INSPIRATION FOR THE CREPUSCULE? WAS IT BASED ON THE TESSERACT IN "AWIT?"
NO.
ARE YOU CONSIDERING WRITING A SEQUEL? MY FRIENDS AND I WOULD LOVE THAT.
WE HAVE STARTED A "HEALERS" CLUB AT MY SCHOOL. WE'VE PLANTED A GARDEN!

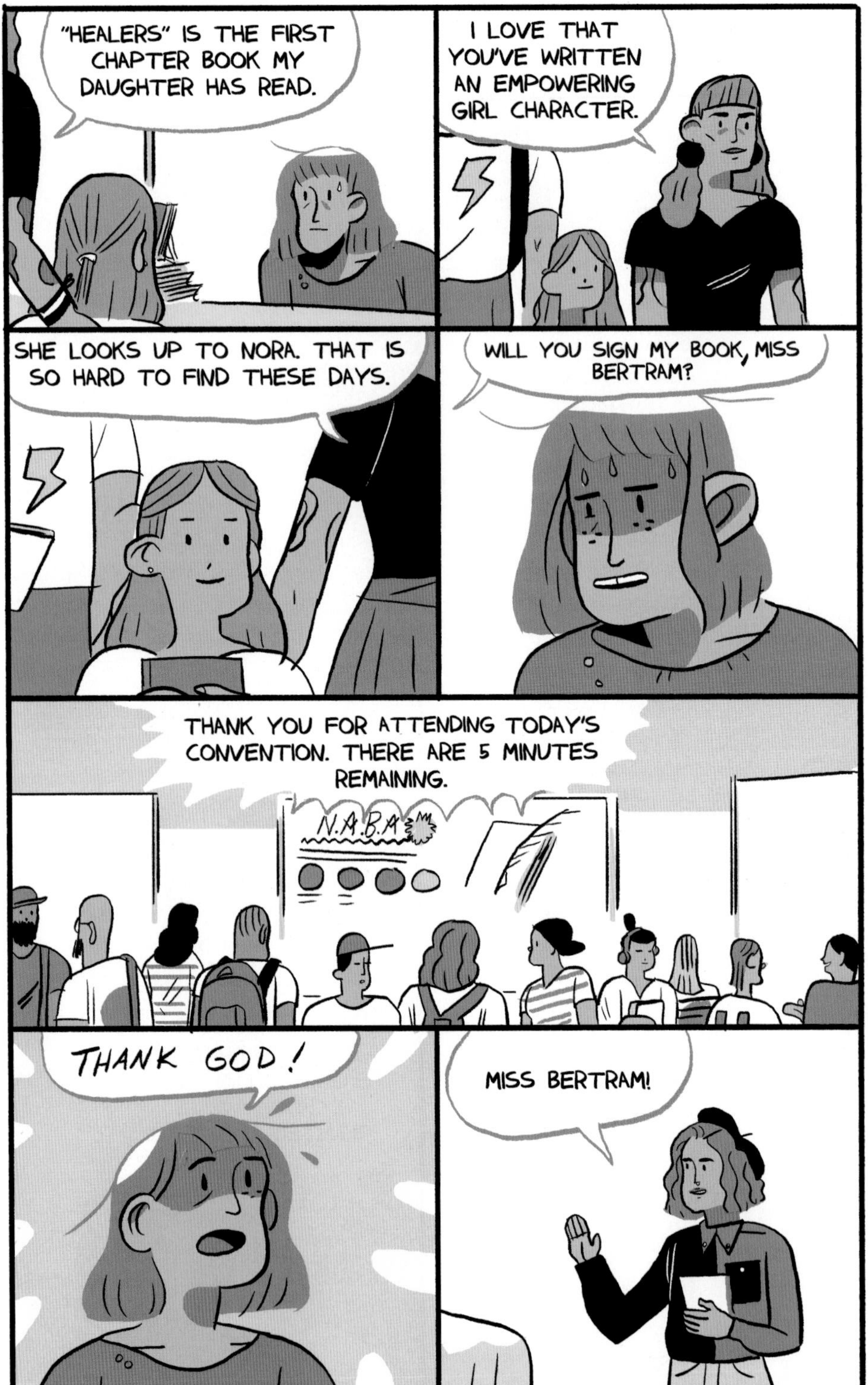
"HEALERS" IS THE FIRST CHAPTER BOOK MY DAUGHTER HAS READ.
I LOVE THAT YOU'VE WRITTEN AN EMPOWERING GIRL CHARACTER.
SHE LOOKS UP TO NORA. THAT IS SO HARD TO FIND THESE DAYS.
WILL YOU SIGN MY BOOK, MISS BERTRAM?
THANK YOU FOR ATTENDING TODAY'S CONVENTION. THERE ARE 5 MINUTES REMAINING.
N.A.B.A.
THANK GOD!
MISS BERTRAM!

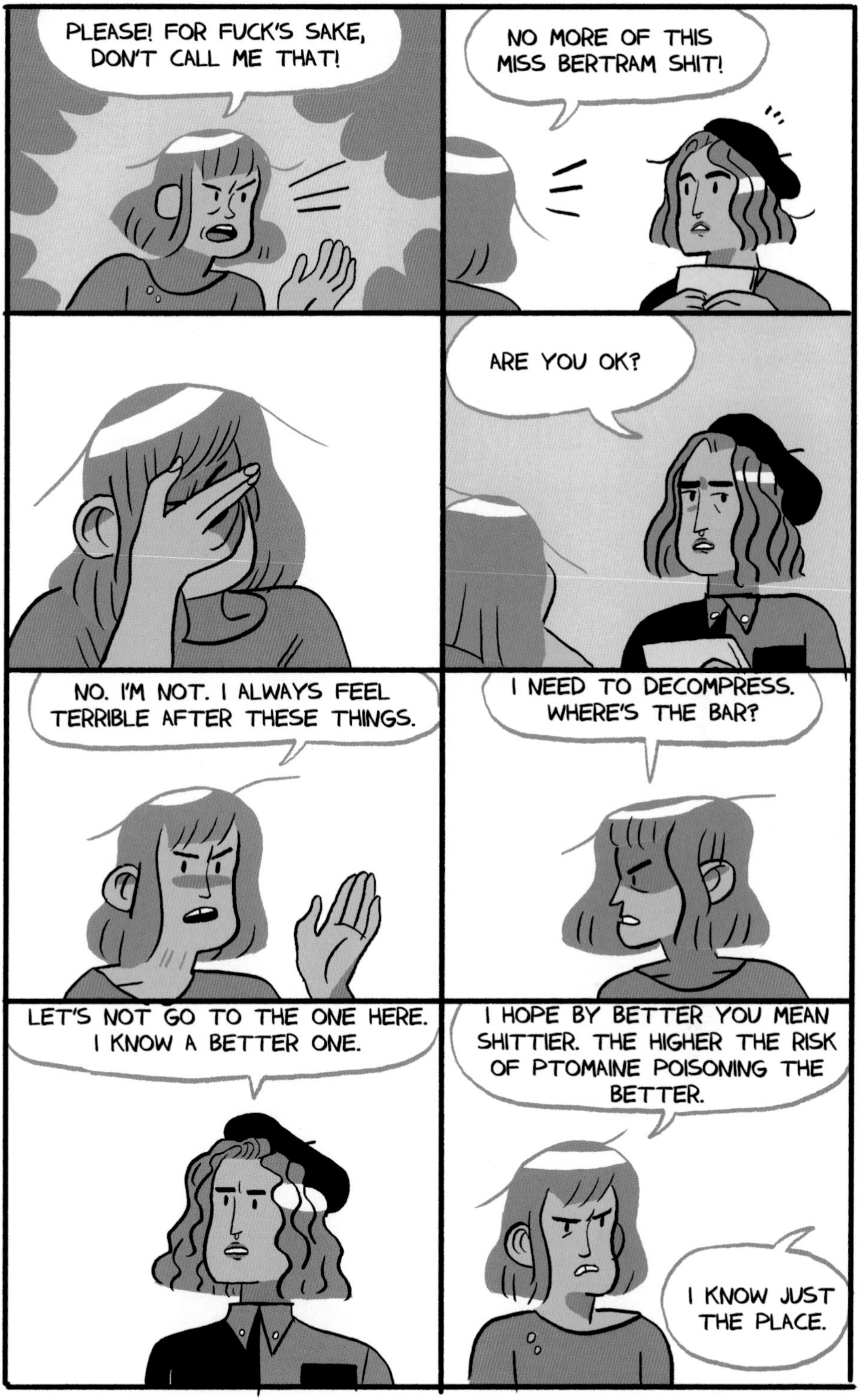
PLEASE! FOR FUCK'S SAKE, DON'T CALL ME THAT!
NO MORE OF THIS MISS BERTRAM SHIT!
ARE YOU OK?
NO. I'M NOT. I ALWAYS FEEL TERRIBLE AFTER THESE THINGS.
I NEED TO DECOMPRESS. WHERE'S THE BAR?
LET'S NOT GO TO THE ONE HERE. I KNOW A BETTER ONE.
I HOPE BY BETTER YOU MEAN SHITTIER. THE HIGHER THE RISK OF PTOMAINE POISONING THE BETTER.
I KNOW JUST THE PLACE.

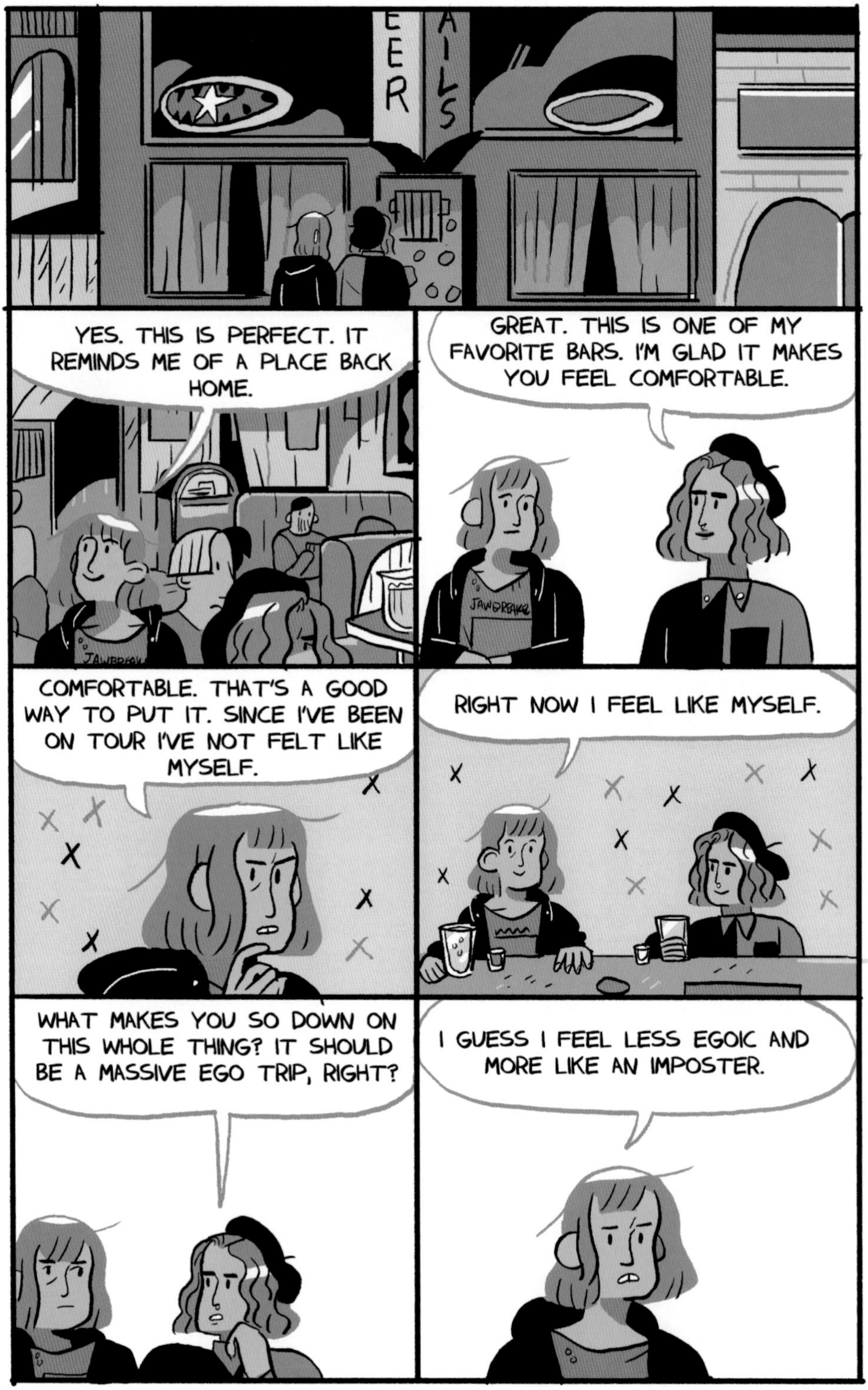
EER
AILS
YES. THIS IS PERFECT. IT REMINDS ME OF A PLACE BACK HOME.
JAWBREAKER
GREAT. THIS IS ONE OF MY FAVORITE BARS. I'M GLAD IT MAKES YOU FEEL COMFORTABLE.
JAWBREAKER
COMFORTABLE. THAT'S A GOOD WAY TO PUT IT. SINCE I'VE BEEN ON TOUR I'VE NOT FELT LIKE MYSELF.
RIGHT NOW I FEEL LIKE MYSELF.
WHAT MAKES YOU SO DOWN ON THIS WHOLE THING? IT SHOULD BE A MASSIVE EGO TRIP, RIGHT?
I GUESS I FEEL LESS EGOIC AND MORE LIKE AN IMPOSTER.

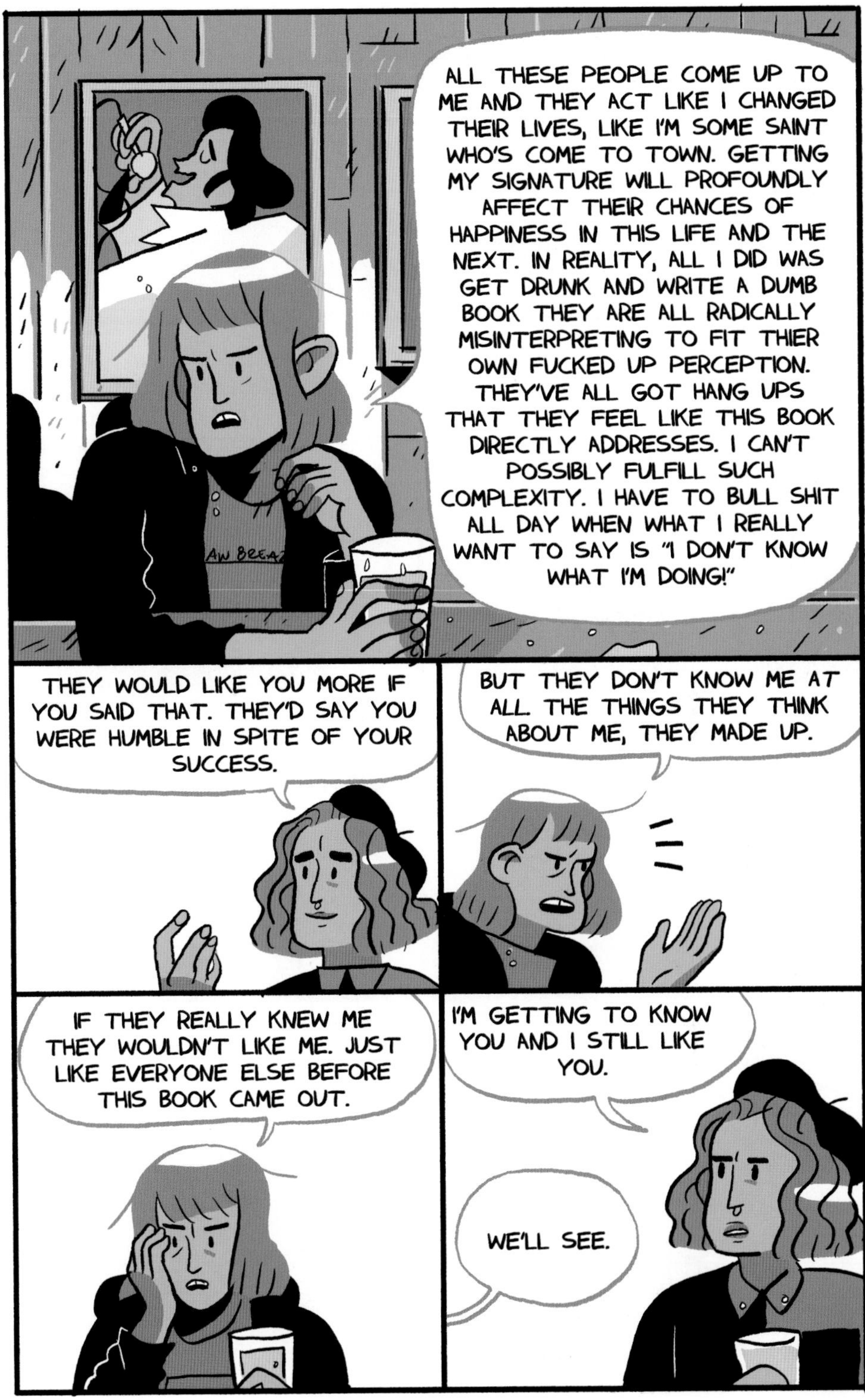
ALL THESE PEOPLE COME UP TO ME AND THEY ACT LIKE I CHANGED THEIR LIVES, LIKE I'M SOME SAINT WHO'S COME TO TOWN. GETTING MY SIGNATURE WILL PROFOUNDLY AFFECT THEIR CHANCES OF HAPPINESS IN THIS LIFE AND THE NEXT. IN REALITY, ALL I DID WAS GET DRUNK AND WRITE A DUMB BOOK THEY ARE ALL RADICALLY MISINTERPRETING TO FIT THIER OWN FUCKED UP PERCEPTION. THEY'VE ALL GOT HANG UPS THAT THEY FEEL LIKE THIS BOOK DIRECTLY ADDRESSES. I CAN'T POSSIBLY FULFILL SUCH COMPLEXITY. I HAVE TO BULL SHIT ALL DAY WHEN WHAT I REALLY WANT TO SAY IS "I DON'T KNOW WHAT I'M DOING!"
THEY WOULD LIKE YOU MORE IF YOU SAID THAT. THEY'D SAY YOU WERE HUMBLE IN SPITE OF YOUR SUCCESS.
BUT THEY DON'T KNOW ME AT ALL. THE THINGS THEY THINK ABOUT ME, THEY MADE UP.
IF THEY REALLY KNEW ME THEY WOULDN'T LIKE ME. JUST LIKE EVERYONE ELSE BEFORE THIS BOOK CAME OUT.
I'M GETTING TO KNOW YOU AND I STILL LIKE YOU.
WE'LL SEE.

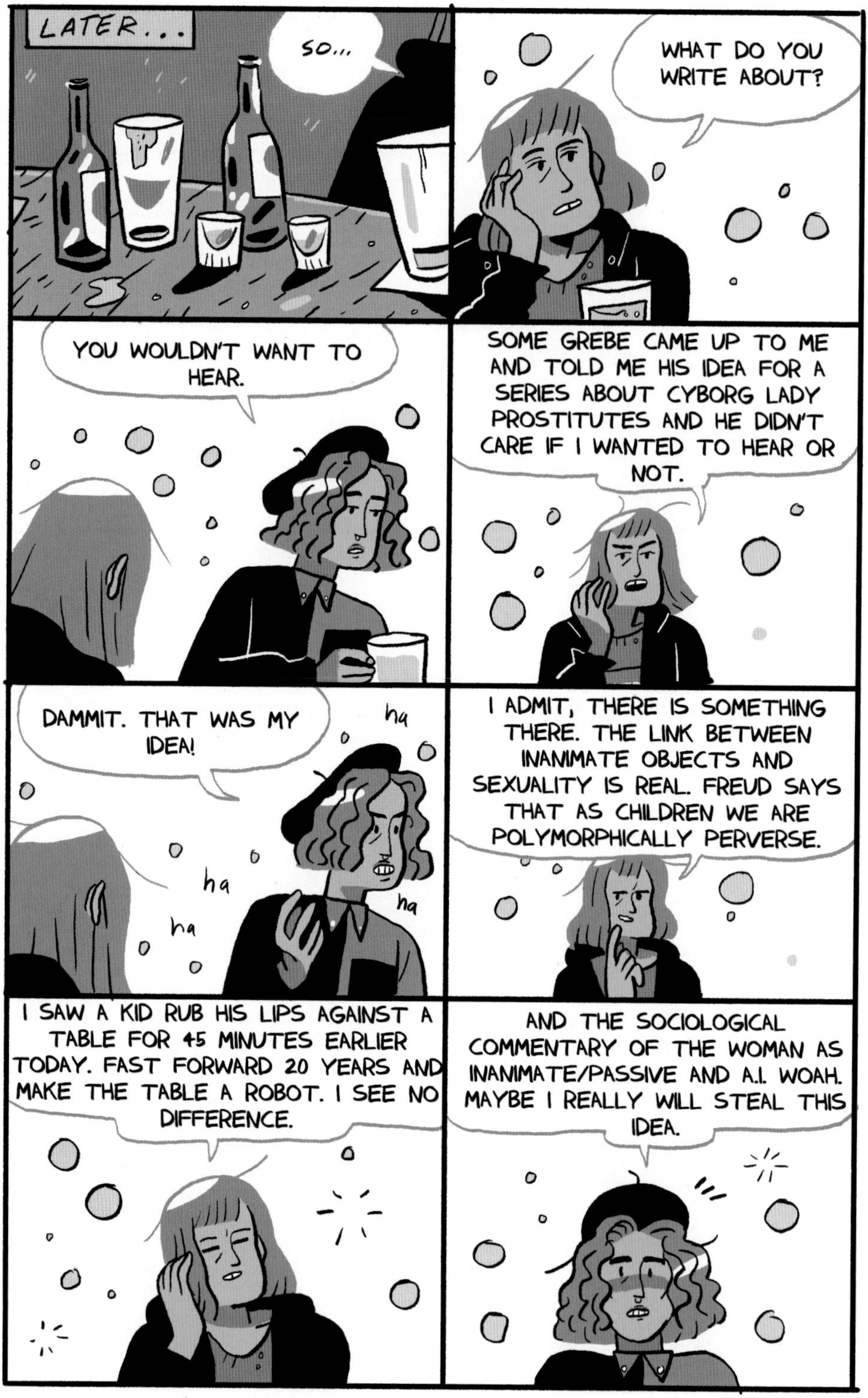
LATER...
SO...
WHAT DO YOU WRITE ABOUT?
YOU WOULDN'T WANT TO HEAR.
SOME GREBE CAME UP TO ME AND TOLD ME HIS IDEA FOR A SERIES ABOUT CYBORG LADY PROSTITUTES AND HE DIDN'T CARE IF I WANTED TO HEAR OR NOT.
DAMMIT. THAT WAS MY IDEA!
ha
ha
ha
ha
I ADMIT, THERE IS SOMETHING THERE. THE LINK BETWEEN INANIMATE OBJECTS AND SEXUALITY IS REAL. FREUD SAYS THAT AS CHILDREN WE ARE POLYMORPHICALLY PERVERSE.
I SAW A KID RUB HIS LIPS AGAINST A TABLE FOR 45 MINUTES EARLIER TODAY. FAST FORWARD 20 YEARS AND MAKE THE TABLE A ROBOT. I SEE NO DIFFERENCE.
AND THE SOCIOLOGICAL COMMENTARY OF THE WOMAN AS INANIMATE/PASSIVE AND A.I. WOAH. MAYBE I REALLY WILL STEAL THIS IDEA.

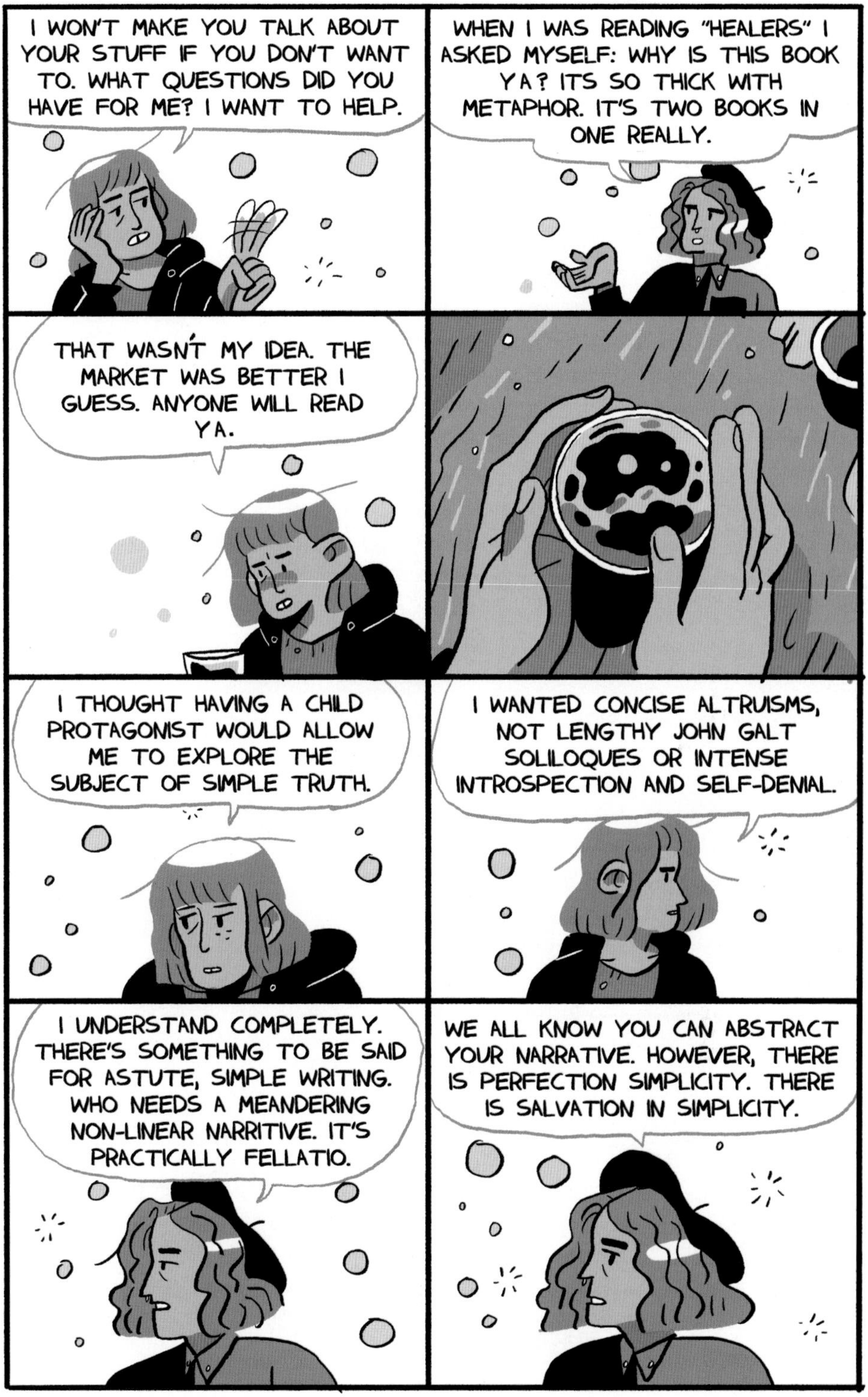
I WON'T MAKE YOU TALK ABOUT YOUR STUFF IF YOU DON'T WANT TO. WHAT QUESTIONS DID YOU HAVE FOR ME? I WANT TO HELP.
WHEN I WAS READING "HEALERS" I ASKED MYSELF: WHY IS THIS BOOK YA? ITS SO THICK WITH METAPHOR. IT'S TWO BOOKS IN ONE REALLY.
THAT WASN'T MY IDEA. THE MARKET WAS BETTER I GUESS. ANYONE WILL READ YA.
I THOUGHT HAVING A CHILD PROTAGONIST WOULD ALLOW ME TO EXPLORE THE SUBJECT OF SIMPLE TRUTH.
I WANTED CONCISE ALTRUISMS, NOT LENGTHY JOHN GALT SOLILOQUES OR INTENSE INTROSPECTION AND SELF-DENIAL.
I UNDERSTAND COMPLETELY. THERE'S SOMETHING TO BE SAID FOR ASTUTE, SIMPLE WRITING. WHO NEEDS A MEANDERING NON-LINEAR NARRITIVE. IT'S PRACTICALLY FELLATIO.
WE ALL KNOW YOU CAN ABSTRACT YOUR NARRATIVE. HOWEVER, THERE IS PERFECTION SIMPLICITY. THERE IS SALVATION IN SIMPLICITY.

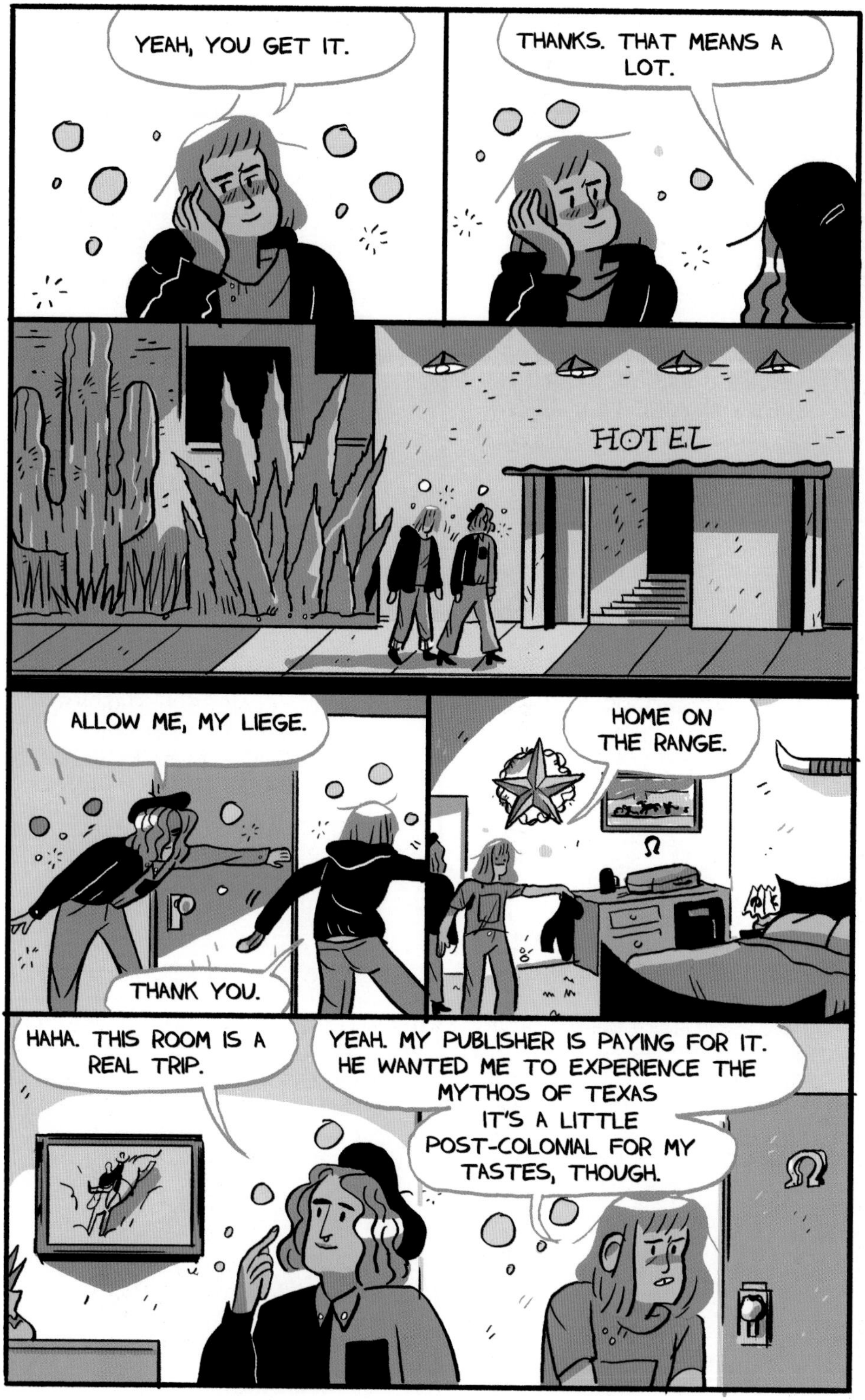
YEAH, YOU GET IT.
THANKS. THAT MEANS A LOT.
HOTEL
ALLOW ME, MY LIEGE.
THANK YOU.
HOME ON THE RANGE.
HAHA. THIS ROOM IS A REAL TRIP.
YEAH. MY PUBLISHER IS PAYING FOR IT. HE WANTED ME TO EXPERIENCE THE MYTHOS OF TEXAS
IT'S A LITTLE POST-COLONIAL FOR MY TASTES, THOUGH.

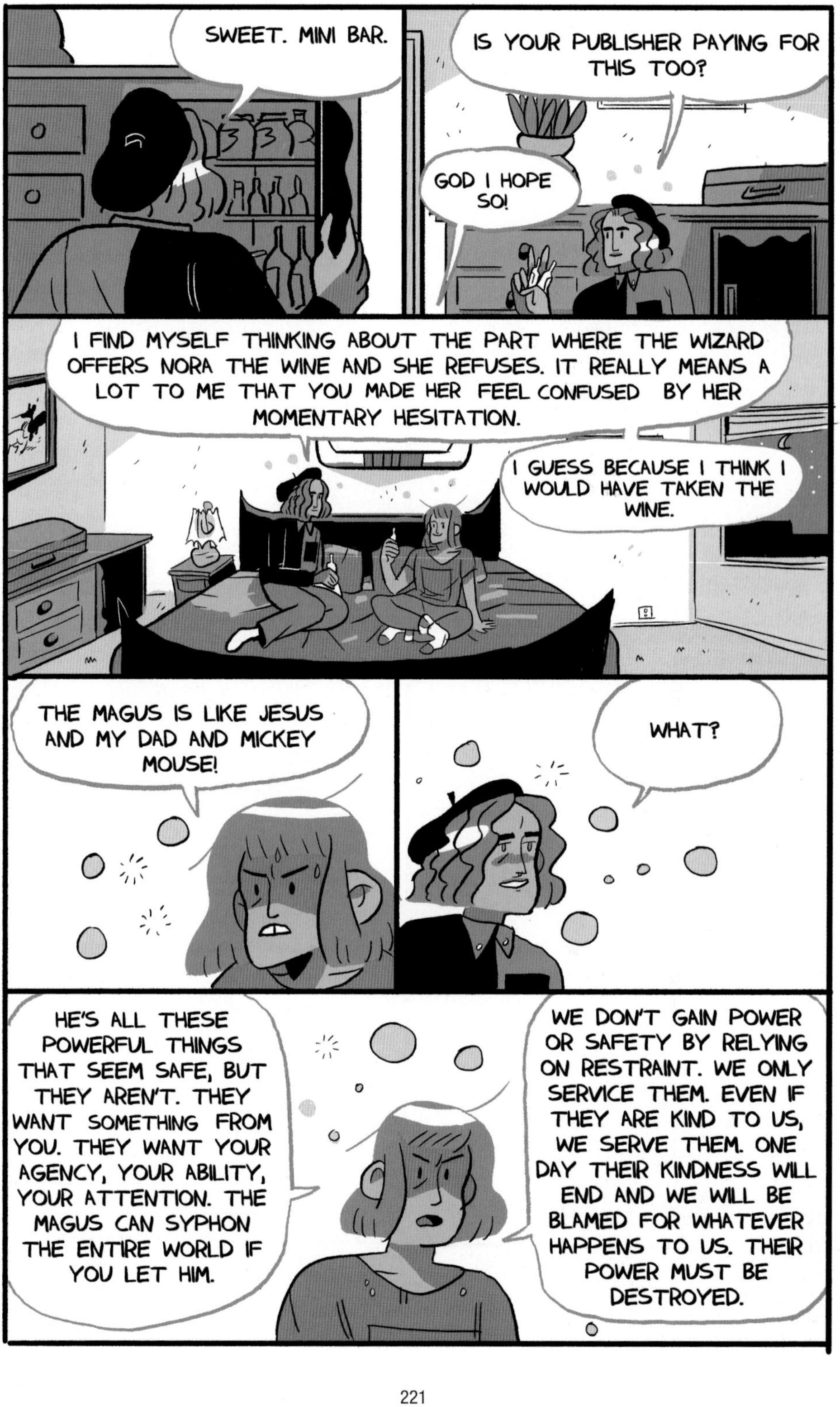
SWEET. MINI BAR.
IS YOUR PUBLISHER PAYING FOR THIS TOO?
GOD I HOPE SO!
I FIND MYSELF THINKING ABOUT THE PART WHERE THE WIZARD OFFERS NORA THE WINE AND SHE REFUSES. IT REALLY MEANS A LOT TO ME THAT YOU MADE HER FEEL CONFUSED BY HER MOMENTARY HESITATION.
I GUESS BECAUSE I THINK I WOULD HAVE TAKEN THE WINE.
THE MAGUS IS LIKE JESUS AND MY DAD AND MICKEY MOUSE!
WHAT?
HE'S ALL THESE POWERFUL THINGS THAT SEEM SAFE, BUT THEY AREN'T. THEY WANT SOMETHING FROM YOU. THEY WANT YOUR AGENCY, YOUR ABILITY, YOUR ATTENTION. THE MAGUS CAN SYPHON THE ENTIRE WORLD IF YOU LET HIM.
WE DON'T GAIN POWER OR SAFETY BY RELYING ON RESTRAINT. WE ONLY SERVICE THEM. EVEN IF THEY ARE KIND TO US, WE SERVE THEM. ONE DAY THEIR KINDNESS WILL END AND WE WILL BE BLAMED FOR WHATEVER HAPPENS TO US. THEIR POWER MUST BE DESTROYED.

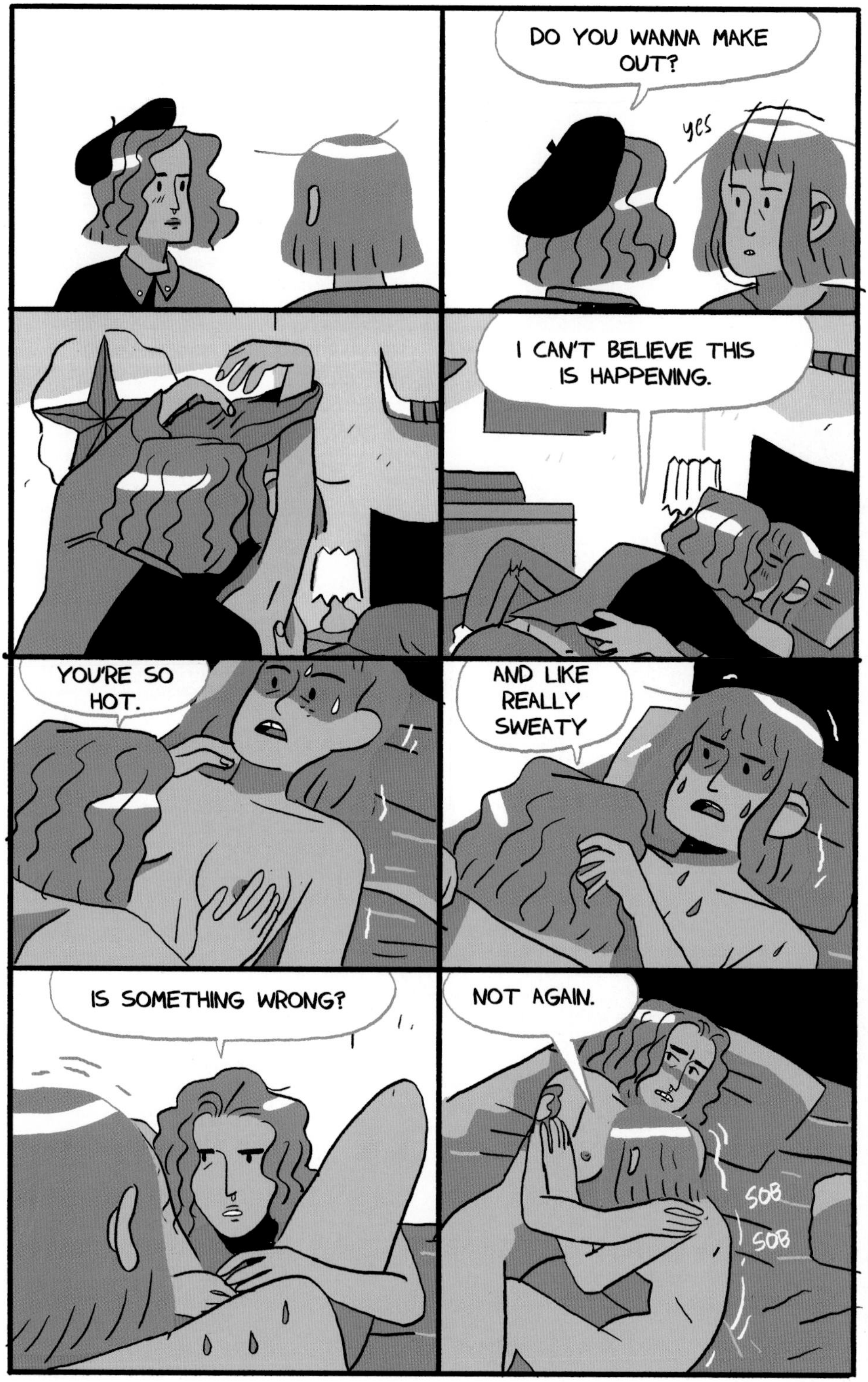
DO YOU WANNA MAKE OUT?
yes
I CAN'T BELIEVE THIS IS HAPPENING.
YOU'RE SO HOT.
AND LIKE REALLY SWEATY
IS SOMETHING WRONG?
NOT AGAIN.
SOB
SOB

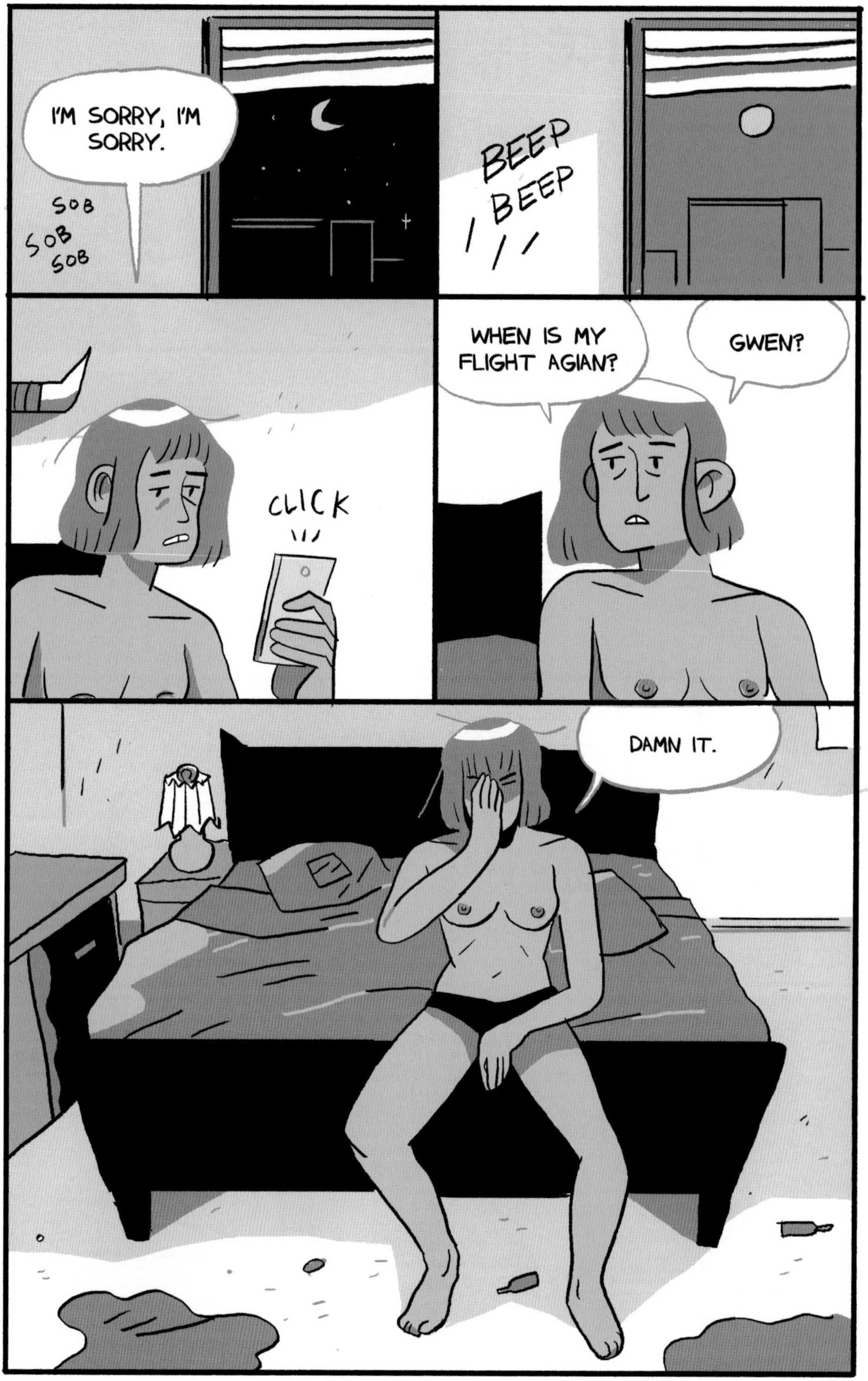
I'M SORRY, I'M SORRY.
SOB SOB SOB
BEEP BEEP
CLICK
WHEN IS MY FLIGHT AGIAN?
GWEN?
DAMN IT.

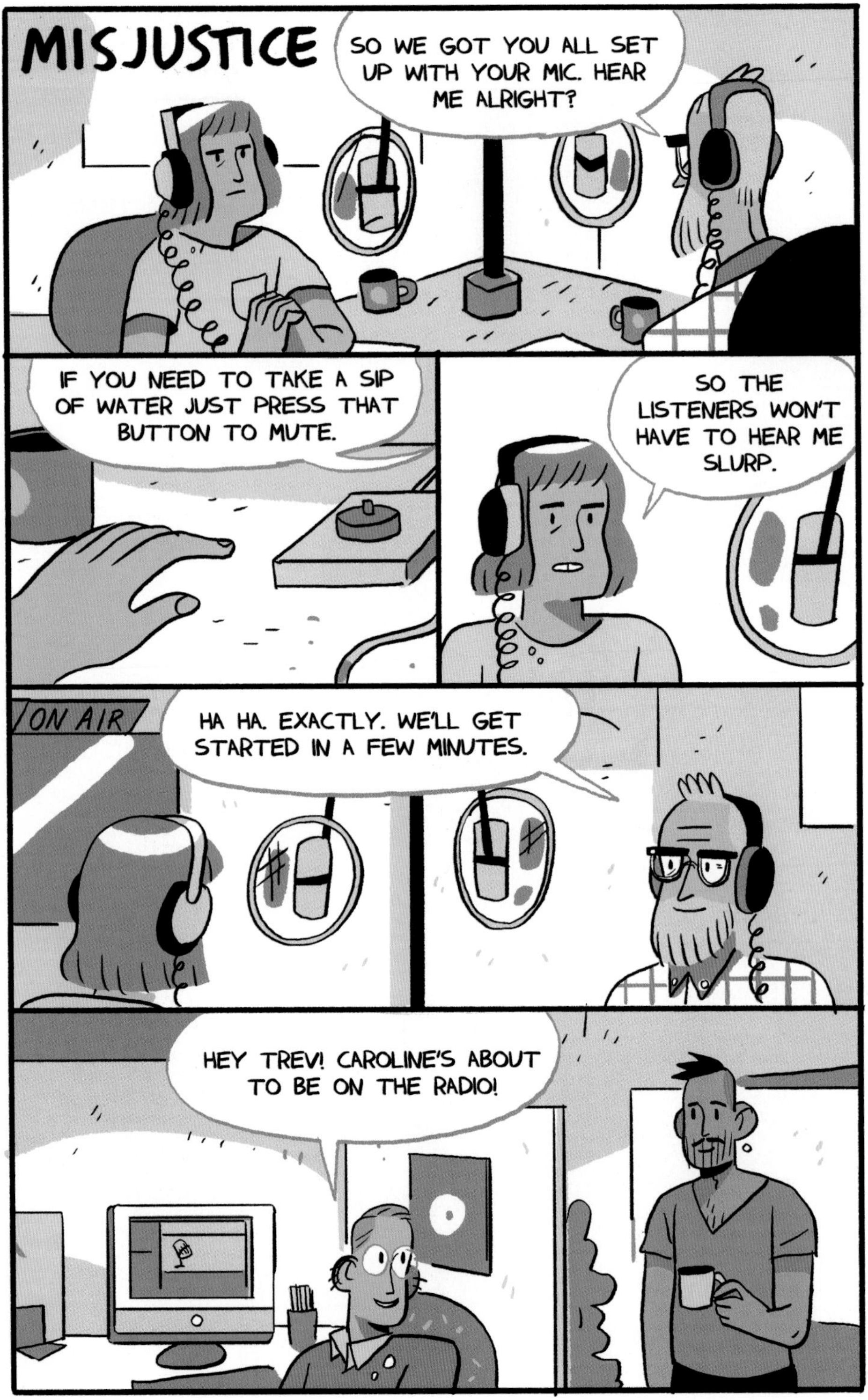
MISJUSTICE
SO WE GOT YOU ALL SET UP WITH YOUR MIC. HEAR ME ALRIGHT?
IF YOU NEED TO TAKE A SIP OF WATER JUST PRESS THAT BUTTON TO MUTE.
SO THE LISTENERS WON'T HAVE TO HEAR ME SLURP.
ON AIR
HA HA. EXACTLY. WE'LL GET STARTED IN A FEW MINUTES.
HEY TREV! CAROLINE'S ABOUT TO BE ON THE RADIO!

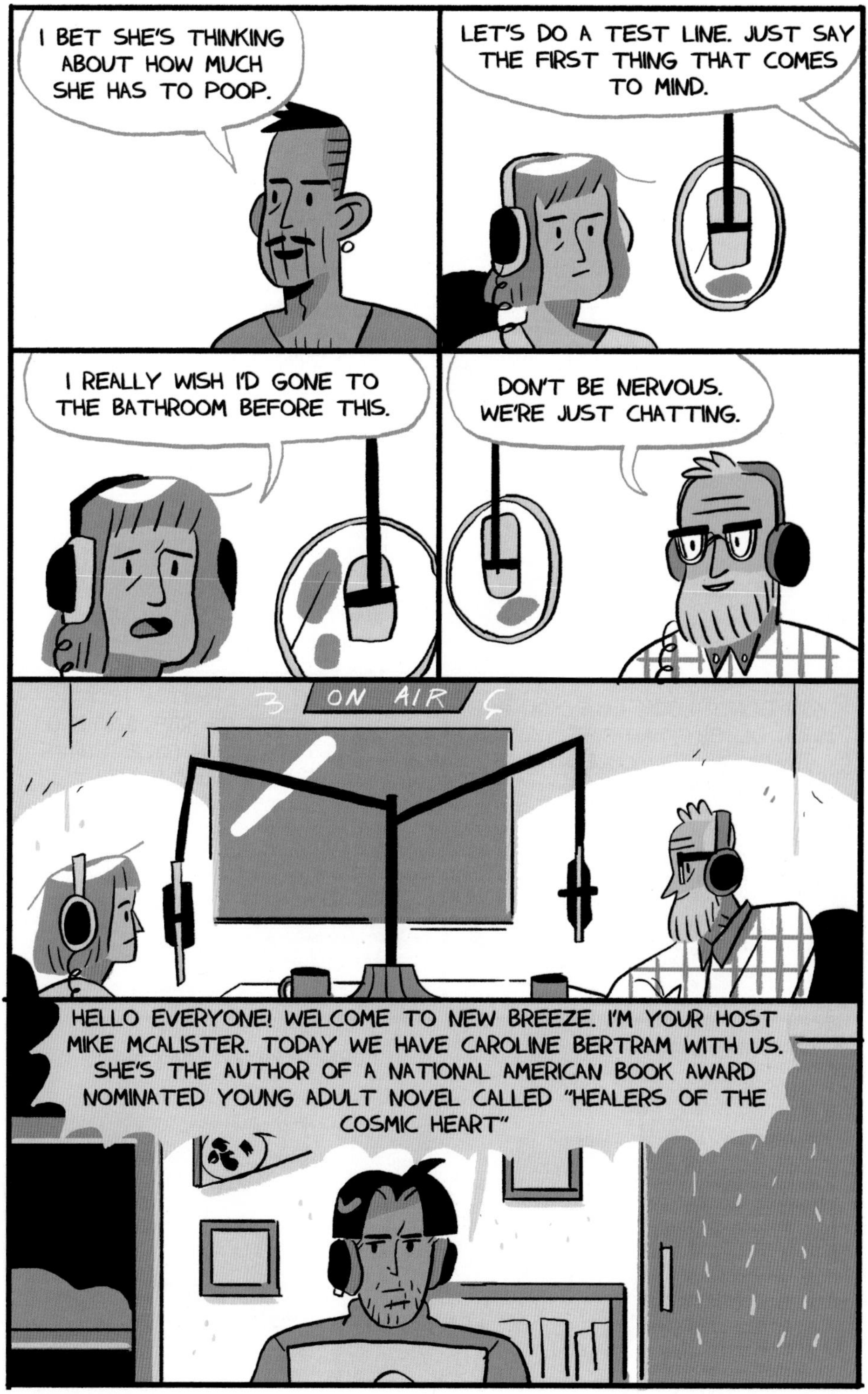
I BET SHE'S THINKING ABOUT HOW MUCH SHE HAS TO POOP.
LET'S DO A TEST LINE. JUST SAY THE FIRST THING THAT COMES TO MIND.
I REALLY WISH I'D GONE TO THE BATHROOM BEFORE THIS.
DON'T BE NERVOUS. WE'RE JUST CHATTING.
ON AIR
HELLO EVERYONE! WELCOME TO NEW BREEZE. I'M YOUR HOST MIKE MCALISTER. TODAY WE HAVE CAROLINE BERTRAM WITH US. SHE'S THE AUTHOR OF A NATIONAL AMERICAN BOOK AWARD NOMINATED YOUNG ADULT NOVEL CALLED "HEALERS OF THE COSMIC HEART"

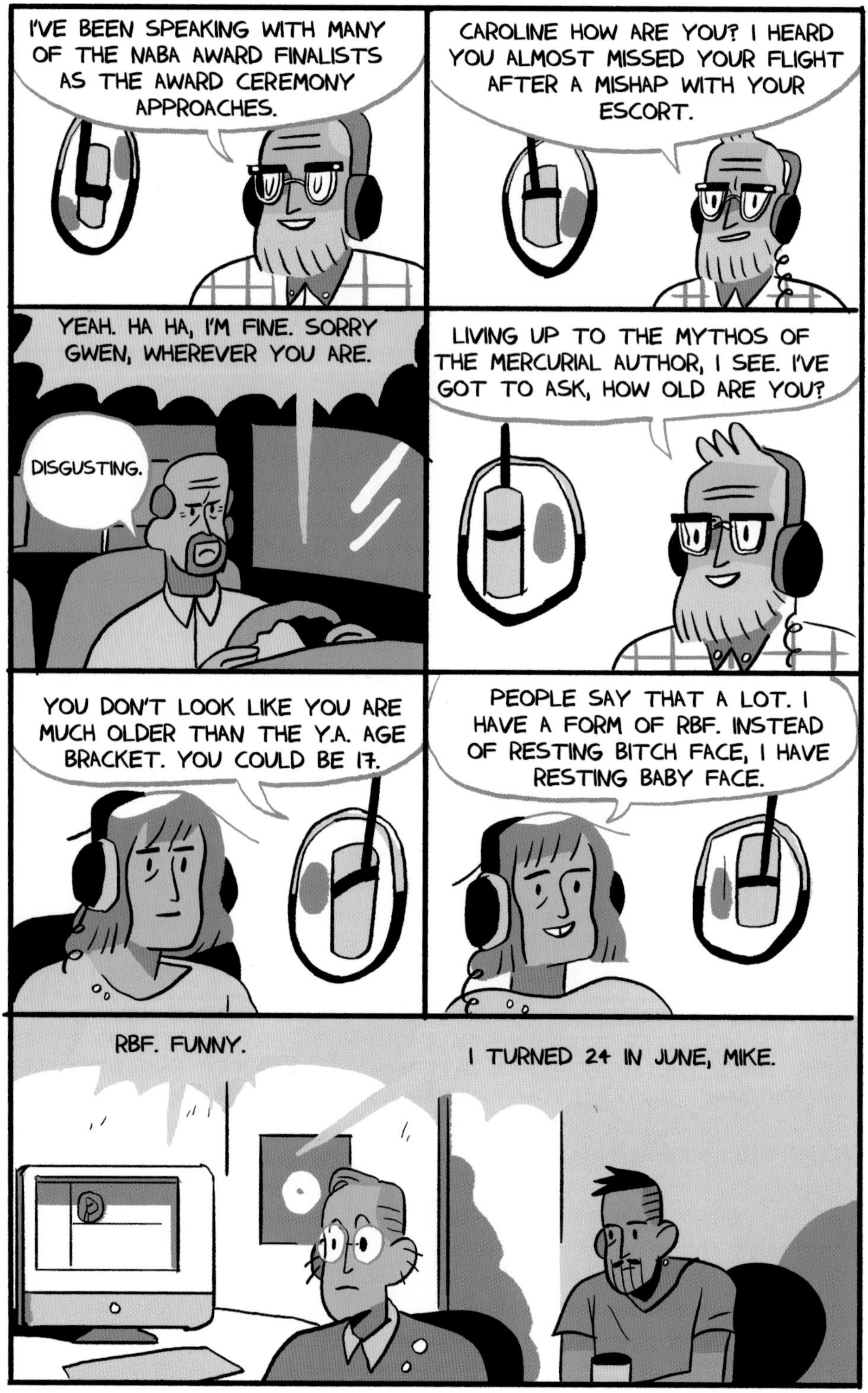
I'VE BEEN SPEAKING WITH MANY OF THE NABA AWARD FINALISTS AS THE AWARD CEREMONY APPROACHES.
CAROLINE HOW ARE YOU? I HEARD YOU ALMOST MISSED YOUR FLIGHT AFTER A MISHAP WITH YOUR ESCORT.
YEAH. HA HA, I'M FINE. SORRY GWEN, WHEREVER YOU ARE.
DISGUSTING.
LIVING UP TO THE MYTHOS OF THE MERCURIAL AUTHOR, I SEE. I'VE GOT TO ASK, HOW OLD ARE YOU?
YOU DON'T LOOK LIKE YOU ARE MUCH OLDER THAN THE Y.A. AGE BRACKET. YOU COULD BE 17.
PEOPLE SAY THAT A LOT. I HAVE A FORM OF RBF. INSTEAD OF RESTING BITCH FACE, I HAVE RESTING BABY FACE.
RBF. FUNNY.
I TURNED 24 IN JUNE, MIKE.

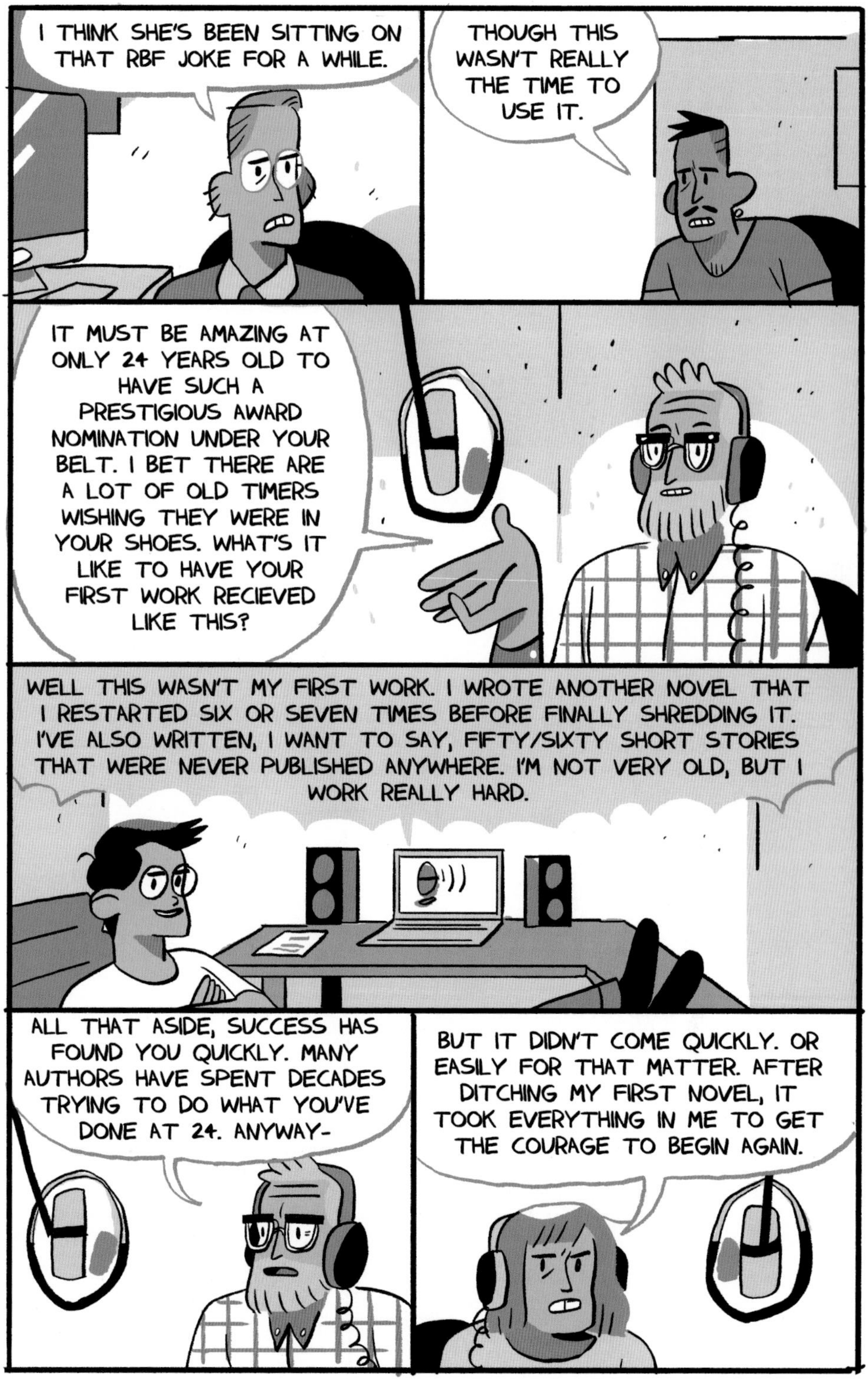
I THINK SHE'S BEEN SITTING ON THAT RBF JOKE FOR A WHILE.
THOUGH THIS WASN'T REALLY THE TIME TO USE IT.
IT MUST BE AMAZING AT ONLY 24 YEARS OLD TO HAVE SUCH A PRESTIGIOUS AWARD NOMINATION UNDER YOUR BELT. I BET THERE ARE A LOT OF OLD TIMERS WISHING THEY WERE IN YOUR SHOES. WHAT'S IT LIKE TO HAVE YOUR FIRST WORK RECIEVED LIKE THIS?
WELL THIS WASN'T MY FIRST WORK. I WROTE ANOTHER NOVEL THAT I RESTARTED SIX OR SEVEN TIMES BEFORE FINALLY SHREDDING IT. I'VE ALSO WRITTEN, I WANT TO SAY, FIFTY/SIXTY SHORT STORIES THAT WERE NEVER PUBLISHED ANYWHERE. I'M NOT VERY OLD, BUT I WORK REALLY HARD.
ALL THAT ASIDE, SUCCESS HAS FOUND YOU QUICKLY. MANY AUTHORS HAVE SPENT DECADES TRYING TO DO WHAT YOU'VE DONE AT 24. ANYWAY-
BUT IT DIDN'T COME QUICKLY. OR EASILY FOR THAT MATTER. AFTER DITCHING MY FIRST NOVEL, IT TOOK EVERYTHING IN ME TO GET THE COURAGE TO BEGIN AGAIN.

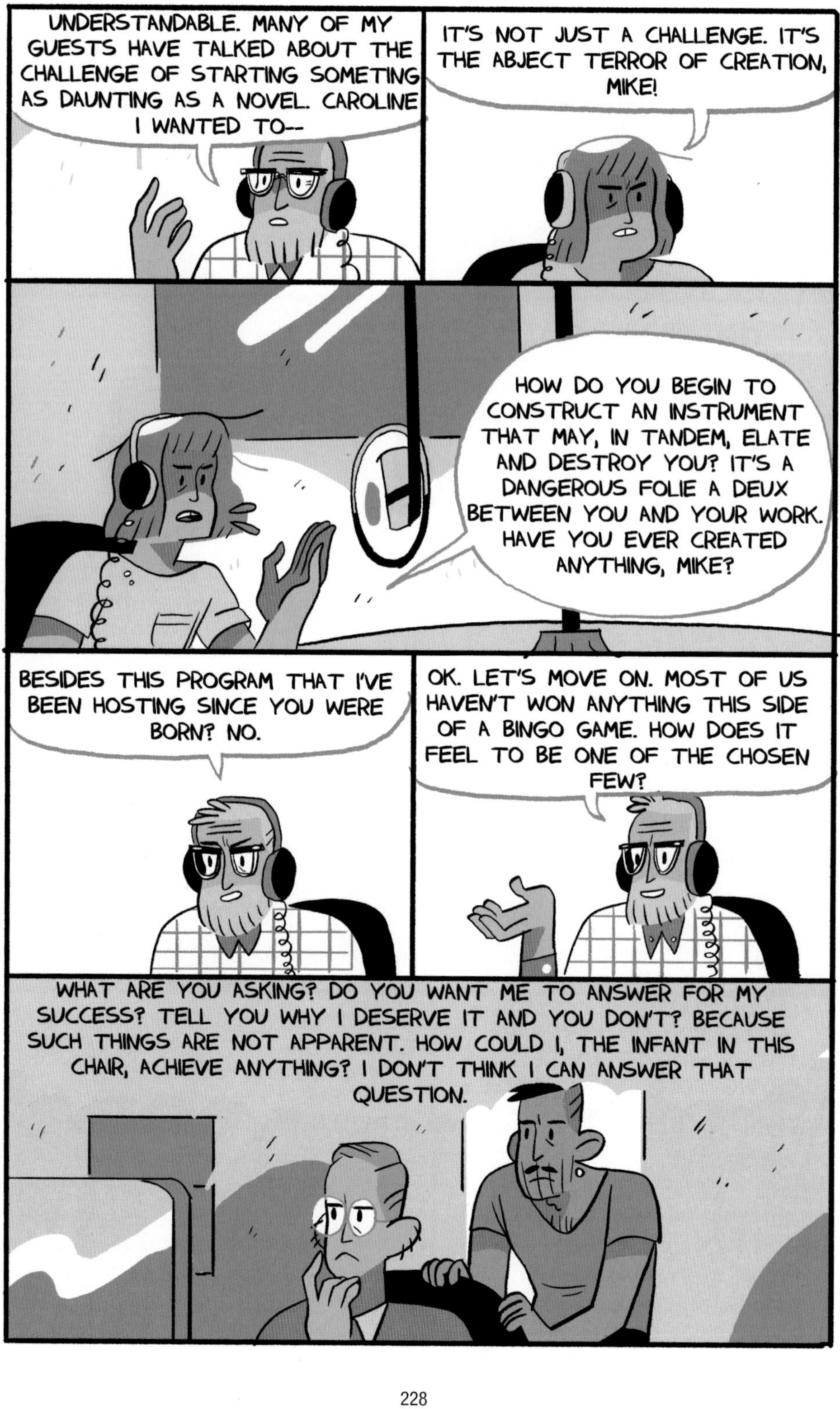
UNDERSTANDABLE. MANY OF MY GUESTS HAVE TALKED ABOUT THE CHALLENGE OF STARTING SOMETING AS DAUNTING AS A NOVEL. CAROLINE I WANTED TO--
IT'S NOT JUST A CHALLENGE. IT'S THE ABJECT TERROR OF CREATION, MIKE!
HOW DO YOU BEGIN TO CONSTRUCT AN INSTRUMENT THAT MAY, IN TANDEM, ELATE AND DESTROY YOU? IT'S A DANGEROUS FOLIE A DEUX BETWEEN YOU AND YOUR WORK. HAVE YOU EVER CREATED ANYTHING, MIKE?
BESIDES THIS PROGRAM THAT I'VE BEEN HOSTING SINCE YOU WERE BORN? NO.
OK. LET'S MOVE ON. MOST OF US HAVEN'T WON ANYTHING THIS SIDE OF A BINGO GAME. HOW DOES IT FEEL TO BE ONE OF THE CHOSEN FEW?
WHAT ARE YOU ASKING? DO YOU WANT ME TO ANSWER FOR MY SUCCESS? TELL YOU WHY I DESERVE IT AND YOU DON'T? BECAUSE SUCH THINGS ARE NOT APPARENT. HOW COULD I, THE INFANT IN THIS CHAIR, ACHIEVE ANYTHING? I DON'T THINK I CAN ANSWER THAT QUESTION.

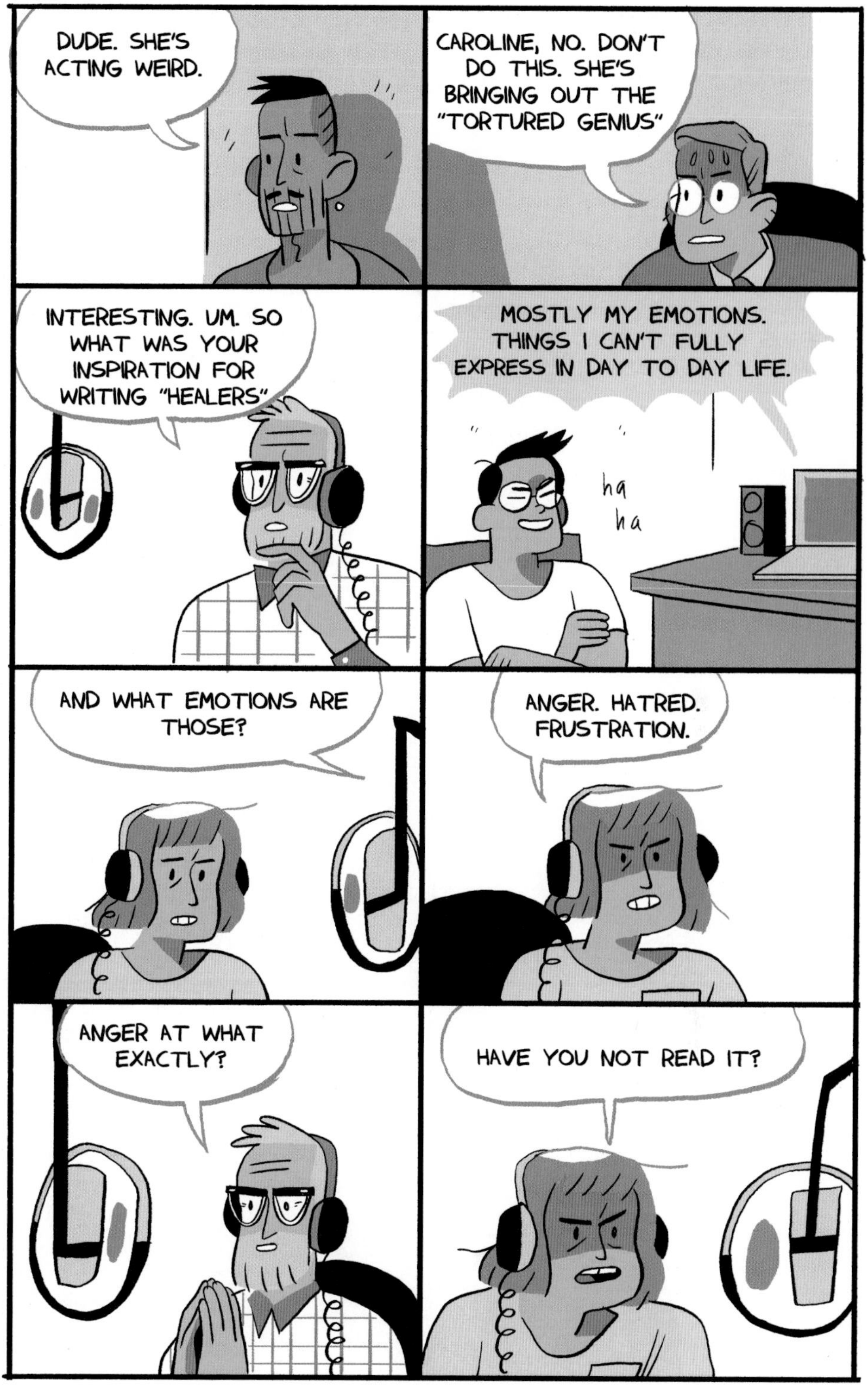
DUDE. SHE'S ACTING WEIRD.
CAROLINE, NO. DON'T DO THIS. SHE'S BRINGING OUT THE "TORTURED GENIUS"
INTERESTING. UM. SO WHAT WAS YOUR INSPIRATION FOR WRITING "HEALERS"
MOSTLY MY EMOTIONS. THINGS I CAN'T FULLY EXPRESS IN DAY TO DAY LIFE.
ha ha
AND WHAT EMOTIONS ARE THOSE?
ANGER. HATRED. FRUSTRATION.
ANGER AT WHAT EXACTLY?
HAVE YOU NOT READ IT?

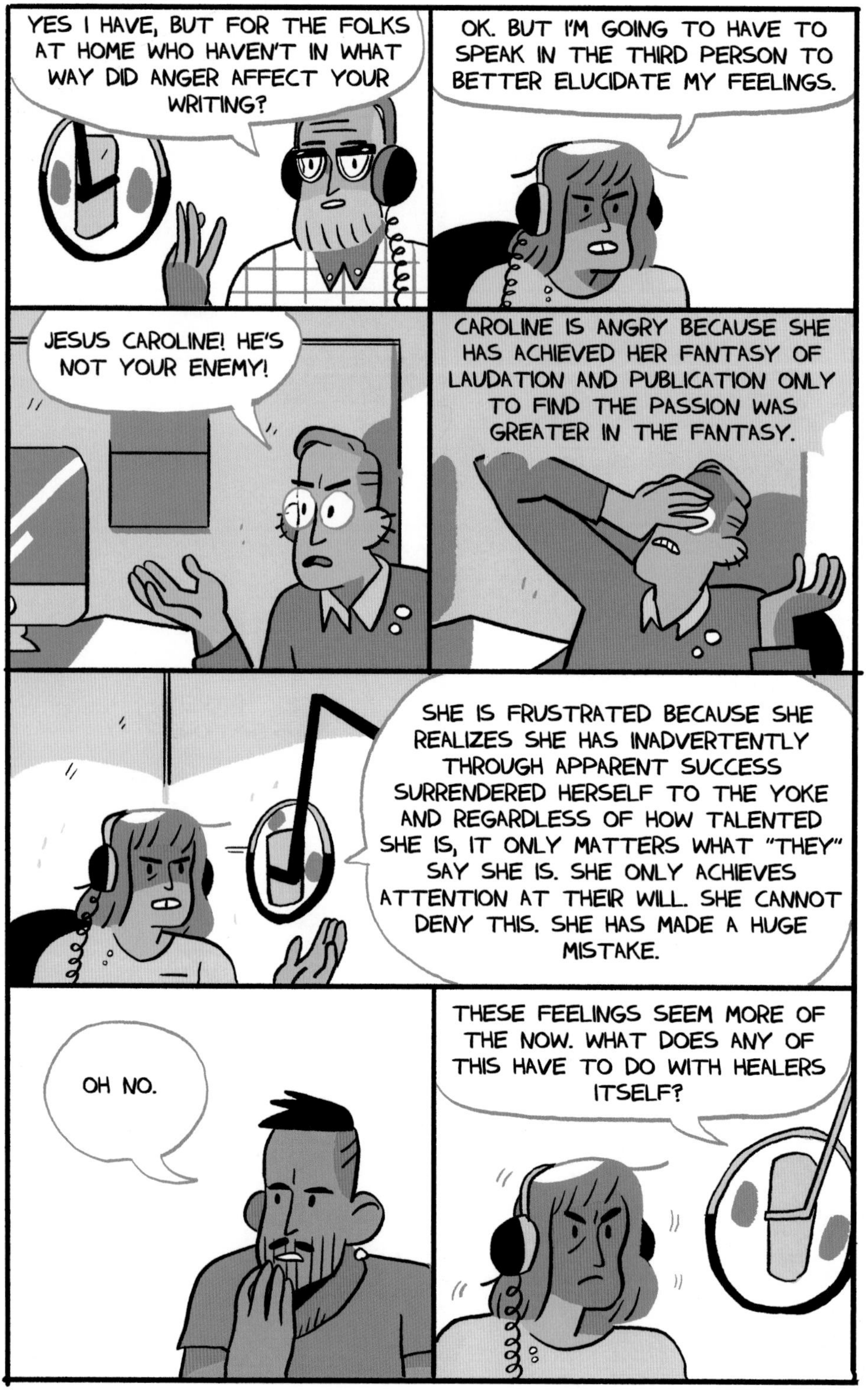
YES I HAVE, BUT FOR THE FOLKS AT HOME WHO HAVEN'T IN WHAT WAY DID ANGER AFFECT YOUR WRITING?
OK. BUT I'M GOING TO HAVE TO SPEAK IN THE THIRD PERSON TO BETTER ELUCIDATE MY FEELINGS.
JESUS CAROLINE! HE'S NOT YOUR ENEMY!
CAROLINE IS ANGRY BECAUSE SHE HAS ACHIEVED HER FANTASY OF LAUDATION AND PUBLICATION ONLY TO FIND THE PASSION WAS GREATER IN THE FANTASY.
SHE IS FRUSTRATED BECAUSE SHE REALIZES SHE HAS INADVERTENTLY THROUGH APPARENT SUCCESS SURRENDERED HERSELF TO THE YOKE AND REGARDLESS OF HOW TALENTED SHE IS, IT ONLY MATTERS WHAT "THEY" SAY SHE IS. SHE ONLY ACHIEVES ATTENTION AT THEIR WILL. SHE CANNOT DENY THIS. SHE HAS MADE A HUGE MISTAKE.
OH NO.
THESE FEELINGS SEEM MORE OF THE NOW. WHAT DOES ANY OF THIS HAVE TO DO WITH HEALERS ITSELF?

DON'T YOU SEE? I WRITE ABOUT THE GRAND MAGUS, THE WIZARD, IN HEALERS AS A WAY TO DISPEL MY HATRED AND ANGER. THE MISJUSTICE HE REPRESENTS IS THE WELL FROM WHICH I DREW STRENGTH!

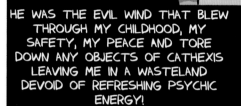

HE WAS THE EVIL WIND THAT BLEW THROUGH MY CHILDHOOD, MY SAFETY, MY PEACE AND TORE DOWN ANY OBJECTS OF CATHEXIS LEAVING ME IN A WASTELAND DEVOID OF REFRESHING PSYCHIC ENERGY!

IMAGINE BEING SURROUNDED BY UNREQUITED EXISTENCE. YOUR PASSIONS SLIDING OFF THE DOME OF HUMAN INTERACTION LIKE EGG YOLKS! I THOUGHT DEFEATING HIM WOULD SAVE ME.

BUT THIS WASN'T TRUE. WHAT I DESTROYED WAS A MERE REFLECTION OF HIS POWER.

THAT IS A LOT OF INTENSE PESSIMISM, CAROLINE. MY FATHER ALWAYS TAUGHT ME NOT TO HATE ANYTHING.

HASN'T ANYONE EVER TOLD YOU, IN THOUGHT WORD OR DEED THAT YOU CAN'T HAVE SOMETHING? SOMETHING YOU DESIRED MORE THAN YOUR OWN LIFE?

OF COURSE YOU'RE GOING TO HATE! YOUR FRIENDS, YOUR PARENTS, YOURSELF! ANYONE THAT DENIES YOU! AND THEY ALL DO, MIKE! WE TRY TO TRUST THEIR KINDNESS, BUT WE CAN'T! IN THE END IT ALL JUST GET'S TOTALLY FUCKED UP MAN! IT'S MEANINGLESS! WHY NOT JUST FUCKING KILL YOURSELF, Y'KNOW?

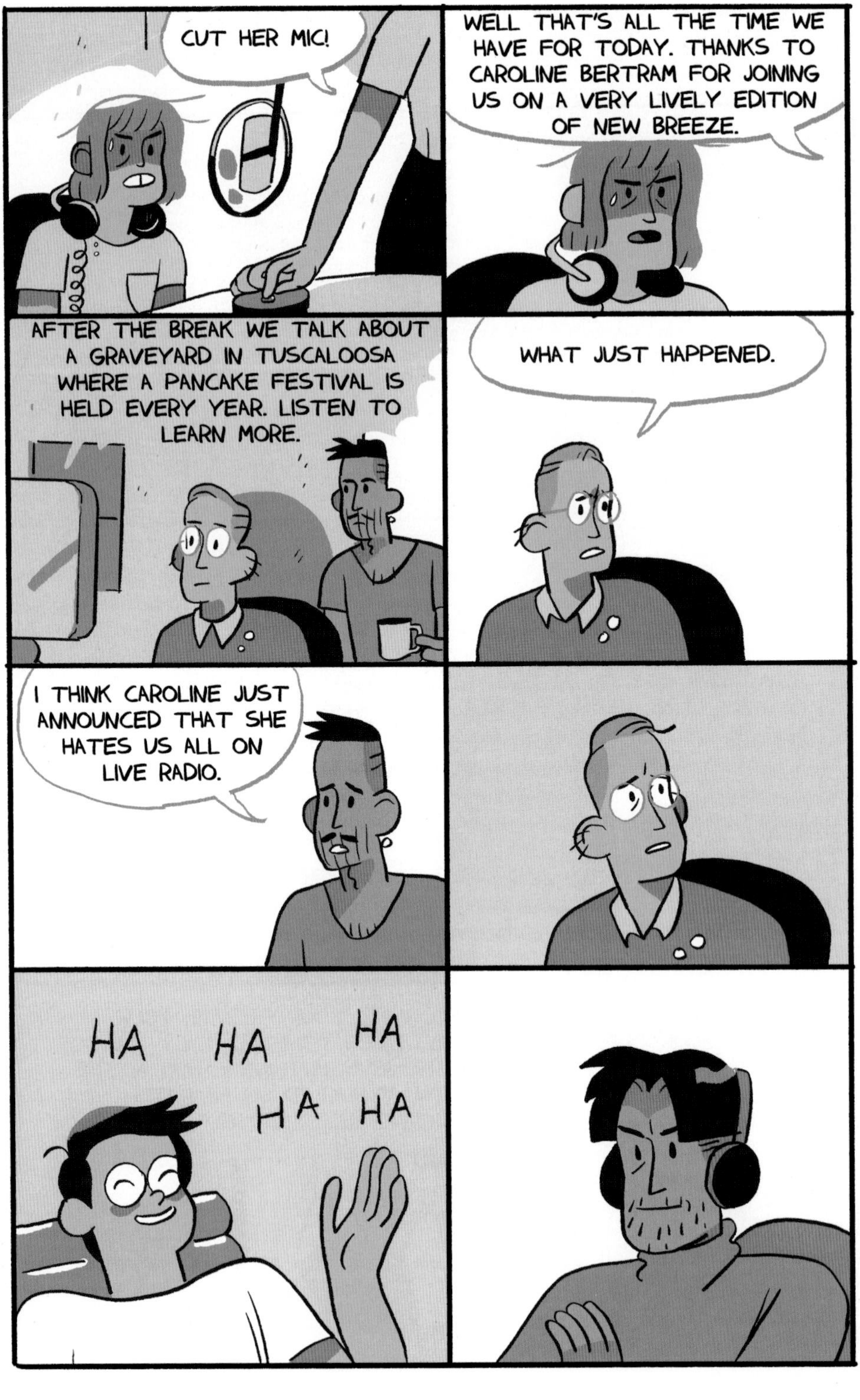
CUT HER MIC!
WELL THAT'S ALL THE TIME WE HAVE FOR TODAY. THANKS TO CAROLINE BERTRAM FOR JOINING US ON A VERY LIVELY EDITION OF NEW BREEZE.
AFTER THE BREAK WE TALK ABOUT A GRAVEYARD IN TUSCALOOSA WHERE A PANCAKE FESTIVAL IS HELD EVERY YEAR. LISTEN TO LEARN MORE.
WHAT JUST HAPPENED.
I THINK CAROLINE JUST ANNOUNCED THAT SHE HATES US ALL ON LIVE RADIO.
HA HA HA
HA HA

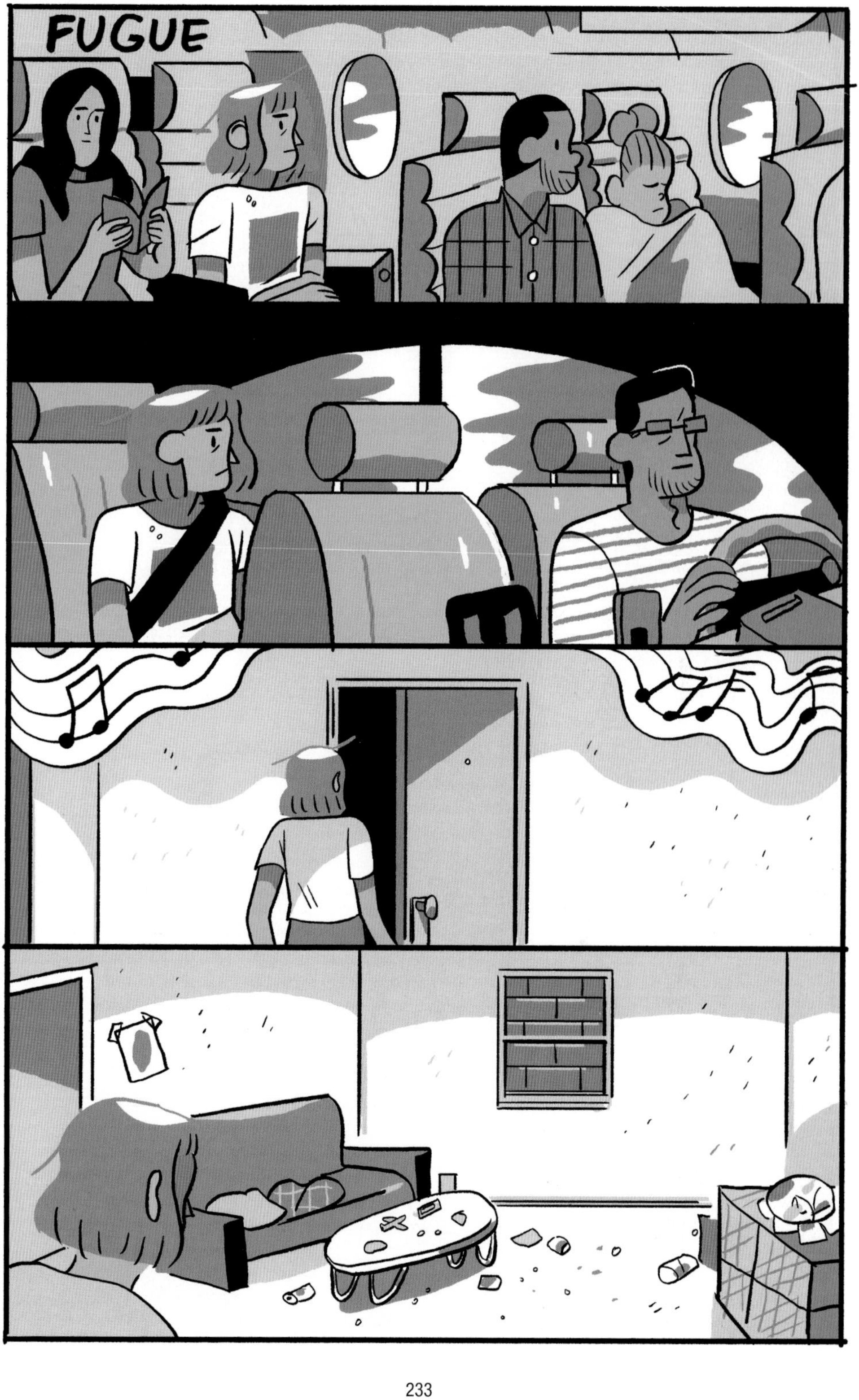
FUGUE

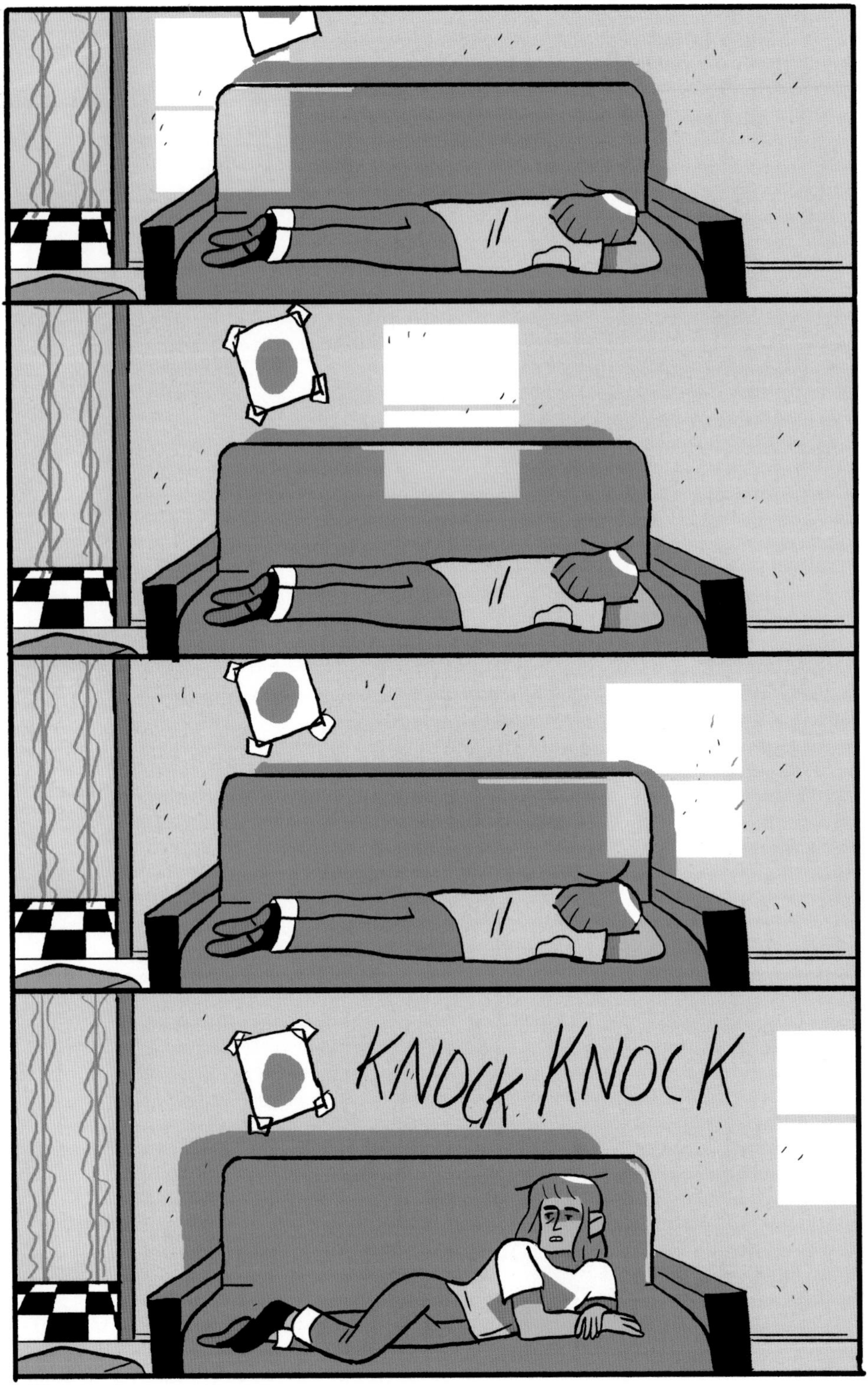
KNOCK KNOCK

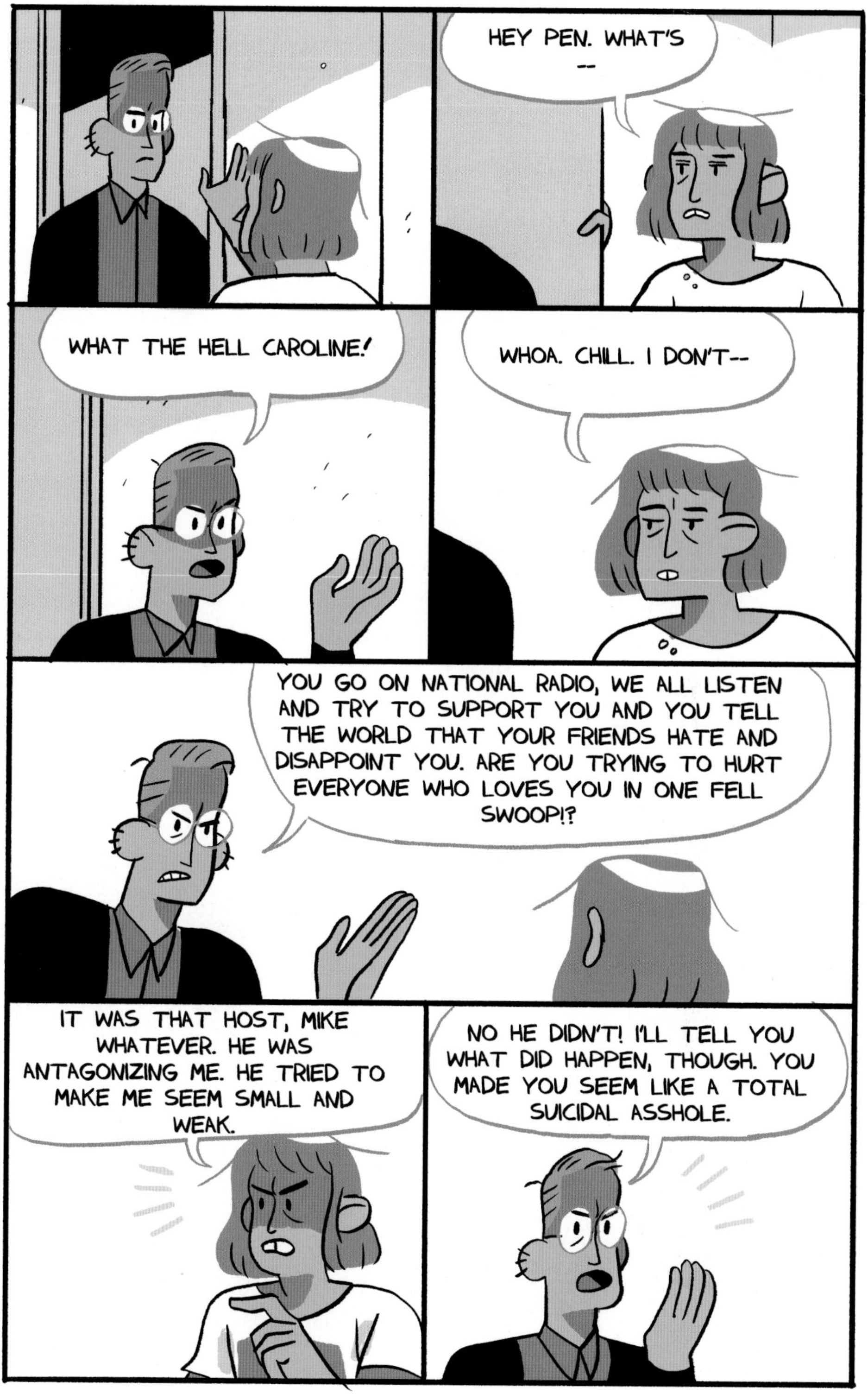
HEY PEN. WHAT'S --
WHAT THE HELL CAROLINE!
WHOA. CHILL. I DON'T--
YOU GO ON NATIONAL RADIO, WE ALL LISTEN AND TRY TO SUPPORT YOU AND YOU TELL THE WORLD THAT YOUR FRIENDS HATE AND DISAPPOINT YOU. ARE YOU TRYING TO HURT EVERYONE WHO LOVES YOU IN ONE FELL SWOOP!?
IT WAS THAT HOST, MIKE WHATEVER. HE WAS ANTAGONIZING ME. HE TRIED TO MAKE ME SEEM SMALL AND WEAK.
NO HE DIDN'T! I'LL TELL YOU WHAT DID HAPPEN, THOUGH. YOU MADE YOU SEEM LIKE A TOTAL SUICIDAL ASSHOLE.

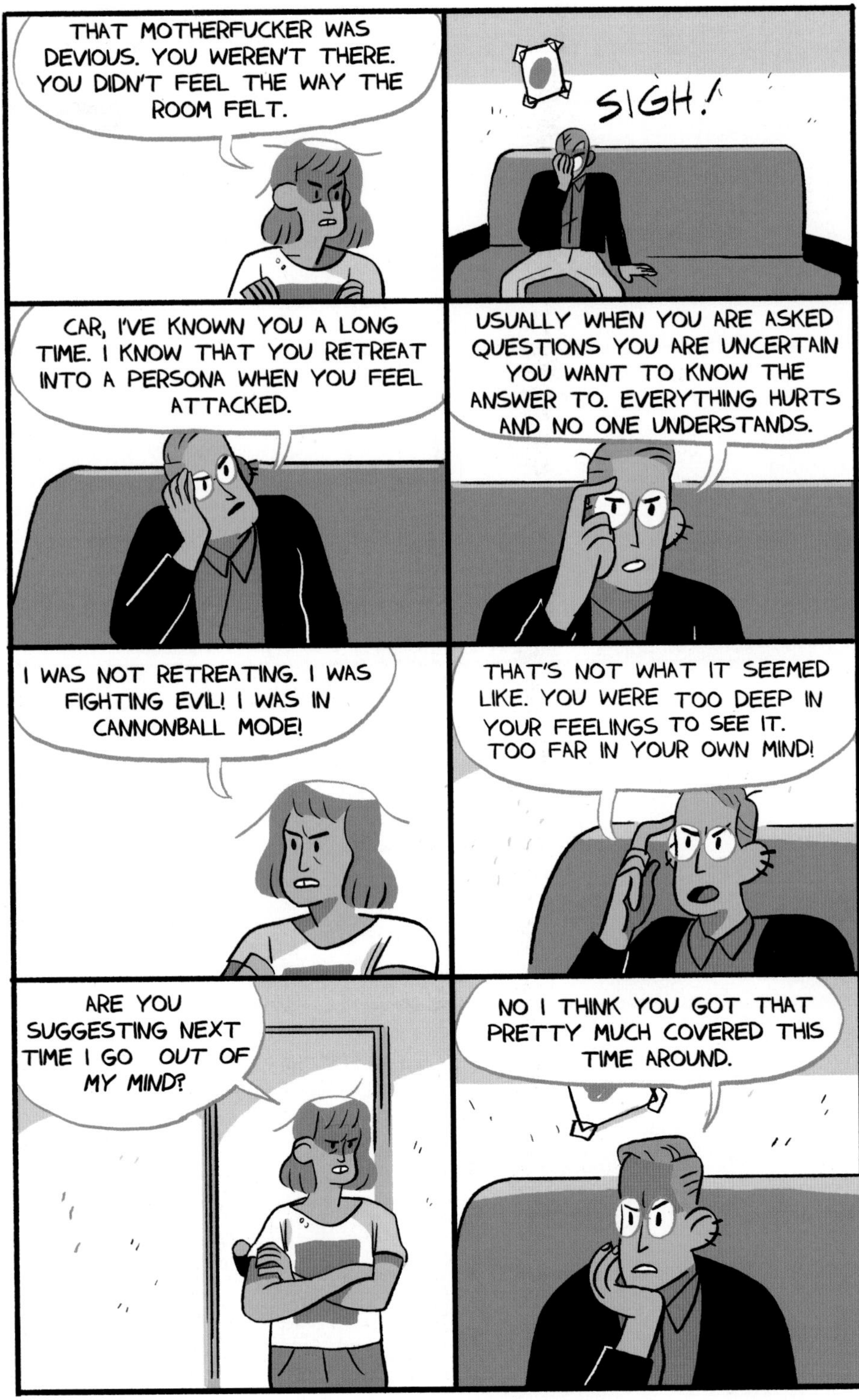
THAT MOTHERFUCKER WAS DEVIOUS. YOU WEREN'T THERE. YOU DIDN'T FEEL THE WAY THE ROOM FELT.
SIGH!
CAR, I'VE KNOWN YOU A LONG TIME. I KNOW THAT YOU RETREAT INTO A PERSONA WHEN YOU FEEL ATTACKED.
USUALLY WHEN YOU ARE ASKED QUESTIONS YOU ARE UNCERTAIN YOU WANT TO KNOW THE ANSWER TO. EVERYTHING HURTS AND NO ONE UNDERSTANDS.
I WAS NOT RETREATING. I WAS FIGHTING EVIL! I WAS IN CANNONBALL MODE!
THAT'S NOT WHAT IT SEEMED LIKE. YOU WERE TOO DEEP IN YOUR FEELINGS TO SEE IT. TOO FAR IN YOUR OWN MIND!
ARE YOU SUGGESTING NEXT TIME I GO *OUT OF MY MIND*?
NO I THINK YOU GOT THAT PRETTY MUCH COVERED THIS TIME AROUND.

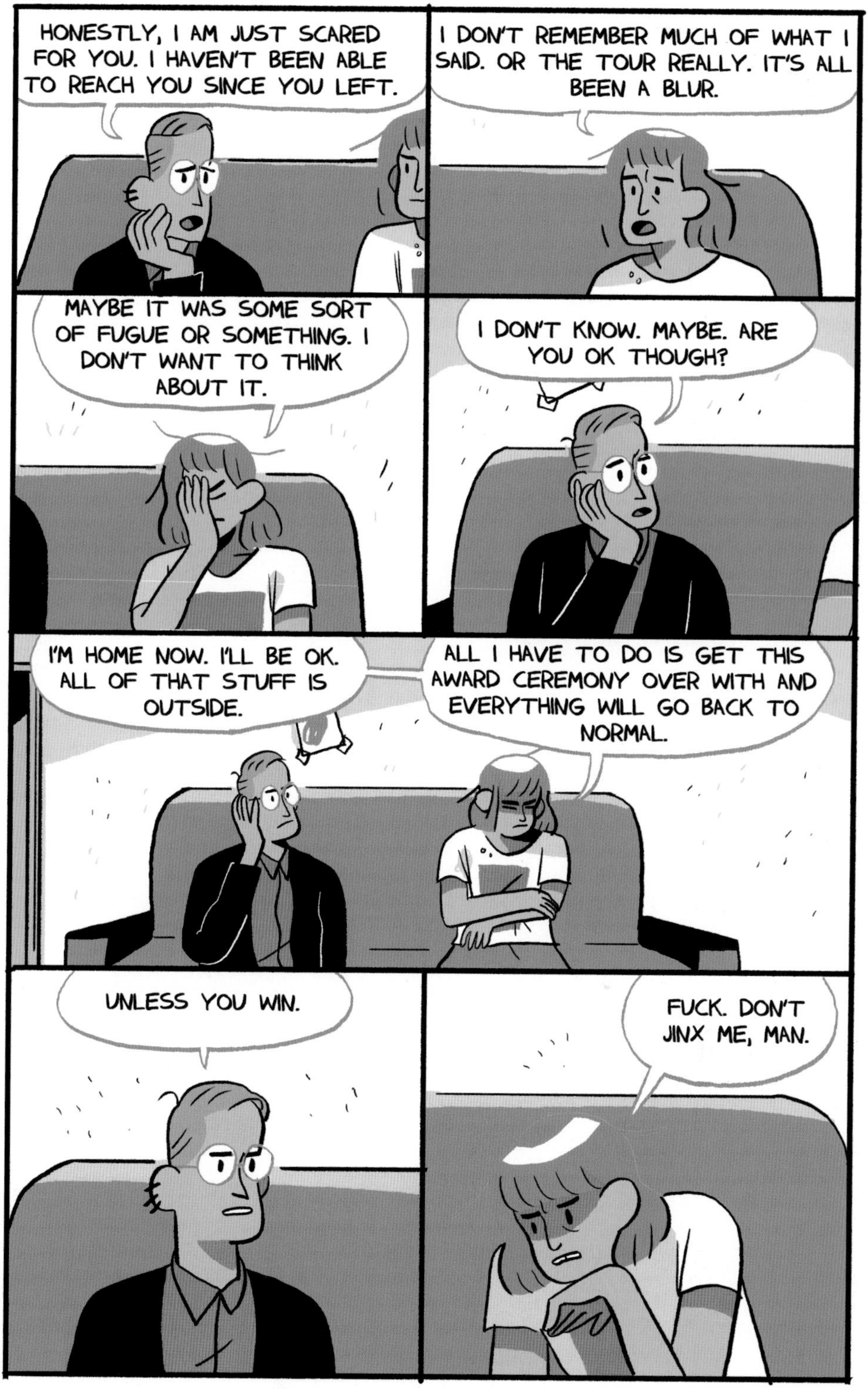
HONESTLY, I AM JUST SCARED FOR YOU. I HAVEN'T BEEN ABLE TO REACH YOU SINCE YOU LEFT.
I DON'T REMEMBER MUCH OF WHAT I SAID. OR THE TOUR REALLY. IT'S ALL BEEN A BLUR.
MAYBE IT WAS SOME SORT OF FUGUE OR SOMETHING. I DON'T WANT TO THINK ABOUT IT.
I DON'T KNOW. MAYBE. ARE YOU OK THOUGH?
I'M HOME NOW. I'LL BE OK. ALL OF THAT STUFF IS OUTSIDE.
ALL I HAVE TO DO IS GET THIS AWARD CEREMONY OVER WITH AND EVERYTHING WILL GO BACK TO NORMAL.
UNLESS YOU WIN.
FUCK. DON'T JINX ME, MAN.

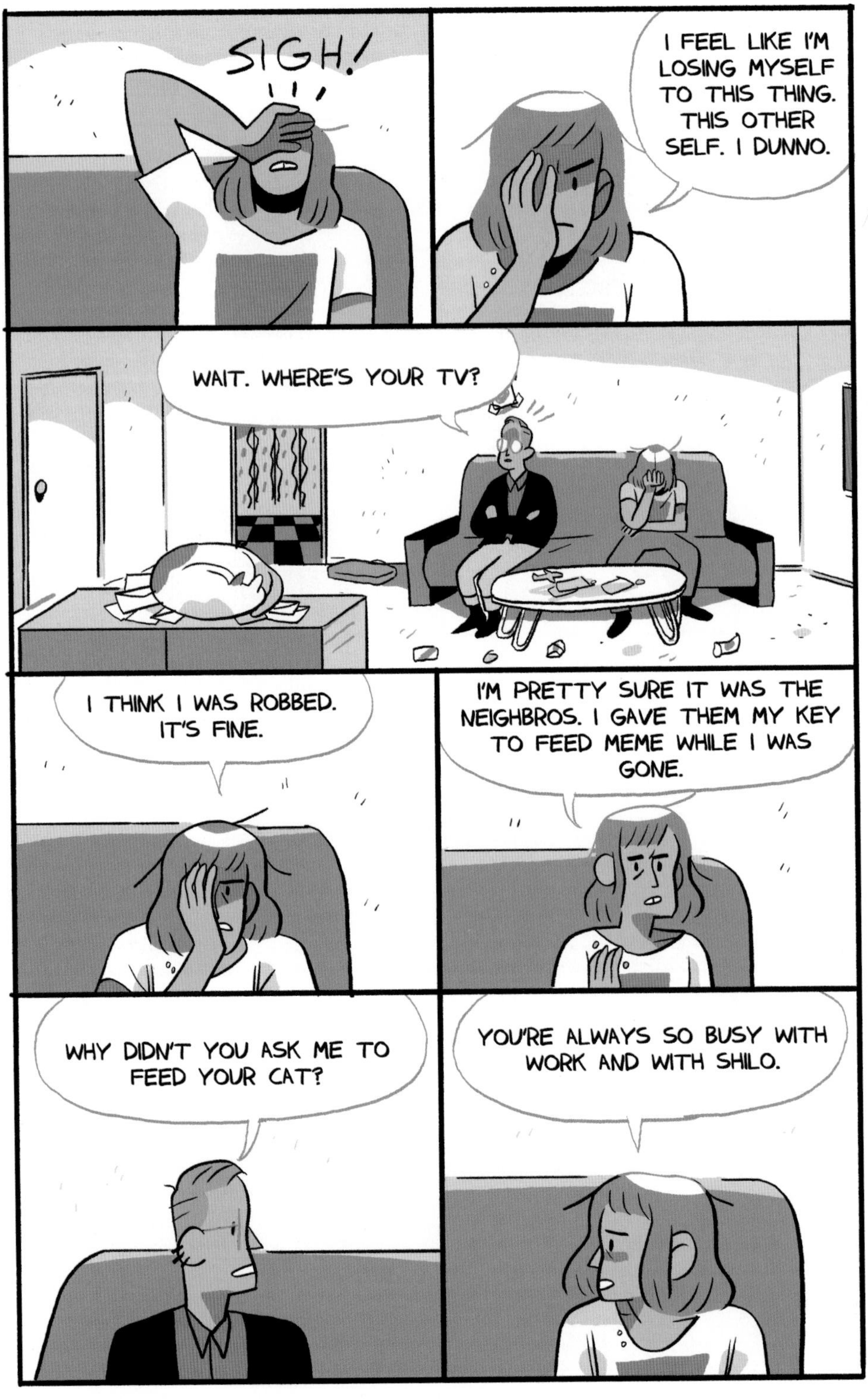
SIGH!
I FEEL LIKE I'M LOSING MYSELF TO THIS THING. THIS OTHER SELF. I DUNNO.
WAIT. WHERE'S YOUR TV?
I THINK I WAS ROBBED. IT'S FINE.
I'M PRETTY SURE IT WAS THE NEIGHBROS. I GAVE THEM MY KEY TO FEED MEME WHILE I WAS GONE.
WHY DIDN'T YOU ASK ME TO FEED YOUR CAT?
YOU'RE ALWAYS SO BUSY WITH WORK AND WITH SHILO.

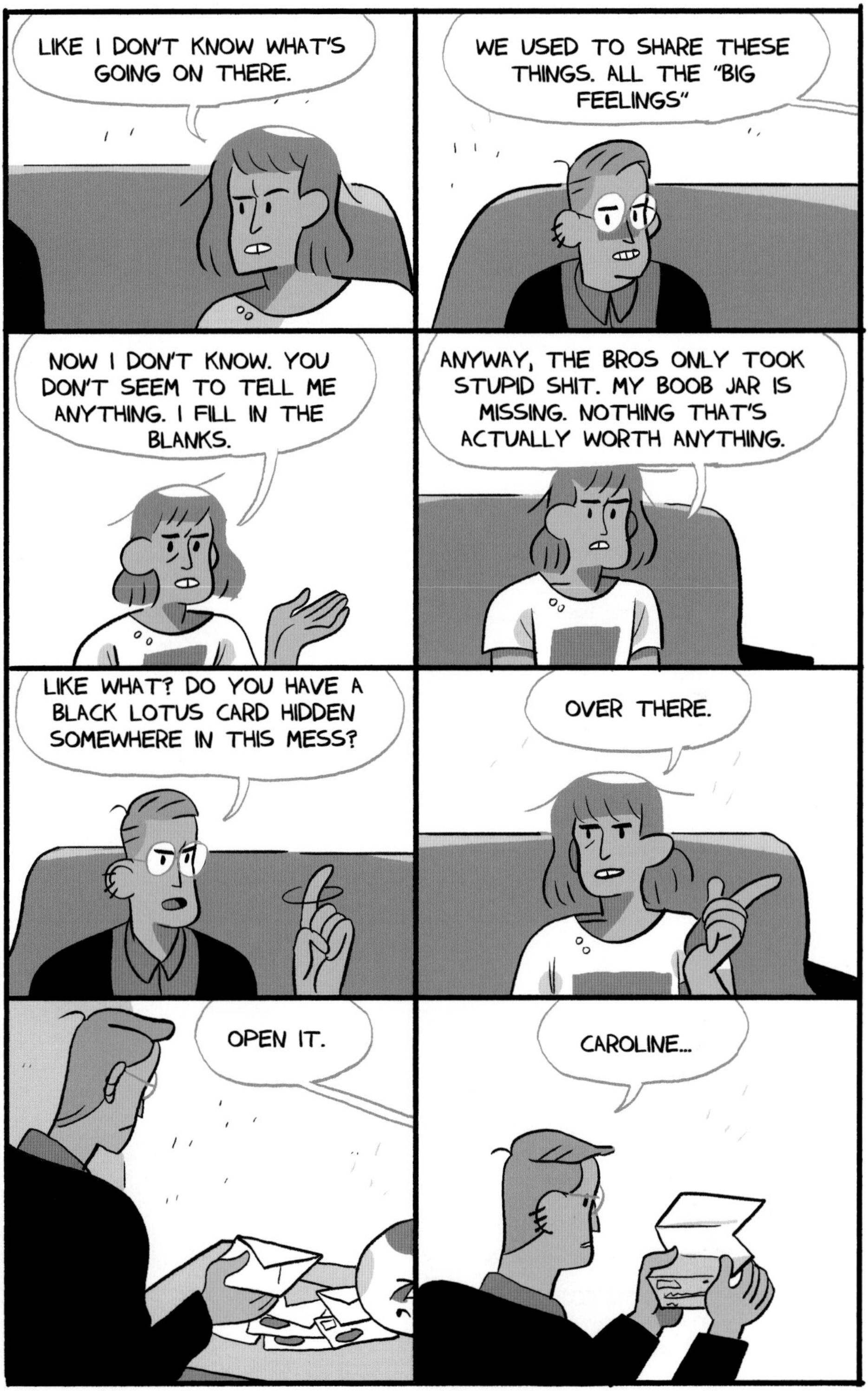
LIKE I DON'T KNOW WHAT'S GOING ON THERE.
WE USED TO SHARE THESE THINGS. ALL THE "BIG FEELINGS"
NOW I DON'T KNOW. YOU DON'T SEEM TO TELL ME ANYTHING. I FILL IN THE BLANKS.
ANYWAY, THE BROS ONLY TOOK STUPID SHIT. MY BOOB JAR IS MISSING. NOTHING THAT'S ACTUALLY WORTH ANYTHING.
LIKE WHAT? DO YOU HAVE A BLACK LOTUS CARD HIDDEN SOMEWHERE IN THIS MESS?
OVER THERE.
OPEN IT.
CAROLINE...

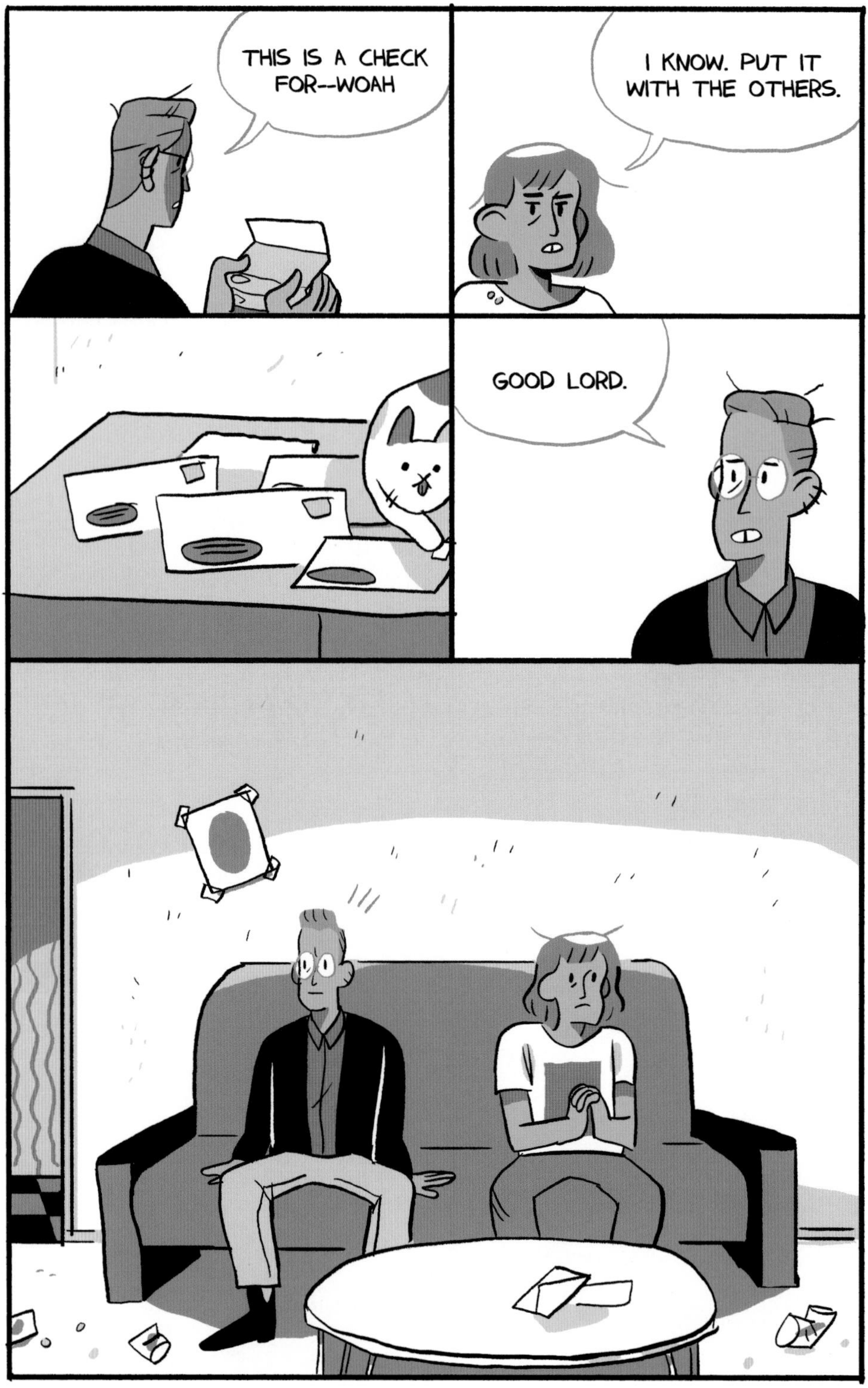
THIS IS A CHECK FOR--WOAH
I KNOW. PUT IT WITH THE OTHERS.
GOOD LORD.

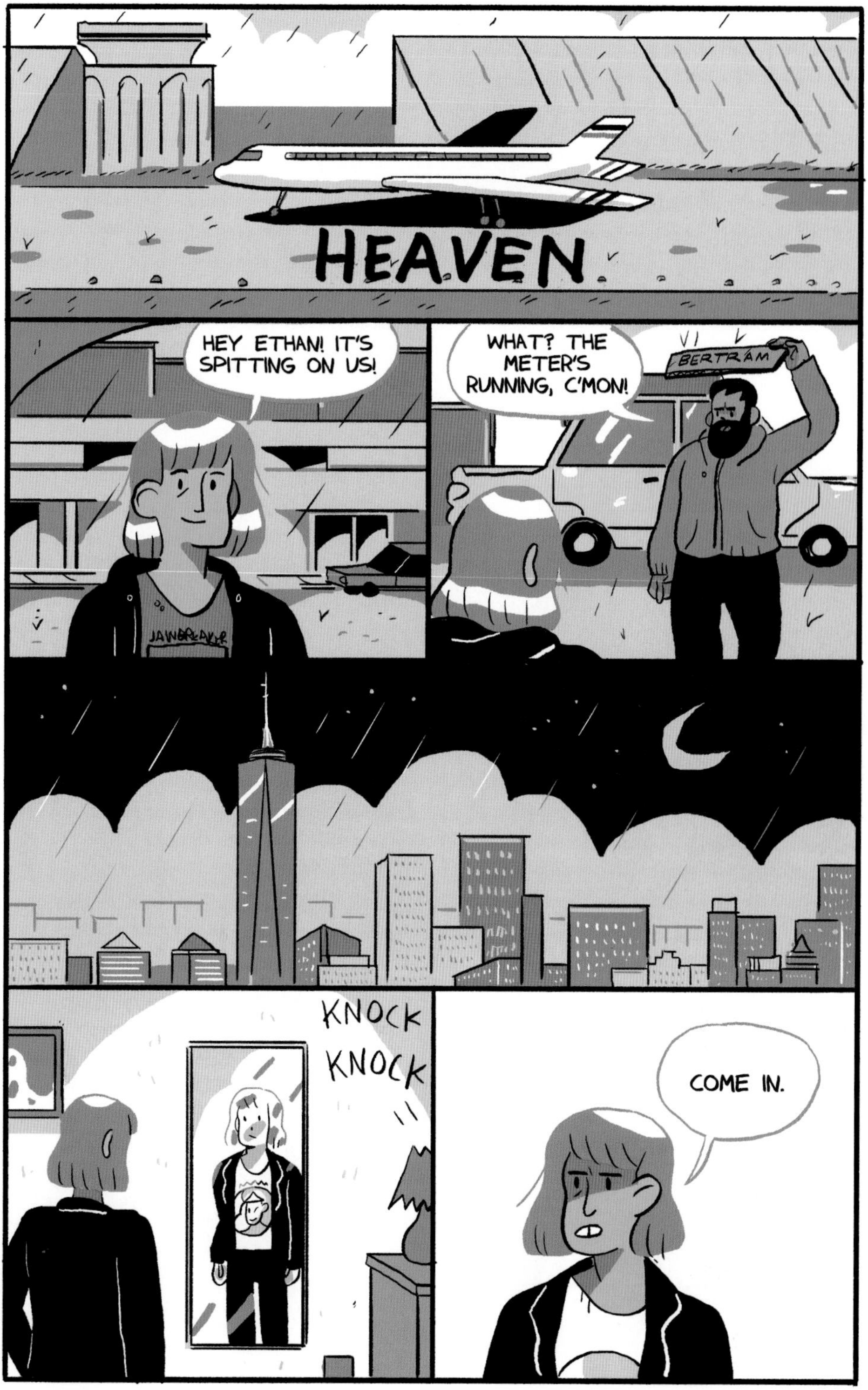
HEAVEN
HEY ETHAN! IT'S SPITTING ON US!
WHAT? THE METER'S RUNNING, C'MON!
BERTRAM
KNOCK
KNOCK
COME IN.

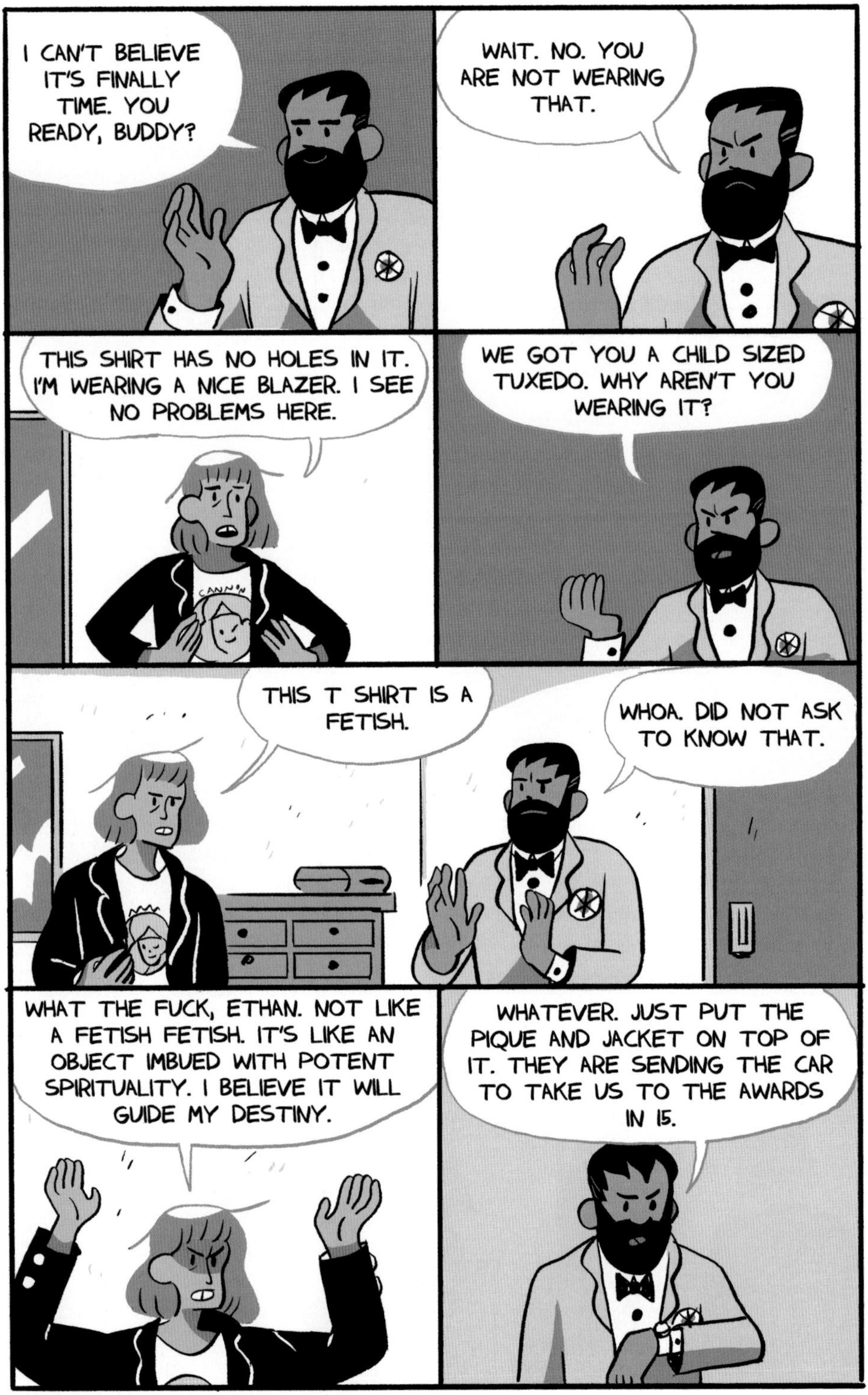
I CAN'T BELIEVE IT'S FINALLY TIME. YOU READY, BUDDY?
WAIT. NO. YOU ARE NOT WEARING THAT.
THIS SHIRT HAS NO HOLES IN IT. I'M WEARING A NICE BLAZER. I SEE NO PROBLEMS HERE.
WE GOT YOU A CHILD SIZED TUXEDO. WHY AREN'T YOU WEARING IT?
THIS T SHIRT IS A FETISH.
WHOA. DID NOT ASK TO KNOW THAT.
WHAT THE FUCK, ETHAN. NOT LIKE A FETISH FETISH. IT'S LIKE AN OBJECT IMBUED WITH POTENT SPIRITUALITY. I BELIEVE IT WILL GUIDE MY DESTINY.
WHATEVER. JUST PUT THE PIQUE AND JACKET ON TOP OF IT. THEY ARE SENDING THE CAR TO TAKE US TO THE AWARDS IN 15.

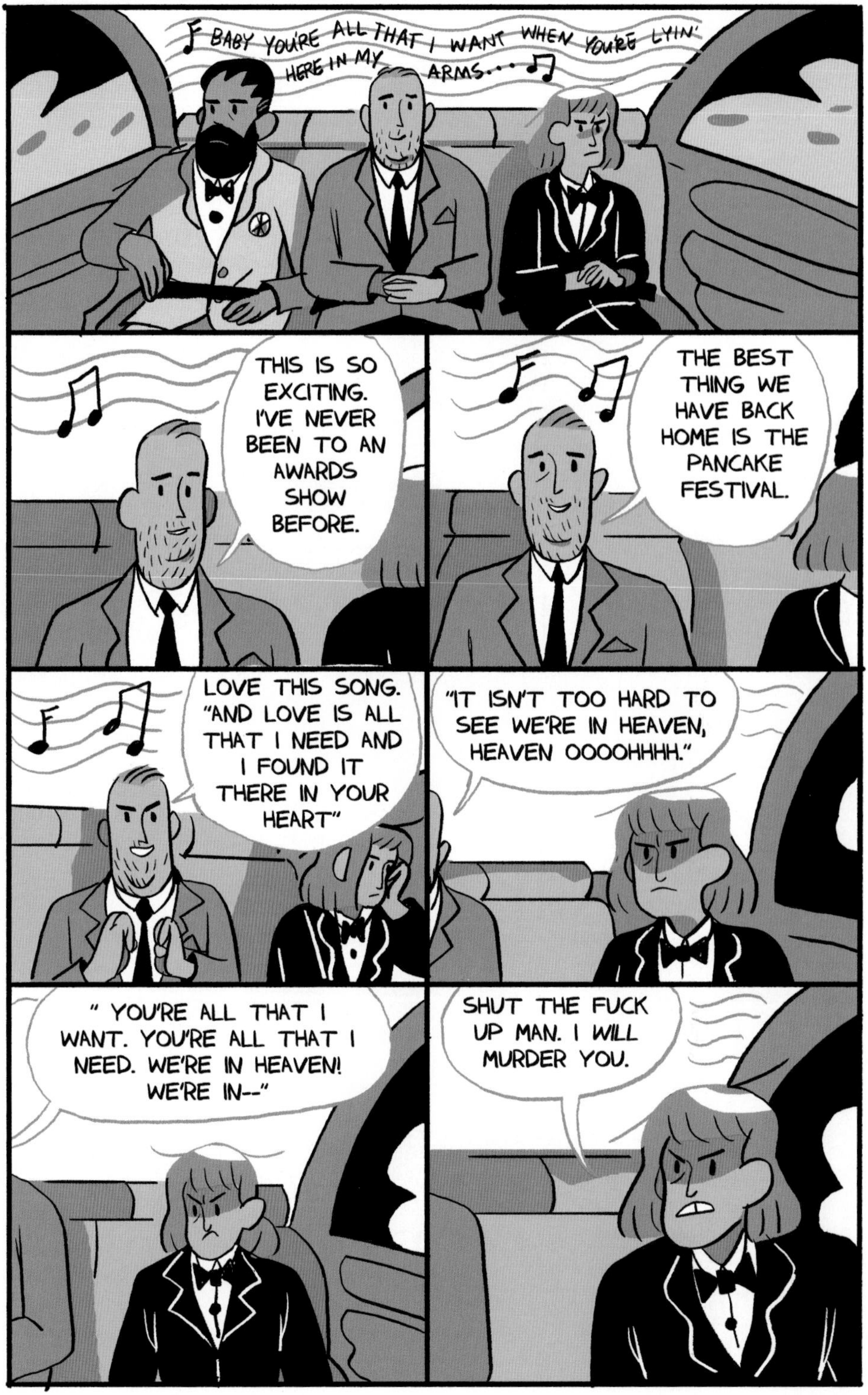
BABY YOU'RE ALL THAT I WANT WHEN YOU'RE LYIN' HERE IN MY ARMS...
THIS IS SO EXCITING. I'VE NEVER BEEN TO AN AWARDS SHOW BEFORE.
THE BEST THING WE HAVE BACK HOME IS THE PANCAKE FESTIVAL.
LOVE THIS SONG. "AND LOVE IS ALL THAT I NEED AND I FOUND IT THERE IN YOUR HEART"
"IT ISN'T TOO HARD TO SEE WE'RE IN HEAVEN, HEAVEN OOOOHHHH."
" YOU'RE ALL THAT I WANT. YOU'RE ALL THAT I NEED. WE'RE IN HEAVEN! WE'RE IN--"
SHUT THE FUCK UP MAN. I WILL MURDER YOU.

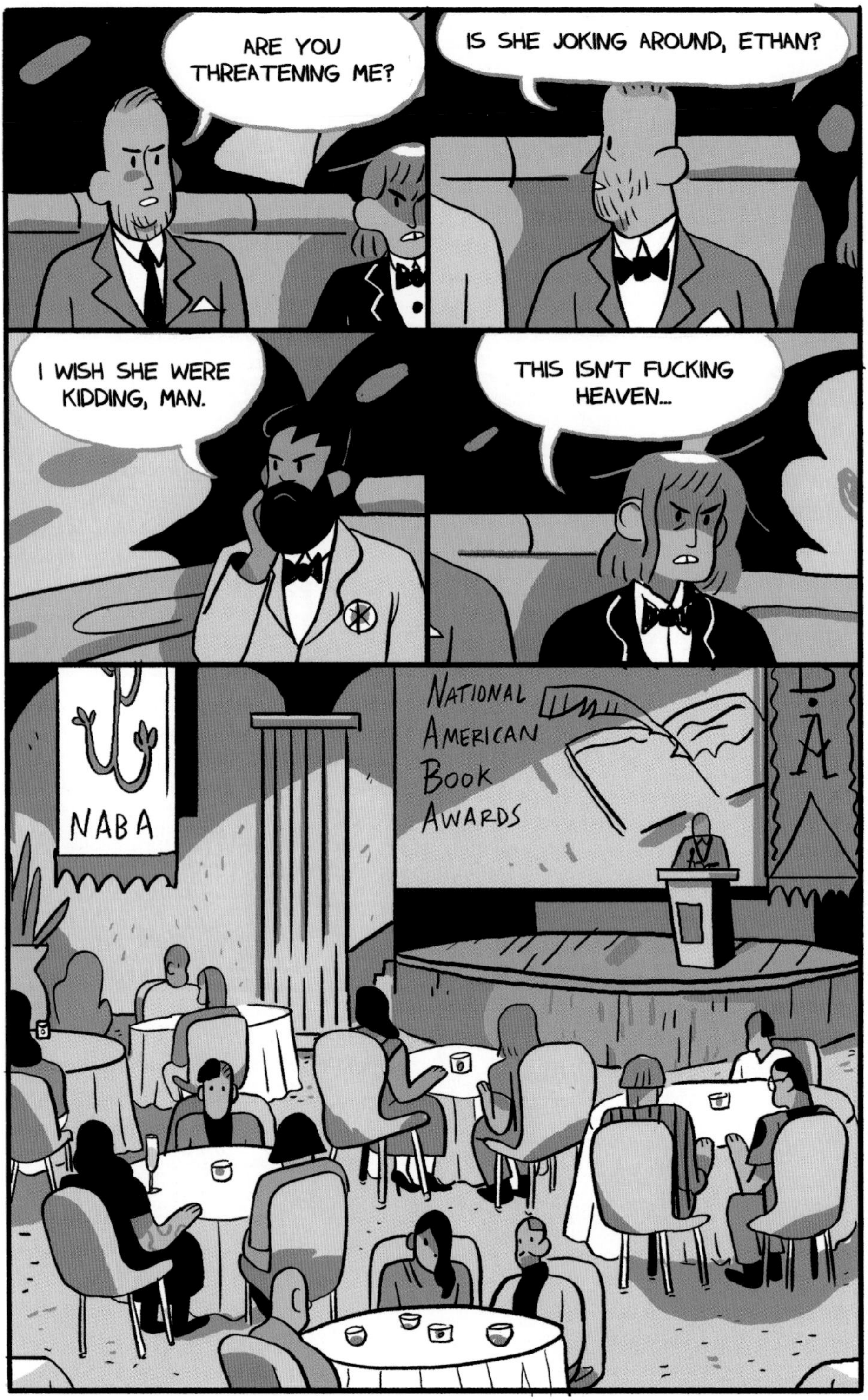

ARE YOU THREATENING ME?
IS SHE JOKING AROUND, ETHAN?
I WISH SHE WERE KIDDING, MAN.
THIS ISN'T FUCKING HEAVEN...
NABA
NATIONAL AMERICAN BOOK AWARDS

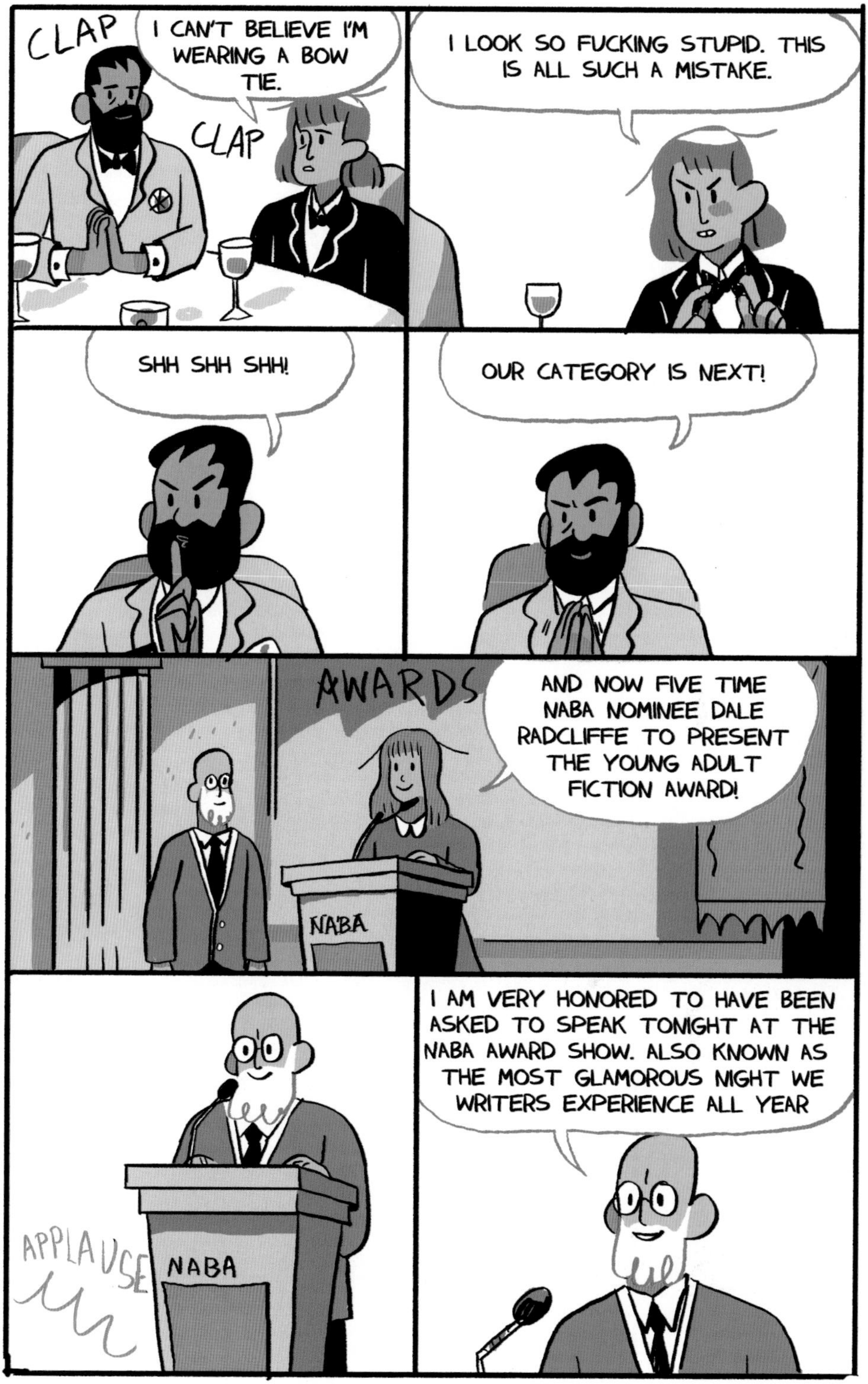
CLAP
I CAN'T BELIEVE I'M WEARING A BOW TIE.
CLAP
I LOOK SO FUCKING STUPID. THIS IS ALL SUCH A MISTAKE.
SHH SHH SHH!
OUR CATEGORY IS NEXT!
AWARDS
AND NOW FIVE TIME NABA NOMINEE DALE RADCLIFFE TO PRESENT THE YOUNG ADULT FICTION AWARD!
NABA
NABA
APPLAUSE
I AM VERY HONORED TO HAVE BEEN ASKED TO SPEAK TONIGHT AT THE NABA AWARD SHOW. ALSO KNOWN AS THE MOST GLAMOROUS NIGHT WE WRITERS EXPERIENCE ALL YEAR

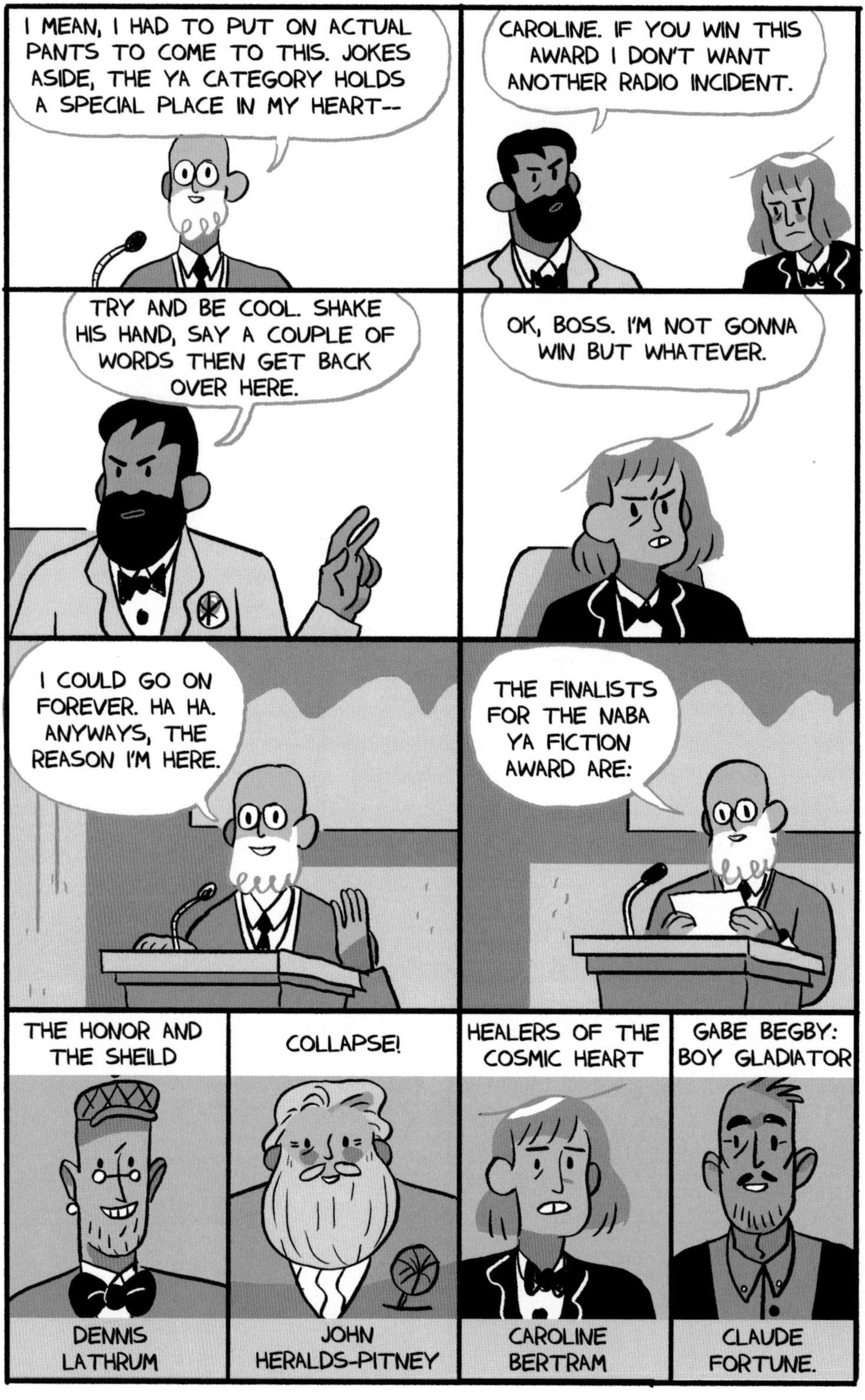
I MEAN, I HAD TO PUT ON ACTUAL PANTS TO COME TO THIS. JOKES ASIDE, THE YA CATEGORY HOLDS A SPECIAL PLACE IN MY HEART--
CAROLINE. IF YOU WIN THIS AWARD I DON'T WANT ANOTHER RADIO INCIDENT.
TRY AND BE COOL. SHAKE HIS HAND, SAY A COUPLE OF WORDS THEN GET BACK OVER HERE.
OK, BOSS. I'M NOT GONNA WIN BUT WHATEVER.
I COULD GO ON FOREVER. HA HA. ANYWAYS, THE REASON I'M HERE.
THE FINALISTS FOR THE NABA YA FICTION AWARD ARE:
THE HONOR AND THE SHEILD
DENNIS LATHRUM
COLLAPSE!
JOHN HERALDS-PITNEY
HEALERS OF THE COSMIC HEART
CAROLINE BERTRAM
GABE BEGBY: BOY GLADIATOR
CLAUDE FORTUNE.

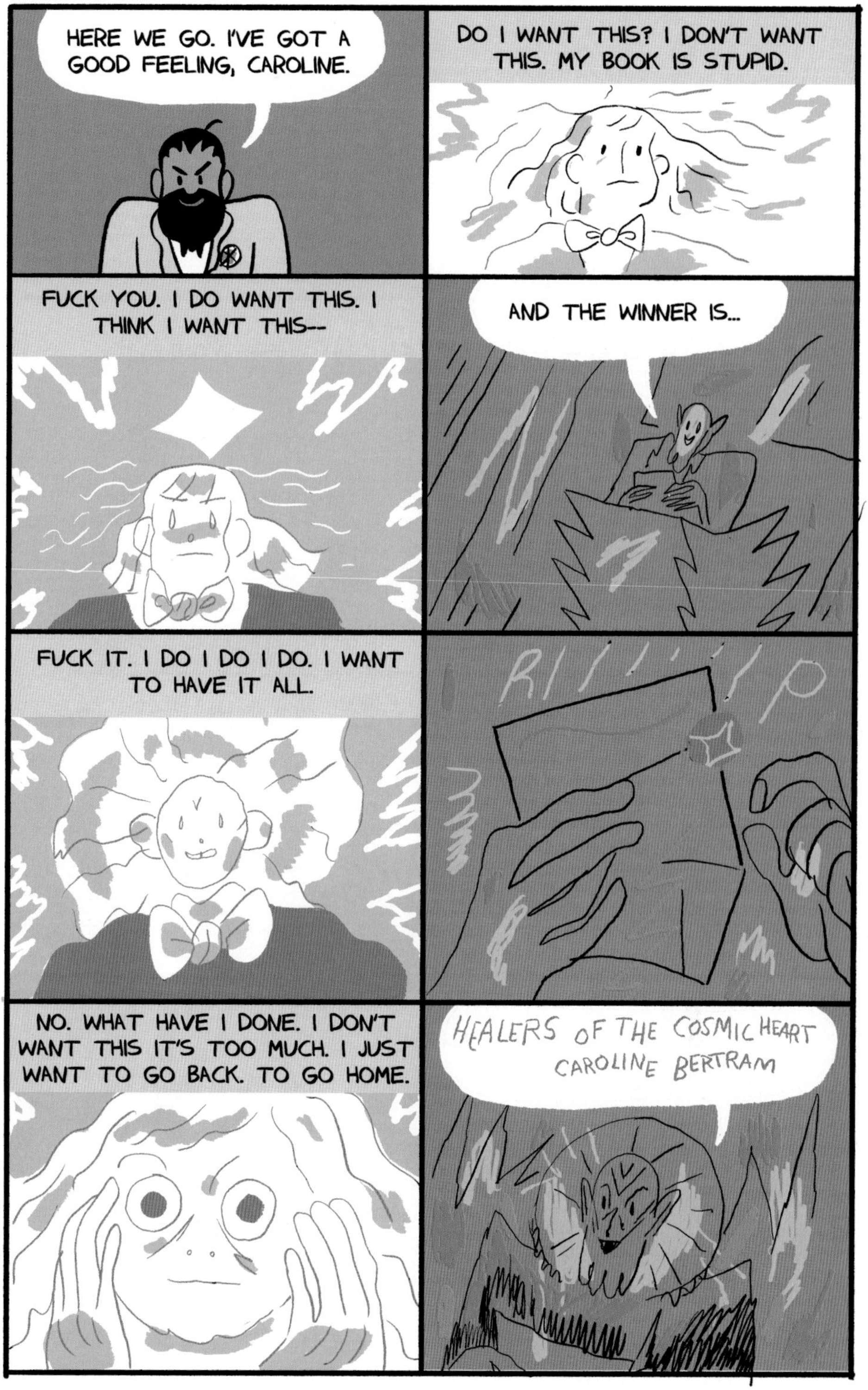
HERE WE GO. I'VE GOT A GOOD FEELING, CAROLINE.
DO I WANT THIS? I DON'T WANT THIS. MY BOOK IS STUPID.
FUCK YOU. I DO WANT THIS. I THINK I WANT THIS--
AND THE WINNER IS...
FUCK IT. I DO I DO I DO. I WANT TO HAVE IT ALL.
RIIIIIP
NO. WHAT HAVE I DONE. I DON'T WANT THIS IT'S TOO MUCH. I JUST WANT TO GO BACK. TO GO HOME.
HEALERS OF THE COSMIC HEART
CAROLINE BERTRAM

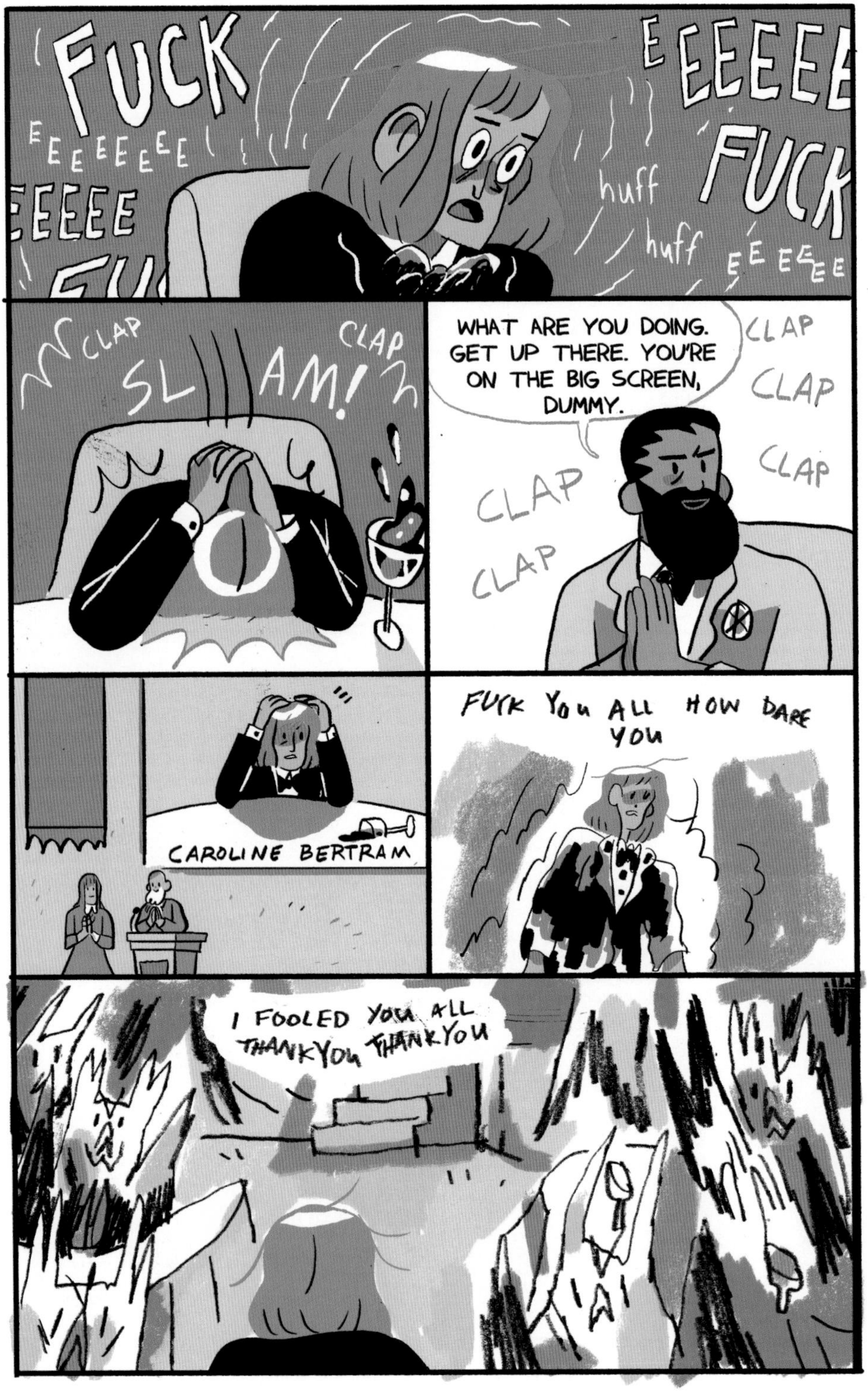
FUCK
EEEEEEEE
EEEEE
EEEEEE
FUCK
huff
huff
EEEEEE
CLAP
SLAM!
CLAP
WHAT ARE YOU DOING. GET UP THERE. YOU'RE ON THE BIG SCREEN, DUMMY.
CLAP
CLAP
CLAP
CLAP
CLAP
CAROLINE BERTRAM
FUCK YOU ALL HOW DARE YOU
I FOOLED YOU ALL
THANKYOU THANKYOU

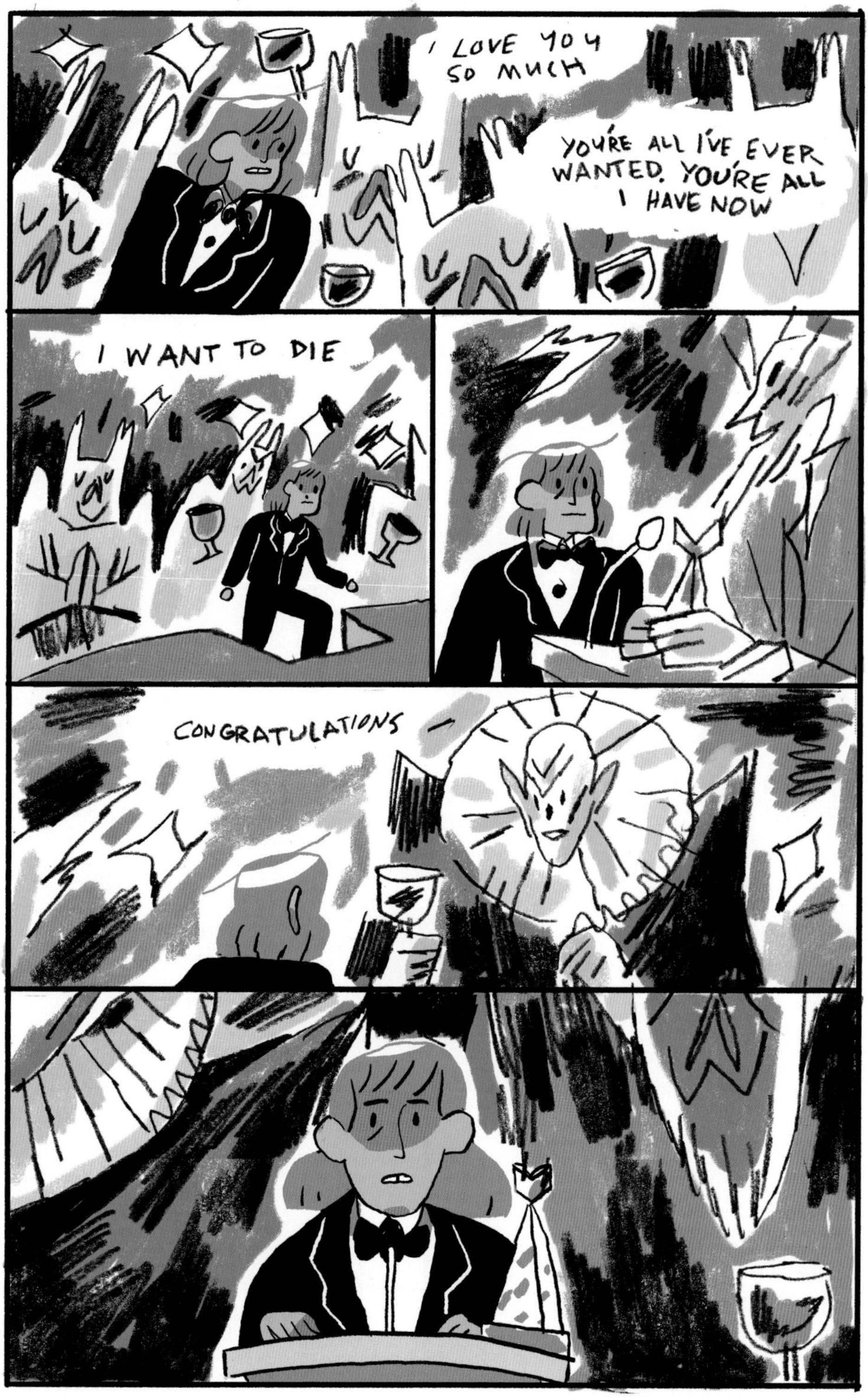
I LOVE YOU SO MUCH
YOU'RE ALL I'VE EVER WANTED. YOU'RE ALL I HAVE NOW
I WANT TO DIE
CONGRATULATIONS

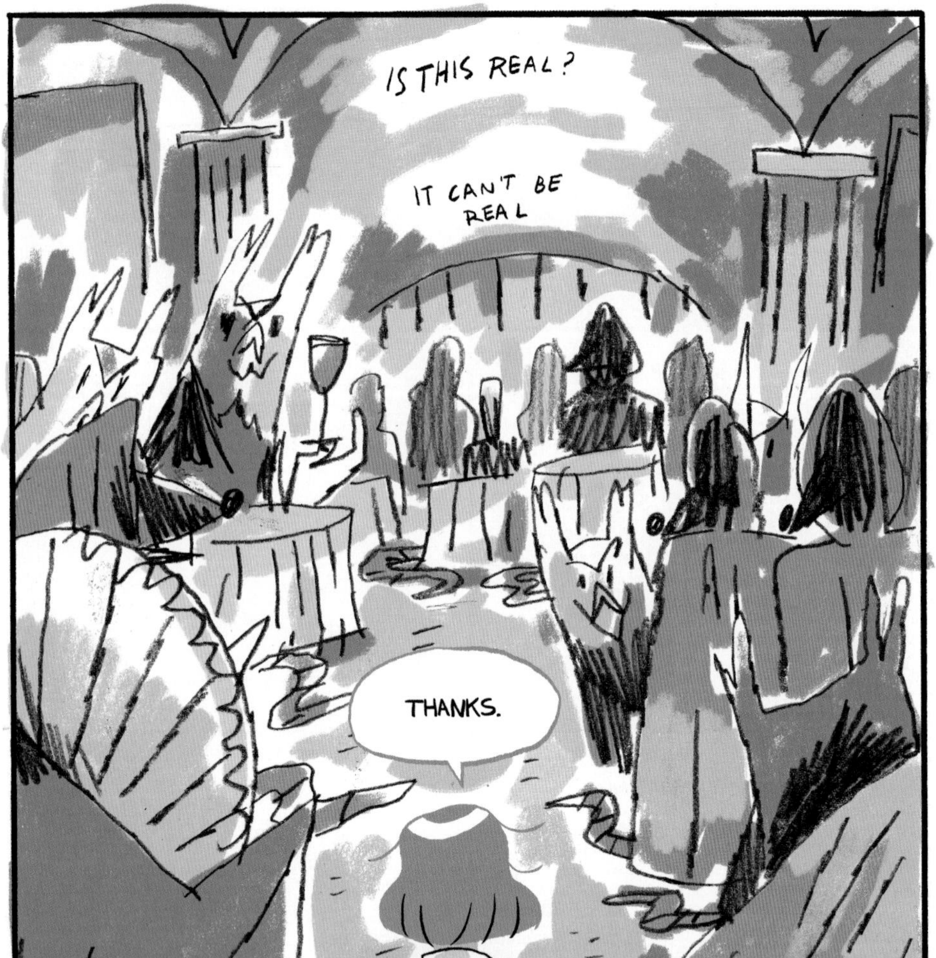
IS THIS REAL?
IT CAN'T BE REAL
THANKS.

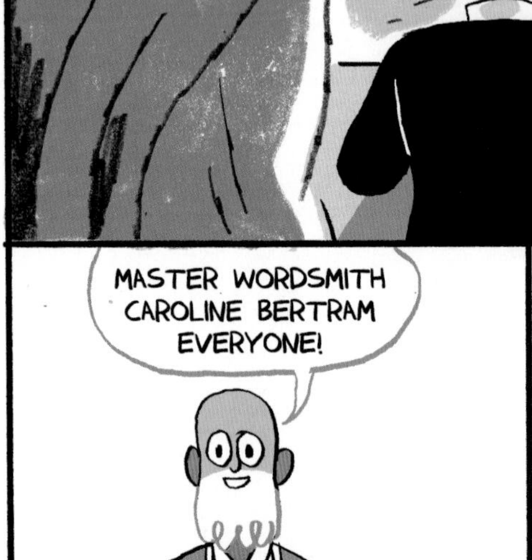
MASTER WORDSMITH CAROLINE BERTRAM EVERYONE!

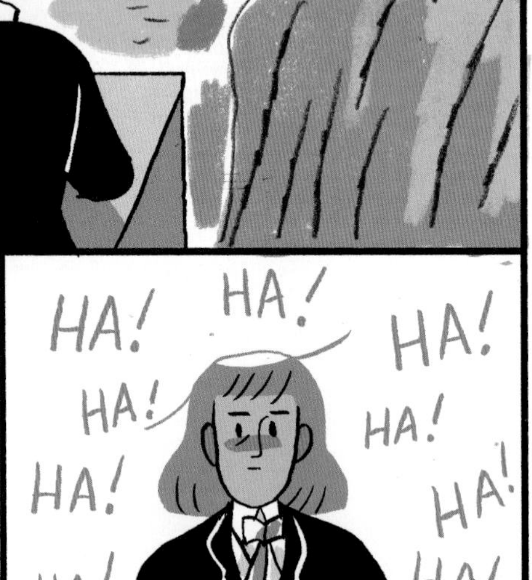
HA! HA! HA! HA! HA! HA! HA! HA! HA!

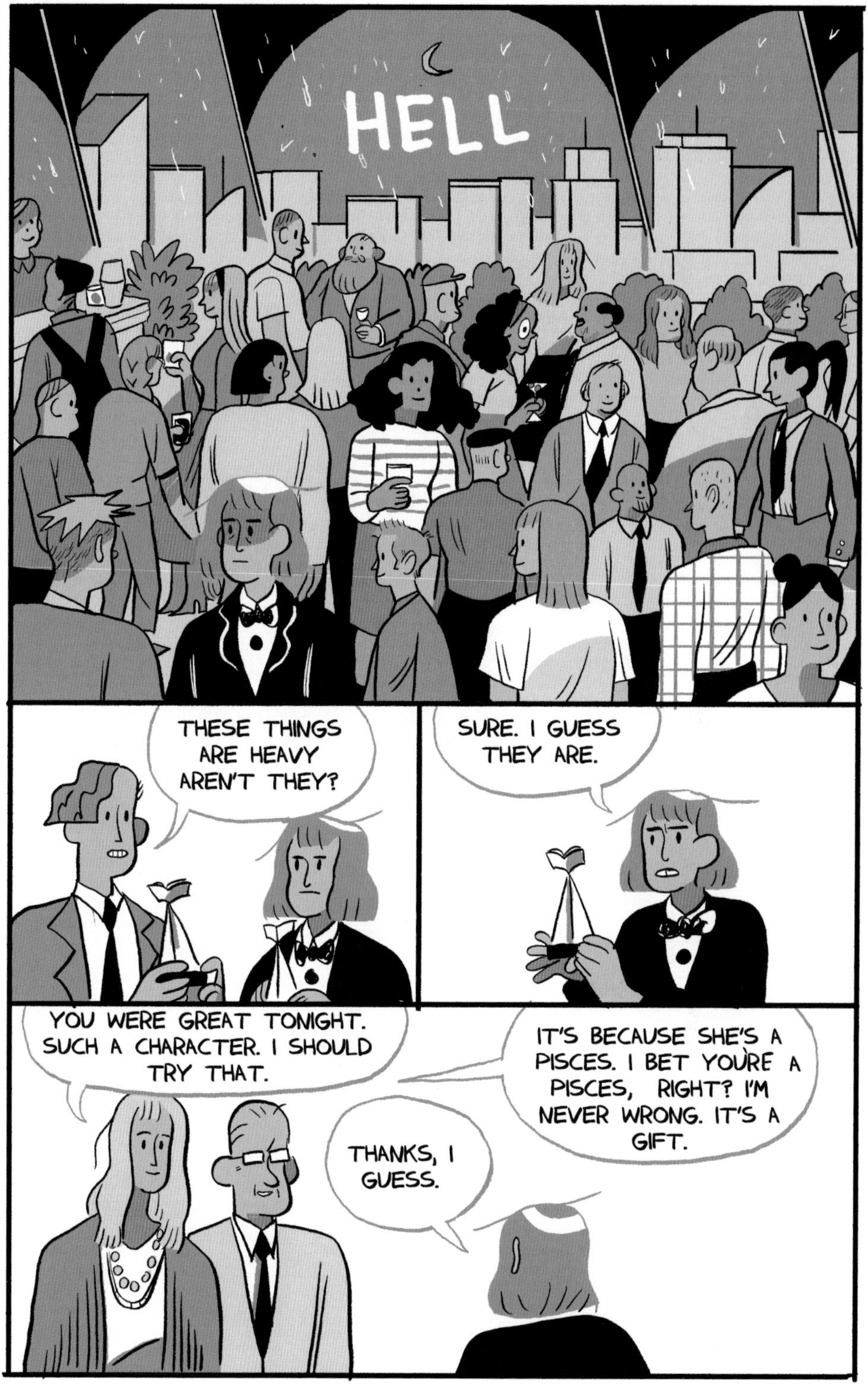
HELL
THESE THINGS ARE HEAVY AREN'T THEY?
SURE. I GUESS THEY ARE.
YOU WERE GREAT TONIGHT. SUCH A CHARACTER. I SHOULD TRY THAT.
IT'S BECAUSE SHE'S A PISCES. I BET YOU'RE A PISCES, RIGHT? I'M NEVER WRONG. IT'S A GIFT.
THANKS, I GUESS.

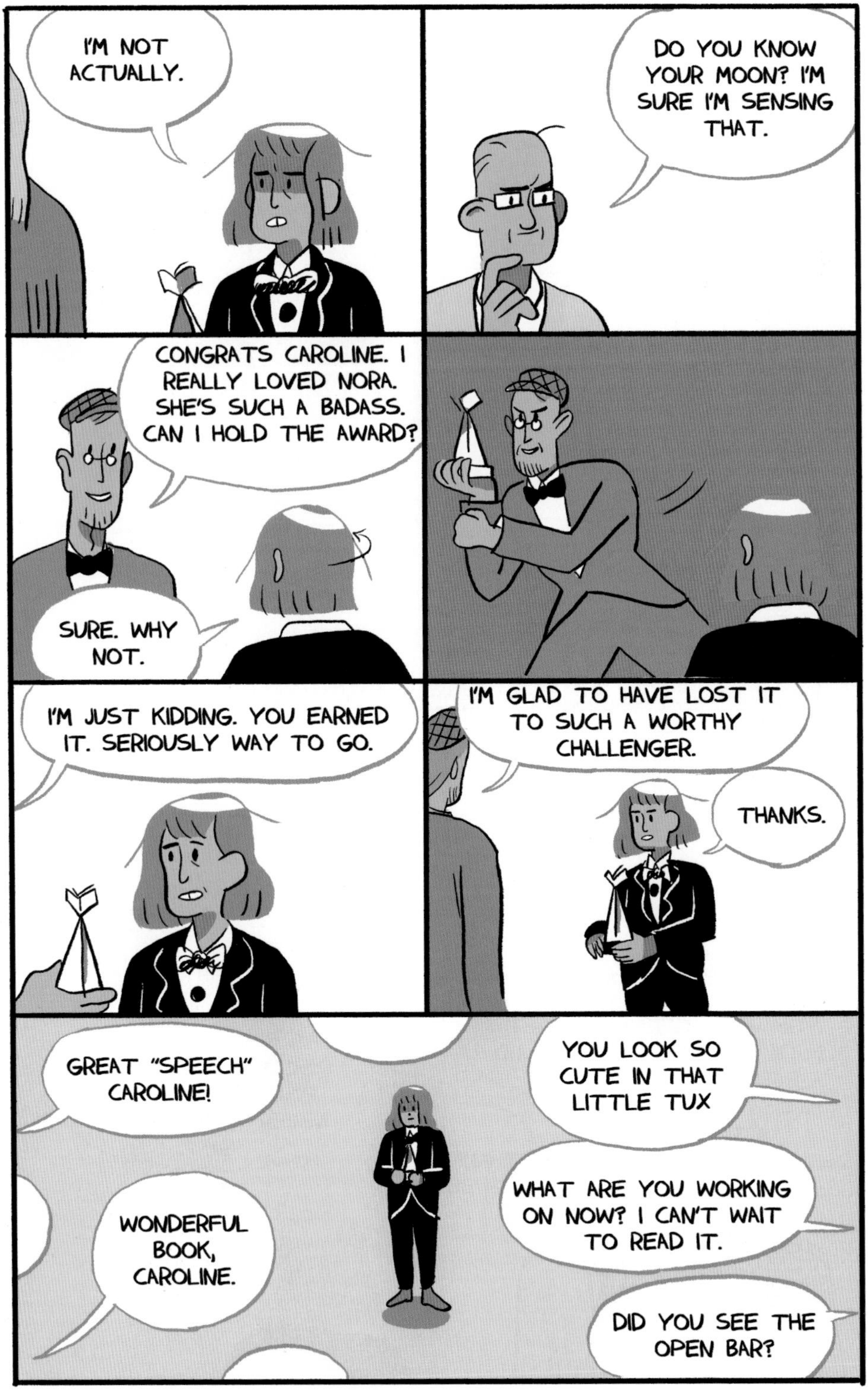
I'M NOT ACTUALLY.
DO YOU KNOW YOUR MOON? I'M SURE I'M SENSING THAT.
CONGRATS CAROLINE. I REALLY LOVED NORA. SHE'S SUCH A BADASS. CAN I HOLD THE AWARD?
SURE. WHY NOT.
I'M JUST KIDDING. YOU EARNED IT. SERIOUSLY WAY TO GO.
I'M GLAD TO HAVE LOST IT TO SUCH A WORTHY CHALLENGER.
THANKS.
GREAT "SPEECH" CAROLINE!
YOU LOOK SO CUTE IN THAT LITTLE TUX
WHAT ARE YOU WORKING ON NOW? I CAN'T WAIT TO READ IT.
WONDERFUL BOOK, CAROLINE.
DID YOU SEE THE OPEN BAR?

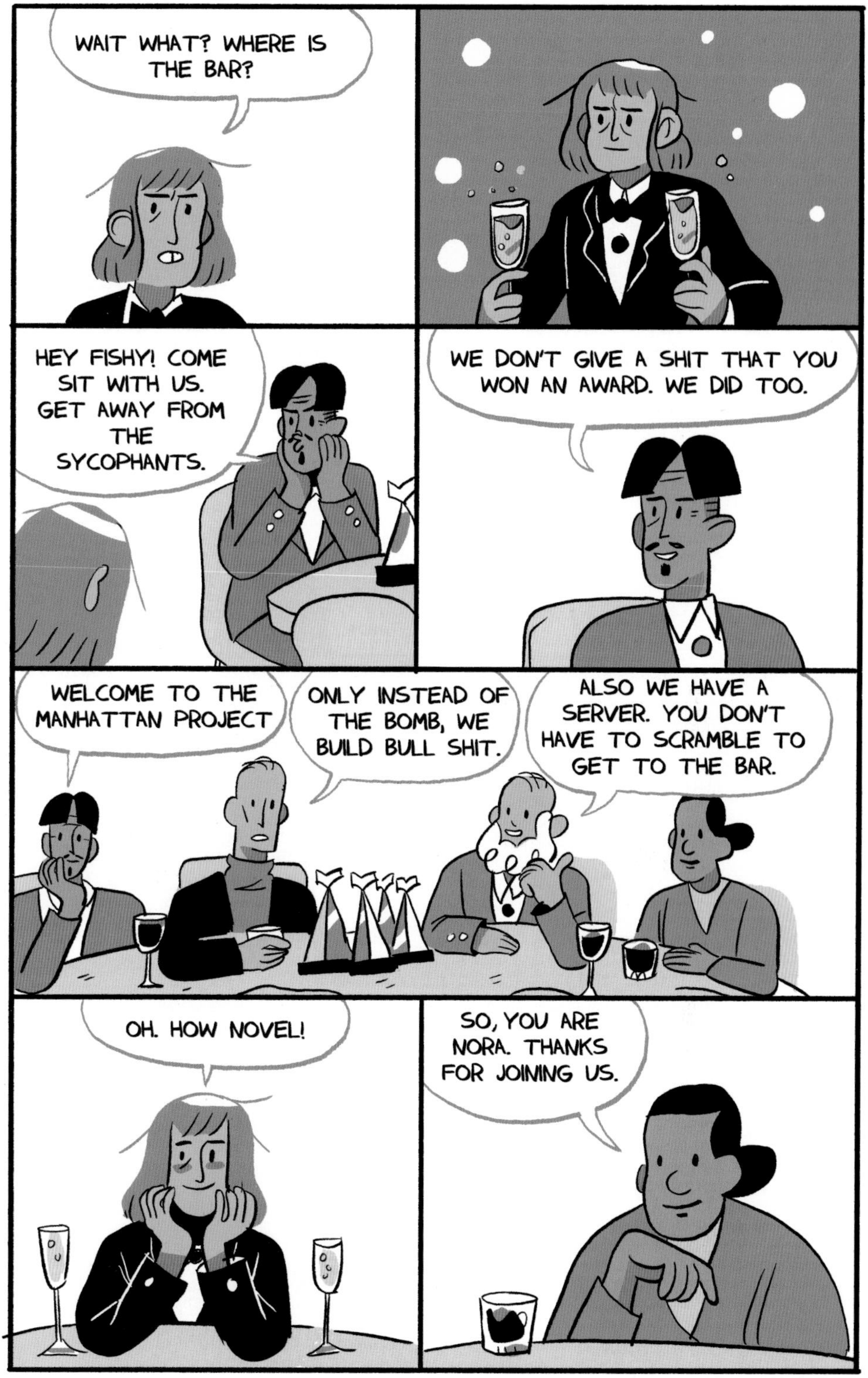
WAIT WHAT? WHERE IS THE BAR?
HEY FISHY! COME SIT WITH US. GET AWAY FROM THE SYCOPHANTS.
WE DON'T GIVE A SHIT THAT YOU WON AN AWARD. WE DID TOO.
WELCOME TO THE MANHATTAN PROJECT
ONLY INSTEAD OF THE BOMB, WE BUILD BULL SHIT.
ALSO WE HAVE A SERVER. YOU DON'T HAVE TO SCRAMBLE TO GET TO THE BAR.
OH. HOW NOVEL!
SO, YOU ARE NORA. THANKS FOR JOINING US.

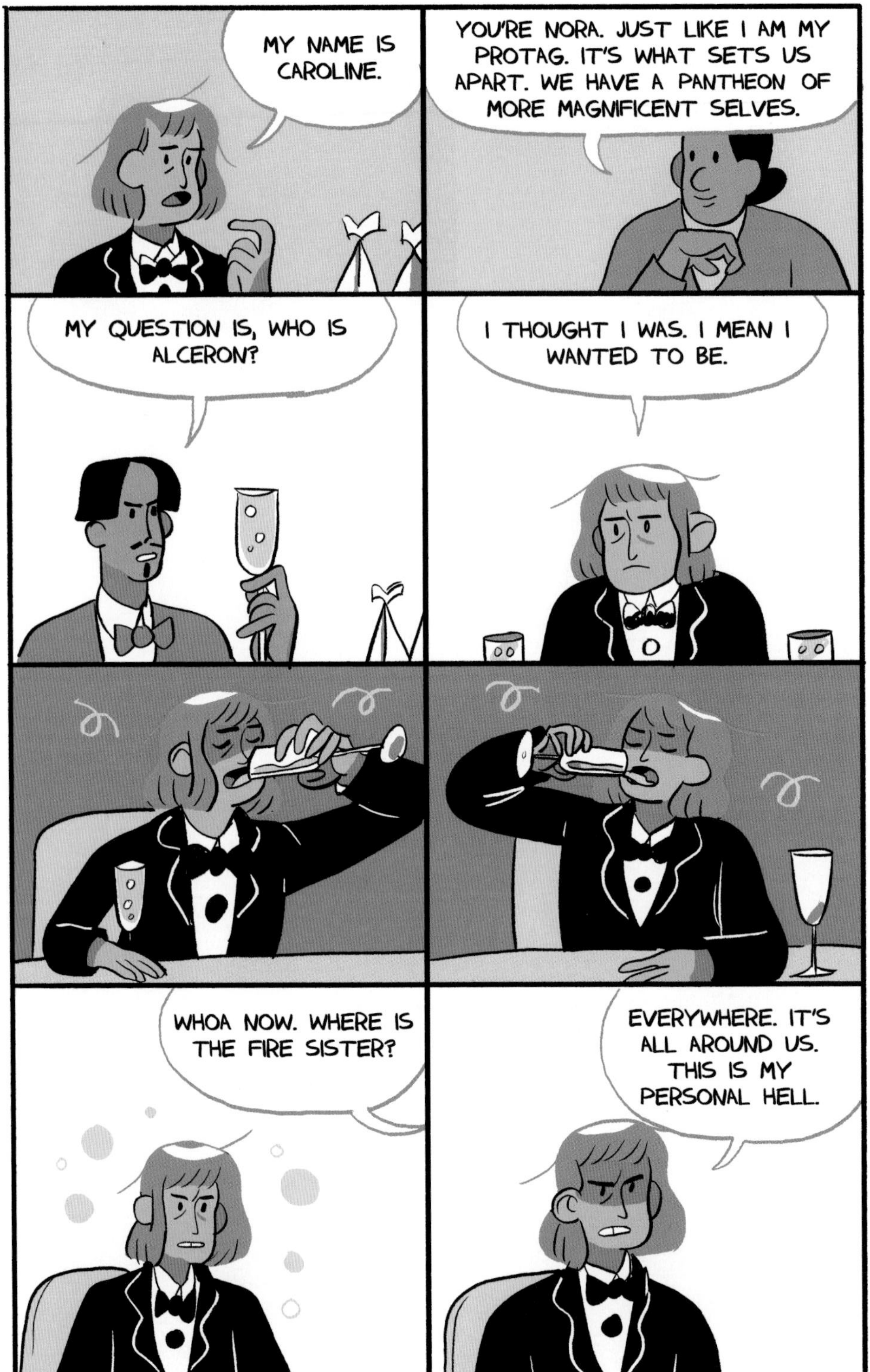
MY NAME IS CAROLINE.
YOU'RE NORA. JUST LIKE I AM MY PROTAG. IT'S WHAT SETS US APART. WE HAVE A PANTHEON OF MORE MAGNIFICENT SELVES.
MY QUESTION IS, WHO IS ALCERON?
I THOUGHT I WAS. I MEAN I WANTED TO BE.
WHOA NOW. WHERE IS THE FIRE SISTER?
EVERYWHERE. IT'S ALL AROUND US. THIS IS MY PERSONAL HELL.

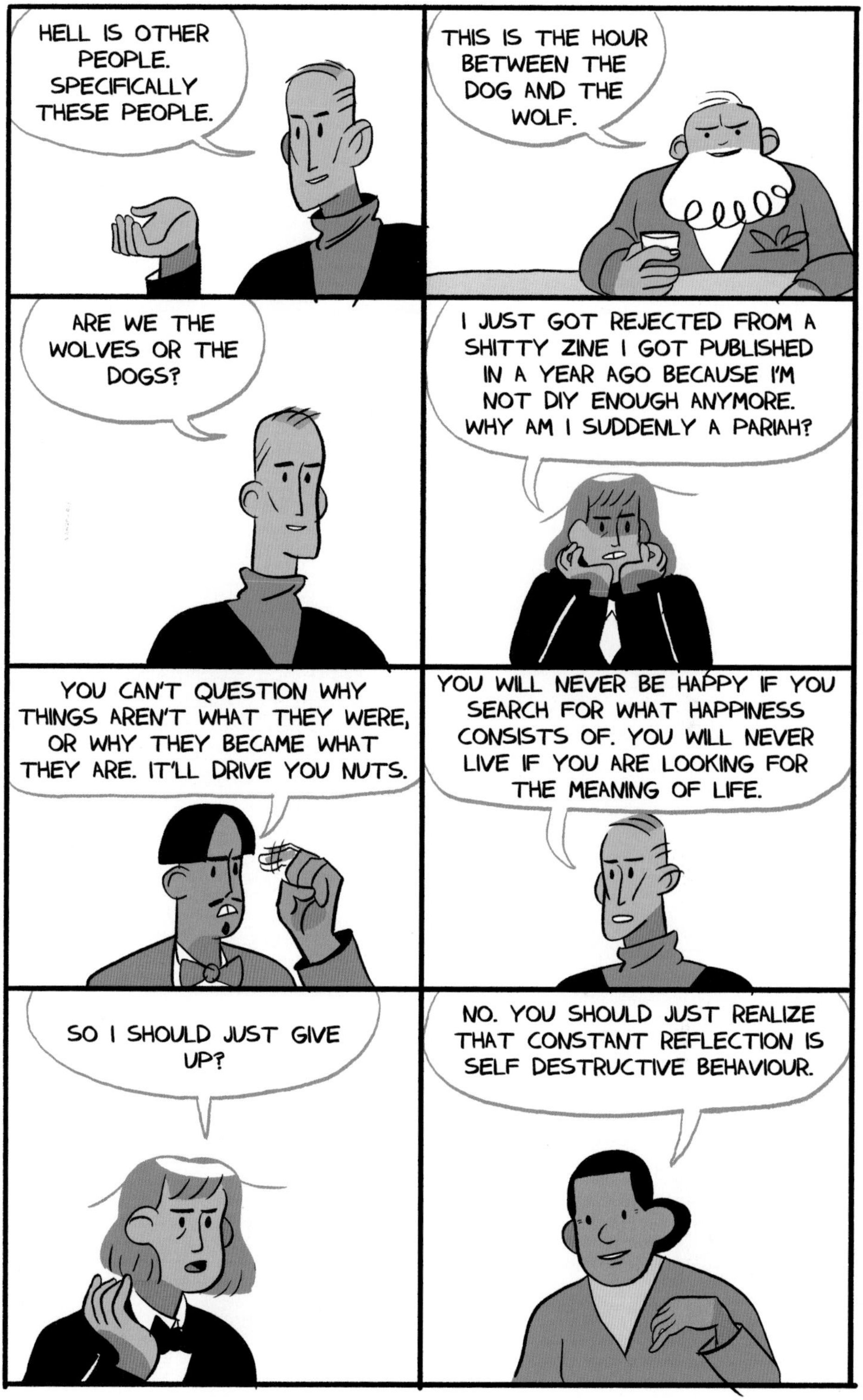
HELL IS OTHER PEOPLE. SPECIFICALLY THESE PEOPLE.
THIS IS THE HOUR BETWEEN THE DOG AND THE WOLF.
ARE WE THE WOLVES OR THE DOGS?
I JUST GOT REJECTED FROM A SHITTY ZINE I GOT PUBLISHED IN A YEAR AGO BECAUSE I'M NOT DIY ENOUGH ANYMORE. WHY AM I SUDDENLY A PARIAH?
YOU CAN'T QUESTION WHY THINGS AREN'T WHAT THEY WERE, OR WHY THEY BECAME WHAT THEY ARE. IT'LL DRIVE YOU NUTS.
YOU WILL NEVER BE HAPPY IF YOU SEARCH FOR WHAT HAPPINESS CONSISTS OF. YOU WILL NEVER LIVE IF YOU ARE LOOKING FOR THE MEANING OF LIFE.
SO I SHOULD JUST GIVE UP?
NO. YOU SHOULD JUST REALIZE THAT CONSTANT REFLECTION IS SELF DESTRUCTIVE BEHAVIOUR.

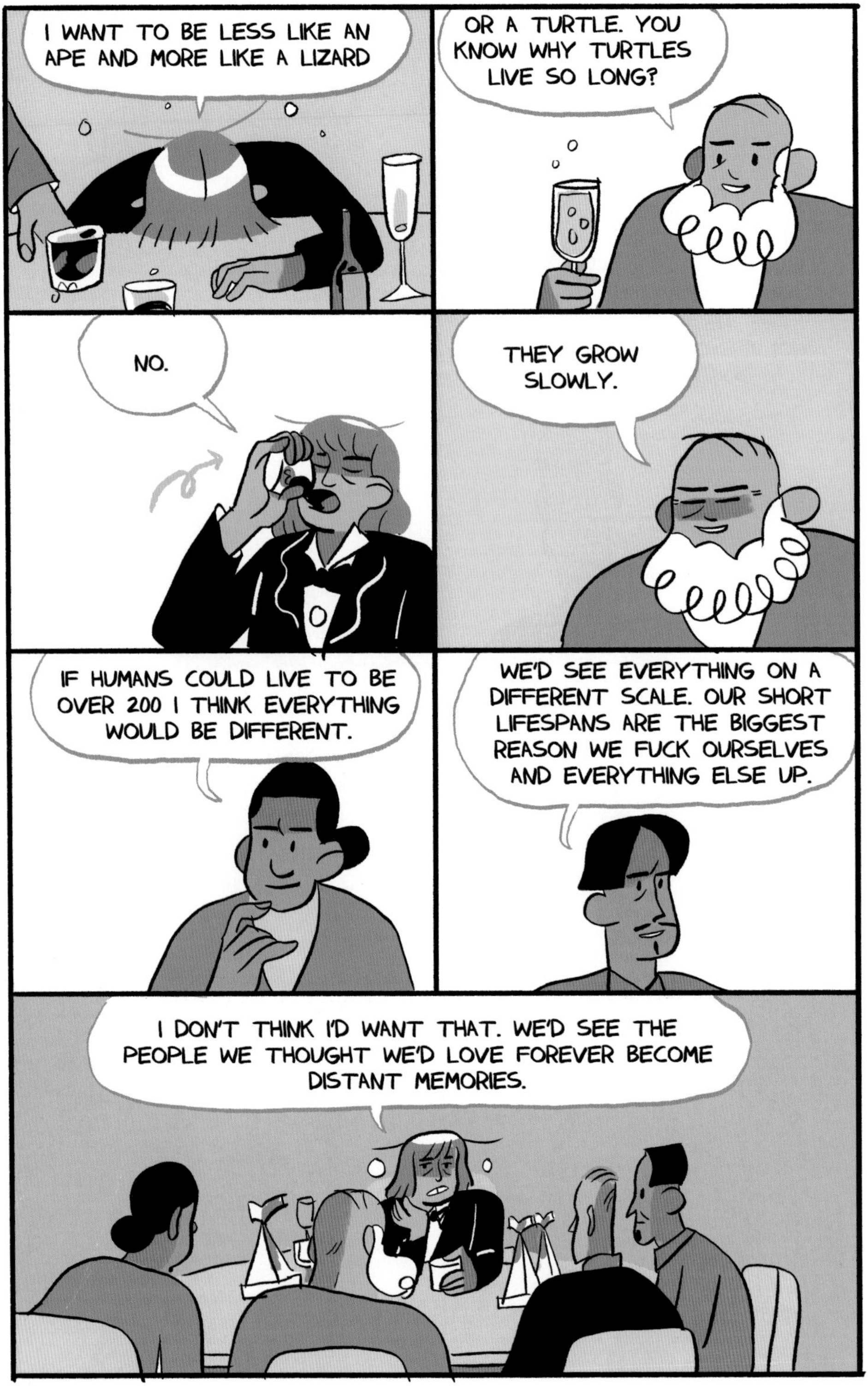
I WANT TO BE LESS LIKE AN APE AND MORE LIKE A LIZARD
OR A TURTLE. YOU KNOW WHY TURTLES LIVE SO LONG?
NO.
THEY GROW SLOWLY.
IF HUMANS COULD LIVE TO BE OVER 200 I THINK EVERYTHING WOULD BE DIFFERENT.
WE'D SEE EVERYTHING ON A DIFFERENT SCALE. OUR SHORT LIFESPANS ARE THE BIGGEST REASON WE FUCK OURSELVES AND EVERYTHING ELSE UP.
I DON'T THINK I'D WANT THAT. WE'D SEE THE PEOPLE WE THOUGHT WE'D LOVE FOREVER BECOME DISTANT MEMORIES.

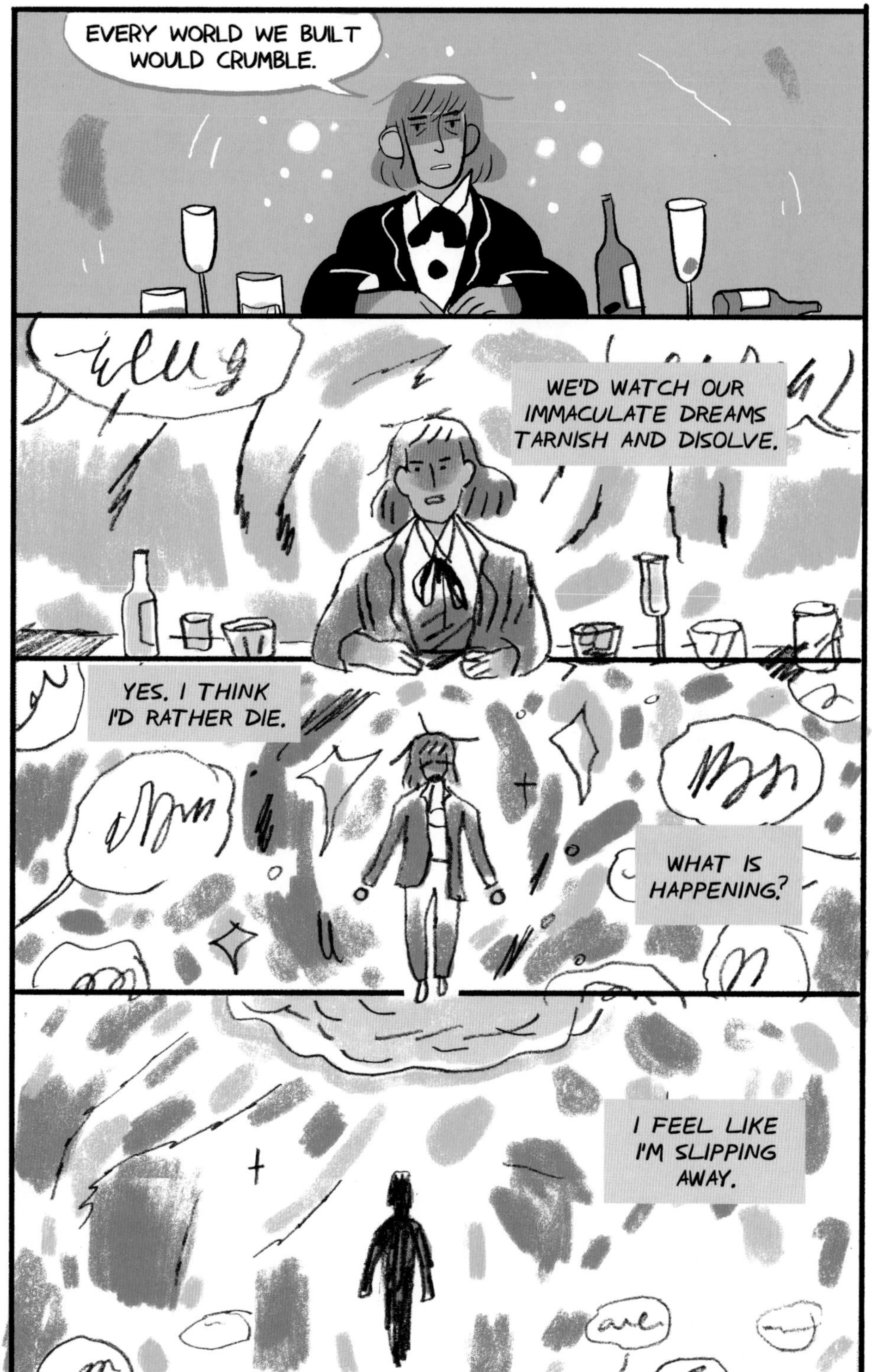
EVERY WORLD WE BUILT WOULD CRUMBLE.
WE'D WATCH OUR IMMACULATE DREAMS TARNISH AND DISOLVE.
YES. I THINK I'D RATHER DIE.
WHAT IS HAPPENING?
I FEEL LIKE I'M SLIPPING AWAY.

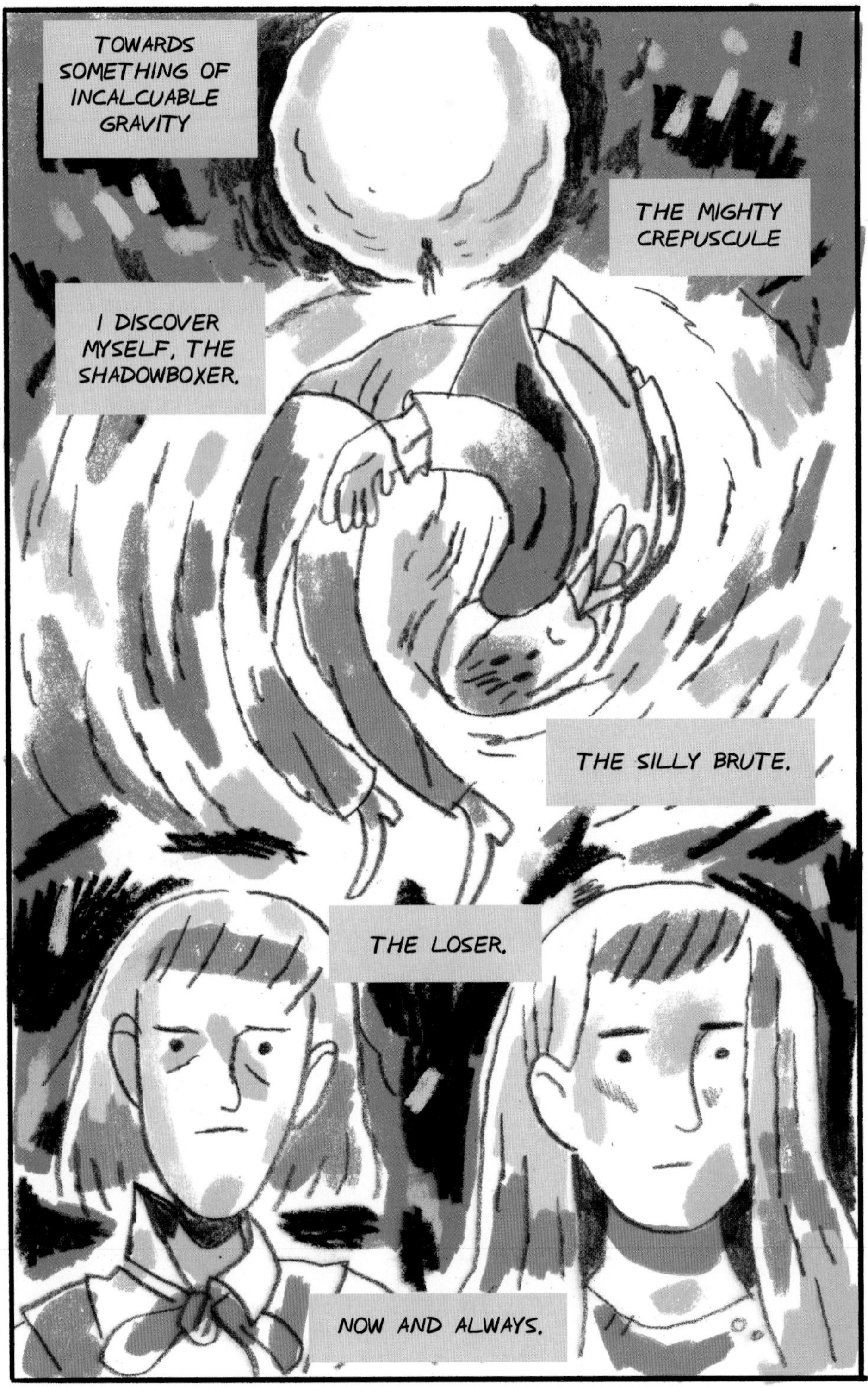
TOWARDS SOMETHING OF INCALCUABLE GRAVITY
THE MIGHTY CREPUSCULE
I DISCOVER MYSELF, THE SHADOWBOXER.
THE SILLY BRUTE.
THE LOSER.
NOW AND ALWAYS.

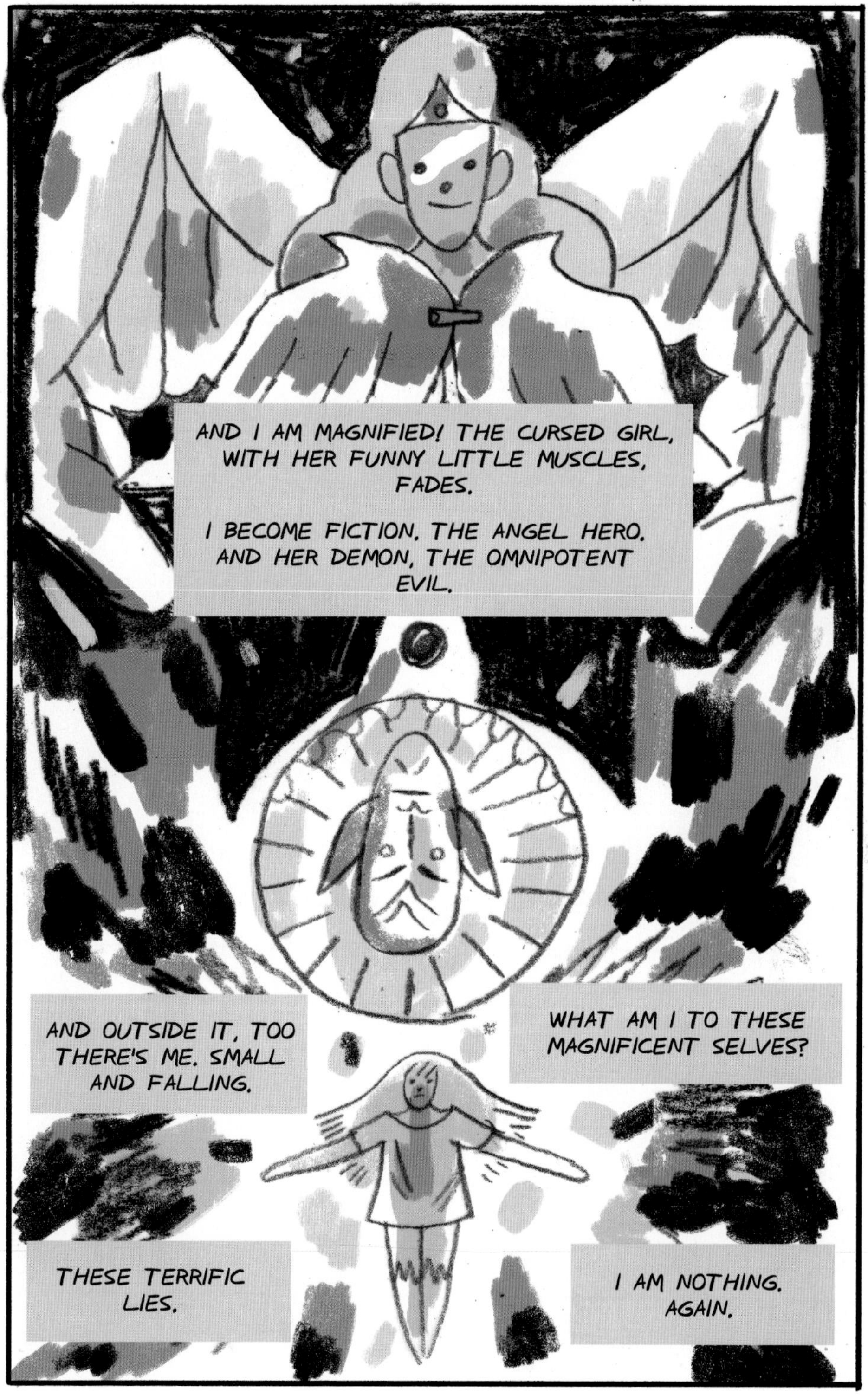
AND I AM MAGNIFIED! THE CURSED GIRL, WITH HER FUNNY LITTLE MUSCLES, FADES.
I BECOME FICTION. THE ANGEL HERO. AND HER DEMON, THE OMNIPOTENT EVIL.
AND OUTSIDE IT, TOO THERE'S ME. SMALL AND FALLING.
WHAT AM I TO THESE MAGNIFICENT SELVES?
THESE TERRIFIC LIES.
I AM NOTHING. AGAIN.

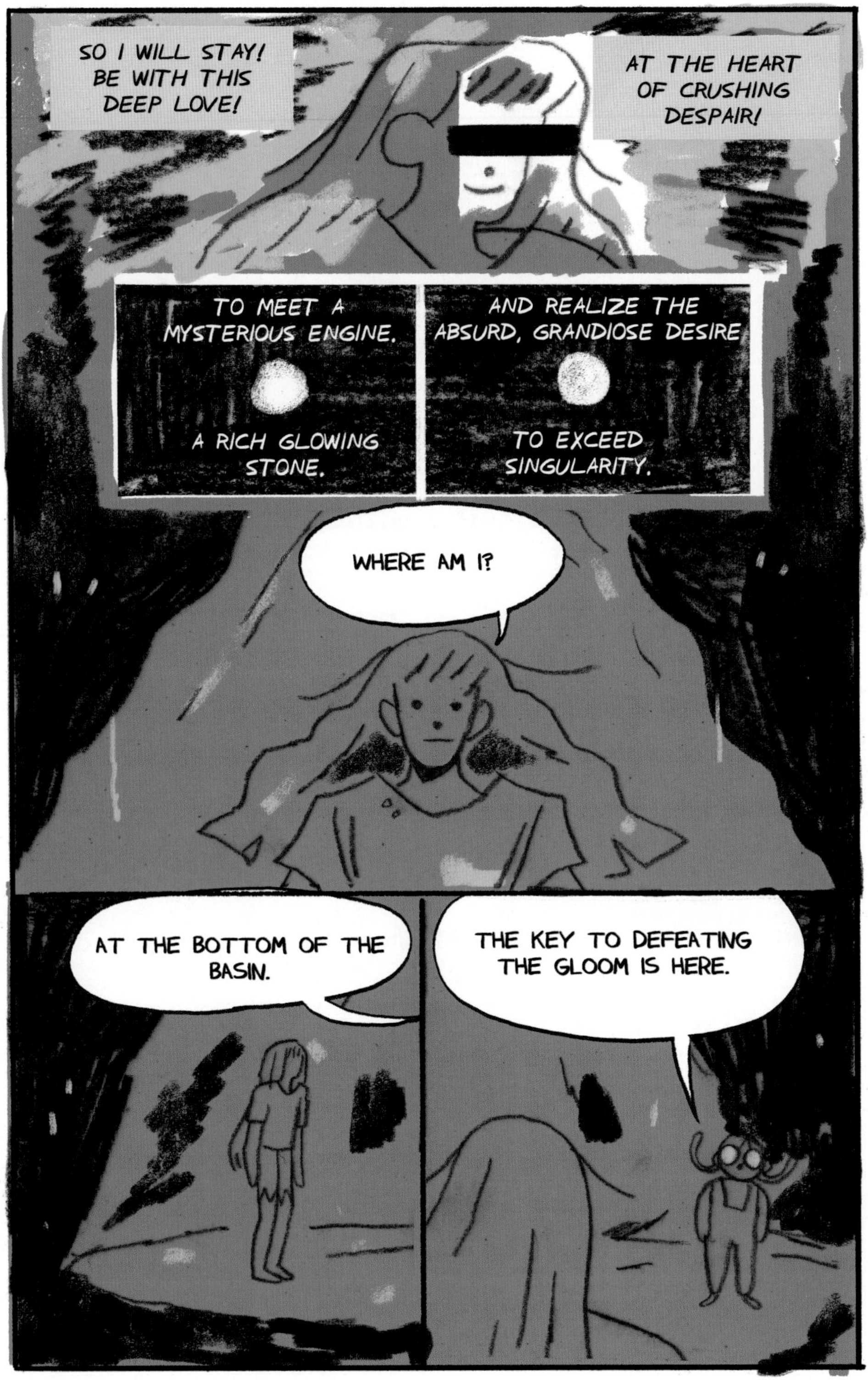
SO I WILL STAY! BE WITH THIS DEEP LOVE!
AT THE HEART OF CRUSHING DESPAIR!
TO MEET A MYSTERIOUS ENGINE.
A RICH GLOWING STONE.
AND REALIZE THE ABSURD, GRANDIOSE DESIRE
TO EXCEED SINGULARITY.
WHERE AM I?
AT THE BOTTOM OF THE BASIN.
THE KEY TO DEFEATING THE GLOOM IS HERE.

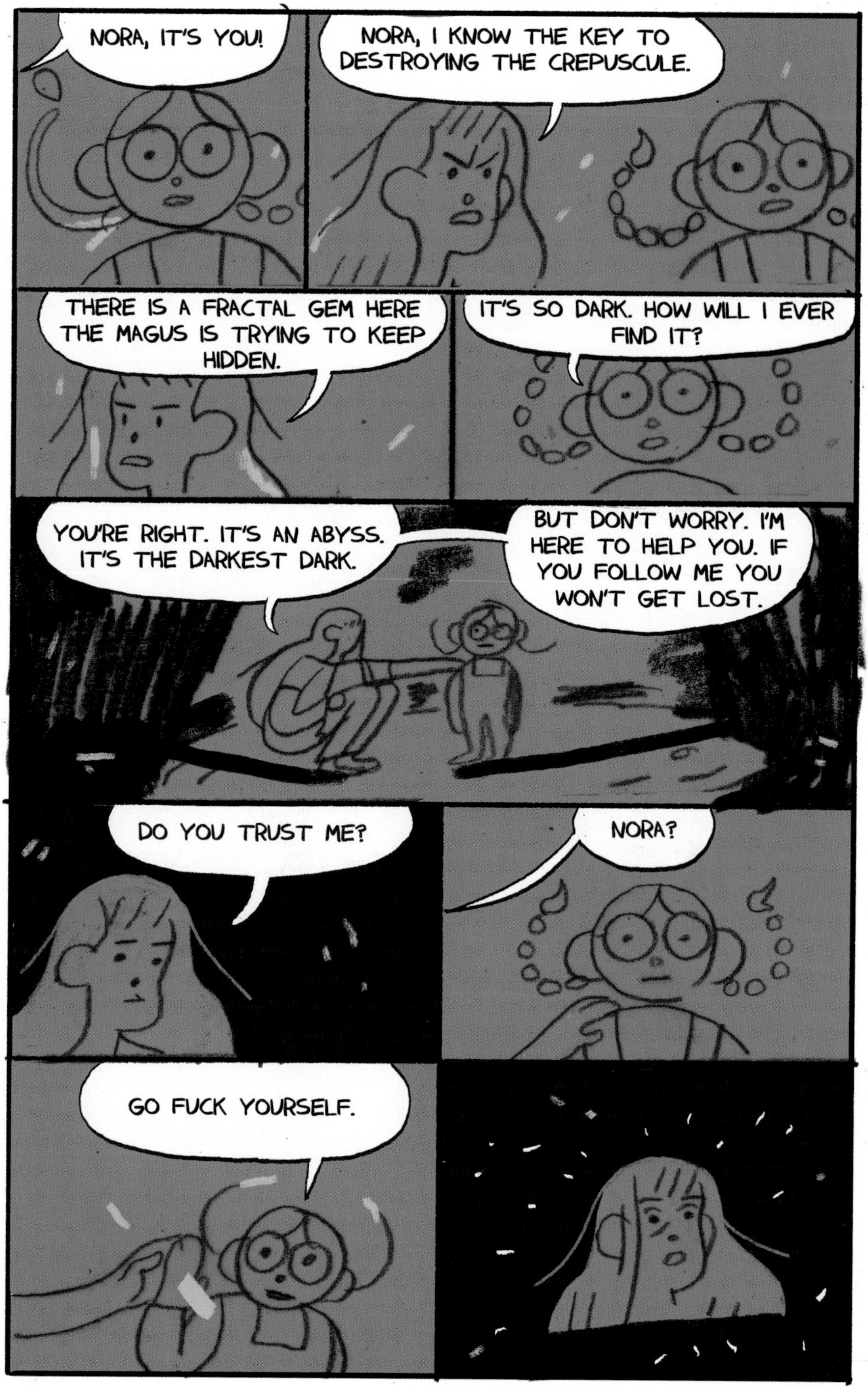
NORA, IT'S YOU!
NORA, I KNOW THE KEY TO DESTROYING THE CREPUSCULE.
THERE IS A FRACTAL GEM HERE THE MAGUS IS TRYING TO KEEP HIDDEN.
IT'S SO DARK. HOW WILL I EVER FIND IT?
YOU'RE RIGHT. IT'S AN ABYSS. IT'S THE DARKEST DARK.
BUT DON'T WORRY. I'M HERE TO HELP YOU. IF YOU FOLLOW ME YOU WON'T GET LOST.
DO YOU TRUST ME?
NORA?
GO FUCK YOURSELF.

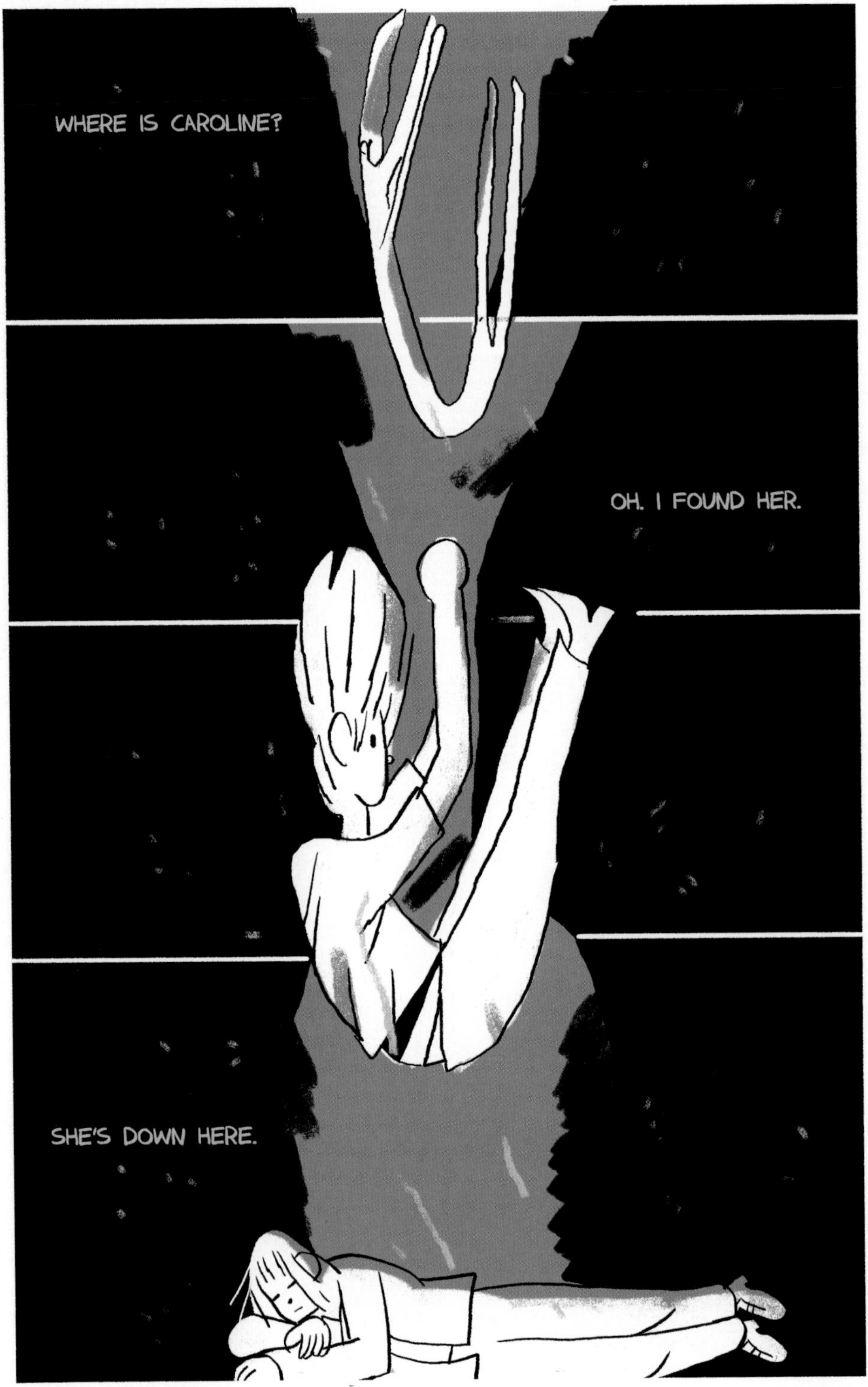
WHERE IS CAROLINE?
OH. I FOUND HER.
SHE'S DOWN HERE.

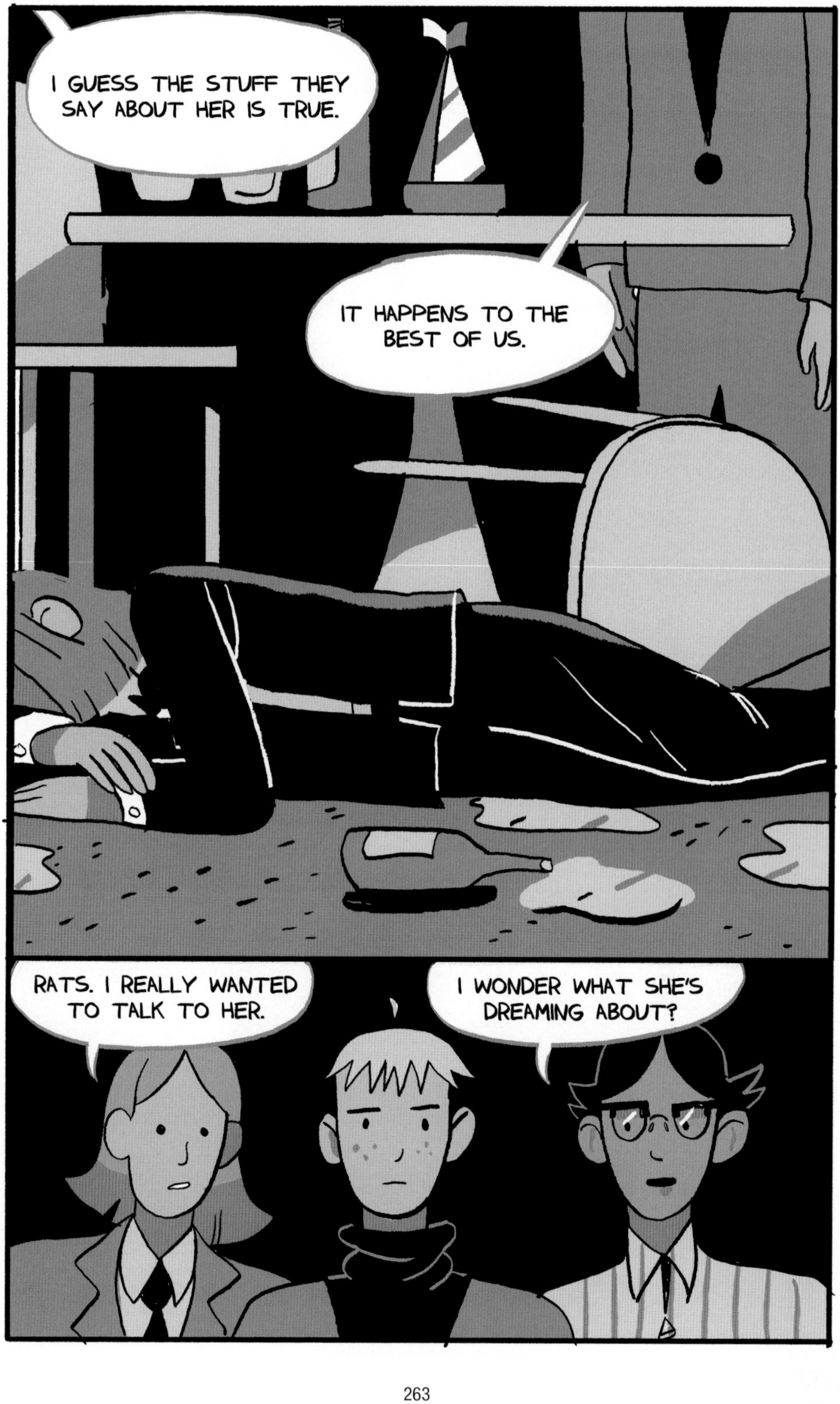
I GUESS THE STUFF THEY SAY ABOUT HER IS TRUE.
IT HAPPENS TO THE BEST OF US.
RATS. I REALLY WANTED TO TALK TO HER.
I WONDER WHAT SHE'S DREAMING ABOUT?

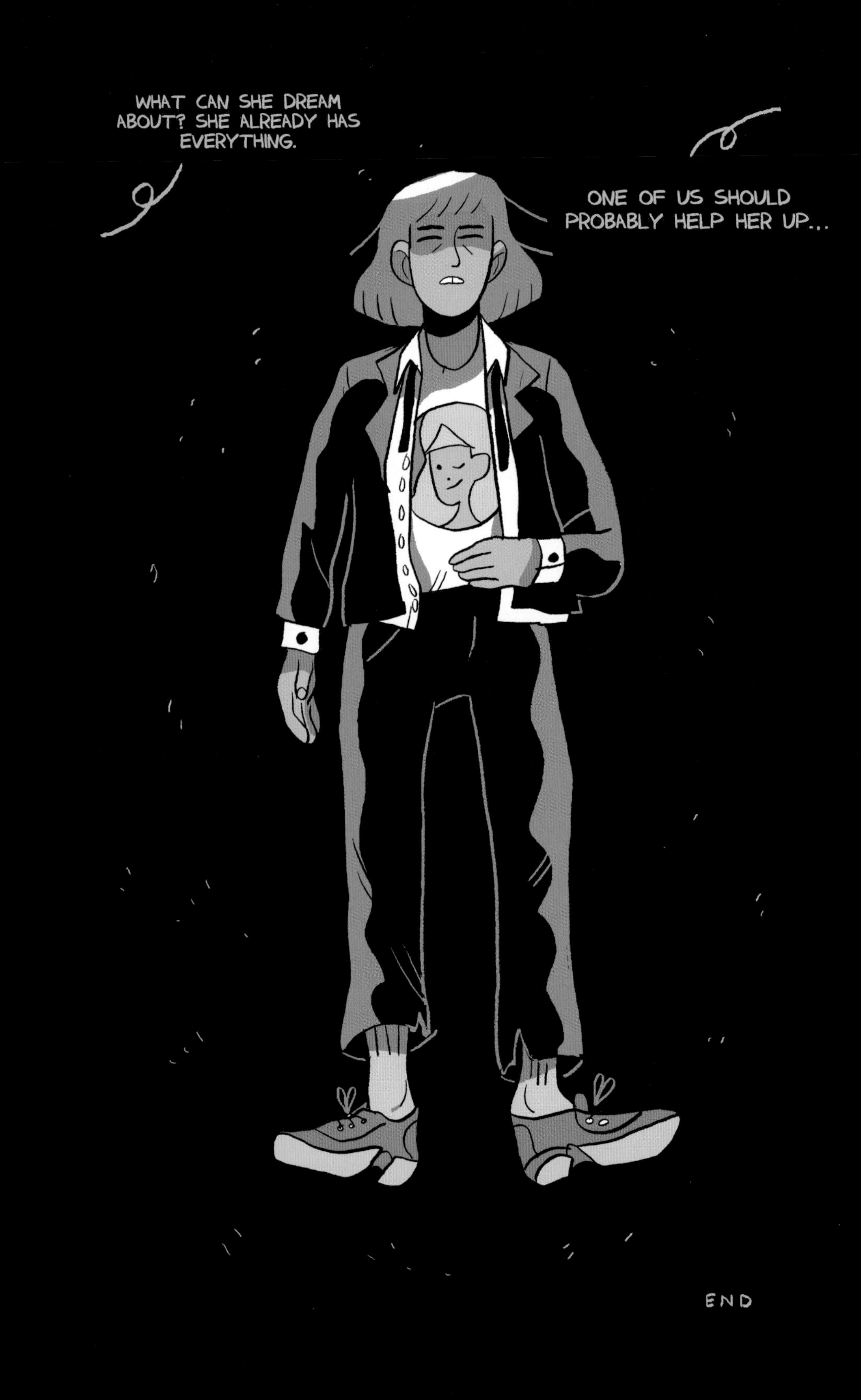
WHAT CAN SHE DREAM ABOUT? SHE ALREADY HAS EVERYTHING.
ONE OF US SHOULD PROBABLY HELP HER UP...
END

KELSEY WROTEN IS AN ILLUSTRATOR AND CARTOONIST BASED OUT OF BROOKLYN.

5-19